The Workings of Kamma

(Second Revised Edition)

The Pa-Auk Tawya Sayadaw

In compliance with the wishes of the author of *The Workings of Kamma (Second Revised Edition)*, the parties involved in organizing this second printing have made sure that the funds used for that purpose are pure:

- the funds do not include any funds, under any whatsoever form, collected by any bhikkhu or *sāmaṇera* in any whatsoever way, direct or indirect.
- the funds do not include any funds, under any whatsoever form, received from any bhikkhu or *sāmaṇera* in any whatsoever way, directly or indirectly.
- the funds do not include any funds, under any whatsoever form, from any fund/foundation or other source administered, founded, or funded by any bhikkhu or *sāmaṇera* in any whatsoever way, direct or indirect.
- the funds include solely funds collected by and received from laity, without prompting or any whatsoever other kind of direct or indirect verbal, written, or other intimation to that effect, by any bhikkhu or *sāmaṇera*.

The parties involved in organizing this printing are furthermore fully aware that unless this condition has been fulfilled, according to the workings of kamma as they are explained by The Buddha, and discussed in *The Workings of Kamma (Second Revised Edition)*, the kamma of organizing the printing this book will be inferior, and the printed book will be impure, in which case the said book will, in accordance with The Buddha's *Vinaya*, be unallowable for a bhikkhu or *sāmaṇera* to accept, possess, and read.

Pa-Auk Meditation Centre (Singapore)
15 Teo Kim Eng Road Singapore 416385
2009, 2012

The Workings of Kamma

(Second Revised Edition)

The Pa-Auk Tawya Sayadaw

Title: *The Workings of Kamma*

WORKINGS: 'the fact or manner of functioning or operating <*the ~s of his mind*>' *Penguin Hutchinson Reference Library*, Helicon Publishing and Penguin Books Ltd: 1996;

WORKING: '~s (of sth) the processes involved in the way a machine, an organization, a part of the body, etc operates: *the workings of the human mind*.' *Oxford Advanced Learner's Dictionary of Current English*, A S Hornby, 6th Edition, Oxford University Press, Oxford: 2000.

Cover Illustration:

The Indian emperor Asoka (ca. 304-232 BC) erected many pillars throughout India, Nepal, Pakistan, and Afghanistan. They were crowned with a horse, a lion, a bull, four bulls, etc. A small number have so far been found. Inscriptions describe his wishes for conduct in his government and among his people that accords with the Dhamma. One such pillar he also erected at Lumbini (249 BC), to mark the birthplace of The Buddha, who had passed away only some two hundred years earlier. At the time this pillar was discovered and the inscription deciphered, it was the first 'historical' evidence of The Buddha's existence.
(Drawn from *The Edicts of King Asoka* by the Venerable S. Dhammika, Wheel Publication No. 386-387, *Buddhist Publication Society*, Kandy, Sri Lanka.)

The Most Venerable Pa-Auk Sayadaw has adopted Asoka's four roaring lions as a symbol for Pa-Auk Tawya Monastery. And recently, he received news from Sri Lanka that the original four lions in fact carried a Dhamma-wheel on their backs, which had broken off: the Pa-Auk symbol was changed accordingly.

Contents

page

Tables

Contents
(Contents in Detail)

Namo Tassa,	**Homage to Him,**
Bhagavato,	**The Exalted One,**
Arahato,	**The Worthy One,**
Sammā-	**The Perfectly**
Sambuddhassa.	**Self-Enlightened One**

I —'THE CLOG-BOUND SUTTA'

('Gaddula·Baddha·Suttaṁ')[1]

In the course of our Dhamma talks, we shall discuss two main suttas. One is called *'Gaddula·Baddha·Suttaṁ'* ('The Clog-Bound Sutta'), the other is called *'Dutiya·Gaddula·Baddha·Suttaṁ'* ('The Second Clog-Bound Sutta'): that is two *'Gaddula·Baddha'* suttas.[2] We shall begin with the first one:

INCONCEIVABLE IS THE BEGINNING, BHIKKHUS

Thus I heard.[3] One time the Exalted One was dwelling in Sāvatthi, in Jeta's Grove, Anāthapiṇḍika's monastery. There the Exalted One addressed the bhikkhus:

Inconceivable is the beginning, bhikkhus, of the round of rebirth*(saṁsāra)*. **A first point is not known of ignorance-hindered beings***(avijjā·nīvaraṇānaṁ sattānaṁ)* **fettered by craving***(taṇhā·saṁyojanānaṁ)*, **rushing on***(sandhāvataṁ)* **and running about***(saṁsarataṁ)*.

Here, The Buddha discusses the round of rebirth*(saṁsāra)*,[4] the rushing on from one world to another (now a human being, then a deva, then an animal, then again a human being, etc.), and the running about within one world (again and again a human being, or again and again a deva, etc.). The Buddha mentions the two main causes for this ongoing process: ignorance*(avijjā)* and craving*(taṇhā)*.

Ignorance and craving are necessary for actions to possess kammic potency. The kammic potency*(kamma·satti)* is the potency by which volitional action through body, speech, or mind is able to produce a kamma result, *kamma·vipāka*. This potency is also called 'other-moment kamma'*(nānā·kkhaṇika kamma)* because we produce the kamma at one particular consciousness moment, and if the kamma matures, the kammic potency produces the result at another moment: either in this life or a future life.[5] But without ignorance and craving, action does not possess kammic potency.

---

[1] Reference numbers in italics refer to sutta quotations, etc. in endnotes beginning p.20.

[2] S.III.I.x.7 and S.III.I.x.8. *Gaddula* (clog) + *baddha* (bound: pp. of *bandhati* = to bind) = clog-bound. In English, a clog is a block of wood that serves to impede the motion of a horse, dog, etc. Here, it is a cubit-long block of hardwood that hangs by a strap from a dog's neck to prevent it from running. The stick is attached by the middle so it hangs horizontally before the dog's knees: when the dog tries to run, the dog's knees strike the stick. The device may be found still in use in rural Myanmar.

[3] Regarding translations and reference to The Buddha, see 'Editor's Note', p.367.

[4] SAṀSĀRO: the noun *saṁsāra* comes from the verb *saṁsārati*, which comes from *saṁ* (in the same way) + *sārati* (run on) = to run on in the same way. (PED)

[5] KAMMIC POTENCY: in the *Paṭṭhāna (Causal Relations)*, The Buddha lists twenty-four types of cause*(paccaya)*. They all produce their result because of their inherent potency*(dhamma·satti)* (*satti* = ability, capacity, potential, power, potency). Thus, while each volitional formation arises and perishes, its inherent kammic-potency*(kamma·satti)* remains in that same mentality-materiality continuity. While kamma is the cause, its inherent potency produces the result*(vipāka)*. This potency is also called *nānā·kkhaṇika kamma*: *nānā* (other/different) + *khaṇika* (moment). The result arises in another consciousness: in this life or another. (P.I.427 *'Kamma·Paccayo'* ('Kamma Cause') & PṬ *'Paccay·Uddesa·Vaṇṇanā'* ('Description of the Kamma Section'). See also footnote 56, p.15, and 'Kammic Potency', p.375.

What is ignorance*(avijjā)*? It is explained in the *Visuddhi·Magga*:[6]

Amongst the ultimately non-existent*(param·atthato a·vijjamānesu)*, **amongst women, men, it** [ignorance] **hurries on; amongst the existent***(vijjamānesu)*, **however, amongst the aggregates, etc., it does not hurry on....**[1]

What does this mean? It means that ignorance sees only conventional truth *(sammuti·sacca)*:[7] women and men, mothers and fathers, wives and husbands, daughters and sons, dogs, cats, pigs, and chickens, etc. It is wrong to see in this way, because these things do not exist according to reality*(yathā·bhūta)*. The things that do exist according to reality, however, are the aggregates*(khandha)*, the elements*(dhātu)*, the bases*(āyatana)*, mentality-materiality*(nāma·rūpa)*, dependent origination*(paṭicca·samuppāda)*, the workings of kamma, the three characteristics*(ti·lakkhaṇa)*,[8] etc.: in brief, the Four Noble Truths.[2] These things, which are ultimate truth*(param·attha·sacca)*, ignorance does not see.[9] That is why, if we think: 'This is a woman, a man, mother, father, daughter, son,' etc., it is the perception of a being*(satta·saññā)*, a manifestation of ignorance*(avijjā)*. And that ignorance is a cause of kamma, a reason why beings run on from life to life, from suffering to suffering.[10/3]

Ignorance is to think there are men, women, fathers, mothers, sons, daughters, etc. It is wrong to think in this way because there are in fact no men, women, etc., there is only ultimate materiality and mentality.[11]

To examine materiality, we need to practise materiality meditation*(rūpa·kamma·ṭṭhāna)*, that is, four-elements definition meditation*(catu·dhātu vavatthāna kammaṭṭhāna)*.

---

[6] VsM.xvii.587 *'Paññā·Bhūmi·Niddesa'* ('Exposition of the Wisdom-Ground') PP.xvii.43. Ibid.591 (PP.xvii.58-59) quotes The Buddha's explanation in DhS.iii.1106 *'Āsava·Gocchakaṁ'* ('The Taints Cluster'): 'Herein, what is the ignorance-taint? Non-knowledge of suffering, of suffering's origin, of suffering's cessation, of the path leading to suffering's-cessation, non-knowledge of the past, of the future, of the past&future, non-knowledge of specifically-caused dependently-originated things.' And VsM explains: 'When [ignorance has] arisen, it keeps the Truth of Suffering concealed, preventing penetration of the true individual function and characteristic of that truth. Likewise, origin, cessation, and the path, bygone five aggregates called the past, coming five aggregates called the future, and both specific causality, and dependently-originated things called specifically-caused dependently-originated things it keeps concealed, preventing their true individual functions and characteristics from being penetrated thus: "This is ignorance, these are formations."'

[7] SAMMUTI·SACCA: also called customary truth*(vohāra·sacca)*.

[8] THREE CHARACTERISTICS: impermanence*(anicca)*, suffering*(dukkha)*, and non-self*(an·atta)*. See quotation at 'Is Materiality Permanent or Impermanent?', p.319.

[9] VbhA.ii.154 *'Āyatana·Vibhaṅgo'* ('Base Analysis') DD.iv.243 explains that the three types of compactness conceal the three characteristics: 'But it is owing to not keeping what in mind, owing to non-penetration of what, and owing to concealment by what, that these characteristics do not appear? Firstly the characteristic of impermanence*(anicca)* does not appear owing to not keeping in mind, not penetrating rise and fall owing to its being concealed by continuity*(santati)*. The characteristic of pain*(dukkha)* does not appear owing to not keeping in mind, not penetrating continuous oppression and owing to its being concealed by the postures*(iriyāpatha)*. The characteristic of non-self does not appear owing to not keeping in mind, not penetrating the resolution into various elements(*nānā·dhātu·vinibbhoga)*.' See also 'The Three Types of Material Compactness', p.95.

[10] See also discussion p.14.

[11] Seeing mothers and fathers as a manifestation of ignorance is not the same as seeing that certain results arise because of unwholesome/wholesome kamma performed towards one's parents. See further explanation endnote 203, p.252.

Then do we see small particles, clusters of materiality *(rūpa·kalāpa)*. If we analyse those small particles, we see ultimate materiality: altogether twenty-eight types of materiality *(rūpa)*.[12] Apart from materiality, there is also mentality, which depends on materiality.[13] To examine mentality, we need to practise mentality meditation *(nāma kammaṭṭhāna)*. Then do we see the consciousness moments of the different types of mental process. If we analyse those consciousness moments, we see ultimate mentality: altogether eighty-one types of consciousness, and their associated mental factors.[14] There is nothing else: only materiality and mentality. As soon as the elements that are materiality and mentality arise, they perish, which means they are impermanent. Since they are impermanent, there can be no permanent entities such as a man, woman, father, mother, son, daughter, etc. If one thinks such things exist, it is a manifestation of ignorance.

When there is such ignorance, craving for those non-existent objects may arise. And when our actions of body, speech, and mind[15] are associated with such ignorance and craving, our actions possess kammic potency: kamma. If that kamma matures, it produces a good or bad result, and we continue rushing on and running about in the round of rebirth. That is why, in this sutta, The Buddha says:

Inconceivable is the beginning, bhikkhus, of the round of rebirth. A first point is not known of ignorance-hindered beings fettered by craving, rushing on and running about.

Then The Buddha explains how, in the future, the world system will come to an end.

THERE WILL COME A TIME, BHIKKHUS

First the great ocean dries up:

There will come a time, bhikkhus, when the great ocean dries up, evaporates, and is no more.

In the distant future the world will be destroyed in one of three ways:[4] destroyed by fire, by water, or by wind.[5] Here, The Buddha describes what happens when the world is destroyed by fire.[6]

First of all, a hundred thousand years beforehand, certain sky-devas will appear before people with dishevelled hair, and pitiful faces, wiping their tears with their hands.[16] They will announce the end of the world, and urge people to develop

---

[12] For a discussion of ultimate materiality, see 'Analysis of Ultimate Materiality', p.96, and table '4: The Twenty-Eight Types of Materiality', p.105.

[13] In the sensual sphere, mentality cannot arise independently of materiality: see 'Things Impossible for Consciousness to Do', p.350.

[14] The eighty-one types of consciousness are eighty-one mundane consciousnesses (unwholesome – 12, wholesome consciousnesses – 17, functional – 20, resultant – 32). The remaining eight supramundane types of consciousness (wholesome – 4, resultant – 4), which all take Nibbāna as object, are not included in mentality-meditation. See also 'Ultimate Mentality', p.105.

[15] ACTIONS OF BODY, SPEECH, AND MIND: physical, verbal, and mental actions.

[16] CERTAIN DEVAS: they are *loka·byūha* (world marshal) *kām·āvacara devā* (sensual-sphere devas) (VsM.xiii.405 *'Pubbe·Nivās·Ānussati·Ñāṇa·Kathā'* ('Discussion of the Past-Abodes-Recollection Knowledge') PP.xiii.34). Some teachers say the devas see many signs *(nimitta)*, which tell them of the destruction of the world-system. Other teachers say Brahmas of the pure abodes *(suddh·āvāsa)* (the Brahma-world plane where Non-Returners spend their last life), who possess superior psychic powers that enable them to look far into the future, see the future destruction of the world system, and ask the devas to inform

(Please see further next page.)

the four divine abidings *(cattāro brahma·vihārā)*: loving-kindness *(mettā)*, compassion *(karuṇā)*, sympathetic joy *(muditā)*, and equanimity *(upekkhā)* up to jhāna. And they will advise people to look after their parents, and to honour their elders.

Most people will take these words to heart, and practise loving-kindness towards each other, and in other ways accomplish wholesome kamma. Those who are able will develop jhāna. Those who are unable to develop jhāna will, because of their past wholesome kamma, be reborn in the deva world: as devas, they will develop jhāna. Dependent on ignorance and craving, the kammic potency *(kamma satti)* of their jhāna causes all these beings to be reborn in the Brahma world.[7]

After a long period, a great cloud appears, and heavy rain falls throughout the hundred thousand million world spheres *(koṭi·sata·sahassa·cakka·vāḷa)*. People sow crops, but when the crops have grown high enough for an ox to graze, the rain stops.[8] With no more rain, all plants dry up and are no more, and there is soon famine. Human beings die, and so do earth devas *(bhumma·devā)*, for they live on flowers and fruits. Owing to their past wholesome kamma, they are reborn in the deva world, and as devas they develop kasiṇa jhāna. Again, dependent on ignorance and craving, the kammic potency of their jhāna causes them to be reborn in the Brahma world.

After a long time, the water in the world begins to evaporate, and fish, turtles, and other creatures that live in water die. Owing to their past wholesome kamma, also they are reborn in the deva world, where they as devas develop jhāna. Dependent on ignorance and craving, the kammic potency of their jhāna causes them to be reborn in the Brahma world. According to a law of nature, also the beings in hell escape from hell and are reborn in the human world.[17] They develop loving-kindness, and are reborn in the deva world, where they as devas develop jhāna. Dependent on ignorance and craving, the kammic potency of their jhāna causes them to be reborn in the Brahma world. But the beings who were reborn in hell as a result of persistent wrong views *(niyata·micchā·diṭṭhi)*[18] do not escape. Dependent on ignorance and craving, the kammic potency of their persistent wrong view causes them to be reborn in a world-interstice hell *(lok·antarika·niraya)*: one of the hells situated in the space between world systems.[19] Thus, even though the world system is coming to an end, the continued rushing on and running about of beings does not come to an end. The Buddha explains:[20]

Not even then, bhikkhus, is the suffering of ignorance-hindered beings fettered by craving (who rush on and run about) brought to an end, I declare.

After a long period without rain, by the time all beings have been reborn elsewhere, a second sun appears.[21] And, as one sun sets, the other rises, so there is no more telling night from day: the world is continuously scorched by the heat of the two suns. Streams and smaller rivers dry up.

---

mankind (VsMṬ).

[17] VsM.xiii.405 *'Pubbe·Nivās·Ānussati·Ñāṇa·Kathā'* ('Discussion of the Past-Abodes-Recollection Knowledge') PP.xiii.33 mentions that according to another teacher, this takes place only at the appearance of the seventh sun.

[18] This is the most serious of the six weighty kammas: see 'Unwholesome Weighty Kamma', p.170.

[19] For details, see endnote 205, p.252.

[20] S.III.I.x.7 *'Gaddula·Baddha·Suttaṁ'* ('The Clog-Bound Sutta')

[21] A.VII.vii.2 *'Satta·Sūriya·Suttaṁ'* ('The Seven-Suns Sutta')

After yet another very long period, a third sun appears, and now also the great rivers dry up.[22] Then, after yet another very long period, a fourth sun appears, and the great lakes that were the source of the great rivers also dry up.[23] Again, after yet another very long period, a fifth sun appears, and also the seas dry up, so that there is not enough water left to wet the joint of a finger.[24] Again, after yet another very long period, a sixth sun appears, and now the great Mount Sineru[25] and the very earth itself begin to burn, and give off clouds of smoke. Eventually, after yet another very long period, a seventh sun appears, and now everything bursts into flames, into one sheet of flame. Great Mount Sineru and the earth burn up and disintegrate, and powerful winds carry the fire right up to the Brahma worlds. And just as burning ghee or oil leave no ashes, so the burning Mount Sineru and earth leave no ashes either.[26]

Even so, explains The Buddha, there is no end to the rushing on and running about of beings in the round of rebirth:[27]

There will come a time, bhikkhus, when Sineru, king of mountains, is burned, destroyed, and is no more. Not even then, bhikkhus, is the suffering of ignorance-hindered beings fettered by craving (who rush on and run about) brought to an end, I declare.

There will come a time, bhikkhus, when the great earth, is burned, destroyed, and is no more. Not even then, bhikkhus, is the suffering of ignorance-hindered beings fettered by craving (who rush on and run about) brought to an end, I declare.

Having explained how beings continue to rush on and run about in the round of rebirth, The Buddha then discusses why they do so.

Suppose, Bhikkhus, a Dog Was Clog-Bound

To explain why beings rush on and run about in the round of rebirth, The Buddha uses a simile, the simile of a clog-bound dog:[9]

Suppose then, bhikkhus, a dog was clog-bound *(sā gaddula·baddho)*, **and to a strong post or pillar was bound close; it would keep going round and circling round that same post or pillar.**

The dog is bound by a clog, and bound close to a strong post or pillar, so it cannot run away: it can only go round and round close to the post or pillar.

---

[22] GREAT RIVERS: The Buddha lists five rivers: the Ganges, the Yamunā, the Aciravatī, the Sarabhū, and the Mahī (ibid.).

[23] GREAT LAKES: The Buddha lists seven lakes: the Anotattā, the Sīhapapātā, the Rathakārā, the Kaṇṇamuṇḍā, the Kuṇālā, the Chaddantā, and the Mandākiniyā (ibid.).

[24] The Buddha gives a detailed explanation of how the waters of the seas recede and become shallower and shallower, till there are mere puddles here and there as in cows' footprints (ibid.).

[25] GREAT MOUNT SINERU: The Buddha explains Mount Sineru: 'Sineru, bhikkhus, king of mountains, is eighty-four thousand leagues in length, eighty-four thousand leagues in breadth, eighty-four thousand leagues immersed in the great ocean. It stands eighty-four thousand leagues out above the waters of the ocean.' (ibid.)

[26] The Buddha concludes by explaining that only a Noble One will believe His teaching about the impermanence of the earth and Mount Sineru. The commentary explains that it is because a Noble One has comprehensive faith in The Buddha, and has discerned dependent origination (ibid.). See 'Faith', p.374.

[27] S.III.I.x.7 *'Gaddula·Baddha·Suttaṁ'* ('The Clog-Bound Sutta')

THE UNEDUCATED ORDINARY PERSON

The image of the clog-bound dog The Buddha uses as a simile to describe what He calls **the uneducated ordinary person** *(assutavā puthu·jjano)*.

THE UNEDUCATED PERSON

What does The Buddha mean when He says a person is **uneducated** *(assutavā)*?[28] He means someone who is uneducated in and ignorant of both the theory and practice of the Dhamma; someone who possesses neither learning *(āgama)*, nor attainment *(adhigama)*. The uneducated person is one who needs to be educated about the Four Noble Truths.

- X The uneducated person has failed to study and inquire about the Texts, and so does not know the difference between the aggregates *(khandha)*, the elements *(dhātu)*, and the sense bases *(āyatana)*, which are the First Noble Truth, the Noble Truth of Suffering *(Dukkha Ariya·Sacca)*.[10]
- X The uneducated person has failed to study and inquire about dependent origination *(paṭicca·samuppāda)*, which is the Second Noble Truth, the Noble Truth of the Origin of Suffering *(Dukkha·Samudaya Ariya·Sacca)*.
- X The uneducated person has failed to study and inquire about the four foundations of mindfulness *(sati·paṭṭhāna)*, which is the Fourth Noble Truth (the Noble Eightfold Path), the Noble Truth of the Practice Leading to the Cessation of Suffering *(Dukkha·Nirodha·Gāminī Paṭipadā Ariya·Sacca)*.
- X The uneducated person has not practised systematically, and so has not discerned any of these things either, and so has attained no Path *(Magga)* or Fruition *(Phala)*. They take as object Nibbāna, the Third Noble Truth, the Noble Truth of the Cessation of Suffering *(Dukkha·Nirodha Ariya·Sacca)*.

That is what The Buddha means when He says a person is **uneducated** *(assutavā)*.

THE ORDINARY PERSON

What then does The Buddha mean when He says one is an ordinary person *(puthu·jjana)*? He means someone who is one of the many *(puthu)*,[11] who are without morality *(sīla)*, who are averse to the Noble Dhamma *(Ariya·Dhamma)*,[12] and who live according to an inferior dhamma *(nīca·dhamma)*.[29] For example:

- X The ordinary person generates many *(puthu)* defilements *(kilese)* such as greed, hatred, delusion, conceit, wrong view, shamelessness, etc.[30]
- X The ordinary person has many identity views *(sakkāya·diṭṭhi)* such as seeing materiality as self, materiality as having self, as in self, etc.[31]
- X The ordinary person looks up to many teachers *(satthā)*,[32] whose teachings are metaphysical and contrary to the Dhamma.[13]

---

[28] The Buddha explains the uneducated ordinary person in very many ways. The analyses that follow have been taken from the synopsis given in DhSA.iii.1007 (E.451-456), and MA.I.i.1 *'Mūla·Pariyāya·Suttaṁ'* ('The Root Theme Sutta').

[29] INFERIOR DHAMMA: here, *dhamma* refers to the values and views according to which one lives. It may therefore refer to values that are based on wrong view, contrary to The Buddha's Teaching.

[30] The Buddha explains it in, for example, 'The Second Clog-Bound Sutta': see p.29.

[31] The Buddha explains it in this 'Clog-Bound' sutta': see 'Regards the Five Aggregates as Self', p.10.

- X The ordinary person accomplishes many kamma formations *(abhi·saṅkhāra)*, through body, speech, and mind.[33]
- X The ordinary person may be reborn in many destinations *(gati)*:[14] the hells, the ghost and animal worlds, and the human and deva worlds.[15]
- X The ordinary person is attached to many pleasures through the five sensual lines *(kāma·guṇa)*: sights through the eye, sounds through the ear, odours through the nose, tastes through the tongue, and touches through the body.[16]
- X The ordinary person is hindered by many hindrances *(nīvaraṇa)*:[17] sensual desire *(kāma·cchanda)*, ill-will *(byāpāda)*, sloth&torpor *(thina·middha)*, restlessness&worry *(uddhacca·kukkucca)*, scepticism *(vicikicchā)*[18] (about The Buddha, Dhamma, Sangha, past and future lives, etc.), and ignorance.[34]

Who Does Not See Noble Ones

The Pali word *puthu* means not only 'many'; it means also 'separate'. Thus, the ordinary person *(puthu·jjana)* can be seen also as separate and distinct from Noble Ones,[19] who possess qualities such as virtue, learning, etc. That is what The Buddha refers to when He describes the uneducated ordinary person further, that is:

The uneducated ordinary person *(assutavā puthu·jjano)*, **who does not see Noble Ones** *(Ariyānaṁ a·dassāvī)*, **who is in their Noble Dhamma unskilled** *(Ariya·Dhammassa a·kovido)*, **who is in the Noble Dhamma undisciplined** *(Ariya·Dhamme a·vinīto)*.

A Noble One *(Ariya)* is a Buddha,[20] a Paccekabuddha, or a Buddha's Disciple *(Buddha·Sāvaka)* who has attained a supramundane state.

The uneducated ordinary person's not seeing Noble Ones is of two types: not seeing with the eye *(cakkhunā a·dassāvī)*, and not seeing with knowledge *(ñāṇena a·dassāvī)*.[35] For even though one may see Noble Ones with one's physical eye, one sees only their exterior, not their Noble state.

There was once a bhikkhu who was mortally ill. When The Buddha asked him if he had anything to regret, he said he regretted not having seen The Buddha for a long time, meaning that he had not seen The Buddha's exterior with his physical eye. The Buddha said to him:[36]

> **Why do you, Vakkali, this stinking body want to see?**
> **Whoever, Vakkali, the Dhamma sees, he Me sees;**
> **whoever Me sees, he the Dhamma sees.**

---

[32] By contrast, see the Noble Disciple's faith in The Buddha, endnote 54, p.28, and analysis of faith at 'Faith', p.374.

[33] KAMMA FORMATIONS: physical, verbal, and mental actions. The Buddha explains this quality of the ordinary person in, for example, 'The Second Clog-Bound Sutta': see p.29.

[34] The Buddha explains it in the phrase 'ignorance-hindered beings', used in, for example, both *'Gaddula·Baddha'* suttas. See also footnote 3, p.20, and 'Unwholesome Consciousness', p.46.

[35] This is how the two types of seeing are explained in MA.ibid./DhSA.ibid. They can also be explained as not seeing Noble Ones with the translucency-eye *(pasāda·cakkhu)* (see under 'Concrete Derived Materiality', p.93) or the knowledge-eye *(ñāṇa·cakkhu)*/wisdom-eye *(paññā·cakkhu)*. These two types of eye are described in, for example, DhSA.II.596 *'Upādā·Bhājanīya·Kathā'* ('Discussion of the Classification of Derived [Materiality]') E.402-403.

[36] DhSA/MA ibid. refer to this incident, from S.III.I.ix.5 *'Vakkali·Suttaṁ'* ('The Vakkali Sutta').

For by the Dhamma seeing, Vakkali, one Me sees;
Me seeing, one the Dhamma sees.

This means that it is not enough merely to see Noble Ones with one's physical eye. One needs also to see the Noble state of the Noble Ones, and the things pertaining to their Noble state: that is, one needs to have known and seen the impermanence*(anicca)*, suffering*(dukkha)*, and non-self*(an·atta)* of ultimate materiality and ultimate mentality through insight meditation practice, and one needs to have attained to the Dhamma that the Noble Ones have attained to. So long as those things remain unseen, so long is one still a person **who does not see Noble Ones**.

Who Is Unskilled and Undisciplined

The Buddha explained also that the uneducated ordinary person is in the Noble Ones' **Noble Dhamma unskilled***(Ariya·Dhammassa a·kovido)*, and in **the Noble Dhamma undisciplined***(Ariya·Dhamme a·vinīto)*.

To be unskilled in the Dhamma of Noble Ones is to be without skill in the four foundations of mindfulness, samatha and vipassanā, etc.

To be undisciplined in the Noble Dhamma is to be without two types of discipline:

1) Restraint discipline*(saṁvara·vinaya)*
2) Abandonment discipline*(pahāna·vinaya)*

There are five types of restraint discipline, and five types of abandonment discipline.

Restraint Discipline

The uneducated ordinary person is undisciplined by the five types of restraint discipline*(saṁvara·vinaya)*:

1) Restraint by morality*(sīla·saṁvara)*: the uneducated ordinary person is not disciplined by the five, eight, or ten precepts, or the *Pāṭimokkha* precepts, and so does not refrain from killing, stealing, sexual misconduct, lying, drinking beer and wine, etc., or taking other intoxicants,etc.[37/21]
2) Restraint by mindfulness*(sati·saṁvara)*: the uneducated ordinary person does not restrain the six faculties: eye, ear, nose, tongue, body and mind.[22]
3) Restraint by knowledge*(ñāṇa·saṁvara)*: that is,[38]
   i) the uneducated ordinary person is undisciplined by the restraint of samatha knowledge*(samatha·ñāṇa)*: knowledge of her or his meditation subject's learning sign*(uggaha nimitta)* or counterpart sign*(paṭibhāga nimitta)* at access-*(upacāra samādhi)* or absorption concentration*(appanā samādhi)*.
   ii) the uneducated ordinary person is undisciplined by the restraint of insight knowledge*(vipassanā·ñāṇa)*: knowledge of the impermanence, suffering, and non-self characteristics of ultimate materiality and ultimate mentality.
   iii) the uneducated ordinary person is undisciplined by the restraint of Path Knowledge*(Magga·Ñāna)*: knowledge of the Four Noble Truths.[23]

---

[37] For an analysis, see 'Beer&Wine Liquor', p.372.

[38] The analysis for restraint by knowledge has been taken from MA.I.i.2 *'Sabb·Āsava·Suttaṁ'* ('The All-Taints Sutta').

iv) the uneducated ordinary person is undisciplined by the restraint of knowledge that arises through wise attention *(yoniso manasikāra)* with regard to the four requisites of life: clothes, food, dwelling, and medicine.[24]

4) Restraint by patience *(khanti·saṁvara)*: the uneducated ordinary person does not patiently endure cold and heat, hunger and thirst, harmful and harmless insects, rude speech, pain, etc.[25]
5) Restraint by energy *(vīriya·saṁvara)*: the uneducated ordinary person does not arouse energy to remove thoughts of sensual desire, ill-will, and cruelty.[26]

The uneducated ordinary person does not know that there are actions through body, speech and mind which should be restrained and disciplined in these five ways.

Abandonment Discipline

The uneducated ordinary person is also undisciplined by the five types of abandonment discipline *(pahāna·vinaya)*:

1) Abandonment by substitution *(tad·aṅga·pahāna)*: the uneducated ordinary person has not practised insight meditation, and so has not substituted the appropriate insight knowledges for the various defiling factors.[27] For example:
   - X the uneducated ordinary person has not substituted the Mentality-Materiality Determining Knowledge *(Nāma·Rūpa·Vavatthāna)*[39] for the identity view *(sakkāya·diṭṭhi)*.[28]
   - X the uneducated ordinary person has not substituted the Cause-Apprehending Knowledge *(Paccaya·Pariggaha)*[40] for the rootlessness view[41] or invalid-root view *(a·hetu·visama·hetu·diṭṭhi)*.[29]
   - X the uneducated ordinary person has not substituted discernment of the arising of formations *(udaya·dassana)* for the annihilation view[42] *(uccheda·diṭṭhi)*.[30]
   - X the uneducated ordinary person has not substituted discernment of the perishing of formations *(vaya·dassana)* for the eternity view[43] *(sassata·diṭṭhi)*.[44]
   - X the uneducated ordinary person has not substituted the contemplation of disenchantment *(nibbid·ānupassanā)* for the perception of delight in formations *(abhirati·saññā)*.[45]
2) Abandonment by suppression *(vikkhambhana·pahāna)*: the uneducated ordinary person has not practised samatha meditation, and so has not suppressed the hindrances *(nīvaraṇa)* through access- or jhāna concentration.[31]

---

[39] Mentality-Materiality Determining Knowledge: a synonym for the Mentality-Materiality Definition Knowledge *(Nāma·Rūpa·Pariccheda·Ñāṇa)*. See 'The Two Preparatory Insight Knowledges', p.90.

[40] CAUSE-APPREHENDING KNOWLEDGE: see 'The Two Preparatory Insight Knowledges', p.90.

[41] See The Buddha's description at 'The Rootlessness View', p.172.

[42] See The Buddha's description at 'Annihilation View', p.12.

[43] See The Buddha's description at 'Eternity View', p.13.

[44] See quotation, endnote 51, p.27.

[45] For The Buddha's explanation of the contemplation of disenchantment that follows insight meditation on the five aggregates, see quotation at 'The Educated Noble Disciple Is Disenchanted', p.327.

3) Abandonment by eradication *(samuccheda·pahāna)*: the uneducated ordinary person has not eradicated any defilements by attainment of one of the Noble Paths *(Ariya·Magga)*.[32]
4) Abandonment by subsiding *(paṭippassaddhi·pahāna)*: the uneducated ordinary person has not attained to the subsiding of any defilements by attainment of one of the Noble Fruits *(phala)*.[33]
5) Abandonment by escape *(nissaraṇa·pahāna)*: the uneducated ordinary person has not escaped from all formations (the formed) by attainment of the Unformed element, Nibbāna.[34]

The uneducated ordinary person often lets go of her or his restraint, and has not abandoned what needs to be abandoned: that is what The Buddha is referring to when He says the uneducated ordinary person is **in the Noble Dhamma undisciplined** *(Ariya·Dhamme a·vinīto)*.

Who Does Not See True Men

Finally, The Buddha explains the uneducated ordinary person as one:

Who does not see True Men, who is in the True Men's Dhamma unskilled, who is in the True Men's Dhamma undisciplined.

In this case, True Men are the same as Noble Ones, for Noble Ones are True Men, and True Men are Noble Ones. The Noble Ones' Dhamma is the same as the True Men's Dhamma, and the Noble Ones' discipline is the same as the True Men's discipline.

That concludes our explanation of what The Buddha means when He speaks of the uneducated ordinary person *(assutavā puthu·jjano)*.

Regards the Five Aggregates as Self

Having explained the qualities of the uneducated ordinary person, The Buddha then explains how such a person regards the five aggregates *(pañca·kkhandha)*.

Since we now understand The Buddha's words better, let us begin again with the image of the clog-bound dog:

Suppose then, bhikkhus, a dog was clog-bound, and to a strong post or pillar was bound close; it would keep going round and circling round that same post or pillar.

So too, bhikkhus, the uneducated ordinary person,

- **who does not see Noble Ones, who is in their Noble Dhamma unskilled, who is in the Noble Dhamma undisciplined,**
- **who does not see True Men, who is in the True Men's Dhamma unskilled, who is in the True Men's Dhamma undisciplined,**

[1] **regards materiality** *(rūpa)* **as self, or self as having materiality, or materiality as in self, or self as in materiality;**

[2] **regards feeling** *(vedanā)* **as self, or self as having feeling, or feeling as in self, or self as in feeling;**

[3] **regards perception** *(saññā)* **as self, or self as having perception, or perception as in self, or self as in perception;**

[4] **regards formations** *(saṅkhāra)*[46] **as self, or self as having formations, or formations as in self, or self as in formations;**

---

[46] FORMATIONS *(saṅkhāra)*: The meaning of this term depends on the context. 1) As the cause of consciousness (in dependent origination), it refers to the formation of kamma: volitional formation by body, speech, or mind (see footnote 107, p.42). 2) As the fourth aggregate of clinging (here), it refers to all the mental factors (except the two mental

(Please see further next page.)

[5] **regards consciousness** *(viññāṇa)* **as self, or self as having consciousness, or consciousness as in self, or self as in consciousness.**

Here, The Buddha explained how the uneducated ordinary person regards the five aggregates.

Each of the five aggregates may in four ways be regarded somehow as self. That gives twenty types of identity view *(sakkāya diṭṭhi)*, the wrong view of identity.

SIMILES ON THE IDENTITY VIEW

The uneducated ordinary person has four types of identity view based on, for example, materiality:[47]

1) One regards materiality as self: one thinks one's self and one's materiality are identical.

   We can compare it to a candle's light and a candle's flame: they are identical. The light is the flame and the flame is the light. In the same way, one may think one's self is one's materiality and one's materiality is one's self. Just as a candle's light and flame are identical, so may one think one's materiality and self are identical.

2) One regards self as possessing materiality: one thinks one's self and one's materiality are different, because one thinks one's self is one's mentality.

   One thinks one's mental aggregates of feeling, perception, formations and consciousness are one's self, and that they possess materiality. One may think one of them is self, or several of them, or all of them.

   We can compare it to a tree and its shadow: they are different. A tree possesses a shadow: the tree is one thing; its shadow is another. In the same way, one may think one's self is one thing and one's materiality is another. Just as a tree possesses a shadow, so may one think one's self (mentality) possesses materiality.

3) One regards materiality as contained in self: one thinks one's materiality is inside one's self, which one thinks is one's mentality.

   We can compare it to the smell of a flower. The smell is in the flower. In the same way, one may think one's materiality is inside one's self (mentality).

4) One regards self as contained in materiality: one thinks one's self is inside one's materiality, and one thinks one's mentality is one's self.

   We can compare it to a box where there is a ruby. The ruby is inside the box. In the same way, one may think one's self (mentality) is inside one's materiality.

These four similes (1) the candle light and flame, 2) the tree and its shadow, 3) the flower and its smell, 4) the box and the ruby) describe the four types of identity view *(sakkāya·diṭṭhi)* based on the materiality aggregate. For each of the four mental aggregates (feeling, perception, formations, and consciousness) there are a similar four types of identity view, which can be explained in the same way. In this way, the five aggregates are each the basis for four types of identity view: that gives altogether twenty types of identity view.

---

factors feeling and perception) associated with any kind of consciousness (resultant-, functional-, or kamma consciousness): formations (See footnote 433, p.157.). In other contexts, the term has yet other meanings.

[47] The similes have been taken from DhSA.iii.1007 *'Tika·Nikkhepa·Kaṇḍaṁ'* ('Section on Summary of the Threes') E.456-457.

The Twenty Types of Identity View

Let us summarize them all. In one case,

1) one regards self as identical to materiality.

In seven cases, one regards self as identical to mentality, that is:

1) One regards self as possessing materiality.
2) One regards materiality as contained in self.
3) One regards self as contained in materiality.
4) One regards feeling as self.
5) One regards perception as self.
6) One regards formations as self.
7) One regards consciousness as self.

In twelve cases, one regards self as identical to both mentality and materiality, that is:

1) One regards self as possessing feeling.
2) One regards feeling as contained in self.
3) One regards self as contained in feeling.
4) One regards self as possessing perception.
5) One regards perception as contained in self.
6) One regards self as contained in perception.
7) One regards self as possessing formations.
8) One regards formations as contained in self.
9) One regards self as contained in formations.
10) One regards self as possessing consciousness.
11) One regards consciousness as contained in self.
12) One regards self as contained in consciousness.

Annihilation View

In five cases, where one regards self as directly identical to either materiality, feeling, perception, formations, or consciousness, it is a manifestation of the annihilation view *(uccheda·diṭṭhi)*;[48] the wrong view that when one dies, one's self is annihilated.

In the *'Brahma·Jāla·Suttaṁ'* ('The Supreme-Net Sutta'), The Buddha explains such an annihilation view:[49]

Here, bhikkhus, some ascetic or Brahmin thus saying holds this view: 'Since in fact, Sir, this self is material, of the four great essentials composed, the product of mother and father, at the break-up of the body, it is annihilated and perishes, and does not exist after death.'

---

[48] ANNIHILATION VIEW: with this view, one believes the self is annihilated at death. It is not to be equated with nihilism/nihilistic view, because in one extreme, nihilism denies all reality, all objective truths; in another extreme, it denies merely any metaphysical reality; and in its tamest form it denies any objective morality and order, advocating only the positivism of modern science (Latin *nihil* = nothing). The annihilation view differs, however, in that it asserts the reality of a material self that is annihilated. See next footnote.

[49] In D.i.1 *'Brahma·Jāla·Suttaṁ'* ('The Supreme-Net Sutta'), The Buddha explains also that there are seven annihilation views: 'When those ascetics and Brahmins who are annihilationists declare on seven grounds the annihilation, destruction and extermination of an existing being, that too is merely the feeling, of those who do not know and do not see; [it is] the anxiety and contortion of those possessed of craving.'

This view arises because one has not discerned ultimate materiality *(paramattha-·rūpa)* and ultimate mentality *(paramattha·nāma)*.[50] Therefore, one does not know that when an aggregate ceases, it is followed by the arising of a new aggregate: wrongly one thinks that when an aggregate ceases, it ceases completely without remainder. The annihilation view arises also because one has not discerned the workings of dependent origination: one does not know that the aggregates arise dependent on past kamma.[35]

ETERNITY VIEW

In the remaining fifteen cases (where one regards self as possessing mentality or materiality, self as containing mentality or materiality, or self as contained in materiality or mentality), it is a manifestation of the eternity view *(sassata diṭṭhi)*: the wrong view that when one dies, one's self lives on into eternity.

Again in the *'Brahma·Jāla·Suttaṁ'* ('The Supreme-Net Sutta'), The Buddha explains how some ascetic or Brahmin is able to develop sufficient concentration as to see many hundreds of thousands of past lives, and on that basis he declares an eternity view:[51]

He says: 'The self and the world are eternal, barren, like a mountain peak, set firmly as a post. These beings rush on and run about, pass away and arise again, but this remains eternally.'[36]

To believe that the self and the world are **barren** *(vañjha)* is to deny that kamma produces a result: for example, to deny that development of jhāna can produce rebirth in the Brahma world.[52]

This view arises also because one has not discerned ultimate materiality *(paramattha·rūpa)* and ultimate mentality *(paramattha·nāma)*. Therefore, even though one regards, for example, materiality as self, one does still not give up the perception of permanence *(nicca·saññā)*. Why? Because one confuses the materiality of one's meditation subject with the mind-made image of it that arises in the mind:[53] one thinks they are the same thing, and one has not seen that they both arise and perish. In the same way, because one has failed to see that feelings, perceptions, formations, or consciousnesses arise and perish, one may think one of them (or several of them) is permanent.[37]

All twenty views of self are obstructions on the Noble Path. But all twenty types of identity view are destroyed when one attains the First Noble Path, the Noble Path of Stream Entry *(Sot·Āpatti Magga)*. Until then, identity view may still arise.

---

[50] The commentary to 'The Clog-Bound Sutta' explains how the twenty views of self are either the annihilation view or eternity view; the subcommentary gives the details.

[51] In D.i.1 *'Brahma·Jāla·Suttaṁ'* ('The Supreme-Net Sutta'), The Buddha explains also that there are four ways in which the eternity view comes to be: 'When those ascetics and Brahmins who are eternalists declare on four grounds the eternity of the self and the world, that is merely the feeling, of those who do not know and do not see; [it is] the anxiety and contortion of those possessed of craving.'

[52] BARREN: *(vañjha)* DA.i.1 explains that it refers to being unable to produce fruit/children, and jhāna being unable to produce rebirth.

[53] The Subcommentary gives as example the material kasiṇa-circle and learning sign *(uggaha·nimitta)* or counterpart sign *(paṭibhāga·nimitta)* that has arisen in the yogi's mind: one is temperature-born materiality *(utuja·rūpa)*, the other is consciousness-born materiality *(citta·ja·rūpa)*.

These twenty types of identity view are all wrong view, and they give rise to further wrong views. The wrong views that the identity view gives rise to are, for example, three views that deny kamma and its results:

1) The inefficacy view *(akiriya·diṭṭhi)*: it denies the action of unwholesome and wholesome kammas.
2) The rootlessness view *(ahetuka·diṭṭhi)*: it denies the root of results.
3) The non-existence view *(n·atthika·diṭṭhi)*: it denies the result of any cause.

These three views all in some way deny the workings of kamma and its result. We shall explain them later, when we discuss the weighty kammas *(garuka·kamma)*.[54]

HE MERELY GOES ROUND THE FIVE AGGREGATES

Having explained how the uneducated ordinary person's identity view *(sakkāya-·diṭṭhi)* manifests in twenty ways, The Buddha explains the result of such a view:

[1] **He goes round and circles round merely materiality,**
[2] **goes round and circles round merely feeling,**
[3] **goes round and circles round merely perception,**
[4] **goes round and circles round merely formations,**
[5] **goes round and circles round merely consciousness.**

[1] **He going round and circling round materiality,**
[2] **going round and circling round feeling,**
[3] **going round and circling round perception,**
[4] **going round and circling round formations,**
[5] **going round and circling round consciousness,**

[1] **he is not released from materiality,**
[2] **he is not released from feeling,**
[3] **he is not released from perception,**
[4] **he is not released from formations,**
[5] **he is not released from consciousness.**

He is not released from birth, from ageing&death, from sorrow, from lamentation, from pain, from displeasure, and from despair.

'He is not released from suffering,' I declare.

The dog is bound with a clog, and bound close to a strong post or pillar, so it is not released, and cannot run away. In the same way, an uneducated ordinary person *(assutavā puthu·jjano)* has much ignorance and craving, and clings to the wrong view of identity: he is in other words bound close by those three factors. Being bound in that way, he is not released, and cannot escape from the five aggregates, from the round of rebirth: he clings to the five aggregates. That is why they are called the five clinging-aggregates *(pañc·upādāna·kkhandha)*.

The wrong view of identity is like the clog that hangs by the neck of the uneducated ordinary person. Craving is like the rope that binds him to the strong post or pillar. The five clinging-aggregates are like the post or pillar. The wrong view of identity, craving, and ignorance cover the uneducated ordinary person's eye of wisdom. Because of this blindness, the uneducated ordinary person is unable to see things according to reality *(yathā·bhūta)*; unable to see ultimate truth; unable to see ultimate materiality and ultimate mentality.[55] Being in that way unable to see things according to reality, the uneducated ordinary person is unable to see that

[54] The Buddha's descriptions of these three views are given at 'The Three Views that Deny the Workings of Kamma', p.171.
[55] ULTIMATE TRUTH: see quotation and discussion, p.2.

they are impermanent*(anicca)*, suffering*(dukkha)*, and non-self*(an·atta)*. This ignorance, and its associated craving is why she or he commits unwholesome and wholesome actions through body, speech and mind. Such actions are called kamma. So long as there is ignorance and craving, the kammic potency of one of those actions will mature at her or his death, to produce the rebirth-linking consciousness*(paṭisandhi·citta)* of her or his next life. When there is a rebirth-linking consciousness again, there will also be disease again, old age again, and death again, and there will also be sorrow again, lamentation again, pain again, displeasure again, and despair again. That way the uneducated ordinary person is not released from suffering, from the round of rebirth.[38]

WISHING FOR REBIRTH

Let us take a practical, everyday example of the identity view in operation. Say, for example, a woman or man offers a lit candle to The Buddha image with the wish to become a bhikkhu in the next life. What they wish for does not exist: there is no bhikkhu, only materiality and mentality. If they regard the five aggregates*(pañca·kkhandha)* as a bhikkhu, it is a manifestation of ignorance*(avijjā)*. Their attachment to life as a bhikkhu is a manifestation of craving*(taṇhā)*. As the craving and attachment accumulate, they become clinging*(upādāna)*. In other words, dependent on ignorance, craving, and clinging, the woman or man offers the lit candle to The Buddha image. The offering is a wholesome action*(kusala kamma)*, a volitional formation*(saṅkhāra)* with kammic potency: a formation of kamma. There are altogether five causes for this formation of kamma: ignorance, craving, clinging, volitional formations, and the kammic potency.

If, however, they practise discernment of mentality*(nāma kammaṭṭhāna)*, they may see that as they offered the lit candle to The Buddha image, there were only thirty-four mental phenomena: as soon as they arose, they perished. No formation is permanent. But there remained the potency by which the wholesome kamma is able to mature and produce a result.[56] If it matures, it may, according to their wish, produce the five aggregates that are a bhikkhu's life. The potency that can

[56] THERE REMAINED THE POTENCY: this does not mean the kamma leaves an imprint or trace in the life continuum, depositing a 'something'. The potency of kamma does not as such 'underlie' the continuity of mentality-materiality. Owing to certain conditions, the individual kamma matures, and only at that moment does the potency of that kamma underlie the continuity of mentality-materiality as an actual, working force. (See also footnote 5, p.1, and 'Kammic Potency', p.375.) The Buddha makes this kind of distinction when He explains that the tune of a lute is not waiting inside the lute, but arises owing to conditions: the physical components of the lute and the musician's playing on it (S.IV.I.xix.9 *'Vīṇ·Opama·Suttaṁ'* ('The Lute-Simile Sutta')). And VsM.xx.723 *'Magg·Āmagga·Ñāṇa-·Dassana·Visuddhi·Niddeso'* ('Exposition of the Path&Non-Path Knowledge&Vision Purification') PP.xx.96 explains also: '...there is no heap or store of unarisen mentality-materiality prior to its arising. When it arises, it does not come from any heap or store, and when it ceases, it does not go in any direction. There is nowhere any depository in the way of a heap or store or hoard of what has ceased. But just as there is no store (prior to its arising) of the sound that arises when a lute is played, nor does it come from any store when it arises, nor does it go in any direction when it ceases, nor does it persist as a store when it has ceased. But, on the contrary, not having been, it is brought into being owing to the lute, the lute's neck, and the man's appropriate effort, and having been, it vanishes. So too all material and immaterial states, not having been, are brought into being; having been, they vanish.' See also 'Where Does the Arahant Go?', p.351.

do such a thing is called the kammic potency*(kamma·satti)*.[57] And so long as ignorance, craving, clinging, and volitional formations exist, so does the round of rebirth continue, and the uneducated ordinary person is not released from suffering.

THE EDUCATED NOBLE DISCIPLE

Having explained the uneducated ordinary person, and such a person's twenty types of identity view, The Buddha then speaks of

The educated Noble Disciple, who sees Noble Ones, who is in their Noble Dhamma skilled, who is in the Noble Dhamma disciplined, who sees True Men, who is in the True Men's Dhamma skilled, who is in the True Men's Dhamma disciplined.

TWO TYPES OF NOBLE DISCIPLE

There are two types of **Noble Disciple***(Ariya·Sāvaka)*:[58]

1) A disciple of The Buddha, the Noble One.[59]
2) A disciple who is a Noble Individual*(Ariya·Puggala)*.

Here in the *'Gaddula·Baddha'* sutta, The Buddha means a disciple who is a Noble Individual.

EIGHT NOBLE INDIVIDUALS

There are eight Noble Individuals:[60/39]

1) The one entered upon realization of the Stream-Entry Fruition*(Sot·Āpatti·Phala·sacchi·kiriyāya paṭipanna)*.
2) The Stream Enterer*(Sot·Āpanna)*.
3) The one entered upon realization of the Once-Return Fruition*(Sakad·Āgāmi·phala·sacchi·kiriyāya paṭipanna)*.
4) The Once Returner*(Sakad·Āgāmī)*.
5) The one entered upon realization of the Non-Return Fruition*(An·Āgāmi·phala·sacchi·kiriyāya paṭipanna)*.
6) The Non-Returner*(An·Āgāmī)*.
7) The one entered upon realization of the Arahant Fruition*(Arahatta·phala·sacchi·kiriyāya paṭipanna)*.
8) The Arahant*(Arahā)*.

Each of the first seven types of Noble Individual is also called a **trainee***(sekha)*, because they have undertaken the threefold training: morality (precepts), concentration (jhāna), and wisdom (insight*(vipassanā)*).[40] The Arahant, however, is

---

[57] *Paṭṭhāna(Causal Relations)*.I. *'Kusala·Ttika'* ('Wholesome Triads')

[58] NOBLE DISCIPLE: this refers only to a disciple of The Buddha, the Noble One. Generally speaking, it may include a disciple who is not a Noble Individual. In, for example, Iti.III.iv.3 *'Deva·Sadda·Suttaṁ'* ('The Deva-Sound Sutta'), The Buddha uses Noble Disciple *(Ariya·Sāvaka)* to refer also to the bhikkhu who has undertaken the threefold training (morality*(sīla)*, concentration*(samādhi)*, and wisdom*(paññā)*), but has not yet become a Noble Individual. Such a person is in the commentaries referred to as the good, ordinary person*(kalyāna·puthu·jjana)*.

[59] For the determining qualities of a devotee*(upāsikā/upāsaka)*, see endnote 104, p.239.

[60] The one entered upon realization of one of the four Frutions refers to the person in whom the Path-consciousness has arisen: the consciousness immediately preceding the Fruition consciousness.

called a **non-trainee***(a·sekha)*,[41] meaning an adept, because he has completed the training; done what had to be done.[61]

The Educated Noble Disciple Trainee

Thus, in the *'Gaddula·Baddha'* sutta, when The Buddha speaks of an educated Noble Disciple*(sutavā Ariya·Sāvako)*, He means one of the seven trainees, or an Arahant.

We may describe the educated Noble Disciple as simply one who possesses those things that an uneducated ordinary person does not possess. The educated Noble Disciple is thus not one of the many, but one of the very few,[62] and is educated in and knowledgeable of both theory and practice of the Dhamma. In other words, the educated Noble Disciple understands the Four Noble Truths.[42]

Let us take some examples of how the educated Noble Disciple trainee differs from the uneducated ordinary person:[63]

- The educated, Noble Disciple trainee possesses conscience and shame;[64] is conscientious of misconduct through body, speech, and mind, and ashamed of it; is conscientiousness not to do wrong, and ashamed of it.[43]
- The educated, Noble Disciple trainee arouses energy to remove thoughts of sensual desire, ill-will, and cruelty.[44]
- The educated, Noble Disciple trainee restrains the eye, ear, nose, tongue, body, and mind, by attending to the four foundations of mindfulness, which is the same as to say samatha or vipassanā.[45]
- The educated, Noble Disciple trainee does not find pleasure in the five sensual lines*(kāma·guṇa)*: does not find pleasure in sights through the eye, sounds through the ear, odours through the nose, tastes through the tongue, and touches through the body.[46/47]
- The educated, Noble Disciple trainee who is a bhikkhu is restrained by scrupulous observance of the bhikkhu *Pāṭimokkha* rule. The educated Noble Disciple who is a layperson is restrained by scrupulous observance of the five precepts. That means she or he does not kill, does not steal, does not engage in sexual misconduct, does not tell lies, does not drink things like beer and wine. The educated Noble Disciple will also once a week observe the eight precepts, she or he may even observe them all the time, likewise the ten precepts. In that case, she or he observes does not eat after noon, etc.[65]
- The educated, Noble Disciple trainee possesses Right Concentration*(Sammā·Samādhi)*, which is access concentration, or the four jhānas.[48]
- The educated, Noble Disciple trainee possesses penetrating wisdom.[66] Until the Noble Disciple becomes a Noble Individual, the wisdom is only mundane insight knowledge*(vipassanā·ñāṇa)*, which suppresses the defilements, and dis-

---

[61] The Buddha explains it, for example, at the end of the second *'Gaddula·Baddha'* sutta: see 'Done Is What Needs to Be Done', p.343.

[62] For The Buddha's explanation of how few are possessed of the eye of wisdom, see endnote 11, p.21.

[63] See also 'Stream Entry', p.336.

[64] CONSCIENCE/SHAME: see quoted analysis at 'Conscience', p.373.

[65] See quotations endnote 284, p.356.

[66] For this analysis of the Noble Disciple's wisdom, see, for example, the commentary to M.II.i.3 *'Sekha·Suttaṁ'* ('The Trainee Sutta').

cerns the arising and perishing of the five aggregates,[67]/[49] as well as their dependent origination and cessation.[50] But once she or he has become a Noble Individual, the wisdom that she or he possesses is supramundane, the Path Knowledge*(Magga·Ñāṇa)*: it takes Nibbāna as object, and eradicates defilements. Owing to that Path Knowledge, she or he does not hold the annihilation view, the eternity view[51] or the identity view.[52]

- The educated, Noble Disciple trainee possesses learning, having studied and inquired about the Texts.[53]
- The educated, Noble Disciple trainee has no scepticism about The Buddha's enlightenment, about the Dhamma, about the Sangha, about past lives, about future lives, about the present life, about other worlds, or about the law of kamma and its effect, etc.: she or he has complete faith[68] in The Buddha,[54] and looks to no other teacher.[55]
- The educated, Noble Disciple trainee is certain no longer to be reborn in the bad destinations*(duggati)*: not in the ghost world, not in the animal world, and not in any of the hells.[56]
- The educated, Noble Disciple trainee is certain to attain full enlightenment *(Sambodhi)* within seven lives: even earlier.[57]

That concludes our explanation of what The Buddha means when He speaks of the educated, Noble Disciple*(sutavā Ariya·Sāvako)*.

Does Not Regard the Five Aggregates as Self

Having explained the qualities of the educated, Noble Disciple, The Buddha then explains how such a person regards the five aggregates.

Since we now understand The Buddha's words better, let us begin again with His description of the educated, Noble Disciple:

But, bhikkhus, the educated Noble Disciple,

- **who sees Noble Ones, who is in their Noble Dhamma skilled, who is in the Noble Dhamma disciplined,**
- **who sees True Men, who is in the True Men's Dhamma skilled, who is in the True Men's Dhamma disciplined,**

[1] **does not regard materiality as self, nor self as having materiality, nor materiality as in self, nor self as in materiality;**
[2] **does not regard feeling as self, nor self as having feeling, nor feeling as in self, nor self as in feeling;**
[3] **does not regard perception as self, nor self as having perception, nor perception as in self, nor self as in perception;**
[4] **does not regard formations as self, nor self as having formations, nor formations as in self, nor self as in formations;**
[5] **does not regard consciousness as self, nor self as having consciousness, nor consciousness as in self, nor self as in consciousness.**

He Does Not Go Round the Five Aggregates

[1] **He does not go round, does not circle round, materiality;**
[2] **does not go round, does not circle round, feeling;**
[3] **does not go round, does not circle round, perception;**
[4] **does not go round, does not circle round, formations;**

---

[67] FIVE AGGREGATES: these are the objects for vipassanā. See quotation at 'Therefore, Bhikkhus, Any Whatsoever Materiality', p.320.

[68] For an analysis of faith*(saddhā)*, see 'Faith', p.374.

[5] **does not go round, does not circle round consciousness.**

[1] **He not going round, and not circling round, materiality;**
[2] **not going round, and not circling round, feeling;**
[3] **not going round, and not circling round, perception;**
[4] **not going round, and not circling round, formations;**
[5] **not going round, and not circling round, consciousness;**

[1] **he is released from materiality;**
[2] **he is released from feeling;**
[3] **he is released from perception;**
[4] **he is released from formations;**
[5] **he is released from consciousness;**

he is released from birth, from ageing&death, from sorrow, from lamentation, from pain, from displeasure, and from despair.
'He is released from suffering,' I declare.

As mentioned before, the Noble Disciple will never again be reborn either in the animal world, in the ghost world, or in any of the hells: she or he is released from the suffering of rebirth in a bad destination. The Noble Disciple who is a Non-Returner is reborn in the fine-material world, and will never again be reborn in the human or sensual deva worlds: she or he is released altogether from the suffering of rebirth in the sensual world. The Noble Disciple who is an Arahant will have done what had to be done, which means that at death, there will be no more existence of materiality, no more existence of feeling, no more existence of perception, no more existence of formations, and no more existence of consciousness: she or he will never again be reborn in any way. She or he is released altogether from the suffering of formations.[69]

What does one need to do to become an educated Noble Disciple, to be released from suffering in this way? We shall discuss that later.[70] Let us first discuss the second *'Gaddula·Baddha'* sutta.

[69] See The Buddha's explanation at the end of the second *'Gaddula·Baddha'* sutta: see 'Done Is What Needs to Be Done', p.343, and the verse p.154.
[70] This is discussed at 'The Unworking of Kamma', p.338*ff.*

ENDNOTES CHAPTER I
(SUTTA REFERENCES ETC.)

[1] The commentary to D.ii.9 *'Mahā·Sati·Paṭṭhāna·Suttaṁ'* ('The Great Mindfulness-Foundation Sutta') explains this with a verse: 'What one sees, that is not seen; What is seen, one does not see; Not seeing, bound is the fool; And, being bound, he is not released.'
[2] The Buddha explains it in, for example, S.II.I.i.2 *'Vibhaṅga·Suttaṁ'* ('The Analysis Sutta'): 'And what, bhikkhus, is ignorance? [1] Non-knowledge of suffering, [2] ... of the origin of suffering, [3] ... of the cessation of suffering, [4] ... of the path leading to the cessation of suffering.'
[3] In Iti.I.ii.4 *'Avijjā·Nīvaraṇa·Suttaṁ'* ('The Ignorance-Hindrance Sutta'), The Buddha explains: 'It is indeed by the hindrance of ignorance *(avijjā·nivaraṇa)*, bhikkhus, that mankind is obstructed and for a long time runs on and rushes about.'
[4] The Buddha explains this process in A.IV.iv.i.6 *'Kappa·Suttaṁ'* ('The Aeon Sutta'): 'When, bhikkhus, the aeon contracts [goes towards destruction]... the contracted aeon persists... the aeon expands [goes towards construction]... the expanded aeon persists, then is it not easy to calculate: so many years, or so many hundreds of years, or so many thousands of years, or so many hundreds of thousands of years. These then, bhikkhus, are the four incalculable aeons.' He explains the duration of such an aeon in, e.g. S.II.IV.i.5 *'Pabbata·Suttaṁ'* ('The Mountain Sutta'): 'Suppose, bhikkhu, there was a great stone mountain a *yojana* [PED: seven miles] long, a *yojana* wide, and a *yojana* high, without holes or crevices: one solid mass of rock. At the end of every hundred years, a man would stroke it once with a piece of Kāsi cloth [very fine cotton]. That great stone mountain might by this effort be worn away and done away with, but the aeon would still not have come to an end. That long is an aeon, bhikkhu. That long, bhikkhu, are the aeons: we have run on not [only] one aeon, we have run on not [only] one hundred aeons, we have run on not [only] one thousand aeons, we have run on not [only] a hundred thousand aeons. Why is that? Because inconceivable, bhikkhu, is the beginning of this round of rebirth.' He explains the reconstruction of the lower Brahma worlds at the beginning of a new aeon in D.i.1 *'Brahma·Jāla·Suttaṁ'* ('The Supreme-Net Sutta'). And He explains the evolution of human beings and their society in D.iii.4 *'Agg·Añña·Suttaṁ'* ('The Beginnings-Knowledge Sutta').
[5] In M.I.iii.8 *'Mahā·Hatthi·Padopama·Suttaṁ'* ('The Great Elephant's-Footprint Sutta'), the Venerable Sāriputta mentions the destruction of 'villages, towns, cities, regions and countries' by the water, fire, and wind elements.
[6] The details are not from 'The Clog-Bound Sutta', but from A.VII.vii.2 *'Satta·Sūriya·Suttaṁ'* ('The Seven-Suns Sutta'), where The Buddha gives a detailed explanation of the world system's destruction by fire. Also, in for example D.i.2 *'Sāmañña·Phala·Suttaṁ'* ('The Asceticism-Fruit Sutta'), The Buddha explains how the bhikkhu develops the direct knowledge *(abh·iññā)* that enables him to see past destructions (contractions) and reconstructions (expansions) of world systems: 'He directs, he inclines, his mind to the knowledge of recollection of past life. He recollects his manifold past life, that is to say, one birth, two births, three births, four births, five births, ten births, twenty births, thirty births, forty births, fifty births, a hundred births, a thousand births, a hundred thousand births, many contraction aeons, many expansion aeons, many contraction&expansion aeons....' Development of this knowledge and what one sees is discussed in VsM.xiii.402-410 *'Pubbe·Nivās·Ānussati·Ñāṇa·Kathā'* ('Discussion of the Past-Abodes-Recollection Knowledge') PP.xiii.34-71, and VsMT, with reference to 'The Seven-Suns Sutta', as well as other details.
[7] In e.g. D.i.1 *'Brahma·Jāla·Suttaṁ'* ('The Supreme-Net Sutta'), The Buddha explains that at the destruction of the world system, most beings are reborn in the world of refulgent devas *(ābhassara·devā)*, which is the Brahma-world that corresponds to the second jhāna.

[8] The Buddha explains it in A.VII.vii.2 *'Satta·Sūriya·Suttaṁ'* ('The Seven-Suns Sutta'): 'For many years, for many hundred years, for many thousand years, for many hundred thousand years, there is no rain.'

[9] In M.III.i.2 *'Pañca·Ttaya·Suttaṁ'* ('The Five&Three Sutta'), The Buddha discusses all the possible wrong views about the future, and to describe those ascetics and Brahmins who declare the annihilation view, He uses the same simile of the clog-bound dog rushing round a post.

[10] In M.I.iv.3 *'Mahā·Gopālaka·Suttaṁ'* ('The Great Cowherd Sutta'), The Buddha explains eleven qualities by which 'a bhikkhu is incapable of growth, increase, and fulfilment in this Dhamma and Vinaya.' The sixth is: 'Here, a bhikkhu does not go from time to time to those bhikkhus of wide learning, versed in the doctrine, masters of the Dhamma, masters of the Vinaya, masters of the Matrices [the bhikkhu/bhikkhunī rule]. And he does not enquire and ask questions of them thus: "How is this, Venerable Sir? What is the meaning of this?" Those venerable ones the unrevealed [they] do not reveal, the unclear [they] do not make clear, the many doubt-based things the doubt [they] do not dispel.'

[11] In, for example, S.V.XII.vii.3 *'Paññā·Suttaṁ'* ('The Wisdom Sutta'), The Buddha puts some grains of soil on his fingernail and compares it to the planet earth. Using that comparison as a simile, He says: 'So too, bhikkhus, trifling are those beings who possess the noble eye of wisdom. But legion are the beings who are possessed of ignorance, and are confused. What is the reason? They have not seen, bhikkhus, the Four Noble Truths.' The commentary explains that the wisdom-eye is mundane/supramundane insight *(vipassanā)*.

[12] In M.I.iv.3 *'Mahā·Gopālaka·Suttaṁ'* ('The Great Cowherd Sutta'), The Buddha explains eleven qualities by which 'a bhikkhu is incapable of growth, increase and fulfilment in this Dhamma and Vinaya.' The seventh is: 'Here, when the Dhamma and Vinaya proclaimed by the Tathāgata is being taught, a bhikkhu does not gain enthusiasm for the meaning, does not gain enthusiasm for the Dhamma, does not gain Dhamma-related joy.'

[13] The Buddha analyses all the wrong views that are taught, in, for example, D.i.1 *'Brahma·Jāla·Suttaṁ'* ('The Supreme-Net Sutta'): 'When those ascetics and Brahmins who are speculators about the past... about the future... about the past and future proclaim various views on the past and future, concerning the past and future (that upon sixty-two premises have been arrived at by inclination), it is merely the sensation of those who do not know and do not see; [it is] the anxiety and contortion of those possessed of craving.'

[14] In M.III.iii.9 *'Bāla·Paṇḍita·Suttaṁ'* ('The Fool&Sage Sutta'), The Buddha explains the present results of bodily-, verbal, and mental bad/good conduct (see 'The Courses of Kamma', p.119), as well as their resultant rebirths: rebirth in hell, the animal world, and a low-class human family; in the sensual heavens and a high-class human family. In M.III.iii.10 *'Deva·Dūta·Suttaṁ'* ('The Divine-Messenger Sutta'), He describes the horrific sufferings of beings in the various hells. And He concludes: 'I tell you this, bhikkhus, not as something I heard from another ascetic or Brahmin. I tell you this as something that I have actually known, seen, and discovered for Myself.' See also quotation, endnote 39, p.25.

[15] The Buddha explains the five destinations in, for example, M.I.ii.2 *'Mahā·Sīha·Nāda·Suttaṁ'* ('The Great Lion's-Roar Sutta'): 'There are, Sāriputta, these five destinations. What five? Hell, the animal world, the ghost world, human beings, devas.' And in S.V.XII.vii.1 *'Aññatra·Suttaṁ'* ('The "Other" Sutta'), He puts some grains of soil on his fingernail and compares it to the planet earth, and using that comparison as a simile, He explains: 'Trifling are the beings who (when they pass away as human beings) are reborn as human beings. But legion are the beings who (when they pass away as human beings) are reborn other than among human beings. What is the reason? They have not seen, bhikkhus, the Four Noble Truths.'

[16] The Buddha explains it in, for example, S.IV.I.xviii.2 *'Dutiya·Samudda·Sutta'* ('The Second Ocean Sutta'): 'There are, bhikkhus, sights cognizable by the eye [sounds cognizable by the ear, odours by the nose, flavours by the tongue, tangibles by the body] that are desirable, lovely, agreeable, pleasing, sensually enticing, tantalizing. This is called the ocean in the Noble One's Discipline. Here this world with its devas, Māras, and Brahmas, this generation with its ascetics and Brahmins, its devas and humans, for the most part is submerged, has become like a tangled skein, like a knotted ball of thread, like matted reeds and rushes, and cannot pass beyond the plane of misery, the bad destinations, the nether world, the round of rebirth.'

[17] The Buddha explains it in, for example, M.II.ii.4 *'Mahā·Mālukyya·Suttaṁ'* ('The Great Mālukyya Sutta'): 'Here, Ānanda, an uneducated ordinary person... abides with a mind obsessed and enslaved by scepticism... by adherence to rule&rite... by sensual lust... by ill-will....'

[18] SCEPTICISM: The Buddha explains it in, for example, M.I.ii.6 *'Ceto·Khila·Suttaṁ'* ('The Mental-Barrenness Sutta'): 'That any bhikkhu, bhikkhus, who has not abandoned five mental barrennesses... should come to growth, increase, and fulfilment in this Dhamma-Vinaya: that is impossible.... [1] Here, a bhikkhu is doubtful, sceptical, undecided, and uncertain about the Teacher... [2] ...the Dhamma ... [3] ...the Sangha... [4] ...the training... and thus his mind does not incline to ardour, devotion, perseverance, and striving.... [5] ...a bhikkhu is angry and displeased with his companions in the holy life, resentful, and callous towards them....' The Buddha then explains the bhikkhu who can come to growth, increase and fulfilment in the Dhamma-Vinaya, because he is not doubtful, not sceptical, etc. about the same objects. And in, for example, M.I.i.2 *'Sabb-·Āsava·Suttaṁ'* ('The All-Taints Sutta'), He explains the scepticism that arises owing to unwise attention *(ayoniso manasikāra)*: 'He in this way attends unwisely: "Was I, I wonder now, really in the past?... not in the past? What... How... What having been, I wonder now, was I in the past?"... "Shall I become... in the future?... not in the future?... What... How... What having been, I wonder now, shall I become in the future?" Or else there is internal talking about manner: "Am I, I wonder, now? ...not now? What... How... This being, I wonder, where has it come from? This being, I wonder, where will it go?"' The Buddha then explains that the Noble Disciple does not entertain these doubts, but attends only to the Four Noble Truths. And in, for example, the M.I.iv.8 *'Mahā·Taṇhā·Saṅkhaya·Suttaṁ'* ('The Great Craving-Destruction Sutta'), He explains that this scepticism about past, future and present disappears with the discernment of dependent origination in regular and negative order.

[19] The Buddha explains the ordinary person's separateness from Noble Ones in, for example, *'Paṭipanna·Suttaṁ'* ('The "Faring" Sutta'): see endnote 39, p.25.

[20] In S.V.XII.iii.8'Loka·Suttaṁ' ('The World Sutta'), The Buddha explains that He is the Noble One: 'In this world with its devas, with its Māras, with its Brahmas, in this generation with its ascetics and Brahmins, devas and men, The Tathāgata is the Noble One *(Tathāgato Ariyo)*.'

[21] In S.V.XII.vii/viii *'Sacca·Saṁyutta'* ('Truth Section') The Buddha puts some grains of soil on his fingernail and compares it to the planet earth. Using that comparison as a simile, He explains: 'So too, bhikkhus, trifling are the beings who abstain from beer&-wine liquor, which is a foundation for carelessness. But legion are the beings who do not abstain from beer&wine liquor, which is a foundation for carelessness.... from killing.... stealing sexual misconduct.... lies.... slander.... abuse.... who do not abstain from prattle. What is the reason? They have not seen, bhikkhus, the Four Noble Truths.' See also endnote 32, p.24.

[22] FACULTY RESTRAINT: see the Venerable Ānanda's explanation endnote 45, p.26.

[23] The Buddha explains ignorance (non-knowledge) of the Four Noble Truths in, for example, S.V.XII.iii.1 *'Paṭhama·Koṭigāma·Suttaṁ'* ('The First Koṭigama Sutta'): 'The Four, bhikkhus, Noble Truths not having been understood, not having been penetrated, there

has thus for a extensively drawn-out time been this running on and rushing about for me and you.' See also endnotes 11, p.21, 15, p.21, and 21, p.22.

[24] The Buddha explains such reflection in, for example, M.I.i.2 *'Sabb·Āsava·Suttaṁ'* ('The All-Taints Sutta'): 'Here a bhikkhu, reflecting wisely, the robe uses only for counteracting cold... heat; [only] for counteracting gadflies, mosquitoes, wind, heat of the sun, contact with creeping things; only for the purpose of covering the pudenda.' And there is also a similar type of reflection with regard to use of food, dwelling, and medicine.

[25] The commentary refers to The Buddha's explanation in M.I.i.2 *'Sabb·Āsava·Suttaṁ'* ('The All-Taints Sutta'): 'Here a bhikkhu, reflecting wisely, bears cold and heat, hunger and thirst, and contact with gadflies, mosquitoes, wind, the sun, and creeping things; he endures ill-spoken, unwelcome words, and arisen physical feelings that are painful, racking, sharp, piercing, disagreeable, distressing, and menacing to life.'

[26] The commentary refers to The Buddha's explanation in M.I.i.2 *'Sabb·Āsava·Suttaṁ'* ('The All-Taints Sutta'): 'Here a bhikkhu, reflecting wisely, does not tolerate an arisen thought of sensual desire: he abandons it, removes it, does away with it, and annihilates it.' This is what The Buddha calls Right Effort *(Sammā·Padhāna)*: 'And what, bhikkhus, is Right Effort? Here, bhikkhus, a bhikkhu rouses his will, makes an effort, stirs up energy, exerts his mind, and strives to prevent the arising of unarisen evil unwholesome states; he rouses his will... to overcome evil unwholesome states that have arisen; he rouses his will ... to produce unarisen wholesome mental states; he rouses his will to maintain wholesome mental states that have arisen, not to let them fade away, to bring them to greater growth, to the full perfection of development. This is called Right Effort.' (D.ii.9 *'Mahā·Sati·Paṭṭhāna·Suttaṁ'* ('The Great Mindfulness-Foundation Sutta')) For a briefer version, see quotations, endnotes 44, p.25, and 178, p.249.

[27] The Buddha explains it in, for example, M.III.v.7 *'Mahā·Saḷ·Āyatanika·Suttaṁ'* ('The Great Sixfold-Base Sutta'): 'Those things that by direct knowledge should be abandoned, those things by direct knowledge he abandons.'

[28] The Buddha explains the knowledge of defining mentality-materiality in, for example, D.ii.9 *'Mahā·Sati·Paṭṭhāna·Suttaṁ'* ('The Great Mindfulness-Foundation Sutta'): 'Here, bhikkhus, a bhikkhu understands: "Such is materiality... such is feeling... such is perception... such are formations... such is consciousness."' See also quotation under 'The Lion's Roar', p.39.

[29] The Buddha explains the Cause-Aapprehending Knowledge in, for example, D.ii.9 *'Mahā·Sati·Paṭṭhāna·Suttaṁ'* ('The Great Mindfulness-Foundation Sutta'): 'Here, bhikkhus, a bhikkhu understands: "Such is materiality, such is its origin... feeling, such is its origin... perception, such is its origin... formations, such is their origin... consciousness, such is its origin...."' See also quotation under 'The Lion's Roar', p.39.

[30] The Buddha explains it in, for example, S.III.I.xiii.1 *'Samudaya·Dhamma·Suttaṁ'* ('The Arising-Phenomenon Sutta'): 'Here, bhikkhu, the uneducated ordinary person according to reality does not understand the phenomenon of materiality's arising as "the phenomenon of materiality's arising".... of materiality's perishing as "the phenomenon of materiality's perishing"... of materiality's arising and perishing as "the phenomenon of materiality's arising and perishing"... feeling's... perception's... formations'... consciousness's... arising... perishing... arising and perishing." This is called, bhikkhu, ignorance, and in this way is there the disposition of ignorance.' He then says the opposite for the educated, Noble Disciple. See also quotation at 'Therefore, Bhikkhus, Any Whatsoever Materiality', p.320, and endnotes 49, p.27, and 50, p.27.

[31] The Buddha explains how one suppresses the five hindrances with concentration in, for example, M.I.iii.7 *'Cūḷa·Hatthi·Pad·Opama·Suttaṁ'* ('The Small Elephant's-Footprint Simile Sutta'): 'Abandoning covetousness [a synonym for sensual desire]... abandoning ill-will... abandoning sloth&torpor... abandoning restlessness&remorse... abandoning scepticism... he purifies his mind of scepticism. Having thus abandoned these five hindrances, defilements of the mind that weaken wisdom, quite secluded from sensual

pleasures, secluded from unwholesome states, he enters and abides upon the first jhāna... This, Brahmin, is called a footprint of the Exalted One.'

[32] The Venerable Ānanda explains some of the defilements that have been eradicated with Stream Entry in S.V.XI.ii.3 *'Ānanda·Tthera·Suttaṁ'* ('The Ānanda-Elder Sutta'): 'One does not have, friend, that displeasure regarding The Buddha which the uneducated ordinary person has, because of which he with the breakup of the body, after death, is reborn in the plane of misery, in a bad destination, in the nether world, in hell .... One does not have that displeasure regarding the Dhamma which the uneducated ordinary person has... does not have that displeasure regarding the Sangha which the uneducated ordinary person has... and one has that perfect confidence in The Buddha which the educated, Noble Disciple has, because of which he, with the breakup of the body, after death is reborn in a good destination, in a heavenly world... Dhamma... Sangha.... One does not have, friend, that immorality [not keeping the five precepts] which the uneducated ordinary person has .... And one has those virtues dear to the Noble Ones which the educated, Noble Disciple has....' See also quotations, endnote 54, p.28.

[33] The Buddha explains subsidence of defilements in, for example, S.IV.II.ii.1 *'Raho·Gata·Suttaṁ'* ('The "Solitude-Gone" Sutta'): 'In one whose taints are destroyed, lust has subsided, hatred has subsided, delusion has subsided.'

[34] The Buddha explains how there is escape from all formations (the formed), to Nibbāna (the Unformed) in U.viii.3 *'Tatiya·Nibbāna·Paṭisaṁyutta·Suttaṁ'* ('The Third Sutta of the Nibbāna Section'): '...since there is an Unborn, Ungrown, Unmade, Unformed, so is escape possible from this born, this grown, this made, this formed.' See also quotation endnote 270, p.354 and 'The Two Types of Parinibbāna', p.343.

[35] In S.II.I.iv.5 *'Avijjā·Paccaya·Suttaṁ'* ('The Ignorance-Cause Sutta'), The Buddha explains that if one holds the annihilation view, there is no holy life: 'The self *(jīva)* is the body, bhikkhus, when there is this view, there is not the holy life.' The commentary explains that practice of the holy life is practice of the Noble Path, which is aimed at annihilation of the going on [annihilation of continued rebirth]; since with the annihilation view the going on is annihilated anyway, practice of the Noble Path would be pointless.

[36] The Buddha explains how identification with the five aggregates gives rise to the eternity view in S.III.III.i.3 *'So·Attā·Suttaṁ'* ('The This-Is-Self Sutta'): 'When there is [materiality/ feeling/perception/formations] consciousness, bhikkhus, by clinging to... adhering to [materiality/feeling/ perception/formations] consciousness, such a view as this [eternity view] arises: "This is the self, this is the world; having passed away, I shall be this: a permanent, stable, eternal, unchangeable entity."

[37] In S.II.I.iv.5 *'Avijjā·Paccaya·Suttaṁ'* ('The Ignorance-Cause Sutta'), The Buddha explains that if one holds the eternity view, there is no holy life: 'The self *(jīva)* is other than the body, bhikkhus, when there is this view, there is not the holy life.' The commentary explains that with this view, only the body is annihilated, while the soul goes free like a bird released from a cage, which is the eternity view; practice of the holy life is practice of the Noble Path, which is aimed at annihilation of the going on [annihilation of continued rebirth]; if there were even one formation that is permanent, stable, and eternal, practice of the Noble Path would not bring about annihilation of the going on, in which case practice of the Noble Path would be pointless. The Buddha makes this point in, for example, S.III.I.x.5 *'Nakha·Sikhā·Suttaṁ'* ('The Nail-Tip Sutta').

[38] In M.III.i.2 *'Pañca·Ttaya·Suttaṁ'* ('The Five&Three Sutta'), The Buddha uses the same simile of the clog-bound dog running round the post or pillar to explain the non-escape of those who believe the self is annihilated after death. And VsM.xiv.455 *'Viññāṇa·Kkhandha·Kathā'* ('Discussion of the Consciousness Aggregate') PP.xiv.124 explains: 'After decease, there is rebirth-linking again; and after rebirth-linking, life continuum. Thus the conscious continuity of beings who hasten through the kinds of existence, destiny, station, and abode, goes on occurring without break. But when a man attains Arahantship here, it ceases with the cessation of his decease consciousness.'

[39] The Buddha explains the Noble Disciple's unshakeable faith in the Sangha of eight Noble Individuals in, for example, D.ii.3 *'Mahā·Parinibbāna·Suttaṁ'* ('The Great-Parinibbāna Sutta'): 'There is perfect faith in the Sangha: "Entered upon the good way is The Exalted One's Sangha of Disciples *(Sāvaka·Saṅgho)*; entered upon the straight way is The Exalted One's Sangha of Disciples; entered upon the true way is The Exalted One's Sangha of Disciples; entered upon the proper way is The Exalted One's Sangha of Disciples: that is to say, the four pairs of men, eight individual men. This, the Exalted One's Sangha of Disciples for gifts is right, for hospitality is right, for offerings is right, for revverential salutation is right: an incomparable field for merit in the world."' In, for example, A.VIII.II.i.9 *'Paṭhama·Puggala·Suttaṁ'* ('The First Individual Sutta'), He explains that the eight individual men are the eight listed here. And in *'Paṭipanna·Suttaṁ'* ('The "Faring" Sutta'), He explains that one possessed of the five faculties (faith, effort, mindfulness, concentration, and wisdom) is one of these eight individuals, whereas one devoid of the five faculties is an outsider who stands 'on the side of ordinary people *(bāhiro puthu·jjana·pakkhe ṭhito)*.' Then in *'Cūḷa·Sīha·Nāda·Suttaṁ'* ('The Small Lion's-Roar Sutta'), The Buddha explains that the Four Noble Individuals are found only in The Buddha's Dispensation: 'Only here, bhikkhus, is there an ascetic, here a second ascetic, here a third ascetic, here a fourth ascetic. Empty are other, contradictory teachings *(parappa·vāda)* of ascetics.' See also quotation endnote 294, p.357.

[40] The Buddha explains the bhikkhu's threefold training in, for example, A.III.II.iv.9 *'Paṭhama·Sikkhattaya·Suttaṁ'* ('The First Training Sutta'): 'Here, a bhikkhu lives morally; with the Pātimokkha-restraint restrained he lives, possessed of conduct and resort; in the slightest faults seeing fearsomeness; undertaking to train in the training precepts. This is called, bhikkhus, the higher-morality training.... a bhikkhu, quite secluded from sensuality, secluded from unwholesome states... enters upon and abides in the first jhāna... second jhāna... third jhāna... fourth jhāna. This is called, bhikkhus, the higher-mind training. A bhikkhu according to reality understands, "This is suffering"... "This is the origin of suffering"... "This is the cessation of suffering"... "This is the path leading to the cessation of suffering." This is called, bhikkhus, the higher-wisdom training.' See also 'The Trainee Sutta', summarized in in footnote 378, p.138.

[41] The Buddha uses this term in, for example, M.II.ii.5 *'Bhaddāli·Sutta'* ('The Bhaddāli Sutta'), when He speaks of the Arahant's ten factors as the factors of the non-trainee. In this classification, the uneducated ordinary person is called a neither-trainee nor non-trainee *(n'eva·sekha·n·ā·sekha)*.

[42] In S.V.XII.vi.1 *'Nakha·Sikha·Suttaṁ'* ('The Nail-Tip Sutta'), The Buddha puts some grains of soil on his fingernail and compares it to the planet earth. Using that comparison as a simile, He explains: 'So too, bhikkhus, for a Noble Disciple, an individual possessing view, who has understood, more is the suffering that has been destroyed and brought to an end, trifling is the remainder. For whoever understands "This is suffering" according to reality; understands "This is the origin of suffering" according to reality; understands "This is the cessation of suffering" according to reality; understands "This is the path leading to the cessation of suffering" according to reality, it is not to be estimated, it is not to be compared, it is not a fractional amount, the former amount of suffering that has been destroyed and brought to an end, compared, that is, with the ending after seven times [seven more lives].'

[43] The Buddha explains it in, for example, A.VII.i.4 *'Vitthata·Bala·Suttaṁ'* ('The Detailed-Power Sutta'): 'Here, bhikkhus, the Noble Disciple has conscience, he is conscientious [not to engage in] bodily misconduct, verbal misconduct, mental misconduct, conscientious [not to engage in] evil, unwholesome deeds. This is called, bhikkhus, the conscience power.... the Noble Disciple has shame, he is ashamed of bodily misconduct, verbal misconduct, mental misconduct, ashamed of evil, unwholesome deeds. This is called the shame power.'

[44] The Buddha explains it in, for example, A.VII.i.4 *'Vitthata·Bala·Suttaṁ'* ('The Detailed Power Sutta'): 'Here, bhikkhus, the Noble Disciple dwells exerting energy to abandon

unwholesome things, and to acquire wholesome things, is resolute, firm in striving, without putting aside this duty regarding wholesome things. This is called, bhikkhus, the energy power.' See also quotation endnote 26, p.23.

[45] The Venerable Ānanda explains it in M.II.i.3 *'Sekha·Suttaṁ'* ('The Trainee Sutta'): 'On seeing a sight with the eye... hearing a sound with the ear... smelling an odour with the nose... tasting a flavour with the tongue... touching a tangible with the body... cognizing a thing with the mind, the Noble Disciple does not grasp at its signs and features. Since, if he left the [eye-, ear-, nose-, tongue-, body-, and] mind faculty unguarded, evil unwholesome states of covetousness and displeasure [greed/hatred] might invade him, he practises the way of its restraint, he guards the [eye-, ear-, etc. and] mind faculty, he undertakes the restraint of the mind faculty. That is how a Noble Disciple guards the doors of his faculties.' And in S.IV.I.xix.3 *'Kumm·Opama·Suttaṁ'* ('The Tortoise-Simile Sutta'), The Buddha advises the bhikkhus to keep in their sense faculties just as the tortoise keeps its limbs inside its shell, when the jackal approaches. SA then explains that the bhikkhu by keeping his mind inside his object's shell *(ārammaṇa·kapāle)* does not give the defilements opportunity to arise. And in S.I.I.ii.7 *'Du·Kkara·Suttaṁ'* ('The Difficult-to-Do Sutta'), where The Buddha gives the same simile, the subcommentary explains that the object's shell of the bhikkhu is his resort *(gocara)*. And the bhikkhu's resort The Buddha explains in S.V.III.i.6 *'Sakuṇagghi·Suttaṁ'* ('The Hawk Sutta'): 'And what is a bhikkhu's resort *(bhikkhuno gocaro)*, his own ancestral domain? It is the four foundations of mindfulness *(cattāro satipaṭṭhāna)* [~ samatha and vipassanā].' See also the Buddha's explanation, footnote 513, p.184.

[46] The Buddha explains it in, for example, M.III.v.10 *'Indriya·Bhāvanā·Suttaṁ'* ('The Faculty-Development Sutta'): 'Here, Ānanda, when a bhikkhu sees a sight with the eye... hears a sound with the ear... smells an odour with the nose... tastes a flavour with the tongue... touches a tangible with the body... cognizes another thing with the mind, there arises in him the agreeable [pleasant feeling]... the disagreeable [unpleasant]... the agreeable-disagreeable [neutral]. He by the arisen agreeable, the arisen disagreeable and the arisen agreeable-disagreeable is bothered, ashamed, and disappointed. Thus, Ānanda, is the trainee who has entered upon the path [thus is a Noble Disciple trainee].' And in M.III.ii.5 *'Bahu·Dhātuka·Suttaṁ'* ('The Many-Elements Sutta'), He explains: 'It is impossible, it cannot happen that a person possessed of view, should treat any formation as happiness *(sukhato)*: no such thing is known. But it is possible, it can happen that a common person should treat some formation as happiness: such a thing is known.'

[47] The Non-Returner Path has destroyed all sensual desire, which is why the Non-Returner is altogether unable to enjoy sensual pleasures. The Stream-Entry Path and Once-Returner Path, however, have only weakened the desire for those grosser sensual pleasures that do not lead to rebirth in the woeful states. Hence, the Stream Enterer and Once Returner may still enjoy sensual pleasures that accord with the Dhamma *(Dhammika)*, do not violate the five precepts, and are not any of the ten courses of unwholesome kamma (see 'The Ten Unwholesome Courses of Kamma', p.119). Thus, for example, The Buddha's chief patroness Visākha was a Stream Enterer who enjoyed household pleasures, with attachment for children and grandchildren: in, for example, U.viii.8 *'Visākha·Suttaṁ'* ('The Visākha Sutta'), she tells The Buddha she would like to have as many children and grandchildren as there are people in Sāvatthi. Then The Buddha brings to her attention the fact that every day people die in Sāvatthi, which would mean she would always be mourning the death of a child or grandchild. And in A.III.II.ii.10 *'Uposatha·Suttaṁ'* ('The Uposatha Sutta'), He explains to her how she is to observe the eightfold Uposatha. Also The Buddha's chief patron, Anāthapiṇḍika was a Stream Enterer who enjoyed sensual pleasures, and The Buddha teaches him a number of suttas on how the householder who enjoys sensual pleasures may do so: for example, in A.IV.II.-ii.2 *'Āṇanya·Suttaṁ'* ('The Debtlessness Sutta'), The Buddha explains the four types of happiness that a householder enjoying sensual pleasures may enjoy: 1) possession

(wealth and property obtained according to the Dhamma*(dhammika)*); 2) wealth (enjoying his wealth and making merit with it); 3) debtlessness; 4) blameless bodily, verbal, and mental kamma. And in A.V.I.v.1 *'Ādiya·Suttaṁ'* ('The Acquisition Sutta'), He explains the five reasons for getting rich: 1) enjoying one's wealth with one's family, slaves and employees; 2) enjoying it with one's friends and companions; 3) guarding one's wealth; 4) the five expenditures (expenditure towards relatives; towards guests; towards the departed; towards the king; towards devas); 5) making offerings to ascetics and Brahmins who strive, are committed to patience and kindness, to taming and calming themselves for the attainment of Nibbāna. A third example is the Sakyan rajah Mahānāma, who was a Once Returner. In M.I.ii.4 *'Cūḷa·Dukkha·Kkhandha·Suttaṁ'* ('The Small Suffering-Mass Sutta'), he explains to The Buddha that although he knows greed, hatred, and delusion are defilements, they still arise and remain in him. The Buddha explains to him that this is because he has not abandoned sensuality. And He explains that if Mahānāma's understanding of the danger of sensual pleasures were supported by experience of pleasures apart from sensual pleasures (1st/2nd jhāna), or something more peaceful than that (3rd/&4th jhāna), he would not be living as a householder enjoying sensual pleasures: see this mentioned in footnote ‡, p.342.

[48] The Venerable Ānanda explains it in M.II.i.3 *'Sekha·Suttaṁ'* ('The Trainee Sutta'): 'Here, Mahānāma, a Noble Disciple, quite secluded from sensual pleasures, secluded from unwholesome states, enters upon and abides in the first... second... third... fourth jhāna.... That is how, Mahānāma, a Noble Disciple possesses the four jhānas, the higher mind, perceptible states of pleasant abidings, at his pleasure to obtain, not difficult to obtain, and not troublesome to obtain.' The Buddha explains it also in, for example, A.VII.i.4 *'Vitthata·Bala·Suttaṁ'* ('The Detailed-Power Sutta'), and in, for example, M.III.-ii.7 *'Mahā·Cattārīsaka·Suttaṁ'* ('The Great-Forty Sutta'), He explains the four jhānas as Right Concentration *(Sammā·Samādhi)*. VsM.xviii.662 *'Diṭṭhi·Visuddhi Niddesa'* ('Exposition of the View-Purification') PP.xviii.1 explains: 'Purification of Consciousness is the eight attainments together with access concentration': purification of consciousness is the same as Right Concentration.

[49] The Buddha explains the Noble Disciple's seeing their arising and perishing in, for example, A.VII.i.4 *'Vitthata·Bala·Suttaṁ'* ('The Detailed-Power Sutta'): 'Here, bhikkhus, the Noble Disciple is knowledgeable, possesses the arise&perish-directed wisdom *(udayattha·gāminiyā paññāya)*, which is Noble, directed towards dispassion, and directed towards complete destruction of suffering.' See also quotation endnote 30, p.23.

[50] The Buddha explains it in, for example, S.II.I.v.9 *'Ariya·Sāvaka·Suttaṁ'* ('The Noble-Disciple Sutta'): 'The educated, Noble disciple has knowledge about this that is independent of others: "That being, this is: with the arising of that, this arises."... He understands thus: "This is how the world originates."... "That not being, this is not: with the ceasing of that, this ceases."... He understands thus: "This is how the world ceases."'

[51] The Buddha explains it in, for example, S.II.I.ii.5 *'Kaccānagotta·Suttaṁ'* ('The Kaccānagotta Sutta'): 'But, Kaccāna, when one sees (according to reality, with Right Wisdom) the origin of the world [dependent origination in regular order], there is no non-existence in regard to the world [annihilation view]. And, Kaccāna, when one sees (according to reality, with Right Wisdom) the cessation of the world [dependent origination in negative order], there is no existence in the world [eternity view].' See also footnote 315, p.110.

[52] The Buddha explains it in, for example, A.I.xv.1 *'Aṭṭhāna·Pāḷi'* ('Impossible Text'): 'It is impossible, it cannot happen that a person possessed of view, should treat any formation as self *(attato)*: no such thing is known. But it is possible, it can happen that an ordinary person should treat some formation as self: such a thing is known.' And He explains it in the continuation of the *'Gaddula·Baddha'* sutta.

[53] The Buddha explains it in, for example, A.VII.i.4 *'Vitthata·Bala·Suttaṁ'* ('The Detailed-Power Sutta'): 'Here, bhikkhus, the Noble Disciple has learned much, remembers what he has learned, and consolidates what he has learned. Such teachings as are lovely in

the beginning, lovely in the middle, and lovely in the end, with the right meaning and phrasing, and as affirm a holy life that is utterly perfect and pure: such teachings as these he has learned much of, remembered, recited, investigated, and penetrated well by view. This is called the learning power.' And in M.III.ii.5 *'Bahu·Dhātuka·Suttaṁ'* ('The Many Elements Sutta'), He gives details: 'When, Ānanda, a bhikkhu is in the elements skilled, is in the bases skilled, is in dependent origination skilled, is in the possible and impossible skilled, in that way he can be called a sage and an enquirer.'

[54] The Buddha explains it in, for example, A.VII.i.4 *'Vitthata·Bala·Suttaṁ'* ('The Detailed-Power Sutta'): 'Here, bhikkhus, the Noble Disciple has faith, has faith in the Exalted One's enlightenment: 'Thus is The Exalted One: Worthy; Perfectly Self-Enlightened; of Knowledge and Conduct Possessed; Accomplished; World Knower; Unsurpassable Trainer of men; Teacher of devas and human beings; Enlightened; Exalted.' See also the Venerable Ānanda's explanation quoted endnote 32, p.24. And in, for example, S.V.XI.i.3 *'Dīghāvu-Upāsaka·Suttaṁ'* ('The Dīghāvu-Devotee Sutta'), the layman Dīghāvu explains to The Buddha: 'Venerable Sir, as to these four factors of Stream Entry that have been taught by the Blessed One, these things exist in me, and I live in conformity with those things. For, Venerable Sir, I possess confirmed confidence in The Buddha... Dhamma... Sangha, I possess the virtues dear to the Noble Ones, unbroken... leading to concentration.'

[55] The Buddha explains it in, for example, S.V.IV.vi.3 *'Sekha·Suttaṁ'* ('The Trainee Sutta'): 'He [the trainee] thus understands: "Indeed, there is outside [The Buddha's Dispensation] not another ascetic or Brahmin who such a real, true, actual dhamma teaches as does the Exalted One."'

[56] The Buddha explains this quality in the Noble Disciple in, for example, S.V.XI.i.7 *'Veḷu-·Dvāreyya·Suttaṁ'* ('The Bamboo-Gate Sutta'): 'If he wishes, he may himself declare of himself: "Destroyed is hell, destroyed is animal birth, destroyed is the ghost world, destroyed are the lower worlds, the bad destinations, the woeful states; I am a Stream Enterer, certain not to fall into states of woe, with full enlightenment as my destination."'

[57] In, for example, A.III.II.iv.7 *'Dutiya·Sikkhā·Suttaṁ'* ('The Second Training Sutta'), The Buddha explains that the Stream Enterer is destined to maximum seven more births, the Once Returner to maximum one more birth as a human being, and the Non-Returner to rebirth in the Brahma world, where he will eventually attain Arahantship. For details on each Noble Disciple, see 'The Four Path Knowledges', p.336.

II — 'The Second Clog-Bound Sutta'
('Dutiya Gaddula·Baddha·Suttaṁ')[71]

The Dog Near the Post

The second *'Gaddula·Baddha'* sutta[72] begins as the first one did. Also here, The Buddha gives the simile of a dog bound by a clog, tied to a post. But here The Buddha speaks not of the dog going round the post; here, He speaks of the dog walking near the post, standing, sitting down, and lying down near the post:

Thus I heard.
One time the Exalted One was dwelling in Sāvatthi, in Jeta's Grove, Anāthapiṇḍika's monastery. There the Blessed One addressed the bhikkhus:

Inconceivable is the beginning, bhikkhus, of the round of rebirth. A first point is not known of ignorance-hindered beings fettered by craving, rushing on and running about.

Suppose then, bhikkhus, a dog was clog-bound, and to a strong post or pillar was bound close. If it walks, then it walks near that same post or pillar; if it stands, then it stands near that same post or pillar; if it sits down, then it sits down near that same post or pillar; if it lies down, then it lies down near that same post or pillar.

As explained before, the dog cannot run away because it is wearing a clog, and is by a rope tied close to a strong post or pillar. Whatever posture it assumes, walking, standing, sitting down, or lying down, it remains near the post or pillar.

This Is Mine, This I Am, This Is My Self

Then, as before, The Buddha compares the dog to the uneducated ordinary person:[73]

So too, bhikkhus, the uneducated ordinary person,
[1] **regards materiality as: 'This is mine***(etaṁ mama)***, this I am***(es·oham·asmi)***, this is my self***(eso me attā)***';**
[2] **regards feeling as: 'This is mine, this I am, this is my self';**
[3] **regards perception as: 'This is mine, this I am, this is my self';**
[4] **regards formations as: 'This is mine, this I am, this is my self';**
[5] **regards consciousness as: 'This is mine, this I am, this is my self.'**

In the first *'Gaddula·Baddha'* sutta, The Buddha explained that the uneducated ordinary person regards the five clinging-aggregates as related to self in twenty ways: that is the twenty types of identity view. But here The Buddha explains that the uneducated ordinary person regards the five clinging-aggregates as related to self in only three ways:

1) The uneducated ordinary person regards the five clinging-aggregates as 'This is mine'*(etaṁ mama)*. That is a manifestation of grasping by craving*(taṇhā·ggāha)*.[74]
2) The uneducated ordinary person regards the five clinging-aggregates as 'This I am'*(eso·ham·asmi)*. That is a manifestation of grasping by conceit*(māna·ggāha)*.

---

[71] Reference numbers in italics refer to sutta quotations, etc. in endnotes p.36.
[72] S.III.I.x.8 *'Dutiya·Gaddula·Baddha·Suttaṁ'* ('The Second Clog-Bound Sutta')
[73] For details with regard to the uneducated ordinary person, see 'The Uneducated Ordinary Person', p.6*ff.*
[74] For the analysis with regard to the three types of grasping, see the commentary to M.I.i.8 *'Sallekha·Suttaṁ'* ('The Discipline Sutta').

3) The uneducated ordinary person regards the five clinging-aggregates as 'This is my self' *(eso me attā)*. That is a manifestation of grasping by view *(diṭṭhi-·ggāha)*, which is the twenty types of identity view *(sakkāya·diṭṭhi)* explained by The Buddha in the first *'Gaddula·Baddha'* sutta.

These three types of grasping are always associated with ignorance *(avijjā)*, and craving *(taṇhā)*: when there is the identity view, there is always ignorance and craving.

The wrong view of identity, craving, and ignorance cover the uneducated ordinary person's eye of wisdom. They prevent her or him from seeing ultimate materiality and ultimate mentality according to reality. Because of this blindness, the uneducated ordinary person is unable to see that ultimate materiality and ultimate mentality is impermanent *(anicca)*, suffering *(dukkha)*, and non-self *(an·atta)*. And she or he develops conceit *(māna)*. Conceit and ignorance and craving, or identity view and ignorance and craving, makes the uneducated ordinary person commit unwholesome and wholesome actions through body, speech and mind. Such action is called kamma: either ***akusala kamma*** or ***kusala kamma***.

He Is Near the Five Clinging-Aggregates

The kammic potency of those actions has the capacity to produce renewed existence after death, which means the uneducated ordinary person is not released from the round of rebirth. When there is production of renewed existence *(puna-·bhav·ābhinipphatti)*, there is also renewed disease, renewed ageing&death, renewed sorrow, renewed lamentation, renewed pain, renewed displeasure, and renewed despair: in short, there are renewed five aggregates *(pañca·kkhandha)*. There being no release from the five aggregates means the uneducated ordinary person is not released from suffering, from the round of rebirth:

- **If he walks, then he walks near those five clinging-aggregates;**
- **if he stands, then he stands near those five clinging-aggregates;**
- **if he sits down, then he sits down near those five clinging-aggregates;**
- **if he lies down, then he lies down near those five clinging-aggregates.**

The dog is wearing a clog, and is tied close to a strong post or pillar by a rope, which means it cannot release itself from the strong post. In the same way, the uneducated ordinary person is wearing the clog of a firmly held identity view *(sakkāya diṭṭhi)*, and is tied close to the strong post or pillar of the five clinging-aggregates by the rope of craving *(taṇhā)*. That means the uneducated ordinary person cannot gain release from the strong post of the five clinging-aggregates *(pañc·upādāna·kkhandha)*:[75/58] cannot get released from the round of rebirth *(saṁsāra)*.

For a Long Time this Mind Has Been Defiled

It is for this reason The Buddha gives the following advice:

Therefore, bhikkhus, one should reflect repeatedly upon one's own mind: 'For a long time this mind has been defiled by lust *(rāga)*, **by hatred** *(dosa)*, **and by delusion** *(moha)*.'

By mental defilement *(citta·saṁkilesā)*, **bhikkhus, beings are defiled; by mental purification** *(citta·vodānā)*, **beings are purified.**

---

[75] FIVE CLINGING-AGGREGATES: this means they are what the uneducated ordinary person clings to: there is nothing else to cling to. Athought possessed of five aggregates, The Noble One *(Ariya)*, does not cling to them with any of the twenty kinds of identity view.

THE FANTASTIC PICTURE

Then The Buddha explains the mind *(citta)* by comparing it to a fantastic picture *(citta)*:

Have you seen, bhikkhus, the 'wandering picture'? (Yes, Venerable Sir.)
Even that 'wandering picture', bhikkhus, owing to only the mind is fantastic. And yet, bhikkhus, the mind is more fantastic than the 'wandering picture'.

The picture mentioned here is the 'wandering picture' *(caraṇa citta)*.[76] It had that name, because Brahmins called Saṅkhas wandered about with it to preach their Dhamma. To illustrate the workings of kamma, they had on a canvas painted fantastic images of the good and bad destinations. And they carried the picture around on their wanderings. Then they would show it to people, and explain: 'If one does this kamma, one gets this result; if one does that, one gets that.'

Such a fantastic picture is very imaginative. But the mind is even more fantastic. That is because one must first imagine what image to paint, and how to compose the image, and then one paints according to one's imagination. And one might imagine, for example, a fantastic ruby that was brighter than the sun, even though such a ruby cannot exist.

Thus, with The Buddha's simile of the wandering picture, we may understand how fantastic the mind is. That is why The Buddha says:

Even that 'wandering picture', bhikkhus, owing to only the mind is fantastic. And yet, bhikkhus, the mind is more fantastic than the 'wandering picture'.

And He adds:

Therefore, bhikkhus, one should reflect repeatedly upon one's own mind: 'For a long time this mind has been defiled by lust, by hatred, and by delusion.'
By mental defilement, bhikkhus, beings are defiled; by mental purification, beings are purified.

THE FANTASTIC ANIMAL REALM

Next, The Buddha explains the mind by comparing it to the fantastic variety of beings in the animal realm:

I do not, bhikkhus, another one order see so fantastic, bhikkhus, as the animal-realm beings. Even they, bhikkhus, the animal-realm beings, owing to only the mind are fantastic. And yet, bhikkhus, the mind is more fantastic than the animal-realm beings.

The point The Buddha is making here is that the fantastic variety of creatures in the animal realm reflects the variety of past kammas that produced their rebirth as animals. That variety of kammas originated from the fantastic variety of craving *(taṇhā)*, a mental factor.

For example,[77] quails and partridges did not in their previous lives accomplish various kammas with the thought: 'We will become a being with such and such characteristics.' It is when the kammic potency of a certain previous kamma has matured, that it produces the result of rebirth into a certain species *(yoni)*, such as a quail, or partridge. And the variety of appearance, way of life etc. in the animal realm depends on the species. Beings that arise in a particular species become the way they do according to the species they have been born into. Thus variety manifests through the order of beings, and reflects the variety of kamma.

---

[76] This analysis is derived from the commentary to the second *'Gaddula·Baddha'* sutta.

[77] This example is given in the commentary to the second *'Gaddula·Baddha'* sutta.

For example, if you in a life accomplish sufficient wholesome kamma to become a human being, then if the kammic potency of that kamma matures, you will appear in the human species *(manussa yoni)*, with the five clinging-aggregates of a human being. That is why parents and children are usually similar to each other.

In the same way, if you in a life accomplish such an unwholesome kamma as to become a quail, then if the kammic potency of that kamma matures, you will appear in the species of quails, with the five clinging-aggregates of a quail. That is how the variety of animals manifests through the species, and the species reflects the variety of previous kamma.

And yet, the mind is more varied. That is why The Buddha says:

Even they, bhikkhus, the animal-realm beings, owing to only the mind are fantastic. And yet, bhikkhus, the mind is more fantastic than the animal-realm beings.

And He adds:

Therefore, bhikkhus, one should reflect repeatedly upon one's own mind: 'For a long time this mind has been defiled by lust, by hatred, and by delusion.'

By mental defilement, bhikkhus, beings are defiled; by mental purification, beings are purified.

The Variety of Temperament

When The Buddha says the mind is more fantastic than the wandering picture, and more fantastic than the beings in the animal realm, He is referring to the fantastic variety of kamma consciousnesses *(kamma·viññāṇa)*, the fantastic variety of consciousnesses associated with kammic potency. It is this kamma that distinguishes beings as inferior and superior.[78]

You see, for example, human beings with different temperaments. A human being's temperament is the result of kamma accomplished in previous lives.[79]

Let us say you, in a previous life, accomplished wholesome kamma *(kusala kamma)*: you made offerings *(dāna)*, observed morality *(sīla)* (the five or eight precepts), or practised meditation *(bhāvanā)*. And you did it with a strong wish for sensual pleasures in the future. Maybe you wished that your wholesome kamma would produce future lives as a rich human being, or you wished that it would produce future lives in the deva world, so you could enjoy deva pleasures. Then if, owing to that wholesome kamma, you are reborn as a human being, you will have great desire to enjoy sensual pleasures. You will have a lustful temperament *(rāga·carita)*.[80/59]

You may also have accomplished wholesome kamma with hatred. For example, you made offerings, but with anger: maybe you did not like the people you were with, maybe you quarreled with the other people about how to conduct the offering, or you were angry with the receivers, or you were dissatisfied with the objects you were offering. You might also, for example, have kept the eight precepts with anger: angry that you could not eat after noon, or bored because you could not watch television. Then if, owing to that wholesome kamma, you are reborn as a human being, you will very easily get angry and bored. You will have a hating temperament *(dosa·carita)*.

---

[78] For these, The Buddha's words, see p.258.

[79] DhSA.i.498 *'Aṭṭha·Mahā·Vipāka·Citta·Vaṇṇanā'* ('Description of the Eight Great Resultant Consciousnesses') E.355-356

[80] For how wholesome phenomena can be cause for the arising of unwholesome phenomena, see The Buddha's explanation quoted in subsequent endnote 59, p.36.

You may also have accomplished the wholesome kamma with conceit: comparing your practice with the practice of others: 'Their offerings are very poor; mine is much better!', 'He always breaks the precepts, but mine are pure!', 'She can never calm her mind, but I can sit in perfect jhāna for six hours!', 'I've seen two hundred past lives, but he's seen only two!', 'She's offering very delicious food; that's unnecessary. I'm offering plain food; that's good enough!', 'I'm a bad person; it's no use for me to try to keep the precepts!', or, 'I think too much; it's impossible for me to meditate. I will just make offerings!' Measuring one's wholesome kamma in this way is conceit: superiority conceit, equality conceit, and inferiority conceit.[81][60] If you, owing to that kamma, are reborn as a human being, you will have a conceited temperament *(māna·carita)*: always comparing yourself with others. This same principle applies also to those who have an envious or jealous temperament. And those with a deluded temperament *(moha·carita)* will have accomplished wholesome kamma without understanding the law of kamma, without understanding that their kamma is wholesome, and without understanding that their kamma can produce rebirth.

Say, on the other hand, you in a previous life accomplished wholesome kamma with determined faith *(okappana·saddhā)* in the Triple Gem (The Buddha, Dhamma, and Sangha), and determined faith in the law of kamma and its results.[82] Then if, owing to that kamma, you are reborn as a human being, you will be one full of faith and devotion. You will have a pious temperament *(saddhā·carita)*.

You may also have accomplished wholesome kamma with strong and powerful loving-kindness *(mettā)*: you may have made offerings with a great desire for the receivers to benefit from your offerings. Or you refrained from killing other beings while also having great loving-kindness for other beings. You may also habitually have practised loving-kindness meditation *(mettā·bhāvanā)*. Then, if owing to the access concentration of that loving-kindness meditation, or owing to a nearby wholesome kamma, you are reborn as a human being, you will have a temperament of loving-kindness *(mettā·carita)*.[83]

Then say you, in a previous life, made offerings with a good understanding of the law of kamma: understanding, 'This kamma can produce rebirth in the human or deva world', 'This kamma can be a supporting cause for the attainment of Nibbāna.' You may even have developed strong and powerful wisdom such as insight knowledge. You may even have practised insight meditation on the receiver's mentality-materiality, on the materiality of the offering, and on your own mentality-materiality. Then if, owing to that kamma, you are reborn as a human being, you will have a wise temperament *(buddhi·carita)*, and a sharp mind. And if the kammic potency that produces its results in this life includes insight

---

[81] VbhA.xvii *'Khuddaka·Vatthu·Vibhaṅga'* ('Minor-Bases Analysis') explains such pride and conceit as many types of infatuation/intoxication *(mada)*: owing to family, name, youth, health, life, gain, skin colour, learning, intelligence, success, fame, virtue, concentration, etc. They are mentioned throughout the Pali Texts.

[82] For an analysis of faith *(saddhā)*, see 'Faith', p.374.

[83] DhSA.I.iii.498 *'Vipāk·Uddhāra·Kathā'* ('Discussion of the Result-Apprehension') E.354, explains that every Buddha's rebirth-linking consciousness is a sensual-sphere, wholesome resultant, joyous, triple-rooted, unprompted loving-kindness consciousness: see table '3b: Mental Phenomena at the Arising of Knowledge-Associated Consciousness', p.69.

knowledge such as the Formations-Equanimity Knowledge *(Saṅkhār·Upekkhā·Ñāṇa)*,[84] you will possess very strong, powerful and sharp wisdom for the realization of Nibbāna. If you practise samatha and vipassanā, you can quickly penetrate the Four Noble Truths.[85]

This role played by the mind is why The Buddha says:[86]

Therefore, bhikkhus, one should reflect repeatedly upon one's own mind: 'For a long time this mind has been defiled by lust, by hatred, and by delusion.'

By mental defilement, bhikkhus, beings are defiled; by mental purification, beings are purified.

The Parsimonious Millionaire

A good example of what we have discussed is the millionaire who died in Sāvatthi, without any children to inherit his fortune.[87] So it went to King Pasenadi of Kosala. And the king told the Buddha how that millionaire had lived like a very poor man, even though he was so rich.

The Buddha then explained that because the millionaire in a past life had offered food to a Paccekabuddha, he was seven times reborn as a deva, and seven times as a human being who became a millionaire. But because he had in that past life regretted offering the food to the Paccekabuddha, in his human lives, his mind did not incline towards spending money on enjoying sensual-pleasures. Even though he was a millionaire, he preferred to eat poor food, dress poorly, and ride in a poor cart.[88/61] Thus, his stinginess and parsimony were because of his own past unwholesome kamma.

The Two Brothers

Another good example is The Buddha's account of one Jotika's past lives.[89]

Once, in the very distant past, there were two brothers. They owned a large field of sugar-cane. One day, the younger brother offered some sugar-cane juice to a Paccekabuddha. After he had offered the juice, he aspired for three things: that his offering would result in his enjoying glory in the human world, that it would result in his enjoying glory in the deva world, and that it would eventually be a supporting cause for him to attain Arahantship. Afterwards, on behalf of his elder brother, he offered some more sugar-cane juice to the Paccekabuddha, which the Paccekabuddha took back to his dwelling, to share with other Paccekabuddhas. When the younger brother told his elder brother about his offering, the elder brother was filled with great joy, and made an aspiration. But he did not aspire for three things. He aspired for only one thing: Arahantship.

---

[84] FORMATIONS-EQUANIMITY KNOWLEDGE: see p.113.

[85] For details regarding the consciousnesses with which one accomplishes wholesome kamma, see 'Inferior and Superior', p.60*ff.* For the relationship between the unwholesome and the wholesome, see also footnote 597, p.205.

[86] S.III.I.x.8 *'Dutiya·Gaddula·Baddha·Suttaṁ'* ('The Second Clog-Bound Sutta'), quoted p.30.

[87] S.I.III.ii.10 *'Dutiya·Aputta·Suttaṁ'* ('The Second Childless Sutta')

[88] The Buddha says: 'Because of that kamma *(tassa kammassa vipākena)*, the mind did not incline *(namati)* towards enjoying superior food... superior clothes... superior vehicles... the five sensual lines.' Further to how past kamma accounts for present attitudes of mind, see The Buddha's analysis from the *'Velāma'* sutta, subsequent endnote 61, p.36.

[89] DhP.xxvi.34 *'Brāhmaṇa·Vagga'* ('Brahman Chapter')

When the two brothers passed away, they were reborn in the deva world. Then, at the time of Buddha Vipassī,[90] they were again reborn as brothers in a good family. When they reached manhood, they married, established a family, and lived as householders. Then, one day, they heard that a Buddha had appeared in the world. Together with many other householders, they went to see The Buddha, to make offerings, and to listen to the Dhamma. As The Buddha was teaching the Dhamma, the elder brother developed a very strong desire to renounce the household life and become a bhikkhu: he was the one who had aspired for only Arahantship. His desire was so powerful that he gave over all his property to his younger brother, ordained as a bhikkhu, and soon put an end to suffering with Arahantship. But his younger brother could not give up the household life: he was still too attached to sensual pleasures, and so could not put an end to suffering. Instead, the younger brother made great offerings of requisites to The Buddha and Sangha: he offered even a magnificent dwelling for The Buddha.

The elder brother had, in that life, put an end to rebirth, but his younger brother continued in the round of rebirth from The Buddha Vipassī's time till our Buddha Gotama's time. For many, many aeons, he continued being reborn. Owing to the many wholesome kammas he had accomplished, he was reborn now in the deva world, now in the human world. Only at our Buddha's time, as the treasurer Jotika, was he finally able to renounce sensual pleasures, and become a bhikkhu. Only in that life was he finally able to put an end to suffering, by becoming an Arahant.

When He had explained how the two brothers had fared differently because of their different thoughts when accomplishing wholesome kamma, The Buddha uttered the following verse:

Whoever, craving *(taṇhā)* **having given up, a wandering homeless one, with craving and existence consumed, such a one do I call a Brahman.**

Craving and existence consumed is the same as to say that the clog-bound dog has severed the rope binding it to the strong post or pillar. And it has managed to throw off the clog that was bound to its neck. That is, with attainment of the Noble Path, and eventually Arahantship, the uneducated ordinary person has severed the rope of craving *(taṇhā)*, has managed to throw off the clog of identity view *(sakkāya diṭṭhi)*, has gained release from the strong post of the five clinging-aggregates *(pañc·upādāna·kkhandha)*: she or he has escaped from the round of rebirth *(saṁsāra)*.

That concludes our example of how the variety of kamma consciousnesses *(kamma·viññāṇa)*, the variety of consciousnesses associated with kammic potency, accounts for the variety in the five aggregates, the variety in beings.

In this regard, we should like to go on to discuss a sutta where The Buddha explains the variety of kamma and its results. It is called the 'The Small Kamma-Analysis Sutta'.[91] But for you better to understand that sutta, we shall at some length first discuss the workings of kamma according to The Buddha's Knowledge of Kamma&Result *(Kamma·Vipāka·Ñāṇa)*.

[90] The Buddha Vipassī: the sixth Buddha before The Buddha Gotama. See 'Appendix 2: The Lineage of Buddhas', p.365.

[91] Discussed at 'IV — 'The Small Kamma-Analysis Sutta', p.257*ff.*

ENDNOTES CHAPTER II
(SUTTA REFERENCES ETC.)

[58] In M.II.iii.5 *'Māgaṇḍiya·Suttaṁ'* ('The Māgaṇḍiya Sutta'), The Buddha explains to one wanderer that if he undertakes the training: 'Then perhaps you might think: "Indeed, I have long been tricked, cheated, and defrauded by this mind. For when clinging, I have been clinging to only matter... feeling... perception... formations... consciousness."'

[59] In P.I.423 *'Upanissaya·Paccayo'* ('Decisive-Cause Cause'), The Buddha explains how wholesome phenomena can become the decisive cause for the arising of unwholesome phenomena: 'Wholesome phenomenon *(kusalo dhammo)* of unwholesome phenomenon *(akusalassa dhammassa)* as decisive cause is the cause *(upanissaya·paccayena paccayo)*: [1] object decisive-cause *(ārammaṇ·ūpanissayo)*, and [2] customary decisive-cause *(pakat·ūpanissayo)*. [1] Object decisive-cause: alms having given; morality having undertaken; the Uposatha observance having done; having made it pre-eminent *(garuṁ katvā)*, one enjoys it *(assādeti)*, delights in it *(abhinandati)*; having made it pre-eminent, lust arises *(rāgo uppajjati)*, view *(diṭṭhi)* arises. Earlier good habits *(su·[ā]ciṇṇāni)* having made them pre-eminent one enjoys them .... Having emerged from jhāna, the jhāna having made pre-eminent, one enjoys it... lust... view arises. [2] Customary decisive-cause: with faith *(saddham)*... morality *(sīlaṁ)*... learning *(sutaṁ)*... generosity *(cāgaṁ)*... wisdom *(paññaṁ)* as decisive-cause, conceit one works up *(mānaṁ jappeti)*, view one grasps *(diṭṭhiṁ gaṇhāti)*. Faith... morality... learning... generosity... lust *(rāgassa)*... hatred *(dosassa)*... delusion *(mohassa)*... conceit *(mānassa)*... view *(diṭṭhāya)*... yearning *(patthanāya)*... as decisive cause is the cause.'

Also in, for example, M.III.ii.10 *'Saṅkhār·Ūpapatti·Suttaṁ'* ('The Formations-Rebirth Sutta'), The Buddha explains how the bhikkhu possessed of faith/morality/learning/generosity/wisdom and yearning for a certain rebirth in the human/sensual-sphere deva worlds will be reborn there. Likewise if he based on those five things yearns for rebirth in the fine-material/immaterial Brahma worlds, and develops the jhānas. But if he based on those five things yearns for Arahantship and develops insight, he 'is not anywhere reborn *(na katthaci upapajjati)*.' Then in M.I.v.1 *'Sāleyyaka·Suttaṁ'* ('The People of Sālā Sutta'), The Buddha explains this same procedure for one who practises the ten wholesome courses of kamma, and in A.VIII.I.iv.5 *'Dān·Ūpapatti·Suttaṁ'* ('The Alms&Rebirth Sutta'), for the virtuous one who makes offerings: see quotaton under, for example, 'One Is Not a Tormentor', p.266.

[60] The Buddha speaks of three types of conceit in, for example, S.I.I.ii.10 *'Samiddhi·Suttaṁ'* ('The Samiddhi Sutta'): 'Equal, superior, or inferior: whoever so thinks, he is therefore likely to quarrel.' And in S.V.I.vii.2 *'Vidhā·Suttaṁ'* ('The Pride Sutta'), He explains: 'Three, bhikkhus, are the [forms of] pride.... The pride of "Better am I", "Equal am I", "Low am I".... It is, bhikkhus, for the direct knowledge, full understanding, and complete destruction of these three [forms of pride] that the Noble Eightfold Path is to be developed.' : for example, infatuation owing to youth, health, and life in A.III.I.iv.9 *'Sukhumāla·Suttaṁ'* ('The "Delicate" Sutta') and A.V.II.i.7 *'Abhiṇha·Paccavekkhitabba·Ṭhāna·Suttaṁ'* ('The Subject Often-to-Be-Reflected Sutta'), and pride/conceit about one's femininity/masculinity in A.VII.v.8 *'Saṁyoga·Suttaṁ'* ('The Bondage Sutta').

[61] In A.IX.I.ii.10 *'Velāma·Suttaṁ'* ('The Velāma Sutta'), The Buddha explains that whether one makes offerings *(dānaṁ deti)* that are coarse or fine, if one offers without care and reverence, and not by one's own hand, if it is leftovers, and if one offers without faith that one's offering will produce a result, then wherever that offering's result is generated, one's mind will be like the mind of the millionaire just mentioned. Furthermore, one's family and those in one's employ will not want to listen to what one says, nor try to understand it. But if one offers with care and reverence, by one's own hand, if it is not leftovers, and if one offers with faith that one's offering will produce a result, then wherever that offering's result is generated, one's mind will incline towards enjoying sensual pleasures: good food, clothes, and modes of transport. Furthermore, one's fami-

ly and those in one's employ will want to listen to what one says, and try to understand it.

III — The Workings of Kamma[92]

The Buddha's Knowledge of Kamma&Result

The workings of kamma and kamma's result is so profound and difficult to see that only a Buddha's Knowledge of Kamma&Result *(Kamma·Vipāka·Ñāṇa)* can see it clearly: His disciples do not possess this knowledge, not even Arahants.[93]

This knowledge of kamma and its result is the second of what The Buddha calls His ten 'Tathāgata Powers' *(Tathāgata·Bala)*.

He explains it to the Venerable Sāriputta:[94]

Again and further, Sāriputta, the Tathāgata understands the result *(vipāka)* **of past, future, and present kamma that has been undertaken, by way of contingency and root, according to reality.**[95]

And whatever, Sāriputta, result of past, future, and present kamma that has been undertaken the Tathāgata by way of contingency and root understands according to reality. This then, Sāriputta, is a Tathāgata's Tathāgata power, because of which power the Tathāgata assumes the bull's stance, roars the lion's roar in the assemblies, and sets in motion the divine wheel.[96]

The Lion's Roar

With this Tathāgata power, The Buddha roars His lion's roar. What is His lion's roar? He explains that it is His teaching of the five aggregates *(pañca·kkhandha)*, their origin *(samudaya)*, and their disappearance *(atthaṅgama)*:[97/*62*]

[1] **Thus materiality, thus materiality's appearance** *(samudaya)*, **thus materiality's disappearance** *(atthaṅgama)*.
[2] **Thus feeling, thus feeling's appearance, thus feeling's disappearance.**
[3] **Thus perception, thus perception's appearance, thus perception's disappearance.**
[4] **Thus formations, thus formations' appearance, thus formations' disappearance.**
[5] **Thus consciousness, thus consciousness's appearance, thus consciousness's disappearance.**

---

[92] Reference numbers in italics refer to sutta quotations, etc. in endnotes beginning p.233.

[93] In A.IV.II.iii.7 *'Acinteyya·Suttaṁ'* ('The "Imponderable" Sutta'), The Buddha explains: 'The result of kamma *(kamma·vipāko)*, bhikkhus, is imponderable.'

[94] M.I.ii.2 *'Mahā·Sīha·Nāda·Suttaṁ'* ('The Great Lion's-Roar Sutta').

[95] CONTINGENCY *(ṭhāna)*: the commentary explains that this refers to the circumstances contingent/dependent upon which a certain kamma produces its result. It is either achievement or failure with regard to four types of circumstance: 1) destination *(gati)*; 2) appearance *(upadhi)*; 3) time *(kāla)*; 4) means *(payoga)*. ROOT *(hetu)*: the kamma is the root of the result. (The four types of contingency are discussed under 'Achievement/Failure', p.209.)

[96] BULL'S *(āsabhaṁ)* STANCE *(ṭhānaṁ)*: the stance is the posture of four feet on the ground, and the bull's stance is the supreme, highest, unshakable stance, adopted by the chief of all bulls. The Tathāgata's four feet are His four intrepidities *(vesārajja)*. DIVINE WHEEL *(Brahma·cakka)*: this refers to the Dhamma-Wheel: *BRAHMA* (divine) means here supreme, highest, superior.

[97] S.II.I.iii.1 *'Dasa·Bala·Suttaṁ'* ('The Ten-Powers Sutta'). This is how, in D.ii.9 *'Mahā·Sati·Paṭṭhāna·Suttaṁ'* ('The Great Mindfulness-Foundation Sutta'), The Buddha describes the meditating bhikkhu's understanding of the five aggregates, before he contemplates them.

The five aggregates are the Noble Truth of Suffering *(Dukkha Ariya·Sacca)*; their appearance is the Noble Truth of the Origin of Suffering *(Dukkha·Samudaya Ariya-·Sacca)*; their disappearance is the Noble Truth of the Cessation of Suffering *(Dukkha·Nirodha Ariya·Sacca)*. And to explain the appearance and disappearance of the five aggregates, The Buddha then gives the formula for dependent origination *(paṭicca·samuppāda)*:

Thus, this being, that is; this arising, that arises.
This not being, that is not; this ceasing, that ceases.

Next, The Buddha explains the twelve links of dependent origination: because of ignorance, volitional formations arise; because of volitional formations, consciousness arises, etc. We shall discuss them later.[98]

THE HEART OF THE BUDDHA'S TEACHING

Having now listened to The Buddha explain His own teaching, we understand that to understand the five aggregates, we need to understand dependent origination and cessation, which means we need to understand the workings of kamma.

Being only disciples of The Buddha, however, we cannot fully understand the workings of kamma: that is impossible. But by practising insight meditation, disciples may be able to see the connections between certain kammas and their result, and thereby gain a partial understanding of the workings of kamma.

In fact, such an understanding is essential. In fact, to be true disciples of The Buddha, the most important thing for us to do is to understand and have deep faith in the actuality of a law of kamma and kamma's result. Why? Because, as we just heard The Buddha explain, the workings of kamma is the heart of The Buddha's Teaching: it is the driving force of dependent origination *(paṭicca·samuppāda)*, which is the Second Noble Truth, the Noble Truth of the Origin of Suffering *(Samudaya Sacca)*, the origin of the five aggregates. So if we do not understand the workings of kamma, we cannot understand the Noble Truth of the Origin of Suffering *(Dukkha·Samudaya Ariya·Sacca)*, the origin of the five aggregates. That means we cannot become a Noble Disciple *(Ariya·Sāvaka)*, and escape suffering.[99] Therefore, we must attend closely to The Buddha's explanations of the workings of kamma. But we must always remember that although we must try to understand The Buddha's explanations of the workings of kamma, such explanations cannot provide true understanding. To gain true understanding of the workings of kamma, we need (as far as it is possible for a disciple) to know and see the workings

---

[98] See 'Dependent Origination', p.109*ff.*

[99] VsM.xix.687 *'Kaṅkhā·Vitaraṇa·Visuddhi·Niddeso'* ('Exposition of the Doubt-Transcendence Purification') PP.xix.17 explains: 'The succession of kamma and its result in the twelve categories of kamma [see p.144*ff*] is clear in its true nature only to The Buddha's Knowledge of Kamma and Its Result [*Kamma·Vipāka·Ñāṇa*], which knowledge is not shared by disciples. But the succession of kamma and its result can be known in part by one practising insight [vipassanā].' VsMṬ explains: 'Because it is a specialty of The Buddha, and because it is the province of the knowledge that is not shared by disciples, it is called "not shared by disciples" *(a·sādhāraṇaṁ sāvakehi)*. That is why only a part can be known; it cannot all be known because it is not the province of such knowledge. A part must be known; knowing it all without remainder cannot be done, is inaccessible. Not knowing it at all, the Cause-Apprehending [Knowledge] *(Paccaya·Pariggaha [·Ñāṇa])* cannot be fulfilled.'

of kamma for ourselves by practising proper insight meditation,[63] and attaining the Cause-Apprehending Knowledge *(Paccaya·Pariggaha·Ñāṇa)*.[100]

THE WORKINGS OF THE MIND

For us properly to understand the workings of kamma, it is first of all necessary to understand something about the workings of the mind. The Buddha explains that when the mind is alert, then within a snap of the fingers, very many thousand million consciousnesses arise and perish: they arise as series, many thousand million mental processes *(citta·vīthi)*.[101] Most of them are mind-door processes: many thousand million mind-door processes arising and perishing like a river in full flow. On our plane (the sensual-sphere plane *(kām·āvacara·bhūmi)*), usually a mind-door process has seven impulsion consciousnesses *(javana)*.[102] When an impulsion consciousness arises that is unwholesome *(akusala)*, there are minimum sixteen mental phenomena *(nāma·dhamma)*, maximum twenty-two; when it is wholesome *(kusala)*, there are minimum thirty-two mental phenomena, maximum thirty-five.[103] In all cases, one of those mental phenomena is volition *(cetanā)*, and it is volition that forms kamma.[104] What is referred to as kamma is specifically the volition of the seven impulsions in an unwholesome or wholesome mental process.[105] But in the 'Kamma Cause' *(Kamma Paccaya)* chapter of the ***Paṭṭhāna***, kamma is also explained as the kammic potency *(kamma satti)* of the volition in those impulsions.[106] Please try to remember this as we explain further.

---

[100] CAUSE-APPREHENDING KNOWLEDGE: see p.91.

[101] The Commentary to S.III.I.x.3 *'Pheṇa·Piṇḍ·Ūpama·Suttaṁ'* ('The Foam-Lump Simile Sutta') explains: 'In one snap of the fingers, the estimate is ten-million *(koṭi)* hundred-thousand *(sata·sahassa)*, having arisen, cease.' (10,000,000 x 100,000 = 1,000,000,000,000 = one billion consciousnesses *(citta)* (one trillion, American English)). These billion consciousnesses do not all comprise five-door and mind-door processes: a great many are life-continuum consciousnesses arising between such mental processes. Thus, in one snap of the fingers, very many thousand million consciousnesses arise and perish (estimated at a billion), which then include many thousand million mental process. For details, see table '5b: The Five-Door Process', p.146, and table '5c: The Mind-Door Process', p.148.

[102] On the sensual plane, usually there arise only sensual-sphere mental processes. But if one develops the fine-material-, immaterial-, or supramundane jhānas, that will constitute fine-material-, immaterial-, or supramundane mental processes: they comprise from one to countless impulsions. See table '5d: The Jhāna-Attainment Process', p.178.

[103] MENTAL PHENOMENA AT THE ARISING OF UNWHOLESOME IMPULSION CONSCIOUSNESSES: see tables 2a/2b/2c, p.48*ff*; AT THE ARISING OF WHOLESOME CONSCIOUSNESSES: tables 3a/3b, p.67*ff*.

[104] All kamma is produced by volition, but not all volition produces kamma. Since volition is one of the seven universal mental factors (see footnote 433, p.157), it means there is volition in all consciousnesses. But kamma is not produced by the volition of resultant consciousnesses (see table '1: The Resultant Consciousnesses', p.46), or functional consciousnesses (see tables '5b: The Five-Door Process', p.146, and '5c: The Mind-Door Process', p.148, and the Arahant's functional volition at 'The Unworking of Kamma', p.338*ff*).

[105] The exception is the Arahant's cognition: it is purely functional *(kiriya)*, neither unwholesome nor wholesome. See previous footnote.

[106] See footnotes 5, p.1, and 56, p.15. (P.I.427 *'Kamma·Paccayo'* ('Kamma Cause') & PṬ *'Paccay·Uddesa·Vaṇṇanā'* ('Description of the Kamma Section'))

DEFINITION OF KAMMA

Literally, the word 'kamma' means action or deed, but in The Buddha's Teaching kamma refers only to volitional action:[107]

It is volition*(cetanā)***, bhikkhus, that is kamma, I declare.**
Having willed, one accomplishes kamma by body*(kāyena)***, by speech***(vācāya)***, and by mind***(manasā)***.**

Volition is the mental factor responsible for kamma.

UNWHOLESOME AND WHOLESOME VOLITION

There are two such types of volition:

1) Unwholesome volition*(akusala cetanā)*
2) Wholesome volition*(kusala cetanā)*

Unwholesome volition is unwholesome kamma, and wholesome volition is wholesome kamma. But the volition of Buddhas and other Arahants is neither unwholesome nor wholesome: it is purely functional*(kiriya)*. It never produces kamma, because they have eradicated the roots of kamma: ignorance and craving.[108] Nevertheless, as long as their mental and material continuity persists, even Buddhas and other Arahants cannot avoid experiencing the results of their past kamma: the results stop arising only when they enter Parinibbāna (final cessation).[109]

IMPOSSIBLE AND POSSIBLE RESULTS

The law of kamma*(kamma niyāma)* is a natural law that is self-sustaining in its operation.[110] It ensures that the result of kamma is similar to the kamma itself *(kamma·sarikkhaka·vipāka)*, just as the seed of a fruit produces a tree that bears the

---

[107] To explain that kamma is volition, DhSA.I.iii *'Kamma·Kathā'* ('Discussion of Kamma') E.117-118 quotes this passage, which can be found in A.VI.vi.9 *'Nibbedhika·Suttaṁ'* ('The Penetrating Sutta'). It quotes also a passage that can be found in S.II.I.iii.5 *'Bhūmija·Suttaṁ'* ('The Bhūmija Sutta'): 'A body there being, Ānanda, there arises in oneself happiness and suffering that is rooted in bodily volition [speech/mind there being, there arises in oneself happiness/suffering that is rooted in verbal-/mental volition]: and with ignorance as cause.' The commentary quotes also a similar passage that is the same as a passage in A.X.xxi.7&8 *'Paṭhama·*[& *Dutiya·*] *Sañcetanika·Suttaṁ'* ('The First [& Second] "Volitional" Sutta'), and another similar passage that can be found in M.III.iv.6 *'Mahā·Kamma·Vibhaṅga·Suttaṁ'* ('The Great Kamma-Analysis Sutta'): see endnote 206, p.252.

[108] ARAHANT'S FUNCTIONAL VOLITION: using the metaphor of black/white kamma, The Buddha explains how with the abandonment of black/white kamma (by the Arahant Path&-Fruition), one's kamma becomes non-black/non-white (see endnote 282, p.355); and He explains that with the destruction of lust, hatred and delusion, there is the destruction of kamma causation (see endnote 300, p.358); and He explains that when a bhikkhu has attained the Arahant Path-Knowledge, he accomplishes neither a meritorious, demeritorious, nor imperturbable formation of kamma (see endnote 315, p.360). In all cases, the Arahant's volition is functional (see also explanation footnote 941, p.349).

[109] See discussion at 'The Two Types of Parinibbāna', p.343*ff.*

[110] DhSA.I.iii *'Vipāk·Uddhāra·Kathā'* ('Discussion of the Result-Apprehension') E.360 explains: 'And here at this stage, they [the ancient Commentary Teachers] include what is called the fivefold order of nature: the seed order, the temperature order, the kamma order, the Dhamma order, the consciousness order.' See also quotation footnote 206, p.73.

same kind of fruit. For example, the fruit of the nimb *(nimba)* tree is bitter. If we plant the seed of a nimb fruit, it produces a tree that bears also nimb fruits: they are also bitter. In the same way, an unwholesome kamma produces a result that is similar to the unwholesome kamma itself.

Unwholesome kamma does not produce an agreeable result. If the unwholesome kamma produces its result, it will always be a disagreeable result:[111]

[1] **Impossible it is, bhikkhus, there is no occasion where bodily bad conduct could produce a desired, pleasant, and agreeable result: such a possibility does not exist. But such a possibility, bhikkhus, does exist where bodily bad conduct could produce an undesired, unpleasant, and disagreeable result: such a possibility does exist.**

[2] **Impossible it is, bhikkhus, there is no occasion where verbal bad conduct could produce a desired, pleasant, and agreeable result: such a possibility does not exist. But such a possibility, bhikkhus, does exist where verbal bad conduct could produce an undesired, unpleasant, and disagreeable result: such a possibility does exist.**

[3] **Impossible it is, bhikkhus, there is no occasion where mental bad conduct could produce a desired, pleasant, and agreeable result: such a possibility does not exist. But such a possibility, bhikkhus, does exist where mental bad conduct could produce an undesired, unpleasant, and disagreeable result: such a possibility does exist.**

Then we can take sugar cane: it is sweet. If we plant the cutting of a sugar cane, it produces cane that is also sweet.[112] In the same way, a wholesome kamma produces a result that is similar to the wholesome kamma itself. Wholesome kamma does not produce a disagreeable result. If the wholesome kamma produces its result, it will always be an agreeable result:[113]

[1] **Impossible it is, bhikkhus, there is no occasion where bodily good conduct could produce an undesired, unpleasant and disagreeable result: such a possibility does not exist. But it is indeed possible, bhikkhus, there is the possibility where bodily good conduct could produce a desired, pleasant, and agreeable result: such a possibility does exist.**

[2] **Impossible it is, bhikkhus, there is no occasion where verbal good conduct could produce an undesired, unpleasant and disagreeable result: such a possibility does not exist. But such a possibility, bhikkhus, does exist where verbal good conduct could produce a desired, pleasant, and agreeable result: such a possibility does exist.**

[3] **Impossible it is, bhikkhus, there is no occasion where mental good conduct could produce an undesired, unpleasant and disagreeable result: such a possibility does**

---

[111] A.I.xv.2 *'Aṭṭhāna·Pāḷi'* ('Text of the Impossible'). In this connection, The Buddha lists a number of impossibilities with their opposite possibility. For example, one of Right View cannot do certain things (but an ordinary person can do them); two Buddhas/Wheel-Turning Kings cannot arise in one world system at the same time (but one can); a woman cannot be a Buddha/Wheel-Turning King/Sakka/Māra/Brahma (a man can); unwholesome kamma cannot lead to a happy destination (wholesome kamma can), and vice-versa. The ability to see this is the first of what The Buddha calls His ten Tathāgata powers *(Tathāgata·Bala)*. See quotation at 'The Buddha's Knowledge of the Possible/Impossible', p.44.

[112] The simile of the bitter nimb fruit (above) and sweet sugar cane is mentioned in AA.I.xv.2 The Buddha uses it in A.X.III.i.4 *'Bīja·Suttaṁ'* ('The Seed Sutta'). There, He explains how the kamma of one with wrong view leads to the unwholesome and painful, whereas the kamma of one with Right View does the opposite.

[113] A.I.xv.3 *'Aṭṭhāna·Pāḷi'* ('Text of the Impossible')

not exist. But such a possibility, bhikkhus, does exist where mental good conduct could produce a desired, pleasant, and agreeable result: such a possibility does exist.

It is impossible for unwholesome kamma to produce an agreeable result just as it is impossible for a seed of the bitter nimb fruit to produce sweet sugar cane; and it is impossible for wholesome kamma to produce a disagreeable result just as it is impossible for a cutting of sweet sugar cane to produce the bitter nimb fruit.

THE BUDDHA'S KNOWLEDGE OF THE IMPOSSIBLE AND POSSIBLE

This knowledge of the impossible and possible is the first of The Buddha's ten 'Tathāgata Powers' *(Tathāgata·Bala)*. He explains it to the Venerable Sāriputta:[114]

Here, Sāriputta, according to reality, the Tathāgata understands the possible as possible, and the impossible as impossible.

And whatever, Sāriputta, possible as possible, and impossible as impossible the Tathāgata understands according to reality. This then, Sāriputta, is a Tathāgata's Tathāgata power, because of which power the Tathāgata assumes the bull's stance, roars the lion's roar in the assemblies, and sets in motion the divine wheel.[115]

The Buddha explains this principle of impossible and possible throughout His Teaching:[64] it is fundamental to His Teaching.

THE RESULTANT DHAMMAS

The results of kamma are the resultant dhammas *(vipāka dhamma)*.[116] They are resultant mentality *(vipāka·nāma)* and kamma-born materiality *(kamma·ja·rūpa)*:[117]

- Resultant mentality is the different types of resultant consciousness *(vipāka·citta)*: for example, the unwholesome resultant consciousness that gives rebirth in one of the hells, in the ghost world, or the animal world. It is called the rebirth-linking consciousness *(paṭisandhi·citta)*.[118] When it is a wholesome resultant consciousness, it gives rebirth in the human world, the deva worlds, the Brahma worlds, and the immaterial worlds.[65] The life-continuum consciousnesses that maintain the mentality of a life are also resultant, and they stop arising only when the kamma that produces them has ceased.

  Other resultant consciousnesses are, for example, the eye-, ear-, nose-, tongue-, and body consciousnesses that arise upon contact with either a desirable object, or an undesirable object.[119]

---

[114] M.I.ii.2 *'Mahā·Sīha·Nāda·Suttaṁ'* ('The Great Lion's-Roar Sutta'). The Most Venerable Sayadaw refers also to the ten Tathāgata powers as The Buddha gives them in Vbh.I.-xvi.10, and as they are explained in VbhA. They are mentioned also in A.I.xv *'Aṭṭhāna Pāḷi'* ('Text of the Impossible'), and M.III.ii.5 *'Bahu Dhātuka·Suttaṁ'* ('The Many Types of Element Sutta').

[115] BULL'S STANCE/DIVINE WHEEL: see footnote 96, p.39.

[116] DHAMMAS: here *dhamma* is equivalent to the English 'thing': any possible object of thought, including animate/inanimate objects, mental/material objects, facts, events, qualities, circumstances, utterances, and acts. Thus, unwholesome/wholesome dhammas, material/mental dhammas, jhāna dhammas, etc.

[117] See 'Dependent Origination', p.109.

[118] REBIRTH-LINKING CONSCIOUSNESS: this resultant consciousness links the past life with the present. For details, see table '5a: Death and Rebirth', p.52.

[119] There are in all thirty-six types of resultant consciousness, see table '1: The Result-

(Please see further next page.)

Resultant mentality includes then also the mental factors *(cetasika)* associated with the resultant consciousnesses:[120] for example, the pain, joy, or equanimity of a resultant consciousness.[66]

- Kamma-Born Materiality *(kamma·ja·rūpa)*[121] is eighteen types of materiality:

1) Earth element 2) Water element 3) Fire element 4) Wind element 5) Colour 6) Odour 7) Flavour 8) Nutritive essence	Inseparable materiality *(avinibbhoga·rūpa)*: the basic eight elements of any type of materiality, whether it is born of kamma, consciousness, temperature or nutriment. When it occurs together with kamma-born materiality, it is kamma-born materiality.
9) Life faculty	The life faculty *(jīvit·indriya)* maintains one's life. All kamma-born materiality arises together with the life faculty.
10) Eye translucency[122] 11) Ear translucency 12) Nose translucency 13) Tongue translucency 14) Body translucency	The five types of translucent materiality *(pasāda·rūpa)* that are the eye-, ear-, nose-, tongue-, and body base *(āyatana)*. They function as the five material doors *(dvāra)* through which the respective objects are cognized (sights, sounds, odours, etc.).[123]
15) Heart-base materiality	The untranslucent materiality *(napasāda·rūpa)* that is the heart base, located in the blood in the heart. It serves as base for the mind door *(mano·dvāra)*, by which all objects are cognized.
16) Female sex-materiality 17) Male sex-materiality	The sex-materiality *(bhāva·rūpa)* determines whether one is a woman or a man, and determines that sex's feminine and masculine appearance, etc.
18) Kamma-born space	The space element *(ākāsa·dhātu)* that defines and delimits kamma-born material clusters *(rūpa·kalāpa)*.

ant Consciousnesses', p.46.

[120] VsMṬ calls them also resultant mental factors *(vipāka·cetasika)*.

[121] For The Buddha's explanation of how the body is born of dependently originated past kamma, see quotation endnote 63, p.233. For further details, see 'Ultimate Materiality', p.92.

[122] TRANSLUCENCY: see dictionary definition, footnote 964, p.367.

[123] Although the beings in the fine-material world possess a nose, tongue, and body, the equivalent translucent elements do not occur, nor does sex-materiality (see footnote 489, p.175). But the beings there appear as males (VbhA.XVI.x.809 *'Paṭhama·Bala·Niddeso'* ('Exposition of the First Power') DD.XVI.x.2191). Beings in the immaterial world possess no materiality at all.

These resultant dhammas all arise when the appropriate kamma meets the right conditions to produce its result.

1: THE RESULTANT CONSCIOUSNESSES *(Vipāka·Citta)*

Sphere of Consciousness	**Result of**	**Roots**	**Number**	**Details** (See table)
Sensual Sphere	Unwholesome	Unrooted	7	1a, p.54
Sensual Sphere	Wholesome	Unrooted	8	1b, p.64
Sensual Sphere	Wholesome	Rooted	8	1c, p.65
Fine Material Sphere	Wholesome	Rooted	5	1d, p.180
Immaterial Sphere	Wholesome	Rooted	4	1d, p.180
Supramundane Sphere	Wholesome	Rooted	4	1e, p.341
			36[124]	

UNWHOLESOME AND WHOLESOME KAMMA

What then, does The Buddha mean by unwholesome and wholesome kamma? *Akusala·kamma* and *kusala·kamma*?

When a consciousness has an unwholesome root *(akusala·mūla)*, it is an unwholesome consciousness *(akusala·citta)*, and when a consciousness has a wholesome root *(kusala·mūla)*, it is a wholesome consciousness *(kusala·citta)*. Thus, when a mental process's impulsions *(javana)* have an unwholesome root, their volition *(cetanā)* is unwholesome, and we have unwholesome kamma. When a mental process's impulsions have a wholesome root, their volition is wholesome, and we have wholesome kamma.

UNWHOLESOME CONSCIOUSNESS

The unwholesome roots are three: greed *(lobha)*, hatred *(dosa)* and delusion *(moha)*. That means there are three main types of unwholesome consciousness:[125]

1) Greed-rooted consciousness *(lobha·mūla·citta)*
2) Hatred-rooted consciousness *(dosa·mūla·citta)*
3) Delusion-rooted consciousness *(moha·mūla·citta)*

Unwholesome consciousnesses can never be associated with good things, only bad.[67] That is why unwholesome consciousnesses are always associated with

[124] VsM.xiv.454 *'Khandha·Niddesa'* ('Exposition of the Aggregates') PP.xiv.94-105

[125] The Buddha explains the roots in, for example, A.III.II.ii.9 *'Akusala·Mūla·Suttaṁ'* ('The Unwholesome-Root Sutta'): 'These three, bhikkhus, are the unwholesome roots. What three? The greed unwholesome root, the hatred unwholesome root, the delusion unwholesome root.... These three, bhikkhus, are the wholesome roots. What three? The non-greed wholesome root, the non-hatred wholesome root, the non-delusion wholesome root.'

consciencelessness *(ahiri)*,[68] shamelessness *(anottappa)*, restlessness *(uddhacca)*,[69] and delusion *(moha)*.[126] This means that a greed-rooted consciousness is always associated also with delusion, and a hatred-rooted consciousness is also always associated with delusion. But a greed-rooted consciousness cannot be associated with hatred, nor can a hatred-rooted consciousness be associated with greed: greed and hatred cannot arise in the same consciousness. The third type of consciousness, the delusion-rooted one, is an unwholesome consciousness associated with delusion alone.

What is that delusion? It is the same as ignorance *(avijjā)*. We explained it in connection with the *'Gaddula·Baddha'* sutta:[127]

Amongst the ultimately non-existent, amongst women, men, it [ignorance] **hurries on; amongst the existent, however, amongst the aggregates, etc., it does not hurry on....**

What does this mean? It means that ignorance (delusion) sees only conventional truth *(sammuti·sacca)*:[128] women and men, mothers and fathers, wives and husbands, daughters and sons, dogs, cats, pigs, and chickens, etc. These things do not exist according to reality *(yathā·bhūta)*.[70]

The things that do exist according to reality, however, are the aggregates *(khandha)*, the elements *(dhātu)*, the bases *(āyatana)*, mentality-materiality *(nāma·rūpa)*, dependent origination *(paṭicca·samuppāda)*, the workings of kamma, the three characteristics, etc.: in brief, the Four Noble Truths.[129] These things, which are ultimate truth *(paramattha·sacca)*, ignorance does not see.[130] And as we also explained in connection with the *'Gaddula·Baddha'* sutta, that is why beings run on from life to life. This ignorance is the delusion associated with unwholesome consciousnesses.

Greed, hatred, and delusion make a consciousness unwholesome, which means the volition is unwholesome: unwholesome kamma.[71] The Buddha calls it also evil *(pāpa)*, and demerit *(apuñña)*.[72] And the accomplishment of unwholesome kamma, He calls also bad conduct *(du·ccarita)*,[73] and demeritorious formation *(apuññ·ābhisaṅkhāra)*.[74] If that kamma produces its result, it will be an unwished for, undesired and disagreeable result,[75] and will lead to continued production of kamma.[71]

Unprompted and Prompted

If the unwholesome kamma is accomplished spontaneously, without hesitation or the urging of another, it is unprompted *(asaṅkhārika)*; if the unwholesome kamma is accomplished with hesitation, or the urging of self or another, it is prompted *(sasaṅkhārika)*.[76]

The volition of unprompted kamma is the stronger, for it is associated with joy *(pīti)*, whereas prompted kamma is weaker, because it is associated with sloth&torpor *(thina·middha)*.[77]

---

[126] The three roots are also three of the ten defilements *(kilesa)*: 1) greed, 2) hatred, 3) delusion, 4) conceit, 5) views (wrong), 6) scepticism, 7) sloth, 8) restlessness, 9) consciencelessness, 10) shamelessness. (DhS.iii.1235 *'Kilesa·Gocchakaṁ'* ('The Defilement Cluster'))

[127] VsM.xvii.587 *'Paññā·Bhūmi·Niddesa'* ('Exposition of the Wisdom-Ground') PP.xvii.43

[128] SAMMUTI·SACCA: also called *vohāra·sacca*.

[129] See quotation endnote 152, p.245.

[130] The three characteristics are: 1) impermanence *(anicca)*, 2) suffering *(dukkha)*, 3) non-self *(an·atta)*. Ignorance does not see them because of the three types of compactness: see quotation, footnote 9, p.2.

GREED-ROOTED CONSCIOUSNESS[131]

What then does it mean that a consciousness is rooted in greed *(lobha)*?

Here, greed has to do with attraction, gross or subtle: for example, craving *(taṇhā)*, lust *(rāga)*, sensual desire *(kāma·cchanda)*, covetousness *(abhijjhā)*, attachment *(āsajjana)*, clinging *(upādāna)*, conceit *(māna)*, vanity *(mada)*, and views *(diṭṭhi)*.

A consciousness that is associated with these things is a greed-rooted consciousness *(lobha·mūla·citta)*. The volition will in that case always be unwholesome. And, as mentioned, when there is greed, there is always also consciencelessness, shamelessness, restlessness, and delusion. But please note that when an unwholesome consciousness is dissociated from wrong view, it is not thereby associated with Right View: an unwholesome consciousness cannot be associated with Right View.

2a: **MENTAL PHENOMENA** *(nāma·dhamma)* **AT THE ARISING OF GREED-ROOTED CONSCIOUSNESS** *(lobha·mūla·citta)*	Unprompted *(asaṅkhārika)*						Prompted *(sasaṅkhārika)*					
CONSCIOUSNESS *(citta)*	■	■	■	■	■	■	■	■	■	■	■	■
MENTAL FACTORS *(cetasika)*												
Universals *(sabba·citta·sādhāraṇa)*												
1. contact *(phassa)*	■	■	■	■	■	■	■	■	■	■	■	■
2. feeling[132] *(vedanā)*	■	■	■	■	■	■	■	■	■	■	■	■
3. perception *(saññā)*	■	■	■	■	■	■	■	■	■	■	■	■
4. volition *(cetanā)*	■	■	■	■	■	■	■	■	■	■	■	■
5. one-pointedness *(ek·aggatā)*	■	■	■	■	■	■	■	■	■	■	■	■
6. life faculty *(jīvit·indriya)*	■	■	■	■	■	■	■	■	■	■	■	■
7. attention *(manasikāra)*	■	■	■	■	■	■	■	■	■	■	■	■
Miscellaneous *(pakiṇṇaka)*												
1. application *(vitakka)*	■	■	■	■	■	■	■	■	■	■	■	■
2. sustainment *(vicāra)*	■	■	■	■	■	■	■	■	■	■	■	■
3. decision *(adhimokkha)*	■	■	■	■	■	■	■	■	■	■	■	■
4. energy *(vīriya)*	■	■	■	■	■	■	■	■	■	■	■	■
5. joy *(pīti)*	■	■	■				■	■	■			
6. desire *(chanda)*	■	■	■	■	■	■	■	■	■	■	■	■
Unwholesome Mental Factors *(akusala·cetasika)*												
1. delusion *(moha)*	■	■	■	■	■	■	■	■	■	■	■	■
2. consciencelessness *(ahiri)*	■	■	■	■	■	■	■	■	■	■	■	■
3. shamelessness *(anottappa)*	■	■	■	■	■	■	■	■	■	■	■	■
4. restlessness *(uddhacca)*	■	■	■	■	■	■	■	■	■	■	■	■
5. greed *(lobha)*	■	■	■	■	■	■	■	■	■	■	■	■
6. wrong view *(diṭṭhi)*	■			■			■			■		
7. conceit *(māna)*		■			■			■			■	
8. sloth *(thina)*							■	■	■	■	■	■
9. torpor *(middha)*							■	■	■	■	■	■
Total	20		19	19		18	22		21	21		20

[131] The tables that follow have been designed according to the combination system *(saṅgaha·naya)*: all combinations of mental phenomena (AbS.ii.43-52 *'Akusala·Citta·Saṅgaha·Nayo'* ('Unwholesome Consciousness Combination System') CMA.ii.26, and AbS.ii.33-34 *'Sobhana·Cetasika·Sampayoga·Nayo'* ('Beautiful Mental-Factor Association System') CMA.ii.17). One column is one type of consciousness, with mental factors shaded.

[132] FEELING: a greed-rooted consciousness is associated with either pleasure *(somanassa)*, or equanimity *(upekkhā)*: both mental feelings. When there is pleasure, there is also joy *(pīti)*; when there is equanimity, there can be no joy.

HATRED-ROOTED CONSCIOUSNESS

Greed has to do with attraction, but hatred *(dosa)* has to do with repulsion, and resistance, gross or subtle: for example, aversion *(paṭigha)*, envy *(issā)*, possessiveness *(macchariya)*,[134] ill-will *(byāpāda)*, anger *(kodha)*, enmity *(vera)*, cruelty *(vihiṁsā)*, and boredom *(kosajja)*, impatience *(akkhanti)*, remorse *(kukkucca)*, sorrow *(soka)*, lamentation *(parideva)*, displeasure *(domanassa)*, and despair *(upāyāsa)*.

A consciousness that is associated with these things is a hatred-rooted consciousness *(dosa·mūla·citta)*. The volition will in that case always be unwholesome. And when there is hatred, there is always also consciencelessness, shamelessness, restlessness, and delusion.

2b: **MENTAL PHENOMENA** *(nāma·dhamma)* **AT THE ARISING OF HATRED-ROOTED CONSCIOUSNESS** *(dosa·mūla·citta)*	Unprompted *(asaṅkhārika)*				Prompted *(sasaṅkhārika)*			
CONSCIOUSNESS *(citta)*	■	■	■	■	■	■	■	■
MENTAL FACTORS *(cetasika)*								
Universals *(sabba·citta·sādhāraṇa)*								
1. contact *(phassa)*	■	■	■	■	■	■	■	■
2. feeling[133] *(vedanā)*	■	■	■	■	■	■	■	■
3. perception *(saññā)*	■	■	■	■	■	■	■	■
4. volition *(cetanā)*	■	■	■	■	■	■	■	■
5. one-pointedness *(ek·aggatā)*	■	■	■	■	■	■	■	■
6. life faculty *(jīvit·indriya)*	■	■	■	■	■	■	■	■
7. attention *(manasikāra)*	■	■	■	■	■	■	■	■
Miscellaneous *(pakiṇṇaka)*								
1. application *(vitakka)*	■	■	■	■	■	■	■	■
2. sustainment *(vicāra)*	■	■	■	■	■	■	■	■
3. decision *(adhimokkha)*	■	■	■	■	■	■	■	■
4. energy *(vīriya)*	■	■	■	■	■	■	■	■
5. joy *(pīti)*								
6. desire *(chanda)*	■	■	■	■	■	■	■	■
Unwholesome Mental Factors *(akusala·cetasika)*								
1. delusion *(moha)*	■	■	■	■	■	■	■	■
2. consciencelessness *(ahiri)*	■	■	■	■	■	■	■	■
3. shamelessness *(anottappa)*	■	■	■	■	■	■	■	■
4. restlessness *(uddhacca)*	■	■	■	■	■	■	■	■
5. hatred *(dosa)*	■	■	■	■	■	■	■	■
6. envy *(issā)*		■				■		
7. possessiveness *(macchariya)*			■				■	
8. remorse *(kukkucca)*				■				■
9. sloth *(thina)*					■	■	■	■
10. torpor *(middha)*					■	■	■	■
Total	18	19			20	21		

[133] FEELING: a hatred-rooted consciousness is associated with either displeasure *(domanassa)*, or equanimity *(upekkhā)*: both mental feelings. Hence, there can be no joy *(pīti)* associated with hatred-rooted consciousness.

[134] For an analysis of this term, see 'Possessiveness', p.376.

Delusion-Rooted Consciousness

Delusion *(moha)*, when alone, has to do with deluded equanimity, indifference towards the workings of kamma. And when there is scepticism *(vicikicchā)*, and restlessness *(uddhacca)*, it is a delusion-rooted consciousness *(moha·mūla·citta)*. Scepticism refers in this case to scepticism, uncertainty, about The Buddha, the Dhamma, the Sangha, the training, dependent origination, past lives, future lives, etc.[136] The volition is in that case always unwholesome. And when there is delusion, there is again always also consciencelessness and shamelessness.

2c: **Mental Phenomena** *(nāma·dhamma)* **at the Arising of Delusion-Rooted Consciousness** *(moha·mūla·citta)*		
Consciousness *(citta)*	■	■
Mental Factors *(cetasika)*		
Universals *(sabba·citta·sādhāraṇa)*		
1. contact *(phassa)*	■	■
2. feeling[135] *(vedanā)*	■	■
3. perception *(saññā)*	■	■
4. volition *(cetanā)*	■	■
5. one-pointedness *(ek·aggatā)*	■	■
6. life faculty *(jīvit·indriya)*	■	■
7. attention *(manasikāra)*	■	■
Miscellaneous *(pakiṇṇaka)*		
1. application *(vitakka)*	■	■
2. sustainment *(vicāra)*	■	■
3. decision *(adhimokkha)*	■	
4. energy *(vīriya)*	■	■
5. joy *(pīti)*		
6. desire *(chanda)*		
Unwholesome Mental Factors *(akusala·cetasika)*		
1. delusion *(moha)*	■	■
2. consciencelessness *(ahiri)*	■	■
3. shamelessness *(anottappa)*	■	■
4. restlessness *(uddhacca)*	■	■
5. scepticism *(lvicikicchā)*		■
Total	16	16

Unwholesome Resultants

When a kamma with one of these three unwholesome roots matures at the time of death, the rebirth-linking consciousness *(paṭisandhi·citta)* will be an unwholesome resultant consciousness *(akusala·vipāka·citta)*, which means there will be rebirth in either the animal world, the ghost world, or in one of the hells. It is impossible otherwise:[137]

[1] **Impossible it is, bhikkhus, there is no occasion where one of bodily bad conduct possessed, due to that, because of that, at the breakup of the body, after death, in a good destination, a heavenly world, could be reborn: such a possibility does not exist.**
But such a possibility, bhikkhus, does exist where one of bodily bad conduct possessed, due to that, because of that, at the breakup of the body, after death, in perdition, in a bad destination, an infernal place, in hell, could be reborn: such a possibility does exist.

[2] **Impossible it is, bhikkhus, there is no occasion where one of verbal bad conduct possessed, due to that, because of that, at the breakup of the body, after death, in a good destination, a heavenly world, could be reborn: such a possibility does not**

---

135 FEELING: a delusion-rooted consciousness is always and only associated with equanimity *(upekkhā)*, hence it can never be associated with joy. Delusion-rooted consciousness can also never be associated with desire *(chanda)*.

136 See quotations endnote 18, p.22.

137 A.I.xv.3 *'Aṭṭhāna·Pāḷi'* ('Text of the Impossible'). AA explains that 'perdition', 'bad destination', etc., are all synonyms for hell. And it explains that when The Buddha says one is 'possessed' of certain bodily-/verbal-/mental conduct, this refers to three types of 'possession': 1) accumulation-possession *(āyūhana·samaṅgitā)*; AṬ: volition-continuity *(cetanā·santati)*. This corresponds to the preceding/succeeding volitions. 2) volition-possession *(cetanā·samaṅgitā)*; AṬ: decisive volition *(sanniṭṭhāpaka·cetanā)*. This corresponds to the conclusive volition *(sanniṭṭhāna·cetanā)*. 3) kamma possession *(kamma·samaṅgitā)*, which is past kamma that can mature. See in this connection also table '1a: Unwholesome Resultant Consciousness', p.54.

exist.

But such a possibility, bhikkhus, does exist where one of verbal bad conduct possessed, due to that, because of that, at the breakup of the body, after death, in perdition, in a bad destination, an infernal place, in hell, could be reborn: such a possibility does exist.

[3] **Impossible it is, bhikkhus, there is no occasion where one of mental bad conduct possessed, due to that, because of that, at the breakup of the body, after death, in a good destination, a heavenly world, could be reborn: such a possibility does not exist.**

But such a possibility, bhikkhus, does exist where one of mental bad conduct possessed, due to that, because of that, at the breakup of the body, after death, in perdition, in a bad destination, an infernal place, in hell, could be reborn: such a possibility does exist.

Kamma with one of the three unwholesome roots leads also always to continued running on from life to life.

In the hells, the ghost world, and the animal world, the consciousnesses that arise are almost only unwholesome, rooted in greed, hatred, and delusion. Delusion is very strong in the lower worlds, and it is very, very rare for wholesome consciousnesses to arise there. That is why it is almost impossible for beings in those lower worlds to escape.[78]

Rebirth in the human world is always because of wholesome kamma. Nonetheless, among the great majority, the uneducated ordinary people, consciousness is rooted predominantly in greed, hatred, and delusion. Only occasionally do wholesome consciousnesses arise. And among the uneducated ordinary people, delusion is very deep. That is why, when human beings pass away, they are almost always reborn either in hell, the ghost world, or the animal world.[79]

Rebirth in the sensual-plane deva-worlds is always because of superior wholesome kamma. That is why sensual-sphere devas enjoy superior sensual pleasures. And their bodies, their faces, their eyes, their complexion, their clothes, and their mansions are very, very beautiful. Because of that, unfortunately, there is very much lust, envy, and possessiveness. That is why, when sensual-sphere devas pass away, they are also almost always reborn either in hell, the ghost world, or the animal world.[138/80]

In the higher deva worlds, the Brahma worlds, no hatred-rooted consciousnesses can arise. But there is often attachment to and craving for life there, which is greed-rooted. A Brahma may also think his life is eternal, and that he is the creator of the universe, an omnipotent and omniscient god:[81] that is wrong view, which is greed-rooted.

When a Brahma passes away, he can never go directly to hell, the ghost world or the animal world. When the kamma that produced rebirth in the Brahma world has finished, he may be reborn in a lower Brahma world, or in the deva- or human world.

---

[138] See, for example, 'Spoilt Devas', p.194.

5a: **Death and Rebirth***

	PREVIOUS LIFE						PRESENT LIFE →	
CONSCIOUSNESS MOMENT *Citta·Kkhaṇa*	Final consciousnesses of ‡ near-death process *(maraṇ·āsanna·vīthi)*					Final consciousness in one life.	First consciousness in one life.	Sixteen Life-Continuum consciousnesses.
	⇒	⇒	⇒	⇒	⇒	⇒	⇒	⇒⇒⇒...⇒⇒⇒
OBJECT *Ārammaṇa*	Near-death object (kamma/kamma sign *(kamma·nimitta)*/destination sign *(gati·nimitta)*)					Previous life's near-death object	Previous life's near-death object	
CONSCIOUSNESS *Citta*	1st Impulsion *Javana* ↑|↓	2nd Impulsion *Javana* ↑|↓	3rd Impulsion *Javana* ↑|↓	4th Impulsion *Javana* ↑|↓	5th Impulsion *Javana* ↑|↓	DECEASE *Cuti* ↑|↓	Rebirth-Linking *Paṭisandhi* ↑|↓	Life-Continuum *Bhavaṅga* ↑|↓
	The volition of these impulsion consciousnesses functions as a bridge into the new life: if the volition is unwholesome, it is a bad rebirth; if wholesome, it is a good rebirth.					Resultant *Vipāka*	Resultant *Vipāka*	Resultant *Vipāka*

CONSCIOUSNESS MOMENT *Citta·Kkhaṇa*	PRESENT LIFE'S FIRST COGNITIVE PROCESS (a mind-door process)								(After the mental process)
	⇒	⇒	⇒	⇒	⇒	⇒	⇒	⇒	⇒⇒⇒...⇒⇒⇒
OBJECT *Ārammaṇa*	New aggregates (For a deva, human being, animal, or being in hell, it is five aggregates)								Previous life's near-death object.
CONSCIOUSNESS *Citta*	Mind-Door Adverting *Mano·Dvār·Āvajjana* ↑|↓	1st Impulsion *Javana* ↑|↓	2nd Impulsion *Javana* ↑|↓	3rd Impulsion *Javana* ↑|↓	4th Impulsion *Javana* ↑|↓	5th Impulsion *Javana* ↑|↓	6th Impulsion *Javana* ↑|↓	7th Impulsion *Javana* ↑|↓	Life-Continuum *Bhavaṅga* ↑|↓
	Functional *Kiriya*	Kamma							Resultant *Vipāka*

* VsM.xiv.455 *'Viññāṇa·Kkhandha·Kathā'* ('Discussion of the Consciousness-Aggregate') PP.xiv.111-114, & VsM.xvii.622-627 *'Saṅkhāra-·Paccayā·Viññāṇa·Pada·Vitthāra·Kathā'* ('Detailed Discussion of the Formations-as-Cause-Consciousness Phase') PP.xvii.133-145

‡ These are the final consciousnesses of either a five-door- or mind-door process: see subsequent notes.

Notes for Table '5a: Death and Rebirth'

- One consciousness lasts one consciousness moment *(citta·kkhaṇa)*, with three stages: arising *(uppāda)* ↑, standing *(ṭhiti)* |, dissolution *(bhaṅga)* ↓.
- Cognition follows a fixed procedure, according to the natural law of the mind *(citta·niyāma)*. The procedure for death and birth is:

Final Mental Process in One Life

One life's final mental process is either a five-door process or a mind-door process.[139] The object of the final mental process is one of three:

1) Kamma: the volitional formations of an unwholesome or wholesome kamma accomplished earlier in the same life or a previous life. For example, one may recollect the hatred associated with slaughtering animals, the happiness associated with offering food to bhikkhus or other receivers, or the happiness and tranquillity associated with meditation.
2) Kamma Sign *(kamma nimitta)*: an object associated with an unwholesome or wholesome kamma accomplished earlier in the same life or a previous life. A butcher may see a butcher's knife or hear the screams of animals about to be slaughtered, an abortionist may see a dead foetus, a doctor may see patients, a devotee of the Triple Gem may see a bhikkhu, a Buddha image or hear chanting of the Pali Texts, and a meditator may see the ***paṭibhāga*** nimitta of his samatha meditation subject, or one of the three characteristics of his vipassanā meditation subject.
3) Destination sign *(gati nimitta)*: a vision of one's destination, where one is about to be reborn. For rebirth in hell, one may see fire; for an animal rebirth, one may see forests or fields; for a deva-rebirth, one may see deva-mansions.

This object serves as the object of the next life's process-separated consciousnesses *(vīthi·mutta·citta)*.[140/82] They arise independently of sense-door processes. They are all life-continuum consciousnesses *(bhavaṅga·citta)*, with the same past object, and same mental factors. The first such consciousness in one life serves as a link between the past existence and the present, so it is called the rebirth-linking consciousness *(paṭisandhi·citta)*. The last life-continuum consciousness in one life is called the decease consciousness *(cuti·citta)*, because it passes the mentality-materiality continuity on/over to the next existence. All such consciousnesses that arise throughout one life, in between the various mental processes, are just called life-continuum consciousnesses *(bhavaṅga·citta)*.[141/83]

The final mental process of a life has always only five impulsions (not the usual seven). Their volition does not alone produce the rebirth-linking consciousness, but functions as a bridge to cross into the new life.[142] They may be followed by two registration consciousnesses. There may also arise life-continuum conscious-

---

[139] See tables '5b: The Five-Door Process' (p.146), and '5c: The Mind-Door Process' (p.148).

[140] lit. 'process-freed', also called door-separated *(dvāra·vimutta)* lit.'door-freed': in English, this means they are without a process/door, which is misleading. There has been the question whether Nibbāna or a Path-/Fruition consciousness can be the object of the process-separate consciousnesses. For the Sayadaw's answer, see subsequent endnote 82, p.235.

[141] For why the life-continuum ***(bhavaṅga)*** and decease consciousness ***(cuti·citta)*** have those names, see subsequent endnote 83, p.236. For further details on the nature of the life continuum, see footnote 306, p.107.

[142] See further 'Reinforcing Kamma', p.189.

nesses before the decease consciousness: they may arise for a shorter or longer time, even up to days or weeks. With the cessation of the decease consciousness, the life faculty is cut off, and there remains only a corpse: dead materiality.

First Mental Process in One Life

Immediately after the rebirth-linking consciousness (the first consciousness of a life),[143] follow sixteen life-continuum consciousnesses with the same object.[144] And then always a mind-door process, which has the new aggregates as object. Release from the suffering of death (17 consciousness moments earlier) gives rise to relief accompanied by attachment *(nikantika)*, which is existence craving *(bhava·taṇhā)*. Hence, the kamma accomplished by the first mental process in one life is always unwholesome *(akusala)*.

1a: **The Unwholesome Resultant Consciousness** *(Akusala·Vipāka·Citta)*

Door	Consciousness	Feeling	Function	Object
eye-	1. **eye-**	equanimity	seeing	colour
ear-	2. **ear-**	equanimity	hearing	sound
nose-	3. **nose-**	equanimity	smelling	odour
tongue-	4. **tongue-**	equanimity	tasting	flavour
body-	5. **body-**	pain	touching	tangible
mind-	6. **receiving**	equanimity	receiving	colour/sound/odour/ flavour/tangible
mind-	7. **investigation**	equanimity	1.investigation	colour/sound/odour/ flavour/tangible
			2.registration	colour/sound/odour/ flavour/tangible/other
			3.rebirth-linking/ life-continuum/death	kamma/kamma-sign/ destination-sign

In the Pali, it is understood that these types of resultant consciousness are unrooted *(ahetuka)* sensual-sphere consciousnesses *(kām·āvacara·citta)*.

Consciousness: see table '5b: The Five-Door Process', p.146.

Feeling: in the act of seeing, derived materiality (colour) strikes upon derived materiality (the eye translucency of an eye decad-kalāpa). Thus the impact is weak. It is like striking

[143] As may be seen in the 'Death and Rebirth' table, rebirth in one of the three realms of existence follows immediately after death in one of those realms. Nonetheless, there are those who speak of an intermediate existence *(antarā·bhava)*. It is hypothesized to be an existence between the arising of the decease consciousness and subsequent rebirth-linking consciousness (where one has been neither reborn nor not reborn). This wrong view is discussed in KV.viii.2 *'Antarā·Bhava·Kathā'* ('Discussion of Intermeditate Existence'). There, it is explained that such a hypothesis amounts to declaring a realm of existence apart from the three stated by The Buddha (see quotation, endnote 313, p.359). Such a wrong view arises owing to a misinformed reading of the different kinds of Non-Returner (see endnote 289, p.356). It arises also because of misunderstanding a brief existence as a ghost *(peta)* (caused by unwholesome kamma) prior to another rebirth, which itself is caused by: 1) an identical unwholesome kamma (see for example, 'The Ghost Nandaka', p.207); 2) another unwholesome kamma; 3) a wholesome kamma. When one has discerned dependent origination with one's own insight knowledge, this wrong view becomes unsustainable.

[144] An exception is the impercipient being *(a·saññā·satta)*, as there is no consciousness. See footnote 937, p.347.

with one ball of cotton upon another ball of cotton that is lying on an anvil. Hence, both the unwholesome and wholesome resultant eye consciousness is accompanied by only equanimity. This is the same for hearing, smelling, and tasting. But in the act of touching, a great essential object *(mahā·bhūt·ārammaṇaṁ)* (tangible = earth-/fire-/wind element) strikes upon derived materiality (the body translucency of a body decad-kalāpa) as well as upon the four great essentials (of the same body decad-kalāpa). It is like striking with a hammer upon a ball of cotton lying on an anvil. Hence, the unwholesome resultant body consciousness is always accompanied by painful feeling, and the wholesome resultant body consciousness is always accompanied by pleasant feeling (DhSA.I.iii *'Abyākata·Padaṁ'* ('Discourse on Unmoral Consciousness') E.349-350: see also table '1b: The Wholesome Resultant Unrooted Consciousness', p.64).

FUNCTION: the type of consciousness called the investigation consciousness may function as one life's life-continuum consciousnesses: the first one is the rebirth-linking consciousness *(paṭisandhi·citta)* and the last one is the decease consciousness *(cuti·citta)*. Such types of consciousness are also called process-separate consciousnesses *(vīthi·mutta·citta)*. See table mentioned below.

OBJECT: for the kamma/kamma sign/destination sign, see notes to table '5a: Death and Rebirth', p.52.

IGNORANCE AND CRAVING AND THE ROOTS

Before we go on to explain the consciousnesses with wholesome roots, perhaps it is better now to explain the connection between ignorance and craving and the three unwholesome roots.

Let us again quote The Buddha in the *'Gaddula·Baddha'* sutta:

A first point is not known of ignorance-hindered beings fettered by craving, rushing on and running about.

This is what The Buddha calls the round of rebirth *(saṁsāra)*. The round of rebirth is just continued rebirth, life after life. At the end of each life, there is death, and immediately after death, an unwholesome or wholesome kamma produces its result: the result is a new rebirth-linking consciousness *(paṭisandhi·citta)*, and new aggregates. As The Buddha explained, this continued process is maintained by ignorance *(avijjā)* and craving *(taṇhā)*.

When there is craving, the consciousness is greed-rooted *(lobha·mūla)*. And, as explained earlier, when there is greed, there is also delusion *(moha)*. Delusion is the same as ignorance. A greed-rooted consciousness is always associated with delusion, which means craving is always associated with ignorance. Craving *(taṇhā)* is the same as greed *(lobha)*, and ignorance *(avijjā)* is the same as delusion *(moha)*.

Why then does The Buddha mention only ignorance and craving? Why does He not mention hatred? It is because not everyone has hatred. When one becomes a Non-Returner *(An·Āgāmi)*, one will have destroyed the hatred root *(dosa·mūla)*. But there remains some very subtle ignorance and craving as latencies *(anusayā)*, very subtle existence-craving *(bhava·taṇhā)*. The Buddha calls it the lust-for-existence latency *(bhava·rāg·ānusaya)*.[145/84] Everyone except the Arahant has ignorance and craving, and they are the most fundamental conditions for continued rebirth.

[145] LATENCY: there are seven: the sensual-lust-, aversion-, views-, scepticism-, conceit-, lust-for-existence-, and the ignorance latency. Until they have destroyed by a Path Knowledge, they will always be latent. VsM.xxii. (PP.xxii.60) explains: 'For it is owing to their inveteracy that they are called latencies *(anusaya)*, since they lie latent *(anusenti)* as cause for the arising of greed for sense desires, etc., again and again.' For example, one may by practising jhāna suppress the hindrances, and be reborn in the Brahma world,

(Please see further next page.)

Let us say, for example, we think: 'I do not want to be reborn anymore! I want to be a true disciple of The Buddha!' And we practise with the desire for Arahantship in this life. But even though we have a strong desire to put an end to rebirth, it depends on our *pāramī*:[146] especially wisdom *(paññā)*. How much samatha and vipassanā practice did we accomplish in past lives. If we accomplished sufficient wisdom in past lives, we may indeed attain Arahantship in this life: otherwise it is impossible. We may practise with a great desire for Arahantship and no more rebirth, but because our wisdom is not yet deep enough, that desire is in fact also not strong enough. There is still the latency of lust for existence, the latent craving to come into existence *(bhava·taṇhā)*.[147] It is only with the Arahant Path-Knowledge *(Arahatta·Magga·Ñāṇa)* that craving to come into existence, and its associated ignorance, is destroyed without remainder. That is why The Buddha speaks of only ignorance and craving: not mentioning hatred.

Let us now discuss the wholesome roots.

WHOLESOME CONSCIOUSNESS

The wholesome roots are also three: non-greed *(a·lobha)*, non-hatred *(a·dosa)* and non-delusion *(a·moha)*.[148] But when discussing the roots, we do not say non-delusion, we say knowledge *(ñāṇa)*.

Just as unwholesome consciousnesses never can be associated with good things, so can wholesome consciousnesses never be associated with bad things.[85] That is why wholesome consciousnesses never can be associated with conscience-lessness *(ahiri)*, shamelessness *(anottappa)*, restlessness *(uddhacca)*, or greed *(lobha)*, hatred *(dosa)* and delusion *(moha)*. Wholesome consciousnesses are associated always with good things such as the nineteen so-called beautiful universals *(sobhana·sādhāraṇa)*: for example, conscience *(hiri)* and shame *(ottappa)*,[149] tranquillity of [mental] body *(kāya·passaddhi)*, and tranquillity of consciousness *(citta·passaddhi)*,[150] mindful-

---

and remain there for a long time. But eventually one will be reborn again in the sensual realm. And even though the hindrances have been absent from one's mentality-materiality continuity for a very long time, when the conditions are right, they will return. VsM.xxii.830 *'Ñāṇa·Dassana·Visuddhi·Niddeso'* ('Exposition of the Knowledge&Vision Purification') PP.xxii.73 explains that the wrong view-, and scepticism latency are uprooted with Stream Entry; the sensual-lust-, and aversion latency, with Non-Return; the conceit-, lust-for-existence-, and ignorance latency only with Arahantship. See also endnote 180, p.249.

[146] PĀRAMĪ: ten things requisite over many lives for the future attainment of Arahantship: 1) offering, 2) morality, 3) renunciation, 4) wisdom, 5) energy, 6) patience, 7) truthfulness, 8) resolution, 9) loving-kindness, 10) equanimity. For the attainment of Buddhahood, they comprise in all thirty: ten standard, ten medium, and ten ultimate *pāramī*. Gotama Buddha developed them over four incalculables, and a hundred thousand aeons. See detailed exposition in commentary to *'Cariyā·Piṭaka'* ('The Basket on Conduct'), chapter iii, *'Pakiṇṇaka·Kathā'* ('Discussion of the Miscellaneous').

[147] See also endnote 180, p.249.

[148] See quotation, footnote 125, p.46.

[149] See quoted analysis at 'Conscience', p.373.

[150] TRANQUILLITY OF BODY/CONSCIOUSNESS: VsM.xiv.470 *'Khandha·Niddesa'* ('Exposition of the Aggregates') PP.xiv.144-149 explains that body = three mental aggregates (feeling, perception, and formations); consciousness = the consciousness aggregate. There are six such modes, attributes, of wholesome mentality: 1) tranquillity (opposite restlessness); 2) lightness (opposite sloth&torpor); 3) flexibility (opposite the mental rigidity of views

(Please see further next page.)

ness*(sati)* and faith*(saddhā)*.[151] In the same way, all wholesome consciousnesses are associated with non-greed*(a·lobha)* and non-hatred*(a·dosa)*. A non-greed rooted consciousness is always associated also with non-hatred, and a non-hatred rooted consciousness is also always associated with non-greed. But not all wholesome consciousnesses are associated with non-delusion, with knowledge: that is the main distinction between them.[86] We have thus two main types of wholesome consciousness:[152]

- Consciousness that is knowledge-dissociated.*(ñāṇa·vippayutta)*: it is double-rooted*(dvi·hetuka)*, rooted in only non-greed and non-hatred.
- Consciousness that is knowledge-associated.*(ñāṇa·sampayutta)*: it is triple-rooted*(ti·hetuka)*, rooted in non-greed, non-hatred, and non-delusion (knowledge*(ñāṇa)*).

Please note that the wholesome consciousness dissociated from knowledge is not thereby associated with delusion*(moha)*. There is merely no knowledge: a wholesome consciousness cannot be associated with delusion.

Non-greed, non-hatred, and knowledge make a consciousness wholesome, which means the volition is wholesome: wholesome kamma.[87] The Buddha also calls it merit*(puñña)*. And the accomplishment of wholesome kamma He also calls meritorious formation*(puññ·ābhisaṅkhāra)*.[153] If that kamma produces its result, it will be a wished for, desired, and agreeable result. And such wholesome kamma is necessary for us to put an end to kamma and rebirth.[88]

Here we should mention that with attainment of the Arahant Path*(Arahatta·Magga)*, all subsequent consciousnesses in one's final life are associated with non-greed and non-hatred. The Arahant's constant abiding*(satata·vihāra)*[89] is namely cognizing the arising and perishing of formations, and their dependent origination. It is almost always knowledge-associated. But at the time of waking up or falling asleep, or when tired, weak, or sick, the Arahant's cognition may be knowledge-dissociated.[90] Nonetheless, the Arahant's consciousnesses are not wholesome as such, for the Arahant's volition does not generate kamma: it is purely functional*(kiriya)*.[154]

NON-GREED AND NON-HATRED ROOTED CONSCIOUSNESS

Wholesome consciousnesses are always rooted in non-greed*(a·lobha)* and non-hatred*(a·dosa)*. What does that mean? Here, non-greed refers to anything that has to do with generosity*(cāga)*, offering*(dāna)*, and renunciation*(nekkhamma)*, gross or subtle. Non-hatred refers to anything that has to do with loving-kindness*(mettā)*, goodwill*(abyāpada)*, amity*(avera)*, pity*(avihiṁsā)*, compassion*(karuṇā)*, and sympathetic

---

and conceit); 4) wieldiness (opposite the remaining hindrances); 5) proficiency (opposite faithlessness, etc.), 6) rectitude (opposite deceit, dishonesty, etc.). VsMṬ explains that when there is tranquillity, etc. of the mental body, there comes to be also tranquillity, etc. of the material body. That is why The Buddha divided these mental attributes into two.

[151] There are twenty-five beautiful mental factors in all, but these nineteen are present in any wholesome consciousness: see tables 3a/3b, p.67*ff.*

[152] In the discussion that follows, about wholesome consciousnesses and the merit-work bases, reference is made only to the wholesome impulsion consciousnesses: those consciousnesses that in a non-Arahant accomplish kamma.

[153] See quotation endnote 74, p.234.

[154] For further details regarding the Arahant's volition, see 'Unwholesome and Wholesome Volition', p.42.

joy*(mūditā)* (rejoicing in another's good fortune) gross or subtle. And they cannot be separated. When there is offering, there is also goodwill. When there is compassion, there is also renunciation. And, of course, such consciousnesses cannot be associated with delusion: they can only be either dissociated from or associated with non-delusion*(a·moha)*.

KNOWLEDGE-DISSOCIATED AND KNOWLEDGE-ASSOCIATED

What then is the non-delusion, the knowledge*(ñāṇa)*, dissociated from or associated with wholesome consciousnesses?

As we explained earlier,[155] the delusion associated with unwholesome consciousnesses is to see and believe in conventional truth*(sammuti·sacca)*, instead of ultimate truth*(paramattha·sacca)*: it is to see women and men, mothers and fathers, dogs, cats, pigs, and chickens, etc., instead of seeing the aggregates *(khandha)*, mentality-materiality*(nāma·rūpa)*, dependent origination*(paṭicca·samuppāda)*, etc. The knowledge dissociated from or associated with wholesome consciousnesses, however, is five types of knowledge*(ñāṇa)*. They are also called wisdom*(paññā)* or Right View*(Sammā·Diṭṭhi)*.[156]

THE FIVE TYPES OF KNOWLEDGE

The first three types of knowledge are mundane*(lokiya)*:

1) Kamma-Ownership Knowledge/Wisdom*(Kamma·Ssakata·Ñāṇaṁ/Paññā)*: knowledge about the workings of kamma, which is knowing that one's rebirth is determined by one's own past kamma, and that throughout one's life, one's own past and present unwholesome kamma produces painful results, whereas one's own wholesome kamma produces pleasant results.[157] This is the basic Right View*(Sammā·Diṭṭhi)*.[158]
2) Jhāna Wisdom[159]*(Jhāna·Paññā)*:[160] this is knowledge absorbed into,[161] fixed onto, one's meditation object.[162] It may be fixed onto, for example, the

[155] See *Visuddhi·Magga* quotation, p.47.

[156] e.g. AA.I.xvi.4 (324) *'Eka·Dhamma·Pāḷi'* ('Single Thing Text'). These five types of knowledge are in AA.ibid.2 (305) also referred to as five types of Right View*(Sammā·Diṭṭhi)*. Thus, Right View, knowledge, and wisdom are synonyms.

[157] See quotation p.258.

[158] BASIC RIGHT VIEW: see quotation 'To Hold Right View', p.135.

[159] See table '3c: Mental Phenomena at the Arising of Exalted Consciousness', p.85*f.*

[160] Jhāna is referred to only as jhāna wisdom/Right View, never as jhāna knowledge *(ñāṇa)*.

[161] ABSORBED INTO: jhāna is also called absorption (see quotation footnote 163, p.58). VsM.iii.39 *'Kamma·Ṭṭhāna·Ggahaṇa·Niddeso'* ('Exposition of the Meditation-Subject Obtainment') PP.iii.5 explains that there are two kinds of concentration: 1) access*(upacāra)* and 2) absorption*(appanā)*. VsMṬ explains absorption: 'Application that occurs as though absorbing associated things in the object is absorption. Accordingly, it is described as "absorption, absorbing".' DhSṬ.I.iii.160 *'Paṭama·Jjhāna·Kathā·Vaṇṇanā'* ('Description of the First-Jhāna Discussion') explains that 'absorption' is in commentarial usage*(aṭṭha·kathā·vohāro)* used to refer to the application's distinctive function*(vitakkassa kicca·visesena)* of stability*(thirabhāva)* gained in first-jhāna concentration*(thirabhāva·ppatte paṭhama·jjhāna·samādhimhi)*, as well as that same stability in the concentration of the second-, third-, and fourth jhāna, even though they are without application*(vitakka·rahitesu)*.

[162] DhSA.i.160 *'Catukka·Nayo Paṭhama·Jjhānaṁ'* ('Fourfold-System First-Jhāna') E.222-223 explains that jhāna is twofold: 1) object scrutiny*(ārammaṇ·ūpanijjhāna)* is scrutiny of the

(Please see further next page.)

counterpart sign in mindfulness-of-breathing and the ten kasiṇas, or the image of happy beings in loving-kindness meditation.

3) Insight Knowledge/Wisdom *(vipassanā·ñāṇa/paññā)*: this is knowledge absorbed into, fixed onto, the three characteristics of ultimate materiality and mentality.[163] When a consciousness is associated with this knowledge, it does not see women and men, mothers and fathers, dogs, cats, pigs, and chickens; it does not see hands and feet, eyes and ears, left and right, etc.:[164] such things are conventional truth *(sammuti·sacca)*, concepts *(paññati)*. They do not exist according to reality *(yathā·bhūta)*: we cannot practise insight meditation *(vipassanā·bhāvanā)* on things that do not exist. The object of insight meditation is ultimate truth *(paramattha·sacca)*: the aggregates *(khandha)*, mentality-materiality *(nāma·rūpa)*, dependent origination *(paṭicca·samuppāda)*, etc. They exist according to reality.

These three types of knowledge are mundane: they know the formed element *(saṅkhata·dhātu)*. The next two types of knowledge are supramundane *(lokuttara)*. They know Nibbāna, the Unformed Element *(Asaṅkhata·Dhātu)*:[165]

4) Path Knowledge/Wisdom *(Magga·Ñāṇaṁ/Paññā)*: it is the first consciousness that knows Nibbāna: the Stream-Entry-, Once-Return-, Non-Return-, or Arahant Path-Knowledge.
5) Fruition Knowledge/Wisdom *(Phala·Ñāṇaṁ/Paññā)*:[166] it is the subsequent consciousness that knows Nibbāna: the Stream-Entry-, Once-Return-, Non-Return-, or Arahant Fruition-Knowledge.

These two supramundane knowledges are superior to all other kinds of knowledge.[167] But outside the Dispensation of a Buddha, they arise only in those who become Paccekabuddhas, nobody else, because Paccekabuddhas are unable to teach the Dhamma. Only a Fully Enlightened Buddha is able to teach others how to attain these two knowledges.

When a wholesome consciousness is associated with one of these five types of knowledges, it is associated with non-delusion *(a·moha)*, which means it is knowledge-associated *(ñāṇa·sampayutta)*: triple-rooted *(ti·hetuka)*. But when a wholesome consciousness is dissociated from one of these five knowledges, it is dissociated

---

samatha object for attaining the jhānas, for example, scrutiny of the earth-kasiṇa. 2) characteristic scrutiny *(lakkhaṇ·ūpanijjhāna)* is then again threefold: i) vipassanā, which is scrutiny of, for example, the impermanence characteristic. ii) Path, because it accomplishes the work to be done by vipassanā. iii) Fruition, because it scrutinizes the cessation-truth, Nibbāna.

[163] VbhA.X.i.467 *'Suttanta·Bhājanīya·Vaṇṇanā'* ('Description of the Suttanta Classification') DD.X.i.1527 explains: '"Becoming concentrated" is rightly centred, is placed immovably upon the object, becomes as though attained to absorption... this one-pointedness of mind which is associated with insight *(vipassanā)* and originates awakening factors is called the concentration awakening factor.'

[164] See quotation footnote 280, p.93.

[165] See 'Path&Fruition', p.334, and table '5e: The Path Process', p.340.

[166] FRUITION KNOWLEDGE/WISDOM: this is the primary result of the Path Kamma. The secondary result is destruction of defilements.

[167] VbhA.XVI.x.3.770 *'Tika·Niddesa·Vaṇṇanā'* ('Description of the Threes Exposition') DD.XVI.x.2084 explains: 'But Path&Fruition wisdom exceeds all types of wisdom. It occurs widely only when a Tathāgata has arisen, not when One has not.'

from non-delusion, which means it is knowledge-dissociated *(ñāṇa·vippayutta)*: double-rooted *(dvi·hetuka)*.

UNPROMPTED/PROMPTED

If the wholesome kamma is accomplished spontaneously, without hesitation or the urging by self or another,[168] it is unprompted *(asaṅkhārika)*; if the wholesome kamma is accomplished with hesitation, or the urging by self or another, it is prompted *(sasaṅkhārika)*.[169/91] The volition of unprompted wholesome kamma is the stronger, although both unprompted and prompted wholesome kamma have the same combination of mental factors.[170] But there are other important factors to be considered.

INFERIOR AND SUPERIOR

Wholesome kamma can also be divided into the inferior *(omaka)* and superior *(ukkaṭṭha)*.[171] It depends on how one performs the wholesome kamma. When accomplishing wholesome kamma, four things decide the quality of the kamma:[172]

1) Desire *(chanda)*: this is one's desire to perform the wholesome kamma: for example, one's desire to make the offering, one's desire to abstain from the unwholesome action, one's desire to concentrate on the meditation subject. If one's desire is low, the wholesome kamma is inferior, whereas if it is high, one's wholesome kamma is superior.

---

168 The Buddha makes this distinction also in S.II.I.iii.5 *'Bhūmija·Suttaṁ'* ('The Bhūmija Sutta'): see quotation endnote 76, p.20.

169 VsM.xiv.452 *'Khandha·Niddesa'* ('Exposition of the Aggregates') PP.xiv.84 explains: 'When a man is happy on encountering an excellent gift to be offered, or recipient, etc., or some such cause for joy, and by placing Right View foremost that occurs in the way beginning "There is offering" [see end of footnote], he unhesitatingly and unurged by others performs such merit as offering, etc., then his consciousness is accompanied by joy, associated with knowledge, and unprompted. But when a man is happy and content in the way aforesaid, and, while placing Right View foremost, yet he does it hesitantly through lack of free generosity, etc., or urged on by others, then his consciousness is of the same kind as the last but prompted; for in this sense "prompting" is a term for a prior effort exerted by himself or, others. But when young children have a natural habit due to seeing the behaviour of relatives and are joyful on seeing bhikkhus and at once give them whatever they have in their hands or pay homage, then the third kind of consciousness arises [knowledge-dissociated, unprompted]. But when they behave like this on being urged by their relatives, "Give; pay homage", then the fourth kind of consciousness arises [as above but prompted].'

170 This as opposed to unwholesome unprompted/prompted consciousnesses: see 'Unprompted and Prompted', p.47. See also Tables 2a/2b/2c pp.48-50.

171 In DhS.i.269-276 *'Te·Bhūmaka·Kusalaṁ'* ('Triple-Planed Wholesome') The Buddha divides wholesome consciousnesses into three: low *(hīna)*/medium *(majjhima)*/high *(paṇīta)* (also DhSA.ibid./E.vii, and DhSṬ). But AbS.v.72-73 *'Kamma·Catukkaṁ'* ('Kamma Tetrad') CMA.-v.29 narrows them down to two: inferior/superior.

172 These four factors are usually discussed only as means to power *(iddhi·pāda)*, related to jhāna practice (see 'The Four Means to Power', p.175). But discussing low, medium, and high meritorious consciousness of the three spheres, The Buddha in DhS.ibid. discusses these factors without referring to them as means to power; as does DhSA.ibid. Also VsM.-i.12 *'Sīla·Ppabheda·Kathā'* ('Discussion of the Morality-Variety') PP.i.33 refers to them as determining low, medium, and high morality. The details here have been taken from The Buddha's explanation in Vbh.ix *'Iddhi·Pāda·Vibhaṅgo'* ('Analysis of Means to Power').

2) Energy*(vīriya)*: this is one's arousing of energy to perform the wholesome kamma, the arousing of effort*(padhāna)*.
3) Consciousness*(citta)*: this is one's concentrating on the wholesome kamma. Without distraction, one makes the offering, undertakes the precepts, concentrates on the meditation subject, etc.
4) Investigation*(vīmaṁsā)*: this is one's knowledge*(ñāṇa)*, wisdom*(paññā)*, and Right View*(Sammā·Diṭṭhi)* when performing the wholesome kamma. We just discussed it.

When either of these factors is low or middling, the wholesome kamma is inferior; when high, the wholesome kamma is superior. For example, if one makes an offering or undertakes the precepts in order to attain future sensual pleasures as a rich human being, or a deva, then the wholesome kamma is inferior. If one does it with the intention to attain Nibbāna, then the wholesome kamma is superior.[173] We shall discuss this in more detail later, when we discuss the three merit-work bases*(puñña·kiriya·vatthu)*.[174]

The inferior is thus associated with unwholesome things before and after the wholesome kamma consciousnesses, whereas the superior is associated with wholesome things before and after the wholesome kamma consciousnesses. They are called the preceding&succeeding volitions*(pubb·āpara·cetanā)*.[175]

What does this mean? When we make knowledge-associated offerings, or train in knowledge-associated morality and meditation, it does not mean we no longer see concepts such as men and women, etc.: we do, but such unwholesome consciousnesses intersperse the wholesome consciousnesses. Generally speaking,[176] during the whole course of a meritwork, many different kinds of consciousnesses will arise: unwholesome as well as wholesome.

When we make an offering, the wholesome consciousnesses of offering that take the wholesome kamma of offering as object may be interspersed by different types of unwholesome consciousness: we discussed them in connection with the different types of temperament.[177] For example, there may be greed-rooted consciousnesses, thinking: 'My offering is better than her offering!' or 'If I make this superior offering, maybe I shall win the lottery!' or 'My business will prosper!' There may be hatred-rooted consciousnesses, thinking: 'My offering is not very good!' or after the offering, 'I made too much food: what a waste!' And there may be delusion-rooted consciousnesses, thinking: 'This is my mother', 'this is my son', 'this is a bhikkhu', etc., or 'Can offerings produce rebirth? Is it true?'

Our offering may, on the other hand, be interspersed by wholesome consciousnesses: rooted in non-greed and non-hatred. For example: 'I want to make very good offerings: that will make me happy!' or 'How good it is that he also makes offerings!' (rejoicing over another's offering). The interspersing wholesome consciousnesses may also be knowledge-associated. For example: 'Making offerings

---

[173] DhSṬ.ibid. explains that the low is dependent on occurrence of rebirth*(vaṭṭa·nissita)*, and the superior is dependent on non-occurrence of rebirth*(vivaṭṭa·nissita)*.
[174] See 'The Merit-Work Bases', p.66.
[175] These differences manifest in the resultant consciousnesses: see table '1f: Inferior & Superior Wholesome Kamma, Their Roots & Resultant Rebirth-Linking', p.63. For the succeeding/preceding volitons, see explanation from MA, footnote 671, p.259.
[176] That is, in some cases excepting a Noble One, and in all cases excepting the Arahant.
[177] See 'The Variety of Temperament', p.32.

will make me happy: it will help my meditation!' or 'This offering can be a supporting cause for my attainment of Nibbāna!'[92]

In the same way, when we attain jhāna, the jhāna consciousnesses will all be associated with knowledge of the meditation object. But before we go into jhāna, or after we have come out of jhāna, there may be unwholesome consciousnesses. For example, greed-rooted consciousnesses may arise, thinking: 'I am a very good meditator!' or 'If I can sit in jhāna for a whole day, I can become famous!' Hatred-rooted consciousnesses may arise, thinking: 'Why is that meditator so noisy!' or 'What is the use of sitting in jhāna?' Delusion-rooted consciousnesses may arise, thinking: 'This is my mother', 'this is my son', 'this is a bhikkhu', etc., or 'Does jhāna enable me to see past and future lives? Is it true?'

Our jhāna may, on the other hand, be interspersed by wholesome consciousnesses, rooted in non-greed and non-hatred. For example: 'I want to develop jhāna: that will make me happy!' or 'How good it is that he is also meditating!' (this is rejoicing over another's practice). The interspersing wholesome consciousnesses may also be knowledge-associated. For example: 'Developing jhāna will enable me to see ultimate truth: then I can practise insight meditation, and attain Nibbāna!'

Teaching of Dhamma may also be interspersed by unwholesome consciousnesses.[178] For example, if one teaches the Dhamma for gain, with the thought, 'By this I will be known as a teacher!' greed-rooted consciousnesses arise. The same if one reads the Dhamma or listens to Dhamma talks with the thought: 'By this people will consider me as one of the faithful!' One's teaching and learning the Dhamma may, on the other hand, be interspersed by wholesome consciousnesses, rooted in non-greed and non-hatred, even in knowledge: for example, if one teaches and learns the Dhamma thinking, 'Teaching the Dhamma will help me understand the Dhamma better, and be a supporting cause for attaining Nibbāna!' and 'Learning the Dhamma is very meritorious, and will be a supporting cause for attaining Nibbāna!'

In this way, we may understand that unless we are in deep concentration, practising samatha or vipassanā, many, many different types of mental process may arise one after the other: wholesome and unwholesome. But please always remember that these analyses are only general guidelines: the workings of kamma is very profound, and there are many variations. Only a Buddha can explain them in detail, and then only case by case.

Inferior and Superior; the Roots and Resultants

Why are these associated things important? Because they help determine the quality of the wholesome kamma's result. The quality of the impulsion consciousnesses *(javana)* determines the quality of the resultant consciousnesses *(vipāka·citta)*: for example, the quality of the rebirth-linking consciousness *(paṭisandhi·citta)*.

[178] The examples in this paragraph are from DhSA.i.156-9 *'Puñña·Kiriya·Vatth·Ādi·Kathā'* ('Discussion of Merit-Work Base Etc.') E.211.

1f: **Inferior & Superior Wholesome Kamma, Their Roots & Resultant Rebirth-Linking**

	KAMMA →		Rebirth-linking	KAMMA →		Rebirth-linking
TRIPLE-ROOTED*(ti·hetuka)*	Superior *(ukkaṭṭha)*		consciousness *(paṭisandhi·citta)*	Inferior *(omaka)*		consciousness *(paṭisandhi·citta)*
1. Non-greed*(a·lobha)*						
2. Non-hatred*(a·dosa)*		→			→	
3. Non-delusion*(a·moha)*						
DOUBLE-ROOTED*(dvi·hetuka)*						UNROOTED*(ahetuka)*
1. Non-greed*(a·lobha)*		→			→	0. ———
2. Non-hatred*(a·dosa)*						

According to inferiority and superiority, and the dissociation or association of knowledge, there are three different types of resultant consciousness:[179]

1) The wholesome resultant consciousness that is unrooted*(ahetuka)*: it may function either as a process consciousness*(vīthi·citta)* or as a process-separate consciousness*(vīthi·mutta·citta)*.
   i) As a process consciousness*(vīthi·citta)*, the wholesome resultant unrooted consciousness is the result of wholesome kamma that is inferior*(omaka)* as well as superior*(ukkaṭṭha)*, knowledge-dissociated*(ñāṇa·vippayutta)* as well as knowledge-associated*(ñāṇa·sampayutta)*, triple-rooted*(ti·hetuka)* as well as double-rooted*(dvi·hetuka)*. How so? Because any type of wholesome kamma may produce eye consciousness, ear consciousness, etc. Also a Buddha sees, hears, smells, tastes, and touches objects that are the result of wholesome kamma: pleasant*(iṭṭha)* or very pleasant*(ati·iṭṭha)*.
   ii) As a process-separate consciousness*(vīthi·mutta·citta)*, the wholesome resultant unrooted consciousness is the result of wholesome kamma that is inferior*(omaka)* and knowledge-dissociated*(ñāṇa·vippayutta)*: inferior double-rooted*(dvi·hetuka)*. If such kamma produces the rebirth-linking consciousness, one will be either a lower deva, a ***rakkha***, a ***nāga*** or ***garūda***, or a human being who is congenitally blind, deaf, mute, or in some other way physically or mentally deficient.

[179] AbS.v.71 *'Kamma·Catukkaṁ'* ('Kamma Tetrad') CMA.v.29)

1b: **The Wholesome Resultant Unrooted Consciousness***(Kusala·Vipāka·Ahetuka·Citta)*

DOOR	CONSCIOUSNESS	FEELING	FUNCTION	OBJECT
eye-	1. **eye-**	equanimity	seeing	colour
ear-	2. **ear-**	equanimity	hearing	sound
nose-	3. **nose-**	equanimity	smelling	odour
tongue-	4. **tongue-**	equanimity	tasting	flavour
body-	5. **body-**	happiness	touching	tangible
mind-	6. **receiving**	equanimity	receiving	colour/sound/odour/ flavour/tangible
mind-	7. **investigation**	pleasure	1. investigation	colour/sound/odour/ flavour/tangible
		equanimity	investigation	colour/sound/odour/ flavour/tangible
		pleasure	2. registration	colour/sound/odour/ flavour/tangible/other
		equanimity	registration	colour/sound/odour/ flavour/tangible/other
		equanimity	3. rebirth-linking/ life-continuum/ death	kamma/kamma-sign/ destination-sign

In the Pali, it is understood that these types of resultant consciousness are sensual-sphere consciousnesses*(kām·āvacara·citta)*.

CONSCIOUSNESS: see table '5b: The Five-Door Process', p.146.

FEELING: see notes to 'Unwholesome Resultant Consciousness', p.54.

FUNCTION: the type of consciousness called the investigation consciousness may function as one life's life-continuum consciousnesses: the first one is the rebirth-linking consciousness *(paṭisandhi·citta)* and the last one is the decease consciousness*(cuti·citta)*. Such types of consciousness are also called process-separate consciousnesses*(vīthi·mutta·citta)*. See table mentioned below.

OBJECT: for the kamma/kamma sign/destination sign, see notes to table '5a: Death and Rebirth', p.52.

2) The resultant consciousness that is double-rooted*(dvi·hetuka)*:[180] it is the result of two types of wholesome kamma. Wholesome kamma that is superior*(ukkaṭṭha)* and knowledge-dissociated (superior double-rooted), and wholesome kamma that is inferior and knowledge-associated*(ñāṇa·sampayutta)*: inferior triple-rooted*(ti·hetuka)*. As we just mentioned, when such kamma produces eye consciousness, ear consciousness, etc., those resultant consciousnesses are unrooted: those types of consciousness are unrooted whatever the wholesome kamma that produces them. But if the double-rooted resultant consciousness becomes a rebirth-linking consciousness, one will be a lower deva, or a low-born human being, but with faculties complete. And one's wisdom will be dull, meaning one will be unable to understand the Dhamma well. And one will in that life be unable to attain either jhāna or Path&Fruition.[93]

[180] See table '1c Rooted Sensual-Sphere Wholesome Resultant Consciousness', p.65.

3) The resultant consciousness that is triple-rooted *(ti·hetuka)*: it is the result of wholesome kamma that is superior and knowledge-associated: superior triple-rooted. And here again, when such kamma produces eye consciousness, ear consciousness, etc., those resultant consciousnesses are unrooted: those types of consciousness are unrooted whatever the wholesome kamma that produces them. But if the triple-rooted resultant consciousness becomes a rebirth-linking consciousness, one will be either a very beautiful high deva with superior deva-pleasures, or a high-born human being with faculties complete, great beauty, good health, enjoying superior sensual pleasures, etc.[94] And one's wisdom will be sharp, meaning one will be able to understand the Dhamma well. And in that life (according to one's *pāramī*), one will be able to attain jhāna and Path&Fruition.

1c: **The Rooted Sensual-Sphere Resultant Consciousness** *(Sahetuka·Kām·Āvacara·Vipāka·Citta)**

DOOR	NO.	FEELING	KNOWLEDGE	PROMPTING	FUNCTION	OBJECT
mind-	1.	pleasure	knowledge-associated	unprompted	1. registration	colour, sound, odour, flavour, tangible, other
	2.	"	"	prompted		
	3.	pleasure	knowledge-dissociated	unprompted		
	4.	"	"	prompted		
	5.	equanimity	knowledge-associated	unprompted	2. rebirth-linking, life-continuum, death	kamma, kamma-sign, destination-sign
	6.	"	"	prompted		
	7.	equanimity	knowledge-dissociated	unprompted		
	8.	"	"	prompted		

The kamma consciousnesses that produce these types of resultant consciousness are also called the great wholesomes *(mahā·kusala)*, and their resultants the great resultants *(mahā·vipāka)*. Even so, the great resultants are usually not called wholesome-resultants *(kusala·vipāka)*, since that term refers usually only to the wholesome resultant unrooted types of consciousness: see table, p.64.

PROMPTING: see 'Unprompted and Prompted', p.60.

KNOWLEDGE: see 'Knowledge-Dissociated and Knowledge-Associated', p.58.

FUNCTION: these eight types of consciousness may function as one life's life-continuum consciousnesses: the first one is the rebirth-linking consciousness *(paṭisandhi·citta)* and the last one is the decease consciousness *(cuti·citta)*. Such types of consciousness are also called process-separate consciousnesses *(vīthi·mutta·citta)*. See table mentioned below.

OBJECT: for the kamma/kamma sign/destination sign, see notes to table '5a: Death and Rebirth', p.52.

Again, please remember that these analyses are general guidelines: there are many variations. Thus, someone with sharp wisdom who is ugly, born into a rich or poor family, may in fact have a triple-rooted rebirth-linking consciousness; or someone who is dull but very beautiful, born into a rich or poor family, may in fact have a double-rooted rebirth-linking consciousness.[181] You will understand it

[181] Such variations may be attributed to frustrating kamma: see 'Frustrating Kamma', p.190. For an example of variation, see also 'Scowling Pañcapāpī' (p.271): she was born very ugly, but with a superior touch.

better when you discern these workings of kamma yourself with your own direct knowledge: when you discern dependent origination, and attain the Cause-Apprehending Knowledge *(Paccaya·Pariggaha·Ñāṇa)*.

In accordance with these guidelines, we shall now discuss wholesome consciousness as the three merit-work bases *(puñña·kiriya·vatthu)*.

The Merit-Work Bases

The three merit-work bases *(puñña·kiriya·vatthu)* are three ways to accomplish wholesome kamma, to develop wholesome consciousness. They are:[95] offering *(dāna)*, morality *(sīla)*, and meditation *(bhāvanā)*.[182/96]

All three merit-work bases can be either knowledge-dissociated *(ñāṇa·vippayutta)* or knowledge-associated *(ñāṇa·sampayutta)*; in other words, double-rooted *(dvi·hetuka)* or triple-rooted *(ti·hetuka)*.

For offering and morality, the associated knowledge is the Kamma-Ownership Knowledge *(Kamma·Ssakata·Ñāṇa)*; for meditation, the associated knowledge is either jhāna-wisdom *(jhāna·paññā)*, or insight meditation-knowledge *(vipassanā·ñāṇa)*. And if our meditation reaches its summit, the associated knowledge is Path Knowledge *(Magga·Ñāṇa)* and Fruition Knowledge *(Phala·Ñāṇa)*.

Offering

The first merit-work base is offering *(dāna)*: the kamma of offering someone something.[183] Such an act is opposite greed; rooted in non-greed *(a·lobha)*. It is also rooted in non-hatred *(a·dosa)*, because hatred cannot arise together with non-greed. If we offer without faith in the Kamma-Ownership Knowledge *(Kamma·Ssakata·Ñāṇa)*, it is knowledge-dissociated *(ñāṇa·vippayutta)*: double-rooted *(dvi·hetuka)*. If we offer with faith or direct knowledge of the Kamma-Ownership Knowledge, it is knowledge-associated *(ñāṇa·sampayutta)*: triple-rooted *(ti·hetuka)*.

As we just mentioned, the Kamma-Ownership Knowledge is the basic Right View: it exists also outside a Buddha's Dispensation. But so long as one has not seen the workings of dependent origination (so long as one has not attained the Cause-Apprehending Knowledge *(Paccaya·Pariggaha·Ñāṇa)*), so long is that Right View based on faith in one's teacher. If one's teacher is The Buddha, one's Right View can be strong. And one may make great offerings that are knowledge-associated.[184]

---

[182] DhSA.i.156-9 *'Puñña·Kiriya·Vatth·Ādi·Kathā'* ('Discussion of Merit-Work Base Etc.') E.212 expands the merit-work bases from three to ten: see subsequent endnote 96, p.238.

[183] For the ten bases for offering *(dasa dāna·vatthu)*, see quotation at 'One Makes Offerings', p.286.

[184] As examples of superior offerings made outside a Buddha's Dispensation, VbhA.XVI.x.3.770 *'Tika·Niddesa·Vaṇṇanā'* ('Description of the Threes-Exposition') DD.XVI.x.2084 refers to the offerings of our Bodhisatta in past lives, as Velāma (A.IX.I.ii.10 *'Velāma·Suttaṁ'* ('The Velāma Sutta')), and Vessantara (JA.xxii.10 (547) *'Vessantara·Jātaka·Vaṇṇanā'* ('Description of the Vessantara Jātaka'). And explaining offerings made when a Tathāgata has arisen, it explains: 'There is no measure of those who undertake great offerings *(mahā·dāna)* by means of that knowledge.'

If one's offering is knowledge-dissociated, however, dissociated from the Kamma-Ownership Knowledge, one makes offerings for a reason other than to accomplish wholesome kamma.

3a: **Mental Phenomena** *(nāma·dhamma)* **at the Arising of Knowledge-Dissociated Consciousness** *(ñāṇa·vippayutta·citta)*[185]
CONSCIOUSNESS *(citta)*
MENTAL FACTORS *(cetasika)*
Universals *(sabba·citta·sādhāraṇa)*
1. contact *(phassa)*
2. feeling[186] *(vedanā)*
3. perception *(saññā)*
4. volition *(cetanā)*
5. one-pointedness *(ek·aggatā)*
6. life faculty *(jīvit·indriya)*
7. attention *(manasikāra)*
Miscellaneous *(pakiṇṇaka)*
1. application *(vitakka)*
2. sustainment *(vicāra)*
3. decision *(adhimokkha)*
4. energy *(vīriya)*
5. joy *(pīti)*
6. desire *(chanda)*
Beautiful Universals *(sobhana·sādhāraṇa)*
1. faith *(saddhā)*
2. mindfulness *(sati)*
3. conscience *(hiri)*
4. shame *(ottapa)*
5. non-greed *(a·lobha)*
6. non-hatred *(a·dosa)*
7. ever-evenness *(tatra·majjhattatā)*

Please continue next page.

THE WORKINGS OF OFFERING

KNOWLEDGE-DISSOCIATED

For example, it is very rare for children to offer with knowledge of the workings of kamma. Usually children will offer because they want to copy their parents, or because their parents have told them to offer, or because they enjoy offering, or enjoy being praised when they offer. Even most adults offer without knowledge of the workings of kamma. One may offer, for example, out of loving-kindness, wishing to help another, such as offering food and other requisites to the poor, the starving, etc. One may also offer to ascetics and monks, etc. because of kindness. One may also offer because it is custom or tradition, or because one's religion says one should. And one may offer because of conceit, wanting to have a good name, and be respected. One may even offer because one is afraid of blame. When parents give something to their children there is usually also much attachment and unwise attention (thinking, 'This is my son', or, 'This is my daughter'): the same when a husband gives something to his wife, a wife to her husband, a friend to a friend, etc. One may even offer with wrong view: offering and believing that there is no result from offering, that there is no rebirth after death, etc.

---

185 The tables that follow (3a & 3b) have been designed according to the combination system *(saṅgaha·naya)*: all combinations of mental phenomena. (AbS.ii.40-42 *'Kām·Āvacara·Sobhana·Citta·Saṅgaha·Nayo'* ('Sensual-Sphere Beautiful-Consciousness Combination-System') CMA.ii.24, and AbS.ii.33-34 *'Sobhana·Cetasika·Sampayoga·Nayo'* ('Beautiful Mental-Factor Association-System') CMA.ii.17.) One column is one arising of consciousness, with mental factors shaded.

186 FEELING: a wholesome consciousness is associated with either pleasure *(somanassa)*, or equanimity *(upekkhā)*: both mental feelings. When there is pleasure, there is also joy *(pīti)*; when there is equanimity, there can be no joy.

Even so, offering is in all cases wholesome: if it is interspersed by wholesome consciousnesses, it can even be superior *(ukkaṭṭha)*. But when it is dissociated from knowledge of the workings of kamma, it is the less superior, for it is only double-rooted *(dvi·hetuka)*: associated with only non-greed *(a·lobha)* and non-hatred *(a·dosa)*. The kamma being less powerful means the result will also be less powerful.

Continued from previous page.

3a: **Mental Phenomena** *(nāma·dhamma)* **at the Arising of Knowledge-Dissociated Consciousness** *(ñāṇa·vippayutta·citta)*

Beautiful Universals *(sobhana·sādhāraṇa)*				
8. tranquillity of [mental] body[187] *(kāya·passaddhi)*				
9. tranquillity of consciousness *(citta·passaddhi)*				
10. lightness of [mental] body *(kāya·lahutā)*				
11. lightness of consciousness *(citta·lahutā)*				
12. flexibility of [mental] body *(kāya·mudutā)*				
13. flexibility of consciousness *(citta·mudutā)*				
14. wieldiness of [mental] body *(kāya·kammaññatā)*				
15. wieldiness of consciousness *(citta·kammaññatā)*				
16. proficiency of [mental] body *(kāya·pāguññatā)*				
17. proficiency of consciousness *(citta·pāguññatā)*				
18. rectitude of [mental] body *(kāy·ujukatā)*				
19. rectitude of consciousness *(citt·ujukatā)*				
Abstinences *(viratī)*				
1. Right Speech *(Sammā·Vācā)*				
2. Right Action *(Sammā·Kammanta)*				
3. Right Livelihood *(Sammā·Ājīva)*				
Immeasurables *(appamaññā)*				
1. compassion *(karuṇā)*				
2. sympathetic joy *(muditā)*				
Total mental phenomena	33	34	32	33

[187] TRANQUILLITY OF [MENTAL] BODY/CONSCIOUSNESS: see footnote 150, p.56.

Knowledge-Associated

Offering with knowledge of the workings of kamma is more powerful. Why? Because the presence of wisdom means the consciousness is triple-rooted *(ti·hetuka)*: rooted in non-greed *(a·lobha)*, non-hatred *(a·dosa)*, and non-delusion *(a·moha)*. That always makes a wholesome kamma more powerful.

A further important factor is whether the offering is inferior *(omaka)* or superior *(ukkaṭṭha)*.

The Inferior Offering

What are the factors for an offering that is inferior *(omaka)*? There are four:[97]

1) The offerer has obtained the requisite by wrong livelihood.
2) The offerer has poor or no morality: she or he keeps only some precepts, or no precepts at all.
3) Before or after the kamma consciousnesses of the actual offering, the offerer's mind is associated with unwholesome things. For example, before offering, she or he may have been angry or impatient; she or he may be dissatisfied with the requisite, or she or he may offer in a casual or distracted manner; after offering, she or he may regret having made the offering.[190] She or he may also have only shallow faith in the workings of kamma. She or he may also make the offering with the wish for some worldly gain, or for sensual pleasures in a future life as a rich human being, or a deva.
4) The receiver has poor or no morality: she or he keeps only some precepts, or no precepts at all.[98]

3b: **Mental Phenomena** *(nāma·dhamma)* **at the Arising of Knowledge-Associated Consciousness** *(ñāṇa·sampayutta·citta)*[188]
Consciousness *(citta)*
Mental Factors *(cetasika)*
Universals *(sabba·citta·sādhāraṇa)*
1. contact *(phassa)*
2. feeling *(vedanā)*
3. perception *(saññā)*
4. volition *(cetanā)*
5. one-pointedness *(ek·aggatā)*
6. life faculty *(jīvit·indriya)*
7. attention *(manasikāra)*
Miscellaneous *(pakiṇṇaka)*
1. application *(vitakka)*
2. sustainment *(vicāra)*
3. decision *(adhimokkha)*
4. energy *(vīriya)*
5. joy *(pīti)*
6. desire *(chanda)*
Beautiful Universals *(sobhana·sādhāraṇa)*
1. faith *(saddhā)*
2. mindfulness *(sati)*
3. conscience *(hiri)*
4. shame *(ottapa)*
5. non-greed *(a·lobha)*
6. non-hatred *(a·dosa)*
7. ever-evenness *(tatra·majjhattatā)*
8. tranquillity of [mental] body[189] *(kāya·passaddhi)*
9. tranquillity of consciousness *(citta·passaddhi)*
10. lightness of [mental] body *(kāya·lahutā)*
11. lightness of consciousness *(citta·lahutā)*
12. flexibility [of mental] body *(kāya·mudutā)*
13. flexibility of consciousness *(citta·mudutā)*

Please continue next page.

[188] See footnote 185, p.67.
[189] TRANQUILLITY OF BODY/-CONSCIOUSNESS: see footnote 150, p.56.
[190] See, for example, 'The Parsimonious Millionaire', p.34.

These are examples of how one's offering can be interspersed by countless thousand million unwholesome consciousnesses rooted in greed *(lobha)*, hatred *(dosa)*, and delusion *(moha)*. That makes one's offering inferior. If in such a case, one does not understand the workings of kamma, it is dissociated from non-delusion, which makes one's offering inferior, double-rooted *(dvi·hetuka)*: that means the resultant consciousness will be unrooted *(ahetuka)*. If one does understand the workings of kamma, it is associated also with non-delusion *(a·moha)*, but even so the interspersion of countless unwholesome consciousnesses make one's offering inferior, triple-rooted *(ti·hetuka)*: that means the resultant consciousness will be only double-rooted *(dvi·hetuka)*.

Continued from previous page.

3b: **Mental Phenomena** *(nāma·dhamma)* **at the Arising of Knowledge-Associated Consciousness** *(ñāṇa·sampayutta·citta)*				
Beautiful Universals *(sobhana·sādhāraṇa)*				
14. wieldiness [of mental] body *(kāya·kammaññatā)*				
15. wieldiness of consciousness *(citta·kammaññatā)*				
16. proficiency [of mental] body *(kāya·pāguññatā)*				
17. proficiency of consciousness *(citta·pāguññatā)*				
18. rectitude [of mental] body *(kāy·ujukatā)*				
19. rectitude of consciousness *(citt·ujukatā)*				
Abstinences *(viratī)*				
1. Right Speech *(Sammā·Vācā)*				
2. Right Action *(Sammā·Kammanta)*				
3. Right Livelihood *(Sammā·Ājīva)*				
Immeasurables *(appamaññā)*				
1. compassion *(karuṇā)*				
2. sympathetic joy *(muditā)*				
Non-Delusion *(a·moha)*				
1. WISDOM FACULTY *(paññ·indriya)*[191]				
Total mental phenomena	34	35	33	34

In the Pali Texts, there is an example of a man who makes such inferior offerings.[192] In one of His past lives, when He was only an unenlightened Bodhisatta, The Buddha was a hermit *(tāpasa)* called Kaṇhadīpayana. One day, a father and mother brought their young son to him, because the boy had been bitten by a snake. And to counteract the poison, they all decided to make declarations of Truth *(Sacca·kiriya)*. After the Bodhisatta had made his declaration, the father made his. He declared that he made offerings without delight, unwillingly: not having faith in the results of making offerings, he made offerings without conviction. That means his offerings were all inferior.

The Superior Offering

The factors for an offering that is superior *(ukkaṭṭha)* are the opposite:

1) The offerer has obtained the requisite by Right Livelihood.
2) The offerer has good morality: she or he keeps the precepts.
3) Before or after the offering consciousnesses, the offerer's mind is associated with wholesome things. For example, before offering, she or he may with joy *(pīti)*[193] have made great effort to get good requisites; she or he may offer in a respectful, concentrated, and joyful manner; after offering, she or he may rejoice over having made the offering. And she or he has deep faith in the

---

[191] WISDOM FACULTY: here, it is the Kamma-Ownership Knowledge *(Kamma·Ssakata·Ñāṇaṁ/-Paññā)*: see 'The Five Types of Knowledge', p.58.

[192] JA.IV.x.6 (444) *'Kaṇhadīpāyana·Jātaka·Vaṇṇanā'* ('Description of the Kaṇhadīpāyana Jātaka')

[193] The feeling is pleasure *(somanassa)*, which arises with joy *(pīti)*: see footnote 186, p.66.

workings of kamma. She or he may make the offering with the wish for Nibbāna.

4) The receiver has good morality: she or he keeps the precepts. The most superior receiver is, of course, a Buddha, another Arahant,[194] a Noble One, or one practising for the attainment of Arahantship. But the even more superior receiver is one or more bhikkhus or novices seen as representatives of the Sangha.[99]

These are examples of how one's offering can be interspersed by countless thousand million wholesome consciousnesses associated with non-greed *(a·lobha)*, non-hatred*(a·dosa)*, and joy*(pīti)*. If one does not understand the workings of kamma, it is dissociated from non-delusion, which makes one's offering superior, double-rooted*(dvi·hetuka)*: that means the resultant consciousness will be double-rooted. If one does understand the workings of kamma, it is associated also with non-delusion*(a·moha)*, which makes one's offering superior, triple-rooted*(ti·hetuka)*: that means the resultant consciousness will be triple-rooted.

Morality

The second merit-work base is morality*(sīla)*: to abstain from certain unwholesome kammas. It comprises the three abstinences*(viratī)*: Right Speech*(Sammā·Vācā)*, Right Action*(Sammā·Kammanta)*, and Right Livelihood*(Sammā·Ājīva)*, which is, livelihood that excludes wrong speech*(micchā·vācā)* or wrong action*(micchā·kammanta)*.[195] These abstinences arise on three occasions:[196]

1) There arises an occasion to do an unwholesome thing*(akusala dhamma)*. But one abstains because one considers it an unsuitable thing to do.[197] This is called occasional-abstinence*(sampatta·virati)*: one abstains as and when the occasion arises.
2) There arises an occasion to do an unwholesome thing. But one abstains because one has undertaken the training precepts*(sikkhā·pada)*: the five, eight, ten precepts, or the *Pātimokkha* rule.[198] This is called undertaken-abstinence *(samādāna·virati)*.
3) There arises an occasion to do an unwholesome thing. But because one has with a Noble Path Knowledge uprooted certain or all defilements, it is impossible for one deliberately to do certain unwholesome things: the Arahant Path-Knowledge makes it impossible for one deliberately to do anything un-

[194] For some examples from the Pali Texts, see 'Present Result from Wholesome Kamma', p.157.
[195] The three abstinences may arise with either knowledge-dissociated or knowledge associated consciousness: see table 3a, p.67*f*, and table 3b, p.69.
[196] DhSA.i.1 *'Kusala·Kamma·Patha·Kathā'* ('Discussion of the Wholesome Kamma-Course') E.136-137
[197] DhSA.ibid gives the example of a young boy who is asked to catch a hare, for his mother to eat as medicine. He chases a hare, and it gets caught in some creepers, crying out in fear. He thinks: 'It is not proper that for the sake of my mother's life, I should take the life of another,' and frees the hare. Coming home, he declares before his mother that he has never intentionally killed any being. With that declaration, his mother recovers from her sickness.
[198] DhSA.ibid gives the example of a man who is caught by a boa-constrictor. Thinking first to kill it with his axe, he remembers that he has taken the precepts from a bhikkhu, and throws the axe away. And the boa-constrictor releases him.

wholesome at all.[199] In this case, one's abstinence is natural, and is called uprooting-abstinence *(samuccheda·virati)*.

The occasional, arbitrary morality is the inferior morality, whereas morality as a training is superior.

Let us then discuss the different types of morality training.

THE FIVE PRECEPTS

Basic morality training is to abstain from the five main unwholesome kammas:[100]

1) From killing to abstain *(pāṇātipātā veramaṇī)*: she or he does not kill any being: human, animal, fish, insect, etc.
2) From taking what is not given to abstain *(a·dinn·ādāṇā veramaṇī)*: she or he obtains things in a lawful way.
3) From sexual misconduct to abstain *(kāmesu micchā·cārā veramaṇī)*: she or he is content with her or his husband or wife.[200]
4) From untrue speech to abstain *(musā·vādā veramaṇī)*: she or he does not tell a lie for any reason. She or he either speaks the truth, or is silent.[101]
5) From beer&wine liquor, which is a foundation for carelessness, to abstain *(surā·meraya·majja·pamāda·ṭṭhānā veramaṇī)*:[201] she or he does not take any type of intoxicant, for any reason. Indulging in intoxicants makes it very difficult to train in morality, leads to harm,[102] and eventually to dementia.[202]

These five abstinences *(pañca veramaṇi)* are what we call training precepts *(sikkhā·pada)*: the five precepts *(pañca·sīla)*. A devotee *(upāsikā/upāsaka)* of The Buddha, Dhamma, Sangha observes minimum these five precepts: that is the devotee's quality of morality achievement *(sīla·sampadā)*.[203]

But included in one's moral training is, of course, also Right Livelihood *(Sammā·Ājīva)*: to abstain from wrong livelihood *(micchā ājīva)*. That is, not to gain one's livelihood by breaking any of one's precepts.[204] To abstain from killing, theft, sexual misconduct and intoxicants is Right Action *(Sammā·Kammanta)*; to abstain from lying, slander, harsh speech, and prattle, is Right Speech *(Sammā·Vācā)*; and to abstain from all of them in one's livelihood is part of Right Livelihood. For devotees *(upāsikā/upāsaka)*, The Buddha includes also abstinence from five types of trade:[103]

1) Arms trade *(sattha·vaṇijjā)*

---

[199] DhSA.ibid explains that when one attains the Noble Path Knowledge, the Noble Eightfold Path arises, with Right Speech, Right Action, and Right Livelihood. Once it has arisen, one can no longer intentionally break any of the five precepts. See 'The Ten Wholesome Courses of Kamma', p.130.

[200] For those who are 'unapproachable ones *(agamanīya·vatthu)*', see quotation at 'To Be One Who Engages in Sexual Misconduct', p.121.

[201] For an analysis, see 'Beer&Wine Liquor', p.372.

[202] See 'The Trivial Results of Unwholesome Kamma', p.127.

[203] The details with regard to the female/male devotee have been taken from DA.i.2 *'Sāmañña·Phala·Suttaṁ'* ('The Asceticism-Fruit Sutta').

[204] DhSA.i.301 *'Lokuttara·Kusala·Vaṇṇanā'* ('Description of the Supramundane Wholesome') E.298 explains: 'For the sake of livelihood, whatever breathers hunters, fishermen, etc., may kill, whatever theft people may commit, however they may wrongly behave themselves: this is known as wrong livelihood... After taking a bribe, whatever lies they may speak, whatever slander they may utter, harsh speech, or prattle: this is known as wrong livelihood; abstinence therefrom is Right Livelihood.'

2) Beings trade *(satta·vaṇijjā)*: selling human beings.
3) Flesh trade *(maṁsa·vaṇijjā)*: rearing pigs and other animals, and selling them for slaughter.
4) Liquor trade *(majja·vaṇijjā)*: any type of intoxicant.
5) Poisons trade *(visa·vaṇijjā)*: herbicide, insecticide, and any other type of poison.

To be a devotee *(upāsikā/upāsaka)*, one's livelihood needs to exclude all these five trades, for one's livelihood needs to be in accordance with the Dhamma *(Dhammena samena)*: that is the devotee's quality of livelihood achievement *(ājīva·sampadā)*. If one engages in any of these types of wrong livelihood, or if one breaks any of the five precepts, of course, one's Triple Refuge *(Ti·Saraṇa)* is broken, and one is no longer a devotee *(upāsikā/upāsaka)* of The Buddha, Dhamma, Sangha:[205] one is then what The Buddha calls an outcast devotee *(upāsaka·caṇḍāla)*, a dirty devotee *(upāsaka·mala)*, and a vile devotee *(upāsaka·patikuṭṭho)*.[104]

The five precepts help prevent the most dangerous acts of greed, hatred, and delusion. When one kills, steals, engages in sexual misconduct, lies, and drinks beer and wine, etc., the volition is unwholesome: it is unwholesome kamma. If that kamma produces its result at the time of death, one will be reborn in hell, the ghost world or the animal world.[105] This causative fixity, the natural order of kamma,[206] is why The Buddha, the bhikkhu-, and bhikkhunī Sangha, and devotees teach the five precepts:[207] not to undertake them is to one's own detriment and harm for a long time. Hence, the five precepts are not unique to a Buddha's Teachings.[208/106] Outside the Dispensation of a Buddha, they are taught by ascetics and wanderers,[209] Bodhisattas bound for Full Enlightenment, and Wheel-Turning Kings.[107]

The Buddha mentions also slander *(pisuṇa·vācā)*, harsh speech *(pharusa·vācā)*, and prattle *(samphappalāpa)*, as kamma that can give such a rebirth, but they become more difficult to do when one observes the five precepts in one's daily life.[108]

If one in this way observes the five precepts in one's daily life, and one makes a living by Right Livelihood, one may avoid an unhappy rebirth, and gain a happy rebirth in the human world or even the deva world.[210]

---

[205] KhPA.i *'Bhed·Ābheda·Phala·Dīpanā'* ('Illumination of the Fruit of Breach/Non-Breach') MR.i.23 explains, for example, that the blameless *(anavajja)* breach of one's refuge takes place at death. The blameful *(sāvajja)* breach takes place when one takes another teacher as refuge, or one takes refuge in an improper way (details are given for the proper ways). The refuge becomes defiled *(saṁkiliṭṭha)* by non-knowledge *(aññāṇa)*, doubt *(saṁsaya)*, and wrong knowledge *(micchā·ñāṇa)* about a Buddha's qualities *(guṇa)* (for example, holding wrong views about what a Buddha is or is not, what He does or does not do, or what He can or cannot do), and is defiled also by disrespect *(anādara)*, etc. towards The Buddha, the Dhamma (Vinaya, Sutta, Abhidhamma), or the Sangha.

[206] To explain this, VbhA.XVI.10.iii.770 *'Tika·Niddesa·Vaṇṇanā'* ('Description of the Threes-Exposition') DD.XVI.iii.2082 quotes S.II.I.ii.10 *'Paccaya·Suttaṁ'* ('The Cause Sutta'): 'Whether there is the appearance of Tathāgatas, or the non-appearance of Tathāgatas, there exists this element, the Dhamma fixity *(Dhamma·ṭṭhitatā)*, the Dhamma order *(Dhamma·niyāmatā)*, causation *(idappaccayatā)*.'

[207] VbhA.XVI.x.3.770 *'Tika·Niddesa·Vaṇṇanā'* ('Description of the Threes-Exposition') DD.-XVI.x.2082

[208] Ibid.

[209] For example, the Brahmins called Saṅkhas: see 'The Fantastic Picture', p.31.

[210] See endnote 124, p.242.

THE EIGHT PRECEPTS

There are also devotees who observe the eight precepts *(aṭṭha·sīla)*. The eight precepts are:[109]

1) From killing to abstain *(pāṇātipātā veramaṇī)*: this is the same as the first of the five precepts.
2) From taking what is not given to abstain *(a·dinn·ādāṇā veramaṇī)*: this is the same as the second of the five precepts.
3) From unchastity to abstain *(abrahma·cariyā veramaṇī)*: this precept is purer than the third precept of the five precepts. There she or he does not engage in sexual misconduct; here she or he does not engage in any type of sexual conduct. It greatly denourishes sensual desire *(kāma·cchanda)*.[110]
4) From untrue speech to abstain *(musā·vādā veramaṇī)*: this is the same as the fourth of the five precepts.
5) From beer&wine liquor, which is a foundation for carelessness, to abstain *(surā·meraya·majja·pamāda·ṭṭhānā veramaṇī)*: this is the same as the fifth of the five precepts.
6) From eating at the wrong time to abstain *(vi·kāla·bhojanā veramaṇī)*: she or he does not eat between noon and the next day's dawn. It greatly denourishes sensual desire *(kāma·cchanda)* and sloth&torpor *(thina·middha)*, and helps nourish contentment *(santosa/santuṭṭhi)*, and moderation in food *(bhojane·mattaññutā)*.
7) From dancing, singing, music, and watching other entertainment *(nacca·gīta-·vādita·visūka·dassanā·)*, from jewellery, perfume, and cosmetics, for the sake of adornment to abstain *(·mālā·gandha·vilepana·dhāraṇa·maṇḍana·vibhūsan·aṭṭhānā vera-maṇī)*: she or he does not indulge actively or passively in music and other entertainment. That greatly denourishes greed, hatred and delusion. And she or he does not beautify the body by appearance or smell. That greatly denourishes sensual desire and vanity *(mada)*.
8) From a high and large bed to abstain *(uccā·sayana·mahā·sayanā veramaṇī)*: she or he does not indulge in a big and luxurious bed, and sleeps alone. It denourishes sensual desire and sloth&torpor.

The eight precepts are also not unique to a Buddha's Teaching.[211] They are practised by good people also outside a Buddha's Dispensation.[111] Some people train in the eight precepts as a way of life, and some train in them only occasionally, especially on the Uposathas: the new moon and full-moon days.[112] The Buddha calls such practice the Uposatha possessed of eight factors *(aṭṭh·aṅga·sam-annāgata Uposatha)*.[113] And He explains that with such practice, one emulates the Arahants.[114] The results of such a practice are, He explains, the complete happiness of rebirth in the deva worlds, with a life span from nine million human years, up to nine thousand, two hundred and sixteen million human years. And He explains that such practice may also be a supporting cause for the Path&Fruition of Non-Return, Once-Return, or Stream Entry.[115]

THE TEN PRECEPTS

Apart from the five and eight precepts, there are also the ten precepts *(dasa·sīla)*. With the ten precepts, abstinence from entertainment becomes the seventh precept, abstinence from beautifying the body becomes the eighth precept, and ab-

---

[211] VbhA.XVI.x.3.770 *'Tika·Niddesa·Vaṇṇanā'* ('Description of the Threes-Exposition') DD.XVI.x.2082

stinence from a high and large bed becomes the ninth. And then there is the tenth precept:

10) From accepting gold and silver to abstain *(jātarūpa·rajata·paṭiggahanā veramaṇī)*: this does not refer only to gold and silver, but to any type of money: cash, cheques, drafts, credit cards, etc.[116]

Possession and use of money is inseparable from greed, hatred, and delusion.[117] That is why not to have money denourishes greed, hatred and delusion.

There are some laypeople who undertake the ten precepts, and a Theravāda novice *(sāmaṇera)* is ordained by the ten precepts. Theravāda nuns are ordained by either the eight precepts, or the ten. Here again, the ten precepts are not unique to a Buddha's Dispensation.[212]

THE BHIKKHU'S MORALITY

The highest training in morality is the bhikkhu's morality *(bhikkhu·sīla)*. It is the first of the bhikkhu's three trainings:[213] The Buddha calls it the higher morality training *(adhi·sīla·sikkhā)*. A bhikkhu's morality is the foundation of his holy life, and is a fourfold purification morality *(catu·pārisuddhi·sīla)*:[214]

1) The *Pātimokkha*-restraint morality *(Pātimokkha·saṁvara·sīla)*:[215] this is the bhikkhu rule laid down by The Buddha. It comprises a chief two hundred and twenty-seven precepts, as well as very many associated precepts.
2) Faculty-restraint morality *(indriya·saṁvara·sīla)*: restraining the eye-, ear-, nose-, tongue-, body-, and mind faculty by attending to one's meditation subject, be it samatha or vipassanā. That way defilements do not arise by way of the six faculties.[118]
3) Livelihood-purification morality *(ājīva·pārisuddhi·sīla)*: just as a layperson must abstain from wrong livelihood, so must a bhikkhu.[119] Wrong livelihood for a bhikkhu is a livelihood that breaks any of the *Pātimokkha* precepts.[120]
4) Requisite-related morality *(paccaya·sannissita·sīla)*. The bhikkhu receives his four requisites from the faithful:
   i) the robe *(cīvara)*
   ii) the almsfood *(piṇḍapāta)*
   iii) the bed&seat *(sen·āsana)*: that is the Pali word for his dwelling.
   iv) the medical requisite to help the sick *(gilāna·paccaya·bhesajja·parikkhāra)*.

   As part of his moral training, the bhikkhu must reflect upon his four requisites with wise attention *(yoniso manasikāra)*. For example, The Buddha advises the bhikkhu to reflect upon his food in the following way:[216]

   With wise reflection the almsfood do I use: '[It is] **neither for fun, nor for intoxication, nor for beautification, nor for embellishment; only for this body's subsistence and maintenance, for harm's prevention, for assisting the holy life.**[217]

---

212 Ibid.

213 THE BHIKKHU'S THREE HIGHER TRAININGS: see quotation endnote 40, p.25.

214 VsM.i.13*ff* *'Sīla·Niddeso'* ('Exposition of Morality') PP.i.42*ff*

215 PĀTIMOKKHA RESTRAINT: see quotations endnotes 40, p.25; 121, p.241; and 284, p.356.

216 The Buddha explains it in, for example, M.I.i.2 *'Sabb·Āsava·Suttaṁ'* ('The All-Taints Sutta') and A.VI.vi.4 *'Āsava·Suttaṁ'* ('The Taints Sutta'). And in S.IV.xii.7 *'Rath·Opama·Suttaṁ'* ('The Chariot-Simile Sutta'), He equates it with moderation in food *(bhojane mattaññutā)*.

217 FUN: as village boys eating for the pleasure of eating, or as a social event. INTOXICA-

(Please see further next page.)

Thus, old feelings [of hunger] **I put an end to; and new feelings** [of overeating] **I do not arouse; and my livelihood will be blameless, and a living in comfort.'**

When the bhikkhu in this way reflects on his requisites,[218] he is able to develop contentment*(santosa/santutti)*. When a bhikkhu develops contentment, he does not ask much from his patrons*(dāyaka)* and stewards*(kappiya)*. That means his holy life*(brahma·cariya)* becomes blameless.

The bhikkhu's four trainings in purification greatly help to control his mind, to prevent much kamma that is greed-, hatred-, and delusion-rooted. In that way the bhikkhu's higher morality training greatly helps him in his development of jhāna (samatha), which The Buddha calls his higher-mind training*(adhi·citta·sikkhā)*.[121] It helps the bhikkhu in also his insight training, which The Buddha calls his higher wisdom training*(adhi·paññā·sikkhā)*.[219] Furthermore, when a bhikkhu observes his morality training scrupulously,[122] the True Dhamma may continue for a long time.[123]

All these different types of morality are opposite greed and hatred; rooted in non-greed*(a·lobha)*, and non-hatred*(a·dosa)*. And if we practise morality without faith in the Kamma-Ownership Knowledge*(Kamma·Ssakata·Ñāṇa)*, it is knowledge-dissociated*(ñāna·vippayutta)*: double-rooted*(dvi·hetuka)*. If we practise in morality with faith or direct knowledge of the Kamma-Ownership Knowledge, it is knowledge-associated*(ñāṇa·sampayutta)*: triple-rooted*(ti·hetuka)*.

The Workings of Morality Training

Knowledge-Dissociated

For example, it is very rare for children to train in morality with knowledge of the workings of kamma. Usually children will train in morality because they want to copy their parents, or because their parents have told them to train in morality, or because they enjoy being praised when they train in morality.

One may also train in the precept of not killing, for example, not because of one's training, but out of loving-kindness, not wishing to harm another. And one may be selective. One may abstain from killing human beings of one race, of one religion, or of one country, yet kill human beings of another race, or religion, or country. One may abstain from killing human beings who have done no wrong to

---

TION: infatuation with health and strength, as in athletes. BEAUTIFICATION: to look attractive, as in concubines and prostitutes etc. EMBELLISHMENT: to look graceful, as in actors, dancers etc. (VsM.i.18*ff 'Sīla·Niddeso'* ('Exposition of Morality') PP.i.89-94)

[218] For The Buddha's advised reflection on the robe, see quotation endnote 24, p.23.

[219] VbhA.XVI.x.3.770 *'Tika·Niddesa·Vaṇṇanā'* ('Description of the Threes-Exposition') DD.-XVI.x.2082 explains: 'But the morality of Pātimokkha restraint exceeds all morality, and arises only when a Tathāgata has arisen, not when one has not arisen; and only the Omniscient Buddhas make it known. For making it known thus: "In respect of this basis, this is the offence" is the field of the Buddhas only, the power of the Buddhas.' Ibid.2085 explains the bhikkhu's threefold higher training: 'Just as, compared to an undersized umbrella or flag, and over-sized one is called a super-umbrella, a super-flag, so, compared to the fivefold morality and the tenfold morality, this Pātimokkha morality is called higher morality, and compared to the round-basis eight attainments [jhāna for the attainment of a higher rebirth], the vipassanā-basis eight attainments [jhāna for the practice of vipassanā] are called the higher mind, and compared to the kamma-ownership wisdom, insight wisdom and Path wisdom and Fruition wisdom are called the higher wisdom.'

oneself, one's family, one's friends or associates, etc., yet one will kill human beings who have done wrong to oneself, one's family, etc.[220] One may also abstain from killing human beings, yet kill other beings such as fish, rats, mice, and insects. And one may wish to protect the life of an animal one considers to be beautiful or interesting: for example, a hawk or eagle, a dolphin or whale, or a lion or tiger, or an elephant or gorilla, or even a butterfly. Yet one may not wish in the same way to protect the life of an animal one considers to be ugly: for example, a vulture or crow, a shark, a jackal or fox, or a rat, a cockroach, a wasp or a mosquito. In the same way, one may out of compassion abstain from eating pork, beef, and poultry, yet not abstain from eating eggs, fish, and other seafood. And one may abstain from eating flesh for reasons of health, rather than out of compassion.

One may also train in morality because of a sense of honour, and abstain from killing, stealing, sexual misconduct, and telling lies, yet one will drink beer and wine, etc. And one may also train in morality because it is custom or tradition, or because one's religion says one should. One may also train in morality because one wants to have a good name, and be respected. And one may even train in morality because one is afraid of blame. In these many ways, one's training in morality may be knowledge-dissociated *(ñāṇa·vippayutta)*.[221]

Even though the consciousnesses by which one abstains from evil actions may be dissociated from knowledge of the workings of kamma, they are not for that reason associated with ignorance and wrong view. As we explained, a wholesome consciousness cannot be associated with ignorance. But one may at other times hold to wrong view. One may believe that there is no result from doing bad and doing good, one may believe that at death, one is annihilated, and one may believe that the deva worlds and the hells are just legends or metaphors for unwholesome consciousnesses. And one may think the five-, eight-, and ten precepts, and the bhikkhus' many precepts, are just cultural things from ancient India. When there is in this way no faith in or knowledge of the workings of kamma, etc., there is, of course, no fear of a bad rebirth, and no fear of the round of rebirth. Then can it be very difficult to train properly in morality.

When one in these ways trains in morality without faith in or knowledge about the workings of kamma, it is much more difficult to do. If there is some inconvenience, one very easily gives up. For example, one may discover vermin in one's house, and choose the easy solution: to kill them or have them killed. One may also want to entertain business associates, or enjoy the company of one's friends, and then drink beer and wine, etc., because it is expected. When declaring one's taxable income, and when doing business, for example, it is very easy to tell lies,

---

[220] VsM.i.12 *'Sīla·Ppabheda·Kathā'* ('Discussion of the Morality-Variety') PP.i.31 explains that there is morality which is restricted *(pariyanta)* by gain, fame, relatives, limbs, and life, and there is morality that is unrestricted *(apariyanta)*. It quotes PsM.I.ii.37 *'Sīlamaya·Ñāṇa·Niddeso'* ('Exposition of Morality-Comprising Knowledge') PD.I.ii.258: 'Here, someone with gain as root, with gain as cause, with gain as reason, transgresses an undertaken training precept: such morality is restricted by gain (see, for example, footnote 222, p.78).' The other restrictions should be understood in the same way. PsM.ibid. explains that such morality is in pieces, is not praised by the wise, is insecure, does not lead to concentration, is not a basis for non-remorse, happiness, knowledge&conduct, etc., and does not lead to Nibbāna. Unrestricted morality is the opposite.

[221] For the mental phenomena at the arising of such consciousness, see table '3a: Mental Phenomena at the Arising of Knowledge-Dissociated Consciousness', p.67*f.*

with the excuse that one must make a living, and the excuse that everyone does it.[222]

Nonetheless, in all cases, abstention from evil actions is wholesome: if it is interspersed by wholesome consciousnesses, it can even be superior *(ukkaṭṭha)*. But when it is dissociated from knowledge of the workings of kamma, it is the less superior, for it is only double-rooted *(dvi·hetuka)*: associated with only non-greed *(a·lobha)* and non-hatred *(a·dosa)*. The kamma being less powerful means the result will also be less powerful.

Knowledge-Associated

When one's training in morality is knowledge-associated *(ñāṇa·sampayutta)*, it is much, much easier to do. With that knowledge, one becomes afraid to do wrong, because one does not want to suffer the results of unwholesome kamma. With knowledge of the workings of kamma, one knows that immoral conduct leads not only to a bad rebirth, but in this life, it leads to restlessness, unhappiness, and low self-confidence.[124] With knowledge of the workings of kamma, one knows that the higher the training one undertakes, the more happiness and self-confidence one gains. One knows it is inevitable. One has experience of the good things that accompany the wholesome consciousness: conscience *(hiri)*, shame *(ottappa)*, tranquillity of consciousness *(citta·passaddhi)*, mindfulness *(sati)*, and faith *(saddhā)*: in short, happiness *(sukha)*. Such happiness is very important if one wants to succeed in the third merit-work base, meditation *(bhāvanā)*.[125] These inevitable benefits from morality, in this life and in the future, are why The Buddha explains that we should reflect on the Kamma-Ownership Knowledge every day:[223/126]

> **Kamma owner am I** *(kamma·ssakomhi)*, **kamma heir** *(kamma·dāyādo)*, **kamma-born** *(kamma·yoni)*, **kamma-bound** *(kamma·bandhu)*, **kamma-protected** *(kamma·paṭisaraṇo)*: **whatever kamma I do, good or bad, of that I shall be heir.**[224]

Morality with such knowledge of the workings of kamma is more powerful.[225] Why? Because the presence of wisdom means the consciousness is triple-rooted *(ti·hetuka)*: rooted in non-greed *(a·lobha)*, non-hatred *(a·dosa)*, and non-delusion *(a·moha)*.[226] That always makes a wholesome kamma more powerful.[127]

Most powerful, of course, is the knowledge-associated morality of the one who has attained a Noble Path Knowledge *(Ariya·Magga·Ñāṇa)* and Fruition Knowledge *(Phala·Ñāṇa)*: a Noble Disciple. The arising of the Path Knowledge is the arising of the Noble Eightfold Path *(Ariya Aṭṭh·Aṅgika Magga)*:[128]

1) Right View .... *(Sammā·Diṭṭhi)*	5) Right Livelihood .... *(Sammā·Ājīva)*
2) Right Intention ...... *(Sammā·Saṅkappa)*	6) Right Effort .... *(Sammā·Vāyāma)*
3) Right Speech .... *(Sammā·Vācā)*	7) Right Mindfulness .... *(Sammā·Sati)*
4) Right Action .... *(Sammā·Kammanta)*	8) Right Concentration ... *(Sammā·Samādhi)*

With the arising of these eight Noble factors, the three morality factors (Right Speech, Right Action, and Right Livelihood) will have eradicated wrong speech, wrong action and wrong livelihood. One is no longer able deliberately to kill be-

---

[222] This is morality restricted by gain. See footnote 220, p.77.

[223] A.V.II.i.7 *'Abhiṇha·Paccavekkhitabbaṭhāna·Suttaṁ'* ('The Often-to-Be-Reflected Sutta')

[224] See also quotation p.258.

[225] THIS IS UNRESTRICTED MORALITY: see footnote 220, p.77.

[226] For the mental phenomena at the arising of such consciousness, see table '3b: Mental Phenomena at the Arising of Knowledge-Associated Consciousness', p.69.

ings, to steal, to engage in sexual misconduct, to tell lies, to drink beer and wine, etc. And above all, Right View will have eradicated wrong view.[129] To attain this Path Knowledge, one will namely have attained also the Cause-Apprehending Knowledge *(Paccaya·Pariggaha·Ñāṇa)*. And with that knowledge, one will have discerned past and future lives, and will have known and seen the workings of kamma: how certain kamma matures after death, to produce the rebirth-linking consciousness and new aggregates. Having in this way known and seen the workings of kamma, one is unable to hold any wrong view.[130] And with the arising of Stream-Entry Path Knowledge, one's morality is not only triple-rooted, but one is certain never again to be reborn in hell, as a ghost, or as an animal. With the arising of the Non-Return Path Knowledge, one is certain never again to be reborn in the sensual world. And with the arising of the Arahant Path-Knowledge, one is certain never ever again to be reborn in any way.[227]

Before that takes place, however, a further important factor in one's morality is whether it is inferior *(omaka)* or superior *(ukkaṭṭha)*.

INFERIOR MORALITY

What makes one's morality inferior *(omaka)*? If, before or after the abstaining consciousness, one's mind is associated with unwholesome things, it is inferior. As we just explained, when one's morality is dissociated from knowledge of the workings of kamma, abstinences may often be selective or arbitrary. Such abstinence is usually inferior. Why? Because immediately before and after abstaining, there will usually be greed-rooted consciousnesses. Farther away, there may be non-abstinence, either greed-rooted or hatred-rooted consciousnesses. For example, one may abstain from killing a butterfly, because one thinks it is beautiful: thinking it is beautiful is greed-rooted consciousness. And one may, on the other hand, make effort to kill mosquitoes and cockroaches: that is hatred-rooted consciousness. That way, one's abstinence is interspersed by greed, hatred and delusion. One may abstain from stealing from a member of one's own family, an inhabitant of one's own village, or someone from one's own country: that is conceit, greed-rooted consciousness. But one may happily steal from a member of another family, an inhabitant of another village, or someone from another country: that is greed, hatred, and delusion. This same principle goes for all the examples we gave for selective or arbitrary morality. Usually, it will be dissociated from knowledge of the workings of kamma. But it can also be associated with such knowledge. One may, for example, think: 'Later, later! I have to look after my family and my property. When I get older, I can train in morality properly.' Or: 'When I go on a retreat, or stay in a monastery, I can train properly in morality.' Such arbitrary morality is interspersed by greed- and hatred-rooted consciousnesses, which makes it inferior.

Then there is the inferior undertaking of the precepts. One may, for example, undertake them unwillingly. Because of a view, one may think undertaking the precepts is old-fashioned and therefore wrong; because of conceit, one may dislike the formal ritual of taking the precepts from a bhikkhu; or because of a view one may dislike having to learn the Pali formula. But one may be prompted by friends or family to undertake the precepts, and one may be ashamed to let them know one does not want to keep all the precepts. So, unwillingly one goes to the bhikkhu, unwillingly one learns the Pali, and unwillingly one undertakes the pre-

[227] For further details, see 'Path&Fruition', p.334.

cepts. Then one's undertaking is interspersed by unwholesome consciousnesses associated with views (greed-rooted), and boredom and dissatisfaction (hatred-rooted). Later, remembering or reminding oneself that one has undertaken the precepts, one may with dissatisfaction continue observing them.

Also, one will in the course of the day meet opportunities to break one's precepts. For example, a mosquito comes, and sits on one's arm. When one consciously refrains from killing it, wholesome consciousnesses arise, but one may do it unwillingly, actually wishing to kill the mosquito. Another good example is the devotee who unwillingly undertakes the eightfold Uposatha training for a day: all day she or he is bored and unhappy, wishing the day was over. She or he trains in morality unwillingly, or impatiently, and without joy.

Here again,[228] there is the example of the Bodhisatta, when he was the hermit called Kaṇhadīpayana: we mentioned before how he made a declaration of truth to save the life of a boy who had been bitten by a snake. His declaration of truth was that only for the first week as a hermit did he live the holy life happily, with the desire for merit *(puññ·atthiko)*. After that, he lived the holy life, and practised jhāna, unwillingly, without conviction. That means he practised both good morality as well as concentration with dissatisfaction: then both those bases for work of merit became inferior, over fifty years.

Inferior is also good morality that one maintains out of a desire to become famous, for some worldly gain, or for a happy existence in the future. And inferior it is too if one becomes proud of one's good morality, and looks down on those whose morality is not as good.

These are examples of how one's morality, the kamma of abstinence, can be interspersed by countless thousand million unwholesome consciousnesses rooted in greed *(lobha)*, hatred *(dosa)*, and delusion *(moha)*. That makes one's morality inferior. If one does not understand the workings of kamma, it is dissociated from non-delusion, which makes one's morality inferior, double-rooted *(dvi·hetuka)*: that means the resultant consciousness will be unrooted *(ahetuka)*. If one does understand the workings of kamma, it is associated also with non-delusion *(a·moha)*, but even so the interspersion of countless unwholesome consciousnesses make one's morality inferior, triple-rooted *(ti·hetuka)*: that means the resultant consciousness will be only double-rooted *(dvi·hetuka)*.

Superior Morality

What then, makes one's morality superior *(ukkaṭṭha)*? If, before or after the abstaining consciousnesses, one's mind is associated with wholesome things, it is superior.[229]

For example, one may abstain from killing a mosquito or cockroach with the same joy as one abstains from killing a butterfly. Why? Because the first precept covers all beings: not just the ones we think are beautiful. Likewise, one abstains from stealing from a member of another family, an inhabitant of another village, or someone from another country, with the same joy as one abstains from stealing from a member of one's own family, an inhabitant of one's own village, or someone from one's own country. This way one's morality is superior, because it

---

[228] See under 'The Workings of Offering: Knowledge-Dissociated', p.67.

[229] See also explanation from MA of how preceding/succeeding abstinence from killing makes one's wholesome kamma superior: footnote 679, p.262.

is neither selective nor arbitrary. That is usually because it is associated with knowledge of the workings of kamma.

Then there is the superior undertaking of the precepts. One may joyfully go to a bhikkhu and respectfully ask to go through the formal ritual of taking the precepts. And with joy one may kneel respectfully before the bhikkhu, hold one's hands in *añjali*, and joyfully and respectfully declare one's taking refuge in The Buddha, Dhamma, and Sangha. Afterwards, one may joyfully, respectfully and with resolution declare one's undertaking of each of the precepts. For example, the first precept:

Pāṇātipātā veramaṇi sikkhā·padaṁ samādiyāmi.
The abstinence-from-killing training precept I undertake.

After one has in this way undertaken the precepts, one may have a mind of joy. Later, remembering or reminding oneself that one has undertaken the precepts, one may with joy and resoluteness reinforce one's undertaking. In the course of the day, one will meet opportunities to break one's precepts. For example, a mosquito comes and sits on one's arm. And with joy one consciously refrains from killing it, but kindly waves it away. There may also arise the desire to tell a lie, but with joy one does not let it manifest in speech. Remembering or reminding oneself of one's abstinences, again there may arise joy. And maintaining good morality is most superior if one does it out of a desire for Arahantship, with the thought: 'This has to be done.'

These are examples of how one's morality can be interspersed by countless thousand million wholesome consciousnesses associated with non-greed*(a·lobha)*, non-hatred*(a·dosa)*, and joy*(pīti)*. If one does not understand the workings of kamma, it is knowledge-dissociated, which makes one's morality superior, double-rooted*(dvi·hetuka)*: that means the resultant consciousness will be double-rooted. If one does understand the workings of kamma, it is associated also with non-delusion*(a·moha)*, which makes one's morality superior, triple-rooted*(ti·hetuka)*: that means the resultant consciousness will be triple-rooted.[230]

We need to remember also that so long as one has not attained a Path&Fruition *(Magga·Phala)*, so long is one's Kamma-Ownership Right View uncertain. Because of greed, hatred or delusion, one may stop holding Right View; one may even hold wrong view.[231] Only the Stream-Entry Path Knowledge*(Sot·Āpatti·Magga·Ñāṇa)* makes one's Right View certain, because one will have known and seen the workings of kamma directly. That is why the Stream Enterer is unable to break any of the five precepts. Thus the most superior morality is associated with at least the Stream-Entry Path Knowledge.[232]

That concludes our explanation of the second merit-work base, morality*(sīla)*.

---

230 For details, see '1f: Inferior & Superior Wholesome Kamma, Their Roots & Resultant Rebirth-Linking', p.62.

231 WRONG VIEW: the absence of Right View does not necessarily mean the presence of wrong view, as wrong view arises only with greed-rooted consciousnesses. See tables 2a/2b/2c, p.48*ff.*

232 See 'Stream Entry', p.336.

MEDITATION

The third merit-work base is meditation *(bhāvanā)*. There are two types of meditation:[131] samatha meditation *(samatha·bhāvanā)*, and insight meditation *(vipassanā·bhāvanā)*.

SAMATHA MEDITATION

Samatha meditation is to develop strong and powerful concentration (one-pointedness[132]) on one object: either access concentration *(upacāra·samādhi)* or absorption concentration *(appanā·samādhi)*. Absorption concentration is also called jhāna.[233] There are eight types of jhāna: the four fine-material jhānas *(rūpa·jjhāna)*, and the four immaterial jhānas *(arūpa·jjhāna)*.[234] They are also called the eight attainments *(aṭṭha samāpatti)*. The eight attainments are not unique to a Buddha's Dispensation. Outside the Dispensation of a Buddha,[235] they are taught by ascetics and wanderers, by Bodhisattas bound for Full Enlightenment, and by Wheel-Turning Kings.[236] For example, our Bodhisatta learned the four material jhānas and first three immaterial jhānas from Āḷāra Kālāma, and then he learned also the fourth immaterial jhāna from Uddaka Rāmaputta.[237] This is called round-basis jhāna *(vaṭṭa·pādikā·jhāna)*: developing jhāna in order to attain a higher rebirth, to continue the rebirth round.[238] Outside a Buddha's Dispensation, there are also those who use their jhāna to develop psychic powers *(abhiññā)*: flying, walking on water, etc.[239] Developing insight-basis jhāna *(vipassanā·pādaka·jjhāna)*[240] (developing jhāna in order

---

[233] See table '5d: The Jhāna-Attainment Process', p.178.

[234] The four immaterial jhānas have the exact same number of mental phenomena as the fourth jhāna; the difference lies in their being based on an immaterial object. Hence, The Buddha describes both the fourth jhāna and the four immaterial jhānas as imperturbable *(āneñja)*. See M.II.ii.6 *'Laṭukik·Opama·Suttaṁ'* ('Quail Simile Sutta')/M.III.i.6 *'Āneñja·sappāya·Suttaṁ'* ('The Imperturbable-Wards Sutta'). Needless to say, the immaterial jhānas are mundane. For details, please see VsM.x *'Ā·Ruppa·Niddesa'* ('Immaterial Description') PP.x.

[235] VbhA.XVI.x.3.770 *'Tika·Niddesa·Vaṇṇanā'* ('Description of the Threes-Exposition') DD.XVI.x.2085

[236] See quotation endnote 111, p.240.

[237] Mentioned at 'Wholesome Weighty Kamma', p.175.

[238] See endnote 198, p.251.

[239] PSYCHIC POWERS: there are six. Five are mundane: 1) being one, becoming many; being many, becoming one; appearing/disappearing; walking through walls and mountains as if through the air; diving into and arising from the earth as if it were water; walking on water as if it were the ground; cross-legged flying through the air; touching sun/-moon with the hand; moving the body up to the Brahma world; 2) the divine ear, which can hear human/ divine sounds far/near; 3) reading the minds of others; 4) recollecting many hundred thousand births, many world expansions/contractions, recollecting also concepts such as name, occupation, pleasures, etc. (see endnote 6, p.20); 5) the divine eye, which can see how beings are reborn according to their kamma. The sixth psychic power is supramundane: destruction of the taints (the sensuality-/existence-/ignorance taint), which is Arahantship. (4, 5, and 6 are also called the three knowledges *(te·vijjā)*). The Buddha explains the psychic powers in, for example, D.i.2 *'Sāmañña·Phala·Suttaṁ'* ('The Asceticism-Fruit Sutta').

[240] VsM.xi.362 *'Samādhi-Ānisaṁsa·Kathā'* ('Discussion of the Concentration-Benefits') PP.xi.121 lists five benefits to be gained from developing concentration. The second one is as the basis for insight meditation: 'When ordinary people and Trainees [non-Arahant Noble Ones] develop it [concentration], thinking "After emerging we shall exercise in-

(Please see further next page.)

to penetrate to ultimate truth for practising insight meditation), however, is unique to a Buddha's Dispensation. Why? Because insight meditation is unique to a Buddha's Dispensation.[241]

The Buddha gives forty meditation subjects for samatha meditation:[242]

- The ten kasiṇas: the earth, water, fire, and wind kasiṇas, the blue, yellow, red, and white kasiṇas, the light kasiṇa, and the space kasiṇa.
- The ten foulnesses *(asubha)*: the ten types of corpse, for example, the bloated corpse, the livid corpse, and the skeleton.
- The ten recollections *(anussati)*: for example, recollection of The Buddha, the Dhamma, and the Sangha, recollection of death, the thirty-two parts of the body, and mindfulness of breathing *(ān·āpāna·ssati)*.
- The four divine abidings *(Brahma·vihāra)*: loving-kindness *(mettā)*, compassion *(karuṇā)*, sympathetic joy *(muditā)*, and equanimity *(upekkhā)*.
- The four immaterials *(āruppa)*:[243] the boundless-space base, the boundless-consciousness base, the nothingness base, and the neither-perception nor non-perception base.
- The one perception: the perception of nutriment.
- The one defining: four elements meditation.

With some of these meditation subjects, one can develop only access concentration. With many of these meditation subjects, for example, the kasiṇas and mindfulness-of-breathing, one can develop both access concentration and absorption concentration. Access concentration is very near jhāna, and absorption concentration is jhāna.[244]

The Fourfold and Fivefold Jhānas

The Buddha classifies the jhānas in two ways: as the fourfold jhāna *(catukka·jjhāna)*, and the fivefold jhāna *(pañcaka·jjhāna)*.

In the suttas, The Buddha usually speaks of the fourfold jhāna. For example, in the *'Mahā·Sati·Paṭṭhāna'* sutta, He describes Right Concentration *(Sammā·Samādhi)* as the fourfold jhāna:[245]

1) First jhāna	*(paṭhama jhāna)*	3) Third jhāna	*(tatiya jhāna)*
2) Second jhāna	*(dutiya jhāna)*	4) Fourth jhāna	*(catuttha jhāna)*

In the Abhidhamma, The Buddha refers only to the fivefold jhāna.

---

sight with concentrated consciousness," the development of absorption concentration provides them with the benefit of insight by serving as the proximate cause for insight, and so too does access concentration.' This is followed by a quotation from S.III.I.i.5 *'Samādhi·Suttaṁ'* ('The Concentration Sutta'): see quotation p.88. See also footnote 247, p.255, and endnote 182, p.250.

241 VbhA.XVI.x.3.770 *'Tika·Niddesa·Vaṇṇanā'* ('Description of the Threes-Exposition') DD.-XVI.x.2085

242 VsM.iii.47 *'Kamma·Ṭṭhāna·Ggahaṇa·Niddeso'* ('Exposition of the Meditation-Subject Obtainment') PP.iii.104-105. For a full list with sutta references, see 'Appendix 1: The Forty Meditation Subjects', p.363.

243 FOUR IMMATERIALS: also called immaterial jhāna *(arūpa·jjhāna)*, and immaterial-sphere jhāna *(arūp·āvacara·jjhāna)*.

244 The Buddha explains the jhānas in many places, for example, D.ii.9: quoted endnote 182, p.250.

245 D.ii.9 *'Mahā·Sati·Paṭṭhāna·Suttaṁ'* ('The Great Mindfulness-Foundation Sutta')

What is the difference between the fourfold jhāna and fivefold? The difference lies in the jhāna factors *(jhān·aṅga)*. The first jhāna has five jhāna factors:

1) application ...... *(vitakka)*
2) sustainment ..... *(vicāra)*
3) joy .... *(pīti)*
4) happiness ...... *(sukha)*
5) one-pointedness *(ek·aggatā)*

To attain the second fourfold-jhāna, one needs to overcome the first two factors: application and sustainment. That way the second fourfold jhāna has only three factors: joy, happiness and one-pointedness. But some meditators are unable to overcome both application and sustainment at once.[246] First they overcome application, and have only four factors: sustainment, joy, happiness, and one-pointedness. That is the second fivefold jhāna. Then they overcome sustainment, and have only three factors: joy, happiness, and one-pointedness. That is the third fivefold jhāna: the third fivefold jhāna is the same as the second fourfold jhāna. The rest of the jhānas are accordingly (please see the chart).[247]

The Fourfold and Fivefold Jhānas

FOURFOLD	1st	—	2nd	3rd	4th
FIVEFOLD	1st	2nd	3rd	4th	5th
vitakka	application	~~application~~	~~application~~	~~application~~	~~application~~
vicāra	sustainment	sustainment	~~sustainment~~	~~sustainment~~	~~sustainment~~
pīti	joy	joy	joy	~~joy~~	~~joy~~
sukha	happiness	happiness	happiness	happiness	~~happiness~~
ek·aggatā	one-pointedness	one-pointedness	one-pointedness	one-pointedness	one-pointedness
upekkhā					equanimity

Please be aware that in the charts we have made of the mental phenomena, and the resultant dhammas, we use the fivefold classification, as in the Abhidhamma.

When there is access concentration or jhāna, the mind is full of bright, brilliant and radiant light: that is what The Buddha calls the light of wisdom *(paññ·āloka)*.[133] The brightest, most brilliant, and most radiant light is achieved with the fourth jhāna.

---

246 See VsM.iv.90 *'Pañcaka·Jjhāna·Kathā'* ('Discussion of Fivefold Jhāna') PP.iv.198-202

247 In S.IV.IX.i.3 *'Sa·Vitakka·sa·Vicāra·Suttaṁ'* ('The with-Application & with-Sustainment Sutta')(also A.VIII.II.ii.3 *'Saṁkhitta·Suttaṁ'* ('The "Brief" Sutta')), The Buddha divides the first two fourfold jhānas into the three fivefold jhānas: 'What then, bhikkhus, is the path leading to the Unformed? Concentration with application and sustainment; concentration without application but with sustainment; concentration without application and without sustainment. This is called, bhikkhus, the path leading to the Unformed.' For details on the jhānas, see notes to table 5d 'The Jhāna-Attainment Process', p.178.

THE WORKINGS OF SAMATHA MEDITATION

Here, with offerings, and morality, one's consciousness may be dissociated from or associated with the Kamma-Ownership Knowledge. But with samatha meditation (jhāna), one's consciousness is always knowledge-associated: always associated with penetrating knowledge of the concentration sign *(samādhi·nimitta)*. It is called jhāna wisdom *(jhāna·paññā)*, or jhāna Right View *(jhāna·Sammā·Diṭṭhi)*. But one's samatha meditation may be inferior *(omaka)* or superior *(ukkaṭṭha)*.

INFERIOR SAMATHA MEDITATION

What makes one's samatha meditation inferior *(omaka)*? If, before or after the jhāna consciousnesses, one's mind is associated with unwholesome things, it is inferior.

For example, one may train in samatha meditation because it is custom or tradition, or because one's religion says one should. And one may also train in samatha meditation because one wants to have a

3c: Mental Phenomena *(nāma·dhamma)* **at the Arising of Exalted Consciousness** *(mahaggata·citta)*[248]

FINE-MATERIAL JHĀNA	1st	2nd	3rd	4th	5th
CONSCIOUSNESS *(citta)*	■	■	■	■	■
MENTAL FACTORS *(cetasika)*					
Universals *(sabba·citta·sādhāraṇa)*					
1. contact *(phassa)*	■	■	■	■	■
2. feeling *(vedanā)*	■	■	■	■	■
3. perception *(saññā)*	■	■	■	■	■
4. volition *(cetanā)*	■	■	■	■	■
5. one-pointedness[249] *(ek·aggatā)*	■	■	■	■	■
6. life faculty *(jīvit·indriya)*	■	■	■	■	■
7. attention *(manasikāra)*	■	■	■	■	■
Miscellaneous *(pakiṇṇaka)*					
1. application *(vitakka)*	■				
2. sustainment *(vicāra)*	■	■			
3. decision *(adhimokkha)*	■	■	■	■	■
4. energy *(viriya)*	■	■	■	■	■
5. joy *(pīti)*	■	■	■		
6. desire *(chanda)*	■	■	■	■	■
Beautiful Universals *(sobhana·sādhāraṇa)*					
1. faith *(saddhā)*	■	■	■	■	■
2. mindfulness *(sati)*	■	■	■	■	■
3. conscience *(hiri)*	■	■	■	■	■
4. shame *(ottapa)*	■	■	■	■	■
5. non-greed *(a·lobha)*	■	■	■	■	■
6. non-hatred *(a·dosa)*	■	■	■	■	■
7. ever-evenness *(tatra·majjhattatā)*	■	■	■	■	■
8. tranquillity of [mental] body[250] *(kāya·passaddhi)*	■	■	■	■	■
9. tranquillity of consciousness *(citta·passaddhi)*	■	■	■	■	■

Please continue next page.

[248] The table has been designed according to the combination system *(saṅgaha·naya)*: all combinations of mental phenomena. (AbS.ii.38-39 *'Mahaggata·Citta·Saṅgaha·Nayo'* ('Exalted-Consciousness Combination-System') CMA.ii.21, and AbS.ii.33-34 *'Sobhana·Cetasika·Sampayoga·Nayo'* ('Beautiful Mental-Factor Association-System') CMA.ii.17.) One column is one type of consciousness, with mental factors shaded.

[249] ONE-POINTEDNESS: DhSA.I.11&15 *'Citt·Uppāda·Kaṇḍaṁ'* ('The Consciousness-Arising Section') E.157 explains that it is a synonym for concentration *(samādhi)*, and it manifests as peace of mind or knowledge. DhSA quotes A.IX.I.i.2 *'Cetanā·Karaṇīya·Suttaṁ'* ('The Necessary-Volition Sutta'): 'The concentrated one according to reality knows and sees.' See also endnote 132, p.243.

[250] TRANQUILLITY OF [MENTAL] BODY/CONSCIOUSNESS: for these and other modes, see footnote 150, p.56.

good name, and be respected: maybe because it has become fashionable. One may even train in samatha meditation because one is afraid of blame.

Then again, one may train in samatha meditation because one wants to attain the Deathless. But one does not have a teacher, or one does not have a properly qualified teacher. In that case, one's training may be wrong. For example, one may attain jhāna, and think the bright, brilliant and radiant light (the light of wisdom) that has arisen is the Deathless. Or one may think that to achieve rebirth in a higher world by samatha meditation is to achieve the Deathless. One may also think that by samatha meditation one may find one's inner and true self, a deathless self.

Continued from previous page.

3c: **Mental Phenomena** *(nāma·dhamma)* **at the Arising of Exalted Consciousness** *(mahaggata·citta)*

FINE-MATERIAL JHĀNA	1st			2nd			3rd			4th			5th
Beautiful Universals *(sobhana·sādhāraṇa)*													
10. lightness of [mental] body *(kāya·lahutā)*	✓	✓	✓	✓	✓	✓	✓	✓	✓	✓	✓	✓	✓
11. lightness of consciousness *(citta·lahutā)*	✓	✓	✓	✓	✓	✓	✓	✓	✓	✓	✓	✓	✓
12. flexibility of [mental] body *(kāya·mudutā)*	✓	✓	✓	✓	✓	✓	✓	✓	✓	✓	✓	✓	✓
13. flexibility of consciousness *(citta·mudutā)*	✓	✓	✓	✓	✓	✓	✓	✓	✓	✓	✓	✓	✓
14. wieldiness of [mental] body *(kāya·kammaññatā)*	✓	✓	✓	✓	✓	✓	✓	✓	✓	✓	✓	✓	✓
15. wieldiness of consciousness *(citta·kammaññatā)*	✓	✓	✓	✓	✓	✓	✓	✓	✓	✓	✓	✓	✓
16. proficiency of [mental] body *(kāya·pāguññatā)*	✓	✓	✓	✓	✓	✓	✓	✓	✓	✓	✓	✓	✓
17. proficiency of consciousness *(citta·pāguññatā)*	✓	✓	✓	✓	✓	✓	✓	✓	✓	✓	✓	✓	✓
18. rectitude of [mental] body *(kāy·ujukatā)*	✓	✓	✓	✓	✓	✓	✓	✓	✓	✓	✓	✓	✓
19. rectitude of consciousness *(citt·ujukatā)*	✓	✓	✓	✓	✓	✓	✓	✓	✓	✓	✓	✓	✓
Immeasurables *(a·ppamaññā)*													
1. compassion *(karuṇā)*		✓			✓			✓			✓		
2. sympathetic joy *(muditā)* [251]			✓			✓			✓			✓	
Non-Delusion *(a·moha)*													
1. WISDOM FACULTY *(paññ·indriya)* [252]	✓	✓	✓	✓	✓	✓	✓	✓	✓	✓	✓	✓	✓
Total mental phenomena	34	35		33	34		32	33		31	32		31

Then again, one may train in samatha meditation because one wishes to practise insight; because one has faith in the training laid down by The Buddha, and one wishes to put an end to suffering: this is called insight-basis jhāna *(vipassanā·pādaka·jjhāna)*.[134] But one does not have a teacher, or one does not have a properly qualified teacher. In that case, one may receive wrong instructions. For example, one may think there is no need to train in morality. One may think one can attain jhāna by observing the breath throughout one's body.[135] Or one may believe one has jhāna even though there is no counterpart sign *(paṭibhāga·nimitta)*. Then again, one may have a right understanding of samatha practice, but one trains unsystematically, without patience and respect for one's meditation subject. (When one meditates, one must regard one's meditation subject with as much respect as one regards one's meditation master.) Scepticism may often arise: 'Is this really necessary?' or 'I

[251] COMPASSION/SYMPATHETIC JOY: these are two of the divine abidings. The divine abiding of loving-kindness *(mettā)*, wishing good for all beings, is the mental factor non-hatred; equanimity *(upekkhā)* is ever-evenness.

[252] WISDOM FACULTY: here, it is jhāna wisdom *(jhāna·paññā)*. See 'The Five Types of Knowledge', p.58.

can't succeed! I don't have enough *pāramī*!' Easily one gets bored and distracted, easily one finds excuses for not to practise: maybe one associates with bad friends, who are without faith, effort, mindfulness, concentration, and wisdom. Thus, if one does sit down for meditation, one does so unwillingly. Eventually, one may give up.

Then again, one may practise diligently, but sometimes one does not properly know one's meditation subject, because one of the hindrances has arisen: in that case the knowledge-associated consciousnesses are interspersed with knowledge-dissociated consciousness. And even if one is successful and attains jhāna, unwholesome consciousnesses may arise, such as pride. And one looks down on those who have not yet succeeded. One may go about boasting about one's achievement, talking about it to impress others.

These are examples of how one's samatha meditation can be interspersed by countless thousand million unwholesome consciousnesses rooted in greed *(lobha)*, hatred *(dosa)*, and delusion *(moha)*: dissociated from or associated with wrong view *(micchā·diṭṭhi)*. That makes one's samatha meditation inferior. double-rooted *(dvi-·hetuka)*: it means the resultant consciousness will be unrooted *(ahetuka)*. If, however, one does understand one's meditation subject well, it is knowledge-associated, but even so the interspersion of countless unwholesome consciousnesses make one's samatha meditation inferior, triple-rooted *(ti·hetuka)*: it means the resultant consciousness will be only double-rooted *(dvi·hetuka)*.

Superior Samatha Meditation

What then, makes one's samatha meditation superior *(ukkaṭṭha)*? If, before or after the jhāna consciousnesses, one's mind is associated with wholesome things, it is superior.

For example, one may train in samatha meditation to develop insight-basis jhāna *(vipassanā·pādaka·jjhāna)*. And one has a properly qualified teacher. One bases one's practice on morality. And one trains systematically, with as much patience and respect for one's meditation subject as for one's meditation master. If success is slow in coming, one perseveres: 'It can be done!' 'I must do it!' 'I can do it!' When one gets bored and distracted, one rouses oneself, or one is encouraged by good friends, who have faith, effort, mindfulness, concentration, and wisdom. When one sits down for meditation, one does so with faith and joy, or at least equanimity. And one does not give up.

These are examples of how one's samatha meditation can be interspersed by countless thousand million wholesome consciousnesses associated with non-greed *(a·lobha)*, non-hatred *(a·dosa)*. If one does not understand one's meditation subject very well, it is sometimes knowledge-dissociated, which makes one's samatha meditation superior, double-rooted *(dvi·hetuka)*: it means the resultant consciousness will be double-rooted. If one does understand one's meditation subject well, it is associated also with non-delusion *(a·moha)*, which makes one's samatha meditation superior, triple-rooted *(ti·hetuka)*: it means the resultant consciousness will be triple-rooted.[253]

Training in this way, slowly or quickly, according to one's present effort and past pāramī, one succeeds.

---

[253] For details, see '1f: Inferior & Superior Wholesome Kamma, Their Roots & Resultant Rebirth-Linking', p.62.

The Light of Wisdom

Why then, does The Buddha teach us to develop the light of wisdom *(paññ·āloka)*? It is because with this light of wisdom, one is able to overcome conceptual reality, and penetrate to ultimate truth: with this light, one is able to see the five clinging-aggregates according to reality *(yathā·bhūta)*. Let us listen to The Buddha's explanation:[254]

Develop concentration, bhikkhus *(Samādhiṁ, bhikkhave, bhāvetha)*. **Concentrated, bhikkhus, a bhikkhu according to reality understands** *(samāhito, bhikkhave, bhikkhu yathā·bhūtaṁ pajānāti)*. **And what according to reality does he understand?**

[1] **Materiality's appearance and disappearance;**
[2] **feeling's appearance and disappearance;**
[3] **perception's appearance and disappearance;**
[4] **formations' appearance and disappearance;**
[5] **consciousness's appearance and disappearance.**

It is only when one has developed sufficient concentration, when one has developed the light of wisdom, that one may know and see the five aggregates according to reality:[255] ultimate materiality *(paramattha·rūpa)* and ultimate mentality *(paramattha·nāma)*. That is what we call the Mentality-Materiality Definition Knowledge *(Nāma·Rūpa·Pariccheda·Ñāṇa)*.[256] And it is only then that one can practise insight meditation *(vipassanā·bhāvanā)*. Why? Because one cannot practise insight on conceptual reality.

Perhaps it is better if we briefly discuss insight meditation, and insight knowledge. That way, when we later discuss the workings of kamma, in relation to the three merit-work bases, our explanation will be easier to understand.

Insight Meditation

There are two types of insight meditation *(vipassanā·bhāvanā)*:[257]

1) Mundane insight *(lokiya·vipassanā)*: it takes as object the formed element *(saṅkhata·dhātu)*, things of the three planes of existence: the sensual plane, the fine-material plane and the immaterial plane. That is, ultimate materiality *(paramattha·rūpa)* and ultimate mentality *(paramattha·nāma)*, the Noble Truth of

---

[254] S.III.I.i.5 *'Samādhi·Suttaṁ'* ('The Concentration Sutta')

[255] In S.IV.I.xvi.5 *'Jīvak·Amba·Vana·Samādhi·Suttaṁ'* ('The Jīvaka's-Mango-Grove Concentration Sutta'), The Buddha explains this in accordance with the six bases: 'Develop concentration, bhikkhus. When concentrated *(samāhitassa)*, bhikkhus, things become manifest to the bhikkhu, according to reality. And what becomes manifest according to reality? The eye becomes manifest according to reality as impermanent. Sights... Eye consciousness... Eye contact... And any feeling that arises because of eye contact, be it pleasant, unpleasant, or neither unpleasant nor pleasant... the ear... nose... tongue... body... mind... dhamma-objects... mind consciousness... mind contact... And any feeling that arises because of mind contact, be it pleasant, unpleasant, or neither unpleasant nor pleasant, becomes manifest according to reality as impermanent.' SA explains that 'become manifest' *(okkhāyati)* means they become discernible *(paccakkhāyati)*, knowable *(paññāyati)*, and evident *(pākataṁ)*: *paccakkha* (discernible/perceivable/manifest/known to the senses) is the opposite of *anumāna* (inference).

[256] For details, see 'The Two Preparatory Insight Knowledges', p.90.

[257] VsM.xiv.427 *'Khandha·Niddesa'* ('Exposition of the Aggregates') PP.xiv.15 explains that knowledge of sensual-, fine-material-, and immaterial sphere things is mundane insight, whereas knowledge of Nibbāna is supramundane insight. See also quotation, endnote 292, p.357.

Suffering and the Noble Truth of the Origin of Suffering. There are eleven knowledges associated with mundane insight.

2) Supramundane insight *(lokuttara·vipassanā)*: it takes as object the Unformed element *(Asaṅkhata·dhātu)*. That is, Nibbāna, the Noble Truth of the Cessation of Suffering. There are five knowledges associated with supramundane insight: three are mundane and two are supramundane.

To practise supramundane insight, we need first to practise mundane insight: we need to know and see the five clinging-aggregates according to reality *(yathā·bhūta)*.

THE THREE CHARACTERISTICS

That means we need to know and see that the five aggregates are possessed of three characteristics *(ti·lakkhaṇa)*:[258]

1) The impermanence characteristic *(anicca·lakkhaṇa)*: the five aggregates arise and perish, and change, which means they are impermanent.[259]
2) The suffering characteristic *(dukkha·lakkhaṇa)*: The Buddha speaks of three types of suffering:[260]
    i) Pain suffering *(dukkha·dukkha)*: it refers to the aggregate of feeling. It is physical and mental painful feeling.
    ii) Changeability suffering *(vipariṇāma·dukkha)*: it also refers to the aggregate of feeling, but pleasant feelings, since they are a cause for suffering when they change.
    iii) Formation suffering *(saṅkhāra·dukkha)*: it refers to the aggregate of feeling: equanimous feeling. It refers also to the remaining four aggregates, because they arise and then perish.
3) The non-self characteristic *(an·atta·lakkhaṇa)*: it refers to all five aggregates. Since they arise and perish, and change, they are suffering, which means they possess no permanent substance.[261]

The purpose of knowing and seeing that the five aggregates are possessed of these three characteristics, is to gain the insight knowledges *(vipassanā·ñāṇa)*: first mundane and then supramundane.

The mundane insight knowledges know and see the five clinging-aggregates and their causes. The supramundane knowledges know and see Nibbāna: first the Path-Knowledge consciousness, and then the Fruition-Knowledge consciousness.[262] The Path Knowledge destroys the appropriate defilements: it destroys the delusion that disabled us from knowing and seeing the Four Noble Truths according to reality *(yathā·bhūta)*, ultimate truth *(paramattha·sacca)*. That means, only when we know and see Nibbāna, only then have we properly known and seen the Four Noble Truths.

---

[258] For The Buddha's analysis, see 'Is Materiality Permanent or Impermanent?', p.319.

[259] VsM.viii.236 *'Anussati·Kamma·Ṭṭhāna·Niddeso'* ('Exposition of the Recollection Meditation-Subjects') PP.viii.234. See also 'Impermanence', p.319.

[260] S.V.I.vii.5 *'Dukkhatā·Suttaṁ'* ('The Sufferings Sutta'), explained in e.g. VsM.xvi.539 *'Indriya·Sacca·Niddeso'* ('Exposition of the Faculties and Truths') PP.xvi.34. See also 'Suffering', p.320.

[261] See 'Non-Self', p.320.

[262] PATH KNOWLEDGE: see table '5e: The Path Process', p.340.

That is:

1) The Noble Truth of Suffering *(Dukkha Ariya·Sacca)*: we will have known and seen the five clinging-aggregates, which is the same as to say ultimate materiality and ultimate mentality.
2) The Noble Truth of the Origin of Suffering *(Dukkha·Samudaya Ariya·Sacca)*: we will have known and seen the dependent origination of the five clinging-aggregates. That is, we will have known and seen how ignorance, volitional formation, craving, clinging, and existence of kammic potency give rise to the rebirth-linking consciousness, mentality-materiality, the six bases, contact and feeling. We will have seen this process take place in past lives, up to the present life, and maybe into future lives.[263]
3) The Noble Truth of the Cessation of Suffering *(Dukkha·Nirodha Ariya·Sacca)*: we will have known and seen the cessation of the five clinging-aggregates, which is Nibbāna.
4) The Noble Truth of the Path Leading to the Cessation of Suffering *(Dukkha·Nirodha·Gāminī Paṭipadā Ariya·Sacca)*: we will have known and seen the Noble Eightfold Path *(Ariya Aṭṭhaṅgika·Magga)*, which takes Nibbāna as object:

i) Right View .... *(Sammā·Diṭṭhi)*	v) Right Livelihood .... *(Sammā·Ājīva)*
ii) Right Intention *(Sammā·Saṅkappa)*	vi) Right Effort .... *(Sammā·Vāyāma)*
iii) Right Speech .... *(Sammā·Vācā)*	vii) Right Mindfulness .... *(Sammā·Sati)*
iv) Right Action .... *(Sammā·Kammanta)*	viii) Right Concentration .. *(Sammā·Samādhi)*

It is a truly great thing to know and see Nibbāna, for it means that the end of suffering and rebirth is within reach.*136* But it is not easy to know and see Nibbāna, for it is not easy to practise insight. In fact, it is very, very difficult, and to succeed we need to make much effort in many ways. Why? Because we cannot practise insight on concepts; we can practise insight only on ultimate materiality and ultimate mentality. Ultimate materiality and ultimate mentality are most profound and difficult to see. And they can be seen only with the light of wisdom. They are the objects for insight.

The Two Preparatory Insight Knowledges

Insight knowledge arises as the result of insight meditation *(vipassanā·bhāvanā)*. And since the object of insight meditation is ultimate mentality and ultimate materiality, they need to be discerned, before one can begin to practise insight. Hence, we may say that the first two of the sixteen insight knowledges are really knowledges preparatory to insight meditation proper. They are the Mentality-Materiality Knowledge and the Cause-Apprehending Knowledge:

1) The Mentality-Materiality Definition Knowledge *(Nāma·Rūpa·Pariccheda·Ñāṇa)*:[264] with the defining knowledge of materiality, one will have known and seen ultimate materiality.[265] One will have known and seen the four elements, and materiality derived from the four elements. With the defining knowledge of mentality,[266] one will have known and seen the individual type of

[263] If one attains Arahantship in this life, there will be no future life.
[264] VsM.xviii *'Diṭṭhi·Visuddhi·Niddesa'* ('Exposition of the View Purification') PP.xviii: View Purification is a synonym for the Mentality-Materiality Definition Knowledge.
[265] See 'Ultimate Materiality', p.92*ff.*
[266] See 'Ultimate Mentality', p.105*ff.*

consciousness: one will have defined the consciousnesses associated with the mental processes. Since it takes the formed as object, it is mundane.[267]

2) The Cause-Apprehending Knowledge *(Paccaya·Pariggaha·Ñāṇa)*:[268] with this knowledge, one will have discerned dependent origination in regular and negative order. One will have apprehended the five causal factors of rebirth and the five resultant factors of rebirth. As we explained earlier,[269] one will have known and seen how ignorance, volitional formation, craving, clinging, and existence of kammic potency from a past life, give rise to the rebirth-linking consciousness, mentality-materiality, the six bases, contact, and feeling of this life. It is usually in this connection that one will have discerned the consciousnesses unassociated with cognition (process-separated *(vīthi·mutta)*): the rebirth-linking consciousness, the life-continuum consciousness, and the death consciousness. One will also have known and seen how the cessation of the five causes in a future life gives rise to the cessation of the five results, at one's Parinibbāna (final cessation). Since this knowledge also takes the formed as object, it too is mundane.[270]

Only once one has attained these two preparatory knowledges is one able to know and see the objects for insight meditation.[271] And only then is one able to develop insight meditation proper. Let us therefore very briefly discuss the objects for insight.

The Objects for Insight

The Five Clinging-Aggregates

In the suttas, The Buddha usually speaks of the object of insight as the five clinging-aggregates *(pañc·upādāna·kkhandha)*:

1) The materiality clinging-aggregate *(rūp·upādāna·kkhandha)*
2) The feeling clinging-aggregate *(vedan·upādāna·kkhandha)*
3) The perception clinging-aggregate *(saññ·upādāna·kkhandha)*
4) The formations clinging-aggregate *(saṅkhār·upādāna·kkhandha)*
5) The consciousness clinging-aggregate *(viññāṇ·upādāna·kkhandha)*

The materiality aggregate is the same as ultimate materiality, and the four immaterial aggregates are the same as ultimate mentality. Thus, to know and see ultimate mentality and ultimate materiality, we need to know and see the five clinging-aggregates: they are all the formed element *(saṅkhata·dhātu)*.

---

[267] See The Buddha's description of this knowledge, endnote 28, p.23.

[268] VsM.xix *'Kaṅkhā·Vitaraṇa·Visuddhi·Niddesa'* ('Exposition of the Doubt-Overcoming Purification') PP.xix: Doubt-Overcoming Purification is a synonym for the Cause-Apprehending Knowledge.

[269] See 'Dependent Origination', p.109*ff.*

[270] See The Buddha's description of this knowledge, endnote 29, p.23

[271] This is what The Buddha calls successively higher distinctions: see quotation and explanation in endnote 151, p.244.

What are the five clinging-aggregates? The Buddha explains them in, for example, the *'Khandha'* sutta:[272/137]

What then, bhikkhus, are the five clinging-aggregates*(pañc·upādāna·kkhandha)***?**

[1] **Whatever, bhikkhus, materiality there is, past, future, or present***(atīt·ānāgata·paccuppannaṁ)***, internal or external***(ajjhattaṁ vā bahiddhā vā)***, gross or subtle***(oḷārikaṁ vā sukhumaṁ vā)***, inferior or superior***(hīnaṁ vā paṇītaṁ vā)***, far or near** *(yaṁ dūre santike vā)***, apprehendable by the taints and clingable, this is called the materiality clinging-aggregate.**

[2] **Whatever, bhikkhus, feeling there is, past, future, or present, internal or external, gross or subtle, inferior or superior, far or near, apprehendable by the taints and clingable, this is called the feeling clinging-aggregate.**

[3] **Whatever, bhikkhus, perception there is, past, future, or present, internal or external, gross or subtle, inferior or superior, far or near, apprehendable by the taints and clingable, this is called the perception clinging-aggregate.**

[4] **Whatever, bhikkhus, formations there are, past, future, or present, internal or external, gross or subtle, inferior or superior, far or near, apprehendable by the taints and clingable, this is called the formations clinging-aggregate.**

[5] **Whatever, bhikkhus, consciousness there is, past, future, or present, internal or external, gross or subtle, inferior or superior, far or near, apprehendable by the taints and clingable, this is called the consciousness clinging-aggregate.**
These are called, bhikkhus, the five clinging-aggregates.

From The Buddha's explanation, we can thus understand that to practise insight meditation, we need to know and see the three characteristics (impermanence*(anicca)*, suffering*(dukkha)*, and non-self*(an·atta)*) of fifty-five categories of mentality-materiality:[273]

1) Eleven categories of materiality: the materiality aggregate
2) Eleven categories of feeling: the feeling aggregate
3) Eleven categories of perception: the perception aggregate
4) Eleven categories of formations: the formations aggregate
5) Eleven categories of consciousness: the consciousness aggregate

This knowledge of the five aggregates is the Mentality-Materiality Definition Knowledge*(Nāma·Rūpa·Pariccheda·Ñāṇa)* that we just discussed.

---

[272] S.III.I.v.6 *'Khandha·Suttaṁ'* ('The Aggregate Sutta'). The eleven categories are explained in no sutta, but are explained in, for example, VsM.xiv.493-503 *'Atīt·Ādi·Vibhāga·Kathā'* ('Discussion of the Past, etc. Classification') PP.xiv.185-210. In this sutta, The Buddha gives these eleven categories for both the aggregates and the aggregates of clinging. And as an example, the Most Venerable Pa-Auk Tawya Sayadaw mentions how the Bodhisatta Gotama could discern the five aggregates of Dipaṅkāra Buddha and the Bodhisatta Sumedha. Dipaṇkāra Buddha's aggregates included past supramundane consciousnesses, since He had attained all four Paths&Fruitions: His aggregates were for that reason not clinging-aggregates. The Bodhisatta's aggregates were without past supramundane consciousnesses: his aggregates were for that reason clinging-aggregates. One cannot, however, discern supramundane aggregates unless one has attained them oneself, and one cannot discern supramundane consciousnesses higher than one's own attainment: the common person cannot discern the Stream Enterer's supramundane consciousnesses, and the Stream Enterer cannot discern the Arahant's Arahant Path&Fruition Consciousnesses. For further details, see 'Therefore, Bhikkhus, Any Whatsoever Materiality', p.320.

[273] See, for example, quotation at 'Therefore, Bhikkhus, Any Whatsoever Materiality', p.320.

Ultimate Materiality

What, then, is the materiality clinging-aggregate that we need to know and see? It is two types of materiality:[274]

1) The four great essentials *(cattāro ca mahā·bhūtā)*
2) Materiality derived from the four great essentials[275] *(catunnañca mahā·bhūtānaṁ upādāya·rūpaṁ)* [138]

The Four Great Essentials

The four great essentials *(cattāro ca mahā·bhūtā)* are: [139]

1) Earth element .... *(pathavī·dhātu)*
2) Water element .... *(āpo·dhātu)*
3) Fire element .... *(tejo·dhātu)*
4) Wind element .... *(vāyo·dhātu)*

The four great essentials are concrete materiality *(nipphanna)*:[276] it is born of kamma, consciousness, temperature, or nutriment (later, we shall explain these four origins of materiality).[277]

Derived Materiality

Materiality derived from the four great essentials *(catunnañca mahā·bhūtānaṁ upādāya·rūpaṁ)* is twenty-four types of materiality.[278] They comprise fourteen types of concrete materiality, and ten types of unconcrete materiality:

1) Concrete Materiality *(nipphanna)*: as just mentioned, it is born of kamma, consciousness, temperature, or nutriment.
2) Unconcrete Materiality *(anipphanna)*: it is so-called because it is not born of the four origins of materiality but arises as an attribute, a mode *(ākāra)* of concrete materiality.

Concrete Derived Materiality

The fourteen types of concrete derived materiality are first of all the four types of field materiality *(gocara rūpa)*:

1) Colour .... *(vaṇṇa)*
2) Sound .... *(sadda)*
3) Odour .... *(gandha)*
4) Flavour .... *(rasa)*

Colour is cognized by the eye, sound by the ear, odour by the nose, and flavour by the tongue. Tangibles, cognized by the body, are not included here, because tangibility is not derived materiality. Tangibility is the three great essentials: either the earth-, fire-, and wind element.

---

[274] The following details have been taken from VsM.xviii.667 *'Diṭṭhi·Visuddhi·Niddesa'* ('Exposition of the View Purification') PP.xviii.13. For an overview, see table '4: The Twenty-Eight Types of Materiality', p.105.

[275] DERIVED MATERIALITY: so-called because it derives from, depends upon, the four great essentials: the Texts compare it to plants, which grow dependent on the earth.

[276] CONCRETE: *(nipphanna)* pp. of *nipphajjati*, is produced; springs forth; results; happens (properly, 'concreted materiality': pp. of 'to concrete' (Latin *cresco*, grow)).

[277] See 'The Four Origins of Materiality', p.97.

[278] The Buddha explains the four great essentials, and mentions materiality derived from the four great essentials, in a number of suttas. But there is no sutta where He explains what materiality derived from the four great essentials is. Such materiality is explained only in the commentaries and Abhidhamma: for example, in VsM.xiv.432-446 *'Khandha·Niddesa'* ('Exposition of the Aggregates') PP.xiv.36-71.

Apart from those four types of field materiality, concrete derived materiality is also:

5) Nutritive essence *(ojā)*: it maintains the physical body. We get it from the food we eat.
6) Life faculty *(jīvit·indriya)*: it maintains animate materiality and is born of kamma. When there is death, it means the life faculty has either been cut off, or the kamma producing it has come to an end.
7) Heart-materiality *(hadaya·rūpa)*: it is in the blood in the heart upon which the mind depends. On the plane of five aggregates, mentality cannot arise independently of materiality.

The two types of sex-materiality *(bhāva·rūpa)*:

8) Male sex-materiality *(purisa bhāva·rūpa)*
9) Female sex-materiality *(itthi bhāva·rūpa)*

Male sex-materiality determines a man's material features, the way he moves, etc., and female sex-materiality determines a woman's.

The five types of translucent materiality *(pasāda rūpa)*:[279]

10) Eye translucency	*(cakkhu pasāda)*	13) Tongue translucency	*(jivhā pasāda)*
11) Ear translucency	*(sota pasāda)*	14) Body translucency	*(kāya pasāda)*
12) Nose translucency	*(ghāna pasāda)*		

The translucency is the element through which objects are cognized by the respective faculty. For example, colour is cognized through the eye translucency, and sounds are cognized through the ear translucency. When The Buddha speaks of the eye, the ear, etc., He is referring to this existent ultimate materiality,[140] not to the conceptual eye:[280] it does not exist according to reality *(yathā·bhūta)*.

Unconcrete Derived Materiality

The ten types of unconcrete derived materiality are:

1) Space element	*(ākāsa·dhātu)*	6) Wieldiness	*(kammaññatā)*
2) Bodily intimation	*(kāya·viññatti)*	7) Generation	*(upacaya)*
3) Verbal intimation	*(vacī·viññatti)*	8) Continuity	*(santati)*
4) Lightness	*(lahutā)*	9) Ageing	*(jaratā)*
5) Softness	*(mudutā)*	10) Impermanence	*(aniccatā)*

It is difficult to explain unconcrete materiality before explaining the rūpa-kalāpas and the four origins of materiality: so please, we shall explain unconcrete materiality only then.[281]

Knowing and Seeing Ultimate Materiality

The four great essentials and derived materiality are ultimate materiality. To practise insight, we need to know and see ultimate materiality. That means we need to practise four-elements meditation: we need systematically to know and

---

[279] TRANSLUCENCY: see dictionary definition, footnote 964, p.367.

[280] VsM.xviii.665 *'Nāma·Rūpa·Pariggaha·Kathā'* ('Discussion of Mentality-Materiality Apprehension') PP.xviii.9 explains: 'Instead of taking the piece of flesh variegated with white and black circles, having length and breadth, and fastened in the eye socket with a string of sinew, which the world terms "an eye", he defines as "eye element" the eye translucency of the kind described among the kinds of derived materiality.... The same method applies to the ear element and the rest.'

[281] See also table '4: The Twenty-Eight Types of Materiality', p.105.

see the four elements throughout our body by concentrating on their twelve characteristics.

The Twelve Characteristics

The twelve characteristics of the four elements are:[282]

Earth element		Water element	Fire element	Wind element
1) hardness	2) softness	7) flowing	9) heat	11) supporting
3) roughness	4) smoothness	8) cohesion	10) cold	12) pushing
5) heaviness	6) lightness			

When we have discerned these twelve characteristics throughout the body, and continue the meditation in the proper manner, we shall eventually reach access concentration *(upacāra·samādhi)*. Then, with further meditation, the body will appear to us as a white form. Eventually it will appear to us as a translucent form, like a block of ice or glass. But that is not yet ultimate materiality: it is still a concept, and we cannot practise insight on concepts. So we need to meditate on the translucent form until we can see the space element *(ākāsa·dhātu)*. When we have discerned the space element, the translucent form will dissolve into small particles, clusters of materiality: they are in Pali called ***rūpa·kalāpas***.[283] They arise and perish with great speed. But they are not ultimate materiality either: they are also only concepts. So we need to analyse the individual ***kalāpa***: we need to know and see the individual elements that comprise the kalāpa. Only then can we say we know and see ultimate materiality.

Why do we need to analyse the individual kalāpa? Why do we need to know and see ultimate materiality? To overcome the self perception *(atta·saññā)*. You will remember that when we discussed the *'Gaddula·Baddha'* sutta, we discussed how the uneducated ordinary person somehow identifies the five clinging-aggregates with a self in twenty ways.[284] This occurs because of the delusion of compactness *(ghana)*.

The Three Types of Material Compactness

The uneducated ordinary person identifies the materiality clinging-aggregate with a self because of the three types of material compactness *(ghana)*. It can be overcome only by compactness resolution *(ghana·vinibbhoga)*, which is to resolve the three types of compactness *(ghana)*:[285]

1) Continuity compactness *(santati·ghana)*: because materiality seems to be one compact continuity, a continuous whole, one may think one's body and

[282] DhS.ii.646-651 *'Duka·Niddeso'* ('Exposition of the Pairs') DhSA.ibid./E.402*ff.* See also VsM.xi.306 *'Catu·Dhātu Vavatthāna Bhāvanā'* ('Four-Elements Definition Meditation') PP.-xi.41-43.

[283] *Rūpa* (materiality) + *kalāpa* (group/cluster). The term is used in, for example, AbS.vi.-45*ff* *'Kalāpa·Yojanā'* ('Cluster Exegesis') CMA.vi.16.

[284] See 'Regards the Five Aggregates as Self', p.10.

[285] In VsM.xi.306 *'Catu·Dhātu·Vavatthāna·Bhāvanā·Vaṇṇanā'* ('Description of the Four-Elements Definition Meditation') PP.xi.30, reference is made to the Buddha's simile of the butcher who has killed a cow and cut it into pieces: in D.ii.9 *'Mahā·Sati·Paṭṭhāna·Suttaṁ'* ('The Great Mindfulness-Foundation Sutta'), and M.I.i.10 *'Sati·Paṭṭhāna·Suttaṁ'* ('The Mindfulness-Foundation Sutta'). The Subcommentaries to these texts explain how this involves resolving the three kinds of compactness. See also quotation, footnote 9, p.2.

limbs have actual existence. And one may think the same self 'migrates' from life to life, taking different forms. To overcome this delusion, we need to resolve the seeming compactness of the body. We need to see that the body comprises rūpa kalāpas that arise and perish. That way, we see that a kalāpa has no continuity: as soon as it arises, it perishes. There is no time for a kalāpa to go anywhere, not from life to life, not even from second to second.

2) Synthesis compactness*(samūha·ghana)*: because materiality seems to be a synthetic whole, one may think the kalāpas are ultimate materiality. And one may think they are one's self. To overcome this delusion, we need to resolve the seeming compactness of the individual type of kalāpa: we need to analyse the individual type of kalāpa. That way, we see that a kalāpa comprises elements: earth element, water element, fire element, wind element, colour, odour, flavour, nutritive-essence, life faculty, etc. There is no synthetic whole anywhere.
3) Function compactness*(kicca·ghana)*: because of insufficient understanding about ultimate materiality, one may think the elements rest upon a self, like seeds and plants rest upon earth.[141] To overcome this delusion, we need to see that each element has its own characteristic*(lakkhaṇa)*, function*(rasa)*, manifestation*(paccupaṭṭhāna)*, and proximate cause*(padaṭṭhāna)*: it does not depend on any external thing such as a self.

The Texts explain that unless we successfully resolve these three types of compactness, we shall be unable to overcome the self perception*(atta·saññā)*, unable to attain the non-self perception*(an·atta·saññā)*.

ANALYSIS OF ULTIMATE MATERIALITY

Let us then briefly discuss how to resolve the three types of compactness, by analysis of ultimate materiality.

Analysing the different types of kalāpa throughout the body, we will find that kalāpas comprise two types of materiality:[286]

1) Translucent materiality*(pasāda rūpa)*
2) Untranslucent materiality*(napasāda rūpa)*

THE OCTAD-, NONAD-, AND DECAD KALĀPA

Then we need to analyse the different types of translucent kalāpa and untranslucent kalāpa. And we shall find that there are three types of kalāpa:

1) The octad kalāpa ...... *(aṭṭhaka·kalāpa)*
2) The nonad kalāpa ..... *(navaka·kalāpa)*
3) The decad kalāpa .... *(dasaka·kalāpa)*

The octad kalāpa comprises eight types of materiality. The four great essentials:

1) Earth element .... *(pathavī·dhātu)*
2) Water element .... *(āpo·dhātu)*
3) Fire element .... *(tejo·dhātu)*
4) Wind element .... *(vāyo·dhātu)*

And four types of derived materiality:

1) Colour .... *(vaṇṇa)*
2) Odour .... *(gandha)*
3) Flavour .... *(rasa)*
4) Nutritive essence .... *(ojā)*

In all, eight types of materiality: that is why it is called an octad kalāpa. It is untranslucent. The nonad kalāpa is so called because it comprises the same eight

286 TRANSLUCENCY: see dictionary definition, footnote 964, p.367.

types of materiality as the octad kalāpa, plus a ninth type of materiality: life faculty *(jīvit·indriya)*. The nonad kalāpa is also untranslucent. The decad kalāpa is so called because it comprises the same nine types of materiality as the nonad kalāpa, plus a tenth. But there are three types of decad kalāpa:

1) Translucent decad-kalāpas, which are:
   i) The eye decad-kalāpa *(cakkhu·dasaka·kalāpa)*
   ii) The ear decad-kalāpa *(sota·dasaka·kalāpa)*
   iii) The nose decad-kalāpa *(ghāna·dasaka·kalāpa)*
   iv) The tongue decad-kalāpa *(jivhā·dasaka·kalāpa)*
   v) The body decad-kalāpa *(kāya·dasaka·kalāpa)*

   They are all translucent because their tenth element is translucent materiality *(pasāda·rūpa)*.
2) Heart decad-kalāpas *(hadāya·dasaka·kalāpa)*: they are untranslucent because their tenth element is the untranslucent heart-materiality *(hadāya·rūpa)*.
3) Sex decad-kalāpas *(bhāva·dasaka·kalāpa)*: they are untranslucent because their tenth element is the untranslucent male or female sex-materiality *(bhāva·rūpa)*.

We need to know and see the octad-, nonad-, and decad kalāpas in the eye, ear, nose, tongue, body and heart. And we need also to know and see the octad kalāpas in inanimate materiality: in, for example, the food in our stomach, the urine in our bladder, the faeces in our intestines, and the clothes we wear. Afterwards we need to know and see the different kinds of materiality of other beings, such as other meditators, other people, animals, devas, and Brahmas. And we need also to know and see the different types of materiality of the building we are in, of the trees outside, of other plants, of stones, etc.

Knowing and seeing how all materiality comprises different kinds of kalāpa is not enough, however. We need also to know and see the origin of those kalāpas, what they are born of, to know and see what produces the materiality.

The Four Origins of Materiality

According to origin, materiality is of four types:[287]

1) Kamma-born materiality *(kamma·ja·rūpa)*
2) Consciousness-born materiality *(citta·ja·rūpa)*
3) Temperature-born materiality *(utu·ja·rūpa)*
4) Nutriment-born materiality *(āhāra·ja·rūpa)*

Let us then briefly discuss the origins of materiality.[288]

Kamma-Born Materiality

Kamma-born materiality *(kamma·ja·rūpa)* comprises eight types of kalāpa:

1) The eye decad-kalāpa *(cakkhu·dasaka·kalāpa)*

---

[287] The information given with regard to the four origins of materiality may be found in e.g., VsM.xi.359 *'Catu·Dhātu Vavatthāna Bhāvanā'* ('Four-Elements Definition Meditation') PP.xi.111, VsM.xviii.664 *'Diṭṭhi·Visuddhi·Niddesa'* ('Exposition of the View Purification') PP.xviii.5-6, VsM.xx.701-704 *'Rūpa·Nibbatti·Passanā·Kāra·Kathā'* ('Discussion of Seeing the Cause of Materiality-Generation') PP.xx.22-42, and AbS.vi.29-44 *'Rūpa·Samuṭṭhāna-·Nayo'* ('Materiality-Origination System').

[288] Discerning these different types of origin is included in the development of The Mentality-Materiality Definition Knowledge *(Nāma·Rūpa·Pariccheda·Ñāṇa)*. See 'The Two Preparatory Insight Knowledges', p.90.

2) The ear decad-kalāpa *(sota·dasaka·kalāpa)*
3) The nose decad-kalāpa *(ghāna·dasaka·kalāpa)*
4) The tongue decad-kalāpa *(jivhā·dasaka·kalāpa)*
5) The body decad-kalāpa *(kāya·dasaka·kalāpa)*
6) The heart decad-kalāpa *(hadāya·dasaka·kalāpa)*
7) The female/male sex decad-kalāpa *(bhāva·dasaka·kalāpa)*
8) The life nonad-kalāpas *(jīvita·navaka·kalāpa)*

They are all animate, concrete materiality. At the time of birth, together with the rebirth-linking consciousness *(paṭisandhi·citta)*, there arise three types of kalāpa: heart-decad kalāpas, body decad-kalāpas, and sex-decad kalāpas. At our very conception, we possess body decad-kalāpas, with the body translucency as the tenth (the body base), through which we experience pleasant and unpleasant physical feelings. Later on, during our gestation, the eye-, ear-, nose-, and tongue decad-kalāpas arise. As explained earlier, these kalāpas are born of wholesome kamma accomplished in a past life: offering *(dāna)*, morality *(sīla)*, or meditation *(bhāvanā)*. It depends on ignorance and craving.

To know and see materiality for the practice of insight, we need to know and see how some materiality is kamma-born, and we need, for example, also to know and see how the rebirth-linking consciousness and the materiality that arises with the rebirth-linking consciousness is kamma-born. It is possible to know and see these things with sufficient skill, effort and light of wisdom from access concentration or jhāna.[289]

CONSCIOUSNESS-BORN MATERIALITY

Consciousness-born materiality *(citta·ja·rūpa)* is not born of eye-, ear-, nose-, tongue-, and body consciousnesses, only of consciousnesses that arise dependent on the heart base *(hadaya·vatthu)*: that is, mind consciousnesses. Consciousness-born materiality comprises eight types of kalāpa:

1) Consciousness-born pure octad kalāpa *(citta·ja·suddh·aṭṭhaka·kalāpa)*: it comprises the basic eight types of materiality, the eighth here being consciousness-born nutritive essence *(citta·ja ojā)*. Hence, it is also called consciousness-born nutritive-essence octad-kalāpa *(citta·ja·oj·aṭṭhamaka·kalāpa)*: it is concrete materiality. Anger and worry, for example, are hatred-rooted *(dosa·mūla)*, and hatred-rooted consciousnesses produces consciousness-born pure octad kalāpas with predominant fire element. That is why, when we are angry or worried, we get hot.
2) Bodily-intimation nonad-kalāpa *(kāya·viññatti·navaka·kalāpa)*: it comprises the basic eight plus a ninth type of materiality: bodily-intimation. It is bodily movements that communicate one's intention to another: for example, beckoning with one's hand, raising one's eyebrows, grimacing, and raising one's hand to strike (even dogs understand that). Indirect bodily intimation is bodily movements by which another may deduce one's intention: for example, if we are walking, another may understand we are going in such and such a direction; if we are running, another may understand we are in a hurry. When we walk, the mind is directed at the leg and foot. That intention pro-

[289] When the meditator develops the Mentality-Materiality Definition Knowledge, kamma-born materiality is discerned. But knowledge of which kind of kamma produced it is developed only at the time of practising for the Cause-Apprehending Knowledge: see p.91.

duces consciousness-born bodily-intimation as ninth kalāpas in the leg and foot, and throughout the body: it has predominant wind element. Just as wind carries objects along, so too the wind element carries the limbs and body along. The movement is a long series of different consciousness-born bodily-intimation kalāpas being produced in different places. The kalāpas that arise at the raising of the foot are different from the kalāpas that arise at the lowering of the foot. Each kalāpa arises and perishes in the same place, and new kalāpas arise elsewhere and perish there.

3) Lightness, etc. undecad-kalāpa*(lahut·ādi·ekā·dasaka·kalāpa)*: it comprises the basic eight plus three more types of materiality: lightness*(lahutā)*, softness*(mudutā)*, and wieldiness*(kammaññatā)*. It arises when the body feels comfortable and light, because of happiness, concentration, health, strength, comfort, etc. Take, for example, strong and powerful samatha and vipassanā consciousnesses, or Path&Fruition consciousnesses. Such consciousnesses are very pure, very powerful and superior, because there are no ***upakkilesa*** (corruptions). It means that, depending on how deep the concentration or how sharp the understanding, these consciousnesses produce very many generations of pure and superior consciousness-born lightness, etc. as undecad kalāpas: those kalāpas' earth-, wind-, and fire element are very soft and subtle. When those soft and subtle kalāpas touch the body base (the tenth element in the body decad-kalāpas) the yogi experiences great bodily comfort, with no heaviness (the earth element): that is why the yogi then can sit easily for many hours.

4) Bodily-intimation & lightness, etc. dodecad-kalāpa*(kāya·viññatti·lahut·ādi·dvā·dasaka·kalāpa)*: it comprises the basic eight plus four more types of materiality: bodily-intimation, lightness, softness, and wieldiness. It arises when, because of happiness, youth, health, strength, comfort, etc., bodily movements are graceful, light, and easy. It can also arise when, because of excitement, anger, fear, etc., one moves very fast and with great ease.

5) Verbal-intimation decad-kalāpa*(vacī·viññatti·dasaka·kalāpa)*: it comprises the basic eight plus two more types of materiality: verbal-intimation and sound. That is, speech or other sounds made with the speech organs to communicate with others, such as shouting, crying, etc. This sound is produced only by animate materiality, beings. The sound arises because the earth element of the consciousness-born kalāpas strikes the earth element of the vocal apparatus.[290] It is unconcrete materiality.

6) Verbal-intimation & sound & lightness, etc. thirteen-factored kalāpa*(vacī·viññatti·sadda·lahut·ādi·terasaka·kalāpa)*: it comprises the basic eight plus five more types of materiality: verbal-intimation, sound, lightness, softness, and wieldiness. Here again, it arises when, because of happiness, health, strength, comfort, etc., speech is smooth and easy. It may also arise because the subject matter is beautiful or profound, such as when explaining the profound Dhamma.

---

[290] VsM.xiv.441 *'Rūpa·Kkhandha·Kathā'* ('Discussion of the Materiality-Aggregate') PP.xiv.62 explains that verbal intimation is the mode and alteration of whatever consciousness-originated earth element that causes speech to be uttered, by which there is the knocking together of clung-to materiality (VsMṬ.452: the vocal apparatus). Its function is to display intention. It is manifested as the cause of the voice in speech.

7) In-breath & out-breath consciousness-born sound nonad-kalāpa *(assāsa·passāsa·citta·ja·sadda·navaka·kalāpa)*: it comprises the basic eight plus a ninth type of materiality: the sound of the breath. And it is concrete materiality. This sound is produced only by breathing beings. Again, the sound arises because the earth element of the consciousness-born kalāpas strikes the earth element of the nasal passage.
8) In-breath & out-breath consciousness-born sound & lightness, etc. dodecad-kalāpa *(assāsa·passāsa·citta·ja·sadda·lahut·ādi·dvā·dasaka·kalāpa)*: it comprises the basic eight plus four more types of materiality: the sound of the breath, lightness, softness, and wieldiness. Here again, it arises when, because of happiness, health, strength, comfort, etc., the breath is smooth and easy: for example, when one practises mindfulness of breathing, and the breath becomes very soft and subtle.

To know and see materiality for the practice of insight, we need to know and see how some materiality is consciousness-born. For example, if we want to practise insight on walking, we need to discern the intention to walk. Then we need to discern the consciousness-born kalāpas that arise owing to that intention. And we need to discern how they arise and perish in one place, and new ones arise and perish in another place. We need to analyse the elements of the kalāpas that produce the rising of the foot, the kalāpas that produce the advancing of the foot, the kalāpas that produce the extending of the foot, the kalāpas that produce the descending of the foot, and the kalāpas that produce the landing of the foot. We need to discern all the elements in those different kalāpas. And we need to see which element is predominant: earth, water, fire or wind. We need, of course, also to see this entire procedure for all other postures: standing, sitting, lying down, moving the limbs, etc.

It is possible to know and see these things with sufficient skill, effort and light of wisdom from access concentration or jhāna.

Temperature-Born Materiality

Temperature-born materiality *(utu·ja·rūpa)* (born of the fire element *(tejo·dhātu)*)[291] comprises four types:

1) Temperature-born pure octad kalāpa *(utu·ja·suddh·aṭṭhaka·kalāpa)*: it comprises the basic eight types of materiality, the eighth here being temperature-born nutritive essence *(utu·ja ojā)*. Hence, it is also called temperature-born nutritive-essence octad-kalāpa *(utu·ja·oj·aṭṭhamaka·kalāpa)*: it is concrete materiality. Food in our bowl, food in our alimentary canal (food in our mouth, newly eaten undigested food in our stomach, semi-digested- and fully digested food in our intestines, and faeces), pus and urine are all inanimate temperature-born nutritive-essence octad-kalāpas.
2) Temperature-born sound nonad-kalāpa *(utu·ja·sadda·navaka·kalāpa)*: it comprises the basic eight plus a ninth type of materiality: sound produced by inanimate matter, for example, sound caused by wind in the stomach or intestines, the sound of bones cracking, the sound of music, or an object breaking. It includes all sound kalāpas except the consciousness-born sound kalāpas of verbal intimation or the breath, which we just explained. Again,

[291] *Tejo* (fire) and *utu* (temperature) refer to the same thing.

the sound arises because of the striking together of the earth element. It is concrete materiality.

3) Lightness, etc. undecad-kalāpa *(lahut·ād·ekā·dasaka·kalāpa)*: it comprises the basic eight plus three more types of materiality: lightness *(lahutā)*, softness *(mudutā)*, and wieldiness *(kammaññatā)*. It arises when the body feels comfortable and light, because of happiness, health, strength, comfort, etc.
4) Sound & lightness, etc. dodecad-kalāpa *(sadda·lahut·ādi·dvā·dasaka·kalāpa)*: it comprises the basic eight plus four more types of materiality: sound, lightness, softness, and wieldiness.

All kalāpas have the fire element *(tejo·dhātu)*. And the fire element of all kalāpas produces temperature-born kalāpas. Those temperature-born kalāpas themselves have the fire element, which then also produces temperature-born kalāpas, which also have the fire element, which also produces temperature-born kalāpas, etc. That is how, according to its power, the fire element produces materiality through a number of generations.[292]

We just mentioned how strong and powerful samatha and vipassanā consciousnesses, and Path&Fruition consciousnesses produce very many generations of pure and superior consciousness-born kalāpas: the fire element of those kalāpas also produces many temperature-born kalāpas inside and outside the body.

The radiance, brilliance, and brightness that arises with those superior consciousnesses is produced by the brilliance of the colour-materiality of the consciousness- and temperature-born materiality. This accounts for the clear and bright nimitta that arises with samatha meditation, and the light of wisdom *(paññ·āloka)* that we use to discern ultimate truth.[293] It accounts also for the clear and bright skin and faculties of yogis who develop these superior consciousnesses.[142] The materiality born of, for example, the Venerable Anuruddha's divine-eye consciousnesses *(dibba·cakkhu abhiññāṇa)* spread throughout a thousand world-systems: they were lit up by the superior consciousness-born materiality and became visible to him. We may also be able to see other planes of existence, etc., if we develop sufficiently concentrated and pure consciousness.

Temperature also produces and maintains inanimate materiality. A good example is plants. Their materiality is temperature-born materiality and is born of the fire element originally in the seed. Their growth is nothing except the continued production of temperature-born materiality through many generations. It takes place with the assistance of the fire element from the soil, sun (hot), and water (cold).

The fire element in, for example, stones, metals, minerals, and hardwood is very powerful, and produces very, very many generations of materiality. That is why that materiality can last a long time. But the fire element in, for example, softwood, tender plants, flesh, food and water is very weak, not very many generations of materiality are produced, which is why the materiality soon falls apart. When materiality falls apart, it is because the fire element no longer produces new materiality but instead consumes itself: the materiality rots, falls apart, and dissolves.

---

292 E.g. The fire element of a kamma-born kalāpa itself produces temperature-born kalāpas: [kamma-born] → [1st temperature-born] → [2nd —] → [3rd —] → [4th —] → [5th —]. This is then called kamma-caused temperature-born materiality.

293 See quotations endnotes 133, p.243 and 151, p.244.

When materiality is consumed by fire, such as when wood is burning, it is because the fire element of the external materiality (the flames that strike the wood) supports the fire element of the internal materiality (the wood), and a large amount of fire element bursts forth, which means the fire element becomes predominant and the materiality is consumed.

To know and see materiality for the practice of insight, we need to know and see how some materiality is temperature-born. We need to know and see how each type of kalāpa has the fire element, which temperature produces temperature-born octad-kalāpas, which again produce temperature-born octad-kalāpas, which again produce temperature-born octad-kalāpas, and so on. We need to see how this process takes place in all the sense organs, and in external materiality.

It is possible to know and see these things with sufficient skill, effort and light of wisdom from access concentration or jhāna.

NUTRIMENT-BORN MATERIALITY

Nutriment-born materiality *(āhāra·ja·rūpa)* comprises two types of kalāpa born of nutriment:

1) Nutriment-born pure octad kalāpa *(āhāra·ja·suddh·aṭṭhaka·kalāpa)*: it comprises the basic eight types of materiality, the eighth here being nutriment-born nutritive essence *(āhāra·ja·ojā)*. Hence, it is also called nutriment-born nutritive-essence octad-kalāpas *(āhāra·ja·oj·aṭṭhamaka·kalāpa)*: it is concrete materiality.
2) Lightness, etc. undecad-kalāpa *(lahut·ād·ekā·dasaka·kalāpa)*: it comprises the basic eight plus three more types of materiality: lightness *(lahutā)*, softness *(mudutā)*, and wieldiness *(kammaññatā)*. It arises when the body feels comfortable and light, because of happiness, health, strength, comfort, etc.: for example, if our digestion is very good, these nutriment-born nutritive-essence kalāpas spread very easily. The same thing may happen if the food is wholesome and delicious.

These two types of nutriment-born materiality are produced in the two-fold process of nutrition: when the body is nourished by the nutriment from food and drink. How?

The body gets nutriment from the food and drink in our alimentary canal: the food and drink in our mouth, newly taken undigested food and drink in our stomach, semi-digested- and fully digested food in our intestines, and faeces. All that is temperature-born nutritive-essence octad-kalāpas *(utu·ja·oj·aṭṭhamaka·kalāpa)*, the same as the food in our bowl. And the nutritive-essence of those kalāpas nourishes the body chiefly with the help of the digestive fire *(pācaka·tejo)*: the fire element of the life-nonad kalāpas, which (as mentioned) are kamma-born, and found throughout the body.

There are then two stages of nutrition. The first stage takes place when the digestive fire meets with the nutritive essence of the food in our alimentary canal. By that meeting, further materiality is generated throughout the body: that is, nutriment-born nutritive-essence octad-kalāpas *(āhāra·ja·oj·aṭṭhamaka·kalāpa)* are generated throughout the body.

The second stage of nutrition is when the digestive fire meets with the nutritive-essence of those nutriment-born nutritive-essence octad-kalāpas as well as the nutritive-essence of other materiality of the body. By that meeting, yet further materiality is generated; that is, yet other nutriment-born nutritive-essence octad-kalāpas:[294]

- four to five generations in the case of kamma-born materiality
- two to three generations in the case of consciousness-born materiality
- ten to twelve generations in the case of temperature-born materiality
- ten to twelve generations in the case of other nutriment-born materiality

That is how the nutriment from food and drink nourishes the body.[295]

For example, in the first stage of nutrition, a nutriment-born nutritive-essence octad-kalāpa reaches the eye. Then, in the second stage, the nutritive-essence of such a nutriment-born nutritive-essence octad-kalāpa (together with the digestive fire) meets with the nutritive-essence of an eye-decad kalāpa, and four to five generations of nutriment-born nutritive-essence octad-kalāpas are generated: the nutriment-born nutritive-essence octad-kalāpa and the life-nonad kalāpa function as supporting cause *(upatthambhaka·paccaya)*, and the eye decad-kalāpa functions as productive cause *(janaka·paccaya)*. And again, the fire element in those four to five generations of nutriment-born nutritive-essence octad-kalāpas generates ten to twelve generations of temperature-born nutritive-essence octad-kalāpas. And this same process takes place with the body decad-kalāpas of the eye, sex decad-kalāpas of the eye, as well as consciousness-born octad-kalāpas, life nonad-kalāpas, and other nutriment-born octad-kalāpas. That is how the nutriment from food and drink nourishes, for example, the eye.

The nutriment of food taken in one day may regenerate in this way for up to seven days. But the number of generations depends on our digestive power, which is determined by our own kamma. It depends also on the quality of the food. If the food is poor, it cannot generate many generations, and we become weak and thin. If the food is rich, it can generate many generations, and we may even become fat. Divine nutriment, most superior nutriment of the deva-world, may regenerate this way for up to one or two months.

Since life nonad-kalāpas are found throughout the body, the digestive fire is found to a weaker degree throughout the body. That is why, for example, when medicinal oil is applied to the skin, or an injection of medicine is made under the skin, the medicine spreads throughout the body (the first stage of nutrition). But if very much oil is applied, the weakness of the digestive fire in the skin may mean it takes longer to absorb. The medicine then takes effect when it goes through the second stage of nutrition.

To know and see materiality for the practice of insight, we need to know and see both stages of nutrition: the first stage by which nutriment-born nutritive-essence octad-kalāpas are generated and spread to the various parts of the body, and the second stage by which yet other generations of nutritive-essence octad kalāpas are generated to nourish the various parts of the body.

---

[294] The materiality produced in the first stage is called nutriment-originated materiality *(āhāra·samuṭṭhāna-rūpa)*. In the second stage, for kamma-born materiality, the first generation is kamma-caused nutriment-born materiality *(kamma·paccay·āhāraja·rūpa)*, whereas the following generations are nutriment-caused nutriment-born materiality *(ahāra·paccay·āhāra·ja·rūpa)*: also called nutriment-caused nutriment-originated materiality *(āhāra·paccaya āhāra·samuṭṭhāna·rūpa)*. In the same way, there is consciousness- and temperature-caused nutriment-born materiality.

[295] Superior consciousness may give rise to many more generations; likewise nutriment-born of deva nutriment.

It is possible to know and see these things with sufficient skill, effort, and light of wisdom from access concentration or jhāna.

Conclusion

That concludes our very brief explanation of how one knows and sees the materiality clinging-aggregate by four elements meditation.

To develop this meditation subject, we need to have strong and powerful concentration: either access concentration or jhāna. If we begin with four elements meditation itself, we reach access concentration *(upacāra·samādhi)*. Access concentration is very near jhāna, which means there is also strong and powerful concentration, and the light of wisdom. But if we have developed jhāna beforehand, for example, with mindfulness-of-breathing, our light of wisdom is much more powerful, and it is much easier to develop and complete four-elements meditation. Without such concentration, however, without the light of wisdom, it is impossible to penetrate the rūpa-kalāpas, and know and see ultimate reality.

Why is it necessary to practise a subject as difficult as four-elements meditation? Because we cannot practise insight on concepts. If we are looking at only concepts, clearly we do not know and see the materiality clinging-aggregate according to reality *(yathā·bhūta)*.[296] To be able to practise insight, and understand materiality according to reality, we need therefore to overcome the concepts, to resolve the seeming compactness of materiality, and penetrate to ultimate materiality.

[296] See quotation p.88.

4: **The Twenty-Eight Types of Materiality**

FOUR GREAT ESSENTIALS *(mahā·bhūta)*:
Concrete Materiality *(nipphanna·rūpa)*
1. Earth element .... *(pathavī·dhātu)*
2. Water element .... *(āpo·dhātu)*
3. Fire element .... *(tejo·dhātu)*
4. Wind element .... *(vāyo·dhātu)*

⇓⇓⇓⇓⇓⇓⇓⇓⇓⇓⇓⇓⇓⇓⇓⇓⇓⇓⇓⇓⇓⇓⇓⇓⇓⇓⇓⇓⇓⇓

TWENTY-FOUR TYPES OF DERIVED MATERIALITY *(upādāya·rūpa)*

Concrete Materiality *(nipphanna·rūpa)*	
FIELD MATERIALITY *(gocara·rūpa)*: (objective materiality)	TRANSLUCENT MATERIALITY *(pasāda·rūpa)*: (subjective materiality)
1. Colour .... *(vaṇṇa)*	1. Eye translucency .... *(cakkhu·pasāda)*
2. Sound .... *(sadda)*	2. Ear translucency .... *(sota·pasāda)*
3. Odour .... *(gandha)*	3. Nose translucency .... *(ghāna·pasāda)*
4. Flavour .... *(rasa)*	4. Tongue translucency .... *(jivhā·pasāda)*
(5. Tangible[297] .... *(phoṭṭhabba)*)	5. Body translucency .... *(kāya·pasāda)*
1. Nutritive Essence[297] .... *(ojā)*	SEX-MATERIALITY *(bhāva·rūpa)*:[297]
1. Life faculty[297] .... *(jīvit·indriya)*	1. Male sex-materiality .... *(purisa·bhāva·rūpa)*
1. Heart-Materiality[297] *(hadaya·rūpa)*	2. Female sex-materiality .... *(itthi·bhāva·rūpa)*
Unconcrete Materiality *(anipphanna·rūpa)*	
1. Space element[298] .... *(ākāsa·dhātu)*	6. Wieldiness[298] .... *(kammaññatā)*
2. Bodily Intimation .... *(kāya·viññatti)*	7. Generation[298] .... *(upacaya)*
3. Verbal Intimation .... *(vacī·viññatti)*	8. Continuity[298] .... *(santati)*
4. Lightness[298] .... *(lahutā)*	9. Ageing .... *(jaratā)*
5. Softness[298] .... *(mudutā)*	10. Impermanence[298] .... *(aniccatā)*

Unconcrete materiality is included in definition of the materiality aggregate, but it is not the object of insight.[299]

ULTIMATE MENTALITY

To practise insight meditation, we need not only to know and see the materiality clinging-aggregate; we need also to know and see the four mental clinging-aggregates: the feeling clinging-aggregate, the perception clinging-aggregate, the formations clinging-aggregate, and the consciousness clinging-aggregate. That is mentality *(nāma)*.

---

297 TANGIBLE: the object of body consciousness is not an element of its own, but three of the four great essentials: earth-, fire-, and wind element. NUTRITIVE ESSENCE: also called nutriment-materiality *(āhāra·rūpa)*. LIFE FACULTY: also life-materiality *(jīvita·rūpa)*. HEART-MATERIALITY: also heart base *(hadaya·vatthu)*. MALE/FEMALE SEX-MATERIALITY: also male/female sex faculty *(puris·/itth·indriya)*. Other names may also be found.

298 SPACE ELEMENT: delimitation, boundary of rūpa-kalāpas, separating one from the other. LIGHTNESS/SOFTNESS/WIELDINESS: only in consciousness-/temperature-/nutriment-born materiality. GENERATION: generation of the foetus's physical faculties: discerned only when discerning dependent origination (see 'Dependent Origination', p.109). CONTINUITY: generation of materiality thereafter. IMPERMANENCE: the dissolution *(bhaṅga)* of materiality.

299 VsM.xviii.667 *'Diṭṭhi·Visuddhi·Niddesa'* ('Exposition of the View Purification') PP.xviii.13

Mentality is consciousness*(citta)* (also called ***viññāṇa)***,[143] and mental factors*(cetasika)*. There are six main types of consciousness:[144]

1) eye consciousness ...... *(cakkhu·viññāṇa)*	5) tongue consciousness ... *(jivhā·viññāṇa)*
2) ear consciousness .... *(sota·viññāṇa)*	6) body consciousness .... *(kāya·viññāṇa)*
3) nose consciousness ..... *(ghāna·viññāṇa)*	7) mind consciousness ...... *(mano·viññāṇa)*

But a consciousness never arises alone. There is no such thing as 'bare' consciousness, for consciousness always arises together with a certain number of associated mental factors.[300] There are in total fifty-two mental factors.[301] We have already mentioned them. For example, the mental factors that arise with all consciousnesses, the seven universals*(sabba·citta·sādhāraṇa)*:[302]

1) contact .... *(phassa)*	4) volition .... *(cetanā)*	6) life faculty ... *(jīvit·indriya)*
2) feeling .... *(vedanā)*	5) one-pointedness ... *(ek·aggatā)*	7) attention ...... *(manasikāra)*
3) perception .... *(saññā)*		

There are also the mental factors that arise with only some consciousnesses, the six miscellaneous*(pakiṇṇaka)*:[302]

1) application .... *(vitakka)*	3) decision .... *(adhimokkha)*	5) joy .... *(pīti)*
2) sustainment .... *(vicāra)*	4) energy .... *(vīriya)*	6) desire .... *(chanda)*

There are also the unwholesome*(akusala)* mental factors. For example:[303]

• delusion .... *(moha)*	• conceit .... *(māṇa)*
• consciencelessness .... *(ahiri)*	• hatred .... *(dosa)*
• shamelessness .... *(anottappa)*	• envy .... *(issā)*
• restlessness .... *(uddhacca)*	• possessiveness .... *(macchariya)*
• greed .... *(lobha)*	• remorse .... *(kukkucca)*
• view .... *(diṭṭhi)*	• scepticism .... *(vicikicchā)*

And then there are the beautiful*(sobhana)* mental factors. For example:[304]

• faith .... *(saddhā)*	• Right Speech .... *(Sammā·Vācā)*
• mindfulness .... *(sati)*	• Right Action .... *(Sammā·Kammanta)*
• conscience .... *(hiri)*	• Right Livelihood .... *(Sammā·Ājīva)*
• shame .... *(ottappa)*	• compassion .... *(karuṇā)*
• non-greed .... *(a·lobha)*	• sympathetic joy .... *(muditā)*
• non-hatred .... *(a·dosa)*	• wisdom faculty .... *(paññ·indriya)*

Knowing and Seeing Ultimate Mentality

With the same light of wisdom (from either access concentration or jhāna concentration) we need to know and see the mind resting in the blood in the heart: the heart base*(hadaya·vatthu)*. We need to know and see the stream of life-continuum consciousnesses and their mental factors: it is called the ***bhavaṅga***.[305] We

---

[300] See quotation endnote 307, p.358. It is included in an extensive discussion, 'Things Impossible for Consciousness to Do', p.350. And for further details about associated mental factors, see also footnote 433, p.157.

[301] VsM.xiv.456-492 *'Khandha·Niddesa'* ('Exposition of the Aggregates') PP.xiv.125-184

[302] See tables 2a/2b/2c, p.48*ff*; 3a/3b, p.69*ff*, 3c, p.85*f*; and 3d, p.335*f*.

[303] For all the unwholesome mental factors, see tables 2a/2b/2c, p.48*ff*.

[304] For all the beautiful mental factors, see tables 3a/3b, p.69*ff*, 3c, p.85*f*, and 3d, p.335*f*.

[305] The Most Venerable Pa-Auk Tawya Sayadaw explains that only beginners with sufficient pāramī are able to analyse the life continuum at this stage. Usually, they are able

(Please see further next page.)

need to know and see how the life-continuum consciousness is interrupted every time there is cognition through one of the five material doors*(dvāra)*: eye-, ear-, nose-, tongue- and body door.[306] We need to know and see how such cognition takes place as a mental process*(citta·vīthi)*: an eye-door-, ear-door-, nose-door-, tongue-door, and body-door process. We need also to know and see how there is cognition through the mind door, as a mind-door process*(mano·dvāra·vīthi)*. We need to know and see the individual consciousnesses and mental factors that comprise the different five-door processes, as well as the individual consciousnesses and mental factors that comprise the mind-door processes: that is ultimate mentality.

THE FOUR TYPES OF MENTAL COMPACTNESS

Why do we need to analyse the different types of mental processes? Again, as in the discernment of materiality, it is to overcome the self perception*(atta·saññā)*. You will remember that when we discussed the *'Gaddula·Baddha'* sutta, we discussed how the uneducated ordinary person somehow identifies not only with the materiality clinging-aggregate, but also the four mentality clinging-aggregates.[307] Again, this occurs because of the delusion of compactness*(ghana)*. It can be overcome only by compactness resolution*(ghana·vinibbhoga)*. In the case of mentality, however, we need to resolve four types of compactness*(ghana)*:[308]

1) Continuity compactness*(santati·ghana)*: because mentality seems to be one compact continuity, a continuous whole, one may think it is the same 'mind' that cognizes objects through the eye, ear, nose, tongue, body, and mind.

---

to do so only after having discerned dependent origination: see 'Dependent Origination', p.109.

306 LIFE-CONTINUUM CONSCIOUSNESS: *(bhav·aṅga·citta)* (lit. existence-constituent consciousness) this does not correspond to the subconscious/unconscious hypothesized in Freudian psychology. No such thing exists, for two consciousnesses cannot arise at the same time. The life-continuum consciousness is a flow of resultant consciousnesses, maintained by the kamma that matured at the time of death. It maintains the continuum of mentality between mental processes. It functions also as the mind-door*(mano·dvāra)*. Once the kamma that produces this life comes to an end, the life-continuum consciousness of this life stops. In the non-Arahant, a new life-continuum consciousness, with a new object, arises as the rebirth-linking consciousness. Hence, the life continuum is not a 'subconscious undercurrent' operating 'below' the mental processes of the six doors. As can be seen in tables 5b ('The Five-Door Process', p.146), and 5c ('The Mind-Door Process', p.148), prior to the arising of a mental process, the flow of life-continuum consciousnesses is arrested. And it is resumed once the mental process is complete. The life continuum cognizes always the same object, which is independent of the objects that enter the six doors: that is why it is called process-separated. VsM.xiv.455 *'Viññāṇa-·Kkhandha·Kathā'* ('Discussion of the Consciousness-Aggregate') PP.xiv.114 explains: 'When the rebirth-linking consciousness has ceased, then, following on whatever kind of rebirth-linking it may be, the same kinds, being the result of that same kamma whatever it may be, occur as life-continuum consciousness with that same object; and again those same [three] kinds. And as long as there is no other kind of arising of consciousness to interrupt the continuity, they also go on occurring endlessly in periods of dreamless sleep, etc., like the current of a river.' For details on the life-continuum consciousness's object, see table '5a: Death and Rebirth', p.52.

307 See 'Regards the Five Aggregates as Self', p.10.

308 VsMṬ.xxi.739 *'Upakkilesa·Vimutta-Udaya·Bbaya·Ñāṇa·Kathā·Vaṇṇanā'* ('Description of Explanation of the Corruption-Freed Arise&Perish Knowledge')

And one may think it is the same self, the same 'mind', the same 'pure consciousness',[309] etc., that 'migrates' from life to life, entering different bodies. To overcome this delusion, we need to resolve the seeming compactness of the mind. We need to see that cognition takes place by way of mental processes that arise and perish. That way, we see that the mind has no continuity: as soon as it arises, it perishes. There is no time for consciousness to go anywhere, not from life to life, not even from second to second.

2) Synthesis compactness *(samūha·ghana)*: because mentality seems to be a synthetic whole, one may think it is pure consciousness that cognizes the object. And one may think it is one's self. To overcome this delusion, we need to resolve the seeming compactness of the individual type of consciousness: we need to analyse the individual type of consciousness in each type of mental process. That way, we see that cognition comprises consciousness and a given number mental factors, such as feeling, perception, and volition; application and sustainment; or hatred, delusion, wrong view, conceit, and scepticism; or non-greed, non-hatred, non-delusion, happiness, mindfulness, faith, and Right View. There is no synthetic whole anywhere.
3) Function compactness *(kicca·ghana)*: because of insufficient understanding about ultimate mentality, one may think the elements rest upon a self, like seeds and plants rest upon earth.[310] To overcome this delusion, we need to see that each consciousness and mental factor has its own characteristic, function, manifestation, and proximate cause: it does not depend on any external thing such as a self.
4) Subject compactness *(ārammaṇa·ghana)*: having penetrated the previous three compactnesses, one may think, for example, '<u>I</u> saw ultimate materiality and mentality', or, '<u>the knowing self</u> saw ultimate materiality and mentality'.[311] To overcome this delusion, we need to resolve the three types of compactness in the insight mental-processes that penetrated the three types of compactness, with subsequent insight knowledge. We need to see that the mentality that is the object of our insight knowledge was also the subject of insight knowledge: it penetrated the three types of compactness of mentality that also was a subject with an object.[145]

The Texts explain that unless we successfully resolve these four types of compactness *(ghana)*, we shall be unable to overcome the self perception *(atta·saññā)*, unable to attain the non-self perception *(an·atta·saññā)*. But it may be achieved with sufficient skill, effort, and light of wisdom from access concentration or jhāna.

But that is still not enough, is it? We have so far seen only materiality and mentality of the present, internal and external. As mentioned earlier, according to The Buddha, to know and see the five clinging-aggregates is to know and see the five-clinging-aggregates of past, future, present, internal, external, gross and subtle, inferior and superior, far and near.[146] For us to understand the First Noble Truth, the Noble Truth of Suffering *(Dukkha Ariya·Sacca)*, we need thus to see also those other categories of five aggregates. Having done so, we shall have attained

---

[309] For an example of this delusion, see 'The Bhikkhu Sāti', p.142.
[310] See endnote 141, p.244.
[311] Other variations of this delusion would be, for example, '<u>the knower</u> knows', '<u>the doer</u> knows', '<u>that which knows</u> knows', etc. One may also think 'ultimate materiality and mentality change, but "the knowing mind" does not change.'

the first of the two preparatory insight Knowledges, the Mentality-Materiality Definition Knowledge *(Nāma·Rūpa·Pariccheda·Ñāṇa)*.[312]

DEPENDENT ORIGINATION

Let us then briefly discuss how we need to see the five clinging-aggregates of past and future:[147] in order to know and see dependent origination and cessation. To practise insight meditation, we need namely also to know and see the origins of materiality and mentality. That is the Second Noble Truth, the Noble Truth of the Origin of Suffering *(Dukkha·Samudaya Ariya·Sacca)*: the origin of the five clinging-aggregates.

With the light of wisdom from access concentration or jhāna, one is able to go back along the line of successive mentality-materiality from the present to the moment of one's rebirth in this life, to the moment of one's death in one's past life.[148] And one can go further back in the same way to as many lives as one can discern. Then one can also look into the future, to the time of one's own Parinibbāna (final cessation). By looking at the individual factors of mentality-materiality, one is able to identify the causes and effects. This means that one is able to know and see the individual factors of dependent origination *(paṭicca·samuppāda)*, and how they are related. That is:[313]

[1] **Because of ignorance** *(avijjā)*, **formations** [arise] *(saṅkhāra)*;
[2] **because of formations, consciousness** *(viññāṇa)*;
[3] **because of consciousness, mentality-materiality** *(nāma·rūpa)*;
[4] **because of mentality-materiality, the six bases** *(saḷ·āyatana)*;
[5] **because of the six bases, contact** *(phassa)*;
[6] **because of contact, feeling** *(vedanā)*;
[7] **because of feeling, craving** *(taṇhā)*;
[8] **because of craving, clinging** *(upādāna)*;
[9] **because of clinging, existence** *(bhava)*;
[10] **because of existence, birth** *(jāti)*;
[11] **because of birth,**
[12] **ageing&death** *(jarā·maraṇa)*, **sorrow** *(soka)*, **lamentation** *(parideva)*, **pain** *(dukkha)*, **displeasure** *(domanassa)* **and despair** *(upāyāsa)* **arise.**

It is not easy to understand the workings of dependent origination: only when one has known and seen it for oneself does it become clear. Then does one know and see how dependent origination describes the five causes that give rise to a new life, which is five results. The five causes in one life are:

1) ignorance	*(avijjā)*	4) formations (of kamma)	*(saṅkhāra)*
2) craving	*(taṇhā)*	5) existence (of kammic potency)	*(bhava)*
3) clinging	*(upādāna)*		

[312] MENTALITY-MATERIALITY DEFINITION KNOWLEDGE: see 'The Two Preparatory Insight Knowledges', p.90.

[313] The Buddha gives this formula for dependent origination throughout His Teaching. See, for example, His description of the Arahant's understanding of dependent origination and cessation in U.i.3 *'Tatiya·Bodhi·Suttaṁ'* ('The Third Enlightenment Sutta'). And in A.III.II.ii.1 *'Titth·Āyatana·Suttaṁ'* ('The Sectarian Doctrines Sutta'), He concludes: 'This is called, bhikkhus, the Noble Truth of the Origin of Suffering *(Dukkha·Samudayaṁ Ariya·Saccaṁ)*.' See also footnote 316, p.110.

These five causes give rise to five results in another life. The five results are then:

1) consciousness .... *(viññāṇa)*	4) contact .... *(phassa)*
2) mentality-materiality ...... *(nāma·rūpa)*	5) feeling[149] .... *(vedanā)*
3) the six bases .... *(saḷ·āyatana)*	

The five results are the same as birth, ageing&death. That is how one may know and see dependent origination, the workings of kamma. That is how one may know and see the causes of kamma, and the causes of the result of kamma: continued birth, ageing&death, the continued arising of suffering *(dukkha)*.[314/150] When one has in this way seen dependent origination, one is unable to sustain either the eternity view or annihilation view.[315]

It is not enough, however, to know and see how suffering arises. Fully to understand dependent origination, one needs to see also how suffering ceases. One needs to know and see one's own attainment of Parinibbāna (final cessation) in the future. That is:[316]

[1] **With ignorance's remainderless fading away and cessation** *(avijjāya tveva asesa·virāga·nirodhā)*, **there is formations' cessation** *(saṅkhāra·nirodho)*.
[2] **With formations' cessation, there is consciousness's cessation.**
[3] **With consciousness's cessation, there is mentality-materiality's cessation.**
[4] **With mentality-materiality's cessation, there is the six bases' cessation.**
[5] **With the six bases' cessation, there is contact's cessation.**
[6] **With contact's cessation, there is feeling's cessation.**
[7] **With feeling's cessation, there is craving's cessation.**
[8] **With craving's cessation, there is clinging's cessation.**
[9] **With clinging's cessation, there is existence's cessation.**
[10] **With existence's cessation, there is birth's cessation.**
[11] **With birth's cessation,**
[12] **ageing&death, sorrow, lamentation, pain, displeasure and despair cease** *(nirujjhanti)*.

Here one knows and sees how the attainment of Arahantship has as result the cessation of the five causes: ignorance, craving, clinging, formation of kamma, and existence of kammic potency. At the end of that life, there is then the remainderless cessation (the non-arising) of the five aggregates, which is the five results: consciousness, mentality-materiality, the six bases, contact, and feeling.

---

314 See table 'Dependent Origination from Life to Life', p.349.

315 VsM.xvii.660 *'Paññā·Bhūmi·Niddesa'* ('Exposition of the Wisdom-Ground') PP.xvii.310-311 explains: 'Herein, the non-interruption of the continuity in this way, "Because of ignorance, formations arise; because of formations, consciousness", just like a seed's reaching the state of a tree through the state of the shoot, etc., is called "The Identity Method *(ekatta·nayo)*". One who sees this rightly abandons the annihilation view by understanding the unbrokenness of the continuity that occurs through the linking of cause and fruit. And one who sees it wrongly clings to the eternity view by apprehending identity in the non-interruption of the continuity that occurs through the linking of cause and fruit. The defining of the individual characteristic of ignorance, etc., is called "The Diversity Method" *(nānatta·nayo)*. One who sees this rightly abandons the eternity view by seeing the arising of each new state. And one who sees it wrongly clings to the annihilation view by apprehending individual diversity in the events in a singly continuity as though it were a broken continuity.' See also quotation endnote 166, p.247.

316 E.g. A.III.II.ii.1 *'Titth·Āyatana·Suttaṁ'* ('The Sectarian Doctrines Sutta'). There, The Buddha concludes: 'This is called, bhikkhus, the Noble Truth of the Cessation of Suffering *(Dukkha·Nirodhaṁ Ariya·Saccaṁ)*.' See also footnote 313, p.109.

Does this mean everyone is going to attain Arahantship? No. But when one is practising diligently, with a mind that is purified by strong and powerful concentration, engaged in the deep and profound practice of discerning ultimate mentality-materiality, the conditions are so that one will see one's own attainment of Parinibbāna in the future: complete cessation. But if one stops meditating etc., the conditions will have changed, in which case the future results will also have changed. That is why seeing one's own Parinibbāna in the future is not the same as seeing Nibbāna. That concludes our brief explanation of the preparatory work that is necessary for one to practise insight.

Knowing and Seeing the Three Characteristics

Actual insight meditation *(vipassanā·bhāvanā)* is to again know and see ultimate materiality (the material aggregate), ultimate mentality (the immaterial aggregates), and their origin and cessation, of past, future, and present, internal and external, gross and subtle, inferior and superior, far and near, but this time one sees how they are possessed of the three characteristics *(ti·lakkhaṇa)*: impermanence, suffering, and non-self. That is:[317]

1) Mentality-materiality and their causes perish as soon as they arise: that is the impermanence characteristic *(anicca·lakkhaṇa)*.
2) Mentality-materiality and their causes are subject to constant arising and perishing: that is the suffering characteristic *(dukkha·lakkhaṇa)*.
3) Mentality-materiality, being possessed of impermanence and suffering, can have no stable or indestructible essence: that is the non-self characteristic *(an·atta·lakkhaṇa)*.

The Sixteen Insight Knowledges

To develop such insight meditation is to progress through the knowledges.[151] And, as we discussed earlier, insight knowledge is mundane *(lokiya)* or supramundane *(lokuttara)*.

To explain the development of insight knowledge, the Pali Texts speak of sixteen knowledges. The first two we discussed earlier:[318]

1) The Mentality-Materiality Definition Knowledge *(Nāma·Rūpa·Pariccheda·Ñāṇa)*: with this knowledge, one will have known and seen the various types of ultimate materiality and ultimate mentality.
2) The Cause-Apprehending Knowledge *(Paccaya·Pariggaha·Ñāṇa)*: with this knowledge, one will have known and seen dependent origination in regular and negative order.

As we discussed earlier, these two knowledges are really preparatory knowledges: knowledges by which one first knows and sees the objects of insight meditation. That leaves then fourteen more insight knowledges:[319]

3) The Comprehension Knowledge *(Sammasana·Ñāṇa)*:[320] with this knowledge, one will have known and seen how all groupings of mentality-materiality are

[317] For The Buddha's analysis, see 'Is Materiality Permanent or Impermanent?', p.319. See also 'The Three Characteristics', p.89.

[318] See 'The Two Preparatory Insight Knowledges', p.90.

[319] For further details on these knowledges, see the last chapter, 'The Unworking of Kamma', p.319*ff.*

[320] VsM.xx.694-722 *'Magg·Āmagga·Ñāṇa·Dassana·Visuddhi·Niddeso'* ('Exposition of the

(Please see further next page.)

possessed of the three characteristics that we just mentioned: iimpermanence, suffering, and non-self. One will have comprehended the three characteristics of the five clinging-aggregates of past, future, and present, internal and external, superior and inferior, gross and subtle, far and near. One will also have comprehended the three characteristics of the six internal bases, the six external bases, the twelve factors of dependent origination, and the eighteen elements.[152] Since this knowledge takes the formed as object, it too is mundane.

4) The Arise&Perish Contemplation Knowledge*(Udaya·Bbay·Ānupassanā·Ñāṇa)*:[321] with this knowledge, one will have known and seen the causal and momentary arising and perishing of kamma-, consciousness-, temperature-, and nutriment-born materiality at every consciousness moment of the mental processes that one has discerned from the rebirth-linking consciousness up to the decease consciousness of every past life one has discerned. One will have known the same for this life, and all the future lives one has discerned, up to one's Parinibbāna (final cessation). And one will have done the same for all consciousnesses that one has discerned of past lives, the present life, and future lives. Practising in this way, one will have known and seen how all formations arise and perish, which means they are possessed of impermanence, suffering, and non-self. Since this knowledge takes the formed as object, it too is mundane.
5) The Dissolution-Contemplation Knowledge*(Bhaṅg·Ānupassanā·Ñāṇa)*:[322] with this knowledge, one will have done the same as with the previous knowledge, except that one will have concentrated on only formations' perishing and dissolution. Seeing formations in this way, one will have gained more powerful knowledge of how all formations are possessed of impermanence, suffering, and non-self. Again, since this knowledge takes the formed as object, it too is mundane.
6) The Fearsomeness-Appearance Knowledge*(Bhayat·Upaṭṭhāna·Ñāṇa)*: with this knowledge, all formations of past, future and present will have appeared to one as fearsome, because of their inevitable dissolution. Since this knowledge takes the formed as object, it too is mundane.
7) The Danger-Contemplation Knowledge*(Ādīnav·Ānupassanā·Ñāṇa)*: with this knowledge, one will have come to regard the arising, standing, and perishing of all formations of past, future, and present as dangerous. Since this knowledge takes the formed as object, it is mundane.
8) The Disenchantment-Contemplation Knowledge*(Nibbid·Ānupassanā·Ñāṇa)*: with this knowledge, one will have ceased in any way to be enchanted with formations of past, future, and present. And one will have regarded only the peace of non-arising, the state of peace, to be desirable. Then will one's mind have inclined naturally towards Nibbāna.[323] Since this knowledge also takes the formed as object, it is mundane.

Path&Non-Path Knowledge&Vision Purification') PP.xx.6-92.

[321] VsM.xx.723-731 ibid./PP.xx.93-104.

[322] For details on this knowledge up to knowledge No.11, 'Formations Equanimity Knowledge', see VsM.xxi.741-803 *'Paṭipadā·Ñāṇa·Dassana·Visuddhi·Niddeso'* ('Exposition of the Practice of Knowledge&Vision Purification') PP.xx.10-127.

[323] The Fearsomeness-Appearance/Danger-Contemplation/Disenchantment-Contemplation Knowledges are discussed at 'The Educated Noble Disciple Is Disenchanted', p.327.

9) The Release-Longing Knowledge *(Muñcitu·Kamyatā·Ñāṇa)*: with this knowledge, one will have developed a desire for escape from all formations. Again, since this knowledge takes formations as object, it is mundane.
10) The Reflection-Contemplation Knowledge *(Paṭisaṅkh·Ānupassanā·Ñāṇa)*: with this knowledge, one will again have discerned all formations of past, future and present as possessed of impermanence, suffering, and non-self, but with greater insight power than ever before. Again, since this knowledge takes all formations as object, it is mundane.
11) The Formations-Equanimity Knowledge *(Saṅkhār·Upekkhā·Ñāṇa)*: with this knowledge, one's perception of all formations will have changed: rather than see them as fearsome or delightful, one will have become indifferent to them, regarding them with a neutral mind.[324] Again, since this knowledge takes all formations as object, it is mundane. And it is the highest mundane insight knowledge.

The remaining five knowledges arise only in connection with the arising of the Path&Fruition Knowledges. Thus even though three of them are mundane, we do not count them among the mundane insight Knowledges:[325]

12) The Conformity Knowledge *(Anuloma·Ñāṇa)*: this knowledge may arise two or three times, and arises only immediately before the Path&Fruition Knowledges. It prepares the way for transition from the eight insight knowledges that have come before (from the Arise&Perish Knowledge to the Formations-Equanimity Knowledge) with the formed as object, to the Path&Fruition Knowledges with the Unformed as object. Thus, even though it is mundane, we do not count it among the mundane insight Knowledges.[326] It is the last knowledge that has formations as its object.
13) The Change-of-Lineage Knowledge *(Gotrabhu·Ñāṇa)*: this is the first knowledge to take the Unformed (Nibbāna) as object. Nonetheless, it is mundane, for it only marks the change from one's being an ordinary person *(puthu·jjana)* to one's becoming a Noble One *(Ariya)*.
14) The Path Knowledge *(Magga·Ñāṇa)*: this is the first of the two supramundane knowledges. It takes the Unformed (Nibbāna) as object, and is the first arising of the supramundane Noble Eightfold Path in one continuity of mentality-materiality. By this knowledge, certain defilements are destroyed or weakened. With the Arahant Path-Knowledge, all defilements will have been destroyed.
15) The Fruition Knowledge *(Phala·Ñāṇa)*: this is the second of the two supramundane knowledges. It may arise two or three times, and is the direct result of the Path Kamma.
16) The Reviewing Knowledge *(Paccavekkhaṇa·Ñāṇa)*:[327] this knowledge arises only after the Path&Fruition Knowledges have arisen. It arises in the very next

[324] The Release-Longing, Reflection-Contemplation, and Formations-Equanimity Knowledges are discussed at 'Equanimity Towards the Five Aggregates', p.330.
[325] For details regarding all these knowledges, see table/notes under '5e: The Path Process', p.340.
[326] THE CONFORMITY KNOWLEDGE *(Anuloma·Ñāṇa)*: this corresponds to the two/three impulsion consciousness that precede the Change-of-Lineage Knowledge: see table referred to in preceding footnote.
[327] In the suttas, this knowledge is referred to with the description of the Arahant: 'Liberated, there is the knowledge: "I am liberated."' See quotation and discussion under 'Done Is What Needs to Be Done', p.343. For details regarding this knowledge, see table

(Please see further next page.)

mental process, and consists of five reviewings: reviewing of the Path, Fruition, Nibbāna, and until one has attained the Arahant Path, there is also reviewing of the defilements that have been destroyed as well as those that remain.

These sixteen insight knowledges we shall discuss in some detail in the last chapter, when we discuss the 'unworking' of kamma.

As we mentioned earlier, insight meditation *(vipassanā·bhāvanā)* is unique to a Buddha's Dispensation: it does not exist otherwise. In the same way, developing samatha as a tool for insight (insight-basis jhāna *(vipassanā·pādaka·jjhāna)*) is unique to a Buddha's Dispensation.[328]

THE WORKINGS OF INSIGHT MEDITATION

Here, when one makes offerings or trains in morality, one's consciousness may be dissociated from or associated with the Kamma-Ownership Knowledge. But just as in samatha meditation, the actual, genuine jhāna consciousness is always knowledge-associated (associated with knowledge of the meditation object), so is the actual, genuine insight consciousness always knowledge associated *(ñāṇa·sampayutta)*:[329] associated with knowledge of the three characteristics of ultimate materiality or ultimate mentality. It is called insight knowledge *(vipassanā·ñāṇa)*, insight wisdom *(vipassanā·paññā)*, or Insight Right View *(Vipassanā·Sammā·Diṭṭhi)*. But one's insight meditation may be inferior *(omaka)* or superior *(ukkaṭṭha)*.

INFERIOR INSIGHT MEDITATION

What makes one's insight meditation inferior *(omaka)*? If, before or after the insight consciousnesses, one's mind is associated with unwholesome things, it is inferior.

For example, one may train in insight meditation because it is custom or tradition, or because one's religion says one should. And one may also train in insight meditation because one wants to have a good name, and be respected: maybe because it has become fashionable. One may even train in insight meditation because one is afraid of blame.[153]

Then again, one may train in insight meditation because one wants to attain the Deathless. But one does not have a teacher, or one does not have a properly qualified teacher. In that case, one's training may be wrong. For example, one may think there is no need to train in morality, and no need to train in concentration *(samādhi)*. Or one may also practise insight on conceptual reality: the pain in one's back or one's knee,[330] the wandering mind, etc. In that case, one has no knowledge of ultimate materiality *(paramattha·rūpa)* and ultimate mentality *(paramattha·nāma)*: the Mentality-Materiality Definition Knowledge *(Nāma·Rūpa·Paricchheda·Ñāṇa)*.[331]

/notes under 'The Reviewing Knowledges', p.342.

[328] VbhA.XVI.x.3.770 *'Tika·Niddesa·Vaṇṇanā'* ('Description of the Threes-Exposition') DD.XVI.x.2085

[329] While practising insight meditation, there may be consciousnesses that do not cognize the object properly with insight wisdom: in that case there is no knowledge. Such consciousnesses are properly speaking not 'actual, genuine' insight consciousnesses. See 'The Five Types of Knowledge', p.58.

[330] According to the Buddha' Teaching, painful feeling is in the mind: in one's back/knee is an imbalance of elements, caused by the earth-, fire-, or wind element.

[331] MENTALITY-MATERIALITY DEFINITION KNOWLEDGE: see 'The Two Preparatory Insight Knowl-

(Please see further next page.)

One may also think insight meditation is to find one's inner and true self, a deathless self: the 'knower' or 'that which knows'. One may also train in insight with the view that one must examine only the present, without discerning dependent origination to attain the Cause-Apprehending Knowledge *(Paccaya·Pariggaha·Ñāṇa)*.[332] In that case, one trains in insight without knowledge of the second Noble Truth, the Noble Truth of the Origin of Suffering, which is the workings of kamma.[333] One may even train in insight meditation disbelieving the workings of kamma.

One may also attain a certain degree of concentration, and then one sinks *(otarati)* into the life-continuum consciousness,[334] and thinks it is the Deathless: 'I know nothing then![335/154] The mind is unconditioned!'[336] Sinking into the life-continuum consciousness happens very easily when one's concentration is yet undeveloped.

With such inferior insight meditation, one may, even so, be very successful. Why? Because one may attain things one mistakenly thinks are insight knowledges: one may attain what The Buddha calls wrong knowledge *(micchā ñāṇa)* and

---

edges', p.90.

[332] CAUSE-APPREHENDING KNOWLEDGE: see further p.91.

[333] See 'The Heart of The Buddha's Teaching', p.40.

[334] SINKING INTO THE LIFE CONTINUUM: VsM.iv.58 *'Bhāvanā·Vidhānaṁ'* ('Meditation Directions') PP.iv.33 explains: 'Herein, the mind becomes concentrated on the ground of access *(upacāra)* by the abandonment of the hindrances, and on the ground of obtainment by the manifestation of the jhāna factors. The difference between the two kinds of concentration is this. The factors are not strong in access. It is because they are not strong that when access has arisen, the mind now makes the sign its object and now re-enters the life continuum *(bhavaṅga)*, just as when a young child is lifted up and stood on its feet, it repeatedly falls down on the ground.' One may through insufficient knowledge think there is consciousness with no object, because one does not know about the life-continuum consciousness, and is unable to discern its object. One may with practice be able to enter into the life-continuum consciousness for many hours, believing it is Fruition Attainment. (For details on the life-continuum consciousness, see footnote 306, p.107, and table '5a: Death and Rebirth', p.52.)

[335] 'I KNOW NOTHING': with the arising of the Path&Fruition Knowledge, the Unformed is cognized by one consciousness with minimum thirty-three mental factors (4th/5th jhāna), and maximum thirty-six mental factors (1st jhāna: see table '3d: Mental Phenomena at the Arising of Supramundane Consciousness', p.335): for example, feeling feels happiness at Nibbāna, perception perceives Nibbāna, volition wills consciousness and the mental factors to cognize Nibbāna, one-pointedness focuses them on Nibbāna, attention makes them attend to Nibbāna, decision decides the object is Nibbāna, effort makes consciousness and the mental factors cognize Nibbāna, joy thrills them, desire wants them to experience Nibbāna, faith believes fully in Nibbāna, mindfulness makes them fully aware of Nibbāna, and the wisdom faculty fully understands Nibbāna, thereby fully understanding the Four Noble Truths. Furthermore, immediately afterwards, there arises the Reviewing Knowledge, which reviews the Path Knowledge, the Fruition Knowledge, and Nibbāna (see table '5e: The Path Process', p.340). Thus, the arising of the Path/Fruition Knowledges is associated with knowing, not associated with unknowing.

[336] According to the Buddha's Teaching, mentality-materiality and their causes are formations *(saṅkhāra)*: the five aggregates. Nibbāna is without either of them: it is the Unformed *(Vi·Saṅkhāra/A·Saṅkhata)* (see quotations endnotes 34, p.24 and 270, p.354). And the realization of Nibbāna requires formation of consciousness that cognizes it: the 'Consciousness directed towards the Unformed *(Visaṅkhāra·gata citta)*' (ref. DhP.xi.9). But consciousness, being one of the five aggregates (the First Noble Truth), cannot itself be unformed. See further 'Things Impossible for Consciousness to Do', p.350.

wrong liberation *(micchā vimutti)*.[155] But because those knowledges are not really insight knowledges, they do not suppress or remove defilements; they do not lead to a Path&Fruition Knowledge *(Magga·Phala·Ñāṇa)*.

That way, one's insight meditation is dissociated from proper knowledge of suffering, proper knowledge of the origin of suffering, proper knowledge of the cessation of suffering, and proper knowledge of the way leading to the cessation of suffering. After years of training, this may become evident, and one may then lose faith in the training; one may think The Buddha's training does not in fact make an end of suffering, and one gives up.

Then again, one may indeed have attained the Cause-Apprehending Knowledge *(Paccaya·Pariggaha·Ñāṇa)*; one may indeed have discerned ultimate materiality and mentality of past, future, and present, internal and external, gross and subtle, inferior and superior, far and near. But one gets bored and careless, training with less and less patience with and respect for one's meditation subject. Scepticism may often arise: 'Is this really necessary?' or 'I can't succeed! I don't have enough pāramī!' Easily one gets bored and distracted, easily one finds excuses for not to practise: maybe one associates with bad friends, who are without faith, energy, mindfulness, concentration and wisdom. Thus, if one does sit down for meditation, one does so unwillingly. Eventually, one may give up.

One may also progress through the insight knowledges, but develop one of the ten insight corruptions *(vipassan·upakkilesa)*:[337]

1) Light	*(obhāsa)*	6) Decision	*(adhimokkha)*
2) Knowledge	*(ñāṇa)*	7) Exertion	*(paggaha)*
3) Joy	*(pīti)*	8) Establishment	*(upaṭṭhāna)*
4) Tranquillity	*(passaddhi)*	9) Equanimity	*(upekkhā)*
5) Happiness	*(sukha)*	10) Attachment	*(nikanti)*

Attachment is a corruption proper: it is in all cases unwholesome. But the remaining nine corruptions are not corruptions proper. Light is materiality, and the eight mental factors are in themselves wholesome. But they are here called corruptions because they may give rise to unwholesome consciousnesses. Owing to one's own or one's teacher's insufficient understanding of the Dhamma, one may think one of these things is the attainment of Path&Fruition Knowledge *(Magga·Phala·Ñāṇa)*. Then may arise wrong view *(diṭṭhi)* or conceit *(māna)*, or craving *(taṇhā)*, making one's insight meditation inferior.

Then again, one may be successful, and actually attain insight knowledges. But pride may arise, and one may go about boasting about one's achievement, talking about it to impress others.

These are examples of how one's insight meditation can be interspersed by countless thousand million unwholesome consciousnesses rooted in greed *(lobha)*, hatred *(dosa)*, and delusion *(moha)*: dissociated from or associated with wrong view *(micchā·diṭṭhi)*. That makes one's insight meditation inferior. If one does not understand one's meditation subject very well, it is sometimes dissociated from wisdom (non-delusion *(a·moha)*), which makes one's insight inferior, double-rooted *(dvi·hetuka)*: that means the resultant consciousness will be unrooted *(ahetuka)*. If one does understand one's meditation subject very well, it is associated with wisdom, but even so the interspersion of countless unwholesome consciousnesses makes

---

[337] See VsM.xx.732-735 *'Vipassan·Upakkilesa Kathā'* ('Discussion of Insight Corruption') PP.xx.105-125

one's insight meditation inferior, triple-rooted *(ti·hetuka)*: that means the resultant consciousness will be only double-rooted *(dvi·hetuka)*.

SUPERIOR INSIGHT MEDITATION

What then, makes one's insight meditation superior *(ukkaṭṭha)*? If, before or after the insight consciousnesses, one's mind is associated with wholesome things, it is superior.

Superior practice is associated with determined faith *(okappana·saddhā)* in the training.[338] And one has a properly qualified teacher. One trains in morality, and in order to be able to train in insight, one develops either strong and powerful access concentration, or jhāna. And one trains to penetrate to ultimate materiality *(param·attha·rūpa)* and ultimate mentality *(param·attha·nāma)*: to attain the Mentality-Materiality Definition Knowledge *(Nāma·Rūpa·Pariccheda·Ñāṇa)*.[339] And one trains to discern dependent origination: to attain the Cause-Apprehending Knowledge *(Paccaya·Pariggaha·Ñāṇa)*.[340]

If one sinks into the life-continuum consciousness, one knows it is not the Deathless, and one's teacher knows how to prevent it from happening: by training systematically, with patience and respect for one's meditation subject. If success is slow in coming, one perseveres: 'It <u>can</u> be done!' 'I <u>must</u> do it!' 'I <u>can</u> do it!' When one gets bored and distracted, one rouses oneself, or one is encouraged by good friends, who have faith, effort, mindfulness, concentration, and wisdom. When one sits down for meditation, one does so with faith and joy, or at least equanimity.

That way one is able to discern the five aggregates of past, future, and present, internal and external, gross and subtle, superior and inferior, far and near. If there arises the ten corruptions of insight, one knows how to overcome them, and progress further.

With such practice, according to one's present effort and past pāramī, slowly or quickly, one may attain a true Path *(Magga)* and Fruition *(Phala)*. That is the highest merit-work base: a merit-work base that is supramundane *(lokuttara)*.

These are examples of how one's insight meditation can be interspersed by countless thousand million wholesome consciousnesses associated with non-greed *(a·lobha)*, and non-hatred *(a·dosa)*. If one does not understand one's meditation subject very well, it is sometimes dissociated from non-delusion, which makes one's insight meditation superior, double-rooted *(dvi·hetuka)*: that means the resultant consciousness will be double-rooted. If one does understand one's meditation subject well, it is associated with also non-delusion *(a·moha)*, which makes one's insight meditation superior, triple-rooted *(ti·hetuka)*: that means the resultant consciousness will be triple-rooted.[341]

That concludes our explanation of the three merit-work bases *(puñña·kiriya·vatthu)*: offering *(dāna)*, morality *(sīla)*, and meditation *(bhāvanā)*. They comprise all wholesome consciousnesses: either double-rooted *(dvi·hetuka)* (non-greed and non-hatred), or triple-rooted *(ti·hetuka)* (non-greed, non-hatred, and non-delusion); either inferior *(omaka)* or superior *(ukkaṭṭha)*.

---

[338] For an explanation of such faith, see 'Faith', p.374.

[339] MENTALITY-MATERIALITY DEFINITION KNOWLEDGE: see 'The Two Preparatory Insight Knowledges', p.90.

[340] CAUSE-APPREHENDING KNOWLEDGE: see further p.91.

[341] For details, see '1f: Inferior and Superior; the Roots and Resultants', p.62.

Wholesome Resultants

When a kamma with wholesome roots matures at the time of death, the rebirth-linking resultant consciousness *(paṭisandhi·citta)* will be wholesome, which means there will be rebirth in either the human world, the deva world, or in one of the Brahma worlds.[342] It is impossible otherwise:[343]

- **Impossible it is, bhikkhus, there is no occasion where one of bodily good conduct possessed, due to that, because of that, at the breakup of the body, after death, in perdition, in a bad destination, an infernal place, in hell, could be reborn: such a possibility does not exist.**
  But such a possibility, bhikkhus, does exist where one of bodily good conduct possessed, due to that, because of that, at the breakup of the body, after death, in a good destination, a heavenly world could be reborn: such a possibility does exist.
- **Impossible it is, bhikkhus, there is no occasion where one of verbal good conduct possessed, due to that, because of that, at the breakup of the body, after death, in perdition, in a bad destination, an infernal place, in hell could be reborn: such a possibility does not exist.**
  But such a possibility, bhikkhus, does exist where one of verbal good conduct possessed, due to that, because of that, at the breakup of the body, after death, in a good destination, a heavenly world could be reborn: such a possibility does exist.
- **Impossible it is, bhikkhus, there is no occasion where one of mental good conduct possessed, due to that, because of that, at the breakup of the body, after death, in perdition, in a bad destination, an infernal place, in hell could be reborn: such a possibility does not exist.**
  But such a possibility, bhikkhus, does exist where one of mental good conduct possessed, due to that, because of that, at the breakup of the body, after death, in a good destination, a heavenly world could be reborn: such a possibility does exist.

Wholesome Kamma and Ignorance/Craving

Now, we know that when there is rebirth, there is also ignorance and craving. So, when a wholesome kamma matures at our death, and we gain a happy rebirth, how can there be ignorance and craving?

The last mental process before death does not have any ignorance and craving, that is correct. And the rebirth-linking consciousness has no ignorance and craving, that is also correct. But you see, because ignorance and craving have not been destroyed, they will for sure arise when the conditions are right. They still exist as latencies *(anusaya)*. That is why, whether one is reborn in an unhappy or happy destination, the first mental process that arises in one life is always unwholesome, associated with ignorance and craving: existence-craving *(bhava·taṇhā)*. It is inevitable. If it was not so, rebirth would not have taken place.[344]

This is why The Buddha always advises us to put a complete end to rebirth.[156] That takes place when a consciousness arises with the most superior non-delusion root: the consciousness with the Arahant Path-Knowledge *(Arahatta·Magga·Ñāṇa)*, which takes Nibbāna as object. But for that Knowledge to arise, we need to have accomplished much superior wholesome kamma: superior triple-rooted kamma. It is only when there is sufficient wholesome kamma from past and present, that we may attain the Arahant Path-Knowledge.[345] With the Arahant Path-Knowledge,

---

342 See wholesome resultant consciousnesses, tables 1b, p.64, 1c, p.65, and 1d, p.180.

343 A.I.xv.2 *'Aṭṭhāna·Pāḷi'* ('Text of the Impossible')

344 See table '5a: Death and Rebirth', p.52.

345 See 'Knowledge and Conduct', p.137.

the unwholesome and wholesome roots are destroyed, which means there is no more production of kamma. The Arahant's volition is purely functional.[346] At her or his Parinibbāna (final cessation), there is no further rebirth.[347]

This explanation of the three unwholesome roots and three wholesome roots has been only brief, but we hope it is sufficient to understand our continued explanation of unwholesome and wholesome kamma.

THE COURSES OF KAMMA

Now that we have discussed the unwholesome and wholesome, we can go on to discuss what The Buddha calls courses of kamma *(kamma·patha)*. When He explains why beings have an unhappy or happy rebirth, The Buddha speaks of the unwholesome and wholesome courses of kamma:[348]

1) Ten unwholesome courses of kamma *(dasa akusala·kamma·patha)*:
   i) three courses of unwholesome bodily kamma *(akusala kāya·kamma)*
   ii) four courses of unwholesome verbal kamma *(akusala vacī·kamma)*
   iii) three courses of unwholesome mental kamma *(akusala mano·kamma)*
2) Ten wholesome courses of kamma *(dasa kusala·kamma·patha)*:
   i) three courses of wholesome bodily kamma *(kusala kāya·kamma)*
   ii) four courses of wholesome verbal kamma *(kusala vacī·kamma)*
   iii) three courses of wholesome mental kamma *(kusala mano·kamma)*

THE TEN UNWHOLESOME COURSES OF KAMMA

THE THREE UNWHOLESOME BODILY KAMMAS

Let us then take His explanation of the ten courses of unwholesome kamma: what they are, and their roots (greed, hatred, or delusion).[349] First, He explains the three types of unwholesome bodily conduct:[350]

And how, bhikkhus, are there three types of bodily kamma, of fault and failure, of unwholesome intention, yielding pain, with a painful result?

TO BE A KILLER

Here, bhikkhus, someone is a killer of beings:
cruel, bloody-handed, engaged in slaying and attacking, without mercy towards all living beings.

Why does someone kill another? It is either because of greed *(lobha)* or because of hatred *(dosa)*. And, as you will remember, whenever there is greed or hatred, there is also always delusion *(moha)*. As we explained earlier, the delusion is to believe that there is in fact another being: a woman, a man, a cow, a fish, etc.

---

[346] For further details regarding the Arahant's volition, see 'Unwholesome and Wholesome Volition', p.42.

[347] See further 'The Unworking of Kamma', p.338*ff.*

[348] A.X.IV.ii.10 *'Cunda·Suttaṁ'* ('The Cunda Sutta')

[349] All details regarding the roots of the ten unwholesome courses of kamma have been taken from DhSA.I.iii.1 *'Akusala·Kamma·Patha·Kathā'* ('Discussion of the Unwholesome Kamma-Course') E.126-135. (See also quotation endnote 159, p.246.) For details regarding the three roots, see quotation p.47, and regarding view-associated/dissociated, see quotation endnote 77, p.20.

[350] A.X.V.i.7 *'Paṭhama·Sañcetanika·Suttaṁ'* ('The First "Intentional" Sutta')

A butcher and fisherman kills beings as a livelihood: it is greed, because she or he wants to enjoy sensual pleasures. A soldier may in the same way kill beings because of greed, but she or he may also kill because of fear or anger. A farmer may also kill to protect his crops: it is greed because she or he also wants to enjoy sensual pleasures, and it is hatred because she or he is angry at the beings who eat his crops. One may also kill beings to make one's house or garden look beautiful: it is greed because one wants one's house or garden beautiful, and it is hatred because one is angry at the insects and other vermin who make it unbeautiful. In the same way, a doctor may as livelihood kill a patient who is incurably sick. The patient's family may agree or request to have the patient killed because they hate seeing the patient so sick. It is the same when one has a sick animal killed: one hates the sight of the animal suffering. A doctor may also perform abortions as her or his livelihood: that is greed. And the mother who asks a doctor to perform the abortion does it because she does not want to look after her child: she is greedy for freedom, and hates her child because she or he endangers that freedom. If the child is deformed, she may hate it because it is abnormal, and because it will require much looking after. If the mother has been raped, she may also have an abortion because she hates the man who raped her, or because she hates her child, whom she identifies with that man. In all cases, there is delusion *(moha)*.[351] And if one thinks there is nothing wrong about killing another, or one thinks it is somehow right to kill another, then the kamma is view-associated *(diṭṭhi·sampayutta)*: associated with a wrong view about the workings of kamma. Otherwise the kamma of killing is view-dissociated *(diṭṭhi·vippayutta)*.

Although there can be either greed or hatred before the killing, at the time of actually killing the other being, there is only hatred and delusion. It is impossible to kill another being without hatred and delusion *(moha)*.

After explaining the unwholesome kamma of killing, The Buddha explains the unwholesome kamma of stealing.

To Be a Thief

One is a stealer of what has not been given:
that which is another's wealth and possessions, in the village or in the forest, by theft one is a stealer of that which has not been given.

Theft is also because of either greed and delusion, or hatred and delusion.

One may steal because of greed for the object, or one may steal because of hatred for the owner. At the time of actually taking the thing, there may be joy *(haṭṭha)* (greed-rooted), or fear *(bhīta)* (hatred-rooted): one may be afraid that someone discovers what one is doing; one may be afraid because one knows one is doing a bad thing. In either case, there is delusion *(moha)*.

And if one thinks there is nothing wrong about stealing another's property, or one thinks it is somehow right to steal another's property, then the kamma is view-associated *(diṭṭhi·sampayutta)*: associated with a wrong view about the workings of kamma. Otherwise the kamma of stealing is view-dissociated *(diṭṭhi·vippayutta)*.

---

[351] Explaining the different types of suffering, VsM.xvi.540 *'Jāti·Niddeso'* ('Exposition of Birth') (PP.xvi.39) describes, for example, the pain of abortion: 'When the mother has an abortion, the pain that arises in him through the cutting and rending in the place where the pain arises, it is not fit to be seen even by friends and intimates and companions: this is the suffering rooted in abortion.' For the arising of consciousness and feelings at conception and during gestation, see explanation, p.98, and 'Birth', p.346.

After explaining the unwholesome kamma of stealing, The Buddha explains the unwholesome kamma of sexual misconduct.

To Be One Who Engages in Sexual Misconduct

One is one who engages in sexual misconduct:
[1] **with those under their mother's guardianship,**
[2] **with those under their father's guardianship,**
[3] **with those under their mother's and father's guardianship,**
[4] **with those under their brother's guardianship,**
[5] **with those under their sister's guardianship,**
[6] **with those under their relative's guardianship,**
[7] **with those under their family's guardianship,**
[8] **with those under a religious community's guardianship,**
[9] **with those having a husband,**
[10] **with those entailing a penalty,**
even with those garlanded with flowers [of betrothal], **one is an offender in such conduct.**[352/*157*]

Sexual misconduct, adultery,[353] is because of either lust and delusion, or hatred and delusion.

---

[352] DhSṬ.ibid. explains: THOSE UNDER A RELIGIOUS COMMUNITY'S GUARDIANSHIP*(dhamma·rakkhitā)*: guardianship by co-religionists*(saha·dhammikehi rakkhitā)* (Vin.PārṬ.303 explains it is, white-clothed wanderers*(paṇḍar·aṅga·paribbājaka)*, etc., who practise under one teacher*(eka satthā)*. It is a wide definition that includes religionists of any religion. Within The Buddha's Dispensation, it would include a bhikkhunī, a bhikkhunī candidate, and a female novice). THOSE ENTAILING A PENALTY*(saparidaṇḍā)*: those upon whom approaching one incurs the king's penalty*(raññā daṇḍo)*(E.ibid's 'a woman undergoing punishment', is misleading).

In Vin.Pār.II.v.303 *'Sañcaritta·Sikkhā·Padaṁ'* ('Go-Between Training-Precept'), The Buddha gives twenty types of unapproachable ones*(agamanīya·vatthu)*. There, He explains THOSE HAVING A HUSBAND as one who is under guardianship*(sārakkhā)* (one betrothed already while in the womb, or, as here, 'garlanded with flowers'), and then gives a separate ten types of married woman (under a husband's guardianship: they are listed in subsequent endnote 157, p.245): the tenth is a momentary wife*(muhuttika/taṅkhaṇika)*, which is a prostitute. Thus, DhSA.ibid./E.ibid also gives these ten types of married woman, and explains that sexual misconduct is committed only by the woman under a husband's guardianship, the woman entailing a penalty, and the ten types of wife. In the case of the eight under guardianship other than a husband's guardianship, only the man commits the offence, not the girl/woman, which corresponds to statutory rape (the passage is mistranslated in E.ibid.)). The offence is also greater, the greater the virtue of one's object. ItiA.-iii.5 *'Putta·Suttaṁ'* ('The Son Sutta'), explains further that the offence is greater the greater the passion in the offending party. The offence is less serious (but still a full course of unwholesome bodily kamma) when both parties consent, but very much more serious when persuasion/force is used by either party. See also next footnote.

[353] SEXUAL MISCONDUCT/ADULTERY: in English, 'adultery' refers properly only to sexual intercourse between a married woman/man and someone other than her/his spouse. But according to the Pali analysis of unapproachable ones*(agamanīya·vatthu)*(see footnote 352, p.121), the unwholesome kamma of sexual misconduct includes intercourse with anyone other than one's spouse (Biblically referred to as 'fornication'). Thus it includes: intercourse by one unmarried regardless of partner's status; statutory rape (intercourse with one under the age of consent); seduction/violation of one chaste; and rape. A professional prostitute, however, is one of the ten types of wife: in English a 'term wife'/ 'temporary wife' (EB: *mut'ah* in Islamic law). But if the prostitute is already under contract, whoever approaches her and she herself commits sexual misconduct.

One's object may be either a female or a male. One may do it because of lust for the object, or one may do it because of hatred, wanting to harm the person, or harm the person's family, etc. But at the time of actually engaging in the misconduct, there is only lust and delusion.

And if one thinks there is nothing wrong about sexual misconduct, or one thinks it is somehow right to commit sexual misconduct, then the kamma is view-associated *(diṭṭhi·sampayutta)*: associated with a wrong view about the workings of kamma. Otherwise the kamma of sexual misconduct is view-dissociated *(diṭṭhi·vippayutta)*.

That is the three unwholesome courses of bodily kamma: to be a killer, to be a thief, and to be an adulterer.

The Four Unwholesome Verbal Kammas

Afterwards, The Buddha explains the four unwholesome courses of verbal kamma.

And how, bhikkhus, are there four types of verbal kamma, of fault and failure, of unwholesome intention, pain-yielding, with a painful result?

To Be a Liar

Here, bhikkhus, someone is a speaker of untruth: at the council, or at a meeting, or amidst his relatives, or amidst a crowd, or amidst the royal family.

Summoned and asked as a witness: 'Now good man, tell whatever you know';

- **he not knowing, says 'I know', or knowing, says 'I do not know';**
- **or not seeing, says 'I see', or seeing, says 'I do not see'.**

Thus, for one's own sake, or another's sake, or some material trifle's sake, one is in full awareness a speaker of untruth.

Untrue speech, lying, is because of either greed and delusion, or hatred and delusion.

One may lie because of greed for an object. It is also greed if one lies to protect oneself or another from harm. One may also lie because of hatred, wanting to harm someone. In either case, there is delusion *(moha)*. And if one thinks there is nothing wrong about telling a lie, or one thinks it is somehow right to tell a lie, then the kamma is view-associated *(diṭṭhi·sampayutta)*: associated with a wrong view about the workings of kamma. Otherwise the kamma of lying is view-dissociated *(diṭṭhi·vippayutta)*.

After explaining the unwholesome kamma of lying, The Buddha explains the unwholesome kamma of slander.

To Be a Slanderer

One is a speaker of slander:

- **from here having heard, there one tells, these to divide,**
- **or there having heard, to these one tells, those to divide.**

Thus of the united one is a divider, one is an originator of divisions, with dissension pleased, dissension enjoying, in dissension delighting, one is a speaker of dissension-making speech.

Slanderous speech is because of either greed and delusion, or hatred and delusion.

One may slander someone because of greed for some object, as when people slander each other in court. One may also wish to gain power, to gain someone's benefits, to get someone's job, or to make someone's friends or devotees one's own. One may also slander someone because of hatred, wanting to harm someone. In either case, there is delusion *(moha)*. And if one thinks there is nothing wrong about slandering another, or one thinks it is somehow right to slander another, then the kamma is view-associated *(diṭṭhi·sampayutta)*: associated with a wrong view about the workings of kamma. Otherwise the kamma of slander is view-dissociated *(diṭṭhi·vippayutta)*.

After explaining the unwholesome kamma of slander, The Buddha explains the unwholesome kamma of harsh speech.

To Be a Speaker of Harshness

One is a speaker of harshness:

- **whatever words that are offensive, rough, sharp, cross, bordering on anger,**
- **that do not lead to concentration, one is a speaker of such speech.**

Harsh speech is because of either greed and delusion, or hatred and delusion.

Just as in the case of slander, one may use harsh speech against someone because of greed for some object: for example, when one speaks harshly to a thief, or a government official who does not give one what one wants. Parents very often speak harshly to their children, because their children are not behaving as they want them to, and children speak rudely to their parents because they have been denied something they wanted.[354] It is also very common for one to speak harshly because one has been spoken to harshly by someone else: one's pride is hurt, and one attacks. In all cases, at the time of actually uttering the harsh words, one wants the other person to feel pain at one's words: there is hatred and delusion only. And if one thinks there is nothing wrong about speaking harshly to another, or one thinks it is somehow right to speak harshly to another, then the kamma is view-associated *(diṭṭhi·sampayutta)*: associated with a wrong view about the workings of kamma. Otherwise the kamma of harsh speech is view-dissociated *(diṭṭhi·vippayutta)*.

After explaining the unwholesome kamma of harsh speech, The Buddha explains the unwholesome kamma of prattle.

To Be a Prattler

A prattler one is:

- **a speaker of the untimely,**
- **a speaker of the unfactual,**
- **a speaker of the useless,**
- **a speaker of non-Dhamma,**
- **a speaker of non-Discipline;**
- **one is an utterer of forgettable speech, untimely, aimless, without end, and connected with no purpose.**

Prattle is because of either greed and delusion, or hatred and delusion.

Explaining prattle, The Buddha speaks of different types of low talk *(tiracchāna·kathā)*.

[354] This may also be because one has a hating temperament *(dosa·carita)*. See 'The Variety of Temperament', p.32.

That is:[355]

to speak	to speak	talk
• of kings • of criminals • of ministers • of armies • of catastrophes • of wars • of food • of drink • of clothes • of furniture	• of jewellery • of perfumes • of one's family • of villages • of towns • of cities • of countries • of women (or men) • of heroes	• of the street • of the well • of the dead • of various other aimless things • of the origin of the world: who created the world, it was a god, etc. • of the origin of the sea, or this or that thing, etc.

This is what we talk about all the time, is it not? We may think it is very important to talk about politics, and about this and that war. But The Buddha says that if one wants to attain Nibbāna, one should not talk about these things: He describes such talk as low, of the village, of ordinary people, ignoble, and unbeneficial. More importantly, He explains prattle as not leading to disenchantment, not leading to dispassion, not leading to cessation, to peace, to direct knowledge, or to enlightenment: not leading to Nibbāna.

When we talk about kings, ministers, catastrophes, food, our family, etc., we nourish greed or hatred, and delusion. For example, we talk a long time about how bad such and such a president is, and how terrible such and such a catastrophe was: that is because of hatred and delusion. Or we talk about how beautiful our house is, about food, and about all the different members of our family: that is because of greed and delusion. To enjoy talking about such things is greed and delusion. It serves no good purpose. And because it serves no good purpose, it is also endless.

If one thinks there is nothing wrong about prattling with another, or one thinks it is somehow right to prattle with another, then the kamma is view-associated *(diṭṭhi·sampayutta)*: associated with a wrong view about the workings of kamma. Otherwise the kamma of prattle is view-dissociated *(diṭṭhi·vippayutta)*.

We shall explain what The Buddha says one <u>should</u> talk about, when we explain the wholesome courses of kamma.[356]

That then is the four unwholesome courses of verbal kamma: to be a liar, to be a slanderer, to be a speaker of harshness, and to be a prattler.

The Three Unwholesome Mental Kammas

Then The Buddha explains the three unwholesome courses of mental kamma:

And how, bhikkhus, are there three types of mental kamma, of fault and failure, of unwholesome intention, pain-yielding, with a painful result?

To Be Covetous

One is a coveter:

that which is another's wealth & possessions, of that one is covetous [thinking]**: 'Oh, that what is another's would be mine!'**

---

[355] Literally *animal talk* (PED). The Buddha gives this list in, for example, S.V.XII.i.10 *'Tiracchāna·Kathā·Suttaṁ'* ('The Low-Talk Sutta').

[356] See 'The Four Wholesome Verbal Kammas', p.132.

Covetousness is again because of either greed and delusion, or hatred and delusion.

One may covet something because of greed for the object, or because of hatred for the owner: one wants to harm him, by taking his property. It may be because of competitiveness: there may be envy involved. But at the time of actually coveting the object, wanting someone else's property in an unlawful way, it is because of greed and delusion only.[357] And if one thinks there is nothing wrong about coveting another's property, or one thinks it is somehow right to covet another's property, then the kamma is view-associated *(diṭṭhi·sampayutta)*: associated with a wrong view about the workings of kamma. Otherwise the kamma of covetousness is view-dissociated *(diṭṭhi·vippayutta)*.

After explaining the unwholesome kamma of covetousness, The Buddha explains the unwholesome kamma of ill-will.

To Harbour Ill-Will

> **One is one with a mind of ill-will, one of malicious mind and intention** [who thinks]**: 'May these beings be slain, or trapped, or annihilated, or** [may they] **perish, or not be** [anymore]**!'**

Ill-will is also because of either greed and delusion, or hatred and delusion.

For example, the butcher and fisherman will always have ill-will towards the beings they are about to slaughter. The soldier will have ill-will towards the enemy, and even the civilian who has had her or his home bombed, and friends and family members killed, will have ill-will. Also, a farmer might be observing the five precepts, meaning that she or he does not kill any beings. But when beings harm her or his crops, ill-will can arise, because of greed and delusion. Even in an ordinary situation, one may be keeping the precepts, and then when there are rats, etc. in one's house or garden, or cockroaches in the kitchen, or mosquitoes in one's bedroom, ill-will arises: there is greed for a beautiful house, etc., and although one does not kill the beings, one may wish that they were dead. The doctor who does not kill his patients and the family who do not allow a sick family member to be killed may also have ill-will: wishing that the person were dead. The same with the mother who has an unwanted child: she may have sufficient understanding of the workings of kamma to abstain from having her child killed by abortion, but she may still wish the child was dead.

Although there can be either greed or hatred before the killing, at the time of actually wishing for the other being's harm or death, it is because of hatred and delusion only. And if one thinks there is nothing wrong about wishing another's harm, or one thinks it is somehow right to wish another's harm, then the kamma is view associated *(diṭṭhi·sampayutta)*: associated with a wrong view about the workings of kamma. Otherwise the kamma of ill-will is view-dissociated *(diṭṭhi·vippayutta)*.

After explaining the unwholesome kamma of ill-will, The Buddha explains the unwholesome kamma of wrong view.

---

[357] DhSA.I.iii.1 *'Akusala·Kamma·Patha·Kathā'* ('Discussion of the Unwholesome Kamma-Course') E.135 explains: 'Life-taking has two roots by virtue of hate and delusion... covetousness by virtue of delusion, has a single root; likewise ill-will. Wrong view has a double root by virtue of greed and delusion.'

To Hold Wrong View

One is one of wrong view, one of perverted view [who thinks]:[358]

[1] **'There is no offering,**
[2] **there is no almsgiving,**
[3] **there is no sacrifice;**
[4] **there is no pleasant or painful fruit or result of kamma;**
[5] **there is no this world,**
[6] **there is no other world;**
[7] **there is no mother,**
[8] **there is no father;**[359]
[9] **there are no beings spontaneously born;**
[10] **there are not in the world any ascetics and Brahmins, rightly faring, rightly practising, who with direct knowledge (having themselves realized this world and the other world) declare it.'**

This is the standard wrong view described by The Buddha. It is called the ten-based wrong view *(dasa·vatthukā micchā·diṭṭhi)*. It denies the workings of kamma, and rebirth, etc. When He speaks of basic wrong view, this is usually the type of view He is referring to. But one may, for example, hold the view that good actions lead to rebirth in heaven, and bad actions lead to rebirth in hell, and that a god controls it. Because one thinks it is controlled by a god, it is wrong view, but because one holds to the efficacy of action (a doctrine of action), it is not a wrong view.

Holding wrong view is because of either greed and delusion, or hatred and delusion.

One may hold wrong view because of craving: greed for sensual pleasure, greed for existence, or greed for non-existence. Clinging to one's wrong view (which is views-clinging) is also because of greed. Such clinging to one's view can be associated with conceit, which is also greed-rooted, and is the cause for much dispute among people. One may also hold a wrong view because of a material advantage: maybe one has been promised a reward. Many take up a wrong view because of attachment for their partner: the girl takes up the boy's wrong view, or the boy takes up the girl's wrong view, because of attachment, which is greed-rooted. A wrong view may also have become fashionable, and one takes it up in order to gain recognition among the fashionable people, to be 'modern' (greed-rooted). One may take up a wrong view because of fear (hatred-rooted): perhaps one is persecuted for holding another view. There are even those who take up a wrong view to take revenge (hatred rooted). We know cases of a man committing adultery, and his wife divorcing him and then, to take revenge, marrying someone with wrong view.

Although there can be either greed or hatred before taking up wrong view, at the time of actually pondering the view, seeing things according to that wrong view, it is because of greed and delusion only.[360]

A wrong view that denies the workings of kamma is the most serious of all the unwholesome courses of kamma. Why? Because when one holds a wrong view, it is very easy to do the other unwholesome things: indeed, it is inevitable.[158]

That concludes The Buddha's explanation of the three unwholesome courses of mental kamma: to be covetous of another's property, to harbour ill-will, and to hold a wrong view that denies the workings of unwholesome and wholesome kamma.

---

358 For further details, see 'The Non-Existence View', p.173.

359 For the difference between non-existent and existent parents, see footnotes 11, p.2, 374, p.135, and endnote 203, p.252.

360 For further details, see 'A Course of Unwholesome Kamma', p.127.

In all, there are ten unwholesome courses of kamma: three unwholesome courses of bodily kamma, four unwholesome courses of verbal kamma, and three unwholesome courses of mental kamma. They all arise because of greed, hatred and delusion.[159]

THE RESULTS OF UNWHOLESOME KAMMA

What is the result of such kamma? The Buddha explained it to the bhikkhus:

THE RESULTS OF UNWHOLESOME BODILY KAMMA

With either the three types of bodily kamma, of fault and failure, with unwholesome intention as root, bhikkhus, beings at the breakup of the body, after death, in perdition, in a bad destination, an infernal place, in hell are reborn.

THE RESULTS OF UNWHOLESOME VERBAL KAMMA

Or with the four types of verbal kamma, of fault and failure, with unwholesome intention as root, bhikkhus, beings at the breakup of the body, after death, in perdition, in a bad destination, in an infernal place, in hell are reborn.

THE RESULTS OF UNWHOLESOME MENTAL KAMMA

Or with the three types of mental kamma, of fault and failure, with unwholesome intention as root, bhikkhus, beings at the breakup of the body, after death, in perdition, in a bad destination, in an infernal place, in hell are reborn.

It is because the ten unwholesome courses of kamma can bring such unhappy results that The Buddha condemns them as unwholesome*(akusala)*, useless*(anattho)*, as blameful*(sāvajja)*, and as things with a painful result*(dukkha·vipāka dhamma)*.[361] And because they lead to rebirth in hell, He condemns them as the dark way *(kaṇha·magga)*.[160]

The Buddha explains further that if we make someone else engage in the ten unwholesome courses of kamma, they become twenty things that take us to a bad destination, even hell;[161] if we also approve of the ten unwholesome courses of kamma, they become thirty things that take us to a bad destination;[162] and if we also speak in praise of the ten unwholesome courses of kamma, they become forty things that take us to a bad destination.[163]

THE TRIVIAL RESULTS OF UNWHOLESOME KAMMA

Here, however, The Buddha is referring to unwholesome kamma producing its result after death: producing the rebirth-linking consciousness in the animal world, the ghost world, or in hell. But kamma can also produce its result in the continuance*(pavatti)* of a human life. Then, although the results are still disagreeable and unwished for, The Buddha describes them as trivial*(sabbalahusa)* in comparison. In that case:[362/164]

- Killing leads only to shortening of one's life.
- Stealing leads only to loss of one's wealth.
- Sexual misconduct leads only to rivalry and hatred.
- Telling lies leads only to slander and lies about one.

[361] For details on the results of these ten courses of unwholesome kamma, see also endnote 14, p.21.

[362] For killing's leading to a short life, see The Buddha's explanation from 'The Small Kamma-Analysis Sutta', under 'One Is a Killer', p.258.

- Slander leads only to breakup of one's friendships.
- Harsh speech only gives one a voice that is unpleasant to listen to.
- Prattle leads only to people not believing what one says, even when one speaks the truth.
- Drinking beer&wine liquor leads only to derangement.

Here again, please remember, for an action to become an accomplished course of kamma, it needs to be intentional: there needs to be the desire to do the unwholesome action. One may, for example, feel an itch on one's arm, and without looking scratch one's arm. Then one may discover it was a mosquito, and that one unintentionally killed it. That action is not unwholesome kamma, because one had no intention to harm the mosquito. But one may also feel an itch on one's arm, look down, see that there is a mosquito, and strike it so it dies. That action is unwholesome kamma, because one had the intention to kill the mosquito. It is the same if one sprays insect poison to kill the insects in one's room, or puts out poison for the rats and mice, etc.

A Course of Unwholesome Kamma

Furthermore, we need to understand that when The Buddha explains that unwholesome kamma produces an unhappy rebirth, He is referring to an unwholesome course of kamma*(kamma·patha)*. The course is reached only when a certain number of factors*(sambhāra)* are complete. For example, in the bodily act of killing *(pāṇātipāta)*, the action becomes a full course of kamma only if five factors are complete:[363]

1) There needs to be a being*(pāṇa)*: for example, an insect, a fish, or a human being.
2) One needs to have the perception that it is a being*(pāṇa·saññitā)*: here, it does not matter whether one perceives the being to be an insect, fish or human being. What matters is that one perceives it to be a thing that is possessed of the life faculty: for example, an embryo in the womb.
3) One needs to have the mind to kill*(vadhaka·citta)*: one's intention is to cut off that being's life faculty.
4) One needs to make an attack*(upakkama)*: one needs to make an effort to kill. For example, one needs to strike, to spray the poison, to apply the knife, or to release the bomb.
5) The being needs to die because of one's action*(tena maraṇanti)*: the being's life faculty must have been cut off because of one's attack, not for any other reason.

When these five factors are complete, the kamma has taken its full course, and the volition is called the conclusive volition*(sanniṭṭhāna·cetanā)*. The kamma has also taken its full course if one makes another do it. If such a course of kamma matures after death, it is certain to produce rebirth in the animal world, the ghost

---

[363] The Buddha gives these analyses also in the *Sutta·Vibhaṅga(Rule Analysis)* of the *Vinaya*, to determine when a bhikkhu has/has not broken the respective precept. The analyses are here derived from DhSA.I.iii *'Akusala·Kamma·Patha·Kathā'* ('Discussion of the Unwholesome Kamma-Course') E.126-135. They may be found also in the commentary to M.I.i.9 *'Sammā·Diṭṭhi·Suttaṁ'* ('The Right-View Sutta').

world, even in hell. If, however, only some of the factors are complete, the result is not certain.[364]

Let us then say all the factors for killing the being are there, except that the being does not die. For example, one sees a mosquito on one's arm, and one strikes, but it escapes. Then, although the action does not become the kamma of killing, it does become an unwholesome mental course of kamma: ill-will *(byāpāda)*. For ill-will to be a course of kamma, only two factors need to be complete:

1) Another being *(para·satta)*
2) The wish for its destruction *(tassa ca vināsa·cintāti)*

When these two factors are complete, the kamma has taken its full course. If it matures after one's death, it is certain to produce rebirth in the animal world, the ghost world, even in hell.

One may also see a mosquito and get angry: 'Oh, now that mosquito wants to bite me! Maybe I will get malaria!' And one may take a fan and chase the mosquito out of one's room. So long as one is merely angry, so long as one does not have any wish for the mosquito's destruction, it becomes neither a kamma of killing nor ill-will. But it is still an unwholesome kamma. If that anger arises at one's death, it can help another unwholesome kamma to produce rebirth in the animal world, the ghost world, even in hell.

If, in any course of kamma, one factor is missing, and the kamma matures, the result is not certain. If the kamma matures after one's death, it may produce an unhappy rebirth, it may not. It depends on also other things: for example, was the desire to kill, and the effort to kill, very strong or not so strong? Did one do it of one's own accord, unprompted, or did one do it upon the prompting of another?[365] Was the being small or big? Was it a virtuous person or an evil person? It depends on many things. We can only explain the workings of kamma in principle. But there is one certain and simple rule: unwholesome kamma such as killing, stealing, etc., be it big or small, will never produce a good result, only a bad result.

Another example is the mental kamma of wrong view *(micchā·diṭṭhi)*. It becomes a full course of unwholesome kamma only when two factors are complete:[366]

1) The base *(vatthuno)* according to which one takes a thing: it is the disposition, the guiding philosophy or science, that is of a nature *(sabhāva)* not to be according to reality *(a·yathā·bhūta)*. It is a philosophy or science that contradicts the truth, but only as one of the three types of wrong view that deny the workings of kamma:[367]
   i) The inefficacy view *(akiriya·diṭṭhi)*: it denies the action of unwholesome and wholesome kammas.
   ii) The rootlessness view *(ahetuka·diṭṭhi)*: it denies the root of results.
   iii) The non-existence view *(n·atthika·diṭṭhi)*: it denies the result of any cause.
2) Taking the thing in the distorted way *(gahitā·kāra·viparītatā)*, in accordance with that base: it is the mental kamma of reasoning, judging, and making decisions according to the base; according to one of those three types of wrong

---

[364] See explanation from MA, footnote 671, p.259

[365] See 'Unprompted and Prompted', p.47.

[366] Some of the details given here are from the subcommentary to M.I.i.9 *'Sammā·Diṭṭhi·Suttaṁ'* ('The Right-View Sutta').

[367] The Buddha's descriptions of these three views are given at 'The Three Views that Deny the Workings of Kamma', p.171.

view.[368] At the time of reasoning in this distorted way, one thinks: 'It is so *(evam·etaṁ)*, it cannot be otherwise*(na ito aññathā)*.'

For example, one may hold the materialist view: it denies that there is unwholesome and wholesome kamma as a cause, and it denies that there is a result of unwholesome and wholesome kamma. With such a view, one may then reason that there is nothing wrong about performing the ten unwholesome courses of kamma. For example, one may reason that there is nothing wrong about going fishing, making war, killing vermin, and killing the child that has been conceived in the womb: one may even think it is right to do such things. One may likewise reason that there is nothing wrong about sexual misconduct, telling lies, and nothing wrong about drinking beer, wine, etc. This is because the base of one's reasoning (of one's logic) makes one judge such unwholesome courses of kamma in a distorted way.

When those two factors are complete, the kamma of holding wrong view has taken its full course. If it matures after one's death, it is certain to produce rebirth in the animal world, the ghost world, even in hell. The kamma is more or less serious according to how strongly one holds the view, and how often one reasons and decides according to that view.

The Buddha explains that with such a wrong view and reasoning based on the wrong view, it is only to be expected that one will abstain from the ten wholesome courses of kamma, and that one will undertake the ten unwholesome courses of kamma. Why so? Because one sees nothing wrong in unwholesome things, nor anything good in wholesome ones.[369] Hence, because of such distorted reasoning and deciding, there is much fighting and quarrelling in the world. For the same reason, one may hold that to restrain one's conduct by undertaking morality is only cultural, belonging only to ancient India, etc., not the modern world. That way one may decide that it is unnecessary and even undesirable to undertake and observe morality, to purify one's conduct through body, speech, and mind, and to hold Right View*(Sammā·Diṭṭhi)*.

The Ten Wholesome Courses of Kamma

The Three Wholesome Bodily Kammas

Let us then take The Buddha's explanation of the ten courses of wholesome kamma: what they are, and their roots (non-greed, non-hatred and non-delusion).[370] First, He explains the three types of wholesome bodily conduct:[371]

And how, bhikkhus, are there three types of bodily kamma achievement, of wholesome intention, yielding happiness, with a happy result?

To Be Kind and Compassionate

Here, bhikkhus, abandoning the killing of beings, someone is an abstainer of the killing of beings:

---

[368] Thus what one thinks is logical/natural/rational depends on one's basic view.

[369] See quotations in endnote 158, p.246.

[370] All details regarding the roots of the ten wholesome courses of kamma have been taken from DhSA.i.1 *'Kusala·Kamma·Patha·Kathā'* ('Discussion of the Wholesome Kamma-Course') E.136-137. Regarding the abstinence of a Noble One, see also 'The Four Path Knowledges', p.336.

[371] A.X.V.i.7 *'Paṭhama·Sañcetanika·Suttaṁ'* ('The First "Intentional" Sutta')

with laid-down rod, laid-down knife, gentle and merciful towards all living beings, he dwells kind and compassionate.

Why does someone abstain from killing another? We explained it earlier. It is because of non-greed *(a·lobha)* and non-hatred *(a·dosa)*. And, as you will remember, it may be knowledge-associated *(ñāṇa·sampayutta)* or knowledge-dissociated *(ñāṇa·vipayutta)*: one may not know about the workings of kamma, or one may know about the workings of kamma.[372]

As we also explained earlier, one may abstain from killing out of kindness, because one thinks the being is beautiful or interesting, because of custom, tradition, or because one's religion says one should abstain. One may also abstain because one wants to have a good name, or because one is afraid to be found out: one is afraid of shame, of blame or of punishment. One may abstain because one thinks it is a dishonourable thing to do, or because one has undertaken the precept to abstain from killing. Lastly, one may abstain because one has attained the Stream-Entry Path Knowledge *(Sot·Āpatti·Magga·Ñāṇa)*: it makes it impossible for one ever again deliberately to kill.

After explaining the wholesome kamma of abstaining from killing, The Buddha explains the wholesome kamma of abstaining from stealing.

Not to Be a Thief

Abandoning the taking of what has not been given, one is an abstainer of the taking of what has not been given:

that which is another's wealth & possessions, in the village or in the forest, one is by theft not a stealer of that which has not been given.

Here again, to abstain from theft is because of non-greed *(a·lobha)* and non-hatred *(a·dosa)*: associated with knowledge of the workings of kamma, or dissociated from knowledge of the workings of kamma.

And again, one may abstain from stealing out of kindness, because of custom, tradition, or because one's religion says one should abstain. One may also abstain because one wants to have a good name, or because one is afraid to be found out: one is afraid of shame, of blame or of punishment. One may abstain because one thinks it is a dishonourable thing to do, or because one has undertaken the precept to abstain from stealing. And again, one may abstain because one has attained the Stream-Entry Path Knowledge *(Sot·Āpatti·Magga·Ñāṇa)*: it makes it impossible for one ever again deliberately to take what has not been given.

After explaining the wholesome kamma of abstaining from stealing, The Buddha explains the wholesome kamma of abstaining from sexual misconduct.

Not to be One Who Engages in Sexual Misconduct

Abandoning sexual misconduct, one is an abstainer of sexual misconduct:

[1] **with those under their mother's guardianship,**
[2] **with those under their father's guardianship,**
[3] **with those under their mother's and father's guardianship,**
[4] **with those under their brother's guardianship,**
[5] **with those under their sister's guardianship,**
[6] **with those under their relative's guardianship,**
[7] **with those under their family's guardianship,**
[8] **with those under a religious community's guardianship,**

---

372 This is Kamma-Ownership Knowledge, see 'The Five Types of Knowledge', p.58.

[9] **with those having a husband,**
[10] **with those entailing a penalty,**
even with those garlanded with flowers [of betrothal], **one is not an offender in such conduct.**

Here again, to abstain from sexual misconduct is because of non-greed*(a·lobha)* and non-hatred*(a·dosa)*: associated with knowledge of the workings of kamma, or dissociated from knowledge of the workings of kamma.

And again, one may abstain from sexual misconduct out of kindness, because one does not wish to harm the other person, or the person's family, etc. One may abstain from sexual misconduct because of custom, tradition, or because one's religion says one should abstain. One may also abstain because one wants to have a good name, or because one is afraid to be found out: one is afraid of shame, of blame, or of punishment. One may abstain because one thinks it is a dishonourable thing to do, or because one has undertaken the precept to abstain from sexual misconduct. And again, one may abstain because one has attained the Stream-Entry Path Knowledge*(Sot·Āpatti·Magga·Ñāṇa)*: it makes it impossible for one ever again deliberately to engage in sexual misconduct.

That is the three wholesome courses of bodily kamma: not to be a killer (to be gentle, kind, and compassionate towards all beings); not to be a thief, and not to be an adulterer.

The Four Wholesome Verbal Kammas

Then The Buddha explains the four wholesome courses of verbal kamma:

And how, bhikkhus, are there four types of verbal kamma achievement, of wholesome intention, yielding happiness, with a happy result?

Not to Be a Liar

Here, bhikkhus, abandoning untrue speech, someone is an abstainer of untrue speech: at the council, or at a meeting, or amidst his relatives, or amidst a crowd, or amidst the royal family.
Summoned and asked as a witness: 'Now good man, tell whatever you know';
- **he not knowing, says 'I do not know', or knowing, says 'I know';**
- **or not seeing, says 'I do not see', or seeing, says 'I see'.**

Thus, for one's own sake, or another's sake, or some material trifle's sake, one is not in full awareness a speaker of untruth.

Here again, to abstain from telling lies is because of non-greed*(a·lobha)* and non-hatred*(a·dosa)*: associated with knowledge of the workings of kamma, or dissociated from knowledge of the workings of kamma.

And again, one may abstain from telling lies because of custom, tradition, or because one's religion says one should abstain. One may also abstain because one wants to have a good name, or because one is afraid to be found out: one is afraid of shame, of blame, or of punishment. One may abstain from telling lies because one has too much respect for the truth, and one thinks it dishonourable to tell lies. One may also abstain because one has undertaken the precept to abstain from telling lies. And again, one may abstain because one has attained the Stream-Entry Path Knowledge*(Sot·Āpatti·Magga·Ñāṇa)*: it makes it impossible for one ever deliberately to tell a lie.

After explaining the wholesome kamma of abstaining from lies, The Buddha explains the wholesome kamma of abstaining from slander.

Not to Be a Slanderer

Abandoning slanderous speech, one is an abstainer of slanderous speech:
- **from here having heard, there one does not tell, these to divide,**
- **and there having heard, to these one does not tell, those to divide.**

Thus of the divided one is a uniter, one is an originator of companionship, by unity pleased, unity enjoying, in unity delighting, one is a speaker of unity-making speech.

Here again, to abstain from slander is because of non-greed*(a·lobha)* and non-hatred*(a·dosa)*: associated with knowledge of the workings of kamma, or dissociated from knowledge of the workings of kamma.

And again, one may abstain from slander because of custom, tradition, or because one's religion says one should abstain. One may also abstain because one wants to have a good name, or because one is afraid to be found out: one is afraid of shame, of blame or of punishment. One may abstain from slander because one does not like dissension and disunity, and one thinks it dishonourable to slander others. One may also abstain because one has undertaken the precept to abstain from slander.[373] And again, one may abstain because one has attained the Non-Return Path Knowledge*(An·Āgāmi·Magga·Ñāṇa)*: it makes it impossible for one ever deliberately to engage in slander.

After explaining the wholesome kamma of abstaining from slander, The Buddha explains the wholesome kamma of abstaining from harsh speech.

Not To Be a Speaker of Harsh Speech

Abandoning harsh speech, one is an abstainer of harsh speech:
- **whatever words that are faultless,**
- **pleasing to the ear, affectionate, that go to the heart, are polite,**
- **that are desirable to very many, that are dear to very many,**

one is a speaker of such speech.

Here again, to abstain from harsh speech is because of non-greed*(a·lobha)* and non-hatred*(a·dosa)*: associated with knowledge of the workings of kamma, or dissociated from knowledge of the workings of kamma.

And again, one may abstain from harsh speech because of kindness: for example, the other person may be a child, and one does not wish to hurt the child. One may abstain from harsh speech also because of custom, tradition, or because one's religion says one should abstain. One may also abstain because one wants to have a good name, or because one is afraid to be found out: one is afraid of shame, of blame or of punishment. One may abstain from harsh speech because one likes peace and quiet, and one thinks it dishonourable to speak harshly. One may also abstain because one has undertaken the precept to abstain from harsh speech. And again, one may abstain because one has attained the Non-Return Path Knowledge*(An·Āgāmi·Magga·Ñāṇa)*: it makes it impossible for one ever again to speak harshly.

After explaining the wholesome kamma of abstaining from harsh speech, The Buddha explains the wholesome kamma of abstaining from prattle.

Not to Be a Prattler

Abandoning prattle, one is an abstainer of prattle:

---

[373] For the precept against slander, see the livelihood-as-eighth morality, endnote 108, p.240.

- **a speaker of the timely,**
- **a speaker of the factual,**
- **a speaker of the useful,**
- **a speaker of Dhamma,**
- **a speaker of Discipline;**
- **one is an utterer of of memorable speech, timely, with an aim, with an end, and with a purpose connected**

Here again, to abstain from prattle is because of non-greed*(a·lobha)* and non-hatred*(a·dosa)*: associated with knowledge of the workings of kamma, or dissociated from knowledge of the workings of kamma.

Here, one may abstain from prattle because of respect: for example, the other person may be a monk, and one does not wish to be rude by prattling with him. One may abstain from prattle also because of custom, tradition, or because one's religion says one should abstain. One may also abstain because one wants to have a good name, or because one is afraid of shame, of blame or of punishment. One may abstain from prattle because one has too much respect for the faculty of speech, and one thinks it dishonourable to prattle. One may also abstain because one has undertaken the precept to abstain from prattle. And again, one may abstain because one has attained the Arahant Path-Knowledge*(Arahatta·Magga·Ñāṇa)*: it makes it impossible for one ever again to prattle.

When we explained the unwholesome verbal courses of kamma, we explained what subjects The Buddha says one should not talk about. But He explains also what subjects one <u>should</u> talk about. He lists ten subjects:[165]

1) talk of wanting little*(app·iccha·kathā)*
2) talk of contentment*(santuṭṭhi·kathā)*
3) talk of seclusion*(paviveka·kathā)*
4) talk of dissociation*(asaṁsagga·kathā)*
5) talk of exerting energy*(vīriy·ārambha·kathā)*
6) talk of morality*(sīla·kathā)*
7) talk of concentration*(samādhi·kathā)*
8) talk of wisdom*(paññā·kathā)*
9) talk of liberation*(vimutti·kathā)*
10) talk of knowledge and vision liberation*(vimutti·ñāṇa·dassana·kathā)*

The Buddha explains that to speak of these subjects is suitable because:

- it leads to complete disenchantment*(ekantanibbidāya)*
- it leads to dispassion*(virāgāya)*
- it leads to cessation*(nirodhāya)*
- it leads to peace*(upasamāya)*
- it leads to direct knowledge*(abhiññāya)*
- it leads to enlightenment*(sambodhāya)*
- it leads to Nibbāna*(Nibbānāya)*

That then is the four wholesome courses of verbal kamma: not to be a liar (to speak only the truth, or remain silent), not to be a slanderer (to speak only as to unite the divided and keep the united united), not to be a speaker of harsh speech (to speak politely and gently), and not to be a prattler (to speak of only things worthwhile, speech that serves a good purpose).

The Three Wholesome Mental Kammas

Then The Buddha explains the three wholesome courses of mental kamma:

And how, bhikkhus, are there three types of mental kamma achievement, of wholesome intention, yielding happiness, with a happy result?

NOT TO BE COVETOUS

Here, bhikkhus, someone is a non-coveter:
that which is another's wealth and possessions, of that one is uncovetous [not thinking]: **'Oh, that what is another's would be mine!'**

Here again, to abstain from covetousness is because of non-greed *(a·lobha)* and non-hatred *(a·dosa)*: associated with knowledge of the workings of kamma, or dissociated from knowledge of the workings of kamma.

And again, one may abstain from covetousness because, instead of wanting another's property, one rejoices over the other one's good fortune: that is sympathetic joy *(muditā)*. Again, one may abstain from covetousness because one has attained the Arahant Path-Knowledge *(Arahatta·Magga·Ñāṇa)*: it makes it impossible for one ever again to covet another's property.

After explaining the wholesome kamma of abstaining from covetousness, The Buddha explains the wholesome kamma of abstaining from ill-will.

NOT TO HARBOUR ILL-WILL

One is one of no ill-will, one of no malicious mind & intention [who thinks]:
'May these beings be without hatred, without ill-will, without vexation, may they happily look after themselves!'

Here again, to abstain from ill-will is because of non-greed *(a·lobha)* and non-hatred *(a·dosa)*: associated with knowledge of the workings of kamma, or dissociated from knowledge of the workings of kamma.

And again, one may abstain from ill-will because, instead of wanting another being to die or be harmed, one wants all beings to live and be happy: that is loving-kindness *(mettā)*, and compassion *(karuṇā)*. Again, one may abstain from ill-will because one has attained the Non-Return Path Knowledge *(An·Āgāmi·Magga·Ñāṇa)*: it makes it impossible for one ever again to engage in ill-will.

After explaining the wholesome kamma of abstaining from ill-will, The Buddha explains the wholesome kamma of abstaining from holding wrong view, of holding Right View *(Sammā·Diṭṭhi)*.

TO HOLD RIGHT VIEW

One is one of Right View, not one of perverted view [and one thinks]:

[1] **'There is offering,**
[2] **there is almsgiving,**
[3] **there is sacrifice;**
[4] **there is a pleasant or painful fruit or result of kamma;**
[5] **there is this world,**
[6] **there is another world;**
[7] **there is a mother,**
[8] **there is a father;**[374]
[9] **there are beings spontaneously born;**
[10] **there are in the world ascetics and Brahmins, rightly faring, rightly practising, who with direct knowledge (having themselves realized this world and the other world) declare it.'**

This is the standard Right View described by The Buddha. It is called the ten-based Right View *(dasa·vatthukā Sammā·Diṭṭhi)*. It affirms the workings of kamma, and rebirth, etc. When He speaks of basic Right View, this is usually the type of view He is referring to.[375]

---

[374] This does not mean that mothers and fathers exist according to reality; it means certain results arise because of unwholesome/wholesome kamma performed towards one's parents. See further explanation footnote 11, p.2, and endnote 203, p.252

[375] RIGHT VIEW: this is what is also called Kamma-Ownership Right View *(Kamma·Ssakata·Sammā·Diṭṭhi)*. Hence, in for example, S.V.III.i.3 *'Bhikkhu·Suttaṁ'* ('The Bhikkhu Sutta'), The

(Please see further next page.)

To hold Right View is because of non-greed, non-hatred, and non-delusion, and it is always knowledge-associated. But so long as one has not seen the workings of dependent origination, one's Right View is based on faith, and is for that reason uncertain: sometimes one holds it, sometimes one does not. Only the Stream-Entry Path Knowledge*(Sot·Āpatti·Magga·Ñāṇa)* makes one's Right View certain, because one will have known and seen dependent origination in regular and negative order: then can one not ever again hold wrong view about kamma, nor any of the twenty types of identity view*(sakkāya·diṭṭhi)*.[166] Then does one also possess the Right View that knows the difference between Right View and wrong view.[167]

To hold the view that affirms the workings of kamma is the most important of all the wholesome courses of kamma. Why? Because when one holds Right View, it is very difficult to do unwholesome things. Indeed, if one has attained to the Right View of a Noble Disciple, many unwholesome things will have become impossible for one ever again to do.[168]

That concludes The Buddha's explanation of the three wholesome courses of mental kamma: not to be covetous of another's property, not to harbour ill-will (but to harbour loving-kindness and compassion), and not to hold a wrong view that denies the workings of unwholesome and wholesome kamma, but to hold Right View, which affirms the workings of unwholesome and wholesome kamma.

In all, there are ten wholesome courses of kamma: three wholesome courses of bodily kamma, four wholesome courses of verbal kamma, and three wholesome courses of mental kamma. They all arise owing to non-greed*(a·lobha)* and non-hatred*(a·dosa)*, and can be knowledge-dissociated*(ñāṇa·vippayutta)* or knowledge-associated*(ñāṇa·sampayutta)*.

The Results of Wholesome Kamma

What is the result of such kamma? The Buddha explained it to the bhikkhus:

The Results of Wholesome Bodily Kamma

With the three types of bodily kamma achievement, with wholesome intention as root, bhikkhus, beings at the breakup of the body, after death, in a good destination, a heavenly world are reborn.

The Results of Wholesome Verbal Kamma

Or with the four types of verbal kamma achievement, with wholesome intention as root, bhikkhus, beings at the breakup of the body, after death, in a good destination, a heavenly world are reborn.

The Results of Wholesome Mental Kamma

Or with the three types of mental kamma achievement, with wholesome intention as root, bhikkhus, beings at the breakup of the body, after death, in a good destination, a heavenly world are reborn.

Buddha explains: 'And what is the beginning of wholesome things*(kusalānaṁ dhammānaṁ)*? Morality well purified*(sīlañ·ca su·visuddhaṁ)*, and view straightened*(diṭṭhi ca ujukā)* [SA: kamma-ownership Right View*(kamma·ssakatā·diṭṭhi)*].' And He explains that once those two things have been achieved, then the bhikkhu can practise the four foundations of mindfulness. And The Buddha says the same with regard to practice of the Noble Eightfold Path (S.V.I), and the seven enlightenment factors (S.V.II). See further 'The Five Types of Knowledge', p.58.

The ten wholesome courses of kamma are praised by The Buddha as the wholesome*(kusala)*, as useful*(attha)*, as blameless*(anavajja)*, as things with a happy result*(sukha·vipāka dhamma)*. And because they lead to rebirth in heaven*(sagga)*, He praises them as the bright way*(sukka·magga)*.[169]

The Buddha explains further that if we make someone else engage in the ten wholesome courses of kamma, they become twenty things that take us to a good destination, even heaven;[170] if we also approve of the ten wholesome courses of kamma, they become thirty things that take us to a good destination;[171] and if we also praise the ten wholesome courses of kamma, they become forty things that take us to a good destination.[172]

Conclusion

That concludes our explanation of the ten unwholesome courses of kamma, and the ten wholesome courses of kamma. The ten unwholesome courses of kamma lead to rebirth in the animal world, the ghost world, even in hell, whereas the ten wholesome courses of kamma lead to rebirth in the human world, or deva worlds.

Rebirth in the human or deva world, however, is not the goal of the Dhamma, is it? Such rebirth can be attained also outside a Buddha's Dispensation. Thus, the wholesome courses of kamma are not unique to a Buddha's Dispensation. Unique to The Buddha's Dispensation is the teaching of the Four Noble Truths:[376]

1) Suffering .... *(dukkha)*	3) Cessation .... *(nirodha)*
2) The origin .... *(samudaya)*	4) The path .... *(magga)*

That is The Buddhas' most superior Dhamma teaching*(Buddhānaṁ sāmukkaṁsikā Dhamma·desanā)*. It can lead to the most wholesome of all wholesome things: the attainment of a Path&Fruition, ultimately to Arahantship, the end of birth, ageing and death.

What is necessary for the attainment of a Path&Fruition*(Magga·Phala)*? Successful samatha and vipassanā meditation is necessary.[173] But for our samatha and vipassanā meditation to be successful, it needs to be supported by much other wholesome kamma. In other words, for us to succeed in our meditation, we need to have accomplished much practice of the three merit-work bases: not only in this life but also in past lives. And that practice needs to have been of a high quality: consistent and continuous. That is what we shall now discuss.

Knowledge and Conduct

The kind of past practice necessary for one to attain a Path&Fruition (even Arahantship), is called knowledge and conduct*(vijjā·caraṇa)*:[174]

1) Knowledge*(vijjā)* is the same as wisdom*(paññā)*, and is insight knowledge *(vipassanā·ñāṇa)*: mundane*(lokiya)* and supramundane*(lokuttara)*.[377] Mundane

---

[376] This is the culmination of what is called The Buddha's progressive instruction*(anupubbi·kathā)* (see 'Tambadāthika the Executioner', p.183). See, for example, D.i.3 *'Ambaṭṭha·Suttaṁ'* ('The Ambaṭṭha Sutta'), and M.II.i.6 *'Upāli·Suttaṁ'* ('The Upāli Sutta').

[377] VsM.vii.133 *'Buddh·Ānussati'* ('Buddha Recollection') PP.vii.30 explains that according to D.i.3 *'Ambaṭṭha·Suttaṁ'* ('The Ambaṭṭha Sutta'), knowledge is eight knowledges: 1) Insight knowledge into mentality-materiality, 2) Mind-made power knowledge, 3) Various-Powers Knowledge, 4) Divine-ear knowledge, 5) Others'-mind knowledge, 6) Former-lives recollection knowledge, 7) Divine-eye knowledge, 8) Taints-Destruction Knowledge (Nos.2-8 are explained at footnote 239, p.82). And according to *'Bhaya·Bherava·Suttaṁ'*

(Please see further next page.)

knowledge takes as object the formed element*(Saṅkhata·dhātu)*, which is the five aggregates or mentality-materiality, of the three planes. Supramundane knowledge takes as object the Unformed element*(Asaṅkhata·dhātu)*, Nibbāna. When discussing the past practice necessary for attaining a Path&Fruition, we do not include supramundane knowledge, because if there is supramundane knowledge, it means one has already attained a Path&Fruition.

2) Conduct*(caraṇa)* is the same as the three merit-work bases*(puñña·kiriya·vatthu)*: offering*(dāna)*, morality*(sīla)* and meditation*(bhāvanā)*: by meditation is meant samatha meditation*(samatha·bhāvanā)* and again insight meditation*(vipassanā·bhāvanā)*. But the three merit-work bases may be called conduct only when they are the proper practice, and are practised consistently and continuously.

To explain knowledge and conduct, we shall (to make it easier) begin by explaining conduct*(caraṇa)*.

CONDUCT

Conduct*(caraṇa)* is fifteen things:[378]

1) Morality*(sīla)*: we discussed morality when we discussed the first merit-work base*(puñña·kiriya·vatthu)*.[379] Let us briefly mention all the factors again.
   i) For laypeople, morality means habitual training in the five and eight precepts, or the ten precepts. It includes Right Livelihood*(Sammā·Ājīva)*, which is a livelihood that does not break any of the precepts, and is not one of the five wrong trades: trade in weapons, beings, flesh, liquor, and poison.[380]
   ii) For bhikkhus, morality means the bhikkhu morality*(bhikkhu·sīla)*, the higher morality*(adhi·sīla)*, which is the fourfold purification morality*(catu·pārisuddhi·sīla)*:[175]
      a) Purification through *Pātimokkha*-restraint morality*(pātimokkha·saṁvara·sīla)*, habitually keeping the two hundred and twenty-seven precepts of the bhikkhu rule.

('The Fear& Dread Sutta'), knowledge is three knowledges*(te·vijjā)*: the above 6, 7 and 8. When speaking of past practice, however, supramundane knowledge (No.8) is usually not included.

378 In the introduction to M.II.i.3 *'Sekha·Suttaṁ'* ('The Trainee Sutta'), The Buddha tells the Venerable Ānanda to instruct the Sakyans of Kapilavatthu about the 'Noble Disciple on the path*(sekho pāṭipado)*'. The Venerable Ānanda explains: 'Here, Mahānāma, the Noble Disciple is attained to morality*(sīla·sampanno)*, in the faculties guarded at the doors*(indriyesu gutta·dvāro)*, in food moderate*(bhojane mattaññū)*, devoted to wakefulness*(jāgariyaṁ anuyutto)*, possessed of seven right things*(sattahi sa·ddhammehi samanāgato)*, one who acquires without difficulty*(nikāma·lābhi)* the four jhānas*(catunnaṁ jhānānaṁ)*, which are the higher mentalities *(ābhi·cetasikānaṁ)*, presently-occurring happy abidings*(diṭṭha·dhamma·sukha·vihārānaṁ)*, one who acquires them without distress*(a·kiccha·lābhī)*, without trouble*(a·kasira·lābhī)*.' The seven right things he then explains as the Noble Disciple's being 1) faithful*(saddho)*, 2) conscientious *(hirimā)*, 3) shameful*(ottappī)*, 4) very learned*(bahu·ssuto)*, 5) of resolute energy*(āraddha·viriyo)*, 6) mindful*(satimā)*, and 7) wise*(paññavā)*. And he explains that these things constitute the Noble Disciple's conduct*(caraṇa)*. At the end of his analysis, The Buddha endorses it with *'Sādhu'*.

379 See 'Morality', p.71.

380 See quotation endnote 103, p.239.

b) Purification through restraint of the sense faculties *(indriya·saṁvara·sīla)*: habitually restraining the eye-, ear-, nose-, tongue-, body-, and mind faculty, by attending to one's meditation subject, be it samatha or vipassanā. That way defilements do not arise by way of the six faculties.[381]

c) Purification through livelihood purification morality *(ājīva·pārisuddhi·sīla)*: Right Livelihood *(Sammā·Ājīva)* for bhikkhus. That is to abstain from wrong livelihood: livelihood that does not break any of the ***Pātimokkha*** precepts.[382]

d) Purification through requisite-related morality *(paccaya·sannissita·sīla)*. Reflecting with wise attention upon the four requisites: robe, almsfood, dwelling, and medicine.

2) Faculty restraint *(indriya·saṁvara)*: it is the same as the bhikkhu's second purification: habitual restraint of the eye-, ear-, nose-, tongue-, body-, and mind faculty, by attending to one's meditation subject, be it samatha or vipassanā. That way defilements do not arise by way of the six faculties.

3) Moderation in food *(bhojane mattaññutā)*: habitually to eat only so much as is necessary to support one's practice, and maintain the body.[383]

4) Devotion to wakefulness *(jāgariy·ānuyoga)*: habitually not to sleep during the day, and never to sleep more than is necessary: in between sleeping, habitually to practise meditation.

5) Faith *(saddhā)*: strong and powerful, deep faith[384] in The Buddha, Dhamma, and Sangha, in the workings of kamma, and in dependent origination, rebirth, and other planes of existence. The habitual practice of offering *(dāna)* is in this classification included under faith.

6) Mindfulness *(sati)*: habitual practice of the four foundations of mindfulness: mindfulness of the body, feelings, consciousness, and dhammas.

7) Conscience *(hiri)*: habitually to be conscientious not to do wrong through body, speech, and mind.

8) Shame *(ottappa)*: habitually to be ashamed of doing wrong through body, speech, and mind.

9) Great learning *(bāhu·sacca)*:[176] habitually to study and inquire about the Texts, so as to know the difference between the five clinging-aggregates *(khandha)*, the elements *(dhātu)*, and the sense bases *(āyatana)*, which are the First Noble Truth, the Noble Truth of Suffering *(Dukkha Ariya·Sacca)*.[177] Also to study and inquire about dependent origination *(paṭicca·samuppāda)*, so as to know the origin of the five aggregates *(pañca·kkhandha)*, the Second Noble Truth, the Noble Truth of the Origin of Suffering *(Dukkha·Samudaya Ariya·Sacca)*. And to study and inquire about the four foundations of mindfulness *(sati·paṭṭhāna)*, so as to know the way to the cessation of suffering, the Fourth Noble Truth, the Noble Truth of the Way Leading to the Cessation of Suffering *(Dukkha·Nirodha·Gāminī Paṭipadā Ariya·Sacca)*.

Great learning includes also knowing and seeing the five aggregates, and knowing and seeing their origin. That is the two knowledges preparatory to

[381] For details, see endnote 118, p.240.

[382] For details regarding wrong livelihood for a bhikkhu, see endnote 120, p.241.

[383] In S.IV.xii.7 ***'Rath·Opama·Suttaṁ'*** ('The Chariot-Simile Sutta'), The Buddha explains this as eating in accordance with the reflection quoted at 'The Bhikkhu's Morality', p.75.

[384] For an analysis of faith *(saddhā)*, see 'Faith', p.374.

vipassanā: the Mentality-Materiality Definition Knowledge*(Nāma·Rūpa·Pariccheda-·Ñāṇa)*, and the Cause-Apprehending Knowledge*(Paccaya·Pariggaha·Ñāṇa)*. We discussed them earlier.[385]

10) Energy*(vīriya)*: this is habitual practice of the four kinds of effort*(padhāna)*:[178]
   i) The effort to restrain*(saṁvara·padhāna)*: with energy and effort to restrain oneself from accomplishing unwholesome kamma through body, speech, and mind.
   ii) The effort to abandon*(pahāna·padhāna)*: any unwholesome kamma that one does through body, speech, and mind, one stops with energy and effort.
   iii) The effort to develop*(bhāvanā·padhāna)*: with energy and effort one tries to develop and undertake new wholesome kamma through body, speech, and mind. That is, one tries to develop more and more knowledge*(vijjā)* and conduct*(caraṇa)*.
   iv) The effort to maintain*(anurakkhaṇa·padhāna)*: any wholesome kamma that one does through body, speech, and mind, one maintains: one continues with one's work.
11) Wisdom*(paññā)*:[179] this is insight knowledge proper. Earlier, we discussed the eleven mundane insight knowledges. The first two are not really insight knowledges, but only preparatory knowledges. The next nine are insight knowledges proper.[386] And insight knowledge is included under conduct, when it produces rebirth. How?

   So long as one is not an Arahant, then even though there is no craving when one practises insight meditation, there is still volition that can produce rebirth; there is still the establishment of kammic consciousness. It is caused by the latencies, and cannot be otherwise.[180]

   Also, insight knowledge may actually be interspersed with very subtle enjoyment*(abhinandana)* for that knowledge: that is sensual craving*(kāma·taṇhā)*. And if one has no jhāna, then at the near-death moment one's insight knowledge may be the strongest wholesome kamma to mature. In that case, it will produce rebirth into either the human or sensual-realm deva world.[181]

12) First jhāna .... *(paṭhama jhāna)*
13) Second jhāna .... *(dutiya jhāna)*
14) Third jhāna .... *(tatiya jhāna)*
15) Fourth jhāna .... *(catuttha jhāna)*

This is samatha practice. The four jhānas are what The Buddha calls Right Concentration*(Sammā Samādhi)*.[182] With the four jhānas, the mind becomes strong and powerful, and there is bright, brilliant, radiant light, which is the light of wisdom: light with which to penetrate to ultimate truth, and practise insight on ultimate mentality and ultimate materiality of past, future, and present, internal and external, gross and subtle, inferior and superior, far and near.

These fifteen things are what is called conduct*(caraṇa)*.[183] Then we have knowledge*(vijjā)*.

---

[385] See 'The Two Preparatory Insight Knowledges', p.90.

[386] See 'The Sixteen Insight Knowledges', p.111.

Knowledge

Knowledge*(vijjā)* is again insight knowledge*(vipassanā·ñāṇa)*, but only such insight knowledge as does not produce rebirth.

That then concludes our explanation of knowledge and conduct*(Vijjā·Caraṇa)*. Knowledge and conduct is the kind of past kamma required for one to attain a Path&Fruition*(Magga·Phala)*. Please try to keep it in mind when we later mention people who developed such knowledge in past lives, attaining the highest of the mundane insight knowledges, the Formations-Equanimity Knowledge*(Saṅkhār·Upekkhā·Ñāṇa)*.

The Results

Properly to conclude our explanation of the wholesome, however, we need also to mention that the practice of knowledge and conduct in past lives needs to be balanced: there needs to be both knowledge and conduct. Why?

To explain it, we may use a simile.[184] Knowledge is like the eyes of a human being, and conduct is like the human being's feet.[387] We have thus four kinds of person:

1) The one who has practised conduct, but has not practised knowledge. That is like someone who can walk but is blind.
2) The one who has practised knowledge, but has not practised conduct. That is like someone who can see but is crippled.
3) The one who has practised neither knowledge nor conduct. That is like someone who is blind as well as crippled. It is the kind of person we discussed in connection with the *'Gaddula·Baddha'* sutta: the uneducated ordinary person*(puthu·jjana)*.
4) The one who has practised both knowledge and conduct. That is like someone who can both see and walk.

Insufficient Knowledge

If our practice constitutes mainly conduct*(caraṇa)*, it is like developing healthy limbs. Such practice makes it possible for us to encounter a Buddha's Dispensation. Such practice helps us get reborn as a human being, in a suitable place, with a healthy body, with fully functioning faculties, with the right kind of parents, where there is a Buddha, Dhamma, and Sangha. But insufficient practice of knowledge is like having poor eyesight. Not having such practice of knowledge, we shall be unable properly to know and see the Dhamma, even when taught by The Buddha Himself.

---

[387] VbhA.iv.205 *'Magga·Sacca·Niddesa·Vaṇṇanā'* ('Description of the Path-Truth Exposition') DD.iv.570 explains how knowledge and conduct are included in the Noble Eightfold Path: Knowledge = Right View/Right Intention (which corresponds to insight wisdom not leading to rebirth); Conduct = the remaining factors. In the same way, Knowledge = vipassanā; Conduct = samatha; Knowledge = the aggregate (training) of wisdom; Conduct = the aggregates (trainings) of morality & concentration. And it explains that endowed with these three aggregates and trainings, the Noble Disciple is like a traveller with eyes that can see and feet that can walk, who eventually realizes Nibbāna, the Deathless.

KING PASENADI

A good example is King Pasenadi of Kosala, one of The Buddha's chief patrons. He had become king, enjoyed royal power and royal pleasures, because of past practice of conduct *(caraṇa)*: offering, keeping the precepts, and other works of merit. And because of that past practice, he met The Buddha, and became a great patron of The Buddha. But because of insufficient practice of knowledge *(vijjā)*, he was unable properly to know and see the Dhamma: he never attained any Path or Fruition knowledge. Thus, even though we can find suttas that describe him discussing the Dhamma with The Buddha, it is only superficial Dhamma: on a conceptual level.[388]

THE BHIKKHU SĀTI

Another example is the bhikkhu Sāti, son of a fisherman.[389] Owing to past practice of conduct *(caraṇa)*, he met The Buddha, gained faith in The Buddha, even ordained as a bhikkhu, and undertook the threefold higher training. But when The Buddha explained His past lives to the bhikkhus, the bhikkhu Sāti could not understand it properly: he thought it was one consciousness that migrated from life to life, one consciousness that experienced the results of past unwholesome and wholesome kamma. Because of insufficient practice of knowledge *(vijjā)*, he was unable properly to understand the Dhamma. Even surrounded by wise bhikkhus, and taught by The Buddha Himself, the bhikkhu Sāti could not understand dependent origination.[185]

SACCAKA THE PHILOSOPHER

A third example is Saccaka,[186] a scholar who went round debating with people. Owing to past practice of conduct *(caraṇa)*, he met The Buddha, discussed the Dhamma with The Buddha, and gained respect for The Buddha. But owing to insufficient practice of knowledge *(vijjā)*, he could not fully accept The Buddha's teaching, and did not take refuge in The Buddha.

There are a number of such examples, of disciples of other teachings discussing the Dhamma with The Buddha, admitting that His teaching was superior, yet being unable to give up their own view.[187]

INSUFFICIENT CONDUCT

Let us then say we have failed to practise conduct: have failed to practise offering, morality, and faculty restraint; have failed to develop sufficiently strong faith in The Buddha, Dhamma, and Sangha; have failed to develop sufficiently strong faith in the workings of kamma, dependent origination, rebirth, and other planes of existence; have failed to develop conscience and shame; have failed to practise the four right efforts; and have failed to develop concentration. That is like having deformed limbs.

Then even if we could understand The Buddha's Teachings, it will never take place, because our conduct is that of an uneducated ordinary person. Such conduct means we accomplish much unwholesome kamma through body, speech, and mind: for example, killing, stealing, engaging in sexual misconduct, telling lies, drinking beer&wine liquor, and, worst of all, holding wrong view. That con-

[388] See, for example, S.I.III *'Kosala Saṁyutta'* ('Kosala Section').

[389] M.I.iv.8 *'Mahā·Taṇhā·Saṅkhaya·Suttaṁ'* ('The Great Craving's-Destruction Sutta')

duct means we shall tend towards rebirth in unhappy destinations. If we are reborn in hell, the animal world, or the ghost world, The Buddha says it is almost impossible for us to escape.[390] In the meantime, a Buddha may arise, and we will have lost the opportunity to encounter His Teachings. It is only as either human beings or devas that we can encounter a Buddha's Dispensation.

Even if we do gain a human rebirth, our insufficient practice of those factors of conduct*(caraṇa·dhamma)* will mean that we shall be reborn at an unsuitable time, when there is no Buddha's Dispensation. Why? Because a Buddha's Dispensation is very, very rare.[391] Many, many aeons can pass without a Buddha arising. And even if there is a Buddha's Dispensation, we shall tend to be reborn in an unsuitable place, with the wrong kind of parents, where wrong view prevails, with no knowledge of or access to The Buddha's Dispensation. And we shall also run into trouble as human beings, and be prone to sickness. In that case, it will be very, very difficult for us to encounter a Buddha's Teachings.

Our eyesight may be good, meaning that we would be able to understand the Dhamma, and maybe even attain Path&Fruition. But because of insufficient conduct, we shall be unable to meet The Buddha's Dispensation, because of 'deformed limbs'.

Mahādhana Lord-Son

A good example is Mahādhana Lord-Son, son of a treasurer.[392] He was born into a very rich family in Bārāṇasī, and married a girl from a very rich family. Because he did not practise morality, he spent his entire fortune on drink, flowers, perfume, song, music and dance, etc., to end up in poverty. When The Buddha arose in the world, Mahādhana and his wife were already approaching old age. And they encountered The Buddha's Dispensation only when they in their old age went to the Isipatana monastery to beg for food.

When The Buddha one day saw Mahādhana and his wife, He told the Venerable Ānanda that if Mahādhana as a young man had applied himself to business, he would have become the chief treasurer in Bārāṇasī. And if as a young man, Mahādhana had become a monk, he would have become an Arahant, and his wife a Non-Returner. In the same way, if as a middle-aged man, Mahādhana had applied himself to business, he could have become the city's second treasurer, and as a monk he would have become a Non-Returner, and his wife a Once Returner. And if he had done these things as an elderly man, he would have become the city's third treasurer, or would as a monk have become a Once Returner, and his wife a Stream Enterer. But because he had failed to practise conduct*(caraṇa)*, he now had nothing at all: neither the wealth of a layman nor the wealth of a monk. And at death, he was destined to be reborn in hell.

---

[390] In this regard, The Buddha uses the simile of the blind turtle: see quotation endnote 78, p.235.
[391] The Buddha explains the rarity of a Buddha in A.I.xiii *'Eka·Puggala·Vaggo'* ('One Person Chapter'), A.V.III.v.3 *'Sārandada·Suttaṁ'* ('The Sārandada Sutta'), and He says in DhP.xiv.4 *'Buddha·Vagga'* ('The Buddha Chapter'): 'Rare it is to become a human being; hard is a mortal's life; hard it is the True Dhamma to hear; rare is a Buddha's arising.'
[392] DhPA.xi.9 *'Mahādhana·Seṭṭhi·Putta·Vatthu'* ('The Case of Mahādhana Lord-Son')

King Ajātasattu

Another good example is King Ajātasattu. We shall mention him many times in the course of our explanations. He was the son of King Bimbisāra, who was a Stream Enterer, and great patron of The Buddha and Sangha. In order to become king, King Ajātasattu had his father killed. Then, one night, he went to see The Buddha, and The Buddha gave him the great teaching that is the *'Sāmañña·Phala'* sutta.[393] The king had all the right conditions for attaining Stream Entry like his father. But because he had failed to practise conduct*(caraṇa)* earlier in his life, he had had his father killed. Killing one's father is one of the weighty, unintervenable kammas: the result is inescapable rebirth in hell in the next life.[394] So, King Ajātasattu was unable to attain a Path&Fruition, and remained a common person*(puthu·jjana)*.

Born in an Unsuitable Place

Another example is people who have not been born in what The Buddha calls a suitable place*(patirūpa·desa)*: that is, people born in a country where there is no Buddha's Dispensation*(Buddha·Sāsana)*.[395] For example, now in the Sangha, there are a growing number of bhikkhus from North America and Northern Europe. There are also a growing number of laypeople from those countries who gain faith in The Buddha, Dhamma and Sangha. But it is very often difficult for them to accept The Buddha's Teachings: that is perhaps because of insufficient practice of knowledge*(vijjā)* in the past and present. It is very often also difficult for them to encounter the True Dhamma*(Saddhamma)*: that is perhaps because of insufficient practice of conduct*(caraṇa)* in the past and present: it is difficult to say for sure. When you discern dependent origination, you will be able to understand the workings of such kamma properly.

That concludes our explanation of unwholesome and wholesome kamma. Next, we shall discuss the twelve categories of kamma*(dvā·dasa kamma)*.

The Twelve Categories of Kamma

The twelve categories of kamma are three sets of four:[396]

- Four categories for when kamma takes effect: time of effect.
- Four categories for which type of kamma takes effect first: order of effect.
- Four categories for how kamma functions: function of effect.

---

[393] D.i.2 *'Sāmañña·Phala·Suttaṁ'* ('The Asceticism-Fruit Sutta')

[394] See 'Unwholesome Weighty Kamma', p.170*ff.*

[395] To reside where there is a Buddha's Dispensation is the fourth blessing listed by The Buddha in SuN.ii.4 *'Maṅgala·Suttaṁ'* ('The Blessing Sutta'): 'In a suitable place to reside *(paṭirūpa·desa·vāsa)*.'

[396] These twelve categories are given in the VsM.xix.685-687 *'Kaṅkhā·Vitaraṇa·Visuddhi·Niddeso'* ('Exposition of the Doubt-Transcendence Purification') PP.xix.14-16, and explained, for example, at AA/AṬ.III.I.iv.4 *'Nidāna·Suttaṁ'* ('The Causation Sutta' quoted endnote 237, p.255), and PaD. A fourth set of four is given in AbS.v.53 *'Kamma·Catukkaṁ'* ('The Kamma Tetrad') CMA.v.21: place of effect, where and how kamma produces its result. 1) unwholesome kamma (which takes effect only on the sensual-/fine-material plane); 2) sensual-sphere wholesome kamma; 3) fine-material sphere wholesome kamma; 4) immaterial-sphere wholesome kamma.

The Buddha explains kamma according to these twelve categories.[397] We shall now explain them one by one.

TIME OF EFFECT

The first four categories of kamma are according to when kamma takes effect:[398/188]

1) Presently-effective kamma *(diṭṭha·dhamma·vedanīya·kamma)*: it takes effect in the same individual existence *(atta·bhāva)*.
2) Subsequently-effective kamma *(upapajja·vedanīya·kamma)*: it takes effect in the very next existence.
3) Indefinitely-effective kamma *(apar·āpariya·vedanīya·kamma)*: it takes effect in some existence after the next one.
4) Lapsed kamma *(ahosi·kamma)*: it fails to take effect. It is is presently- or subsequently-effective kamma that is defunct, kamma only by name. After one's Parinibbāna (final cessation), it includes also indefinitely-effective kammas, because after one's Parinibbāna, no kammas take effect anymore.

Before we continue, please remember that within a snap of the fingers, very many thousand million consciousnesses arise and perish: they include many thousand million mental processes *(citta·vīthi)*.[399] Most of them are mind-door processes: many thousand million mind-door processes arising and perishing like a river in full flow. In our world (the sensual world), usually a mind-door process includes seven impulsion consciousnesses *(javana)*.[400] When an impulsion consciousness arises that is unwholesome *(akusala)*, there are minimum sixteen mental phenomena *(nāma·dhamma)*, maximum twenty-two; when it is wholesome *(kusala)*, there are minimum thirty-two mental phenomena, maximum thirty-five.[401] In all cases, one of those mental phenomena is volition *(cetanā)*, and it is volition that forms kamma.[402] Thus, whenever an unwholesome or wholesome kamma is accomplished, we may say that the series of seven impulsion consciousnesses associated with kamma-forming volition arises billions of times.

---

[397] TIME OF EFFECT: discussed just below; ORDER OF EFFECT: discussed p.170*ff*; Function of Effect: discussed p.186*ff.*

[398] VsM.xix.685 (and VsMṬ) *'Kaṅkhā·Vitaraṇa·Visuddhi·Niddeso'* ('Exposition of the Doubt-Transcendence Purification) PP.xix.14, and AbS.v.52 *'Kamma·Catukkaṁ'* ('The Kamma Tetrad') CMA.v.20. For the literal translation of the Pali terms, see subsequent endnote 188, p.250.

[399] For an estimated number, see footnote 101, p.41. The continuity of consciousnesses is made up of countless life-continuum consciousnesses interrupted by set series of consciousnesses called mental processes.

[400] See footnote 102, p.41.

[401] MENTAL PHENOMENA AT THE ARISING OF UNWHOLESOME IMPULSION CONSCIOUSNESSES: see tables 2a/2b/2c, p.48*ff*; OF WHOLESOME SENSUAL-REALM IMPULSION CONSCIOUSNESSES: see tables 3a/3b, p.67*ff.*

[402] But not all volition produces kamma: see footnote 104, p.41.

5b: **The Five-Door Process** *(pañca·dvāra·vīthi)* (eye/ear/nose/tongue/body-door process: example is eye-door process.)*

CONSCIOUSNESS MOMENT *Citta·Kkhaṇa*	(Before the mental process) ⇒⇒...⇒⇒	1⇒	2⇒	3⇒	4⇒	5⇒	6⇒	7⇒	8⇒
OBJECT *Ārammaṇa*	Previous life's near-death object				Sight/Colour Object *Rūp·Ārammaṇa*				
CONSCIOUSNESS *Citta*	Life-Continuum *Bhavaṅga* ↑|↓	Past Life-Continuum *Atīta·Bhavaṅga* ↑|↓	Trembling Life-Continuum *Bhavaṅga·Calana* ↑|↓	Arrest Life-Continuum *Bhavaṅg·Upaccheda* ↑|↓	Five-Door Adverting *Pañca·Dvār·Āvajjana* ↑|↓	Eye Consciousness *Cakkhu·Viññāṇa* ↑|↓	Receiving *Sampaṭi·Cchana* ↑|↓	Investigation *Santīraṇa* ↑|↓	Determining *Voṭṭhapana* ↑|↓
	Resultant *Vipāka*				Functional *Kiriya*	Resultant *Vipāka*			Functional *Kiriya*

CONSCIOUSNESS MOMENT *Citta·Kkhaṇa*	9⇒	10⇒	11⇒	12⇒	13⇒	14⇒	15⇒	16⇒	17⇒	(After the mental process) ⇒⇒⇒...⇒⇒⇒
OBJECT *Ārammaṇa*	Sight/Colour Object *Rūp·Ārammaṇa*									Previous life's near-death object
CONSCIOUSNESS *Citta*	1st Impulsion *Javana* ↑|↓	2nd Impulsion *Javana* ↑|↓	3rd Impulsion *Javana* ↑|↓	4th Impulsion *Javana* ↑|↓	5th Impulsion *Javana* ↑|↓	6th Impulsion *Javana* ↑|↓	7th Impulsion *Javana* ↑|↓	1st Registration *Tad·Ārammaṇa* ↑|↓	2nd Registration *Tad·Ārammaṇa* ↑|↓	Life-Continuum *Bhavaṅga* ↑|↓
	Kamma							Resultant *Vipāka*		Resultant *Vipāka*

* VsM.i.15 *'Indriya·Saṁvara·Sīlaṁ'* ('Faculty-Restraint Morality') PP.i.57; VsM.xiv.455 *'Viññāṇa·Kkhandha·Kathā'* ('Discussion of the Consciousness-Aggregate') PP.xiv.114-123; DhSA.i.1 *'Kām·Āvacara·Kusala·Pada·Bhājanīyaṁ'* ('Sensual-Sphere Wholesome Section Classification') E.96; DhSA.I.iii *'Vipāk·Uddhāra·Kathā'* ('Discussion of the Result-Apprehension') E.359-360; & AbS.iv.10 *'Pañca·Dvāra·Vīthi'* ('Five-Door Process') CMA.iv.6.

Notes for Table 5b 'The Five-Door Process'

- The material object that is cognized by a five-door process lasts 17 consciousness moments.
- One consciousness lasts one consciousness moment *(citta·kkhaṇa)*, with three stages: arising *(uppāda)* ↑, standing *(ṭhiti)* |, dissolution *(bhaṅga)* ↓.
- Before and after a mental process, arises a number of life-continuum consciousnesses (see footnote 306, p.107).
- All five-door processes (eye-, ear-, nose-, tongue-, body door) follow the same procedure, according to the natural law of the mind *(citta·niyāma)*. Thus, the five-door process only 'picks up' the object (the eye-door process only cognizes that there is colour), does not yet 'know' the object (colour). The 'knowing' takes place at the fourth and subsequent mental processes (See table 'The Mind-Door Process', p.148). The volition of the impulsion consciousnesses is here only weak, which means the kamma can produce a result only in a future life's continuance *(pavatti)*:it cannot produce a rebirth-linking consciousness *(paṭisandhi·citta)*.

Mental Phenomena *(nāma·dhamma)* **of the Five-Door Process** *(pañca·dvāra·vīthi)*
(eye/ear/nose/tongue/body-door process: example is eye-door process.)

CONSCIOUSNESS / MENTAL PHENOMENA	5-Door Adverting	Eye Consciousness	Receiving	Investigation		Determining	Impulsion	Registration
CONSCIOUSNESS *(citta)*	1	1	1	1	1	1	1	1
SEVEN UNIVERSALS *(sabba·citta·sādhāraṇa)*	7	7	7	7	7	7	UNWHOLESOME *(akusala)** Greed-rooted *(lobha·mūla)* 17/18/19/20/21 Hatred-rooted *(dosa·mūla)* 17/18/19/20 Delusion-rooted *(moha·mūla)* 15 WHOLESOME *(kusala)** Knowledge Dissociated *(ñāṇa·vippayutta)* 31/32/33 Knowledge Associated *(ñāṇa·sampayutta)* 32/33/34	Mental factors as of the investigation consciousness, or the sensual-sphere beautiful resultant-consciousness *(vipāka·citta)*.‡
SIX SUNDRIES *(pakiṇṇaka)*								
1. application *(vitakka)*	1		1	1	1	1		
2. sustainment *(vicāra)*	1		1	1	1	1		
3. decision *(adhimokkha)*	1		1	1	1	1		
4. energy *(vīriya)*						1		
5. joy *(pīti)*					1			
6. desire *(chanda)* ⅄								
Total	11	8	11	11	12	12	16/18/19/20/21/22/ 32/33/34/35	11/12/ 32/33/34

* For the mental phenomena at the arising of the consciousnesses with unwholesome roots, see tables, p.48*ff*, and the wholesome roots, tables p.67*ff*.
‡ The mental factors at the arising of the sensual-sphere beautiful resultant consciousness correspond to the mental factors at the arising of the wholesome sensual-sphere impulsion, excluding the illimitables and abstinences: see previous column 'Impulsion' under 'Wholesome'.
⅄ The five-door-, eye-, receiving-, investigating-, and determining consciousness is unrooted *(ahetuka)*, and never associated with desire *(chanda)*.

5c: **The Mind-Door Process** *(Mano·Dvāra·Vīthi)* (with colour object as example)*

CONSCIOUSNESS MOMENT *Citta·Kkhaṇa*	(Before the mental process) ⇒⇒...⇒⇒	⇒	⇒	⇒	⇒	⇒	⇒	⇒	⇒	⇒	⇒	(After the mental process) ⇒⇒...⇒⇒
OBJECT *Ārammaṇa*	Previous life's near-death object.	Sight/Colour Object *Rūp·Ārammaṇa*										Previous life's near-death object.
CONSCIOUSNESS *Citta*	Life-Continuum	Mind-Door Adverting	Impulsion *Javana*							1st Registration	2nd Registration	Life-Continuum
			1st	2nd	3rd	4th	5th	6th	7th			
	Bhavaṅga ↑|↓	*Mano·Dvār·Āvajjana* ↑|↓	↑|↓	↑|↓	↑|↓	↑|↓	↑|↓	↑|↓	↑|↓	*Tadārammaṇa* ↑|↓	*Tadārammaṇa* ↑|↓	*Bhavaṅga* ↑|↓
	Resultant *Vipāka*	Functional *Kiriya*	Presently-Effective Kamma *Diṭṭha·Dhamma·Vedanīya·Kamma*	Indefinitely-Effective Kamma *Aparāpariya·Vedanīya·Kamma*					Subsequently-Effective Kamma *Upappajja·Vedanīya·Kamma*	Resultant *Vipāka*	Resultant *Vipāka*	Resultant *Vipāka*

*DhSA.I.iii.1 *'Kām·Āvacara·Kusala·Pada·Bhājanīyaṁ'* ('Sensual-Sphere Wholesome Section Classification') E.97-99; AbS.iv.17 *'Mano·Dvāra·Vīthi'* ('Mind-Door Process') CMA.iv.12

Notes for Table 5c 'The Mind-Door Process'

- One consciousness lasts one consciousness moment *(citta·kkhaṇa)*, with three stages: arising *(uppāda)* ↑, standing *(ṭhiti)* |, dissolution *(bhaṅga)* ↓.
- Before and after a mental process, arises a number of life-continuum consciousnesses.[403]
- Before this type of mind-door process, there is a five-door process or other mind-door process.[404]
- Cognition follows a fixed procedure, according to the natural law of the mind *(citta·niyāma)*. For example, visual cognition:[405]
  1) Eye-door process that 'picks-up' the object; cognizes colour. (See above table '5b: The Five-Door Process', p.146.)
  2) Mind-door process that perceives the colour; knows the past colour, the object of the eye-door process.
  3) Mind-door process that knows which colour it is; knows the colour's name.
  4) Mind-door process that knows the object's 'meaning'; sees the whole image, a concept determined by past experience (perception *(saññā)*).
  5) Mind-door process that judges and feels. This is the beginning of true cognition. In the preceding mental processes, the volition of the impulsions is only weak, which means the kamma can produce a result only in that life's continuance *(pavatti)*: it cannot produce a rebirth-linking consciousness *(paṭisandhi·citta)*.

It is from the fourth mind-door process onwards that the concept is known: 'a man', 'a woman', 'a pot', 'a sarong', 'gold', 'silver' etc. And it is from that mental process onwards that there is mental proliferation *(papañca)*, and the accomplishment of kamma: accomplished by the mental factor volition *(cetanā)* of each impulsion consciousness, which takes the same object.

With wise attention *(yoniso manasikāra)*, wholesome kamma is accomplished with, for example, respect for and worship of one's teacher, a Buddha-statue or a bhikkhu; knowing one's samatha meditation subject, and with insight knowledge seeing formations as impermanence *(anicca)*, suffering *(dukkha)*, and non-self *(an·atta)*.

With unwise attention *(ayoniso manasikāra)*, unwholesome kamma is accomplished when one sees self, husband, wife, children, property, etc. as existing according to reality: as permanence *(nicca)*, happiness *(sukha)*, and self *(atta)*. With this same object and perception arise countless mental processes (mental formations *(saṅkhāra)*), reinforcing the cognition, until again the mind adverts to a new object.[406]

---

[403] LIFE-CONTINUUM CONSCIOUSNESS: for details, see footnote 306, p.107, and table '5a: Death and Rebirth', p.52.

[404] This mind-door process is five-door post-positional *(pañca·dvār·ānu·bandhakā)*. A mind-door process that arises independently of a five-door process is singly occurring *(visuṁ·siddhā)*.

[405] This procedure is described in DAṬ.ii.439-443 *'Poṭṭhapāda·Sutta·Vaṇṇanā'* ('Description of the Poṭṭhapāda Sutta'): 'First the sound through the ear *(paṭhamaṃ saddaṃ sotena)*; Past [sound] through the second thought *(tītaṃ dutiya·cetasā)*; name through the third consciousness *(nāmaṃ tatiya·cittena)*; meaning through the fourth thought *(atthaṃ catuttha·cetasa)*.'

[406] For details on the volition of the seven impulsions, see following discussion of presently-, subsequently-, and indefinitely-effective kamma.

Mental Phenomena *(nāma·dhamma)* **of the Mind-Door Process** *(mano·dvāra·vīthi)*

Consciousness / Mental Phenomena	Mind-Door Adverting *(Mano·Dvār·Āvajjana)*	Impulsion *(Javana)*	Registration *(Tadārammaṇa)*
Consciousness *(citta)*	1	1	1
Seven Universals *(sabba·citta·sādhāraṇa)*	7	**Unwholesome** *(akusala)** Greed-rooted *(lobha·mūla)* 17/18/19/20/21 Hatred-rooted *(dosa·mūla)* 17/18/19/20 Delusion-rooted *(moha·mūla)* 15 **Wholesome** *(kusala)* Sensual-Sphere *(kām·āvacara)** Knowledge Dissociated *(Ñāṇa·vippayutta)* 31/32/33 Knowledge Associated *(Ñāṇa·sampayutta)* 32/33/34 Fine-Material *(rūp·āvacara)** Fine-Material Jhāna *(rūpa·jjhāna)* 30/31/32/33/34 Immaterial-Sphere *(ārūp·āvacara)** Immaterial Jhāna *(arūpa·jjhāna)* 30 Supramundane *(lokuttara)** Path *(Magga)* } Fruition *(Phala)* } 33/34/35/36	Mental factors as of the investigation consciousness, or the sensual-sphere beautiful resultant-consciousness *(vipāka·citta)*.‡
Six Sundries *(pakiṇṇaka)*			
1. application *(vitakka)*	1		
2. sustainment *(vicāra)*	1		
3. decision *(adhimokkha)*	1		
4. energy *(vīriya)*	1		
5. joy *(pīti)* ⅄			
6. desire *(chanda)* ⅄			
Total	12	16/18/19/20/21/22 — 31/32/33/34/35/36/37	11/12 — 32/33/34

* For the mental phenomena at the arising of the unwholesome impulsions, see tables 2a/2b/ 2c, p.48*ff*; of the sensual-sphere wholesome, tables 3a/3b, p.67*ff*; the fine-material /immaterial sphere, table 3c, p.85*ff*; and the supramundane, table 3d, p.333.

‡ The mental factors at the arising of the sensual-sphere beautiful resultant consciousness correspond to the mental factors at the arising of the wholesome sensual-sphere impulsion, excluding the illimitables and abstinences: see previous column 'Impulsion' under 'Wholesome'.

⅄ The feeling *(vedanā)* (one of the seven universals) associated with the mind-door adverting consciousness is equanimity *(upekkhā)*: hence it cannot be associated with joy *(pīti)*. The mind-door adverting consciousness is furthermore an unrooted consciousness *(ahetuka·citta)*, and they are never associated with desire *(chanda)*.

PRESENTLY-EFFECTIVE KAMMA

The first category of kamma is presently-effective kamma *(diṭṭha·dhamma·vedanīya·kamma)*. It is the unwholesome *(akusala)* or wholesome *(kusala)* volition of the first of the seven impulsions in the fifth mental process onwards.[407]

1st Impulsion *Javana*	2nd Impulsion *Javana*	3rd Impulsion *Javana*	4th Impulsion *Javana*	5th Impulsion *Javana*	6th Impulsion *Javana*	7th Impulsion *Javana*

During just one particular kamma, there arise and perish many billion volitions of these first impulsions. Those that meet the right conditions produce their result in the same continuity of mentality-materiality *(atta·bhāva nāma·rūpa)*, the present life.

Any kamma may produce such presently-effective results. The pleasant, unpleasant, and neutral resultant feelings that arise before, during or after a certain kamma may be the result of presently-effective kamma. For example, the happiness that arises in connection with an offering *(dāna)*, or with training in morality *(sīla)* or meditation *(bhāvanā)*, etc.: we cannot say for sure. Only by discerning dependent origination can one be sure. For sure, however, is the consciousness that arises after a Path Consciousnesses *(Magga·Citta)*. It is presently-effective kamma, because its result arises in the next mind moment as the Fruition Consciousness *(Phala·Citta)*.[408]

At the end of the present life, all the presently-effective kammas that have not matured become lapsed kamma *(ahosi·kamma)*.[409]

SUBSEQUENTLY-EFFECTIVE KAMMA

The second category of kamma is subsequently-effective kamma *(upapajja·vedanīya·kamma)*. It is the unwholesome or wholesome volition of the seventh of the seven impulsions in the fifth mental process onwards.[410] It is called the impulsion

1st Impulsion *Javana*	2nd Impulsion *Javana*	3rd Impulsion *Javana*	4th Impulsion *Javana*	5th Impulsion *Javana*	6th Impulsion *Javana*	7th Impulsion *Javana*

that 'the aim accomplishes' *(attha·sādhaka)*, because as the last of the series of seven identical impulsions, it completes the action. This impulsion accomplishes one's aim to break or keep the precepts, to make offerings, to meditate etc. The repetition of the previous six impulsions *(āsevana)* reinforces this seventh impulsion, so the kamma acquires sufficient strength to be kamma proper, subsequently-effective kamma that produces a result.

During just one particular kamma, there arise and perish many billion volitions of these seventh impulsions. Those that meet the right conditions produce their result in the next life.

Let us say, for example, one has accomplished one of the unwholesome weighty kammas *(garuka·kamma)*. They are called unintervenable kamma *(ān·antariya·kamma)*,[411] because one is certain to be reborn in hell in one's subsequent life. When one accomplished that kamma, there arose and perished many billion volitions of the

[407] See table '5c: The Mind-Door Process' and notes, p.148*f.*

[408] PATH KNOWLEDGE: see table '5e: The Path Process', p.340.

[409] Presently-effective kamma is discussed further at 'Conditions for Present Result', p.157.

[410] See table '5c: The Mind-Door Process' and notes, p.148*f.*

[411] UNINTERVENABLE KAMMA *(ān·antariya kamma)*: see 'Unwholesome Weighty Kamma', p.170.

seventh impulsions: they were certain to become subsequently-effective kammas. But, of those many billion seventh impulsions, only one produces the five aggregates in hell, no more. The remaining volitions of those seventh impulsions may, however, support one's five aggregates in hell. They become subsequently-effective kamma that makes one's suffering's in hell even greater. And they prolong one's life and sufferings in hell. Then, at the end of that life, the remaining subsequently-effective kammas become lapsed kamma. The same principle applies for the seventh volitions of lesser unwholesome kammas that produce rebirth in hell, the animal world or the ghost world.

Let us then say one has accomplished one of the wholesome weighty kammas: one of the eight jhānas.[412] All the impulsions of a jhāna attainment are the same: there are no first, middle five or seventh impulsion: they can all function in any way. But only one volition of that kamma's impulsions produces the five aggregates in the Brahma world, no more. The remaining volitions of those impulsions may, however, support one's five aggregates in the Brahma world.

With the attainment of the Stream-Entry and Once-Return Paths, all subsequently-effective kammas lapse in their capacity to produce rebirth in a woeful state. With the attainment of the Non-Return Path, all subsequently-effective kammas lapse in their capacity to produce their result in the sensual world. Of course, with the attainment of the Arahant Path, there will be no subsequent life: at the end of that life (at one's Parinibbāna: final cessation), absolutely all subsequently-effective kammas lapse in every capacity.

As long as subsequently-effective kamma has not produced its result, its potency can produce an effect at any time in one's subsequent continuity of mentality-materiality: it can produce its result at any time in one's next life.[413] So long as the kamma meets the right conditions, no one, not even a Buddha or other Arahant, avoids experiencing the results of subsequently-effective kamma from their previous life.[414]

At the end of the subsequent life, all the subsequently-effective kammas from the previous life that have not matured become lapsed kamma *(ahosi·kamma)*.

The Venerable Devadatta

A good example of subsequently-effective kamma is the Venerable Devadatta, The Buddha's cousin. We shall mention him many times in the course of our explanations. He accomplished two unwholesome weighty kammas.[415/*189*] First, he pushed a large rock off a cliff, with the intention that it should hit The Buddha

---

[412] The eight jhānas are the four material jhānas, and four immaterial jhānas. See 'Wholesome Weighty Kamma', p.175.

[413] This does not mean, however, that there is a 'store' of subsequently-effective kamma which 'underlies' one's mentality-materiality. See footnote 56, p.15.

[414] Certain kamma of one life may be unable to produce its result because, at the time of death, an earlier kamma produces rebirth in a world where the kamma is unable to produce its result. For example, offering, morality, and meditation of one life may be unable to produce its result in the next life because an earlier kamma has produced rebirth in a woeful state. See quotation, endnote 206, p.252, and 'Achievement and Failure', p.209.

[415] His entire career, from the time he ordained as a bhikkhu till his death and subsequent rebirth in the great Unremitting Hell *(Avīci)*, is explained in Vin.Cv.vii *'Saṁgha·Bhedaka·Kkhandhakaṁ'* ('Sangha-Schismatic Division'), and DhPA.i.12 *'Devadatta·Vatthu'* ('The Case of Devadatta'). He is discussed also p.177, p.194, and p.204.

and kill Him. But the rock hit the ground and split into pieces. One piece struck The Buddha's foot. Although the skin was unbroken, there was a serious bruise because of bleeding within The Buddha's foot. Thus the Venerable Devadatta had with evil intent drawn the blood of a Buddha.[416/*190*] Second, he made a schism in the Sangha: that was the weightier of the two kammas. One of the seventh impulsions of his 'schism kamma' produced his five aggregates in the great Unremitting Hell *(Avīci)*. No other seventh impulsion of that kamma would produce rebirth in hell. But his sufferings in hell are intensified, maintained, and prolonged by other seventh impulsions of that kamma, as well as by the seventh impulsions of his kamma of having with evil intent drawn the blood of a Buddha. And, of course, while he is in hell, there will also be indefinitely-effective kammas from the infinite past which will also intensify, maintain, and prolong his sufferings in hell. But, as we explained in connection with the *'Gaddula·Baddha'* sutta, when the world system is destroyed, he will escape, and be reborn in the human world. And the Pali Texts explain that a hundred thousand aeons later, he will attain Arahantship as a Paccekabuddha called Aṭṭhissara.[417]

Indefinitely-Effective Kamma

The third category of kamma is indefinitely-effective kamma *(aparāpariya·vedanīya·kamma)*. It is the unwholesome or wholesome volition of the five middle impulsions:

1st Impulsion *Javana*	2nd Impulsion *Javana*	3rd Impulsion *Javana*	4th Impulsion *Javana*	5th Impulsion *Javana*	6th Impulsion *Javana*	7th Impulsion *Javana*

the five impulsions between the first and the seventh.[418]

Again, during just one particular kamma, there arise and perish many billion volitions of these middle five impulsions. If, in some life after the subsequent life, one such impulsion meets the right conditions, it produces its result. It may, for example, produce the five aggregates at the rebirth-linking moment in some future life.

Now, as we explained earlier, of all the seventh impulsions of a kamma, only one is able to produce rebirth. But it is different with the middle five impulsions: indefinitely-effective kamma. Each one of them can produce a result. That is why, as explained above, one can owing to one particular kamma be reborn in hell again and again, or be reborn as an animal or ghost again and again, or be reborn as a human being or deva again and again.

With the attainment of the Stream-Entry and Once-Return Paths, all indefinitely-effective kammas lapse in their capacity to produce rebirth in a woeful state. With the attainment of the Non-Return Path, all indefinitely-effective kammas lapse in their capacity to produce their result in the sensual world. Of course, with the attainment of the Arahant Path, there will be no more rebirth: at the end of that last life (at one's Parinibbāna: final cessation), absolutely all indefinitely-effective kammas lapse in every capacity.

Otherwise, so long as indefinitely-effective kamma does not produce its result, it can take effect at any time in one's mentality-materiality continuity: it can pro-

---

[416] In Ap.XXXIX.x.78-79 *'Pubba·Kamma·Pilotika·Buddha-Apadānaṁ'* ('Tatters of Previous Kamma Buddha-Narrative'), The Buddha explains that He suffered this attack because in a past life, He for the sake of wealth threw a step-brother into a ravine, and then crushed him with a rock.

[417] DhPA.i.7 *'Devadatta·Vatthu'* ('The Case of Devadatta')

[418] See table '5c: The Mind-Door Process' and notes, p.148*f.*

duce its result in any future life after the next one.[419] However long one's running on from life to life, this kamma lapses only at one's Parinibbāna (final cessation). Before the attainment of Parinibbāna, no one (not even a Buddha) avoids experiencing the results of indefinitely-effective kamma from past lives.

Lapsed Kamma

The fourth category of kamma is lapsed kamma *(ahosi·kamma)*. It does not designate a special class of kamma: it is simply kamma that has not met the conditions to produce its result: it is defunct, kamma only by name. For non-Arahants, it is simply presently-effective kamma of the present life, and subsequently-effective kamma of the preceding life, that at one's death have not met the right conditions to produce its result. At the Arahant's Parinibbāna, it is all three types of kamma. At the Arahant's Parinibbāna, the innumerable unwholesome and wholesome kammas that she or he accomplished throughout the infinite past, which might have matured in the subsequent life or any time later, become every one of them lapsed kamma *(ahosi·kamma)*.[191] That is why The Buddha says:[420]

> **Consumed is the old, there is no new existence;**
> **With disimpassioned mind for future existence,**
> **They the seed consumed** [have] **no growth-desire:**
> **Steadfast, they expire as this lamp.**[421]

Now, before we continue discussing the workings of kamma, we need to recall what we discussed earlier about the mind: we need to remember the workings of kamma according to ultimate truth.

Uncountable Kammas

The Buddha explains that when the mind is alert, then within a snap of the fingers, very many thousand million consciousnesses arise and perish like a river in full flow: they arise as series, many thousand million mental processes *(citta·vīthi)*.[422]

Human beings exist on what we call the sensual-sphere plane *(kām·āvacara bhūmi)*. The sensual-sphere plane comprises the hells, the ghost and demon worlds, the

---

[419] This does not mean, however, that there is a 'store' of indefinitely-effective kamma which 'underlies' one's mentality-materiality. See footnote 56, p.15.

[420] SuN.ii.1 *'Ratana·Suttaṁ'* ('The Jewel Sutta') (also KhP.v.6)

[421] The commentary to the sutta explains that even though past kamma has arisen and ceased, that kamma is still capable of conveying a rebirth-link, because in ordinary beings, the moisture of craving *(taṇhā·sineha)* is unabandoned. But in those for whom the moisture of craving has dried up because of the Arahant Path, that past kamma is incapable of giving any result in the future, like seeds burned up by fire. Any kamma they now perform is called 'new', and is no more capable of giving a result in the future than a flower is capable of appearing on a plant that has been uprooted, which means it is unable to give any result ('there is no new kamma existence'). Kamma thus having been consumed, the seed of rebirth-linking has been consumed (and SuNA quotes: 'kamma is the field; consciousness the seed.' See endnote 313, p.359). And because there is no longer the desire for 'growth' (for renewed existence) they expire like this lamp, and go beyond the range of concepts, such as any 'material or immaterial'. The lamp referred to is a lamp that expired as The Buddha had been speaking. See also the seed-simile mentioned in endnote 237, p.255.

[422] For an estimated number, see footnote 101, p.41.

human world, and the bottom five deva-worlds. The sensual-sphere plane is where the five material sense bases operate:[423]

1) When a sight base*(rūp·āyatana)* meets an eye base*(cakkh·āyatana)*, there arises eye consciousness*(cakkhu·viññāṇa)*.
2) When a sound base*(sadd·āyatana)* meets an ear base*(sot·āyatana)*, there arises ear consciousness*(sota·viññāṇa)*.
3) When an odour base*(gandh·āyatana)* meets a nose base*(ghān·āyatana)*, there arises nose consciousness*(ghāna·viññāṇa)*.
4) When a flavour base*(ras·āyatana)* meets a tongue base*(jivh·āyatana)*, there arises tongue consciousness*(jivhā·viññāṇa)*.
5) When a tangible base*(phoṭṭhabb·āyatana)* meets a body base*(kāy·āyatana)*, there arises body consciousness*(kāya·viññāṇa)*.

These events take place by the mental process called a five-door process*(pañca·dvāra·vīthi)*.[424] But there is also a sixth sense base, the mind base:

6) When a sight-, sound-, odour-, flavour-, or tangible base, or base of other things*(dhamm·āyatana)*, meets the mind base*(man·āyatana)*, there arises mind consciousness*(mano·viññāṇa)*.

The mental processes by which these events take place are mind-door processes.[425] In each of those mental processes there are seven impulsion consciousnesses*(javana)*. When an impulsion consciousness arises that is unwholesome*(akusala)*, there are minimum sixteen mental phenomena *(nāma·dhamma)*, maximum twenty-two; when it is wholesome*(kusala)*, there are minimum thirty-two mental phenomena, maximum thirty-five.[426] In all cases, one of those mental phenomena is volition*(cetanā)*, and it is volition that forms kamma.[427]

What does this mean in practical terms? It means that during just one particular kamma,[428] there arise and perish many billion volitions of the first impulsions, there arise and perish many billion volitions of the seventh impulsions, and there arise and perish many billion volitions of the middle five impulsions. In other words, during just one particular kamma, there arise and perish many billion volitions that can produce their result in this life (presently-effective kamma); there arise and perish also many billion volitions that can produce their result in the next life (subsequently-effective kamma); and there arise and perish also many billion volitions that can produce their result in some future life after that, even a life many aeons in the future (indefinitely-effective kamma).

This means that throughout one's life, one accomplishes billions of unwholesome or wholesome kammas, billions and billions of times. In fact, you may realize that in one life, the number of unwholesome or wholesome kammas that one accomplishes are without number. That is why, when The Buddha speaks of beings in hell, He speaks of their being tormented for **hundreds of years, many thousands of years, and many hundreds of thousands of years**.[192] Take for example, a butcher who kills cows as her or his livelihood. Over maybe thirty, forty, or even

[423] See e.g. M.III.v.6 *'Cha·Chakka·Suttaṁ'* ('The Six-Sixes Sutta').
[424] See table '5b: The Five-Door Process', p.146.
[425] See table '5c: The Mind-Door Process', p.148.
[426] MENTAL PHENOMENA AT THE ARISING OF UNWHOLESOME IMPULSION CONSCIOUSNESSES: see tables 2a/2b/2c, p.48*ff*; OF WHOLESOME CONSCIOUSNESSES: tables 3a/3b, p.67*ff*.
[427] For details, see 'The Workings of the Mind', p.41.
[428] For the principle of identity, see 'The Principle of Identity', p.203.

fifty years, she or he kills cows. At each particular kamma, each time she or he kills a cow, the unwholesome kammas that are produced are uncountable. Likewise, the devotee who every day offers food to the Sangha. Maybe she or he does it for twenty, thirty, forty, fifty years, or more. Each time she or he makes an offering, at each particular kamma, the wholesome kammas that are produced are uncountable.

Even though human beings and devas exist in the sensual sphere, they can still accomplish kamma of the fine-material- and immaterial sphere. That is when a human being or deva enters into either a fine-material jhāna or immaterial jhāna. As mentioned earlier, such kamma cannot be unwholesome: only wholesome. The impulsion consciousnesses of jhāna are called exalted *(mahaggata)*.

When we accomplish sensual-sphere kamma, many billion consciousnesses arise and perish: they include many thousand million mental processes *(citta·vīthi)*.[429] In each of those mental processes there are seven impulsion consciousnesses *(javana)*. But the number of exalted impulsion consciousnesses that arise and perish when one is in jhāna varies: there is no fixed number. It depends on how long one is in the attainment.[430] Maybe only some billion arise and perish, maybe very, very many billion. According to one's determination, they may arise and perish in such numbers one after the other for an hour, for two hours, even for a whole day, or a whole week. When a beginner enters jhāna, however, only one mental process of absorption with only one jhāna impulsion-consciousness arises and perishes, after which one sinks back into the life continuum.

Of the fine-material or immaterial jhānas that one has attained in one life, only the one that one has been able to maintain up to the near-death moment will produce rebirth in the Brahma world; the rest of one's attainments are without result. If, however, one developed those attainments for the ultimate attainment of Nibbāna, they become what is called pāramī.

We need also remember that the round of rebirth has no beginning. This means that everyone has accomplished countless unwholesome and wholesome kammas during lives that are also countless. But we need to remember that even though we have produced countless kammas over countless lives, not all of them will produce their result. As we have also discussed, not all the impulsions of a kamma produce their result.[431]

The Pali Texts give many examples of how kamma works. And when we do not properly understand the workings of kamma, those examples may sometimes seem too fantastic to be true. But when we understand the workings of the mind, and thereby the workings of kamma, it becomes very easy to understand the extreme power of evil actions, and the supreme power of good actions. Then it becomes very difficult to disbelieve the examples of how kamma works. Then, for example, it becomes very easy for us to believe The Buddha, when He speaks of beings who enjoy sublime happiness in the deva worlds for very many hundred thousand years.[193]

Of course, if we develop the power to discern many past lives, then do we see the workings of kamma for ourselves, and any scepticism we may have is dispelled by our personal knowing and seeing.

---

[429] For an estimated number, see footnote 101, p.41.

[430] In the same way, the number of life-continuum consciousnesses varies.

[431] VbhA.xvi.10.810 *'Dutiya·Bala·Niddeso'* ('Exposition of the Second Power') DD.xvi.-2251-2254, and MA.II.iv.6 *'Aṅgulimāla·Suttaṁ'* ('The Aṅgulimāla Sutta').

Conditions for Present Result

Here, we should like further to discuss presently-effective kamma. Under which conditions does presently-effective kamma produce its result, and under which conditions does it lapse? As mentioned earlier, presently-effective kamma is produced by the volition of the first impulsion: it becomes effective when two conditions are met:[432]

1) It has met no opposition *(paṭipakkhehi anabhibhūtatāya)*: that is, no stronger kamma has overpowered it.
2) It has met the right conditions *(paccaya·visesena paṭiladdha·visesatāya)*: that is, the producing kamma was of the type to produce such a result.

Even so, although it may meet the conditions necessary to mature, and although it supports associated phenomena in the impulsion continuity,[433] it is the weakest of all the impulsions. This is because, being the first impulsion, it is alone. Unlike subsequently- and indefinitely-effective kamma, it has no preceding impulsions to give it power; it has not been reinforced by repetition *(āsevana)*. Its result is therefore only weak, and the right conditions for it to mature are not found beyond the present life. Like a mere flower, it matures only in this life: just as the flower does not produce a fruit, so does this type of kamma not produce a future rebirth. By contrast, subsequently- and indefinitely-effective kamma gain power from repetition. That means they can produce their results either in the next life or in some subsequent life, and they have the power to produce rebirth even in the hells or the deva worlds.

Furthermore, for kamma to produce its result, it needs to meet what is called achievement *(sampatti)* and failure *(vipatti)*.[434] If they are not met, it lapses.

Present Result from Wholesome Kamma

Take, for example, the wholesome kamma of offering *(dāna)*. It can become presently-effective kamma that produces material wealth in this life.[194] But there are four things that need to be fulfilled, four types of achievement *(sampadā)*:[435]

---

[432] This and the following details have been taken from VsMṬ.685 *'Kaṅkhā·Vitaraṇa·Visuddhi·Niddeso'* ('Exposition of the Doubt-Transcendence Purification').

[433] SUPPORTS ASSOCIATED MENTAL PHENOMENA IN THE IMPULSION CONTINUITY: kamma is volition, and volition is a mental factor *(cetasika)*. A mental factor cannot arise independently of a consciousness *(citta)*, and a consciousness cannot arise independently of mental factors. And the mental phenomena necessary for a consciousness to arise are eight: the consciousness, and the seven universal mental factors *(sabba·citta·sādhāraṇa)* (There may be more mental factors, but these seven are the minimum.): 1) contact *(phassa)*, 2) feeling *(vedanā)*, 3) perception *(saññā)*, 4) volition *(cetanā)*, 5) one-pointedness *(ek·aggatā)*, 6) life faculty *(jīvit·indriya)*, 7) attention *(manasikāra)*. In one consciousness moment, the consciousness and its mental factors support each other, as mutuality cause *(aññām·añña paccaya)*: they arise together, cease together, take the same object, and have the same basis (in the material worlds either the eye-, ear-, nose-, tongue-, body-, or heart base; in the immaterial world no base). That is why they are called 'associated phenomena' *(sampayutta·dhamma)*. In the same way, if one of the constituent mental factors is absent, the remaining mental factors cannot arise either, which means the consciousness cannot arise. For details, see the tables for 'The Accomplishment of Kamma' under 'Tables', p.v.

[434] ACHIEVEMENT/FAILURE: destination-, appearance-, time-, and means achievement/failure. They are explained at 'Achievement and Failure', p.209*ff.*

[435] DhPA.x.17 *'Sukha·Sāmaṇera·Vatthu'* ('The Case of the Happy Novice'). See also ex-

(Please see further next page.)

1) Object achievement*(vatthu·sampadā)*: the object of one's offering (the receiver) must be an Arahant or Non-Returner who is able to enter the cessation-attainment*(nirodha·samāpatti)*: the temporary cessation of mentality and consciousness-born materiality.[436]
2) Requisite achievement*(paccaya·sampadā)*: the requisite that is offered must have been obtained in accordance with the Dhamma: according to Right Speech*(Sammā·Vācā)*, Right Action*(Sammā·Kammanta)*, and Right Livelihood *(Sammā·Ājīva)*.
3) Volition achievement*(cetanā·sampadā)*: the offerer's volition must be taintless. She or he must have a happy mind before offering, while offering and after offering, untainted by attachment or anger, etc. expecting nothing in return from the receiver.
4) Extra-factor achievement*(guṇ·ātireka·sampadā)*: the receiver must be an Arahant[437] or Non-Returner who has just emerged from the cessation attainment*(nirodha·samāpatti)*.

If these four types of achievement are present, the volition of the first impulsion consciousness associated with the offering may function as presently-effective kamma. But these four factors alone are not sufficient: the offerer needs also have accomplished sufficient wholesome kamma in past lives, that is, the practice of conduct*(caraṇa)*.[438] Especially, the offerer needs in past lives to have made superior offerings: we discussed such offerings earlier.[439]

What makes an offering superior*(ukkaṭṭha)*? The Buddha explains that five things need to be fulfilled:[440]

1) The offerer must be virtuous, one who observes morality*(sīla)*, who observes the precepts: abstinence from killing, stealing, sexual misconduct, lying, drinking beer and wine, etc., and taking other intoxicants.
2) The gift must have been obtained in accordance with the Dhamma: according to Right Speech*(Sammā·Vācā)*, Right Action*(Sammā·Kammanta)* and Right Livelihood*(Sammā·Ājīva)*.
3) The offerer must have a taintless and happy mind before offering, while offering and after offering, untainted by attachment or anger, etc., expecting nothing in return from the receiver.
4) The offerer must have full faith in the law of kamma and its result.[441]
5) The receiver must also be virtuous, someone who observes the precepts. If the receiver's virtue is accompanied by jhāna, insight knowledge or a Path& Fruition knowledge, that makes the offering even more superior.

---

ample at endnote 195, p.251.

[436] CESSATION ATTAINMENT: it can last up to seven days, depending on the meditator's determination. For details, see S.IV.vii.6 *'Dutiya Kāmabhū·Suttaṁ'* ('The Second Kāmabhū Sutta'), S.IV.II.ii.1 *'Rahogata·Suttaṁ'* ('The Solitude Sutta'), and VsM.xxiii.879 *'Nirodha-·Samāpatti·Kathā'* ('Discussion of the Cessation-Attainment') PP.xxiii.43.

[437] This includes all Buddhas, since they too are Arahants.

[438] See 'Conduct', p.138.

[439] See '2) The Superior Offering', p.70.

[440] M.III.iv.12 *'Dakkhiṇā·Vibhaṅga·Suttaṁ'* ('The Gift-Analysis Sutta')

[441] This makes the offering triple-rooted.

The Field of Gold

The Pali Texts give an example of an offering that took present effect, in the same life: the offering of one Puṇṇa, father of Uttarā-Nandamāta from Rājagaha. The event took place in our Buddha's time:[442]

Puṇṇa and his wife were poor people with deep faith in the Venerable Sāriputta. One festival day, even though Puṇṇa's employer had given him the day off, Puṇṇa went out to plough, because he was too poor to take a holiday.

That day, the Venerable Sāriputta emerged from the cessation attainment *(nirodha·samāpatti)*. And he reviewed the world with his divine eye to see who would benefit most from offering him alms. He saw that Puṇṇa had such accomplished wholesome kamma from a past life, that if he offered alms to the Venerable Sāriputta, that past kamma would function as a decisive supporting cause *(upanissaya·paccaya)* for the offering to produce a result in this life: Puṇṇa would become a rich man, and then make a big offering to The Buddha and Sangha. After listening to The Buddha's inspirational talk he and his wife would also become Stream Enterers.

So, at the suitable time, the Venerable Sāriputta took his bowl and double robe, and went to where Puṇṇa was ploughing. And then he stood at a small distance so Puṇṇa could see him. When Puṇṇa saw him, he became very happy, stopped ploughing, approached the Venerable Sāriputta, and with respect and happiness made the fivefold obeisance. Then the Venerable Sāriputta asked him where some good water might be had. Puṇṇa thought the venerable one wanted to wash his face,[443] so he made a tooth stick out of a creeper nearby, and offered it to the Venerable Sāriputta. While the Venerable Sāriputta was brushing his teeth, Puṇṇa took his bowl and water-strainer, and filled the bowl with fresh, properly strained, clear water, which he then offered to the Venerable Sāriputta.

After washing his face, the Venerable Sāriputta went on his way for alms. Then it occurred to Puṇṇa: 'The Venerable One never came this way before. He probably came today for my benefit. If my wife had come with my food, how good it would have been to offer it to the Venerable One!'

At that time, Puṇṇa's wife was on her way with her husband's food, and met the Venerable Sāriputta. She thought: 'Sometimes we have had alms to offer, but there has been no receiver; sometimes there has been a receiver, but owing to our poverty we have had no alms to offer. How fortunate I am now that I have this Venerable One as the receiver, and this food to offer!'[444] So with much happiness, she offered the food to the Venerable Sāriputta. Then she went home again, prepared fresh food again, and took it to her husband. He was overjoyed to hear of her offering to the Venerable Sāriputta. He took his meal and then had a nap.

When he woke up, he saw the field he had ploughed had turned into gold. Then he reported the matter to the king, who sent carts to collect the gold. But as soon as his men touched the gold, saying it was for the king, it turned back into earth. So the gold was collected in Puṇṇa's name, and the king conferred on him the title of *Bahu·Dhana·Seṭṭhi* (Lord of Much Wealth). Puṇṇa built a new house,

---

[442] AA.I.xiv.7 *'Uttarā·Nanda·Mātā·Vatthu'* ('The Case of Uttarā, Nanda's Mother')

[443] This is sometimes a Pali equivalent to the English euphemism 'ablutions'.

[444] In the past, the object achievement was absent, or the requisite achievement: now all four achievements were present.

and as the house-warming, he held a great alms-offering for The Buddha and Sangha. And with The Buddha's inspirational talk,[445] Puṇṇa and his wife and daughter Uttarā became Stream Enterers *(Sot·Āpanna)*.

Here,

1) Puṇṇa and his wife were virtuous.
2) Their offerings had been obtained in accordance with the Dhamma.
3) They had clear, taintless and happy minds before, during and after their offering.
4) They had strong faith in the law of kamma and its result.

And,

5) The receiver (the Venerable Sāriputta) was an Arahant who had just emerged from the cessation attainment *(nirodha·samāpatti)*. His virtue was perfect, his jhāna attainments were perfect, and his insight knowledge was perfect, for he had attained the Arahant Path&Fruition knowledges.

The decisive factor, however, was that Puṇṇa and his wife had in a past life accomplished a superior wholesome kamma that now matured to support their present offering to the Venerable Sāriputta: that past kamma was the decisive supporting cause *(upanissaya·paccaya)*. Owing to the presence of the right conditions, the volition of the first impulsion of Puṇṇa's mind-door process while offering to the Venerable Sāriputta produced a great result in that very life. This was presently-effective kamma *(diṭṭha·dhamma·vedanīya·kamma)*.[195]

Now, we may find it difficult to believe this story; the present result of Puṇṇa's kamma seems too fantastic to be true. But the result was in fact not fantastic. If we compare it with the result that could have matured as subsequently-effective kamma *(upapajja·vedanīya·kamma)*: as kamma experienced upon rebirth (a result of the volition in the seventh impulsion), the presently-effective kamma was in fact only a paltry result. Why? Because if Puṇṇa's offering matured at his time of death *(maraṇa·kāle)*, it would produce rebirth in the deva-world, with the most superior deva pleasures and the long, long life span of a deva:[446] a field of gold bringing wealth to a human being, with a human being's only short life span, bears no comparison. Puṇṇa's offering could also mature as indefinitely-effective kamma *(aparāpariya·vedanīya·kamma)*: as kamma experienced in some subsequent life, a result of the volition in the middle five impulsions. In that case, it would produce sublime results in very, very many succeeding future lives. Again, the field of gold that he gained as a human being bears no comparison.

All these powerful results could arise because he had accomplished billions of wholesome kammas before, during, and after making his offering to the Venerable Sāriputta. Please remember the workings of the mind. On our plane, the sensual-sphere plane *(kām·āvacara·bhūmi)*, within a snap of the fingers, very many thousand million consciousnesses arise and perish: they include many thousand million mental processes *(citta·vīthi)*.[447] In each of those mental processes there are

---

[445] INSPIRATIONAL TALK: a talk given after an offering, such as is the case here, is in Pali called an *anumodana* talk: *modana* means rejoicing; *anu* means repeatedly. An *anu·modana* talk is thus a talk intended to inspire the minds of the offerers with repeated rejoicing, thereby increasing the good kamma and merit of their action, and making it more memorable.

[446] For The Buddha's explanation of the life spans of devas, see endnote 193, p.251.

[447] For an estimated number, see footnote 101, p.41.

seven impulsion consciousnesses *(javana)*.[448] Each of those impulsion consciousnesses is associated with volition: it produces kamma. If you remember this, you may understand how Puṇṇa could have accomplished so many wholesome kammas, and the story becomes easy to understand.*[196]*

PRESENT RESULT FROM UNWHOLESOME KAMMA

THE VENERABLE AṄGULIMĀLA

Presently-effective kamma can also be unwholesome. There is, for example, Aṅgulimāla.[449] He was a bandit in the kingdom of King Pasenadi of Kosala. He killed very many people. Then, one day, The Buddha saw with His divine eye that Aṅgulimāla would on that day either kill his own mother, or, if The Buddha went to see him, he would ordain as a bhikkhu. And seeing that Aṅgulimāla had sufficient pāramī to become an Arahant in that very life, The Buddha went to see him. Aṅgulimāla ordained, and undertook the bhikkhu's threefold higher training: the higher morality training (observing the bhikkhu's *Pātimokkha*), higher mind training (samatha meditation), and higher wisdom training (insight meditation).

At that time, King Pasenadi was trying to catch Aṅgulimāla. But when he saw Aṅgulimāla had become a peaceful bhikkhu with The Buddha as his teacher, King Pasenadi promised the Venerable Aṅgulimāla to provide him with the four requisites: robes, food, dwelling, and medicine. The Venerable Aṅgulimāla's ordination under The Buddha was the presently-effective kamma that gave this result.

Later, under The Buddha's instruction, the Venerable Aṅgulimāla attained Arahantship. The next day, when he went to Sāvatthī on his almsround, people attacked him. They could remember what he had done as the bandit Aṅgulimāla, and one threw a stone, another threw a stick, and another threw a potsherd. And the Venerable Aṅgulimāla returned to The Buddha with his head bleeding, his bowl broken, and his outer robe torn. When The Buddha saw it, He said to Aṅgulimāla:

Bear it, Brahmin! Bear it Brahmin!
You are experiencing here and now the result of deeds owing to which you might have been tortured for many years, for many hundreds of years, for many thousands of years!

The Buddha was here explaining to him that the attack was the present result of Aṅgulimāla's evil kamma in the present life. If that kamma had produced its result as subsequently-effective, or indefinitely-effective kamma, he would instead have been reborn in hell, and would have suffered for very many thousands of years. But because he had attained Arahantship, his past evil kamma lapsed as subsequently- and indefinitely-effective kamma: it could take effect only in this life as attacks from people.

THE CATTLE BUTCHER

Another example of presently-effective unwholesome kamma is the case of a cattle butcher in Sāvatthi.[450] He would kill cows, select the best cuts for himself and his family, and then sell the rest. Killing cows was his livelihood for fifty-five years. And he would never eat rice unless he had beef to go with it.

---

[448] The Most Venerable Pa-Auk Tawya Sayadaw is here referring only to sensual-sphere mental processes: see footnote 102, p.41.

[449] M.II.iv.6 *'Aṅgulimāla·Suttaṁ'* ('The Aṅgulimāla Sutta')

[450] DhPA.xviii.1-4 *'Mala·Vagga'* ('Stain Chapter')

One day, while it was still light, after he had finished his day's work, he gave his wife some beef to cook for his supper, and then went to the pond to bathe. In the meantime, a friend came to his house, and although the butcher's wife protested, the friend took the piece of beef meant for the butcher's supper.

When the butcher returned, and discovered that his dinner had gone, he took a knife, and went out to the back of his house, where a cow was tethered. The butcher put his hand into the cow's mouth, pulled out the cow's tongue, cut it off at the root, and went back inside. He had the cow's tongue cooked on a bed of coals, placed it on the boiled rice, and sat down to eat. First he took a mouthful of rice, and then a piece of meat. At that very moment, his own tongue was severed at the root, and fell out of his mouth onto the dish of rice. Then, with blood streaming from his mouth, he went into the courtyard of his house, and crawled about on his hands and knees, bellowing just like an ox. His kamma of cutting out the cow's tongue functioned as presently-effective kamma, and produced a present result of terrible pain and sorrow.

After he had crawled about for some time, bellowing like an ox, he died. Owing to his subsequently-effective kamma (he had killed cows for fifty-five years), he was reborn in the great Unremitting Hell *(Avīci)*. And he was destined to experience horrific sufferings in that great and terrible hell for a very, very long time because of uncountable other subsequently-effective unwholesome kammas, as well as uncountable indefinitely-effective unwholesome kammas that now met the right conditions to mature: the round of rebirth has no beginning, so every being has accomplished much evil kamma. When the conditions are right, that evil kamma from past lives matures, and one's suffering is prolonged.

Sometimes, a being in hell reaches the end of the kamma that produced rebirth in hell, and he passes away in hell. But he does not escape from hell, because another indefinitely-effective kamma of that same kamma produces rebirth in hell again, and when he again passes away in hell, another indefinitely-effective kamma of that same kamma does it again, and so on.[451] And even when he does escape from hell, and is reborn as a ghost, that same kamma functions as indefinitely-effective kamma, so that he as a ghost is tormented in some similar way.[197]

That concludes our discussion of kamma according to the time of effect (when it takes effect): presently-effective-, subsequently-effective-, indefinitely-effective-, and lapsed kamma. But in order to get the whole picture, we need also to understand that these four types of kamma work over three periods: the past, the present, and the future.

The Workings of Kamma Past — Present — Future

In one continuity of mentality-materiality, there is always past kamma, present kamma, and unless one attains Arahantship, there is also always future kamma. In the same way, there are past results of kamma, present results of kamma, and future results of kamma. According to result, we have thus six workings of past kamma, four workings of present kamma, and two workings of future kamma.

---

[451] This is an example of how the kamma that produces the rebirth-linking consciousness may also be from another past life. See mention of The Buddha's explanation, footnote 460, p.170.

THE SIX WORKINGS OF PAST KAMMA

The *Paṭisambhidā·Magga*,[452] by the Venerable Sāriputta, describes the six workings of past kamma *(atīta·kamma)*:[453]

[1] **There was kamma, there was kamma result.**
[2] **There was kamma, there was no kamma result.**
[3] **There was kamma, there is kamma result.**
[4] **There was kamma, there is no kamma result.**
[5] **There was kamma, there will be kamma result.**
[6] **There was kamma, there will be no kamma result.**

Let us try to see how this is with regard to the different kinds of kamma that we have discussed: presently-effective kamma, subsequently-effective kamma, indefinitely-effective kamma, and lapsed kamma.

PAST KAMMA, PAST RESULT

The first working of past kamma has a past result. How? In all one's past lives, uncountable unwholesome and wholesome presently-effective kammas were accomplished: they were the volitions of the first impulsions of each kamma. Those kammas that met the right conditions produced their result in that same life.

For example, the pleasant, unpleasant, and neutral resultant feelings that arose in connection with a certain kamma in a past life may have been the result of a presently-effective kamma: for example, the feelings that arose in connection with an offering *(dāna)* in that same past life, or with training in morality *(sīla)* or meditation *(bhāvanā)*. Another example is the arising of one of the three lower Path Consciousnesses *(Magga·Citta)* in a past life: its result arose in the next mind moment as the Fruition Consciousness *(Phala·Citta)*.

Also, in all one's past lives, uncountable unwholesome and wholesome subsequently-effective kammas were accomplished: they were the volitions of the seventh impulsions of each kamma. Those kammas that met the right conditions produced their result in the subsequent life: the very next life. But again, if in a past life, one such volition produced the subsequent life's rebirth-linking consciousness and mentality-materiality, the remaining volitions of that kamma's seventh impulsions either lapsed, or supported those aggregates throughout the subsequent life: prolonging one's life and sufferings in a woeful state, or happiness in the human or heavenly world.

Furthermore, in all one's past lives, uncountable unwholesome and wholesome indefinitely-effective kammas were accomplished: they were the volitions of the middle five impulsions of each kamma. Those kammas that met the right conditions produced their results in a certain past life after the subsequent past life.

In these cases, the kamma is past, and fulfilled its function; its result is also past, and fulfilled its function. The kamma came to be and ceased to be in the past; its result came to be and ceased to be in the past. As it says in the *Paṭisambhidā·Magga*: **There was kamma, there was kamma result.**

---

[452] *PAṬISAMBHIDĀ·MAGGA*: a text by the Venerable Sāriputta, which explains in great and purely practical detail how understanding is produced by undertaking the training laid down by The Buddha.

[453] PsM.I.vii.234 *'Kamma·Kathā'* ('Discussion of Kamma') PD.I.vii.1

Past Kamma, No Past Result

The second working of past kamma has no past result. That is, at the end of each past life, all the presently-effective and subsequently-effective kammas that failed to meet the right conditions to produce their result became lapsed kamma.

For example, with rebirth in the human or heavenly world in a past life, all subsequently-effective kammas from the previous life that could have produced their result in a woeful state failed to meet the right conditions to produce their result, and became lapsed kamma at the end of that life. With the attainment of the Stream-Entry Path, or Once-Return Path in the past, however, all subsequently, and indefinitely-effective kammas that were accomplished before that attainment, and which afterwards could have produced their result in a woeful state became lapsed kamma at once. Also, with rebirth in the fine-material or immaterial world in a past life, all subsequently-effective kammas from the previous life that could have produced their result in the sensual world, became lapsed kamma at the end of that life. And with attainment of the Non-Return Path in the past, all subsequently and indefinitely-effective kammas that afterwards could have produced their result in the sensual world became lapsed kamma at once.

In these cases, the kamma was in the past, and fulfilled its function; its result lapsed, and did not fulfil its function. The kamma came to be and ceased to be in the past; its result never came to be. As it says in the *Paṭisambhidā·Magga*: **There was kamma, there was no kamma result.**

Past Kamma, Present Result

The third working of past kamma has a present result: in this life. That is, in the previous life, uncountable unwholesome and wholesome subsequently-effective kammas were accomplished: they were the volitions of the seventh impulsions of each kamma. Those kammas that meet the right conditions produce their result in the present life: this life.

Also, in all one's past lives, uncountable unwholesome and wholesome indefinitely-effective kammas were accomplished: they were the volitions of the middle five impulsions of each kamma. Those kammas that meet the right conditions produce their results in this life.

In these cases, the kamma is past, and fulfilled its function; its result is present, and fulfils its function. The kamma came to be and ceased to be in the past; its result comes to be and ceases to be in the present. As it says in the *Paṭisambhidā·Magga*: **There was kamma, there is kamma result.**

Past Kamma, No Present Result

The fourth working of past kamma has no present result. That is, at the end of this life, all the subsequently-effective kammas from the previous life that fail to meet the right conditions to produce their result in this life become lapsed kamma.[454]

[454] The Most Venerable Sayadaw refers to two clear examples. The first example, is the Venerable Devadatta: he was reborn in hell because of making a schism in the Sangha: that is the weighiest of the five unwholesome weighty kammas. And since weighty kammas are subsequently-effective, his unwholesome weighty kamma of drawing the blood of (bruising) a living Buddha with evil intent, as well as his wholesome kamma of jhāna, and other subsequently-effective unwholesome and wholesome kamma, lapsed in

(Please see further next page.)

For example, with rebirth in the human or a heavenly world in this life, all subsequently-effective kammas from the previous life that could have produced their result in a woeful state fail to meet the right conditions to produce their result, and become lapsed kamma at the end of this life. With the attainment of the Stream-Entry- or Once-Return Path in the previous life, however, all subsequently-effective kammas that could have produced their result in a woeful state in this life became lapsed kamma at once. Also, with rebirth in the fine-material or immaterial world in this life, all subsequently-effective kammas from the previous life that could have produced their result in the sensual world in this life become lapsed kamma at the end of this life. And with attainment of the Non-Return Path in the previous life, all subsequently and indefinitely-effective kammas that could have produced their result in the sensual world in this life became lapsed kamma at once.

In these cases, the kamma was in the past, and fulfilled its function; its result has lapsed, and has not fulfilled its function. The kamma came to be and ceased to be in the past; its result has never come to be. As it says in the *Paṭisambhidā-·Magga*: **There was kamma, there is no kamma result.**

Past Kamma, Future Result

The fifth working of past kamma has a future result. That is, in all one's past lives, unwholesome and wholesome indefinitely-effective kamma was accomplished. That which meets the right conditions will produce its result in the subsequent life, or a later life. The kamma is past, and fulfilled its function; its result is in the future, yet to be experienced, yet to fulfil its function. The kamma came to be and ceased to be in a certain past life; its result will come to be and cease to be in the future. As it says in the *Paṭisambhidā·Magga*: **There was kamma, there will be kamma result.**

Past Kamma, No Future Result

The sixth working of past kamma has no future result. That is, with the attainment of the Stream-Entry Path, or the Once-Return Path in a past life or this life, all indefinitely-effective kammas that in the future could have produced their result in a woeful state became lapsed kamma. With the attainment of the Non-Return Path in a past life or this life, all indefinitely-effective kammas that in the

their capacity to give rebirth. If, however, they meet the right conditions, they will function as subsequently-effective reinforcing, frustrating, and interceptive kamma in his subsequent life in hell. If they do not meet the right conditions, they lapse at the end of that subsequent life. But the indefinitely-effective potency of those kammas (and any other unwholesome and wholesome kammas of the infinite past) may still function as productive, reinforcing, frustrating, and interceptive kamma until he attains Parinibbāna as a Paccekabuddha, at the end of a hundred thousand aeons: see further 'The Venerable Devadatta', p.152. The second example is Brahma Sahampati: he specialized in the first jhāna, and one such first jhāna gave him rebirth in the Brahma world: all the remaining jhānas, including other first jhānas, lapsed in their capacity to give rebirth in the Brahma world. But they did not lapse in their capacity as pāramī. Also other jhāna kammas of the past, as well as sensual-sphere wholesome kammas of, for example, offering, morality, and samatha [before jhāna] and vipassanā practice, accomplished in that life and in previous lives, may function as pāramī, reinforcing other wholesome kammas, and frustrating and intercepting unwholesome kammas: see further 'Brahmā Sahampati', p.177, and 'Non-Return', p.337).

future could have produced their result in the sensual world became lapsed kamma. And with the attainment of the Arahant Path in this life, there will be no future life after this: at one's Parinibbāna, at the end of this life, absolutely all subsequently and indefinitely-effective kammas will lapse.

In these cases, the kamma is past, and fulfilled its function; its result has lapsed, and will not fulfil its function. The kamma came to be and ceased to be in a certain past life; its result will never come to be. As it says in the *Paṭisambhidā-·Magga*: **There was kamma, there will be no kamma result.**

The Four Workings of Present Kamma

The *Paṭisambhidā·Magga* describes also the four workings of present kamma *(paccuppanna·kamma)*:[455]

[1] **There is kamma, there is kamma result.**
[2] **There is kamma, there is no kamma result.**
[3] **There is kamma, there will be kamma result.**
[4] **There is kamma, there will be no kamma result.**

Let us try to see how this is with regard to presently-effective-, subsequently-effective-, and indefinitely-effective kamma.

Present Kamma, Present Result

The first working of present kamma has a present result: in this life. That is, in this life, uncountable unwholesome and wholesome presently-effective kammas are accomplished: they are the volitions of the first impulsions of each kamma. Those kammas that meet the right conditions produce their result in this life.

For example, the pleasant, unpleasant, and neutral resultant feelings that arise before, during, and after a certain kamma in this life may be the result of presently-effective kamma: again for example, the feelings arising in connection with an offering *(dāna)* in this life, or with training in morality *(sīla)* or meditation *(bhāvanā)*. Another example is the arising of a Path Consciousness *(Magga·Citta)* in this life: the result arises in the next mind moment as the Fruition Consciousness *(Phala·Citta)*.

In these cases, the kamma is present, and fulfils its function; its result is also present, and fulfils its function. Both come to be and cease to be in this life. As it says in the *Paṭisambhidā·Magga*: **There is kamma, there is kamma result.**

Present Kamma, No Present Result

The second working of present kamma has no present result. At the end of this life, all the presently-effective kammas that fail to meet the right conditions to produce their result in this life become lapsed kamma.[456]

Now, the kamma is present, and has fulfilled its function; its result has lapsed, and has not fulfilled its function. The kamma has come to be and ceased to be in this life; its result has never come to be. As it says in the *Paṭisambhidā·Magga*: **There is kamma, there is no kamma result.**

Present Kamma, Future Result

The third working of present kamma has a future result. That is, in this life, uncountable unwholesome and wholesome subsequently-effective kammas are ac-

---

[455] PsM.I.vii.234 *'Kamma·Kathā'* ('Discussion of Kamma') PD.I.vii.1

[456] For two clear examples, see footnote 454, p.164.

complished: they are the volitions of the seventh impulsions of each kamma. Those kammas that meet the right conditions will produce their results in the subsequent life: the very next life.

Also, in this life, uncountable unwholesome and wholesome indefinitely-effective kammas are accomplished: they are the volitions of the middle five impulsions of each kamma. Those kammas that meet the right conditions will produce their results in a certain future life after the subsequent life.

In these cases, the kamma is present, and fulfils its function; its result is in the future, yet to be experienced, yet to fulfil its function. The kamma comes to be and ceases in this life; its result will come to be and cease to be in the future. As it says in the *Paṭisambhidā·Magga*: **There is kamma, there will be kamma result.**

Present Kamma, No Future Result

The fourth working of present kamma has no future result. That is, at the end of the subsequent life, all the subsequently-effective kammas from this life that fail to meet the right conditions to produce their result in the subsequent life become lapsed kamma.

For example, with rebirth in the human or a heavenly world in the subsequent life, all subsequently-effective kammas from this life that could have produced their result in a woeful state in the subsequent life, will become lapsed kamma at the end of the subsequent life. With the attainment of the Stream-Entry- or Once-Return Path in this life, however, all subsequently and indefinitely-effective kammas that could have produced their result in a woeful state in the subsequent life have become lapsed kamma at once. Also, with rebirth in the fine-material or immaterial world in the subsequent life, all subsequently-effective kammas from this life that could have produced their result in the sensual world in the subsequent life will have become lapsed kamma at the end of that life. With the attainment of the Non-Return Path in this life, all subsequently and indefinitely-effective kammas that could have produced their result in the sensual world in the subsequent life become lapsed kamma at once. Finally, with the attainment of the Arahant Path in this life, there will be no future life: at one's Parinibbāna, at the end of this life, absolutely all subsequently and indefinitely-effective kammas will lapse.

In these cases, the kamma is present, and fulfils its function; its result will lapse, and will not fulfil its function. The kamma comes to be and ceases to be in this life; its result will never come to be. As it says in the *Paṭisambhidā·Magga*: **There is kamma, there will be no kamma result.**

The Two Workings of Future Kamma

The *Paṭisambhidā·Magga* describes also the two workings of future kamma *(anāgata·kamma)*:[457]

[1] **There will be kamma, there will be no kamma result.**
[2] **There will be kamma, there will be kamma result.**

Let us try to see how this is with regard to presently-effective-, subsequently-effective-, and indefinitely-effective kamma. Again, we shall discuss them only in the case of someone who is still alive: a common person, a Noble One, or an Arahant who has not yet attained Parinibbāna.

---

[457] PsM.I.vii.234 *'Kamma·Kathā'* ('Discussion of Kamma') PD.I.vii.1

FUTURE KAMMA, FUTURE RESULT

The first working of future kamma has a future result. That is, unless one attains Arahantship, one will, in all one's future lives, accomplish uncountable unwholesome and wholesome presently-effective kammas: they will be the volitions of the first impulsions of each kamma. Those kammas that meet the right conditions will produce their result in that same life.

For example, the pleasant, unpleasant, and neutral resultant feelings that arise in connection with a certain kamma in a future life may be the result of a presently-effective kamma: again, for example, the feelings arising in connection with an offering *(dāna)* in a future life, or with training in morality *(sīla)* or meditation *(bhāvanā)*. Another example is the arising of a Path Consciousness *(Magga·Citta)* in a future life: its result will arise in the next mind moment as the Fruition Consciousness *(Phala·Citta)*.

Also, unless one attains Arahantship, one will, in all one's future lives, accomplish uncountable unwholesome and wholesome subsequently-effective kamma: they will be the volitions of the seventh impulsions of each kamma. Those kammas that meet the right conditions will produce their result in the subsequent life: the very next life.

Furthermore, unless one attains Arahantship, one will, in all one's future lives, accomplish unwholesome and wholesome indefinitely-effective kamma: they will be the volitions of the middle five impulsions of each kamma. Those kammas that meet the right conditions will produce their results in a certain future life after the subsequent future life.

In these cases, the kamma will be in the future, and will fulfil its function; its result will be in the future, yet to be experienced, yet to fulfil its function. The kamma will come to be and cease to be in the future; its result will come to be and cease to be in the future. As it says in the *Paṭisambhidā·Magga*: **There will be kamma, there will be kamma result.**

FUTURE KAMMA, NO FUTURE RESULT

The second working of future kamma has no future result. That is, at the end of each future life, all the presently-effective kammas that in that life fail to meet the right conditions to produce their result will become lapsed kamma. In the same way, at the end of each future life, all the subsequently-effective kammas from the previous future life that fail to meet the right conditions to produce their result will become lapsed kamma.

For example, with rebirth in the human or heavenly world in a future life, all subsequently-effective kammas from the previous future life that could have produced their result in a woeful state will become lapsed kamma at the end of that future life. With the attainment of the Stream-Entry Path, or Once-Return Path in a future life, however, all subsequently and indefinitely-effective kammas that could have produced their result in a woeful state in that future life will become lapsed kamma at once. Likewise, with the attainment of the Non-Return Path in a future life, all subsequently and indefinitely-effective kammas that could have produced their result in the sensual world in the future, will become lapsed kamma. Finally, with the attainment of the Arahant Path in the future, there will be no more future: at one's Parinibbāna, at the end of that future life, absolutely all subsequently and indefinitely-effective kammas will lapse.

In these cases, the kamma will be in the future, and will fulfil its function; its result will lapse, and will not fulfil its function. The kamma will come to be and cease to be in the future; its result will never come to be. As it says in the *Paṭi-sambhidā·Magga*: **There will be kamma, there will be no kamma result.**

That concludes our discussion of the workings of kamma, past, present, and future kamma. We have also given some examples of how it works: no doubt, one could think of more examples.

CONCLUSION

As we discuss kamma further, please keep this principle in mind: that unwholesome and wholesome kamma was accomplished in the past, is accomplished in the present, and (so long as we are not Arahants) will be accomplished in the future. Certain past unwholesome or wholesome kamma produced its unwholesome or wholesome result in the past; certain past and present unwholesome or wholesome kamma produces its unwholesome or wholesome result in the present; and certain past, present, and future unwholesome or wholesome kamma will produce its unwholesome or wholesome result in the future. Lastly, in the past, certain unwholesome or wholesome kamma lapsed, in the present certain unwholesome or wholesome kamma lapses, and in the future, certain unwholesome or wholesome kamma will lapse.[458] It is the same with blameful kamma *(s·āvajjaṁ kammaṁ)* and blameless kamma *(anavajjaṁ kammaṁ)*; dark kamma *(kaṇhaṁ kammaṁ)* and bright kamma *(sukkaṁ kammaṁ)*; happiness-producing kamma *(sukh-·udrayaṁ kammaṁ)* and pain-producing kamma *(dukkh·udrayaṁ kammaṁ)*; happiness-resulting kamma *(sukha·vipākaṁ kammaṁ)* and pain-resulting kamma *(dukkha·vipākaṁ kammaṁ)*. Please remember, these workings of kamma work for everybody. Only the Arahant is exempt from accomplishing kamma. But until her or his Parinibbāna, even the Arahant is not exempt from experiencing happiness and pain because of past kamma. Even if he is a Buddha, this will take place.[459]

That concludes our explanation of the first four categories of kamma: presently-effective-, subsequently-effective-, indefinitely-effective-, and lapsed kamma.

---

[458] PsM.I.vii.235 *'Kamma·Kathā'* ('Discussion of Kamma') PD.I.vii.2-3

[459] For details, see 'The Two Types of Parinibbāna', p.343.

ORDER OF EFFECT

The second four categories of kamma we shall discuss are according to which type of kamma takes effect first:[460]

1) Weighty kamma........ *(garuka·kamma)*
2) Habitual kamma........ *(āciṇṇa·kamma)*
3) Near-death kamma....... *(āsanna·kamma)*
4) Accomplished kamma... *(katattā·kamma)*

Weighty kamma is so called because it matures first of all. When there is no weighty kamma, a habitual kamma or near-death kamma matures, depending on which is the stronger at the time of death. When there is none of those two, an accomplished kamma from that very life or a previous life matures.

WEIGHTY KAMMA,

When weighty kamma *(garuka·kamma)* is unwholesome, it is reprehensible, and very unskilful kamma; when weighty kamma is wholesome, it is superior, and very skilful kamma. When there is only one weighty kamma, it will always be subsequently-effective kamma of great power. It is certain to produce a correspondingly powerful result in the form of a very unhappy or very happy rebirth in the next life. The result of weighty kamma cannot be avoided. And when there are several weighty kammas, the weightiest (unwholesome or wholesome) will work as subsequently-effective kamma: any other weighty kamma will be indefinitely-effective kamma.

UNWHOLESOME WEIGHTY KAMMA

The unwholesome weighty kammas are six:

1) To deprive one's mother of life *(mātaraṁ jīvitā voropeti)*
2) To deprive one's father of life *(pitaraṁ jīvitā voropeti)*
3) To deprive an Arahant of life *(Arahantaṁ jīvitā voropeti)*
4) With evil intent to draw a Tathāgata's blood *(duṭṭhena cittena Tathāgatassa lohitaṁ uppādeti)*
5) To make a schism in the Sangha *(Saṅghaṁ bhindati)*
6) To hold a persistent wrong view *(niyata·micchā·diṭṭhi)*: that is, at the time of death to hold to a wrong view that denies the workings of kamma.

If in one life, one has accomplished one of these six kammas alone, it will always be subsequently-effective kamma. Its result is certain rebirth in hell:[461] it cannot

[460] VsM.xix.686 (and VsMṬ) *'Kaṅkhā·Vitaraṇa·Visuddhi·Niddeso'* ('Exposition of the Doubt-Transcendence Purification') PP.xix.15, and AbS.v.51 *'Kamma·Catukkaṁ'* ('The Kamma Tetrad') CMA.v.19. The explanation that follows is from VsMṬ. It quotes M.III.iv.6 *'Mahā-·Kamma·Vibhaṅga·Suttaṁ'* ('The Great Kamma-Analysis Sutta'). There The Buddha explains how the incomplete knowledge of other teachers leads to misleading statements about the workings of kamma, because they do not realize that the kamma which produces the rebirth-linking consciousness is not necessarily the kamma that they have observed: it may be an earlier kamma. See quotation endnote 206, p.252.

[461] AA.I.XVI.iii *'Tatiya·Vaggo'* ('Third Chapter') explains that those who have accomplished the first four (killing one's father, killing one's mother, killing an Arahant, with evil intent drawing a Buddha's blood) escape from hell when their kamma has ceased, which is no later than the end of the aeon *(kappa)*. Those who have caused a schism in the Sangha, escape from hell only at the end of the aeon (See A.X.I.iv.9 *'Paṭhama-Ānanda·Suttaṁ'* ('The First Ānanda Sutta')). The latter three kammas cannot be accomplished very early or late in the aeon, because there is at that time no Buddha's Dispensation *(Buddha-*

(Please see further next page.)

be intervened by any other kamma.[462] That is why these kammas are also called **unintervenable kamma***(ān·antariya kamma)*.[463] The first five types take effect as weighty kammas as soon as one has accomplished the unwholesome volitional act. But the sixth (holding a persistent wrong view) takes effect as weighty kamma only if one holds the wrong view up to the time of death *(maraṇa·kāla)*: up to the last mental process before the decease consciousness arises.[464]

Not all wrong views, however, lead to rebirth in hell. One may, for example, hold the view that the self is eternal, and that according to one's conduct one is reborn in either good or bad destinations. The view that the self is eternal is an eternity view: that is a wrong view. But the view that unwholesome kamma leads to an unhappy destination, and wholesome kamma leads to a happy destination, is a doctrine of action*(kiriya·vādī)*: it does not deny the workings of kamma. This is why, if one with such a view has accomplished wholesome kamma, one may be reborn in either the human world, the deva world or Brahma world.[198]

The persistent, strongly held wrong view that alone can lead to rebirth in hell is the view that somehow denies kamma and its result: either an annihilation view or an eternity view.

The Three Views that Deny the Workings of Kamma

There are three types of view that in this way deny the workings of kamma and its result:[465]

1) Inefficacy View*(akiriya·diṭṭhi)*: it denies the workings of unwholesome and wholesome kammas.
2) Rootlessness View*(ahetuka·diṭṭhi)*: it denies the root, a cause, of results.
3) Non-Existence View*(n·atthika·diṭṭhi)*: it denies the result of any cause.

The Inefficacy View

The inefficacy view*(akiriya·diṭṭhi)* denies the workings of unwholesome and wholesome actions, which is to deny ***akusala*** and ***kusala kamma***. In The

---

·Sāsana). The outcome of holding a persistent wrong view is explained at 'The Weightiest Unwholesome Kamma', p.173.

[462] See, for example, The Buddha's words with regard to King Ajātasattu (who killed his father), quoted p.174.

[463] To explain what a Noble Disciple cannot do, this term appears in MA.III.ii.5 *'Bahu·Dhātuka·Suttaṁ'* ('The Many Types of Element Sutta'), AA.I.xv.1 *'Aṭṭhāna·Pāḷi'* ('Impossible Text'), and DhSA.iii.1035 *'Tika·Nikkhepa·Kaṇḍaṁ'* ('Threes Summarizing Section') E.462: 'In the triplet on wrongfulness, 'immediate' [here translated as 'unintervenable'] means giving results without intervening [time]. This is an equivalent term for such acts [kamma] as matricide [here translated directly as 'mother-killing'], etc. Indeed, when one such act is done, another act is not able, by ejecting it, to find opportunity for its own result. For even the action of one who all his lifetime gives the four requisites to the Order [Sangha] with The Buddha as the head, lodged to its full capacity in a monastery which he may have caused to be built, with golden shrines the size of Mount Meru and jewelled walls as ample as a world-system, cannot inhibit the [subsequent] result of these kammas.'

[464] The decease consciousness's object is the object of that life's life continuum. See table '5a: Death and Rebirth', p.52.

[465] These three views arise from the same basic wrong view: the view that denies kamma and its result. How they arise from the identity view is explained p.14.

Buddha's time, this view was taught by one Pūraṇa Kassapa.[199] The Buddha explains how the identity view gives rise to such a wrong view:[466]

When there is [materiality... feeling... perception... formations]**, consciousness, bhikkhus, by clinging to** [materiality...] **consciousness, by adhering to** [materiality...] **consciousness, such a view as this** [inefficacy view] **arises:**

'If, with a razor-rimmed wheel, one were to make living beings of this earth into one mass of flesh, into one heap of flesh, because of this there would be no evil, and no outcome of evil.

If one were to go along the south bank of the Ganges killing and slaughtering, mutilating and making others mutilate, torturing and making others torture, because of this there would be no evil, and no outcome of evil.

If one were to go along the north bank of the Ganges offering gifts and making others give gifts, making offerings and making others make offerings, because of this there would be no merit, and no outcome of merit.

By offering, by taming oneself, by self-control, by speaking truth, there is no merit, and no outcome of merit.'

This wrong view *(micchā·diṭṭhi)* denies the efficacy of unwholesome and wholesome actions, which is to deny the efficacy of kamma: The Buddha calls it the inefficacy view *(akiriya·diṭṭhi)*. Next we shall discuss the rootlessness view.

The Rootlessness View

The rootlessness view *(ahetuka·diṭṭhi)* holds that events are determined by fate, or by circumstance, or by nature (biology), denying that events have a root or cause.[467] In The Buddha's time, it was taught by one Makkhali Gosāla.[199]

Also here, The Buddha explains how the identity view gives rise to such a wrong view:[468]

When there is [materiality... feeling... perception... formations]**, consciousness, bhikkhus, by clinging to** [materiality...] **consciousness, by adhering to** [materiality...] **consciousness, such a view as this** [rootlessness view] **arises:**

'There is no root and there is no cause for the defilement of beings; without root and without cause beings are defiled.

There is no root and there is no cause for the purification of beings; without root and without cause beings are purified.[200]

There is no power, there is no energy, there is no manly strength, there is no manly endurance.

All beings, all breathers, all creatures, all living beings, are without ability, without power, and without energy: moulded by fate, circumstance, and nature, they experience pleasure and pain in the six classes.'

The six classes of pleasure and pain taught here by Makkhali Gosāla are a sixfold system of purification that he said has no cause either.

This wrong view *(micchā·diṭṭhi)* denies that events have a root or cause, which is to deny that there are causes such as kamma:[469] The Buddha calls it the rootlessness view *(ahetuka·diṭṭhi)*. Next we shall discuss the non-existence view.

---

[466] S.III.III.i.6 *'Karoto·Suttaṁ'* ('The "Doing" Sutta')

[467] These three determinants are equivalent to the wrong views of: 1) fatalism, 2) determinism, 3) biological determinism. See details in the commentary to D.i.2 *'Sāmañña-·Phala·Suttaṁ'* ('The Asceticism-Fruit Sutta')

[468] S.III.III.i.7 *'Hetu·Suttaṁ'* ('The Root Sutta')

[469] In the *Paṭṭhāna (Causal Relations)*, The Buddha enumerates and elaborates twenty-four types of cause: kamma is the thirteenth.

THE NON-EXISTENCE VIEW

The non-existence view *(n·atthika·diṭṭhi)* holds that only materiality has true existence, and denies that actions have any result. For that reason, it denies also that there is rebirth, that there are other planes of existence, and denies that there are teachers such as The Buddha who know and see these things. In The Buddha's time, it was taught by one Ajita Kesakambali.*[201]*

Here again, The Buddha explains how the identity view gives rise to such a wrong view:[470]

When there is [materiality... feeling... perception... formations], **consciousness, bhikkhus, by clinging to** [materiality...] **consciousness, by adhering to** [materiality...] **consciousness, such a view as this** [non-existence view] **arises:**

'There is no offering, there is no almsgiving, there is no sacrifice; there is no fruit or result of good and bad kamma; there is no this world, there is no other world; there is no mother, there is no father; there are no beings born spontaneously; there are not in the world any ascetics and Brahmins, rightly faring, rightly practising, who (with direct knowledge) having themselves realized this world and the other world declare it.

This person consists of the four great essentials. When one dies, earth enters and rejoins the earth-body; water enters and rejoins the water-body; fire enters and rejoins the fire-body; wind enters and rejoins the wind-body: the faculties are transformed into space. With the bier as the fifth, men carry away the corpse. As far as the cemetery is the body known;*[202]* the bones whiten. Sacrifices end in ashes. A stupid wisdom is this offering.*[203]*

When anyone maintains the existence-doctrine [that there is offering, there is a result of good and bad actions, etc.], **it is false, idle talk. Fools and the wise with the breakup of the body are annihilated, perish and do not exist after death.'**

This wrong view *(micchā·diṭṭhi)* The Buddha calls the non-existence view *(n·atthika·diṭṭhi)*. It is an annihilation view *(uccheda·diṭṭhi)*, and is the same as the materialist view.[471] It is also called a non-existence doctrine *(n·atthi·vāda)*, and is the opposite of the existence-doctrine *(atthi·vāda)*, basic Right View *(Sammā·Diṭṭhi)*.*[204]*

THE WEIGHTIEST UNWHOLESOME KAMMA

Grasping such wrong views at the time of death is the weightiest of the six unwholesome weighty kammas, and results in one's suffering in hell for aeons. As long as that kamma's potency is still working, one will not escape from hell even at the destruction of the world system.[472] At that time, (as mentioned when we discussed the *'Gaddula·Baddha'* sutta) all beings in hell are reborn in the human or deva world, and there develop jhāna, which results in their being reborn in the Brahma world. But the ones who are in hell because of grasping one of these wrong views are reborn in one of the woeful states that lie in the interstices between other world systems that are not undergoing destruction.[473/*205*]

---

[470] S.III.III.i.5 *'N·Atthi·Dinna·Suttaṁ'* ('The There-Is-No-Offering Sutta')

[471] For the materialist view described by The Buddha in D.i.1 *'Brahma·Jāla·Suttaṁ'* ('The Supreme-Net Sutta'), see quotation at 'Annihilation View', p.12.

[472] The destruction of the world system is discussed at 'There Will Come a Time, Bhikkhus', p.3*ff.*

[473] AA.I.XVI.iii *'Tatiya·Vaggo'* ('Third Chapter') explains that as the entire cosmos burns up, the beings who have been born in the interstices between world systems suffer accordingly. And when a new cosmos system is formed, they take rebirth again in hell.

If, however, one gives up that wrong view before the time of death, it does not become an unwholesome weighty kamma.[206] An example of this is the Venerable Sāriputta's nephew, Dīghanakha, a wandering ascetic *(paribbājaka)*. He held to the wrong view of annihilation, but after talking with The Buddha, he gave it up. This was one reason why he was able to become a Stream Enterer after listening to what is called 'The Dīghanakha Sutta'.[474]

Attaining to Stream Entry, however, is impossible if one has accomplished one of the first five unwholesome weighty kammas. They present an insurmountable obstruction to one's attaining any type of jhāna, and any type of supramundane attainment.

An example of this is King Ajātasattu: we mentioned him earlier.[475] His father was King Bimbisāra, who was a Stream Enterer, and great patron of The Buddha and Sangha. To gain kingship, King Ajātasattu had his father killed. A present result of this kamma was that he could not sleep. Then, one night, he went to see The Buddha, and The Buddha gave him the great teaching that is the *'Sāmañña-·Phala'* sutta.[476] The king had all the right conditions (pāramī) for attaining Stream Entry like his father, but because he had killed his father, they were obstructed, and he remained a common person *(puthu·jjana)*. The Buddha explained it to the bhikkhus:

Dug up, bhikkhus, is this king;[477] ruined, bhikkhus, is this king. If, bhikkhus, this king had not deprived his father of life (a righteous man, a righteous king), then in this very seat the incorrupt, stainless Dhamma-eye would have arisen.

Through his kamma of listening with respect to a teaching by The Buddha Himself, the king still gained great benefit: he gained the most supreme faith in The Buddha, Dhamma, and Sangha that a common person can attain. His faith was so powerful that he was thereafter able to sleep. And The Buddha saw that his destined time in hell was reduced from many hundred thousand years to sixty thousand years.[478]

---

474 M.II.iii.4 *'Dīgha·Nakha·Suttaṁ'*

475 See 'King Ajātasattu', p.144.

476 D.i.2 *'Sāmañña·Phala·Suttaṁ'* ('The Asceticism-Fruit Sutta')

477 The subcommentary explains that he had dug up the wholesome roots *(kusala·mūlāna)* which he attained in the past, which could have brought their results in this present existence itself: see 'Inferior/Superior; the Roots/Resultants', p.62.

478 For these details, see the commentary and subcommentary to 'The Asceticism-Fruit Sutta'.

Wholesome Weighty Kamma

As we mentioned earlier, weighty kammas are not only unwholesome; there are also wholesome weighty kammas: the eight attainments, maintained up to the time of death. The eight attainments are eight types of concentration *(samādhi)*:[479]

1-4) The four fine-material sphere jhānas *(rūp·āvacara·jhāna)*
5-8) The four immaterial sphere jhānas *(arūp·āvacara·jhāna)*

They are exalted kamma *(mahaggata·kamma)*. But to become wholesome weighty kamma, they need to be maintained up to the time of death: the near-death process *(maraṇ·āsanna·vīthi)* must cognize the jhāna object.[480]

The result of these weighty jhāna kammas is rebirth in the Brahma world: either as a Brahma in the fine-material world *(rūpa·loka)* or as an immaterial being in the immaterial world *(arūpa·loka)*. It can take place only as the result of subsequently-effective kamma; never as the result of indefinitely-effective kamma.

Which Brahma world one is reborn into depends on which jhāna one has emphasized.[481] But we need perhaps to explain what that means.

One may attain all eight jhānas, but usually one will prefer one of them. Usually one will devote one's practice especially to that jhāna. And with the desire for rebirth in that particular plane of the Brahma world, one may develop such mastery of one's jhāna as to be reborn there. Such mastery of concentration is what The Buddha calls 'means to power' *(iddhi·pāda)*.

The Four Means to Power

He explains a means to power as concentration where the volitional formations of striving have one volitional formation that is predominant.[482] And He gives four such means to power:[207]

1) The means to power of concentration that has formations of striving by desire *(chanda·samādhi·ppadhāna·saṅkhāra·samannāgata iddhi·pāda)*.
2) The means to power of concentration that has formations of striving by energy *(vīriya·samādhi·ppadhāna·saṅkhāra·samannāgata iddhi·pāda)*.
3) The means to power of concentration that has formations of striving by consciousness *(citta·samādhi·ppadhāna·saṅkhāra·samannāgata iddhi·pāda)*.
4) The means to power of concentration that has formations of striving by investigation *(vīmaṁsa·samādhi·ppadhāna·saṅkhāra·samannāgata iddhi·pāda)*.

One who attains the eight jhānas, and is not the disciple of a Buddha, may develop the means to power: but not to the same degree as the disciple of a Buddha. Why? Because only the disciple of a Buddha will have penetrated to ultimate mentality-materiality, and only the disciple of a Buddha will with that as object have practised insight meditation *(vipassanā·bhāvanā)*. Such practice does not

---

479 VsM.xix.686 *'Kaṅkhā·Vitaraṇa·Visuddhi·Niddeso'* ('Exposition of the Doubt-Transcendence Purification') PP.xix.15. For the jhānas, see 'Samatha Meditation', p.82.

480 See also tables '5a: Death and Rebirth', p.52, and '5d: The Jhāna-Attainment Process', p.178.

481 The Buddha explains the Brahma planes of rebirth, according to the jhāna one has developed, in, for example, *'Paṭhama·Nānā·Karaṇa·Suttaṁ'* ('The First Various-Activities Sutta').

482 STRIVING: the four types of striving. See quotation endnote 26, p.23.

exist outside a Buddha's Dispensation.[483] Unless one's samatha practice is supported by such strong and powerful insight knowledge *(vipassanā·ñāṇa)*, the means to power that one may develop will be only weak, and one's psychic powers will also be only weak. For that reason, one will be unable to specialize in one jhāna, and attain rebirth on the plane of one's desire.

Those who attain the eight jhānas outside a Buddha's Dispensation think that one can be reborn only on the plane of one's highest jhāna: and if their jhāna produces their rebirth-linking consciousness, they are reborn accordingly.

Āḷāra Kālāma and Uddaka Rāmaputta

For example, when our Buddha was still a Bodhisatta, he learned the seven jhānas from a teacher called Āḷāra Kālāma. Later he learned the eight jhānas from another teacher called Uddaka Rāmaputta.[208] Realizing that these attainments did not lead to the end of suffering, our Bodhisatta then went to the forest and tried austerities. After doing that for six years, he gave it up, took food again, and then sat under the Bodhi Tree by the Nerañjarā river, and attained enlightenment.

Out of gratitude, and because He could see they possessed sufficient wisdom to attain a Path&Fruition, He decided to go and teach his two former teachers the Dhamma He had realized, but he discovered they had both passed away. Āḷāra Kālāma had been reborn on the immaterial plane of the seventh jhāna, the base of nothingness *(ākiñcaññ·āyatana)*, and Uddaka Rāmaputta had been reborn on the immaterial plane of the eighth jhāna, the base of neither-perception nor non-perception *(neva·saññā nā·saññ·āyatana)*.

So, even though The Buddha knew they could understand the Dhamma, He could not teach them the Dhamma. Why? Because in the immaterial world there is no materiality, and beings there have only four aggregates: feeling, perception, formations, and consciousness. They do not have the material aggregate, which means they do not have eyes or ears: Āḷāra Kālāma and Uddaka Rāmaputta could not see The Buddha, nor hear His Dhamma.[484]

Kāḷadevila the Hermit

The same thing happened to Kāḷadevila the hermit:[485] it was he who examined the new-born Prince Siddhattha, and foresaw that He would become a Buddha.

Kāḷadevila mastered all eight jhānas and the mundane psychic powers *(abhiññā)*.[486] He would, for example, spend the day in the Tāvatimsa deva world, because it was more comfortable there than in the human world. And it was there that he heard a Buddha-to-be had been born.

---

[483] For an example of such practice, see the ascetic Nanda's practice under The Buddha Padumuttara, p.276.

[484] In Vbh.XVIII.ii.3 *'Arūpa·Dhātu'* ('Immaterial Element'), The Buddha explains that in the immaterial world there is no seeing or hearing: 'Therein, what are the two bases in the immaterial element? Mind base, dhamma base [all objects cognized by only the mind].' Hence, the commentary to M.I.iii.6 *'Ariya·Pariyesanā·Suttaṁ'* ('The Noble-Search Sutta') explains that Āḷāra Kālāma and Uddaka Rāmaputta had no ears to listen to The Buddha, nor any feet to go and see The Buddha.

[485] BvA.xxvii *'Gotama·Buddha·Vaṁsa·Vaṇṇanā'* ('Description of the Gotama-Buddha Lineage')

[486] PSYCHIC POWERS: see footnote 239, p.82.

When he had told King Suddhodana, and Queen Mahāmāyā, (our Bodhisatta's parents) that their son would become Buddha, he wept. He wept because he was already old, and knew he would pass away before the Bodhisatta became Buddha. But if he had known about the means to training the mind, he need not have wept. He could have made sure to be reborn on one of the planes of the fine-material world, where the beings have eyes and ears.[487] From the fine-material world, he would have been able to see The Buddha, and hear The Buddha's Teachings. Instead, just like Uddaka Rāmaputta, he was reborn on the highest immaterial plane, the base of neither-perception nor non-perception*(neva·saññā nā·saññ·āyatana)*, because he did not know about training of the mind.

Brahmā Sahampati

Then there was Brahmā Sahampati: being a disciple of a Buddha, he knew about the means to power.[209] Under Kassapa Buddha, as the bhikkhu Sahaka, he became a Non-Returner with all eight attainments, having specialized in the first fine-material jhāna.[488] So at death he was reborn in the fine-material world on the Great Brahma plane*(Mahā·Brahmā·bhūmi)*, the highest of the first jhāna planes. That meant he had eyes to see our Buddha, and ears to hear our Buddha's Dhamma.[489]

The Venerable Devadatta

If, however, one does not maintain one's jhāna up to the time of death, it is not weighty wholesome kamma. The Venerable Devadatta, for example, our Buddha's cousin, learned the eight attainments, and five mundane psychic powers from Him.[490] But when he developed the desire to lead the Sangha instead of The Buddha, he lost his jhānas. So at his death, no jhāna became wholesome weighty kamma. Instead, the unwholesome weighty kamma of making a schism in the Sangha took effect, and he was reborn in the great Avīci Hell.

That concludes our explanation of the unwholesome and wholesome weighty kammas*(garuka·kamma)*: they take effect before all other kammas.

---

[487] See quotation, footnote 489, p.177.

[488] He explains this to The Buddha in S.V.IV.vi.7 *'Sahampati·Brahma·Suttaṁ'*. The details are from the commentary to S.I.VI.i.1 *'Brahmā·Yācana·Suttaṁ'* ('The Brahma's-Request Sutta').

[489] In Vbh.XVIII.ii.2 *'Rūpa·Dhātu'* ('Fine-Material Element') BA.XVIII.ii.994, The Buddha explains that in the fine-material (Brahma) world there is seeing and hearing: 'Therein, what are the six bases in the fine-material element? Eye base, sight base, ear base, sound base, mind base, dhamma base [all objects cognized by only the mind].'

[490] The Venerable Devadatta accomplished also the weighty unwholesome kamma of drawing The Buddha's blood with evil intent: see 'The Venerable Devadatta', p.152.

5d: **The Jhāna-Attainment Process** *(Jhāna·Samāpatti·Vīthi)**

CONSCIOUSNESS MOMENT *Citta·Kkhaṇa*	(Before the mental process) ⇒⇒⇒…⇒⇒⇒	⇒	⇒	⇒	⇒	⇒	⇒⇒⇒⇒⇒⇒⇒…⇒⇒⇒⇒⇒⇒⇒	(After the mental process) ⇒⇒⇒…⇒⇒⇒
OBJECT *Ārammaṇa*	Previous life's near-death object.	Jhāna Object *Jhān·Ārammaṇa*						Previous life's near-death object.
CONSCIOUSNESS *Citta*	Life-Continuum *Bhavaṅga* ↑|↓	Mind-Door Adverting *Mano·Dvār·Āvajjana* ↑|↓	Impulsion *Javana*				Very Many Thousand Million Impulsions *Javana* ↑|↓↑|↓↑|↓↑|↓…↑|↓↑|↓↑|↓↑|↓	Life-Continuum *Bhavaṅga* ↑|↓
			1st ↑|↓	2nd ↑|↓	3rd ↑|↓	4th ↑|↓		
			Preparation *Parikamma*	Access *Upacāra*	Conformity *Anuloma*	Change-of-Lineage *Gotrabhu*	Absorption *Appanā*	
	Resultant *Vipāka*	Functional *Kiriya*	Kamma				**WEIGHTY KAMMA** *GARUKA·KAMMA*	Resultant *Vipāka*
	Sensual-/ Fine-Material-/ Immaterial Sphere *Kām·/Rūp·/Arūp·Āvacara*	Sensual Sphere *Kām·Āvacara*					Fine-Material-/ Immaterial Sphere *Rūp·/Arūp·Āvacara*	Sensual-/ Fine-Material-/ Immaterial Sphere *Kām·/Rūp·/Arūp·Āvacara*

* The jhāna-attainment process may take place on any of three planes: the sensual-, fine-material-, or immaterial plane. All details given here are based on VsM.iv.69 *'Paṭhama·Jjhāna·Kathā'* ('Discussion of the First Jhāna') PP.iv.74-78.

Notes to table 5d 'The Jhāna-Attainment Process'

- The object of the fine-material jhāna attainment is always a concept *(paññatti)*, for example, the counterpart sign *(paṭibhāga·nimitta)* of mindfulness-of-breathing *(ānāpāna·ssati)*, or one of the kasiṇas.[491] With some objects only the first jhāna can be attained, with others all four jhānas, taking the same object.
  The four immaterial jhānas are all the fourth fourfold-jhāna (fifth fivefold), and depend on previous attainment of the fourth jhāna, taking a material kasiṇa object. Each subsequent immaterial jhāna takes then a different object, dependent on the previous jhāna:[492]
  - ▶ 1st immaterial jhāna: the boundless space left after removal of the boundless kasiṇa object, which is the space concept *(ākāsa·paññatti)*. The Buddha calls this jhāna the base of boundless space *(ākāsanañc·āyatana)*.
  - ▶ 2nd immaterial jhāna: the consciousness of the first immaterial jhāna, which had boundless space as object, and is an exalted consciousness *(mahaggata·citta)*: it is an ultimate phenomenon *(paramattha·dhamma)*. The Buddha calls this jhāna the base of boundless consciousness *(viññāṇañc·āyatana)*.
  - ▶ 3rd immaterial jhāna: the absence of the consciousness that had boundless space as its object (and which was itself the object of the base of boundless consciousness): it is the concept of not being *(n·atthi·bhava·paññatti)*. The Buddha calls this jhāna called the base of nothingness *(ākiñcaññ·āyatana)*.
  - ▶ 4th immaterial jhāna: the consciousness of the third immaterial jhāna, which has nothingness as object, and is an exalted consciousness: it is an ultimate phenomenon. The Buddha calls this jhāna called the base of neither-perception nor non-perception *(neva·saññā·n·āsaññ·āyatana)*.
- One consciousness lasts one consciousness moment *(citta·kkhaṇa)*, with three stages: arising *(uppāda)* ↑, standing *(ṭhiti)* |, dissolution *(bhaṅga)* ↓.
- Before and after a mental process, arises a number of life-continuum consciousnesses.[493]
- Cognition follows a fixed procedure, according to the natural law of the mind *(citta·niyāma)*. Thus, the procedure of the fine-material jhāna process is:
  - ▶ A mind-door adverting consciousness: it cognizes the jhāna-object.
  - ▶ Three preparatory impulsions cognizing the same object:
    i) Preparation- ii) Access- iii) Conformity Consciousness

    Their application, sustainment, happiness, joy, and one-pointedness are stronger than normal sensual-sphere consciousnesses. Thus they prepare the way for absorption, are in the access of jhāna, and conform to the consciousness preceding them, and the succeeding Change of Lineage. (In one of keen faculties, the preparation consciousness does not arise: there are only three preparatory impulsions.)
  - ▶ Change of Lineage Knowledge: it is a fourth impulsion, which marks the transition from consciousness of the limited lineage *(paritta·gotta)* of sensual-sphere consciousness to the exalted lineage *(mah·aggata·gotta)*, of fine-material- or immaterial-sphere jhāna consciousness.

---

[491] See 'Appendix 1: The Forty Meditation Subjects', p.363.
[492] VsM.x.289-290 *'Āruppa·Niddeso'* ('Exposition of the Immaterial') PP.x.58-59 & AbS.v.-71 *'Ālambaṇa·Saṅgaho'* ('Appendage [appendant object] Compendium') CMA.iii.18
[493] LIFE-CONTINUUM CONSCIOUSNESS: for details, see footnote 306, p.107, and table '5a: Death and Rebirth', p.52.

- ▸ Countless absorption impulsion-consciousnesses (formations*(saṅkhāra)*) cognizing the same object; each cognition reinforcing the next.[494] The number of absorption impulsions depends on how long the jhāna attainment lasts, which depends on the yogi's practice and skill: it may last only some fractions of a second, it may last an hour, it may last several days. The yogi who has developed the five masteries of jhāna determines beforehand how long the jhāna attainment will last. But when the beginner first attains jhāna, there arises only one jhāna consciousness.
- In a five-door-, and mind-door process of the sensual sphere, the impulsions are all the same, but in a jhāna-attainment process (which is of the fine-material- or immaterial sphere) the impulsions are different. The first four are all sensual-sphere consciousnesses, whereas only the fifth is the actual jhāna consciousnesses. It is not only one, but many thousand million, and they are all the same. If one is in the same jhāna for a longer period (several hours, up to a week), the number of fifth impulsions is uncountable.
- The yogi enters the jhāna attainment in accordance with the way the mind is conveyed*(yathābhinīhāravasena)*: the yogi decides which jhāna to attain.
- The wholesome kamma of a jhāna attainment becomes a wholesome weighty kamma when it is maintained up to the near-death mental process.
- This same procedure is followed when one enters into the supramundane Fruition Attainment.[495]

1d: **The Fine-Material Sphere***(Rūp·Āvacara)* **and Immaterial Sphere***(Arūp·Āvacara)* **Resultant Consciousness***(Vipāka·Citta)*

Door	Jhāna	Function	Object	
	1st fine-material jhāna			(concept)
	2nd fine-material jhāna			(concept)
	3rd fine-material jhāna			(concept)
	4th fine-material jhāna	rebirth-linking		(concept)
mind-	5th fine-material jhāna	life continuum	kamma sign	(concept)
	1st immaterial jhāna	death		(concept)
	2nd immaterial jhāna			(ultimate phenomenon)
	3rd immaterial jhāna			(concept)
	4th immaterial jhāna			(ultimate phenomenon)

Even though these types of resultant consciousness are the result of wholesome kamma, they are in the Pali never called wholesome-resultants*(kusala·vipāka)*, since that term refers only to the unrooted wholesome resultants: see table, p.64.

Function: these nine types of consciousness may function as one life's life-continuum consciousnesses: the first one is the rebirth-linking consciousness*(paṭisandhi·citta)* and the last one is the decease consciousness*(cuti·citta)*. Such types of consciousness are also called process-separate consciousnesses*(vīthi·mutta·citta)*.

Object see notes to table 5d 'The Jhāna-Attainment Process'. For the kamma, kamma sign, or destination sign, and the process-separate consciousnesses, see notes to table 5a 'Death and Rebirth', p.52.

[494] For the mental phenomena of the absorption process, see 'Mental Phenomena of the Mind-Door Process', p.150. And of the jhāna-attainment consciousness, see table '3c: Mental Phenomena at the Arising of Exalted Consciousness', p.85*f.*
[495] See table '5e: The Path Process', p.340.

Habitual Kamma

Next in order of effect is habitual kamma *(āciṇṇa·kamma)*: unwholesome or wholesome kamma that is done habitually, frequently, and continuously. Habitual kamma matures before unusual kamma *(abahula·kamma)*.[496] And of several habitual kammas, the most habitual unwholesome or wholesome kamma matures first.

Unwholesome Habitual Kamma

As examples of habitual unwholesome kamma we may refer to the Venerable Mahāmoggallāna. He was chief disciple in psychic powers *(abhiññā)*. At one time, he was living together with the Venerable Lakkhaṇa on the Vulture-Peak Mountain *(Gijjha·Kūṭa Pabbata)*.[497] And once,[210] as they were descending the mountain, the Venerable Mahāmoggallāna smiled. His companion asked him why he smiled, and he said please to ask this only in The Buddha's presence. So, in The Buddha's presence, the Venerable Lakkhaṇa asked him again. The Venerable Mahāmoggallāna explained that he had seen a skeleton moving through the air. Vultures, crows, and hawks were attacking it, and tearing it apart, and it was giving out cries of pain. He had smiled because he thought it was amazing that such a being could exist. Then The Buddha turned to the bhikkhus and explained:

With the [divine] **eye developed indeed, bhikkhus, disciples dwell; with** [the higher] **knowledge developed indeed, bhikkhus, disciples dwell, by which the disciple speaks of such a thing, knows it, and sees it, and can witness it.**

In the past for me, bhikkhus, there was sight of that being,[498] **although I did not speak of it. Had I spoken of it, others would not have believed me. If they had not believed me, that would for a long time be to their detriment and suffering.**

That being, bhikkhus, in this very Rājagaha was a butcher. He having suffered that kamma's result for many years, for many hundred years, for many thousand years, for many hundred thousand years in hell, owing to that same kamma's power, such an individual existence has acquired and is experiencing.

Here, the butcher's livelihood was to kill cattle. That was his habit: habitual kamma. Owing to that kamma, he suffered for a long time in hell. But when he passed away from hell, his near-death mental process took as object a heap of meatless cattle bones. So, owing to the same kamma *(kamma·sabhāgatāya)*, or the same object *(ārammaṇa·sabhāgatāya)*, he was reborn as a ghost in the form of a skeleton. In his next existence, he still suffered torment for his habitual kamma as a butcher.

---

[496] Also called 'accomplished kamma' *(katattā·kamma)*.

[497] Vin.Pār.i.4 *'Catuttha·Pārājikaṁ'* ('The Fourth Defeat'), and S.II.VIII.i.1 *'Aṭṭhi·Suttaṁ'* ('The Skeleton Sutta'). The commentaries explain that the Venerable Lakkhaṇa was one of the thousand former matted-hair fire-ascetics who attained Arahantship with The Buddha's teaching of the 'The "Burning" Sutta' (mentioned at 'Happy Uruvela Kassapa', p.282*ff*).

[498] The Commentaries explain that The Buddha saw this on the night of His enlightenment: when He developed the divine eye *(dibba·cakkhu)*: mentioned also endnote 158, p.246.

The Venerable Mahāmoggallāna reported seeing also more such beings, and again The Buddha confirmed seeing them Himself. In each case, it was beings who suffered because of habitual unwholesome kamma:

- A cattle-butcher suffered in hell for many hundred thousand years.[499] He was reborn as a ghost in the form of a piece of meat crying out in pain as it was being torn at by vultures, crows, and hawks.
- A woman who committed adultery suffered in hell for many hundred thousand years.[500] She was reborn as a ghost in the form of a flayed woman crying out in pain, as she was being torn at by vultures, crows, and hawks.
- A bad bhikkhu, who in The Buddha Kassapa's Dispensation received the four requisites from the faithful,[501] had been without restraint in body and speech, and had practised wrong livelihood, enjoying himself as he pleased: he suffered in hell for many hundred thousand years. Then he was reborn as a ghost in the form of a bhikkhu crying out in pain because his outer robe, bowl, girdle, and body were burning and blazing.

Wholesome Habitual Kamma

A happier example is the example of the householder Dhammika.[211] As a habit throughout his life, he made offerings to The Buddha and Sangha. At the time of death, the destination sign *(gati nimitta)* of that wholesome habitual kamma appeared as devas of the six deva planes in shining chariots come to take him away.[502] Having aspired to it beforehand, he chose to go to the Tusitā deva plane.[503]

Near-Death Kamma

Next in order of effect is near-death kamma *(āsanna·kamma)*: an unusual kamma that at the time of death is recollected very vividly. An unusual kamma is itself not strong enough to overpower a habitual kamma. But if at death, one recollects the unusual kamma very vividly, the act of vivid recollection may give it enough strength to overpower the habitual kamma. Then can the unusual kamma produce its result, and one is reborn accordingly.

Unwholesome Near-Death Kamma

Queen Mallikā

A good example of this process is Queen Mallikā, queen to King Kosala.[504] She was a devout Buddhist, and every day in the palace she gave almsfood to five hundred bhikkhus: that was her habitual kamma. But at death, she was unable to control her mind, and recollected very vividly one unusual unwholesome kamma she had done. For that reason, she was reborn in hell. Nevertheless, the

---

[499] S.II.VIII.i.2 *'Pesi·Suttaṁ'* ('The "Piece" Sutta')

[500] S.II.VIII.ii.3 *'Ni·Cchav·Itthi·Suttaṁ'* ('The Skinless-Woman Sutta')

[501] S.II.VIII.ii.7 *'Pāpa·Bhikkhu·Suttaṁ'* ('The Bad-Bhikkhu Sutta')

[502] DESTINATION SIGN: see table '5a: Death and Rebirth', p.52.

[503] The commentary explains that he chose Tusitā heaven, because it is the plane of existence for the last life for all Bodhisattas, before they go down to the human world to become an Enlightened One.

[504] For other examples of people who recollect an unwholesome kamma, and thereby have an unhappy rebirth, see 'The Envious Venerable Tissa', p.279, and 'The Jealous Venerable Jambuka', p.309.

unusual unwholesome kamma was not very severe, meaning it was quite weak, and after seven days it was overpowered by her habitual kamma: she escaped from hell and was reborn in the deva world.

We may thus understand that it is very dangerous to dwell on one's unwholesome deeds at the time of death. That is why it is custom for those with faith in The Buddha to remind a dying person of his good deeds, or to urge him to arouse good thoughts in the final moments of his life. Even a person of bad character (who has accomplished unwholesome habitual kamma) should just before dying try to recollect a wholesome kamma, or try to accomplish a wholesome kamma, for then may she or he be reborn according to that kamma instead.

WHOLESOME NEAR-DEATH KAMMA

TAMBADĀṬHIKA THE EXECUTIONER

A good example is Tambadāṭhika, the king's executioner.[505] For fifty-five years, he beheaded criminals, but in his old age he could no longer behead a man with a single blow, and was made to retire. On the day he retired, he offered the Venerable Sāriputta some sweet milk-porridge with fresh ghee. Afterwards, the Venerable Sāriputta gave him the progressive instruction *(anupubbi·kathā)* in four stages:[506]

- Instruction on offering *(dāna·kathā)*.
- Instruction on morality *(sīla·kathā)*.
- Instruction on the heavens *(sagga·kathā)*: that is the results of offering and morality.
- Instruction on the danger, depravity, and defilement of sensual pleasure *(kāmānaṁ ādīnavaṁ okāraṁ saṁkilesaṁ)*, and the advantage of renunciation *(nekkhamme ānisaṁsaṁ pakāsesi)*.

Then, when the Venerable Sāriputta could see that Tambadāṭhika's mind was calm, ready, and full of faith, he instructed him in the most superior Dhamma teaching of Buddhas *(Buddhānaṁ sāmukkaṁsikā Dhamma·desanā)*:

1) Suffering .... *(dukkha)*	3) Its cessation .... *(nirodha)*
2) Its origin .... *(samudaya)*	4) The path .... *(magga)*

Tambadāṭhika listened with wise attention *(yoniso manasikāra)*. And owing to sufficient past practice of knowledge and conduct *(vijjā·caraṇa)*,[507] he was able now to attain the Formations-Equanimity Knowledge *(Saṅkhār·Upekkhā·Ñāṇa)*,[508] very close to the Stream-Entry Path Knowledge *(Sot·Āpatti·Magga)*. Then he accompanied the Venerable Sāriputta some of the way, and returned home. But on his way home, a demon in the guise of a cow gored him to death.[509] At the time of death, he recollected the two wholesome kammas with great vividness: offering milk-porridge

[505] DhPA.viii.1 *'Tambadāṭhika·Cora·Ghātaka·Vatthu'* ('The Case of Tambadāṭhika the Bandit-Executioner'). See also 'Tambadāṭhika the Executioner', p.211.

[506] PROGRESSIVE INSTRUCTION: see footnote 376, p.137.

[507] See 'Knowledge and Conduct', p.137.

[508] VERY CLOSE TO THE STREAM-ENTRY PATH KNOWLEDGE: The Buddha explains that he attained the Conformity Knowledge *(Anuloma·Ñāṇa)*. It takes the same object as the Formations-Equanimity Knowledge (for the Conformity Knowledge, see table '5e: The Path Process', p.340).

[509] This demon killed him because of past unwholesome kamma he had accomplished. See 'The Avenging Courtesan', p.272.

to the Venerable Sāriputta, and listening to Dhamma. That became his near-death kamma, and he was reborn in the Tusitā deva world.

THE MIND AT DEATH

Now, please do not misunderstand this example. Please do not think that one can accomplish many unwholesome kammas throughout one's life, and then just recall a wholesome kamma at death in order to gain a happy rebirth. Tambadāthika attained the Formations-Equanimity Knowledge by listening to a Dhamma talk: that requires strong and powerful pāramī. Such a case is quite exceptional, for The Buddha makes it clear that only a very, very, very small number of ordinary people *(puthujjana)* are reborn as human beings after death.[510]

Please remember that it is very difficult to control one's mind at death. For example, if one is killed in a catastrophe like an earthquake or a tsunami, or if one is killed in a war or an accident, or if one is attacked by someone, then fear will inevitably arise. It is very difficult to control one's mind when there is much fear: fear is hatred-rooted, and if one dies with a hatred-rooted consciousness, one will be reborn either in the ghost world, the animal world, or hell. Also if one dies of a terrible disease with much pain, it is difficult to control one's mind. And if one has been given heavy drugs by the doctor, how is one going to control one's mind? Even if one dies under peaceful circumstances, it can be difficult to control one's mind, because the mind changes so quickly. And if one has never practised sense-restraint, or if one has not meditated properly, if one has always engaged in sensual pleasures, then how is one going to be able to control one's mind?

Say one reflects on the beauty of one's children, the beauty of one's husband or wife, the beauty of one's house or garden, or the beauty of a flower, and other such things: that is rooted in greed and delusion. It is a perverted perception *(saññā·vipallāsa)*,[511] based on unwise attention. If one has habitually looked upon such objects with such unwise attention, it will be very difficult at death suddenly to reflect upon them with wise attention. One may also never have reflected on death. Then, on one's deathbed, one may worry about dying and be unhappy: that is rooted in hatred and delusion. One may also never have practised contentment and patience, and frequently be discontent and impatient on one's deathbed: that is also rooted in hatred and delusion. One may also die harbouring a grudge against someone, or one may die with remorse for something bad one has done, or something good one has failed to do: that is also rooted in hatred and delusion. One may be confused about what happens after death: that is rooted in delusion. If one dies with such consciousness (rooted in greed and delusion, hatred and delusion, or delusion alone),[512] one cannot avoid being reborn in a woeful state.[513]

---

[510] See quotation, endnote 15, p.21.

[511] See 'The Four Perversions', p.330.

[512] This refers solely to the delusion-rooted consciousness associated with scepticism *(vicikicchā)*: not the one associated with restlessness *(uddhacca)*. For the two types of delusion-rooted consciousness, see table '2c: Mental Phenomena at the Arising of Delusion-Rooted Consciousness', p.50.

[513] In S.IV.I.xviii.8 *'Āditta·Pariyāya·Suttaṁ'* ('The Fire-Theme Sutta'), The Buddha explains that it were better for one to have one's eye faculty extirpated by a burning, glowing iron spike than for one to grasp the sign of a sight's features, because if one were to die while enjoying such a sign, one may be reborn either in hell or the animal world. He says the

(Please see further next page.)

That is why The Buddha, His disciples, and others who teach the workings of kamma, encourage people to practise the three merit-work bases: to help people avoid being reborn in a woeful state.[514] But if one's merit-work is inferior, or it is a wrong practice, maybe based on wrong view, then it will not be of much help, will it?

Accomplished Kamma

Let us then discuss the last type of kamma to mature: accomplished kamma *(katattā·kamma)*. It is simply kamma that has been completed, any of the twenty courses of kamma that we discussed earlier. Let us just mention them again briefly:[515]

Ten unwholesome courses of kamma *(dasa akusala·kamma·patha)*

Three Unwholesome Bodily Courses of Kamma	Four Unwholesome Verbal Courses of Kamma	Three Unwholesome Mental Courses of Kamma
1) to kill 2) to steal 3) to commit sexual misconduct	1) to lie 2) to slander 3) to use harsh speech 4) to prattle	1) to covet 2) to harbour ill-will 3) to hold wrong view (to deny the workings of kamma, rebirth, other worlds of existence, etc.)

Ten wholesome courses of kamma *(dasa kusala·kamma·patha)*

Three Wholesome Bodily Courses of Kamma	Four Wholesome Verbal Courses of Kamma	Three Wholesome Mental Courses of Kamma
1) from killing to abstain (to be merciful and kind towards beings) 2) from stealing to abstain 3) from sexual misconduct to abstain	1) from lying to abstain (to speak only the truth) 2) from slander to abstain 3) from harsh speech to abstain (to speak gently and politely) 4) from prattle to abstain (to speak only of things worth listening to, things of value)	1) not to covet 2) to have goodwill towards all beings 3) to hold Right View (affirming the workings of kamma, rebirth, other worlds of existence, etc.)

Such unwholesome or wholesome kamma one may have done in this life, in the previous life, or in the infinite past. It brings about rebirth, when the previous three types of kamma either do not exist or fail to arise. Accomplished unwholesome kamma brings about rebirth in the animal world, in the ghost world or in hell, and accomplished wholesome kamma brings about rebirth in the human world or the deva worlds.

---

same for the remaining five faculties. And He explains that the educated Noble Disciple instead practises vipassanā on the six faculties and their objects and consciousness.

[514] For a sutta reference, see endnote 124, p.242.

[515] For a detailed analysis of these ten courses of unwholesome/wholesome kamma, see 'The Courses of Kamma', p.119*ff.*

That concludes our explanation of the order in which kamma takes effect: first weighty kamma, then habitual kamma, then near-death kamma, and last accomplished kamma.

FUNCTION OF EFFECT

The third four categories of kamma we shall discuss are according to kamma's function *(kicca)*. When kamma matures, it may take one of four functions:[516]

1) Productive kamma *(janaka·kamma)*
2) Reinforcing kamma *(upatthambhaka·kamma)*
3) Frustrating kamma *(upapīḷaka·kamma)*
4) Interceptive kamma *(upaghātaka·kamma)*

As we discussed earlier, an unwholesome or wholesome kamma is properly accomplished only with the fulfilment of certain factors: that includes the either unwholesome or wholesome volition to accomplish the kamma. It is called the conclusive volition *(sanniṭṭhāna cetanā)*. The volitions that come before and after the conclusive volition are then called the preceding&succeeding volitions *(pubb·āpara-·cetanā)*.[517]

Only the conclusive volition functions as rebirth-producing productive kamma, whereas the preceding&succeeding volitions function as reinforcing-, frustrating-, and interceptive kamma, as well as other productive kamma.

PRODUCTIVE KAMMA

The function of productive kamma *(janaka·kamma)* is to produce the five aggregates[518] (mentality-materiality),[519] at rebirth *(paṭisandhi)*, and in that life's continuance *(pavatti)*.[520] Productive kamma is unwholesome or wholesome.

---

[516] VsM.xix.687 (and VsMṬ) *'Kaṅkhā·Vitaraṇa·Visuddhi·Niddeso'* ('Exposition of the Doubt-Transcendence Purification') PP.xix.16, and AbS.v.50 *'Kamma·Catukkaṁ'* ('The Kamma Tetrad') CMA.v.18. The explanations are derived from AA/AṬ.III.I.iv.4 *'Nidāna·Suttaṁ'* ('The Causation Sutta'); quoted endnote 237, p.255).

[517] For the conclusive volition, see also 'A Course of Unwholesome Kamma' (p.128). It is also called the decisive volition *(sanniṭṭhāpaka·cetanā)*: see footnote 137 (p.50). For the preceding&succeeding volitions, see under 'Inferior/Superior' (p.60).

[518] The Most Venerable Pa-Auk Tawya Sayadaw is here referring to beings in the sensual- and fine-material world. Beings in the immaterial world comprise only the four mentality aggregates (no materiality aggregate), and impercipient beings only the materiality aggregate (no mentality aggregates) (VsM.xvii.638 *'Paññā·Bhūmi·Niddesa'* ('Exposition of the Wisdom-Ground') PP.xvii.192).

[519] FIVE AGGREGATES: materiality-, feeling-, perception-, formations-, and consciousness aggregate. The material aggregate may be seen also as merely materiality, and the four mental aggregates may also be seen as merely mentality: mentality-materiality.

[520] Included in the materiality aggregate is kamma-caused temperature-born materiality (see footnote 292, p.101): for example, certain mansions in the deva-world (see e.g. 'The Kaṇṇamunda Devī', p.188), the instruments of torture in the hells (see e.g. 'Unwholesome Habitual Kamma', p.181), and the wheel-treasure of a Wheel-Turning King (e.g. M.III.iii.9 *'Bāla·Paṇḍita·Suttaṁ'* ('The Fool&Sage Sutta')).

Productive kamma produces rebirth only if its result arises immediately after the decease consciousness in the previous life.[521] Rebirth is the simultaneous arising of three things:[522]

1) The rebirth-linking consciousness *(paṭisandhi·citta)*: that is the consciousness aggregate.
2) The rebirth-linking mental factors *(paṭisandhi·cetasika)*:[523] that is the mental factors of the rebirth-linking consciousness; the feeling-, perception-, and formations aggregate.
3) The material body of the new being, the materiality aggregate, which is the kamma-born types of materiality *(kamma·ja·rūpa)*.

   At a human being's conception, there arises only body-, heart-, and sex decad-kalāpas. After conception (during gestation) arise the remaining types of materiality, including eye-, ear-, nose-, and tongue materiality, which are also kamma-born.[524]

The five aggregates produced at rebirth are the result of any of the ten unwholesome or wholesome courses of kamma *(kamma·patha)*. We discussed them earlier: killing or abstaining from killing, theft or abstaining from theft, engaging in sexual misconduct or abstaining from it, etc.[525]

Apart from producing the five aggregates at rebirth, productive kamma produces the five aggregates also in the course of life. But it cannot be the same kamma as the one that produced the rebirth consciousness: it is always another kamma.[526] And again, it is the arising of three things:

1) The different types of resultant consciousness *(vipāka citta)*: that is the consciousness aggregate, which is made of the eye, ear, nose, tongue, and body consciousnesses, as well as the receiving, investigating, and registering consciousnesses.[527]
2) Their different types of associated phenomena *(sampayutta dhamma)*, the mental factors *(cetasika)* associated with the different types of resultant consciousness: that is the feeling-, perception-, and formations aggregate.
3) The material body of the being: that is the material aggregate, which is the continuity of kamma-born materiality: the six sense bases, etc.

Any type of unwholesome and wholesome kamma without exception can produce results in that life's continuance *(pavatti)*.

---

[521] For details, see table '5a: Death and Rebirth', p.52.

[522] VsM.xvii.638 *'Paññā·Bhūmi·Niddesa'* ('Exposition of the Wisdom-Ground') PP.xvii.188-196

[523] Also called *paṭisandhi·nāma* (rebirth-linking mentality).

[524] For an explanation of decad kalāpas, see 'Ultimate Materiality', p.92.

[525] See 'The Courses of Kamma', p.119.

[526] It may, however, be another kamma of the same identity (ThīG.xvi.1 *'Sumedhā·Therī·Gāthā'* ('Verses of the Elderess Sumedhā')). See 'The Principle of Identity', p.203.

[527] For details, see table '5b: The Five-Door Process', p.146.

THE COMFORTABLE ELEPHANT

Such kamma The Buddha explains, for example, in connection with someone who has been reborn as an elephant:[528]

Suppose one is a killer; one is a stealer of what has not been given; one is a wrong-doer in sensual pleasure; one is a speaker of untruth; one is a speaker of slander; one is a speaker of harshness: one is a prattler; one is a coveter; one is one with a mind of ill-will; one is one of wrong view, but to ascetics and Brahmins one has been an offerer of food, drink, clothing, transport, garlands, scents, ointments, beds, dwellings and lamps.

At the breakup of the body, after death, among elephants one is reborn. There one enjoys food and drink, flowers and various adornments. In so far as one was a killer [etc.], **on the breakup of the body, after death, one was reborn among elephants. But because to ascetics and Brahmins one had offered food, drink, clothing, transport, garlands, scents, ointments, beds, dwellings, and lamps, for that reason one received food and drink, flowers, and various adornments.**

Here, that person's unwholesome kamma functioned as productive kamma, to produce her or his rebirth as an elephant. But the wholesome kamma functioned as productive kamma in the course of that life, to help keep the elephant healthy, provide a happy living, and maintain the elephant's happy life.[529]

RICH THROUGH WRONG LIVELIHOOD

In the same way, someone who has been reborn as a human being may become rich through wrong livelihood: for example, killing, stealing, and selling weapons. Then you may ask: 'But how can unwholesome kamma produce a desired, pleasant and agreeable result? The Buddha says it is impossible.'[530]

Here, it is not that person's unwholesome kamma that provides the wholesome result; it is still only wholesome kamma that does it. In a previous life she or he made money and acquired possessions by killing, stealing, and selling weapons, etc. Using that money, she or he accomplished wholesome kammas, for example, making offerings to ascetics and Brahmins. While making such wholesome kammas, there may also have been the wish to be successful in business. And one of those wholesome kammas functioned now as the productive kamma that produced a human rebirth. But other of those 'offering kammas' function as productive kamma only when she or he again accomplishes such unwholesome kamma: she or he becomes rich only by wrong livelihood. Such cases we may have seen in any country: someone who is unsuccessful in Right Livelihood, but very successful in wrong livelihood.

That does not mean, however, that one will not suffer for one's unwholesome deeds: no. One's unwholesome kamma may in some subsequent life function as unwholesome productive kamma to produce an unhappy rebirth, as well as function as unwholesome reinforcing kamma in the course of such a life.

Another example of how productive kamma functions in the course of a life is a so-called mansion-ghost *(vimāna·peta)*:[531] wholesome productive kamma produces a beautiful body, etc., and heavenly pleasures for such a being, but unwhole-

---

528 A.X.IV.ii.11 *'Jāṇussoṇi·Suttaṁ'* ('The Jāṇussoṇi Sutta')

529 PaD.145 *'Vīthi·Mutta Saṅgaha Param·Attha·Dīpanī'* ('Ultimate-Reality Manual on the Process-Separated Summary')

530 See quotation at 'Impossible and Possible Results', p.42*f.*

531 PaD.ibid.

some productive kamma produces some type of torment related to the accomplished unwholesome kamma.

The Kaṇṇamuṇḍa Devī

An example of this is the case of the devī and the crop-eared dog *(kaṇṇa·muṇḍa sunakha)*.[532] In The Buddha Kassapa's Dispensation,[533] there was a group of devotees, husbands and wives, who practised offering *(dāna)*, morality *(sīla)*, and meditation *(bhāvanā)*. Then once, a gambler wagered with his friends that he could make one of those virtuous wives break her virtue, and make her commit adultery. And he succeeded. His friends paid the wager, and then told her husband. When her husband asked her if she had committed adultery, she denied it. And, pointing at a dog, she made an oath: 'If I did such a wicked deed, may this crop-eared, black dog eat me wherever I am born!'

Full of remorse, that woman then passed away. Her unwholesome kamma of lying about her adultery gave her rebirth as a mansion-ghost *(vimāna·peti)*. But because of wholesome kamma, she was beautiful, and had many mansions made of gold and silver,[534] on the shores of Lake Kaṇṇamuṇḍa in the Himalayas.[535] And she had five hundred women slaves.[536] She would enjoy heavenly pleasures through the five senses: heavenly clothes, jewellery, garlands, and scents, heavenly food and drink, heavenly couches of gold and silver, her mansion had steps of gold, there were beautiful and fragrant flowers, and trees bearing many kinds of fruit, and there was the sound of many kinds of bird, trees and flowers everywhere, giving off all kinds of pleasant smells, and very beautiful surroundings. But beside her mansion, an unwholesome kamma had produced a lotus pond. And every night at midnight, she would rise from her bed and go down to the lotus pond. There, her adultery kamma and lying kamma would produce a great black dog with shorn ears, of most fearsome appearance. He would attack her, and devour her. When there was only her bones left, he would throw them into the pond, and disappear. And she would revert to her normal state, and return to bed. Every day this would happen: identical meritorious kammas *(puñña·kamma)* would produce heavenly pleasures, and identical bad kammas *(pāpa·kamma)* would produce the torment of being attacked and devoured by the black dog.[537]

Reinforcing Kamma

The function of reinforcing kamma *(upatthambhaka·kamma)* is not to produce its own result, but to reinforce the result of a productive kamma:[538] to reinforce the quality of the result (the pleasure or pain that has arisen), or to reinforce the duration of

---

[532] PvA.ii.12 *'Kaṇṇamuṇḍa·Peti·Vatthu·Vaṇṇanā'* ('Description of the Case of the Kaṇṇamunda Ghost') *Kaṇṇamunda* is both the name of a lake, and means also 'ear-cropped'.
[533] THE BUDDHA KASSAPA: the first Buddha before The Buddha Gotama. See 'Appendix 2: The Lineage of Buddhas', p.365.
[534] This is kamma-caused temperature-born materiality: see footnote 520, p.186.
[535] LAKE KAṆṆAMUṆḌA: one of the lakes mentioned by The Buddha in A.VII.vii.2 *'Satta·Sūriya·Suttaṁ'* ('The Seven-Suns Sutta'): see footnote 23, p.5.
[536] The other wives in the group, when asked, also denied all knowledge, and also made an oath: they said that if they did know of it, they would be her slaves in future lives.
[537] IDENTICAL KAMMAS: see the 'The Principle of Identity', p.203.
[538] AA.III.I.iv.4 *'Nidāna·Suttaṁ'* ('The Causation Sutta'), and VsM.xix.687 *'Kaṅkhā·Vitaraṇa·Visuddhi·Niddeso'* ('Exposition of the Doubt-Transcendence Purification') PP.xix.16.

the result (to make it last). Reinforcing kamma is also unwholesome or wholesome: unwholesome kamma reinforces unwholesome kamma, and wholesome kamma reinforces wholesome kamma.

Thus, for example, the near-death impulsions *(maraṇa·sanna·javana)*, the impulsions of the near-death process *(maraṇ·āsanna·vīthi)* are only five: that means they are too weak to produce rebirth.[539] They only reinforce the rebirth-producing productive kamma, thereby helping it produce the appropriate rebirth. If the rebirth-producing kamma is unwholesome, the impulsions of the near-death process will also be unwholesome: they will give unwholesome reinforcement to the productive kamma, to produce rebirth as a ghost, animal, or in hell. If the productive kamma is wholesome, the impulsions of the near-death process will also be wholesome, and give it wholesome reinforcement, to produce rebirth as a human being or heavenly being. That way reinforcing kamma reinforces a productive kamma.

Reinforcing kammas also reinforce the results of productive kamma: they reinforce the resultant feelings of pleasure or pain, and make them endure. For example,[540] when a wholesome kamma has functioned as productive kamma, to produce rebirth as a human being, wholesome reinforcing kammas help maintain the resultant dhammas, the continuity of aggregates: they help keep the human being healthy, provide a happy living, etc. That way, for example, by accomplishing wholesome kamma such as offering, morality, and meditation, one may prolong one's health, strength, and life span. On the other hand, when an unwholesome kamma has functioned as productive kamma in the course of a life, to produce a painful ailment for a human being, reinforcing unwholesome kamma may prevent medical treatment from working, thereby prolonging the ailment. That way, for example, by accomplishing unwholesome kamma such as killing, theft, sexual misconduct, lying, prattle, drinking beer and wine, etc., one may help weaken one's faculties, undermine one's health, and shorten one's life span.

Similarly, when unwholesome kamma has functioned as a productive kamma, to produce rebirth as an animal, unwholesome reinforcing kamma may reinforce other unwholesome kamma so it matures and functions as productive kamma to produce painful results. Unwholesome reinforcing kamma may also prolong the animal's unhappy life, so that the continuity of unwholesome results will endure.

Frustrating Kamma

The function of frustrating kamma *(upapīḷaka·kamma)* is to frustrate and obstruct. It frustrates the result of another kamma but does not produce a result of its own. It is also unwholesome or wholesome: unwholesome kamma frustrates wholesome kamma, and wholesome kamma frustrates unwholesome kamma.

For example, when someone's wholesome kamma functions as productive kamma to produce rebirth as a human being, unwholesome frustrating kamma may give rise to congenital ailments that prevent that person from enjoying the happy results that the wholesome productive kamma otherwise would have produced. Thus, even the results of powerful productive kamma may be frustrated by kamma that is directly opposed to it.

---

[539] For details, see table '5a: Death and Rebirth', p.52.

[540] PaD.145 *'Vīthi·Mutta Saṅgaha Param·Attha·Dīpanī'* ('Ultimate-Reality Manual on the Process-Separated Summary')

Unwholesome kamma may frustrate wholesome kamma productive of rebirth in a higher plane of existence so one is reborn on a lower plane, and wholesome kamma may frustrate an unwholesome kamma productive of rebirth in one of the great hells, so one is instead reborn in one of the minor hells or in the world of ghosts *(peta)*. Unwholesome kamma may also frustrate a wholesome kamma productive of a long life so one has instead an only short life. Unwholesome kamma may frustrate wholesome kamma productive of beauty so one instead has an ugly or plain appearance.[541] Lastly, for example, unwholesome kamma may frustrate wholesome kamma productive of rebirth in a high-class family so one instead is reborn into a low-class family.

KING BIMBISĀRA

An example of unwholesome kamma frustrating the plane of rebirth is King Bimbisāra: King Ajātasattu's father. He was a Stream Enterer and great patron to The Buddha and Sangha: much loved by his people. For all his good deeds, he could have been reborn as a high deva. But because he was attached to life as a deva, he was reborn as a low deva, in the entourage of King Vessavaṇa, one of the Four Great Kings *(Cātu·Mahā·Rājikā)*.[542]

BHIKKHUS REBORN AS HEAVENLY MUSICIANS

Then, as an example of unwholesome kamma frustrating the plane of rebirth, we have the three virtuous bhikkhus mentioned in the *'Sakka·Pañhā'* sutta.[543] Based on the bhikkhus' morality, they practised samatha and vipassanā successfully, but they did not attain a Noble state. Their morality was so pure that they were sure to be reborn in whatever deva world they wanted. Furthermore, since they had attained the jhānas, they could also have been reborn in one of the Brahma worlds. But at death, they were not reborn in one of the Brahma worlds: they were reborn as musicians and dancers in the deva world *(gandhabba)*. Why? Because they had been such devas in many past lives. So their superior wholesome kammas were frustrated by their attachment for life as musicians and dancers in the world of the Four Great Kings *(Cātu·Mahā·Rājikā)*.

KING AJĀTASATTU

Then, as an example of wholesome kamma frustrating the plane of rebirth, we can again mention King Ajātasattu. He had his father killed: King Bimbisāra, whom we just mentioned. Killing one's father is one of the six unwholesome weighty kammas *(akusala garuka kamma)*.[544] They are productive of rebirth in Avīci Hell. Later, however, King Ajātasattu gained tremendous faith in The Buddha and His Dispensation. His faith was of such wholesome power that it frustrated the unwholesome weighty kamma, and instead of being reborn in Avīci Hell, he was reborn in a minor hell *(ussada)*, for a reduced period.[545] And in the future, he will

---

[541] For an example, see 'Scowling Pañcapāpī', p.271

[542] He explains this to The Buddha in D.ii.5 *'Janavasabha·Suttaṁ'* ('The Janavasabha Sutta'): details from the commentary.

[543] D.ii.8 'The Sakka's-Questions Sutta'. Their case is discussed in more detail at 'The Three Bhikkhus', p.205.

[544] See 'Unwholesome Weighty Kamma', p.170.

[545] DA.i.2 *'Sāmañña·Phala·Sutta·Vaṇṇanā'* ('Description of the Asceticism-Fruit Sutta')

(Please see further next page.)

become a Paccekabuddha called Vijitāvī. At his Parinibbāna, he will then escape from all suffering.

THE SLAVE-WOMAN KHUJJUTTARĀ

As an example of unwholesome kamma frustrating the status of one's human birth, we can mention the slave-woman Khujjuttarā: she was slave to Queen Sāmāvatī.[546]

Once, in a past life, she mimicked a Paccekabuddha because he was slightly hunchbacked. That unwholesome kamma had now frustrated her human rebirth, so she was hunchbacked.

In The Buddha Kassapa's Dispensation, she was the daughter of a treasurer, and had a friend who was a bhikkhunī Arahant. One day, while Khujjuttarā was adorning herself, the bhikkhunī visited her. Khujjutara's maid-servant was not there, so Khujjuttarā asked the bhikkhunī Arahant to hand her a basket of adornments. The Arahant bhikkhunī knew that if she refused, Khujjuttarā would bear her ill-will, which would lead to rebirth in hell. On the other hand, if she obeyed, Khujjutara would be reborn as a maid-servant. That being the better of the two, the Arahant bhikkhunī handed her the basket of adornments. Khujjutara's unwholesome kamma of asking a bhikkhunī Arahant to serve her now frustrated her human rebirth, and she was born to be a maid-servant.[547]

KAMMA FRUSTRATES IN THE COURSE OF LIFE

In the course of life there are innumerable instances of frustrating kamma in operation.[548] For example, unwholesome kamma will in the human world frustrate the wholesome kamma that produces the aggregates: it will help mature such unwholesome kammas that produce suffering and failure in regard to health, in regard to property and wealth, and in regard to family and friends.[549] In the ghost or animal worlds, on the other hand, wholesome frustrating kamma may counteract the unwholesome productive kamma that produced the unhappy rebirth, and contribute towards occasions of ease and happiness.

CERTAIN KAMMAS FRUSTRATE — OTHERS REINFORCE

QUEEN MALLIKĀ

As an example of frustrating- and reinforcing kamma operating in the same life, we can mention, Queen Mallikā. She was originally a poor flower-girl, of very plain appearance.[550] One day, she was going to the park, carrying some pudding to eat.

---

explains that he will escape after sixty thousand years, rather than the customary many hundred thousand years.

[546] Khujjuttarā's story is related at the end of the story of her mistress Queen Sāmāvati, DhPA.ii.1 *'Sāmāvatī·Vatthu'* ('The Case of Sāmāvatī').

[547] For other cases of such disrespect towards one's elders/betters, see 'One Is Stubborn and Proud', p.289.

[548] MA.III.iv.5 *'Cūḷa·Kamma·Vibhaṅga·Suttaṁ'* ('The Small Kamma-Analysis Sutta')

[549] For examples, see how past cruelty towards animals frustrates health in 'The Cruel Bird-Catcher', p.266, past bad action towards an Arahant motivated by envy frustrates food and drink in 'The Envious Venerable Tissa', p.279, and past adultery frustrates relations with family and spouse in 'Mahāpaduma Paccekhabuddha's Picture', p.314.

[550] JA.vii.10 (415) *'Kummāsa·Piṇḍi·Jātaka·Vaṇṇanā'* ('Description of the Pudding-Alms

(Please see further next page.)

Then she saw The Buddha on His almsround. Great faith arose, and spontaneously, with great joy, she put all the pudding in His bowl.[551] Then she did obeisance. Afterwards, The Buddha smiled. And He told the Venerable Ānanda that as a result of her offering, Mallikā would that very day become King Pasenadi's chief queen.

King Pasenadi was riding back to Sāvatthi from battle with King Ajātasattu: he had lost the battle, and was unhappy. Mallikā was in the park, singing because of joy over her offering. King Pasenadi heard her singing, and approached her. He talked to her, and discovered she was unmarried. Then he stayed with her for some time, and she comforted him. Afterwards, he obtained permission from her parents to marry her, and that very day, he made her his chief queen. Mallikā's joyous offering and doing obeisance to The Buddha had functioned as presently-effective kamma.[552]

One day, Queen Mallikā went to see The Buddha, to ask Him four questions about the workings of kamma:[553]

1) First, Queen Mallikā asked why some women are ugly, poor, and without influence. The Buddha explained that the past kamma of being angry and irritable has made them ugly; the past kamma of not making offerings, of being stingy, has made them poor; and the past kamma of envying others their gain and honour has made them uninfluential. Here, all those unwholesome kammas have frustrated the wholesome kamma that gave rebirth as a human being.[554]

   We can see that in Queen Mallikā's case, unwholesome kamma had frustrated her human rebirth, so she was born with a plain appearance, was born into a poor garland-maker's family, and was uninfluential.

2) Second, Queen Mallikā asked why some women are ugly, yet are rich and have great influence. The Buddha explained that the past kamma of being angry and irritable has made them ugly, whereas making offerings, generosity, has made them rich, and not envying others their gain and honour (experiencing sympathetic joy *(mūditā)*) has made them influential. Here, the unwholesome kamma of being angry and irritable has frustrated the wholesome kamma that gave rebirth as a human being, whereas the wholesome kammas of generosity and non-envy have reinforced it.

   We can see that in Queen Mallikā's case, the wholesome kamma of offering The Buddha all her food had reinforced the wholesome kamma that gave her a human rebirth, so she became King Pasenadi's chief queen, with very much influence.

3) Third, Queen Mallikā asked why some women are beautiful, yet are poor and uninfluential. The Buddha explained that the past kamma of not being angry and irritable has made them beautiful, whereas stinginess has made them poor, and envy has made them uninfluential. Here, the wholesome kamma of not being angry and irritable has reinforced the wholesome kamma that gave rebirth as a human being, whereas the unwholesome kammas of stinginess and envy have frustrated it.

Jātaka')

[551] This makes the kamma unprompted *(a·saṅkhārika)*: see 'Unprompted/Prompted', p.60.

[552] For other cases of an offering with immediate result, see endnote 196, p.251.

[553] A.IV.IV.v.7 (197) *'Mallikā·Devī·Suttaṁ'* ('The Queen Mallikā Sutta')

[554] These explanations The Buddha gives in more detail in the 'The Small Kamma-Analysis Sutta', discussed at p.257*ff.*

4) Fourth, Queen Mallikā asked why some women are beautiful, rich, and of great influence. The Buddha explained that the past kamma of not being angry and irritable has made them beautiful, generosity has made them rich, and non-envy has made them influential. Here, all the wholesome kammas have reinforced the wholesome kamma that gave rebirth as a human being.

After The Buddha's teaching, Queen Mallikā vowed never again to be angry and irritable, always to make offerings, and never to envy others their gain and honour. And she took refuge in The Buddha.

Interceptive Kamma

Interceptive kamma *(upaghātaka·kamma)* functions in three ways:[555]

1) It intercepts weaker kamma, produces no result, and forbids another kamma to produce its result.
2) It intercepts weaker kamma, produces no result, and allows another kamma to produce its result.
3) It intercepts weaker kamma, and produces its own result.

Interceptive kamma is also either unwholesome or wholesome. Interceptive kamma is like a force that stops a flying arrow, and makes the arrow drop. For example, wholesome productive kamma may produce rebirth as a deva, but certain unwholesome interceptive kamma may suddenly mature and cause the deva to die, and be reborn as an animal, ghost, or in hell.

Sometimes, interceptive kamma works as frustrating kamma works: it intercepts the result of a weaker kamma only within one life. That means the weaker kamma can still produce results in some subsequent life.

Spoilt Devas

Devas who fall from their deva existence are, for example, the devas whose minds are spoilt by excessive enjoyment or envy.[212] The devas spoilt by play *(khiḍḍa·padosika)* engage in excessive play and enjoyment. Doing so, they become as if drunk, with no control. For that reason, an unwholesome kamma intercepts the wholesome kamma that produced their deva-rebirth, so they perish and get an unhappy rebirth. And the devas spoilt by mind *(mano·padosika)* become very envious when they see another beautiful deva, another beautiful deva-mansion, etc. There again, an unwholesome kamma intercepts the wholesome kamma that produced their deva-rebirth, so they perish, and get an unhappy rebirth.

King Ajātasattu

Then again we can mention King Ajātasattu. The Buddha taught him the great teaching that is the *'Sāmañña·Phala'* sutta.[556] And the king had sufficient pāramī to attain Stream Entry there and then.[557] But the unwholesome heavy kamma *(akusala garuka·kamma)* of killing his father intercepted his pāramī, so he remained a

---

[555] MA.III.iv.5 *'Cūḷa·Kamma·Vibhaṅga·Sutta·Vaṇṇanā'* ('Description of the Small Kamma-Analysis Sutta') & AA.III.I.iv.4 *'Nidāna·Sutta·Vaṇṇanā'* ('Description of the Causation Sutta')

[556] D.i.2 *'Sāmañña·Phala·Suttaṁ'* ('The Asceticism-Fruit Sutta')

[557] See the Buddha's words, quoted p.174.

common person*(puthu·jjana)*. In the distant future, however, those pāramī will enable him to become a Paccekabuddha called Vijitāvī.[558]

THE VENERABLE DEVADATTA

We can also mention the Venerable Devadatta again.[559] He was skilled in the eight attainments: the four material jhānas, and the four immaterial jhānas. He was also skilled in the five mundane psychic powers.[560] But he had not attained any Path&Fruition: he was still a common person*(puthu·jjana)*. And when he developed the desire to take over The Buddha's position as leader of the Sangha, that unwholesome kamma intercepted his jhāna wholesome kamma, so he lost his jhānas and psychic powers.*[213]* In the distant future, however, his jhāna wholesome kamma will produce or reinforce the production of jhānas for him again, and will help him become a Paccekabuddha.

BĀHIYA DĀRUCĪRIYA

Then again, interceptive kamma may indeed cut off another kamma completely, so it no longer produces its own results. Here, an example is Bāhiya Dārucīriya.[561] In The Buddha Kassapa's Dispensation, he and six other bhikkhus had climbed up to the top of a mountain to meditate. They threw away the ladder that they had used, in order that they would not be able to escape. One of them became an Arahant, another a Non-Returner, whereas the remaining five (including Bāhiya) passed away with no Path&Fruition. They were reborn in the heavenly realms, and in our Buddha's Dispensation, they were reborn as human beings.

Bāhiya became a merchant, and was one day shipwrecked, but floated ashore on a plank. Having lost all his clothes, he put on a piece of bark, and went for alms. People thought he must be an Arahant, and eventually he also thought he might be an Arahant. And he became a much-honoured ascetic. But the Non-Returner from his past life in The Buddha Kassapa's Dispensation (who had been reborn in a Brahma world) told him he neither was an Arahant, nor was practising the way to Arahantship. Then Bāhiya asked the Brahma if there was anyone in the world who was an Arahant, and taught the way to Arahantship. The Brahma told him to go and see The Buddha.

So Bāhiya went to Jetavana, the monastery in Sāvatthi, where The Buddha was staying. But The Buddha was on His almsround. So Bāhiya went into Sāvatthi to find The Buddha. When he found The Buddha, he asked The Buddha to teach him the Dhamma. But The Buddha could see that Bāhiya was too excited to understand the Dhamma. So He said it was an unsuitable time, and refused. Then Bāhiya asked again, and said that The Buddha might die before Bāhiya got a teaching, or Bāhiya himself might die. The Buddha saw that indeed Bāhiya would die that very day, but again He refused. And a third time Bāhiya asked Him. By then, Bāhiya's mind was sufficiently calm, and The Buddha taught him the famous and very brief teaching:

'In the seen, the seen merely will be, in the heard, the heard merely will be, in the sensed, the sensed merely will be, in the cognized, the cognized merely will be.' Thus indeed, Bāhiya, should you train.

---

[558] See the commentary to that sutta.

[559] See 'The Venerable Devadatta', p.152.

[560] PSYCHIC POWERS: see footnote 239, p.82.

[561] U.i.10 *'Bāhiya·Suttaṁ'* ('The Bāhiya Sutta')

When then for you, Bāhiya, in the seen, the seen merely will be, in the heard, the heard merely will be, in the sensed, the sensed merely will be, in the cognized, the cognized merely will be, therefore you, Bāhiya, are not because of that; since you, Bāhiya, are not because of that, therefore you, Bāhiya, are not there; since you, Bāhiya, are not there, therefore you, Bāhiya, are neither here, nor beyond, nor between the two. Just this is the end of suffering.

Do you understand it?[214] Bāhiya Dārucīriya not only understood this brief teaching, there and then, he even attained Arahantship: that is how very powerful his pāramī were.[215] But shortly afterwards (as The Buddha had known) Bāhiya was killed by a cow. In spite of his having such superior pāramī, the kamma that produced his rebirth as a human being was intercepted, cut off by a past unwholesome kamma of killing a courtesan, so his life span was shortened.[562] Because of his Arahant Path-Knowledge *(Arahatta·Magga·Ñāṇa)*, all defilements had been destroyed, however, so he passed into Parinibbāna.[563]

THE VENERABLE AṄGULIMĀLA

Another example of how interceptive kamma may cut off another kamma completely is the case of the Venerable Aṅgulimāla.[564] Before ordaining as a bhikkhu, he killed very many people: he accomplished uncountable unwholesome kammas. But after he had ordained as a bhikkhu, he undertook the bhikkhu's higher morality-training. Then, with The Buddha as his teacher, he practised the bhikkhu's higher mind-training (samatha meditation), and higher wisdom-training (insight meditation), and attained the Arahant Path-Knowledge and Fruition-Knowledge. The Arahant Path-Knowledge functioned as wholesome presently-effective interceptive kamma, to cut off all the unwholesome and wholesome kamma capable of producing rebirth that he had accomplished in that life, and previously in the infinite past: they all lapsed. That meant he would never again be reborn.

THE HUNTER SUNAKHAVĀJIKA

Another example is from ancient Sri Lanka.[565] There was a hunter called Sunakhavājika: he went hunting with dogs. His son was a bhikkhu called the Venerable Soṇa. And he was unable to make his father undertake Right Livelihood. But when his father got old, he managed to persuade the old man (against his will) to ordain as a bhikkhu. Then, when the old man was on his death-bed, there appeared a destination sign *(gati·nimitta)*:[566] enormous dogs surrounded him, as if to eat him. The old man became very frightened, and cried out in fear.

Then the Venerable Soṇa had many flowers brought by novices, and had them all offered to The Buddha statue, and strewn about the shrine and the Bodhi Tree. And he had his father brought in his bed. He told him all the flowers were an offering to the Blessed One, on his behalf. And he told his father to do obeisance to The Buddha, and to set his mind at rest. His father did as instructed, and his mind settled down. And there appeared to him a new destination sign: deva palaces, and the beautiful gardens in the deva world, etc. In that way, his wholesome kamma of worshipping The Buddha (reinforced by other wholesome

---

562 For details, see 'The Avenging Courtesan', p.272.

563 See 'The Two Types of Parinibbāna', p.343.

564 M.II.iv.6 *'Aṅgulimāla·Suttaṁ'* ('The Aṅgulimāla Sutta')

565 VbhA.XVI.x.809 *'Paṭhama·Bala·Niddeso'* ('Exposition of the First Power') DD.XVI.x.2194-6

566 This example becomes clearer if one refers to table '5a: Death and Rebirth', p.52.

kamma) intercepted his unwholesome kamma of having hunted innocent beings in the forest.

Let us then discuss the three ways in which interceptive kamma functions.

INTERCEPTS — NO RESULT — FORBIDS

The first way in which interceptive kamma may function is to only intercept weaker kamma, to produce no result, and to forbid another kamma to produce its result.

THE VENERABLE MAHĀMOGGALLĀNA

For example, The Venerable Mahāmoggallāna. In a past life, he had beaten his parents, with the intention to kill them. Over many lives, that unwholesome kamma produced its results: it produced results also in his last life. Over seven days, hired bandits came to his dwelling to kill him. But the Venerable Mahāmoggallāna knew their intention with his psychic power, and with his psychic power, he disappeared from his dwelling: he went out of the keyhole. On the seventh day, however, he was unable to disappear: his parricide kamma functioned as frustrating kamma to stop him from attaining jhāna, and he could not exercise his psychic powers. Then an identical kamma functioned as interceptive kamma, and the bandits beat him to death, till his bones were smashed completely. And then they left him. But he did not die. The interceptive kamma did not cut off his present five aggregates and produce rebirth. He was able again to enter jhāna, and exercise his psychic powers. And using his psychic powers, he was then able to go and ask The Buddha for permission to enter Parinibbāna, to return to his dwelling, and to enter Parinibbāna there.

THE VENERABLE CAKKHUPĀLA

Then another example from our Buddha's time is the bhikkhu called the Venerable Cakkhupāla.[216] He was an Arahant. Wholesome kamma that he had accomplished in a past life produced his five aggregates as a human being at rebirth, as well in the course of this his last life. The materiality aggregate includes the five material sense faculties: they are the translucent element by which the eye sees sights, the translucent element by which the ear hears sounds, the translucent element by which the nose smells odours, etc.[567] When a human being can see, hear, smell, etc., it is owing to past wholesome kamma. But in a past life, as a doctor, the Venerable Cakkhupāla had accomplished a very unwholesome kamma. One of his patients had been a woman with failing eyesight. And she had promised him that if he cured her, she and her children would become his slaves. When her eyesight was restored, however, she changed her mind, and pretended her eyes were worse than before. To take revenge, the doctor then gave her some ointment to make her blind. When she applied it to her eyes, she went completely blind.

That happened in one of the Venerable Cakkhupāla's past lives. Now, in his last life, as a bhikkhu, he undertook to spend one rains retreat in only the three postures: walking, standing, and sitting down. He was not going to lie down for three months: that is one of the thirteen ascetic practices taught by The Buddha. After doing this for one month, the Venerable Cakkhupāla's eyes began to trou-

[567] For details, see table '1: The Resultant Consciousnesses', p.46.

ble him. And on the night he attained Arahantship, he went blind. The unwholesome productive kamma of blinding the woman in a past life matured now to function as interceptive kamma that cut off his eye faculty. But it produced no result of its own, and forbade another kamma to produce its result. So no wholesome kamma was able to give the Venerable Cakkhupāla his eye-sight again.

INTERCEPTS — NO RESULT — ALLOWS

The second way in which interceptive kamma may function is to intercept weaker kamma, to produce no result, but to allow another kamma to produce its result.

QUEEN SĀMĀVATĪ

Here, we can take as example, King Udena's queen Sāmāvatī, and his consorts.[568] In a previous life Sāmāvatī and her friends had been concubines in the king of Bārāṇasī's harem. One day, having bathed with the king in the river, they felt cold, and set fire to a tangle of grass nearby. When the grass had burned down, they found a Paccekabuddha seated there. Since they had had no intention to burn him, it was not unwholesome kamma. But the king held the Paccekabuddha in great reverence, and he might punish them for having burnt the Paccekabuddha to death. So Sāmāvatī and her companions gathered grass, placed it round the Paccekabuddha's body, poured oil on it, and set fire to it so as to destroy all traces of their crime. This act, of burning the Paccekabuddha with evil intention, was unwholesome kamma. The Paccekabuddha, however, had entered the cessation attainment *(nirodha·samāpatti)*, an attainment that is the temporary cessation of mentality and consciousness-born materiality, and nothing could therefore harm him.[569] Nonetheless, even though the Paccekabuddha had not died, Sāmāvatī and her companions had accomplished much unwholesome kamma by their action, and they experienced the result in a subsequent life.[570]

In our Buddha's time, a past wholesome kamma produced their rebirth as human beings. And Sāmāvatī became King Udena's queen, and her former companions became his consorts. They became also devout Buddhists who offered many requisites to The Buddha and Sangha, studied the Dhamma, and with success practised samatha and vipassanā. Because of that practice, Sāmāvatī became a Stream Enterer *(Sot·Āpanna)*, and the consorts attained various Noble attainments. But one day, the kamma of burning the Paccekabuddha matured as interceptive kamma to cut off their life faculty: they were burned to death in their own quarters.[217] The interceptive kamma's own result did not arise, but allowed the wholesome kammas that each one of them had accomplished in our Buddha's time to produce rebirth in the deva and Brahma worlds respectively.

---

[568] DhPA.ii.1 *'Sāmāvatī·Vatthu'* ('The Case of Sāmāvatī'); UA.vii.10 *'Utena·Suttaṁ'* ('The [King] Utena Sutta')

[569] CESSATION ATTAINMENT: see footnote 436, p.158.

[570] The fifth factor for killing to be a full course of unwholesome kamma is that the being dies: that was not the case here. Nonetheless, having had the intention to kill the Paccekabuddha, and having fulfilled the other four factors, means they accomplished very much unwholesome kamma. For details, see 'A Course of Unwholesome Kamma', p.128.

THE FIVE HUNDRED BHIKKHUS

Another example is the five hundred bhikkhus who were killed, either by themselves or another.[571] The Buddha knew that they all shared a common unwholesome kamma: in the distant past, they had all been hunters in the same forest. Using weapons and traps, they had made hunting their livelihood. With keen pleasure *(haṭṭha·tuṭṭha)*, they had throughout their lives killed animals and birds. At their death, that kamma produced rebirth in hell. Then a wholesome kamma gave them rebirth as human beings. And, dependent on a good friend, they came into the presence of The Buddha, and ordained as bhikkhus. Some of them became Arahants, some became Non-Returners, some became Once Returners, some became Stream Enterers, whereas some remained ordinary people *(puthu·jjana)*.

One morning, as The Buddha was surveying the world with His Buddha-Eye *(Buddha·Cakkhu)*, He saw that within two weeks those five hundred bhikkhus would die: indefinitely-effective 'hunting-as-livelihood' kamma would intercept the wholesome kamma that had given them their human rebirth. The Buddha also saw it was impossible to stop this result from arising. And He saw that the Arahants would not be reborn; the other Noble Ones would have a happy rebirth; but those who were still ordinary people *(puthu·jjana)* would die with lustful desire *(chanda·rāga)*, with attachment for their human life, and would die with fear: that would produce a bad rebirth. If, however, He taught them to practise foulness meditation, they would remove their attachment for life, and fear of death. And with that wholesome kamma, they would attain rebirth in the deva world: The Buddha saw that He could help them only that way. And that way, their ordination as bhikkhus would still turn out beneficial to them. So The Buddha told them to take foulness *(asubha)* (the thirty-two parts of the body *(dva·ttiṁs·ākāra)*) as their main meditation subject:[572] in many ways He spoke in praise of that meditation.

The Buddha also knew that in those two weeks, the bhikkhus would come and report: 'Today one bhikkhu died', 'Today two bhikkhus died', etc. Knowing He could not stop it, knowing there was no purpose in His hearing those things, and to protect those who might criticize Him for not stopping it, The Buddha went into seclusion for those two weeks. And two weeks later, all five hundred bhikkhus had died.

There was an ascetic known as Migalaṇḍika the fake ascetic *(samaṇa·kuttaka)*: he lived off the bhikkhus' leftovers. And those bhikkhus who were still ordinary people *(puthujjana)*, either got him to kill them, or got another unenlightened bhikkhu to kill them, or committed suicide. Why? Because even though The Buddha says suicide is blameable *(sāvajja)* in one who is not an Arahant, they thought it was blameless *(anāvajja)*: even though it was unwholesome kamma, they thought it was wholesome kamma.[573/*218*]

Even Migalaṇḍika the fake ascetic thought it was wholesome kamma. How? First he killed a number of bhikkhus because they asked him to, and because they told him he could have their requisites. And when he then got remorse, a deva told him he should have no remorse. The deva told him he was doing the

---

[571] Vin.Pār.i.3 *'Tatiya·Pārājikaṁ'* ('The Third Defeat') & S.V.X.i.9 *'Vesālī·Suttaṁ'* ('The Vesali Sutta') and their commentaries.

[572] The commentary points out that The Buddha did not glorify death.

[573] In the *'Channa'* sutta, The Buddha declares suicide by an Arahant to be blameless, and by a non-Arahant blameful. But after this incident with the five hundred bhikkhus, The Buddha declares that it is improper, etc.

bhikkhus a favour. And because he believed the deva, he then went back and killed more bhikkhus, including the Noble Ones who had not asked him to kill them.[574] That was how all five hundred bhikkhus then died.

And when all the bhikkhus had died, The Buddha returned. And He asked the Venerable Ānanda why the Sangha was so diminished. The Venerable Ānanda told Him it was because the bhikkhus had practised foulness meditation. And the Venerable Ānanda suggested The Buddha teach another meditation subject. The Buddha asked the Venerable Ānanda to have the remaining bhikkhus assembled, and then explained and spoke in praise of mindfulness of breathing *(ān·āpāna·ssati)*.

Here we need to be very careful to understand this story properly. Just earlier, we mentioned how the Venerable Bāhiya was killed by a cow, and the Venerable Mahāmoggallāna was beaten to death by bandits. That cow and those bandits accomplished their unwholesome kamma by their own volition. But their victim died because of past unwholesome kamma intercepting the wholesome kamma that had given him his human rebirth.

Please always remember that if one is attacked by someone, or one is killed in an accident, etc., one is experiencing the result of one's own past kamma. The being who attacks one, or the accident that takes place, etc., is merely the instrument by which one's past unwholesome kamma intercepts the wholesome kamma that gave one a human rebirth.[575]

It is maybe difficult to understand, but please remember that according to The Buddha, the workings of kamma cannot be understood by mere reasoning. You can properly understand them only when you yourself discern the workings of dependent origination. Until then you must depend on faith: not doubt.

The unenlightened bhikkhus had to die within those two weeks, one way or another. That was because of their own past unwholesome kamma. But they did not do as they did because of their own past unwholesome kamma. They did it because of the strong loathing for life they had developed through foulness meditation, and because they did not understand that what they wanted to do was blameable.[576] In the same way, as we just explained, Migalaṇḍika the fake ascetic did not do as he did because of the bhikkhus' past unwholesome kamma. And The Buddha did not do as He did because of the bhikkhus' past unwholesome kamma either. He did as He did because He knew their past kamma would intercept one way or another, and that they would all die. And The Buddha knew also that the best way for the unenlightened bhikkhus to die was to die without lust for life, because that wholesome kamma would then give them rebirth in the deva world.[577/*219*]

---

[574] The commentary points out that the Noble Ones neither killed themselves, nor asked anyone to kill them, nor killed anyone else. And the *Vimativinodanī* subcommentary explains that all the Noble Ones were killed by Migalaṇḍika the fake ascetic.

[575] See in this connect VsM's discussion of timely/untimely death, endnote 241, p.303.

[576] The subcommentary to Vin.Pār.i.3 *'Tatiya·Pārājikaṁ'* ('The Third Defeat') explains that the bhikkhus who were ordinary people did what they did with the perception of blamelessness *(anavajja·saññino)*.

[577] Further to explain the story of the five hundred bhikkhus should be understood, the Most Venerable Sayadaw refers to the kamma because of which the Bodhisatta had to practise austerities *(dukkara)* for six years: see subsequent endnote 219, p.254.

INTERCEPTS — OWN RESULT

The third way in which interceptive kamma may function is to intercept weaker kamma, and produce its own result.

MĀRA DŪSĪ

An example is the case of Māra Dūsī, during The Buddha Kakusandha's Dispensation.[578] The Buddha's two chief disciples were the Venerable Vidhura and the Venerable Sañjīva.[579/220] One day, the Venerable Sañjīva sat down under a tree, and entered into the cessation attainment *(nirodha·samāpatti)*. Some cowherds, goatherds, and farmers passed by, and saw him sitting under the tree: they thought he was dead. So they covered his body with grass and wood, etc., and set fire to it. Then they left.

Now, when one enters into the cessation attainment, it is impossible for one to suffer any harm: and it is impossible for one's requisites to be ruined.[580] So at dawn the next day, the Venerable Sañjīva emerged unharmed from the attainment. He shook out his robe, and with bowl went for alms in the village. When those same cowherds, goatherds, and farmers saw him going for alms, they thought the dead bhikkhu had come back to life: they were filled with wonder and faith.

The Māra at that time was called Māra Dūsī. Like all Māras, he did not like such virtuous, well-behaved bhikkhus, because he did not know their coming and going *(āgatiṁ vā gatiṁ vā)*; he did not know where they were going to be reborn. Why did he not know? Because the Arahant attains Parinibbāna with consciousness *(viññāṇa)* unestablished *(appatiṭṭhita)*.[581] Since the Arahant has put an end to craving and ignorance, there is no subsequent rebirth.

To try to prevent this, Māra Dūsī created images of the bhikkhus misbehaving, for the Brahmin householders to see. And he encouraged the Brahmins to criticize, abuse, scold, and trouble the virtuous bhikkhus. Māra Dūsī thought unpleasant feelings would then arise in the bhikkhus' minds, associated with ill-will, anger, dissatisfaction, dejection of the mind, etc.,[221] which would hinder their practice. That way, he would then be able to know their coming and going. But when the Brahmin householders criticized, abused, scolded and troubled the bhikkhus, The Buddha Kakusandha told the bhikkhus to practise the four divine abidings *(cattāro brahma·vihāra)*: 1) loving-kindness *(mettā)*, 2) compassion *(karuṇā)*, 3) sympathetic joy *(muditā)*, and 4) equanimity *(upekkhā)*. And He told them to use the four divine abidings as their basis for insight meditation, to attain Arahantship. So the bhikkhus would go to the forest or an empty place, and practise according to His instructions. That way, Māra Dūsī's plan fell through: he did still not know their coming and going. Then he encouraged the Brahmin householders to do the opposite: to honour, respect, revere, and pay homage to the virtuous bhikkhus. Māra Dūsī thought pleasant feelings would then arise in the bhikkhus' minds, associated with delight, pleasure, elation of mind, etc.,[222] which would hinder

---

[578] THE BUDDHA KAKUSANDHA: the third Buddha before The Buddha Gotama. See 'Appendix 2: The Lineage of Buddhas', p.365.

[579] M.I.v.10 *'Māra·Tajjanīya·Suttaṁ'* ('The Blameable-Māra Sutta') and commentary.

[580] CESSATION ATTAINMENT: see footnote 436, p.158.

[581] Māra's not knowing where the Arahant goes is discussed at 'Consciousness Unestablished', p.349.

their practice. But here again, The Buddha Kakusandha had a remedy. He told the bhikkhus instead to practise the four types of perception *(saññā)*:[582] 1) the foulness perception *(asubha·saññā)*, 2) the food-repulsiveness perception *(āhāre paṭikū-la·saññā)*, 3) the entire-world disenchantment perception *(sabba·loke an·abhirati·saññā)*, and 4) the impermanence perception *(anicca·saññā)*. And again, the bhikkhus would go to the forest, etc., and practise according to His instructions: they would use these four meditation subjects to counteract lust, hatred, and delusion, develop insight, and attain Arahantship. Again, Māra Dūsī's plan fell through: again, he did not know their coming and going.

Then one day, when The Buddha Kakusandha went for alms together with His chief disciple Vidhura, Māra took possession of a boy. The boy picked up a pot-sherd and threw it at the Venerable Vidhura. It cut his head and drew blood. And now The Buddha Kakusandha turned about with a Buddha's elephant look *(nāgā-·palokita)*. He then said: 'This Māra Dūsī the limit does not know *(na vāyaṁ dūsī māro matta·m·aññāsi)*.' And then Māra Dūsī fell from there and was reborn in the Great Hell. There he was cooked for many thousand years. He was even reborn in the worst of all hells (a smaller hell attached to the Great Hell), where he was cooked for ten thousand years: there, he had a human body and a fish's head.

Dūsī Māra's kamma of harassing a Chief-Disciple intercepted the wholesome kamma that gave him rebirth in the deva world. And it produced its own result, which was rebirth in the Great Hell, even in the worst of all the hells there.

We need here understand that Māra Dūsī's rebirth in hell was not caused by The Buddha Kakusandha's elephant look, or his words. It was caused solely by Māra Dūsī's unwholesome kamma of harassing the chief disciple of a Buddha.[583] Thus are the workings of kamma.

King Kalābu

Another example is the king of Bārāṇasī, King Kalābu, many aeons before our Buddha's time.[584] He had the five aggregates of a human being because of past wholesome kamma. And he became king also because of past wholesome kamma. But one day, he got angry at an ascetic Khantivādī, who taught patience *(khanti)*, and who was our Bodhisatta. To test the Venerable Khantivādī's patience, King Kalābu had Khantivādī's nose cut off, then his ears, then his hands, and then his feet. Those unwholesome kammas matured presently, for the earth opened up and sucked Kalābu down to Avīci Hell. His present unwholesome kamma intercepted the wholesome kamma that had produced his five aggregates as King Kalābu, and produced its own result, which was the five aggregates of a being in hell.[585] We may thus say that the kamma of killing the ascetic functioned both as interceptive kamma and as productive kamma. Looking at it another way, we may also say that one kamma of killing the ascetic intercepted the kamma that produced his five aggregates as King Kalābu, and another identical kamma pro-

---

582 The commentary quotes A.VII.v.6 (49) *'Dutiya·Saññā·Suttaṁ'* ('The Second Perception Sutta'): it is explained endnote 281. p.355.

583 This point is discussed also on p.296.

584 JA.III.IV.ii.3 (313) *'Khanti·Vādī·Jātaka·Vaṇṇanā'* ('Description of the Patience-Speaker Jātaka')

585 For other such cases, see 'Mischievous Nanda', p.265, and 'Ciñcamāṇavikā's Picture', p.311.

duced his five aggregates as a being in Avīci Hell:[586] that is, the interceptive kamma and the productive kamma had the same identity *(ek·attanaya)*.[587]

Let us then discuss the principle of identity.

THE PRINCIPLE OF IDENTITY

According to the principle of identity, the series of kammas that constitute one accomplished action are the same: all the different impulsions have the same identity.[588]

We may understand this principle if we look at the process of dependent origination *(paṭicca·samuppāda)*:[223]

[1] **Because of ignorance, formations** [arise];
[2] **because of formations, consciousness;**
[3] **because of consciousness, mentality-materiality;**
[4] **because of mentality-materiality, the six bases.**

This process is similar to the process of a seed going through the stages of shoot, seedling, sapling, etc., eventually to become a tree. The seed, shoot, seedling, sapling, etc. are not the same as the tree, but the continuity is the same: the different stages have the same identity.

When one accomplishes the wholesome kamma of making an offering *(dāna)*, of undertaking and observing morality *(sīla)*, and of practising samatha and vipassanā meditation, then according to the principle of identity, each such action is considered to be one kamma. In the same way, when one accomplishes the unwholesome kamma of killing, of stealing, of engaging in sexual misconduct, of telling a lie, or of drinking beer and wine, etc., each such action is considered to be one kamma. But it does not mean that one of those actions comprises only one volition *(cetanā)*, for in the course of just one of those actions, many billion unwholesome or wholesome mental processes arise and perish. As we have explained before, on our plane (the sensual-sphere plane *(kām·āvacara·bhūmi)*), within a snap of the fingers very many thousand million consciousnesses arise and perish: they include many thousand million mental processes *(citta·vīthi)*.[589] In each of those mental processes there are seven impulsion consciousnesses *(javana)*.[590] So, when we speak of one kamma, we are in fact referring to the series of kammas that comprise the completed action, such as making an offering. If we consider actions in this way, we may understand that one kamma can function in several ways.

[586] VsMṬ.687 *'Kaṅkhā·Vitaraṇa·Visuddhi·Niddeso'* ('Exposition of the Doubt-Transcendence Purification') denies that interceptive kamma can produce its own result: 'If interceptive kamma acts in this way, it is not interceptive kamma, but productive kamma.' The Most Venerable Pa-Auk Tawya Sayadaw is here explaining that even though it looks as if the *Visuddhi·Magga*'s explanation is contradicted by this denial, it depends on one's point of view. While it is correct that one kamma intercepts and another kamma produces, they can be said to be the same kamma, since they have the same identity. The difference is point of view.

[587] VsM.xvii *'Paññā·Bhūmi·Niddesa'* ('Exposition of the Wisdom-Ground') PP.xvii.309*f*

[588] This matches the logical proposition: A = B. A is not B, and B is not A, yet they are identical.

[589] For an estimated number, see footnote 101, p.41.

[590] The Most Venerable Pa-Auk Tawya Sayadaw is here referring only to sensual-sphere mental processes: see footnote 102, p.41.

Before we discuss the principle of identity further, let us first summarize the different functions that kamma can exercise:[591]

1) When a kamma produces the resultant mentality and materiality at rebirth and in the course of a life, it has functioned as productive kamma *(janaka-·kamma)*.
2) When a kamma facilitates the maturing of the result of an unwholesome or wholesome productive kamma, and makes the result endure, it has functioned as reinforcing kamma *(upatthambhaka·kamma)*.
3) When a kamma obstructs the result of an unwholesome or wholesome productive kamma, it has functioned as frustrating kamma *(upapīḷaka·kamma)*.
4) When a kamma takes over, and cuts off the result of an unwholesome or wholesome productive kamma, it has functioned as interceptive kamma *(upaghātaka·kamma)*.

All these four functions may be exercised by one kamma, that is, different kammas of the same identity may exercise different functions. When, for example, you make an offering to a virtuous person, many billion mind-door processes arise and perish in your mentality-materiality continuity: before you make the offering, while you are making the offering, and after you have made the offering. In each mental process, there are seven wholesome impulsions: some of them will function as productive kammas; some will function as reinforcing kammas; some will function as frustrating kammas; some will function as interceptive kammas; and many of them will not function at all, because they will lapse.

The Venerable Devadatta

A good example of these four functions operating within one identical course of mentality-materiality is the Venerable Devadatta.[592] A wholesome kamma functioned as productive kamma to produce his rebirth into a royal family. That wholesome kamma functioned also as productive kamma and reinforcing kamma to produce continued happiness in his royal life, and later as a bhikkhu. But when he as a bhikkhu later was suspended by the Sangha for his evil deeds, he lost people's respect and was despised: then was his wholesome kamma obstructed by unwholesome kamma that functioned as frustrating kamma. And because he made a schism in the Sangha, he was reborn in hell: his unwholesome, weighty schism kamma functioned as interceptive kamma to cut off the wholesome productive and reinforcing kammas that had produced and sustained his life as a human being.

Here, no one kamma functioned as both interceptive and productive kamma. When Devadatta made a schism in the Sangha, many, many billions of unwholesome mind-door processes arose in him, each with seven impulsions, that is, billions and billions of unwholesome impulsions arising from the one action of making a schism. Those billions of impulsions all had the same identity, yet they exercised different functions: one schism kamma functioned as interceptive kamma to cut off the kamma that produced his human rebirth,[593] and another schism kamma functioned as subsequently-effective productive kamma to produce his

---

[591] VsMṬ.680-681 *'Kaṅkhā·Vitaraṇa·Visuddhi·Niddeso'* ('Exposition of the Doubt-Transcendence Purification')

[592] See 'The Venerable Devadatta', p.152.

[593] In also his case, the earth opened up and he was sucked down to Avīci Hell.

rebirth in Avīci Hell. Other 'schism' kammas, as well as unwholesome weighty kammas from his act of drawing our Buddha's blood with evil intent, and yet other unwholesome kammas of other identities subsequently functioned as reinforcing kammas to increase his suffering in hell, and prolong it so it would last till the destruction of the world system.[594]

The Venerable Ledi Sayadaw's Explanation

Another example of one identical series of kammas exercising all four functions is the Venerable Ledi Sayadaw's[595] explanation of intentional killing.

He explains that when one person takes another's life, the volitions of that act of killing have sufficient power to function as productive kamma, which means they have sufficient power to produce results in the course of a life (as presently-effective kamma), or to produce the rebirth-linking mentality-materiality of a being in hell (as subsequently- or indefinitely-effective kamma). But this will take place only when they meet the right conditions to mature. Until then, however, the volitions of that act of killing may (as subsequently- and indefinitely-effective kamma) exercise one of the three other functions:

1) They may reinforce the results of other unwholesome kammas.
2) They may frustrate the results of wholesome kammas.
3) They may intercept wholesome kammas.

The volitions of an unwholesome or wholesome act may exercise one of these three functions for as long as a hundred thousand aeons or longer into the future.

Having now explained the principle of identity, we shall explain how one kamma may function as what is called identical interceptive kamma *(ekatta·naya·upaghātaka·kamma)*.

Identical Interceptive Kamma

The Three Bhikkhus

Strong and powerful wholesome interceptive kamma may not only intercept the result of weaker unwholesome kamma, but it may also intercept the result of weaker wholesome kamma. A good example of this is Deva Gopaka and the three bhikkhus.[596]

Deva Gopaka was son of Sakka, the king of devas. Deva Gopaka had in his former life been a Sakyan princess called Gopikā, who had faith in The Buddha, Dhamma, and Sangha. She observed the five precepts at all times, and every day three bhikkhus came to her house for alms, and they taught her Dhamma. The result was that, based on her morality, and her knowledge of the Dhamma, she was able to practise samatha and vipassanā so successfully that she became a Stream Enterer *(Sot·Āpanna)*. And being disgusted with her life as a woman, she accomplished many wholesome kammas, with the aspiration to be reborn as a

---

[594] The unwholesome weighty kammas are explained at 'Unwholesome Weighty Kamma', p.170.
[595] The Most Venerable Ledi Sayadaw (1846-1923) was a renowned sayadaw who wrote many books on the Dhamma. This explanation is from his PaD.
[596] They are mentioned also at 'Bhikkhus Reborn as Heavenly Musicians', p.191. The information here is taken from D.ii.8 *'Sakka·Pañhā·Suttaṁ'* ('The Sakka's-Questions Sutta'), and its commentary.

male. At death, she was reborn in the Tāvatiṁsā deva world as the son of King Sakka: her name was now Deva Gopaka.

The three bhikkhus she had fed as Princess Gopikā had also been virtuous: they had practised the bhikkhu's morality. Based on their morality, they also practised samatha and vipassanā successfully, except they did not attain a Noble state. But their morality, concentration, and wisdom were strong and powerful decisive supporting causes*(upanissaya·paccaya)* for the attainment of a Noble state.[597] Their morality was so pure that they were sure to be reborn in whatever deva world they wanted. Furthermore, since they had attained the jhānas, they could also have been reborn in one of the Brahma worlds. But at death, they were not reborn in one of the Brahma worlds: they were reborn as *gandhabba* devas, musicians and dancers in the deva world. Why? Because they had been *gandhabba* devas in many past lives, which meant they inclined towards that type of life. *Gandhabba* devas belong to the world of the Four Great Kings*(Cātu-·Mahā·Rājika)*.

One day, the three *gandhabbas* came to the assembly hall to entertain the devas, and Deva Gopaka thought: 'They are very shiny and beautiful. What was their past kamma?' He saw they had been the three bhikkhus who had come daily to his house for alms-food. Examining further, he discovered also that their morality, concentration and wisdom had been very high. So he said: 'When you listened to the Teachings, and practised the Dhamma, what were your eyes and ears directed at? You were bhikkhus who practised the threefold higher training under the guidance of The Buddha, yet now you have been reborn as *gandhabba* devas, inferior to Tāvatiṁsā devas. We think that is most unsatisfactory.'

On hearing these words of rebuke, which sounded as a warning to the three *gandhabba* devas, two of them remembered their past noble practices, and were ashamed. Immediately, they developed samatha, attained the first jhāna, practised insight meditation based on that jhāna, became Non-Returners*(An·Āgāmi)*, and died. They were reborn on the plane of Brahma's Ministers*(Brahmā Purohita)*. But the third *gandhabba* deva was not ashamed: he remained a *gandhabba* deva.

How then to explain the workings of kamma for the two *gandhabba* devas who became Non-Returners? In their previous life as bhikkhus, they had accomplished wholesome kamma that produced their rebirth in the deva world as male *gan-*

---

[597] DECISIVE SUPPORTING CAUSE: past mental or material things*(dhamma)* that play a decisive part in the subsequent arising of mental phenomena, which would not have arisen otherwise. Unholesome things can be a decisive supporting cause for either unwholesome or wholesome mental phenomena, and vice-versa: wholesome things may be a decisive supporting cause for either unwholesome or wholesome mental phenomena. (P.I.423 *'Upanissaya·Paccayo'* ('Decisive-Supporting Cause')) For example, practice of the three merit-work bases may be caused by faith (wholesome); by the wish for Nibbāna (wholesome); by the wish to become a Buddha, a certain type of Arahant, a deva, a rich human being, a woman/man (unwholesome); by attachment (unwholesome), for example, parents may be attached to their ordained daughter/son, and go and visit them many times, practise, etc. (For two examples by Venerable Ānanda, see endnote 291, p.357). Contrariwise, unwholesome things may arise when one practises the three merit-work bases: arguing about how to conduct an offering, comparing offerings, comparing meditation, etc. (for examples, see 'The Variety of Temperament', p.32). The term is very wide, and includes a good friend, faith, good health, honesty, energy, and knowledge leading to successful practice, and their opposites leading to failure (see 'Good and Bad Friendship', p.212, and footnote 975, p.374).

dhabbas. But that kamma was then cut off, intercepted by the more powerful first-jhāna kamma (a weighty kamma), with which they attained Non-Returnership. And the interceptive kamma gave its own result, which was rebirth on the plane of Brahma's Ministers.

Thus, according to the principle of identity, their first-jhāna wholesome kamma functioned as both a interceptive kamma and a productive kamma. More exactly, within the very short time that they were in the first jhāna, they accomplished billions of first-jhāna kammas (volition),[598] and of those billions of kammas, one functioned as a interceptive kamma, another as a productive kamma: the remaining billions of kammas became lapsed kamma.

The Ghost Nandaka

Just as a wholesome interceptive kamma may intercept weaker wholesome productive kamma, so may an unwholesome interceptive kamma intercept weaker unwholesome productive kamma. The interceptive kamma may also produce its own result, and other identical unwholesome reinforcing kammas may prolong the result. A good example is the ghost *(peta)* Nandaka.[599]

In his former human life, he was the general of a King Piṅgala in Suraṭṭha. Nandaka held firmly what The Buddha calls the Great View *(Mahā·Diṭṭhi)*. According to the Great View, there is no root or cause for the purification of beings; every being's time in *saṁsāra* is fixed, and one's happiness and suffering is predetermined: just as a ball of string unwinds until there is no more string left, so does everyone's time in *saṁsāra* unwind until at a fixed time they are annihilated. Thus, the Great View is a fatalistic view with elements of both an eternity view and an annihilation view.[224] Since the general held this view, he accomplished billions and billions of unwholesome kammas during his lifetime. How strongly he held this view at death, we do not know, but according to the Texts, he was reborn as a ghost.[600]

His daughter Uttarā, however, held Right View, for she was a Stream Enterer. And after her father's death, she offered alms-food to an Arahant who was on his almsround in the village, and she dedicated the merit of that kamma to her late father. When the offering had been accomplished, Nandaka was able to call out *'Sādhu!'* ('It is good!'). Although that wholesome kamma was too weak to intercept the unwholesome productive kamma that maintained the ghost's unhappy life, it was powerful enough to function as productive kamma in the course of that life, to produce the pleasures of a *vemānika* (a being like a deva). But it lasted only six months, for then a more powerful wrong-view kamma (of the same identity as the unwholesome productive kamma that held him in the ghost world) functioned as unwholesome interceptive kamma, and made its own result arise, and now the ghost Nandaka was reborn in Avīci Hell. Other wrong-view kammas then functioned as reinforcing kammas to make his existence in Avīci Hell endure.

---

[598] See further table '5d: The Jhāna-Attainment Process', p.178.

[599] Pv.iv.3 *'Nandaka·Peta·Vatthu'* ('The Case of the Ghost Nandaka')

[600] Holding a view that denies the workings of kamma is the weightiest of the six unwholesome weighty kammas, which leads inevitably to rebirth in hell. For details, see 'Unwholesome Weighty Kamma', p.170.

That concludes our explanation of interceptive kamma, which concludes our explanation of the twelve categories that The Buddha uses to explain the workings of kamma.

Conclusion

Let us conclude by summarizing the twelve categories. First we discussed the workings of kamma according to the time of effect: when does the kamma take effect. We discussed four categories:[601]

1) Presently-effective kamma *(diṭṭha·dhamma·vedanīya·kamma)*: it takes effect in the same individual existence *(atta·bhāva)*.
2) Subsequently-effective kamma *(upapajja·vedanīya·kamma)*: it takes effect in the very next existence.
3) Indefinitely-effective kamma *(apar·āpariya·vedanīya·kamma)*: it takes effect in some existence after the next one.
4) Lapsed kamma *(ahosi·kamma)*: it fails to take effect. It is is presently- or subsequently-effective kamma that is defunct, kamma only by name. After one's Parinibbāna (final cessation), it includes also indefinitely-effective kammas, because after one's Parinibbāna, no kammas take effect anymore.

Then we discussed the workings of kamma according to the order of effect: which type of kamma takes effect first. Again, we discussed four categories:[602]

1) Weighty kamma *(garuka·kamma)*: there are six unwholesome weighty kammas:
   i) killing one's mother
   ii) killing one's father
   iii) killing an Arahant
   iv) with evil intent drawing a Buddha's blood
   v) making a schism in the Sangha
   vi) holding a persistent wrong view (denying the workings of kamma)

   These six weighty kammas are sure to lead to rebirth in hell in the subsequent life. That is why they are also called unintervenable kamma. Then there are the eight wholesome weighty kammas: the four fine-material sphere jhānas and four immaterial sphere jhānas. If held up to the time of death, they are sure to lead to rebirth in the Brahma world.
2) Habitual kamma *(āciṇṇa·kamma)*: that is unwholesome or wholesome kamma which is done habitually, frequently, and continuously. For example, habitually a butcher kills beings, and habitually a thief steals, habitually a patron of the Sangha gives alms, and habitually a meditator practises samatha and vipassanā meditation.
3) Near-death kamma *(āsanna·kamma)*: that is an unusual kamma that at the time of death is recollected very vividly. For example, the habitually virtuous person may vividly recollect an unusual unwholesome action, and a habitually unvirtuous person may vividly recollect an unusual wholesome action.
4) Accomplished kamma *(katattā·kamma)*: that is any other kamma that has been completed: any of the ten courses of unwholesome kamma (killing, theft, sexual misconduct, etc.), or the ten courses of wholesome kamma (to abstain from killing, to abstain from theft, to abstain from sexual misconduct, etc.).

---

601 See 'Time of Effect', p.145.
602 See 'Order of Effect', p.170.

Lastly, we discussed the workings of kamma according to the function of effect: how does the kamma function. And also here there are four categories:[603]

1) Productive kamma *(janaka kamma)*: it is unwholesome kamma that produces the mentality-materiality at the rebirth of an animal, ghost, or being in hell, and in the course of that being's life, or wholesome kamma that produces the mentality-materiality at the rebirth of a human being or heavenly being, and in the course of that being's life.
2) Reinforcing kamma *(upatthambhaka kamma)*: it is unwholesome or wholesome kamma that reinforces a productive kamma. For example, the wholesome kamma that gave one rebirth as a human being may be reinforced so that the human being is healthy, and lives a trouble-free life. Likewise, the unwholesome kamma that gave one rebirth as an animal may be reinforced so that the animal is unhealthy, and lives a troubled life.
3) Frustrating kamma *(upapīḷaka kamma)*: it is unwholesome or wholesome kamma that frustrates and obstructs the result of another kamma. For example, the wholesome kamma that gave one rebirth as a human being may be frustrated so that the human being has many problems with health, property and wealth, or family and friends. Likewise, the unwholesome kamma that gave one rebirth as an animal may be frustrated so that the animal enjoys times of ease and happiness.
4) Interceptive kamma *(upaghātaka kamma)*: it is unwholesome or wholesome kamma that intercepts weaker kamma. For example, the wholesome kamma that gave one rebirth as a human being may be intercepted so that one dies before one has reached the end of one's life span. If it is unwholesome, one may be reborn as an animal, a ghost, or in hell; if it is wholesome, one may be reborn in the deva world or Brahma world.

That concludes our summary of the twelve categories by which The Buddha explains kamma. Next, we shall discuss the workings of achievement and failure.

ACHIEVEMENT AND FAILURE

To explain the workings of kamma, we began by discussing the two *'Gaddula·Baddha'* suttas. There, The Buddha explains why beings are unable to find release from suffering: because of clinging to the five aggregates as self, they go on producing new aggregates life after life. The aggregates arise at the rebirth moment, and they are determined by the kamma that ripened at the time of death in the previous life. In the second *'Gaddula·Baddha'* sutta, The Buddha also discusses how the variety of kamma and the variety of results produces the variety of beings in the different worlds. That variety of past kamma produces also a variety of results throughout the course of existence in those worlds.

This knowledge we have because of what The Buddha calls His Second Tathāgata Power. Let us again listen to Him explain it:[604]

Again and further, Sāriputta, the Tathāgata understands the result of past, future, and present kamma that has been undertaken, by way of contingency and root, according to reality.

And whatever, Sāriputta, result of past, future, and present kamma that has been undertaken the Tathāgata by way of contingency and root understands according to reali-

---

[603] See 'Function of Effect', p.186.

[604] See quotation 'The Buddha's Knowledge of Kamma&Result', p.39

ty. This then, Sāriputta, is a Tathāgata's Tathāgata power, because of which power the Tathāgata assumes the bull's stance, roars the lion's roar in the assemblies, and sets in motion the divine wheel.

The Buddha speaks of the contingency *(ṭhānaso)* and the root *(hetuso)* of the result *(vipāka)*. The root of the result is the kamma accomplished. And we have discussed the variety of kamma and the variety of results according to the twelve categories of kamma. Now, we shall discuss the contingency upon which the kamma produces its result. What does that mean?

As we have discussed, the basic workings of kamma is that unwholesome kammas (rooted in ignorance, craving, and clinging) produce painful results, while wholesome kammas (rooted in ignorance, craving, and clinging) produce good, pleasurable results. But unwholesome and wholesome kammas do not produce their results in every case: they do so only according to circumstances. Those circumstances are the contingency upon which the kamma produces its results. If those circumstances exist, the kamma produces its result; if those circumstances do not exist, the kamma does not produce its result. Thus, even though The Buddha makes it clear that we are the owners of our good and bad kamma, the maturing of such kamma depends on conditions. Just as certain conditions are necessary for the accomplishment of certain good and bad kammas, so are certain conditions necessary for the maturing of such kamma.

To explain this aspect of The Buddha's Second Tathāgata Power, the Pali Texts speak of four kinds of achievement *(sampatti)*,[605] and four kinds of failure *(vipatti)*.[606] Achievement disables bad kamma, and enables good kamma, whereas failure disables good kamma, and enables bad kamma.[607]

Achievement

The four types of achievement *(sampatti)* are:

1) Destination achievement *(gati·sampatti)*: that is rebirth in a happy destination: a divine- or human world.
2) Appearance achievement *(upadhi·sampatti)*: that is an attractive, well-formed, and unimpaired physical body and appearance.
3) Time achievement *(kāla·sampatti)*: that is rebirth at a time when there is good government and good people.
4) Means achievement *(payoga·sampatti)*: that is the right means, which The Buddha also calls kamma achievements *(kammanta·sampatti)*: bodily, verbal, and mental.[225] We discussed them earlier:[608] not to kill (but to be kind and compassionate), not to steal, not to engage in sexual misconduct, not to drink beer and wine, etc., not to tell lies, not to slander, to speak politely, not to prattle, not to covet, not to harbour ill-will, and to hold Right View.

---

605 SAMPATTI: this being the opposite of *vipatti* (failure) should ideally be 'success'. But 'destination success', 'appearance success', or 'success of destination, etc., is inapt if not unacceptable English. Hence 'achievement', which means also 'success', and matches the exact Pali.

606 This and subsequent explanations (excluding examples), and similes have been taken from the analysis of The Buddha's Second Tathāgata Power in VbhA.XVI.x *'Dutiya·Bala·Niddeso'* ('Exposition of the Second Power').

607 For clarity, 'enabled' and 'disabled' are here used, although the Pali is the less symmetrical 'prevented by' and 'by means of', 'on account of'.

608 See 'The Ten Wholesome Courses of Kamma', p.130.

These four types of achievement may disable certain unwholesome kammas from producing their result, and conversely these four types of achievement may enable certain wholesome kammas to produce their result. In other words, contingent upon achievement, some unwholesome kammas do not produce their result, and some wholesome kammas produce their result.

Failure

The four types of failure *(vipatti)* are:

1) Destination failure *(gati·vipatti)*: that is rebirth in a woeful destination: a hell, or an animal-, ghost- or demon world.
2) Appearance failure *(upadhi·vipatti)*: that is an unattractive, ill-formed, and impaired physical body and appearance.
3) Time failure *(kāla·vipatti)*: that is rebirth at a bad time, with bad government and bad people.
4) Means failure *(payoga·vipatti)*: that is the wrong means, which The Buddha also calls kamma faults and failures *(kammanta·sandosa·byāpatti)*: bodily, verbal, and mental. We discussed them earlier: to kill, to steal, to engage in sexual misconduct, to drink beer and wine, etc., to tell lies, to slander, to speak harshly, to prattle, to covet, to harbour ill-will, and to hold wrong view.

These four types of failure may disable certain wholesome kammas from producing their result, and conversely these four types of failure may enable certain unwholesome kammas to produce their result. In other words, contingent upon failure, some wholesome kammas do not produce their result, and some unwholesome kammas do produce their result.

The Workings of Achievement and Failure

We shall now explain the four types of achievement and four types of failure one by one. First how the four types of achievement *(sampatti)* (destination-, appearance-, time-, and means achievement) disable certain unwholesome kammas from producing their result, whereas the four types of failure *(vipatti)* enable them.[609]

Achievement Disables Unwholesome Kammas

Destination Achievement Disables Unwholesome Kammas

There are some bad kamma undertakings that, stopped by destination achievement *(gati·sampatti)*, do not mature.[610]

Someone's unwholesome kamma may function as productive kamma to produce rebirth in a bad destination: hell, the animal world, or the ghost world. That is destination failure *(gati·vipatti)*. Contingent upon that failure, certain of her or his unwholesome kammas are enabled to produce their result. But because of a single wholesome kamma she or he may be reborn in a good destination: the human or heavenly worlds. That is destination achievement *(gati·sampatti)*. Contingent upon

---

[609] VbhA.xvi.810 *'Dutiya·Bala·Niddeso'* ('Exposition of the Second Power') DD.xvi.2202-2205

[610] All the introductory quotations are from The Buddha's explanation in Vbh.XVI.x.810 *'Ñāṇa·Vibhaṅgo'* ('Knowledge Analysis').

that achievement, the unwholesome kammas are disabled, and wholesome kammas are enabled to produce their result instead.

TAMBADĀṬHIKA THE EXECUTIONER

A good example is the executioner Tambadāṭhika: we discussed his case earlier.[611] He had for fifty-five years habitually accomplished the unwholesome kamma of beheading criminals. If he at death was reborn in a lower world such as hell, that destination failure would enable his unwholesome kammas to produce their result. Instead, at his death, the single wholesome kamma of attaining the Formations-Equanimity Knowledge *(Saṅkhār·Upekkhā·Ñāṇa)* functioned as productive kamma to produce rebirth in the deva world: destination achievement. Contingent upon that achievement, his unwholesome kammas were disabled, and enabled were only his wholesome kammas.

APPEARANCE ACHIEVEMENT DISABLES UNWHOLESOME KAMMAS

There are some bad kamma undertakings that, stopped by appearance achievement *(upadhi·sampatti)*, **do not mature.**

Someone may have ill-shaped limbs and an unattractive and ugly appearance: that is appearance failure *(upadhi·vipatti)*. Contingent upon that failure, certain of her or his unwholesome kammas are enabled to produce their result. But because of a single wholesome kamma, she or he may develop well shaped limbs, and be attractive, beautiful and radiant like Brahma: that is appearance achievement *(upadhi·sampatti)*. Contingent upon that achievement, the unwholesome kammas are disabled, and wholesome kammas are enabled to produce their result instead.

The Commentary explains that if such a person is born to a slave, he will not be made to do the work of an elephant keeper, a groom, or cowherd. Because of his beauty, his owners will think: 'Such a one should not do dirty work.' And they dress him in fine clothes, and make him storekeeper, or some such thing. If it is a woman, they do not make her prepare food for the elephants etc.: they give her clothes and ornaments, and make her guard beds, or make her a favourite.

The Commentary gives as example a Queen Sāmā. Once, in the time of King Bhātiya, a number of people were caught eating beef, and were taken to the king. Unable to pay a fine, they were then made cleaners in the king's court. But one of their daughters was attractive and beautiful, and the king took her into his harem, and made her a favourite. Through the influence of her wholesome kamma, she and her family lived happily.

TIME ACHIEVEMENT DISABLES UNWHOLESOME KAMMAS

There are some bad kamma undertakings that, stopped by time achievement *(kāla·sampatti)*, **do not mature.**

Someone may be reborn at the time of bad government, and evil people: that is time failure *(kāla·vipatti)*. Contingent upon that failure, certain of her or his unwholesome kammas are enabled to produce their result. But because of a single wholesome kamma, she or he may be reborn at the time of good government, and good people, for example, when people begin to appear at the beginning of an aeon,[612] when there is a Wheel-Turning King,[613] or a Buddha: that is time

[611] See 'Tambadāṭhika the Executioner', p.183.

[612] BEGINNING OF AN AEON: in D.iii.4 *'Agg·Añña·Suttaṁ'* ('The Beginnings-Knowledge Sutta'),

(Please see further next page.)

achievement *(kāla·sampatti)*. Contingent upon that achievement, the unwholesome kammas are disabled, and wholesome kammas are enabled to produce their result instead.

Let us then discuss what it means to be born at the time of bad and good government, at the time of bad and good people, and how bad and good people may influence our conduct, especially our associates, teachers, and leaders.

GOOD AND BAD FRIENDSHIP

Once the Venerable Ānanda reflected on how one may succeed in the holy life *(brahma·cariya)*.[614] He decided that success in the holy life depends half on good friendship, and half on one's own effort. But when he said this to The Buddha, The Buddha corrected him:

Not so, Ānanda, not so, Ānanda!

The entire holy life, Ānanda, is just this, namely: good friendship *(kalyāṇa·mittatā)*, **good association** *(kalyāṇa·sahāyatā)*, **good companionship** *(kalyāṇa·sampavaṅkatā)*.

With a good friend, Ānanda, this is to be expected of the bhikkhu: that he with a good companion, with a good associate, the Noble Eightfold Path will develop, the Noble Eightfold Path much will practise.

This is the principle of the good friend *(kalyāṇa·mitta)*. When we have good friends, good associates, and good companions, then may we practise the Noble Eightfold Path *(Ariya Aṭṭhaṅgika Magga)*: that is, the merit-work bases, the threefold training, knowledge and conduct, etc. Contingent upon good friendship, it is possible for us to practise these good things, to accomplish such wholesome kamma *(kusala·kamma)*. Contingent upon bad friendship, however, to practise these things is impossible.[226] If we have bad friends, we practise bad things, we accomplish unwholesome kamma *(akusala·kamma)*.

This principle applies also to the ruler and government of a country: if the ruler is virtuous, and government accords with the Dhamma (based on Right View) then may we say it is a good ruler and government. To be born at such a time is time achievement *(kāla·sampatti)*.

THE WHEEL-TURNING KING

An example of good government and how it disables unwholesome kammas from maturing is when the ruler is a Wheel-Turning King. In the *'Mahā·Sudassana'* sutta,[615] The Buddha describes how He was once a Wheel-Turning King called Mahāsudassana. His life span was three-hundred and thirty-six thousand years. To such a king appears the Wheel Treasure *(cakka·ratana)*, and it enables him to establish a great empire ruled by the Dhamma. Why does such a wheel appear to such a king? Because of past and present kamma. The Buddha explains that the Wheel Treasure appeared to King Mahāsudassana because of the king's past and present wholesome kamma of offering *(dāna)*, his past and present wholesome kamma of restraint *(dama)* (keeping the five precepts), and his past and present wholesome kamma of abstinence *(saṁyama)* (keeping the eight precepts on full-moon, new moon, and half-moon days), as well as his governing

---

The Buddha explains the evolution of man, and the first establishment of a king. This is an auspicious time, for the king rules according to the Dhamma.

613 See below, 'The Wheel-Turning King', p.213.

614 S.V.I.i.2 *'Upaḍḍha·Suttaṁ'* ('The "Half" Sutta')

615 D.ii.4 *'Mahā·Sudassana·Suttaṁ'* ('The Great-Sudassana Sutta')

according to the Dhamma. Past kamma accounts also for such a king's superior beauty, long life, good health, and the devotion he receives from his people. In the latter quarter of his life, such a king practises the four divine abidings *(cattāro brahma·vihārā)* (loving-kindness *(mettā)*, compassion *(karuṇā)*, sympathetic joy *(muditā)*, and equanimity *(upekkhā)*): for King Mahāsudassana, it was the latter eighty-four thousand years of his life. Because of that practice, such a king is at death reborn in the Brahma world.

A Ruler's Good Example

The Buddha discussed this principle also with King Pasenadi of Kosala.[616] He told the king he should train himself to have good friends, good associates, and good companions. And having good friends, he should dwell with diligence in wholesome things *(appamādo kusalesu dhammesu)*: offering *(dāna)*, morality *(sīla)* and meditation *(bhāvanā)*.[227]

Then The Buddha explained how this example set by the king (the ruler) would affect the people of the kingdom: the king's wives, the noblemen at court, the troops, and all the people in the towns and in the countryside would see how the king was diligent in wholesome things, and then they would be inspired also to be diligent in wholesome things. The Buddha explained that when everyone in that way were diligent in doing wholesome things, the king, his wives, and his property would be well protected.

To be reborn at the time of such virtuous kings is time achievement *(kāla·sampatti)*, because at such a time, the people are taught not to kill, not to steal, not to engage in sexual misconduct, not to tell lies, not to drink intoxicants, and they are taught to be moderate in eating.[617] And seeing that their ruler is in this way virtuous, they also become virtuous; seeing how their ruler practises offering, etc., they also practise such things.[228] In that way, contingent upon time achievement, there is means achievement *(payoga·sampatti)*, and certain unwholesome kammas do not produce their results.[229]

Deterioration of Human Life

In the *'Cakka·Vatti·Sīha·Nāda'* sutta,[618] The Buddha describes how time achievement can become time failure because the king does not rule according to the Dhamma. The Buddha explains that there was a lineage of Wheel-Turning Kings under whose rule the people prospered and were happy. But after seven generations, it changed. The seventh king did not ask the court sage about his royal duties, but ruled according to his own ideas. Then, because he failed to support the people in society that needed support, poverty arose in the kingdom. As a result, more and more bad things arose: theft, the use of weapons, the taking of life, the telling of lies, harsh speech, prattle, covetousness and ill-will, wrong view, incest, excessive greed, wrong sexual practices, and disrespect for parents, ascetics and Brahmins, and the head of the clan. All these unwholesome things arose because the king (the ruler) was not diligent in wholesome things: he was no longer a good friend to his people. This is what the *Abhidhamma* commentary

---

616 S.I.III.ii.8 *'Kalyāṇa·Mitta·Suttaṁ'* ('The Good Friend Sutta')

617 For another example of such a king, see endnote 111, p.240.

618 D.i.8 *'Cakka·Vatti·Sīha·Nāda·Suttaṁ'* ('The Wheel-Turning Lion's-Roar Sutta')

refers to as being reborn at the time of bad government, and bad, nasty and feeble people,[619] which is time failure *(kāla·vipatti)*.

This deterioration is still going on. And at the same time as these things arise, the human life span is becoming shorter and shorter, and people are becoming less and less beautiful. Also, the quality of food is deteriorating: high quality food is becoming more and more difficult to get.[619] This deterioration occurs over many, many thousands of years.

The Buddha explains that the deterioration will continue until there is no morality left at all, and the human life span is only ten years. At that time, all people will see each other as enemies, and will all be killing each other. But some people will escape to the wilderness, and live on roots and fruits. Realizing that all the bad things happened because of immorality, those people will again undertake the precepts, etc. As they do so, gradually the human life span will increase up to many thousand years, and people will become more beautiful. That way, contingent upon morality, etc., time failure will again become time achievement. Then again, the life span will decrease. When the life span reaches eighty-thousand years, again a Wheel-Turning King will arise, and the last Buddha of this aeon, The Buddha Metteya. A Buddha is the Supreme Good Friend.

The Supreme Good Friend

The Buddha explained it to the Venerable Ānanda:[620]

It may also in this way be understood, Ānanda, how the entire holy life is just this, namely, good friendship, good association, good companionship.

Since it is, Ānanda, due to Me as a good friend, that (subject to birth) beings from birth escape; (subject to ageing) beings from ageing escape; (subject to death) beings from death escape; (subject to sorrow, lamentation, suffering, displeasure, and despair) beings from sorrow, lamentation, suffering, displeasure, and despair escape.

By this method then, Ānanda, it should be understood how the entire holy life is just this, namely, good friendship, good association, good companionship.

When there is a Supremely Enlightened Buddha, beings may practise under His instructions. If their pāramī are sufficiently developed, they may attain a Path&-Fruition: they may even escape from birth, ageing, and death, in that very life. In our Buddha's time, the number of human beings who achieved these supreme benefits were many, and the number of devas and Brahmas who achieved it were beyond counting. That is why The Buddha explains that the arising of a Buddha is for the many's welfare *(bahujana hitāya)*, for the many's happiness *(bahujana sukhāya)*, out of compassion for the world *(lok·ānukampāya)*, for the benefit *(atthāya)*, well being *(hitāya)*, and happiness *(sukhāya)* of devas and men *(deva·manussānaṁ)*.[621]

Without a Buddha, there can be no escape from birth, ageing, and death. Many beings have sufficient pāramī to accomplish the wholesome kamma of a Path Knowledge, but they cannot do it alone: they need to receive instructions from a Supremely Enlightened Buddha, or a learned and competent disciple of a Buddha.[230]

---

[619] See 'Time Failure Enables Unwholesome Kammas', p.221.

[620] S.V.I.i.2 *'Upaḍḍha·Suttaṁ'* ('The "Half" Sutta')

[621] A.I.xiii *'Eka·Puggala·Vaggo'* ('One Person Chapter')

THE VENERABLE AÑÑĀSIKOṆḌAÑÑA

A good example is the Venerable Aññāsikoṇḍañña.[231] He was still young when our Buddha Gotama was born. And he was the first human being to attain the Stream-Entry Path&Fruition Knowledges in this our Buddha's Dispensation *(Buddha-·Sāsana)*: that was when The Buddha taught the *'Dhamma·Cakka·Ppavattana'* sutta.

Aññāsikondañña practised as an ascetic for many years, but he could not attain any Path or Fruition Knowledge. It became possible only with the help of The Buddha.

THE VENERABLE SĀRIPUTTA AND THE VENERABLE MAHĀMOGGALLĀNA

Also, for example, the Venerable Sāriputta and the Venerable Mahāmoggallāna practised for many years, but to no avail.[622] The Venerable Sāriputta attained Stream Entry only when the Venerable Assaji had explained the Dhamma to him. And the Venerable Mahāmoggallāna attained Stream Entry only when the Venerable Sāriputta repeated the explanation to him. This principle applies for all disciples of a Buddha: they are not able to learn the Dhamma, practise the Dhamma, and attain a Path&Fruition without the help of a good friend *(kalyāṇa·mitta)*.

KING AJĀTASATTU

Here again, King Ajātasattu is a good example. When he associated with the Venerable Devadatta, he did many bad things.[623] It was under the Venerable Devadatta's influence he developed the desire to kill his father King Bimbisāra, to become king. Then, when his father handed the kingdom over to him, it was again under the Venerable Devadatta's influence that King Ajātasattu, even so, had his father put in prison, tortured, and killed. It was also under Venerable Devadatta's influence that he arranged for a soldier to kill The Buddha, and then for an elephant to kill The Buddha. To King Ajātasattu, the Venerable Devadatta was not a good friend.

Later, however, King Ajātasattu did many, many good things under the influence of The Buddha. How did that come about? It came about through his association with Jīvaka Komārabhacca.[624] Jīvaka Komārabhacca was physician to the royal household, and to The Buddha and Sangha. And he was a Stream Enterer *(Sot·Āpanna)*. One night, upon King Ajātasattu's request, he took King Ajātasattu to his own *Amba·Vana* (Mango Grove). The Buddha was residing there with a large Sangha of bhikkhus. Then The Buddha taught King Ajātasattu the great sutta, the *'Sāmañña·Phala'* sutta. After that teaching, King Ajātasattu gained tremendous faith in The Buddha. He took refuge in The Buddha, Dhamma and Sangha, and confessed to The Buddha that his killing his father was a fault. From that time onwards, King Ajātasattu extended great hospitality to the Triple Gem as a devotee *(upāsaka)*. And when the First Council was convened, it was in Rājagaha, under King Ajātasattu's patronage. Thus, to King Ajātasattu, Jīvaka Komārabhacca was a good friend. And through him, King Ajātasattu met the Supreme Good Friend, The Buddha.

---

[622] Vin.Mv.i.14 *'Sāriputta·Moggallāna·Pabbajjā·Kathā'* ('Discussion of Sāriputta-Moggallāna's Going-Forth')

[623] For source references, please see footnote 415, p.152.

[624] See DA.i.2 *'Sāmañña·Phala·Suttaṁ'* ('The Asceticism-Fruit Sutta')

The Devotee Gavesī

Another example is the devotee called Gavesī.[625] He was a devotee of The Buddha Kassapa, and was the leader of a group of five hundred men. But he did not observe the five precepts: he had only taken refuge in The Buddha, the Dhamma, and the Sangha. And his followers had done the same: they also took the three refuges.

Then one day, Gavesī decided he wanted to outdo his five hundred followers. So he declared he would from then on undertake morality: the five precepts.[232] When his followers realized he was observing the five precepts, they did the same. So he decided to undertake the chaste way of life *(Brahma·cārī)*. And again they followed him. Then he decided to abstain from eating at the wrong time *(virataṁ vikālabhojana)*: and they followed him. Then he went to Kassapa Buddha and asked to become a bhikkhu, to obtain the higher ordination *(upasampadā)*: and his followers did the same. And finally, he strove hard, with the intention to attain Arahantship in that very life: and his followers did the same. Eventually, they all escaped from future birth, ageing, and death.

That way Gavesī was a good friend *(kalyāṇa·mitta)* to his five hundred followers. And it was all made possible only because of the presence of the supreme good friend, Kassapa Buddha: they began by taking the three refuges *(ti·saraṇa)*.

That concludes our brief explanation of how other people may exert an influence on our conduct: our friends and companions, especially our teachers and leaders. In very many places, The Buddha explains that such good friends are essential for one to accomplish wholesome kamma; and with such good friends there will be certain unwholesome kammas that are disabled from producing their result.

Let us then go on to explain how unwholesome kamma can be disabled by means achievement *(payoga·sampatti)*

Means Achievement Disables Unwholesome Kammas

There are some bad kamma undertakings that, stopped by means achievement *(payoga·sampatti)*, **do not mature.**

Someone's conduct may be bad. She or he may kill, steal, engage in sexual misconduct, tell lies, engage in slander, harsh speech, and prattle, be covetous, have ill-will, and hold wrong view. That is the ten courses of unwholesome kamma that we have mentioned several times: means failure *(payoga·vipatti)*. Contingent upon that failure, certain of her or his unwholesome kammas are enabled to produce their result. But because of associating with good friends such as The Buddha and His disciples, she or he gains faith in the Triple Gem, and faith in the workings of kamma, and accomplishes many wholesome kammas.[626] That way, her or his conduct becomes good: that is means achievement *(payoga·sampatti)*. Contingent upon that achievement, the unwholesome kammas are disabled, and wholesome kammas are enabled to produce their result instead. She or he may refrain from killing beings, etc., which is to purify one's morality, and based on that purified morality, she or he may succeed in samatha and vipassanā.[233]

Suppose a son of good family *(kula·putta)* has accomplished many unwholesome kammas in his previous life. But now he accomplishes many wholesome kammas:

---

[625] A.V.IV.iii.10 *'Gavesī·Suttaṁ'* ('The Gavesī Sutta')

[626] See 'Good and Bad Friendship', p.212.

he purifies his morality, and based on that virtue, practises samatha and vipassanā successfully under the guidance of a skilful teacher up to the attainment of the Stream-Entry Path Knowledge*(Sot·Āpatti·Magga·Ñāṇa)* or Non-Return Path Knowledge *(An·Āgāmi·Magga·Ñāṇa)*. Such practice is means achievement*(payoga·sampatti)*, and it disables those of his unwholesome kammas that could have produced destination failure*(gati·vipatti)*: such practice disables kammas productive of rebirth in a woeful state. The only kammas that can now produce rebirth are wholesome kammas: his means achievement*(payoga·sampatti)* produces only happiness, such as destination achievement*(gati·sampatti)*. At death he may be reborn in a deva world because of a wholesome kamma of the sensual sphere,[627] or in the Brahma world because of a jhāna kamma as was the case with, for example, Pukkusāti.

Pukkusāti

Pukkusāti was very skilful in the jhāna attainments. They are means achievement*(payoga·sampatti)*:[628] Right Effort*(Sammā·Vāyāma)*, Right Mindfulness*(Sammā·Sati)*, and Right Concentration*(Sammā·Samādhi)*. And while listening to The Buddha teach him the *'Dhātu·Vibhaṅga'* sutta,[629] he attained the Non-Returner Path&Fruition Knowledges: the Non-Returner Path Knowledge is a superior means achievement.

Afterwards, he went looking for a bowl and robes to obtain the higher ordination from The Buddha. But he was gored to death by a demon in the guise of a cow.[630] At death, Pukkusāti's Non-Returner Path Knowledge*(An·Āgāmi·Magga·Ñāṇa)*, based on the fourth jhāna, functioned as productive kamma to produce rebirth in the Avihā Brahma world, the lowest plane of the Pure Abodes*(Suddh·Āvāsa)*.[631] His Path Knowledge disabled his innumerable unwholesome kammas from producing their result, and disabled also his innumerable wholesome kammas that could have produced rebirth in the sensual sphere: he would never again be reborn in the four woeful states, nor in the human or deva worlds. That was all the result of his means achievement*(payoga·sampatti)*.

Tambadāṭhika the Executioner

Here, Tambadāṭhika the executioner (whom we mentioned earlier)[632] is again a good example. He had for fifty-five years habitually accomplished the unwholesome kamma of beheading criminals: that is means failure*(payoga·vipatti)*. If that kamma were to produce its result at death, he would have been reborn in a lower world such as hell. But when the Venerable Sāriputta passed his house, Tambadāṭhika invited him inside, offered milk-rice, and then listened with respect to the Venerable Sāriputta's Dhamma, and attained the Formations-Equanimity Knowledge*(Saṅkhār·Upekkhā·Ñāṇa)*: all those actions were means achievement*(payoga·sampatti)*. And contingent upon the attainment of the Formations-Equanimity Knowledge, Tambadāṭhika's unwholesome kammas were disabled, because it functioned as productive kamma to produce rebirth in the deva world: destination achievement*(gati·sampatti)*.

---

627 For the results of sensual-, fine-material-, and immaterial-sphere kamma, see table '1: The Resultant Consciousnesses', p.46.

628 They are also wholesome weighty kammas, and exalted kamma*(mahaggata·kamma)*.

629 M.III.iv.10 *'Dhātu·Vibhaṅga·Suttaṁ'* ('The Elements-Analysis Sutta')

630 For the background for this demon's actions, see 'The Avenging Courtesan', p.272*f.*

631 Ibid.A

632 See 'Tambadāṭhika the Executioner', p.183.

THE VENERABLE AṄGULIMĀLA

Another example is the Venerable Aṅgulimāla: we discussed him earlier.[633] He had not only accomplished innumerable unwholesome kammas in his past lives, but in his last life, as the bandit Aṅgulimāla, he killed many people. Then he ordained as a bhikkhu under The Buddha (Unsurpassable Guide of Men to be Trained *(Anuttaro Purisa·Damma·Sārathi)*).[634] Under The Buddha's guidance, Aṅgulimāla observed the higher morality of a bhikkhu: that is means achievement *(payoga·sampatti)*. Based on that morality, he practised samatha and vipassanā: that is also means achievement. And he practised with such success that he attained the Arahant Path-Knowledge *(Arahatta·Magga·Ñāṇa)*: that is the supreme means achievement.

THE SUPREME MEANS ACHIEVEMENT

Why then is the Arahant Path-Knowledge *(Arahatta·Magga·Ñāṇa)* the supreme means achievement *(payoga·sampatti)*? Because although, in the course of an Arahant's life, certain unwholesome and wholesome kammas function as reinforcing-, frustrating- or interceptive kamma, there are no unwholesome or wholesome kammas whatsoever that can function as productive kamma to produce new five aggregates after the decease consciousness of this life. The Arahant Path-Knowledge has disabled absolutely all kammas from producing rebirth: those kammas productive of an unhappy rebirth (destination failure *(gati·vipatti)*), as well as those kammas productive of a happy rebirth (destination achievement *(gati·sampatti)*). Then at the Arahant's final cessation (her or his Parinibbāna), all whatsoever kammas lapse: they are all disabled from functioning in any way whatsoever. The Arahant will never ever again in any whatsoever way be reborn, which means she or he has escaped suffering forever. That is why the Arahant Path-Knowledge is the supreme means achievement.

If one's Path Knowledge is one of the three lower ones, this same principle applies to a lesser degree. Although, during the life of a Noble Person *(Ariya Puggala)*, certain unwholesome and wholesome kammas will function as reinforcing-, frustrating- and interceptive kammas, there are now no unwholesome kammas that can function as productive kamma to produce new five aggregates after the decease consciousness of this life. The Noble Path Knowledge *(Ariya·Magga·Ñāṇa)* has disabled absolutely all unwholesome kammas from producing rebirth. For Noble Ones, there will never again be an unhappy rebirth (destination failure *(gati·vipatti)*): never again will they be reborn in the ghost world, the animal world, or in hell. For Noble Ones, there will be only a limited number of happy rebirths (destination achievement *(gati·sampatti)*): only wholesome kammas are enabled to produce rebirth, either in the human world, or the deva- or Brahma worlds. And the three Noble Ones are assured Arahantship within a limited number of lives.

---

[633] See 'The Venerable Aṅgulimāla', p.161.

[634] Explaining the nine qualities of a Perfectly Self-Enlightened Buddha *(Sammā·Sam·Buddha)*, The Buddha gives Arahantship as the first: e.g. D.II.3 *'Mahā·Parinibbāna·Suttaṁ'* ('The Great-Parinibbāna Sutta'). This quality of His is explained in VsM.vii.138-139 *'Buddh·Ānussati'* ('Buddha Recollection') PP.vii.46-48.

The Venerable Mahāmoggallāna

An example of this principle is the Venerable Mahāmoggallāna. In a past life, he tried to kill his parents.[635] In his last life (as the Venerable Mahāmoggallāna) that kamma produced its result, when his body was smashed to pieces by hired bandits. Afterwards, he attained Parinibbāna. With his Parinibbāna, his parricide kamma, all other unwholesome kammas of the infinite past, and all wholesome kammas of the infinite past, lapsed: his Arahant Path-Knowledge intercepted them all.

Means Achievement Produces Only Happiness

From our explanation, you may now understand that means achievement produces only happiness.

This we explained also when explaining The Buddha's First Tathāgata Power:[636]

[1] **Impossible it is, bhikkhus, there is no occasion where bodily good conduct could produce an undesired, unpleasant, and disagreeable result: such a possibility does not exist. But such a possibility, bhikkhus, does exist where bodily good conduct could produce a desired, pleasant, and agreeable result: such a possibility does exist.**

[2] **Impossible it is, bhikkhus, there is no occasion where verbal good conduct could produce an undesired, unpleasant, and disagreeable result: such a possibility does not exist. But such a possibility, bhikkhus, does exist where verbal good conduct could produce a desired, pleasant, and agreeable result: such a possibility does exist.**

[3] **Impossible it is, bhikkhus, there is no occasion where mental good conduct could produce an undesired, unpleasant, and disagreeable result: such a possibility does not exist. But such a possibility, bhikkhus, does exist where mental good conduct could produce a desired, pleasant, and agreeable result: such a possibility does exist.**

That concludes our explanation of how unwholesome kammas are disabled from producing their result because of the four types of achievement: destination-, appearance-, time-, and means achievement.

Failure Enables Unwholesome Kammas

Let us then discuss how unwholesome kammas are enabled because of the opposite four failures.[637]

Destination Failure Enables Unwholesome Kammas

There are some bad kamma undertakings that mature at having come to destination failure *(gati·vipatti)*.[638]

Someone's wholesome kamma may function as productive kamma to produce rebirth in a good destination: the human world, or a heavenly world. That is destination achievement *(gati·sampatti)*. Contingent upon that achievement, certain of her or his unwholesome kammas are disabled from producing their result. But

---

[635] A detailed account is given at 'The Venerable Mahāmoggallāna's Past Parricide', p.259.

[636] A.I.xv.3 *'Aṭṭhāna·Pāḷi'* ('Text of the Impossible')

[637] VbhA.xvi.810 *'Dutiya·Bala·Niddeso'* ('Exposition of the Second Power') DD.xvi.2206-2210.

[638] All the introductory quotations are from The Buddha's explanation in Vbh.XVI.x.810 *'Ñāṇa·Vibhaṅgo'* ('Knowledge Analysis').

because of a single unwholesome kamma, she or he may be reborn in a bad destination: hell, the animal world, or the ghost world. That is destination failure *(gati·vipatti)*. Contingent upon that failure, the unwholesome kammas are enabled to produce their result, one after the other.

At one time they produce rebirth in hell; at another time in the world of animals; at another time in the world of ghosts; at another time in the world of demons *(asura)*. For a long time unwholesome kammas do not allow such a person to raise her or his head above the bad destinations. A good example is the Venerable Losaka Tissa. Because of very deep envy, he threw an Arahant's food away. That kamma, supported by the kamma of subsequent remorse over many years, functioned as productive kamma to produce prolonged rebirth in hell, many rebirths as a demon*(asura)*,[639] and many as a dog.[640]

Appearance Failure Enables Unwholesome Kammas

There are some bad kamma undertakings that mature at having come to appearance failure*(upadhi·vipatti)*.

Someone may have well shaped limbs, and be attractive, beautiful and radiant like Brahmā: that is appearance achievement*(upadhi·sampatti)*. Contingent upon that achievement, certain unwholesome kammas are disabled from producing their result. But because of a single unwholesome frustrating kamma, she or he may develop ill-shaped limbs, and have an unattractive appearance, ugly and unsightly like a goblin: that is appearance failure*(upadhi·vipatti)*. Contingent upon that failure, the unwholesome kammas are enabled to produce their result.

The Commentary explains that if such a person is born to a slave, he will be made to do dirty work, even removing rubbish. Because of his ugliness, his owners will think: 'Such a one can do dirty work.' If it is a woman, they make her prepare food for the elephants etc. And even if the woman is born in a good family, the king's tax collectors may think she is a house slave, and bind her and take her away. The Commentary gives an example from ancient Sri Lanka, where this happened to a great landowner's ugly wife.

Time Failure Enables Unwholesome Kammas

There are some bad kamma undertakings that mature at having come to time failure*(kāla·vipatti)*.

Someone may be reborn at the time of good government, and good people, for example, when people begin to appear at the beginning of an aeon, when there is a Wheel-Turning King, or a Buddha: that is time achievement*(kāla·sampatti)*.[641] Contingent upon that achievement, certain of her or his unwholesome kammas are disabled from producing their result. But because of a single unwholesome frustrating kamma, she or he may be reborn at the time of bad government, and bad, nasty, and feeble people.[642] She or he may also be reborn at the time when

[639] VsM.xiii.411 *'Cut·Ūpapāta·Ñāṇa·Kathā'* ('Discussion of the Decease&Reappearance Knowledge') PP.xiii.93

[640] A detailed account is given at 'The Envious Venerable Tissa', p.279.

[641] For details in this regard, see 'Good and Bad Friendship', p.212.

[642] NASTY*(kasape)*: bitter, acrid; FEEBLE*(niroje)*: *nir* (without) + *oje* (nutrition). Thus, sapless, spineless, without character, without principles, decadent.

the life span is down to ten years,[234] when dairy products[643] no longer exist, and ***kudrūsaka*** grains are the best food available. Then, although one is reborn as a human being, one lives like cattle do, or wild animals. To be reborn at such a time is time failure*(kāla·vipatti)*. Contingent upon that failure, the unwholesome kammas are enabled to produce their result.

MEANS FAILURE ENABLES UNWHOLESOME KAMMAS

There are some bad kamma undertakings that mature at having come to means failure *(payoga·vipatti)*.

Someone's conduct may be good. She or he may refrain from killing beings, stealing, engaging in sexual misconduct, etc.: the ten courses of wholesome kamma that we have mentioned several times. That is means achievement*(payoga·sampatti)*. Contingent upon that achievement, certain unwholesome kammas are disabled from producing their result. But then she or he may undertake bad conduct. She or he may kill, steal, engage in sexual misconduct, etc.: the ten courses of unwholesome kamma. That is means failure*(payoga·vipatti)*. Contingent upon that failure, the unwholesome kammas are enabled to produce their result. The Commentary explains that such a person is caught, brought before the king, and tortured and executed.[235]

The Venerable Devadatta, whom we have discussed, is a good example.[644]

THE KING'S FAVOURITE

That concludes our explanation of how the four types of achievement*(sampatti)* (destination-, appearance-, time-, and means achievement) disable certain unwholesome kammas from producing their result, whereas the four types of failure*(vipatti)* enable them.

To explain it, the commentary gives a simile. Suppose a man pleases the king by some act, and the king rewards him with a post and a province. And the man abuses his office, bringing the province to ruin. By force, he takes other people's property: chariots, beasts of burden, slave-girls, parks, and fields. But because he is the king's favourite, people do not complain.

Then one day, he offends a minister to the king. That minister is in greater favour with the king, and has the man seized and beaten. And the minister goes to the king, and tells him the man is bringing the province to ruin. The man is arrested and chained up in prison. Then the king has drums beaten in the city, with the proclamation: 'Who has had something taken by so-and-so?' And people come and raise a thousand cries: 'This property of mine was seized!' 'That property of mine was seized!' And the king, much more angry now, has the man tortured in many ways, and then has him executed, and says: 'Throw the body on the charnel ground, and bring back his chain.'

Here, first the man performed some act that pleased the king, and in return received a post and province: that is like when a certain wholesome kamma gives an ordinary person rebirth in heaven. The people were unable to complain about the man's misconduct because he was the king's favourite: that is like when unwholesome kammas are unable to produce their result because the ordinary per-

---

[643] DAIRY PRODUCTS (the five cow products*(pañca gorasā)*): milk*(khīra)*, curds*(dadhi)*, ghee*(ghata)*, buttermilk*(takka)*, butter*(navanīta)*

[644] See 'The Venerable Devadatta', p.204.

son is in heaven. Then the man offended someone in greater favour with the king, and fell out of favour with the king, and was chained up and imprisoned: that is like when the ordinary person falls from heaven, and is reborn in hell. Once the man had fallen out of favour with the king, and was in prison, then did the people cry: 'This property of mine was seized!' 'That property of mine was seized!' that is like, once the ordinary person has fallen from heaven, and is reborn in hell, then do all his unwholesome kammas gather, and produce their result. The man's corpse was thrown onto the charnel ground, and only his chain was brought back: that is like the ordinary person's suffering for the whole aeon in hell, unable to raise his head from hell: each time one kamma's result has been exhausted, another produces its result.[236]

The Commentary concludes by explaining that there is not just one, or two, or a hundred, or a thousand beings who have accomplished unwholesome kammas that can and do continue producing results for a whole aeon in hell: the beings who suffer for that long in hell cannot be counted. That is how dangerous it is to meet with the four failures.

Failure Disables Wholesome Kammas

Let us then discuss how the same four types of failure disable wholesome kammas from producing their result.[645]

Destination Failure Disables Wholesome Kammas

There are some good kamma undertakings that, stopped by destination failure*(gati·vipatti)*, **do not mature.**[646]

Someone's wholesome kamma may function as productive kamma to produce rebirth in a good destination: the human or heavenly worlds. That is destination achievement*(gati·sampatti)*. Contingent upon that achievement, certain wholesome kammas are enabled to produce their result. But because of a single unwholesome kamma, she or he may be reborn in a bad destination: hell, the animal world or the ghost world. That is destination failure*(gati·vipatti)*. Contingent upon that failure, the wholesome kammas are disabled from producing their result.

King Ajātasattu

A good example is King Ajātasattu: we mentioned him in connection with knowledge and conduct*(vijjā·caraṇa)*.[647] He was the son of King Bimbisāra, who was a Stream Enterer, and great patron of The Buddha and Sangha. To gain kingship, King Ajātasattu had his father killed. Then, one night, he went to see The Buddha, and The Buddha gave him the great teaching that is the *'Sāmañ-ña·Phala'* sutta.[648] The king had accomplished sufficient wholesome kammas (pāramī) to attain Stream Entry like his father. But because of that single unwholesome kamma (having his father killed: means failure*(payoga·vipatti)*) the wholesome kamma of listening to The Buddha was disabled from producing its

---

645 VbhA.xvi.810 *'Dutiya·Bala·Niddeso'* ('Exposition of the Second Power') DD.xvi.2211-2216.
646 All the introductory quotations are from The Buddha's explanation in Vbh.XVI.x.810 *'Ñāṇa·Vibhaṅgo'* ('Knowledge Analysis').
647 See 'King Ajātasattu', p.144.
648 D.i.2 *'Sāmañña·Phala·Suttaṁ'* ('The Asceticism-Fruit Sutta')

result: he was unable to attain a Path&Fruition, and remained a common person *(puthu·jjana)*. Also, having listened to The Buddha's teaching, King Ajātasattu gained tremendous faith in The Buddha, and became a great, great patron of The Buddha and Sangha. But at death all the wholesome kamma he had performed was disabled from producing its result, because inevitably his parricide kamma functioned as productive kamma to produce rebirth in hell. Once he was reborn in hell (destination failure*(gati·vipatti)*), again all his wholesome kammas continued (and still continue) to be disabled from producing their result.

Appearance Failure Disables Wholesome Kammas

There are some good kamma undertakings that, stopped by appearance failure*(upadhi-·vipatti)*, do not mature.

Someone may have well shaped limbs, and be attractive, beautiful, and radiant like Brahmā: that is appearance achievement*(upadhi·sampatti)*. Contingent upon that achievement, certain wholesome kammas are enabled to produce their result. But because of a single unwholesome frustrating kamma, she or he may develop ill-shaped limbs and an unattractive and ugly appearance: that is appearance failure*(upadhi·vipatti)*. Contingent upon that failure, the wholesome kammas are disabled from producing their result.

If, for example, he is reborn into a royal family, he is not anointed king, because they will think: 'What will become of the kingdom of one so unfortunate?' And if he is reborn in a general's house, he does not take over his father's post either, and so on.

The Island King

The Commentary gives an example from ancient Sri Lanka. There was once a king who at his son's birth granted the mother a favour. She kept it for later. Then once, when he was seven or eight years old, the prince was making cocks fight in the royal court: that is means failure*(payoga·vipatti)*. A cock jumped up and blinded him in one eye. Then, when he was fifteen or sixteen years old, his mother wanted to rule the kingdom through her son. So she asked the king to grant her his favour by giving over the kingdom to her son. But he refused because the boy had only one eye. The queen complained, and to please her, the king gave her son rule over the small island of Nāgadīpa. But if he had had two eyes instead of only one, he would have become king over all of Sri Lanka.

Time Failure Disables Wholesome Kammas

There are some good kamma undertakings that, stopped by time failure*(kāla·vipatti)*, do not mature.

Someone may be reborn at the time of good government, and good people, for example, when people begin to appear at the beginning of an aeon, when there is a Wheel-Turning King, or a Buddha: that is time achievement*(kāla·sampatti)*. Contingent upon that achievement, certain of her or his wholesome kammas are enabled to produce their result. But because of a single unwholesome frustrating kamma, she or he may be reborn at the time of bad government, and bad, nasty and feeble people.[649] She or he may also be reborn at the time when the life span

[649] NASTY, ETC.: see footnote 642, p.221.

is down to ten years,[650] when dairy products[651] no longer exist, and ***kudrūsaka*** grains are the best food available. Then, although one is reborn as human being, one lives like cattle do, or wild animals. To be reborn at such a time is time failure *(kāla·vipatti)*. Contingent upon that failure, the wholesome kammas are disabled.

MEANS FAILURE DISABLES WHOLESOME KAMMAS

There are some good kamma undertakings that, stopped by means failure*(payoga·vipatti)***, do not mature.**

Someone's conduct may be good. She or he may refrain from killing beings, stealing, engaging in sexual misconduct, etc.: the ten courses of wholesome kamma. That is means achievement*(payoga·sampatti)*. Contingent upon that achievement, certain wholesome kammas are enabled to produce their result. But then she or he may undertake bad conduct. She or he may kill, steal, engage in sexual misconduct, etc.: the ten courses of unwholesome kamma. That is means failure*(payoga·vipatti)*. Contingent upon that failure, the wholesome kammas are disabled from producing their result.

The Commentary explains that such a man is not sought for in marriage by families of his own class. They think: 'This bad man is intemperate with women, intemperate with drink, intemperate with dice,' and they keep their distance.

MAHĀDHANA LORD-SON

A good example is Mahādhana Lord-Son, son of a treasurer: we mentioned him in connection with knowledge and conduct*(vijjā·caraṇa)*.[652] He was born into a very rich family in Bārāṇasī, and married a girl from a very rich family. But he spent his entire fortune on drink, flowers, perfume, song, music and dance, etc.: that is means failure*(payoga·vipatti)*. It enabled certain unwholesome kammas to produce their result, and he ended up in extreme poverty, having to beg for food. The Buddha told the Venerable Ānanda that if Mahādhana as a young man had applied himself to business, he would have become the chief treasurer in Bārāṇasī. And if as a young man, Mahādhana had become a monk, he would have become an Arahant, and his wife a Non-Returner. In both cases, that would have been means achievement*(payoga·sampatti)*, enabling wholesome kammas to produce their result. In the same way, if as a middle-aged man, Mahādhana had applied himself to business, he could have become the city's second treasurer, and as a monk he would have become a Non-Returner, and his wife a Once Returner: again means achievement*(payoga·sampatti)*, enabling wholesome kammas to produce their result. And if he had done these things as an elderly man, he would have become the city's third treasurer, or would as a monk have become a Once Returner, and his wife a Stream Enterer: again means achievement*(payoga·sampatti)*, enabling wholesome kammas to produce their result. But because of means failure*(payoga·vipatti)*, those wholesome kammas were disabled from producing their result, and he had nothing at all: neither the wealth of a layman nor the wealth of a monk. And at death, he was destined to be reborn in hell, which is destination failure*(gati·vipatti)*, disabling wholesome kammas from producing their result, and enabling unwholesome kammas to produce their result, one after the other.

---

[650] life-span is down to ten years: see 'Deterioration of Human Life', p.214.
[651] DAIRY PRODUCTS: see footnote 643, p.221.
[652] See 'Mahādhana Lord-Son', p.143.

Both husband and wife had accomplished sufficient wholesome kammas to become even more rich than they already were, and even to become Noble Ones. But those wholesome kammas would produce their result only so long as there was means achievement, not so long as there was means failure.

How You Avoid Failure

Now we have explained how the four types of failure disable certain wholesome kammas from producing their results. Keeping these facts in mind, you may understand how dangerous the four types of failure are. How to avoid them? By avoiding unwholesome kammas. Unwholesome kammas will only help you meet with the four types of failure in your future lives. They are always ready to give you a warm welcome, and provide a fertile ground for your unwholesome kammas to produce their results: undesired, unpleasant and disagreeable results.[237] How then, do you avoid unwholesome kammas? By undertaking wholesome kammas. Wholesome kammas will only help you meet with the four types of achievement in your future lives. The four types of achievement provide fertile ground for your wholesome kammas to produce their results: desired, pleasant, and agreeable results.

Within any life, there are, of course, three types of achievement or failure that are beyond one's control, that is, destination achievement or failure, appearance achievement or failure, and time achievement or failure. Within one life, only means achievement are within one's control. In your case, however, the three that are beyond one's control are all achievements. You have in this life attained a human rebirth: that is the first one, destination achievement. Then, even though you may not be as beautiful or radiant as Brahmā, you do have well-shaped limbs, with well-developed faculties: you can see, hear, etc. That is the second one, appearance achievement. Lastly, here and now The Buddha's Teachings still exist in the human world; that is the third one, time achievement. Those three achievements you have acquired because of past and present means achievement. And having those three means you have ample opportunity to continue with means achievement. We can then say you abide with all four achievements, and they will welcome with warm hospitality all the wholesome kammas that you accomplished in the infinite past as well as in this life. The results of those many wholesome kammas will be only desired, pleasant, and agreeable. So please try to avoid means failure, and abide with only means achievement. How do you do so?

Please remember what The Buddha said in the second *'Gaddula·Baddha'* sutta:

Therefore, bhikkhus, one should reflect repeatedly upon one's own mind: 'For a long time this mind has been defiled by lust, by hatred, and by delusion.'

By mental defilement, bhikkhus, beings are defiled; by mental purification, beings are purified.

Lust, hatred, and delusion defile the mind, whereas non-lust, non-hatred, and non-delusion purify it. When there is non-lust, non-hatred, and non-delusion, the volition of one's actions are wholesome. So you need to purify your actions by accomplishing only the ten wholesome courses of kamma *(dasa kusala·kamma·patha)*. We discussed them earlier:[653]

1) The three wholesome courses of bodily kamma *(kāya kamma)*:
   i) not to kill, but to be kind and compassionate

[653] For details, see 'The Ten Wholesome Courses of Kamma', p.130*ff.*

  ii) not to steal
  iii) not to engage in sexual misconduct
2) The four wholesome courses of verbal kamma *(vacī kamma)*:
  i) not to tell lies
  ii) not to slander
  iii) not to speak harshly, but to speak politely
  iv) not to prattle
3) The three wholesome courses of mental kamma *(mano kamma)*:
  i) not to covet
  ii) not to harbour ill-will
  iii) not to hold wrong view, but to hold Right View *(Sammā·Diṭṭhi)*
  The last one is the most important: to have full faith in the workings of kamma.

These ten courses are mundane wholesome kamma. We have in several ways explained how to accomplish them. For example, as what The Buddha calls the three merit-work bases *(puñña·kiriya·vatthu)*:[654]

1) Offering *(dāna)*
2) Morality *(sīla)*: for monks the Vinaya precepts, for nuns the eight or ten precepts, and for laypeople the five, eight, or ten precepts.
3) Meditation *(bhāvanā)*: samatha meditation, which is either access concentration or jhāna, and vipassanā meditation, which is to know and see the impermanence, suffering, and non-self of ultimate mentality *(paramattha·nāma)* and ultimate materiality *(paramattha·rūpa)* of past, future, and present, internal and external, gross and subtle, superior and inferior, far and near.

The Buddha explains these three merit-work bases also as knowledge and conduct *(vijjā·caraṇa)*. Also that we discussed earlier:[655]

1) Conduct *(caraṇa)* is fifteen things: morality, faculty restraint, moderation in food, devotion to wakefulness, faith (which includes habitual practice of offering), mindfulness, conscience, shame, great learning, energy, wisdom, and the four jhānas.
2) Knowledge *(vijjā)* is insight knowledge *(vipassanā·ñāṇa)*, up to the Formations-Equanimity Knowledge *(Saṅkhār·Upekkhā·Ñāṇa)*.

   As we discussed earlier, insight meditation that produces rebirth is included under the wisdom factor of conduct, and insight meditation that does not produce rebirth is included under knowledge.

Knowledge and conduct is also the threefold training of morality *(sīla)*, concentration *(samādhi)*, and wisdom *(paññā)*.[656] The training of morality is to train in three things:[238]

1) Right Speech *(Sammā·Vācā)*
2) Right Action *(Sammā·Kammanta)*
3) Right Livelihood *(Sammā·Ājīva)*

When you train in morality, you achieve morality purification *(sīla·visuddhi)*.[239]

---

[654] For details, see 'The Merit-Work Bases', p.66*ff.*
[655] For details, see 'Knowledge and Conduct', p.137.
[656] For these equivalences between the different categorizations, see footnote 387, p.141.

Then, based on your now purified morality, you can go on to the training of concentration *(samādhi)*. That is samatha, to train in three things:

1) Right Effort *(Sammā·Vāyāma)*
2) Right Mindfulness *(Sammā·Sati)*
3) Right Concentration *(Sammā·Samādhi)*

When you train in concentration, if you attain access concentration and the eight attainments, you achieve mind purification *(citta·visuddhi)*.[657]

Then, based on your now purified virtue and purified mind, you can go on to the training in wisdom *(paññā)*. That is insight meditation, to train in two things:

1) Right View *(Sammā·Diṭṭhi)*
2) Right Intention *(Sammā·Saṅkappa)*

When you train in wisdom, you may (depending on your pāramī) achieve view purification *(diṭṭhi·visuddhi)*: the attainment of Right View *(Sammā·Diṭṭhi)*.

What is Right View? The Buddha explains it in the *'Mahā·Sati·Paṭṭhāna'* sutta:[658]

What then, bhikkhus, is Right View *(Sammā·Diṭṭhi)* **? Whatever, bhikkhus, is**
[1] **knowledge of suffering** *(Dukkhe Ñāṇaṁ)*,
[2] **knowledge of suffering's origin** *(Dukkha·Samudaye Ñāṇaṁ)*,
[3] **knowledge of suffering's cessation** *(Dukkha·Nirodhe Ñāṇaṁ)*,
[4] **knowledge of the way leading to suffering's cessation** *(Dukkha·Nirodha·Gāminiyā Paṭipadāya Ñāṇaṁ)*:
it is called, bhikkhus, Right View.

That means, if you know the Four Noble Truths completely, your mind is also purified completely, and you have attained Arahantship.[659] That is because your Noble Path Knowledge *(Ariya·Magga·Ñāṇa)* (which knows the Four Noble Truths), will have eradicated the defilements stage by stage. When your mind is thus completely pure, we can say that you abide fully in the four types of achievement. After your Parinibbāna, there will no longer be any ground for your unwholesome or wholesome kammas to produce their results.

You may not, however, be able to attain such purification of mind in this life. Nevertheless, as long as you practise the threefold training with diligence and perseverance as far as you can, we may still say you are abiding in the four types of achievement. When this is so, your wholesome kammas will be enabled to produce their results, which will be only beneficial results.

Achievement Enables Wholesome Kammas

That is what we shall now discuss: how the four types of achievement enable wholesome kammas to produce their result.[660]

---

[657] VsM.xviii.587 *'Diṭṭhi·Visuddhi·Niddesa'* ('Exposition of the View Purification') PP.xviii.1-2 explains: 'morality purification is the quite purified fourfold morality beginning with Pāṭimokkha restraint ...mind purification, namely, the eight attainments [the jhānas] together with access concentration ...view purification is the correct seeing of mentality-materiality.'

[658] D.ii.9 'The Great Mindfulness-Foundation Sutta'

[659] See also quotation, endnote 166, p.247.

[660] VbhA.xvi.810 *'Dutiya·Bala·Niddeso'* ('Exposition of the Second Power') DD.xvi.2217-2250.

Destination Achievement Enables Wholesome Kammas

There are some good kamma undertakings that mature, having come to destination achievement*(gati·sampatti)*.[661]

Someone's unwholesome kamma may function as productive kamma to produce rebirth in a bad destination: hell, the animal world, or the ghost world. That is destination failure*(gati·vipatti)*. Contingent upon that failure, certain of her or his wholesome kammas are disabled from producing their result. But because of a single good kamma, she or he may be reborn in a good destination: the human world, or a heavenly world. That is destination achievement*(gati·sampatti)*. Contingent upon that achievement, the wholesome kammas are enabled to produce their result, one after the other. At one time they produce rebirth in the human world, at another time in a heavenly world. For a long time wholesome kammas do not allow such a person to lower her or his head below the good destinations.

The Venerable Pañcasīla samādaniya

A good example is the Venerable Pañcasīla Samādaniya.[662] In Buddha Anomadassī's Dispensation, he observed the five precepts for a hundred thousand years, without breaking a single precept. Based on that virtue, he developed strong, powerful concentration, and practised insight meditation up to the Formations-Equanimity Knowledge*(Saṅkhār·Upekkhā·Ñāṇa)*. As a result, he was reborn in the deva world, going from one deva world to another, and up and down between the heavenly worlds and the human world.

Appearance Achievement Enables Wholesome Kammas

There are some good kamma undertakings that mature at having come to appearance achievement*(upadhi·sampatti)*.

Someone may have ill-shaped limbs, and have an unattractive appearance, ugly and unsightly like a goblin: that is appearance failure*(upadhi·vipatti)*. Contingent upon that failure, certain wholesome kammas are disabled from producing their result. But because of a single wholesome kamma, she or he may develop well shaped limbs, and be attractive, beautiful and radiant like Brahmā: that is appearance achievement*(upadhi·sampatti)*. Contingent upon that achievement, the wholesome kammas are enabled to produce their result.

The Commentary explains that if such a person is born to a royal family, even if he has elder brothers, they will say: 'He is blessed and fortunate; if his umbrella is raised, there will be happiness in the world.' And he is the one they anoint. Likewise, if he is reborn into the house of a viceroy or general, he will be the one to take over his father's post.

Good examples of someone with appearance achievement are Wheel-Turning Kings, such as Mahāsudassana.[663]

Time Achievement Enables Wholesome Kammas

There are some good kamma undertakings that mature at having come to time achievement*(kāla·sampatti)*.

---

661 All the introductory quotations are from The Buddha's explanation in Vbh.XVI.x.810 *'Ñāṇa·Vibhaṅgo'* ('Knowledge Analysis').

662 For details, see 'The Virtuous Venerable Pañcasīlasamādaniya', see p.262*ff.*

663 WHEEL-TURNING KING MAHĀSUDASSANA: see 'The Wheel-Turning King', p.213.

Someone may be reborn at the time of bad government, and bad, nasty, and feeble people: that is time failure*(kāla·vipatti)*. Contingent upon that failure, certain of her or his wholesome kammas are disabled from producing their result. But because of a single good kamma, she or he may be reborn at the time of good government, and good people, for example, when people begin to appear at the beginning of an aeon, when there is a Wheel-Turning King, or a Buddha: that is time achievement*(kāla·sampatti)*.[664] Contingent upon that achievement, the wholesome kammas are enabled to produce their result.

The Venerable Mahāsoṇa

The commentary gives an example of how time failure disables wholesome kammas to produce their result, and then when the times change to time achievement, those wholesome kammas are enabled to produce their result. It is the case of the Venerable Mahāsoṇa. It takes place in ancient Sri Lanka, when there was much unrest owing to a bandit called Brahman Tissa. There was famine, invasion, and the king went into hiding. Almost all bhikkhus fled to India, but some of the most senior bhikkhus stayed behind. Two of them were the Venerable Isidatta and the Venerable Mahāsoṇa.

On their wanderings, they lived on the skins of fruits, and on lotus stalks that were offered to them. And at one village, the daughter of a faithful family invited them to receive alms. Having no proper food, she pounded up some bark and leaves, and made it into three lumps. One lump she put into the senior Venerable Isidatta's bowl, the other she put into the Venerable Mahāsoṇa's bowl. Then, as she was stretching out her hand to put the third lump into the Venerable Isidatta's bowl, she moved her hand, and put it instead into the Venerable Mahāsoṇa's bowl. Then the Venerable Isidatta said, 'The kamma that produces lumps of bark and leaves as its result during the Brahman Tissa Troubles, how great a result will it not produce when there is place and time achievement*(desa·kāla·sampadāya)*!' That faithful family then took the two bhikkhus to a certain dwelling place, and looked after them for the duration of the troubles: so long as there was time failure.

When the robber Brahman Tissa had died, and the king had returned from exile, the Sangha returned from abroad, and five hundred bhikkhus brought the Venerable Mahāsoṇa to a certain Maṇḍalārāma monastery.

That night, devas told the resident seven hundred families of the village that they should next day make offerings to the Sangha: each person offering a measure of food worth a kahāpana, and a piece of cloth nine hands long. And the next day, when the bhikkhus went for their almsround, they were invited to sit and receive rice-gruel. The most senior bhikkhu of the Maṇḍalārāma monastery was a Venerable Tissabhūti. A prominent lay devotee paid homage to him, and asked, 'Venerable Sir, who is the Venerable Mahāsoṇa?' At that time the Venerable Mahāsoṇa, being yet a junior bhikkhu was seated at the end of the line. The senior bhikkhu indicated him, and said: 'He is called Mahāsoṇa, lay devotee.'

The lay devotee paid homage to the Venerable Mahāsoṇa, and wanted to take his bowl. But the venerable one thought: 'How come I am known to him? Perhaps somebody has pointed out something,' and did not hand over his bowl. Being a junior bhikkhu, he did not wish to be singled out.

---

664 See 'Good and Bad Friendship', p.212.

The senior bhikkhu, the Venerable Tissabhūti said to him: 'Friend Soṇa, just as you do not know why, so do we not know why. The devas cause merit to mature for those who have it. Please hand over your bowl, and help your companions in the holy life.' So the Venerable Mahāsoṇa handed over his bowl. The prominent lay devotee took the bowl, went and filled it with almsfood worth a kahāpaṇa, and making the cloth into a bowl-stand, he brought it and placed it in the venerable one's hand. And another lay devotee did the same, and another, and so on, till the Venerable Mahāsoṇa alone had received seven hundred measures of food. He shared it with the other bhikkhus.

Later, when the Venerable Mahāsoṇa returned to the capital city Anurādhapura, he went for alms together with the Sangha of bhikkhus, and received many alms, and great honour.

Thus, when there was time failure, even the skin of *madhuka* fruits, and white lotus stalks were hard to get, but when there was time achievement, there was great gain.

The Venerable Vattabbaka Nigrodha

The commentary gives another example from the times of the Brahman Tissa troubles in ancient Sri Lanka. It is about a Venerable Vattabbaka Nigrodha, who was then a novice. Just like the Venerable Mahāsoṇa, he and his preceptor did not leave the country. On their wanderings, they lived on the occasional fruits they were able to get, and finally they found an abandoned monastery in the country of the leaf-eating people. There, they stayed, being supported by devotees with tubers, roots, fruits, and leaves. When the troubles were over, and the novice had obtained higher ordination, to become the Venerable Vattabbaka, he received many requisites and much honour.

Thus, when there was time failure*(kāla·vipatti)*, fruits, tubers, roots and leaves were hard to get: many wholesome kammas were disabled from producing their result. But when the time failure changed to time achievement*(kāla·sampatti)*, the Venerable Vattabbaka received many requisites: many wholesome kammas were enabled to produce their result.

Means Achievement Enables Wholesome Kammas

There are some good kamma undertakings that mature at having come to means achievement*(payoga·sampatti)*.

Someone's conduct may be bad. She or he may kill, steal, engage in sexual misconduct, etc.: the ten courses of unwholesome kamma. That is means failure *(payoga·vipatti)*. Contingent upon that failure, certain wholesome kammas are disabled from producing their result. But then she or he may undertake good conduct. She or he may undertake the five precepts, the eight precepts, the ten precepts, etc. She or he may refrain from killing beings, stealing, engaging in sexual misconduct, etc.: the ten courses of wholesome kamma that we have mentioned several times. That is means achievement*(payoga·sampatti)*. Contingent upon that achievement the wholesome kammas are enabled to produce their result.

She or he may be reborn at a time of good government and a virtuous king: that is time achievement*(kāla·sampatti)*. Then, because of his own good conduct, the virtuous king will be pleased, and think: 'My daughters are fit for him.' The king will send them to him adorned with every type of ornament. Thinking, 'They are fit for him', the king will send him various special gifts such as chariots, beasts of burden, gems, gold, silver, etc. And if he becomes a monk, he becomes very famous and mighty.

THE VENERABLE CŪḶASUDHAMMA

Also here, the commentary gives an example from ancient Sri Lanka. There was a king called Kūṭakaṇṇa. He was devoted to one Venerable Cūḷasudhamma. Once he summoned the bhikkhu, who then took up residence in a monastery nearby. The king asked the bhikkhu's mother what he liked. She said a certain type of tuber *(kanda)*. The king had them brought, and went to the monastery. But when he offered them to the bhikkhu, he was unable to see his face. When he had come out, he asked the queen: 'What is the Venerable One like?' She answered: 'You, being a man, are unable to make him out; how should I be able to? I do not know what he is like.' The king said: 'In my kingdom I am not even able to look upon a tax-paying householder's son *(bali·kāra·gahapati·putta)*; great indeed is The Buddha's Dispensation!' And out of delight, he clapped his hands.

Why could the king not see the Venerable Cūḷasudhamma's face? Because of the king's great respect for him; because the Venerable Cūḷasudhamma was eminent *(mahesakkha)*, a most respected person. And according to the workings of kamma, one should not look upon such a person in the face.[665]

THE INNOCENT MINISTER

That concludes our explanation of how the four types of failure *(vipatti)* (destination-, appearance-, time-, and means failure) disable certain wholesome kammas from producing their result, whereas the four types of achievement *(sampatti)* enable them.

To explain it, the commentary gives a simile. Suppose the king gets angry with a minister, and has him removed from his post, and chained up in prison. The minister's relatives know the king did it out of anger, and say nothing. When the sharpness of the king's anger has abated, they let him know that the minister is innocent. The king has the minister released, and restored to his post. After that, there is no end to the gifts that the minister receives from various quarters: so much so that people are unable to cope with all the gifts.

Here, first the king got angry with the minister, and had him removed from his post, and chained up in prison: that is like when a certain unwholesome kamma gives an ordinary person rebirth in hell. The minister's relatives did not declare his innocence because the king was angry: that is like when wholesome kammas are unable to produce their result because the ordinary person is in hell. Then the king's anger abated, and the minister's relatives let him know that the minister was innocent, and the minister was released from prison, and restored to his

[665] This is a reference to what was once respectful conduct in both East and West: not to look eminent people in the face. Being in accordance with the Dhamma-Vinaya, it is still practised in parts of the East. When talking to his teacher, the respectful Myanmarese bhikkhu does not refer to his teacher by his personal name, nor by the second person singular 'you' (only the third person); does not sit very close; holds his hands in *añjali* at all times; speaks with the utmost respect and propriety; and does not look his teacher in the face. Such behaviour is found also among the faithful outside the bhikkhu Sangha. For how to become a *mahesakkha*, see The Buddha's explanation under 'One Does Not Harbour Envy', p.282. The Most Venerable Sayadaw refers also to the DhP verse quoted under 'Āyuvaḍḍhana Kumāra Lives Long', p.263, and The Buddha's explanation of the results of an offering made with care/respect: see endnote 61, p.36.

post: that is like when the ordinary person escapes from hell and is reborn in heaven. Once the minister had regained the king's favour, and been restored to his post, he received so many gifts he could not cope with them: that is like, once the ordinary person has escaped from hell, and is reborn in heaven, then do all his wholesome kammas gather, and produce their result. She or he goes from happy rebirth to happy rebirth, up and down between the human world and the heavenly worlds, each time attaining the four types of achievement. And this may go on for as much as a hundred thousand aeons. Eventually, his wholesome kammas will help produce the supramundane kammas, and he attains the supreme means achievement, Arahantship.[240]

That concludes our explanation of kamma's contingency: the different types of contingency upon which the kamma produces its result. Destination-, time-, appearance-, and means achievement *(sampatti)* disables bad kamma, and enables good kamma, whereas failure disables good kamma, and enables bad kamma.

Next we shall discuss a sutta where The Buddha explains seven types of unwholesome kammas and their result, and seven types of wholesome kammas and their result. Now that we have explained the technical aspects of the workings of kamma, The Buddha's explanations, and the examples we shall give, will be easier to understand. The sutta is the *'Cūḷa·Kamma·Vibhaṅga'* sutta ('The Small Kamma-Analysis Sutta').

ENDNOTES CHAPTER III
(SUTTA REFERENCES ETC.)

[62] Also in S.III.I.viii.6 *'Sīha·Suttaṁ'* ('The Lion Sutta'), The Buddha explains that this teaching is His lion's roar *(sīha·nāda)*. And in A.IV.I.iv.3 *'Sīha·Suttaṁ'* ('The Lion Sutta'), He explains it as identity/personality *(sakkāya)*, its origin, cessation, and the way leading to its cessation.

[63] In, for example, S.II.I.iv.7 *'Na·Tumha·Suttaṁ'* ('The Not-Yours Sutta'), The Buddha explains how the Noble Disciple discerns that the body is dependently originated by past kamma: 'This body, bhikkhus, is not your own, nor others'. This thing, bhikkhus, is to be regarded as by past kamma formed, willed, and experienced. There indeed, bhikkhus, the educated Noble Disciple attends well and wisely to only dependent origination: "Thus, this being, that is; this arising, that arises. This not being, that is not; this ceasing, that ceases. That is, ignorance is the cause of formations...[+12 factors of dependent origination/cessation: see 'Dependent Origination', p.109] displeasure and despair cease."' In S.IV.I.xv.1 *'Kamma·Nirodha·Suttaṁ'* ('The Kamma-Cessation Sutta'), The Buddha explains that the six faculties may as a metaphor be regarded as 'old kamma', since kamma is the cause for their arising: 'And what, bhikkhus, is old kamma? The eye is old kamma, to be seen as accomplished, and willed, and to be experienced. The ear... nose... tongue... body... mind.... This is called old kamma.'

[64] For example, in DhP.i.1&2 *'Yamaka·Vagga'* ('Pairs Chapter'), He explains: 'Mind is the forerunner of things; mind is their chief, mind has made them. If with a corrupted mind, one speaks or acts, afterwards one is followed by suffering, as the wheel follows the [ox's] foot.... If with a pure mind, one speaks or acts, afterwards one is followed by happiness, as one's shadow never-departing.'

[65] The Buddha explains it in, for example, A.III.II.iii.6 *'Paṭhama·Bhava·Suttaṁ'* ('The First Existence Sutta') (see quotation endnote 313, p.359), and in, for example, A.VI.vi.9 *'Nibbedhika·Suttaṁ'* ('The Penetrating Sutta'): 'There is, bhikkhus, kamma that is experienced in hell... experienced in the animal birth... in the ghost realm ... the human world... there is kamma that is experienced in the deva world. This is called, bhikkhus, kamma's variety.'

[66] The Buddha explains this in, for example, A.III.I.iii.3 *'Saṅkhāra·Suttaṁ'* ('The Formations Sutta'): 'Here, bhikkhus, someone... having accomplished harmful bodily... verbal... mental formations is reborn in a harmful world. When he is reborn in a harmful world, harmful contacts touch him. Being touched by harmful contacts, he experiences harmful feelings, wholly suffering, as is the case of beings in hell... someone having accomplished harmless bodily... verbal... mental formations is reborn in a harmless world.... he experiences harmless feelings, wholly happiness, as is the case of the lustrous devas... harmless&harmful... formations... in a harmless&harmful world... as is the case with human beings, some devas [sensual sphere devas], and some beings in the woeful states.' See also, for example, quotations footnote 107, p.42, and endnote 206, p.252.

[67] The Buddha explains it in, for example A.VI.I.iv.9 *'Nidāna·Suttaṁ'* ('The Causation Sutta'): 'Not, bhikkhus, from greed, does non-greed arise: it is, bhikkhus, rather greed that arises from greed.... hatred arises from hatred.... delusion arises from delusion.'

[68] CONSCIENCELESSNESS *(a·hiri)*/SHAMELESSNESS *(an·ottappa)*: VsM.xiv.478 *'Saṅkhāra·Kkhandha·Kathā'* ('Discussion of the Formations Aggregate') PP.xiv.160 explains: 'Herein, it [consciencelessness] has no conscientious scruples, thus it is consciencelessness. It [shamelessness] is unashamed, thus it is shamelessness. Of these, consciencelessness has the characteristic of absence of disgust at bodily misconduct, etc., or it has the characteristic of immodesty. Shamelessness has the characteristic of absence of dread on their account, or it has the characteristic of absence of anxiety about them. This is in brief here. The detailed, however, is the opposite of what was said above under conscience and shame. Thus, the proximate cause for consciencelessness is no respect for self; for shamelessness no respect for others.' See also quoted analysis at 'Conscience', p.373.

[69] RESTLESSNESS *(uddhacca)*: VsM.xiv.482 *'Saṅkhāra·Kkhandha·Kathā'* ('Discussion of the Formations Aggregate') PP.xiv.165 explains: 'Being restless is restlessness. It has the characteristic of disquiet, like water whipped by the wind. Its function is unsteadiness, like a flag or banner whipped by the wind. It is manifested as turmoil, like ashes flung up by pelting with stones. Its proximate cause is unwise attention to mental disquiet. It should be regarded as distraction of consciousness.'

[70] The commentary to D.II.9 *'Mahā·Sati·Paṭṭhāna·Suttaṁ'* ('The Great Mindfulness-Foundation Sutta') describes this with a verse: 'What one sees, that is not seen; what is seen, one does not see; Not seeing, bound is the confused one; and, being bound, one is not released.

[71] The Buddha explains it in A.III.III.i.9 *'Paṭhama·Nidāna·Suttaṁ'* ('The First Causation Sutta'): 'These three, bhikkhus, are the causes for kamma's arising. What three? Greed, hatred, and delusion are the causes for the arising of kamma.... [any such kamma is] unwholesome, blameful, has sorrow for result, and leads to kamma's [further] arising, not to kamma's cessation.' For the roots of specific unwholesome acts, see quotation endnote 159, p.246.

[72] See, for example, A.X.IV.v.5 *'Na·Sevitabb·Ādi·Suttāni'* ('The "Not-to-Be-Followed" Etc. Suttas'), and A.III.III.v.5. *'Paṭhama·Khata·Suttaṁ'* ('The First "Uprooted" Sutta').

[73] See A.I.xv.3 *'Aṭṭhāna·Pāḷi'* ('Text of the Impossible'): quoted p.43.

[74] The Buddha uses this term in S.II.I.vi.1 *'Pari·Vīmaṁsana·Suttaṁ'* ('The Thorough-Investigation Sutta'): 'If of ignorance disposed, bhikkhus, a person accomplishes a meritorious formation, consciousness fares on to the meritorious; if he accomplishes a demeritorious formation, consciousness fares on to the demeritorious; if he accomplishes an imperturbable formation [immaterial jhāna], consciousness fares on to the imperturbable [immaterial plane].'

[75] The Buddha explains it in, for example, A.VI.iv.9 *'Nidāna·Suttaṁ'* ('The Causation Sutta'): 'Not, bhikkhus, of greed-born kamma, of hatred-born kamma, of delusion-born kamma are devas known, are human beings known, and known any other happy existence. On the contrary, of greed-born kamma, of hatred-born kamma, of delusion-born kamma, the hells are known, animal birth is known, the ghost realm is known, and known other types of unhappy existence.'

[76] In S.II.I.iii.5 *'Bhūmija·Suttaṁ'* ('The Bhūmija Sutta') (also A.IV.IV.iii.1 *'Cetanā·Suttaṁ'* ('The Volition Sutta')), The Buddha explains: 'By oneself, bhikkhus, one performs that body-formation because of which arises happiness or suffering in oneself; or by another one performs that body-formation. Knowingly, bhikkhus, one performs that body-formation, because of which arises happiness or suffering in oneself. Or unknowingly [etc. and likewise for the performance of verbal-, and mental formations]. These things, bhikkhus, with ignorance occur.' The commentary explains that 'by oneself' *(sāmaṁ)* refers to unprompted kamma, whereas 'by another' *(pare)* refers to prompted kamma. 'Knowingly' *(sampajāna)* refers to kamma associated with the Kamma-Ownership Knowledge, whereas 'unknowingly' *(a·sampajāna)* refers to kamma so dissociated.

[77] E.g. VsM.xiv.453 *'Khandha·Niddesa'* ('Exposition of the Aggregates') PP.xiv.91 explains unprompted/prompted greed-rooted consciousness: 'When a man is happy and content in placing wrong view foremost of the sort beginning "There is no danger in sense desires" [see end of endnote], and either enjoys sense desires with consciousness that in its own individual essence is eager without being urged, or believes auspicious sights, etc. have a core, then the first kind of unprofitable consciousness arises [wrong-view associated, unprompted]; when it is with consciousness that is sluggish and urged on, it is the second kind [as before but prompted]. But when a man is happy and content only, without placing wrong view foremost, and indulges in sexual intercourse, or covets others' good fortune, or steals others' goods, with consciousness that in its own individual essence is eager without being urged, it is the third kind [wrong-view dissociated, unprompted]. When it is with consciousness that is sluggish and urged on, it is the fourth kind. But when they behave like this on being urged by their relatives, "Give; pay hom-

age", then the fourth kind of consciousness arises [as before but prompted].' 'There is no danger in sense desires' refers to M.I.v.5 *'Cūḷa·Dhamma·Samādāna·Suttaṁ'* ('The Small Way-of-Undertaking Sutta'). There, The Buddha explains how certain ascetics and Brahmins believe there is no harm in their enjoying sensual pleasures with female ascetics, disbelieving those who say there is: only when they are reborn in hell do they realize the harm. See Tables 2a/2b/2c, just following.

[78] The Buddha explains how human beings are reborn among the different types of animal in, for example, M.III.iii.9 *'Bāla·Paṇḍita·Suttaṁ'* ('The Fool&Sage Sutta'). Then he gives the simile of the yoke that has been thrown into the great sea of the world, and the blind turtle that arises once every hundred years. And He explains: 'Sooner, do I declare, would that blind turtle (coming to the surface once every hundred years) stick its neck into that yoke with the single hole than the fool who has gone to the nether world [would regain] the human state. Why is that? Because there is not, bhikkhus, any conduct according to the Dhamma, no righteous conduct, no wholesome work, no meritorious work.'

[79] The Buddha explains it in, for example, S.V.XII.xi.1 *'Manussa·Cuti·Niraya·Suttaṁ'* ('The Human-Decease Hell Sutta'), ibid.2 *'-Tiracchāna·Suttaṁ'* ('- Animal-'), ibid.3 *'-Petti Visaya-'* ('- Ghost Realm-'). He puts some grains of soil on his fingernail and compares it to the planet earth. Using that comparison as a simile, He says: 'So too, bhikkhus, trifling are those beings who, when they decease as human beings, are reborn among human beings. But those beings are legion who, when they decease as human beings, are reborn in hell. ... animal birth... the ghost realm....'

[80] In, for example, S.V.XII.xi.7 *'Deva·Cuti·Nirayādi·Suttaṁ'* ('The Deva-Decease Hell Sutta'), ibid.8 *'-Tiracchāna·Suttaṁ'* ('- Animal-'), ibid.9 *'-Petti Visaya-'* ('- Ghost Realm-'), The Buddha explains that a trifling number of devas are reborn as devas, whereas almost all are reborn in hell, the ghost-, or animal world: for His simile, see previous endnote. In, for example, S.V.XII.xi.10 *'Deva·Manussa·Niray·Ādi·Suttaṁ'* ('The Deva-Human-Hell-Etc. Sutta'), ibid.11 *'-Tiracchāna·Suttaṁ'* ('- Animal-'), ibid.12 *'-Petti Visaya-'* ('- Ghost Realm-'), He explains that in the same way only a trifling number of devas are reborn as human beings, whereas almost all are reborn in the lower realms.

[81] The Buddha explains such a case in M.I.v.9 *'Brahma·Nimantanika·Suttaṁ'* ('The Brahma-Invitation Sutta'), where He says: 'The worthy Baka the Brahma has lapsed into ignorance.' And in D.i.1 *'Brahma·Jāla·Suttaṁ'* ('The Supreme-Net Sutta'), He explains how at the beginning of the world system, when Brahmas begin to appear, the first one to appear thinks it is his work. He thinks: 'I am Brahmā, the Great Brahmā, Transcendent, Untranscended, All-Seeing, Master Mover, the Lord Maker, and Creator [MA: 'I am the world's lord, I am the world's maker and creator, the earth, the Himalayas, Mount Sineru, the world-system, the great ocean, the moon, the sun by me were made.'], Supreme Ordainer [MA: 'I am the world's Chief and Ordainer: "You be called a noble, you a Brahmin, a commoner, menial, householder, a monk be called. Even you a camel be, a cow be."'], Omnipotent Father of those that are and shall be.' Then, when one of the other Brahmas is reborn as a human being, he recollects that life in the Brahma world, and concludes the same about the first one who was there. As a human being, he teaches that wrong view.

[82] A Path Consciousnesses is a kamma consciousness, which has as its result the Fruition Consciousness, in the very next consciousness moment: they both take Nibbāna as object. Therefore, a Path Consciousness cannot also produce a rebirth-linking consciousness or any other process-separate consciousnesses.

In AbS.iii.58-59 & 62 *'Ālambaṇa·Saṅgaho'* ('Appendage [appendant object] Compendium') CMA.iii.18 i (which summarizes The Buddha's analyses in DhS) is an analysis of which types of consciousness have either Nibbāna or a supramundane consciousness as object: 1) The knowledge-associated sensual-sphere wholesome (consciousnesses) *(ñāṇa·sampayutta·kām·āvacara·kusalāni)*, and 2) the direct knowledge made up of the fifth-jhāna (consciousness) *(pañcama·jjhāna·saṅkhātaṁ abhiññā·kusalañ·ceti)*, take all objects except the Arahant

Path&Fruition *(Arahatta·Magga·Phala·vajjita·sabb·ārammaṇāni).*) 3) The knowledge-associated sensual-sphere functional consciousnesses *(ñāṇa·sampayutta·kām·āvacara·kiriyāni)*, 4) the functional direct-knowledge and 5) the determining consciousnesses *(kiriy·ābhiññā·voṭṭhabbanañ·ceti)* all also *(sabbath·āpi)* take all objects. 6) The supramundane consciousnesses *(lokuttara·cittāni)* [take] the Nibbāna object.' (See 'The Path Process', p.340, and notes).

Thus, the consciousnesses with Nibbāna as object are the four supramundane Path and Fruition consciousnesses (see No.6 above); the mundane Change-Of-Lineage consciousness *(Gotrabhu·citta)* that precedes the Stream-Entry Path (see No.1), and the mundane Cleansing consciousness *(Vodāna·citta)* that precedes the Once-Return (see No.1)/Non-Return (see No.1)/Arahant (see No.3) Path/Fruition Consciousnesses; the mind-door adverting *(mano·dvār·āvajjana)* that precedes (see No.5), and the impulsion consciousnesses *(javana·citta)* (see Nos.1/3) that perform one's mundane Reviewing Knowledge *(Paccavekkhaṇa·Ñāṇa)* of Nibbāna; the mundane direct-knowledge consciousnesses *(abhiññā·citta)* (see Nos. 2/4) by which a Noble One may read another's Path/Fruition (not higher than her/his own).

The only consciousnesses with a supramundane consciousness as object are the mind-door adverting consciousness (see No.5) that precedes, and the impulsion consciousnesses (see Nos.1/3) that perform one's mundane reviewing knowledge of one's Path and Fruition, as well as the mundane direct knowledge consciousnesses (see Nos.2/4) by which a Noble One may read another's Path/Fruition (not higher than her/his own).

The Noble One's rebirth-linking consciousness is either a knowledge-associated sensual-sphere resultant consciousness, or a fine-material/immaterial-sphere resultant consciousness, with a kamma/kamma sign/destination sign as object, neither of which include any of the nine supramundane phenomena.

[83] VsM.xiv.455 *'Ahetuka·Kusala·Vipāko'* ('The Unrooted Wholesome Resultant') PP.xiv.-123 explains that with the cessation of the rebirth-linking consciousness, there arises the life-continuum consciousness *(bhavaṅga·viññāṇaṁ)*, as the result of the same kamma and with the same object as the rebirth-linking consciousness. And there not being any interruption of that continuity by the arising of another type of consciousness, then life-continuum consciousnesses of unlimited reckoning *(aparimāṇa·saṅkhyam·pi)* just continue to occur *(pavattati·yeva)*. VsMṬ then explains that the life-continuum *(bhavaṅga)* is so called because of its occurring as a continuum factor *(aṅga·bhāvena)* of rebirth existence *(upapatti·bhavassa)* (as a factor maintaining the continuum of consciousnesses in between the various types of mental processes throughout one existence). VsM then explains that in one existence, the last life-continuum consciousness of all is called 'passed on/over *(cuti)* (decease)', because of passing on/over *(cavanattā)* to another existence. (The English 'decease' may be analysed in the same way: PHR 'decease: Latin *decessus* departure/ death, pp of *decedere* to depart/ die, from *de* from + *cedere* to go.)' For an analysis of the various terms for death/decease used by The Buddha, see VbhA.IV.i.193 *'Dukkha·Sacca·Niddesa·Vaṇṇanā'* ('Description of the Suffering-Truth Exposition') DD.iv.475-479.

[84] LATENCY: The Buddha explains the seven latencies in, for example, A.VII.ii.1 *'Paṭhama Anusaya·Suttaṁ'* ('The First Latency Sutta'): 'These seven, bhikkhus, are the latencies. What seven? The sensual-lust latency... aversion-... views-... scepticism-... conceit-... lust-for-existence-... the ignorance latency.'

[85] The Buddha explains it in, for example A.VI.I.iv.9 *'Nidāna·Suttaṁ'* ('The Causation Sutta'): 'Not, bhikkhus, from non-greed, does greed arise: it is, bhikkhus, rather non-greed that arises from non-greed.... non-hatred that arises from non-hatred.... non-delusion that arises from non-delusion.'

[86] The Buddha makes this distinction also in S.II.I.iii.5 *'Bhūmija·Suttaṁ'* ('The Bhūmija Sutta'): see quotation endnote 76, p.20.

[87] In, for example, M.III.iii.9 *'Bāla·Paṇḍita·Suttaṁ'* ('The Fool&Sage Sutta'), The Buddha uses four terms for wholesome kamma: 1) conduct according to the Dhamma *(Dhamma·cariyā)*, 2) righteous conduct *(sama·cariyā)*, 3) wholesome work *(kusala·kiriyā)*, 4) meritorious work *(puñña·kiriyā)*. See quotation endnote 78, p.235.

[88] The Buddha explains it in A.III.III.i.9 *'Paṭhama·Nidāna·Suttaṁ'* ('The First Causation Sutta'): 'These three, bhikkhus, are the causes for the arising of kamma. What three? Non-greed, non-hatred, non-delusion are the causes for the arising of kamma. ...[any such kamma is] wholesome, praiseworthy, has happiness for result, and leads to the ending of kamma, not to the arising of kamma.' For details, see 'The Unworking of Kamma', p.338*ff.*

[89] In S.III.I.vi.5 *'Satta·Ṭṭhāna·Suttaṁ'* ('The Seven-Standpoints Sutta'), The Buddha explains the Arahant's continuously seeing only the arising and perishing of formations: 'And what, bhikkhus, is one who has examined in three ways *(ti·vidh·ūpaparikkhī)*: the elements he examines *(dhātuso upaparikkhati)*, the bases he examines *(āyatanaso upaparikkhati)*, and dependent origination he examines *(paṭicca·samuppādaso upaparikkhati)*.' SA explains that this is the Arahant's constant abiding *(satata·vihāra)*. The Arahant does not see a being *(satto)* or a person *(puggalo)*, but sees only by way of the individual nature of the elements *(dhātu·sabhāvena)*, etc., and sees only that having done such and such kamma, one comes to such an existence. The Buddha explains this abiding also in, for example, A.IV.IV.v.5 *'Vappa·Suttaṁ'* ('The Vappa Sutta'): 'Thus by the bhikkhu of liberated mind *(vimutta·cittassa)* then, Vappa, six constant abidings *(cha satata·vihārā)* are attained. He seeing a sight with the eye is neither glad *(sumano)* nor sad *(dummano)*: equanimous he abides *(upekkhako viharati)*, mindful and discerning *(sato sampajāno)*... hearing a sound with the ear... [etc.].' In AA this is called the Arahant's permanent abiding *(nicca·vihāra)*, continuous abiding *(nibaddha·vihārā)*. And in, for example, S.II.I.vi.1 *'Pari·Vīmaṁsana·Suttaṁ'* ('The Full Investigation Sutta'), The Buddha explains: 'If he a happy feeling feels, detached he feels it *(visaṁyutto naṁ vedayati)*... painful feeling, detached... neither painful nor happy feeling, detached he feels it.' VsM.xii.375 *'Dasa-Iddhi·Kathā'* ('Discussion of the Tenfold Success ') PP.xii.36-38 discusses this abiding, and quotes the Venerable Sāriputta's explanation of PsM.III.xxii.17 *'Dasa-Iddhi·Niddeso'* ('Exposition of the Tenfold Success'): 'What is a Noble One's success *(Ariyā iddhi)*? Here if a bhikkhu should wish, "May I abide perceiving the unrepulsive *(appaṭikkūla·saññī)* in the repulsive *(paṭikkūle)*," he abides perceiving the unrepulsive in that... equanimous *(upekkhako)* he abides towards that, mindful *(sato)* and discerning *(sampajāno)*.' And VsM explains: 'Because this is brought about only in mind-mastery attained *(ceto·vasi·ppattānaṁ)* Noble Ones, it is called "Noble Ones' success".' And VsM explains that the Arahant is perceiving the unrepulsive *(appaṭikūla·saññī)*, when he practises *(karonto)* loving-kindness pervasion *(mettā·pharaṇaṁ)* or the elements-attention *(dhātu·manasikāraṁ)* towards a repulsive *(paṭikkūle)* and disagreeable *(aniṭṭhe)* object; he is perceiving the repulsive, when he practises foulness pervasion *(asubha·pharaṇaṁ)* or the impermanence perception *(aniccanti manasikāraṁ)* towards an unrepulsive *(appaṭikkūle)*, beautiful *(iṭṭhe)* object; and he is perceiving either when he practises the appropriate towards either the repulsive or unrepulsive in an object. And he may also pay attention neither to the repulsive nor the unrepulsive, but abide just with the six-factored equanimity *(chaḷ·aṅg·upekkhaṁ)* (mentioned above), mindful and discerning.

[90] Discussing the difference between understanding gained by perception, consciousness, and wisdom, VsMṬ.xiv.423 *'Paññā·Kathā·Vaṇṇanā'* ('Description of the Discussion of Wisdom') explains that just as one may recite a familiar passage from the Texts without paying attention to the meaning, so, because one has many times again and again penetrated the three characteristics of one's vipassanā object, one will have developed expertise in their occurrence, and they will have become familiar, which means one may sometimes know the object without actually penetrating *(paṭivijjhanaṁ)* its characteristics *(lakkhaṇānaṁ)*.

[91] The commentary refers to M.I.v.1 *'Sāleyyaka·Suttaṁ'* ('The People of Sālā Sutta'), where The Buddha cites the ten unwholesome/wholesome courses of kamma, with this view as Right View: see quotation 'To Hold Right View', p.135.

[92] In A.VII.v.9 *'Dāna·Maha·Pphala·Suttaṁ'* ('The Great-Fruit from Offering Sutta'), The Buddha discuss the various motives for offering, from the most inferior to the most superior: to gain sensual pleasures → because it is good to do → because it is a family

tradition → because the receivers do not cook themselves → because great sages of ancient times received offerings → because it calms the mind, and gives rise to joy and happiness → to adorn the mind, to equip the mind for samatha and vipassanā meditation.

93 This The Buddha mentions in, for example, DhP.xxv.13 *'Bhikkhu·Vagga'* ('Bhikkhu Chapter'): 'There is no jhāna for one without wisdom, there is no wisdom for one without jhāna, but the one with both jhāna and wisdom, he is indeed close to Nibbāna.' Discussing the roots of the rebirth-linking consciousness, the commentary to PsM.I.6 *'Gati·Kathā'* ('Discussion of Destination') PD.271 explains that for the one with a double-rooted rebirth-link *(du·hetuka·paṭisandhikassa)* jhāna does not arise *(na uppajjati)*, and quotes the first sentence of this verse: 'There is no jhāna for one without wisdom.'

94 See endnote 248, p.303.

95 The Buddha explains it in, for example, A.VIII.I.iv.6 *'Puñña·Kiriya·Vatthu·Suttaṁ'* ('The Merit-Work Base Sutta'): 'These three, bhikkhus, are the merit-work bases. What three? The merit-work base consisting in offering... in morality... in meditation.'

96 DhSA.i.156-9 *'Puñña·Kiriya·Vatth·Ādi·Kathā'* ('Discussion of Merit-Work Base Etc.') E.212 expands the three merit-work bases to ten merit-work bases: 1) Offering *(dāna)*; 2) morality *(sīla)*; 3) meditation *(bhāvanā)*; 4) reverence *(apaciti)*; 5) service *(veyyāvacca)*; 6) merit sharing *(pattānuppadāna)*; 7) rejoicing [in another's merit] *(abbhanumodana)*; 8) teaching *(desanā)*; 9) listening/learning *(savana)*; 10) view-rectification *(diṭṭh·ijukamma)*. As the threefold bases, their grouping is: offering = 1/6/7; morality = 2/4/5; meditation = 3/8/9/10.

97 The Buddha discusses these things in very many places (the details that follow have been taken from several of these sources): for example, factors for inferior/superior offerings, and superior/inferior receivers in M.III.iv.12 *'Dakkhiṇā·Vibhaṅga·Suttaṁ'* ('The Gifts-Analysis Sutta'), A.IV.II.iv.8 *'Dakkhiṇa·Suttaṁ'* ('The Gift Sutta'), A.V.III.v.7 *'A·Sa·Ppurisa·Dāna·Suttaṁ'* ('The Untrue Man's Offering Sutta') & A.V.III.v.8 *'Sa·Ppurisa·Dāna·Suttaṁ'* ('The True Man's Offering Sutta'); also M.III.i.10); making merit even though it is troublesome in A.IV.III.ii.5 *'Thāna·Suttaṁ'* ('The Occasion Sutta'); one who offers good things will receive good things in A.V.V.3 *'Manāpa·Dāyī·Suttaṁ'* ('The Good Offerer Sutta'); the factors for offering of immeasurable merit in A.VI.iv.7 *'Chaḷ·Aṅga·Dāna·Suttaṁ'* ('The Six-Factored Offering Sutta'); example of how to offer with a pure mind in A.VIII.I.iii.2 *'Dutiya Ugga·Suttaṁ'* ('The Second Ugga Sutta'); family unsuitable/suitable for a bhikkhu to associate with in A.IX.I.ii.7 *'Kula·Suttaṁ'* ('The Family Sutta'); the main results of respectful offering in DhP.viii.9 *'Sahassa·Vaggo'* ('Thousands Chapter'); and DhSA.i.156-9 *'Puñña·Kiriya·Vatth·Ādi·Kathā'* ('Discussion of Merit-Work Base Etc.') E.209-215. See also endnote 194, p.251, and Princess Sumana's questions to the Buddha, mentioned 'Princess Sumanā's Picture', p.316.

98 Thus, in M.III.iv.12 *'Dakkhiṇā·Vibhaṅga·Suttaṁ'* ('The Gifts-Analysis Sutta'), The Buddha lists the merit gained from offering a meal according to the receiver: if the offerer fulfils all the superior factors, and offers to an animal, it can produce a hundredfold result (MA: life, beauty, happiness, strength, and intelligence in a hundred lives (see end of this endnote)); to an immoral ordinary person, a thousandfold; to a moral ordinary person, a hundred-thousandfold; to one outside The Buddha's Dispensation who has jhāna a hundred thousand a hundred-thousandfold; to a Noble One an increasingly immeasurable amount of merit, culminating in an offering to a Fully Enlightened Buddha, which offering is surpassed only by an offering to the Sangha. In Dhp.viii.9 *'Sahassa·Vaggo'* ('Thousand Chapter'), The Buddha explains also: 'To one ever respectfully serving, these four things increase: life *(āyu)*, beauty *(vaṇṇo)*, happiness *(sukhaṁ)*, and strength *(balaṁ)*.' This latter verse is often chanted by bhikkhus upon receiving an offering.

99 The commentary to M.III.iv.12 *'Dakkhiṇā·Vibhaṅga·Suttaṁ'* ('The Gifts-Analysis Sutta') explains that one young novice is sufficient for this factor to be fulfilled. See also previous endnote.

100 In, for example, A.IV.II.v.9 *'Sikkhā·Pada·Suttaṁ'* ('The Training-Precept Sutta'), The Buddha explains that the person who undertakes the five precepts practises for his own

benefit. And the one who encourages another to undertake the five precepts practises for the other's benefit.

[101] This means one should know the right occasion for speaking the truth, and for keeping silent. Thus, in M.II.i.8 *'Abhaya·Rāja·Kumāra·Sutta'* ('The Abhaya King-Son Sutta') The Buddha explains that He does not utter speech that is 1) unfactual, useless, and displeasing to others; 2) factual but useless, and displeasing to others; 3) unfactual, useless, and pleasing to others; 4) factual but useless, and pleasing to others. On the other hand, He knows the right occasion for uttering speech that is 5) factual, useful, and displeasing to others; 6) factual, useful, and pleasing to others. In the same way, in A.IV.ii.5.10 *'Potaliya·Suttaṁ'* ('The Potaliya Sutta'), The Buddha explains that the ones to be less respected are: the one who criticizes that which should be criticized but does not praise that which should be praised; the one who praises that which should be praised but does not criticize that which should be criticized; and the one who neither praises that which should be praised nor criticizes that which should be criticized. He explains that the one to be respected is the one who on the right occasion criticizes that which should be criticized and praises that which should be praised.

[102] The Buddha explains drink's harm in D.iii.8 *'Siṅgālaka·Suttaṁ'* ('The Siṅgālaka Sutta').

[103] DA.i.2 *'Sāmañña·Phala·Suttaṁ'* ('The Asceticism-Fruit Sutta') quotes The Buddha's explanation in A.V.IV.iii.5 *'Vaṇijjā·Suttaṁ'* ('The Trades Sutta'): 'Five, bhikkhus, are the trades not to be plied by a lay-disciple. What five? Arms trade, beings trade, flesh trade, liquor trade, poisons trade.' Details from AA.ibid.

[104] DA.ibid. quotes S.V.XI.iv.7 *'Mahānāma·Suttaṁ'* ('The Mahānāma Sutta'). There, The Buddha explains that the devotee is one gone for refuge to The Buddha, Dhamma, and Sangha. And He defines the devotee's four qualities as: possessed of morality *(sīla·sampanna)* by observing the five precepts; possessed of faith *(saddhā·sampanna)* by faith in The Buddha's enlightenment; possessed of generosity *(cāga·sampanna)* by delighting in offering/sharing; and possessed of wisdom *(paññā·sampanna)* by the Arise&Perish Contemplation Knowledge. DA.ibid. quotes also A.V.IV.iii.5 *'Caṇḍāla·Suttaṁ'* ('The "Outcast" Sutta'). There, The Buddha speaks of the jewel devotee, lotus devotee, who has five qualities: 1) faith in The Buddha, Dhamma and Sangha; 2) moral training (the five precepts/abstinences); 3) not resorting to luck, fortune telling, etc.; 4) faith in kamma; 5) not seeking giftworthy ones outside The Buddha's Dispensation, and to provide services first there. In the same sutta, The Buddha speaks also of the outcast devotee, the dirty, and the vile devotee who has the five opposite qualities: such a one has broken her/his status as devotee, thereby her/his triple refuge. See also footnote 58, p.16.

[105] The Buddha explains the results of breaking the five precepts in, for example, *'Du·Ccarita·Vipāka·Suttaṁ'* ('The Result of Bad-Conduct Sutta'). See quotation endnote 164, p.247.

[106] Here, the commentaries distinguish between two kinds of fault *(vajja)*: 1) a universal fault *(loka·vajja)* (such as the five precepts, which are included in the ten unwholesome courses of kamma (see 'The Ten Unwholesome Courses of Kamma', p.119), and which are unwholesome *per se*, regardless of any views to the contrary: see previous endnote); 2) a legal fault *(paṇṇatti·vajja)* (breach of a prescribed regulation, as in the third, sixth, seventh, and eighth precepts of the eight/ten precepts, and the precepts laid down by The Buddha for bhikkhus). Thus, in MiP.V.ii.3 *'Khīṇ·Āsava·Sati·Sammosa·Pañho'* ('Question about the Consumed-Taints Mindfulness-Confusion'), the Venerable Nāgasena explains that an Arahant cannot commit a universal fault, although she/he can commit a legal fault. For example, she/he may eat after noon, thinking it is before noon, in which case an offence against the bhikkhus' rule has been committed.

[107] In for example, M.III.iii.9 *'Bāla·Paṇḍita·Suttaṁ'* ('The Fool&Sage Sutta'), The Buddha explains that the Wheel-Turning King (who may appear independently of a Buddha's dispensation) advises his people: 'You should not kill living beings; ...take what has not been given... engage in sexual misconduct... speak falsehood... drink liquor....' Many examples are found also in The Buddha's accounts of His past lives, the so-called *Jātakas*.

[108] Precepts to abstain from these three types of unwholesome speech are included in the livelihood-as-eighth morality *(ājīv·aṭṭha·maka·sīla)*: it is to abstain from 1) killing; 2) theft; 3) sensual (sexual) misconduct (incl. beer&wine liquor); 4) lies; 5) slander; 6) harsh speech; 7) prattle; 8) wrong livelihood. But this is a daily morality, not a special Uposatha morality *(Uposatha·sīla)*: such morality includes always not eating after noon.
[109] The Buddha explains the undertaking of these eight precepts in, e.g., A.III.II.ii.10 *'Uposatha·Suttaṁ'* ('The Uposatha Sutta').
[110] In, for example, S.V.II.vi.1 *'Āhāra·Suttaṁ'* ('The Nourishment Sutta'), The Buddha speaks of the things that serve as nourishment *(āhāra)* for the hindrances (sensual desire, ill-will, sloth&torpor, restlessness&remorse, scepticism), and those that serve as denourishment *(an·āhāra)* for them.
[111] The Buddha explains it in, for example, M.II.iv.3 *'Maghadeva·Suttaṁ'* ('The Maghadeva Sutta'): 'He was a righteous king who ruled by the Dhamma, a great king who was established in the Dhamma. He conducted himself by the Dhamma, among Brahmins and householders, among townspeople and countryfolk, and he observed the Uposatha days on the fourteenth, fifteenth, and eighth of the fortnight [and after two-hundred and fifty-two thousand years] he led the holy life....' The Buddha explains also that He was Himself that king in a past life. And the commentary explains that the king was established in the ten wholesome courses of kamma (see 'The Ten Wholesome Courses of Kamma', p.130). See also endnote 198, p.251, and 'The Wheel-Turning King', p.213*ff.*
[112] In A.X.I.v.6 *'Sakka·Suttaṁ'* ('The "Sakyan" Sutta'), The Buddha asks some Sakyans whether they observe the eightfold Uposatha. They say that sometimes they do, and sometimes they do not. And The Buddha explains to them that it is to their detriment not to observe it regularly. After He has explained the benefits from observing the Uposatha, they undertake to do it regularly.
[113] In Myanmar, the traditional Uposatha undertaking is the ninefold Uposatha. According to A.IX.I.ii.8 *'Nav·Aṅg·Uposatha·Suttaṁ'* ('The Ninefold-Uposatha Sutta'), it should comprise the eight precepts plus loving-kindness meditation *(mettā·bhāvanā)*.
[114] The Buddha explains it in A.III.II.ii.10 *'Uposatha·Suttaṁ'* ('The Uposatha Sutta').
[115] The Buddha explains it in A.X.I.v.6 *'Sakka·Suttaṁ'* ('The "Sakyan" Sutta').
[116] It is explained in KhPA.ii *'Dasa·Sikkhā·Padaṁ'* ('The Ten Training-Precepts') MR.ii.63 explains: '"Gold" is the precious metal *(su·vaṇṇaṃ)*. "Silver" is a *kahāpaṇa* [basic unit of money], a metal *māsaka (loha·māsaka)* [smaller unit], wooden *māsaka (dāru·māsaka)*, lac *māsaka (jatu·māsaka)*, etc., of any type *(yaṃ yaṃ)*, that serves as currency *(vohāraṃ gacchati)* anywhere *(tattha tattha)*.... "Accepting" is consenting to it *(sādiyanaṃ)* in any whatsoever way *(yena kenaci pakārena)*; it is not proper *(vaṭṭati)* by any whatsoever method *(yena kenaci pariyāyena)*.'
[117] The Buddha explains it in, for example, S.IV.viii.10 *'Maṇicūḷaka·Suttaṁ'* ('The Maṇicūḷaka Sutta'): 'For whomever, chief, gold&silver are allowable, for him the five lines of sensuality are allowable. For whomever the five sensual lines are allowable, for certain such a one, chief, you may consider as not of the ascetic nature *(a·ssamaṇa·dhammo)*, not of the Sakya-son nature *(a·sakya·puttiya·dhammo)*.'
[118] FACULTY-RESTRAINT MORALITY: as an example of the bhikkhu who restrains his mind by attending to his meditation subject, the Most Venerable Sayadaw refers to the elder Mahātissa mentioned in VsM.i.15 *'Indriya·Saṁvara·Sīlaṁ'* ('Faculty-Restraint Morality') PP.i.55, who went for alms attending only to skeleton meditation. See also quotation and discussion regarding faculty-restraint, endnote 45, p.26.
[119] The Buddha explains it in, for example, A.IV.I.v.10 *'Upakkilesa·Suttaṁ'* ('The Corruption Sutta'): 'There are four corruptions *(upakkilesa)* by which ascetics and Brahmins do not glow, do not shine, and do not radiate. What four? Drinking alcohol... indulging in sexual conduct ... accepting gold and silver... obtaining requisites through a wrong mode of livelihood.'
[120] WRONG LIVELIHOOD: In M.III.ii.7 *'Mahā·Cattārīsaka·Suttaṁ'* ('The Great-Forty Sutta'), The Buddha explains (analyses derived from VsM.i.16-17 *'Ājīva·Pārisuddhi·Sīlaṁ'* ('Livelihood

Purification Morality') PP.i.60-84): 'And what, bhikkhus, is wrong livelihood? [1] Scheming. [One speaks and acts so as to invite admiration and devotion, by assuming a particular kind of deportment, and one speaks of one's own practice.] [2] Talking. [One wants to please the laity: one talks indiscriminately, one initiates talk, about oneself, even prattle, one fondles children, etc.] [3] Hinting. [One makes unallowable hints so as to receive requisites.] [4] Belittling. [One reproaches the laity, criticizes them, ridicules them, tells tales about them etc.] [5] Pursuing gain with gain. [One gives food, flowers etc. to the laity, to gain devotion.]' VsM.ibid. refers also to the Buddha's explanation in D.i.2 *'Samañña·Phala·Suttaṁ'* ('The Asceticism-Fruit Sutta') He explains, for example: 'Whereas some ascetics and Brahmins, while living on the food offered by the faithful, earn their living by a wrong means of livelihood, by such debased arts as [for example] interpreting ominous dreams... determining whether the site for a proposed house or garden is propitious or not ... laying ghosts on a charnel-ground ... the composing of poetry, and speculations about the world... reciting charms to make people lucky or unlucky... invoking the goddess of good fortune... giving ceremonial bathings... practising surgery... practising as a children's doctor... administering medicines to cure bodily diseases, and balms to counter their after-effects, he [the bhikkhu] abstains from such wrong means of livelihood, from such debased arts.' Also DhSA.i.301 *'Lokuttara·Kusala-·Vaṇṇanā'* ('Description of the Supramundane Wholesome') E.299 explains wrong livelihood for a bhikkhu: '"The enjoyment of the four requisites, which have been produced in dependence upon the threefold deceit is livelihood." But this is the height of wrong livelihood, abstinence from which is Right Livelihood.' The Sub-sub commentary explains the threefold deceit as to display make-believe powers, to wear coarse robes, etc. (as a ploy to suggest fewness of wishes), and to hint at possessing or pretend to possess the qualities of a Noble One.

[121] The Buddha explains it in, for example, A.III.II.iv.6 *'Paṭhama·Sikkhā·Suttaṁ'* ('The First Training Sutta'): 'More, bhikkhus, than one and a half hundred training precepts [the *Pāṭimokkha*] twice a month come up for recital, in which men of good family who are eager for their own welfare are trained. Now all these combine to make these three trainings. What three? The higher morality training, the higher mind training, and the higher wisdom training. Herein are combined one and all of these precepts.' (Later, The Buddha made the *Pātimokkha* two-hundred and twenty-seven precepts.) See also quotation endnote 40, p.25, and endnote 284, p.356.

[122] The Buddha explains how scrupulous a bhikkhu's morality training should be in, for example, M.I.i.6 *'Ākaṅkheyya·Suttaṁ'* ('The Should-One-Wish Sutta'): 'Live possessed of morality, bhikkhus, possessed of the Pātimokkha; live restrained by the Pātimokkha-restraint; possessed of conduct and resort; in the slightest faults seeing fearsomeness, undertake to train in the training precepts.'

[123] In A.X.I.iv.1 *'Upāli·Suttaṁ'* ('The Upāli Sutta'), The Buddha explains it to the Venerable Upāli, His foremost disciple in the bhikkhu rule: 'For ten reasons, Upāli, were training precepts for disciples of the Tathāgata laid down, and the Pāṭimokkha established. What ten? [1] For the welfare of the Sangha, [2] for the comfort of the Sangha, [3] for the control of evil-minded men, [4] for the comfort of well-behaved bhikkhus, [5] to restrain the taints in this life, [6] to ward off taints liable to arise in a future life, [7] to inspire faith in the faithless, [8] to increase the faith in the faithful, [9] for the perpetuation of the True Dhamma, [10] for the good of the Discipline.'

[124] In, for example, D.ii.3 *'Mahā·Pari·Nibbāna·Suttaṁ'* ('The Great-Parinibbāna Sutta'), The Buddha explains the five immediate dangers in not training in morality: 1) One loses one's wealth because of carelessness; 2) One gets a bad reputation; 3) One has low self-confidence and self-esteem; 4) One dies confused; 5) One gets a bad rebirth, even in hell. He gives the opposite five advantages in training in morality.

[125] In , for example, A.X.I.i.1 *'Kimatthiya·Suttaṁ'* ('The What-Aim Sutta'), The Buddha explains the aims and rewards of wholesome morality: 'Happiness [→] non-remorse [→] gladness [→] joy [→] tranquillity [→] happiness [→] concentration [jhāna concentra-

tion] [→] knowing and seeing according to reality [vipassanā knowledge][→] disenchantment [the Disenchantment Knowledge (see p.327)] and dispassion [Arahant Path-Knowledge] [→] liberation by knowing and seeing [Arahant Fruition/Reviewing knowledge].' In A.X.I.i.2 *'Cetanā·Karaṇīya·Suttaṁ'* ('The Necessary-Volition Sutta'), He explains that the practiser need not wish for these things to arise one by one: they will inevitably arise. And in A.X.I.i.3 *'Paṭhama·Upanisa·Suttaṁ'* ('The First Presence Sutta'), He explains that without this succession of factors, there can be no successful meditation. See also quotation from the *'Bhikkhu'* sutta, footnote 375, p.135.

[126] Also, in M.III.iii.10 *'Deva·Dūta·Suttaṁ'* ('The Divine-Messenger Sutta'), The Buddha describes also how King Yama, the ruler of the hells explains the ownership of kamma to the evil-doer: 'Good man, through negligence have you failed good to do by body, speech and mind. Certainly you, good man, will be dealt with in such a way according to that negligence. But for sure, that your evil action neither by your mother was done, nor by your father was done, nor by your brother was done, nor by your sister was done, nor by your friends and companions was done, nor by kinsmen and relatives was done, nor by ascetics and Brahmins was done, nor by devas was done: by you yourself this evil action was done, and you yourself the result shall experience.' See also quotation footnote 670, p.258.

[127] In D.i.4 *'Soṇadaṇḍa·Suttaṁ'* ('The Soṇadaṇḍa Sutta'), The Buddha explains that wisdom is purified by morality, and morality is purified by wisdom; the moral man is wise, and the wise man is moral.

[128] The Buddha explains it in, for example, S.V.I.i.1 *'Avijjā·Suttaṁ'* ('The Ignorance Sutta'): 'In a wise person who has arrived at knowledge, Right View occurs. In one of Right View, Right Intention occurs. In one of Right Intention, Right Speech occurs. In one of Right Speech, Right Action occurs. In one of Right Action, Right Livelihood occurs. In one of Right Livelihood, Right Effort occurs. In one of Right Effort, Right Mindfulness occurs. In one of Right Mindfulness, Right Concentration occurs.' See table '3d: Mental Phenomena of Supramundane Consciousness', p.335.

[129] The Buddha explains it in, for example, M.III.ii.7 *'Mahā·Cattārīsaka·Suttaṁ'* ('The Great-Forty Sutta'): 'In one whose mind is noble, whose mind is taintless, who possesses the Noble Path, who is developing the Noble Path, wisdom, the faculty of wisdom, the power of wisdom, the investigation-of-states enlightenment factor, the path factor of Right View *(Sammā·Diṭṭhi) (Sammā·Diṭṭhi)*, is Right View that is Noble, taintless, supramundane, a factor of the Path.'

[130] See, for example, 'Abandonment Discipline', p.9, and quotation from S.II.I.ii.5 *'Kaccānagotta·Suttaṁ'* ('The Kaccānagotta Sutta'), endnote 51, p.27.

[131] In M.I.i.6 *'Ākaṅkheyya·Suttaṁ'* ('The Should-One-Wish Sutta'), The Buddha explains, for example, that if a bhikkhu should wish to become a Noble One, and an Arahant, he should do four things: '[1] let him fulfil the precepts, [2] to internal serenity of mind be devoted, not neglect jhāna, [3] be possessed of vipassanā, and [4] dwell in lonely places.' The commentary explains: 1 = training in higher morality; 2 = training in the higher mind, samatha; 3 = training in higher wisdom; 4 = the place where one accomplishes the latter two higher trainings. In S.V.I.vi.11 *'Āgantuka·Suttaṁ'* ('The Guest Sutta'), He explains, for example: 'And what, bhikkhus, are the things to be developed by direct knowledge? samatha and vipassanā.' And in DhP.xxv.13 *'Bhikkhu·Vagga'* ('Bhikkhu Chapter'), He says: 'In whom are jhāna and wisdom, he is indeed Nibbāna near.'

[132] In M.I.v.4 *'Cūḷa·Vedalla·Suttaṁ'* ('The Small Catechism Sutta'), the Arahant Dhammadinnā explains: 'Mental one-pointedness *(cittassa ekaggatā)*, this is concentration.'

[133] The Buddha explains it in, for example, A.IV.III.v.3 *'Āloka·Suttaṁ'* ('The Light Sutta'): 'There are, bhikkhus, these four lights. What four? The light of the moon; the light of the sun; the light of fire; the light of wisdom.' See also the ten insight corruptions discussed under 'Inferior Insight Meditation', p.114, and endnote 151, p.244.

134 The Buddha explains the necessity for developing concentration in order to practise vipassanā in, for example, S.III.I.i.5 *'Samādhi·Suttaṁ'* ('The Concentration Sutta'). See quotation p.88, and endnote 151, p.244.

135 This misunderstanding arises because of misreading The Buddha's instructions on mindfulness-of-breathing: '"Experiencing the whole body *(sabba·kāya·paṭisaṁvedī)*, I shall breathe in... out" thus he trains. "Tranquillizing the body-formation *(passambhayaṁ kāya·saṅ-khāraṁ)*, I shall breathe in... out": thus he trains.' *Kāya* does not, however, refer to the body as such, but to the 'body' of breath. The Buddha explains it in, for example, M.III.-ii.9 *'Ānāpāna·Ssati·Suttaṁ'* ('The Mindfulness-of-Breathing Sutta'): 'Whenever, bhikkhus, a bhikkhu... trains thus: "Experiencing the whole body... tranquillizing the bodily formation, I shall breathe in ...." on that occasion the bhikkhu dwells contemplating the body in the body.... Among the bodies, a certain body, bhikkhus, I declare this, that is, the in&out breath *(Kāyesu kāy·aññatar·āhaṁ, bhikkhave, evaṁ vadāmi yadidaṁ, assāsa·passāsā)*.' And in, for example, S.IV.vii.6 *'Dutiya·Kāmabhū·Suttaṁ'*, the Venerable Arahant Kāmabhu explains to the layman Citta: 'The in&out breath, householder, is the bodily formation *(kāya·saṅkhāro)*.' It is explained also in the commentary to, for example, D.ii.9 *'Mahā·Sati·Paṭṭhāna·Suttaṁ'* ('The Great Mindfulness-Foundation Sutta').

136 In S.II.ii.1 *'Nakha·Sikhā·Suttaṁ'* ('The Nail-Tip Sutta'), The Buddha compares grains of earth on the tip of His fingernail to the great earth. And He says that in the same way (for the Stream Enterer with seven lives to go), the suffering that remains is as the grains of earth, and the suffering that has been destroyed is as the great earth. He concludes: 'Thus great indeed, bhikkhus, is Dhamma penetration, thus great is Dhamma-Eye obtainment.'

137 In M.III.i.9 *'Maha·Puṇṇama·Suttaṁ'* ('The Great Fullmoon-Night Sutta'), a bhikkhu asks The Buddha why the aggregates are called aggregates, and He explains that the eleven categories constitute the aggregation of each aggregate.

138 The Buddha explains it in, for example, M.I.iv.3 *'Mahā·Gopālaka·Suttaṁ'* ('The Great Cowherd Sutta'): 'And how does a bhikkhu have knowledge of materiality? Here, bhikkhus, a bhikkhu as it really is understands, "Any whatsoever materiality, all materiality, consists of the four great essentials, and materiality derived from the four great essentials." That is how a bhikkhu has knowledge of materiality.'

139 The Buddha explains it in, for example, S.II.I.i.2' *Vibhaṅga·Suttaṁ'* ('The Analysis Sutta'): 'There are, bhikkhus, these four elements. What four? The earth element, the water element, the fire element, the wind element.'

140 In, for example, D.ii.9 *'Mahā·Sati·Paṭṭhāna·Suttaṁ'* ('The Great Mindfulness-Foundation Sutta'), The Buddha explains: 'And how then, bhikkhus, does a bhikkhu dwell dhammas as dhammas contemplating in terms of the six internal and external bases? Here, bhikkhus, a bhikkhu the eye discerns, and colour discerns... the ear discerns, and sound discerns [etc.].' And in, for example, M.III.ii.5 *'Bahu·Dhātuka·Suttaṁ'* ('The Many-Elements Sutta'), He explains: 'There are, Ānanda, these eighteen elements: the eye element, the colour element, the eye-consciousness element, the ear element, the sound element, the ear-consciousness element... [the nose-/odour-/nose-consciousness-, tongue-/flavour-/tongue-consciousness-, body-/tangible-/body-consciousness-, mind-/(other-) things-/mind-consciousness element]. When he knows and sees these eighteen elements, a bhikkhu can be called in the elements skilled.' The eye-/ear-/nose-/tongue-/body-translucent element *(pasāda·rūpa)* correspond to the eye-/ear-/nose-/tongue-/body base *(āyatana)*: the five internal bases that are material. They are also called the five material doors *(dvāra)*.

141 M.I.iv.5 *'Cūla·Saccaka·Suttaṁ'* ('The Small Saccaka Sutta') describes a debate between The Buddha and a philosopher Saccaka who held this view. He is mentioned at 'Saccaka the Philosopher', p.142.

142 Frequently referred to in the Texts, e.g. the ascetic who meets the newly enlightened Buddha says: 'Clear, friend, are your faculties, pure and bright the colour of your skin.'

(M.I.iii.6 *'Pāsa·Rāsi·Suttaṁ'* ('The Mass of Snares Sutta'), also called *'Ariya·Pariyesanā-·Suttaṁ'* ('The Noble-Search Sutta'))

[143] The Buddha explains this synonymity in S.II.I.vii.1 *'Assutavā·Suttaṁ'* ('The "Unlearned" Sutta'): 'Just as a monkey roaming through the forest grabs hold of one branch, lets that go and grabs another, then lets that go and grabs yet another, so too that, bhikkhus, which is called "thought" *(citta)*, and "mind" *(mana)*, and "consciousness" *(viññāṇa)*, arises as one thing and ceases as another day and night.' The commentary explains that all three terms are synonyms for 'mind base' *(man·āyatana)*, the sixth internal base.

[144] The Buddha explains it in, for example, S.II.I.i.2 *'Vibhaṅga·Suttaṁ'* ('The Analysis Sutta').

[145] This procedure is explained by The Buddha in S.II.I.iv.4 *'Dutiya·Ñāṇa·Vatthu·Suttaṁ'* ('The Second Knowledge-Subject Sutta'). There, He explains how there is knowledge of each of the factors of dependent origination as operating in accordance with the Dhamma in the present, the past, and the future. And: 'And also that knowledge of the fixity of the Dhamma *(Dhamma·ṭṭhiti·ñāṇaṁ)*, that too is a destructible thing *(khaya·dhammaṁ)*, perishable thing *(vaya·dhammaṁ)*, a fading thing *(virāga·dhammaṁ)*, and ceasing thing *(nirodha·dhammaṁ)*.' SA describes this as counter-insight insight *(vipassanā·paṭi·vipassanā)*.

[146] See for example, quotation footnote 6, p.1, and M.II.iii.10 *'Vekhanasa·Suttaṁ'* ('The Vekhanasa Sutta'): 'If, Kaccāna, any ascetics and Brahmins, without knowing the past, without seeing the future, claim "Birth is destroyed, the holy life has been lived, what had to be done has been done, there is no more coming into any state of being,", such with this, in accordance with the Dhamma, are confuted.' See also next endnote.

[147] In very many suttas (for example, M.III.iv.1 *'Bhaddeka·Ratta·Suttaṁ'* ('The One Excellent-Night Sutta')), The Buddha advises the bhikkhus not to go after past or future five aggregates. He is in such cases referring to the uneducated ordinary person, who does so with craving and views, because of holding the identity view: she/he does so also with regard to present five agregates. He is in such cases not referring to vipassanā meditation on past and future aggregates. Here, He is referring to vipassanā meditation, however, which is necessary for the destruction of craving and views. See also quotation previous endnote.

[148] In S.III.I.viii.7 *'Khajjanīya·Suttaṁ'* ('The Being-Devoured Sutta'), The Buddha discusses ascetics and Brahmins (practising under a Buddha or a Buddha's disciple) who recollect the five aggregates of past lives. The commentary explains that they do not do it by psychic-power (by which one can see also concepts, etc.) but by vipassanā power *(vipassanā·vasena)*.

[149] In S.IV.I.xv.1 *'Kamma·Nirodha·Suttaṁ'* ('The Kamma-Cessation Sutta'), The Buddha explains explicitly that the six bases are the product of past kamma: quoted endnote 63, p.233. And in, for example, A.IV.V.iv.2 *'Vitthāra·Suttaṁ'* ('The Detailed Sutta'), He explains explicitly that contact and feelings are the result of past kamma: see endnote 282, p.355.

[150] In A.III.II.iii.6 *'Paṭhama·Bhava·Suttaṁ'* ('The First Existence Sutta'), The Buddha explains that with kamma result, and kamma (accomplished owing to ignorance and craving), there is the coming-into existence of the rebirth consciousness in the three spheres of existence. See quotation, endnote 313, p.359.

[151] Explaining knowledge in, for example, D.i.3 *'Ambaṭṭha·Suttaṁ'* ('The Ambaṭṭha Sutta'), The Buddha explains how the bhikkhu's mind is purified by jhāna concentration, and full of light, after which he directs it to knowledge and vision *(ñāṇa·dassana)*: he discerns the origination and cessation of the materiality that is his body, and then his consciousness, which is bound up with his body. This refers to vipassanā knowledge of mentality-materiality and their causes. And in S.V.III.i.10 *'Bhikkhun·Upassaya·Suttaṁ'* ('The Bhikkhunī Quarters Sutta'), The Buddha explains how one who abides with a mind well established in the four foundations of mindfulness will know (gain) successively higher distinctions *(uḷāraṁ pubben·āparaṁ visesaṁ sañjānissati)*. SA then explains the successive distinctions: apprehension of the great essentials → of derived materiality; apprehension

of all materiality→of mentality; apprehension of materiality&mentality→of cause; apprehension of mentality-materiality and their causes→ attribution of the three characteristics.

[152] In, for example, M.III.ii.5 *'Bahu·Dhātuka·Suttaṁ'* ('The Many-Elements Sutta'), The Buddha explains the things that need to be known for insight knowledge to arise: 'When, Ānanda, a bhikkhu is in the elements skilled, is in the bases skilled, is in dependent origination skilled, is in the possible and impossible skilled, in that way he can be called a sage and an enquirer.' And He explains that skill in the elements is to know and see the eighteen elements (the elements of eye, ear, nose, tongue, body, and mind, their six objects, and their six types of consciousness); the three elements (the three planes of existence: sensual-, fine-material-, and immaterial element); and the two elements (all formations: the conditioned element; Nibbāna: the unformed element). He explains that when a bhikkhu knows and sees these elements: 'a bhikkhu can be called in the elements skilled.' Skill in the bases He explains as to know and see the six internal and external bases (eye/colours, ear/sounds, nose/odours, tongue/flavours, body/tangibles, mind/ other objects). Skill in dependent origination He explains as to know the twelve factors of dependent origination in regular and negative order. And skill in the possible and impossible He explains as to understand that certain things are impossible, although their opposite is possible: see footnote 111, p.43.

[153] In DA.ii.9 *'Mahā·Sati·Paṭṭhāna·Suttaṁ'* ('The Great Mindfulness-Foundation Sutta'), it is explained how in the Kuru country (where The Buddha taught the sutta), the people were of such wisdom that if a woman was asked by another woman which mindfulness-foundation she was practising, and she said none, the other woman would scold her.

[154] In, for example, A.XI.i.7 *'Saññā·Suttaṁ'* ('The Perception Sutta'), The Buddha explains that with the attainment of Nibbāna, there is perception and knowledge of Nibbāna: 'Here, Ānanda, the bhikkhu is percipient thus: "This is the Peaceful *(Santaṁ)*, this is the Superior *(paṇitaṁ)*, that is, the calming of all formations *(sabba·saṅkhāra·samatho)*, the forsaking of all grounds [for rebirth] *(sabb·ūpadhi·paṭinissaggo)*, the destruction of craving, dispassion *(virāgo)*, cessation, Nibbāna." That then, Ānanda, is how a bhikkhu may acquire such concentration that neither of the earth is he percipient of earth... water... fire... wind... the infinite-space-... infinite-consciousness-... nothingness-... neither-perception nor non-perception base... this world...the other world, and of the seen *(diṭṭhaṁ)*, heard *(sutaṁ)*, sensed *(mutaṁ)*, cognized *(viññātaṁ)*, obtained *(pattaṁ)*, sought after *(pariyesitaṁ)*, the range of the mind *(anuvicaritaṁ manasā)*, not of that either is he percipient, but still he is percipient.'

[155] In S.V.I.iii.6 *'Dutiya A·Sa·Ppurisa·Suttaṁ'* ('The Second Untrue-Man Sutta'), The Buddha discusses the one who possesses the wrong tenfold path: wrong view, -intention, -speech, -action, -livelihood, -effort, -mindfulness, -concentration, -knowledge, -liberation.

[156] In A.I.XVI.iii *'Eka·Dhamma·Pāḷi: Tatiya Vaggo'* ('One Thing Text: Third Chapter'), The Buddha uses powerful similes to make this clear. For example: 'Just as, bhikkhus, even a tiny speck of excrement stinks, so do I not commend existence even for a moment, not even for as long as a snap of the fingers.'

[157] In Vin.Pār.II.v.303 *'Sañcaritta·Sikkhā·Padaṁ'* ('Go-Between Training-Precept'), The Buddha lists ten types of married woman: 1) one money-bought *(dhana·kkītā)*; 2) a desire cohabitant *(chanda·vāsinī)*: she lives with the man of her own desire and his agreement: ('the beloved with the beloved lives *(piyo piyaṃ vāseti)*' (with parental consent)); 3) a wealth cohabitant *(bhoga·vāsinī)*: a country woman becomes the man's wife by receiving certain property; 4) a cloth cohabitant *(paṭa·vāsinī)*: a destitute woman becomes his wife by receiving merely an outer cloth; 5) a water-bowler *(oda·pattakinī)*: family elders dip her and his two hands into a bowl of water, wishing that they be joined like the water, not to part; 6) one with removed (carrying) pad *(obhaṭa·cumbaṭā)*: she becomes his wife by having her head pad (for carrying loads) removed by him; 7) a slave and wife *(dāsī ca bhariyā ca)*: she is both his slave and his wife; 8) a worker and wife *(kammakārī ca bhariyā ca)*; 9) one flag-

brought*(dhaj·āhatā)*: a captive taken in conquered territory, where the flag has been raised; 10) a momentary wife*(muhuttikā)*: a prostitute. DhSA.I.iii.1 *'Akusala·Kamma-·Patha·Kathā'* ('Discussion of the Unwholesome Kamma-Course') E.133 lists these same ten types of wife as unapproachable ones*(agamanīya·vatthu)*.

[158] In M.I.i.4 *'Bhaya·Bherava·Suttaṁ'* ('The Fear&Dread Sutta'), The Buddha explains how He (on the night of His enlightenment, with the divine eye) saw the results of holding a wrong view: 'I understood how beings pass on according to their kamma thus... "These dear beings, of wrong bodily conduct... wrong verbal conduct... wrong mental conduct possessed, critcizers of Noble Ones, holders of wrong view, undertakers of kamma based on wrong view, with the breakup of the body, after death, have been reborn in the plane of misery, in a bad destination, in the nether world, in hell."' (See also quotation endnotes 14, p.21, 168, p.247, and The Buddha's many explanations in, for example, S.V.XII *'Sacca·Saṁyutta'* ('Truth Section'). The inevitability of doing wrong when holding a wrong view He explains in, for example, M.II.i.10 *'Apaṇṇaka·Suttaṁ'* ('The "Incontrovertible" Sutta'): 'Now, householders, of those ascetics and Brahmins whose doctrine and view is this: "There is no offering, there is no almsgiving [etc.]", it is to be expected that they will avoid these three wholesome things, namely, bodily good conduct, verbal good conduct, and mental good conduct, and that they will undertake and practise these three unwholesome things, namely bodily misconduct, verbal misconduct, and mental misconduct. Why is that? Because those good ascetics and Brahmins do not see in unwholesome things the danger of degradation and defilement, nor do they see in wholesome things the blessing of renunciation, the aspect of cleansing.' And in, for example, S.V.I.i.1 *'Avijjā·Suttaṁ'* ('The Ignorance Sutta'), He explains: 'In an unwise person of ignorance disposed, wrong view occurs; in one of wrong view, wrong intention... in one of wrong intention, wrong speech ... wrong action... wrong livelihood ... wrong effort... wrong mindfulness... In one of wrong mindfulness, wrong concentration occurs.' In S.V.I.iii.6 *'Dutiya A·Sa·Ppurisa·Suttaṁ'* ('The Second Untrue-Man Sutta'), He explains also that apart from these eight wrong factors, one may also have wrong knowledge and wrong liberation.

[159] The Buddha explains the roots of the ten unwholesome courses of kamma in, for example, A.X.IV.ii.8 *'Kamma·Nidāna·Suttaṁ'* ('The Kamma-Causation Sutta'): 'Killing I declare, bhikkhus, is of three types: rooted in greed... rooted in hatred... rooted in delusion. Taking what is not given.... Sexual misconduct.... Untrue speech.... Slanderous speech.... Harsh speech.... Prattle.... Covetousness.... Ill-will.... Wrong view I declare, bhikkhus, is of three types: rooted in greed, rooted in hatred, rooted in delusion. Thus, bhikkhus, greed is an origin of kamma causation; hatred... delusion is an origin of kamma causation.'

[160] The Buddha speaks of them as the unwholesome in A.X.IV.iii.3 *'Kusala·Suttaṁ'* ('The "Wholesome" Sutta'); as useless in A.X.IV.iii.4 *'Attha·Suttaṁ'* ('The "Useful" Sutta'); as blameful in A.ibid.7 *'Vajja·Suttaṁ'* ('The "Blameable" Sutta'); as things with a painful result in A.X.IV.iv.11 *'Vipāka·Suttaṁ'* ('The Result Sutta'), as the dark way in A.ibid.2 *'Kaṇha-·Magga·Suttaṁ'* ('The Dark Way Sutta'), and as leading to hell in A.X.V.i.1&2 *'Paṭhama [&Dutiya]·Niraya·Sagga·Suttaṁ'* ('The First [& Second] Hell&Heaven Sutta').

[161] The Buddha explains it in A.X.V.ii.222 *'Sāmañña·Vaggo'* ('Asceticism Chapter'): 'Possessed of twenty things, bhikkhus, one is accordingly, as it were, put in hell... oneself is a killer of beings, and incites another into killing... oneself is a holder of wrong view, and incites another into holding wrong view.'

[162] The Buddha explains it in ibid.223: 'Possessed of thirty things, bhikkhus, one is accordingly, as it were, put in hell... oneself is a killer of beings, and incites another into killing, and one is an approver of killing [etc.].'

[163] The Buddha explains it in ibid.224: 'Possessed of forty things, bhikkhus, one is accordingly, as it were, put in hell... oneself is a killer of beings, and incites another into killing, and one is an approver of killing, also one speaks of the beauty of killing [etc.].'

[164] In M.III.iii.9 *'Bāla·Paṇḍita·Suttaṁ'* ('The Fool&Sage Sutta'), The Buddha describes the fool as one who thinks ill thoughts, speaks ill speech, and does ill actions. He then describes how such a fool suffers when he hears people discuss killing, theft, sexual misconduct, lying, and drinking beer&wine liquor, because he does those things himself. The fool suffers also when he recalls the types of bodily-, verbal, and mental misconduct that he has performed. Thus, in this sutta, The Buddha includes the drinking of beer and wine, etc. under ill actions and bodily misconduct. Furthermore, explaining the results of unwholesome kamma in A.VIII.I.iv.10 *'Du·Ccarita·Vipāka·Suttaṁ'* ('The Result of Bad-Conduct Sutta'), The Buddha includes the trivial results such kamma: 'The killing of beings... taking what has not been given... sexual misconduct... untrue speech... slanderous speech... harsh speech... prattle... drinking beer&wine liquor, monks, pursued, practised, often done, leads one to hell... animal birth... the ghost realm. What is the trivial result of killing is the leading to a human being's shortened life span... what is the trivial result of drinking beer&wine liquor is the leading to a human being's becoming deranged *(ummatta)*.' (See also quotation, endnote 14, p.21.) These eight courses of kamma differ from the customary ten given by The Buddha in that they include only unwholesome courses of bodily/verbal kamma, not the three unwholesome courses of mental kamma. And here the unwholesome course of kamma of drinking beer&wine liquor is given specifically, whereas in the list of ten, it is implied. Hence, explaining the courses of kamma that are abstained from with the five precepts, VbhA.xiv.704 *'Sikkhā·Pada·Vibhaṅgo'* ('Training-Precept Analysis') DD.xiv.1912-1916 explains that drinking beer&wine liquor is a course of kamma *(kamma·patha)*, being bodily kamma rooted in greed/delusion. And VbhṬ.ibid. quotes this sutta to explain that although drinking beer&wine liquor is not specifically mentioned in the ten unwholesome courses of bodily kamma, it is included in them, producing the same results. And the sub-sub-commentary explains that all ten unwholesome courses of kamma are common (part&parcel) *(sabhāga)* to the drinking of beer&wine liquor: it is a support *(upakāra)* for all ten unwholesome courses of kamma. And since it is a sensual pleasure(kāma·guṇa), it should thus be included under 'sensual misconduct' *(kāmesu micchā·cārā)* (here translated 'sexual misconduct').

[165] The Buddha gives this list in, for example, M.III.iii.2 *'Mahā·Suññata·Suttaṁ'* ('The Great Voidness Sutta'), and S.V.XII.i.10 *'Tiracchāna·Kathā·Suttaṁ'* ('The Low-Talk Sutta').

[166] The Buddha explains it in, for example, S.II.I.ii.5 *'Kaccānagotta·Suttaṁ'* ('The Kaccānagotta Sutta'): 'But, Kaccāna, when one sees (as it really is, with Right Wisdom) the origin of the world, there is no non-existence in regard to the world. And, Kaccāna, when one sees (as it really is, with Right Wisdom) the cessation of the world, there is no existence in the world.... this [Noble] one does not... take a stand about "my self". He has no perplexity or doubt that what arises is only suffering's arising, what ceases is only suffering's ceasing.... It is in this way, Kaccāna, that there is Right View.' And He explains also that it is impossible for a person so possessed of view to treat any formation as self: see quotation, endnote 52, p.27. See also 'Stream Entry', p.336.

[167] The Buddha explains it in M.III.ii.7 *'Mahā·Cattārīsaka·Suttaṁ'* ('The Great-Forty Sutta'): 'One understands wrong view as wrong view, and Right View as Right View: this is one's Right View.'

[168] In M.I.i.4 *'Bhaya·Bherava·Suttaṁ'* ('The Fear&Dread Sutta'), The Buddha explains how He (on the night of His enlightenment, with the divine eye) saw the results of holding Right View: 'I understood how beings pass on according to their kamma thus... "These dear beings, of good bodily conduct... good verbal conduct... good mental conduct possessed, not critcizers of Noble Ones, holders of Right View, undertakers of kamma based on Right View, with the breakup of the body, after death, have been reborn in a good destination, in a heavenly world."' (See also quotation endnotes 14, p.21, and 158, p.246.) And in, for example, A.X.III.ii.9 *'Pubbaṅ·Gama·Suttaṁ'* ('The Forerunner Sutta'), He explains: 'Of the sunrise, bhikkhus, this is the forerunner, this is the foretoken, namely, the rise of dawn. So too, bhikkhus, for the wholesome things, this is the

forerunner, this is the foretoken, namely, Right View. With Right View, bhikkhus, Right Intention occurs; with Right Intention, Right Speech occurs; with Right Speech, Right Action occurs; with Right Action, Right Livelihood occurs; with Right Livelihood, Right Effort occurs; with Right Effort, Right Mindfulness occurs; with Right Mindfulness, Right Concentration occurs; with Right Concentration, Right Knowledge occurs; with Right Knowledge, Right Liberation occurs.' (The last two factors are the ninth and tenth factors of the Arahant's tenfold Noble Path.)

[169] The Buddha speaks of them as the wholesome in A.X.IV.iii.3 *'Kusala·Suttaṁ'* ('The "Wholesome" Sutta'); useful in A.ibid.4 *'Attha·Suttaṁ'* ('The "Useful" Sutta'); as blameless in A.ibid.7 *'Vajja·Suttaṁ'* ('The "Blameable" Sutta'); as things with a happy result in A.X.IV.iv.11 *'Vipāka·Suttaṁ'* ('The Result Sutta'), as the bright way in A.ibid.2 *'Kaṇha-·Magga·Suttaṁ'* ('The Dark Way'), and as leading to heaven in A.X.V.i.1&2 *'Paṭhama [&Dutiya]·Niraya·Sagga·Suttaṁ'* ('The First [&Second] Hell&Heaven Sutta').

[170] The Buddha explains it in A.X.V.ii.222 *'Sāmañña·Vaggo'* ('Asceticism Chapter'): 'Possessed of twenty things, bhikkhus, one is accordingly, as it were, put in heaven... one is oneself an abstainer from the killing of beings, and one incites another into killing-abstention... one is oneself a holder of Right View, and one incites another into holding Right View.'

[171] The Buddha explains it in ibid.223: 'Possessed of thirty things, bhikkhus, one is accordingly, as it were, put in heaven... one is oneself an abstainer from the killing of beings, and one incites another into killing-abstention, and one is an approver of killing-abstention....'

[172] The Buddha explains it in ibid.224: 'Possessed of forty things, bhikkhus, one is accordingly, as it were, put in heaven... one is oneself an abstainer from the killing of beings, and one incites another into killing-abstention, and one is an approver of killing-abstention, one speaks also of the beauty of killing-abstention....'

[173] The Buddha explains it in, for example, S.IV.IX.i.2 *'Samatha·Vipassanā·Suttaṁ'* ('The Samatha-Vipassanā Sutta'): 'The Unformed, bhikkhus, I shall teach you, and the path to the Unformed.... And what is the Unformed? The destruction of lust, the destruction of hatred, the destruction of delusion. And what, bhikkhus, is the path to the Unformed? samatha and vipassanā....'

[174] Explaining the nine qualities of a Perfectly Self-Enlightened Buddha *(Sammā-·Sam·Buddha)*, The Buddha gives knowledge and conduct as the third: 'Possessed of Knowledge and Conduct *(Vijjā-Caraṇa Sampanno)*.' It is explained in VsM.vii.133 *'Buddh-·Ānussati'* ('Buddha Recollection') PP.vii.30. And The Buddha explains knowledge and conduct in, for example, D.i.3 *'Ambaṭṭha·Suttaṁ'* ('The Ambaṭṭha Sutta').

[175] Explaining conduct *(caraṇa)* in D.i.3 *'Ambaṭṭha·Suttaṁ'* ('The Ambaṭṭha Sutta'), The Buddha gives a more detailed listing of the bhikkhu's morality: the same as in D.i.2 *'Sāmañña·Phala·Suttaṁ'* ('The Asceticism-Fruit Sutta').

[176] The Venerable Ānanda says the Noble Disciple is very learned *(bahu·ssuto)*, the Texts having been practised verbally, mentally reflected, and well penetrated by view. ApA.I.-3-1 (366) *'Sāriputta·Tthera-Apadāna·Vaṇṇanā'* ('Description of the Sāriputta-Elder Narrative') explains that there are two types of very learned person *(bahu·sutto puggalo)*: one learned in scholarship *(pariyatti)*, one learned in penetration *(paṭivedha)*. In the standard sutta description, the Texts having been practised verbally *(vacasā paricitā)* and mentally reflected *(manas·ānupekkhitā)* refers to scholarship. Their having been well penetrated by view *(diṭṭhiyā su·paṭividdhā)* refers to penetration. Learning as penetration is explained in, for example, the commentary to A.IV.IV.v.1 *'Sot·Ānugata·Suttaṁ'* ('The Come-through-the-Ear Sutta'): 'the effect *(atthato)* and the reason/cause *(kāraṇato)* [five aggregates & their origin], with wisdom well penetrated *(paññāya suṭṭhu paṭividdhā)*, made evident *(paccakkhaṁ katā)*.' This explanation is given also in the commentary to M.I.iv.2 *'Mahā·Gosiṅga·Suttaṁ'* ('The Great Gosiṅga Sutta'), where the sub-commentary adds: 'with fondness for meditation *(nijjhāna·kkhantibhūtāya)*, having resolved *(vavatthapetvā)* material and mental phenomena *(rūp·ārūpa·dhamme)* by the so-called known full-knowledge *(ñāta·pariññā·saṅkhātāya)*: "Thus is

materiality, so much is materiality" *(iti rūpaṁ, ettakaṁ rūpan'ti ādinā)*(this being the five aggregates, their origin, and cessation, see quotation under 'The Lion's Roar', p.39).' Likewise, VbhA.iv.205 *'Magga·Sacca·Niddesa·Vaṇṇanā'* ('Description of the Path-Truth Exposition') DD.iv.551 explains: 'Thus for him, in the preliminary stage *(pubba·bhāge)*, with regard to two truths [1st/2nd], there comes to be acquisition-*(uggaha·)*, inquiry-*(paripucchā·)*, listening/learning-*(savana·)*, bearing in mind-*(dhāraṇa·)*, and comprehension-penetration *(sammasana·paṭivedho)* [vipassanā knowledge], with regard to two [3rd/4th] only listening-penetration *(savana·paṭivedhoy·eva)* [the Nibbāna and the Path are penetrated only at the subsequent stage *(apara·bhāge)*].'

177 In M.I.iv.3 *'Mahā·Gopālaka·Suttaṁ'* ('The Great Cowherd Sutta'), The Buddha explains eleven qualities by which 'a bhikkhu is capable of growth, increase, and fulfilment in this Dhamma and Vinaya.' The sixth is: 'Here, a bhikkhu goes from time to time to those bhikkhus of wide learning, versed in the doctrine, masters of the Dhamma, masters of the Vinaya, masters of the Matrices [the bhikkhu/bhikkhunī rule]. And he enquires and asks questions of them thus: "How is this, Venerable Sir? What is the meaning of this?" Those venerable ones the unrevealed reveal, the unclear make clear, of the many doubt-based things the doubt dispel.'

178 The Buddha explains it in, for example, A.IV.I.ii.4 *'Saṁvara·Suttaṁ'* ('The Restraint Sutta'): 'There are, bhikkhus, these four efforts. What four? [1] The effort to restrain; [2] the effort to abandon; [3] the effort to develop; [4] the effort to maintain.' For a more detailed version, see quotation endnote 26, p.23.

179 The Venerable Ānanda says the Noble Disciple is wise *(paññavā)*: 'He is possessed of wisdom regarding arising&disappearance *(uday·atthagāminiyā)* that is Noble *(Ariyāya)*, penetrating *(nibbedhikāya)*, leading to the complete destruction of suffering *(sammā dukkha·kkhaya·gāminiyā)*.' MA explains that this means he is able to penetrate the arising&disappearance of the five aggregates, by way of suppression *(vikkhambhana·vasena)* with insight-wisdom *(vipassanā·paññā)*, and by way of uprooting *(samuccheda·vasena)* with Path-wisdom *(Magga·paññā)*.

180 The Buddha explains this in S.II.I.iv.8 *'Cetanā·Suttaṁ'* ('The Volition Sutta'): 'If, bhikkhus, one does not will, and one does not design, but it is still latent, this is an object for the standing of [kamma] consciousness *(viññāṇassa ṭhitiyā)*. There being an object, there is the establishment of [kamma] consciousness *(patiṭṭhā viññāṇassa hoti)*. When established consciousness develops, there is future generation of re-existence.' SA.ibid. explains that so long as the latencies exist, there is no preventing kamma consciousness *(kamma·viññāṇa)* from arising. SṬ.ibid. explains that insight meditation of the meditator who has attained the Danger knowledge still produces kamma, caused by the latencies. Kammic consciousness stops arising only when the latencies have been destroyed by the Arahant Path-Knowledge: not before. The Buddha explains the same thing in the next two suttas. For the latencies, see footnote 145, p.55.

181 In M.III.i.6 *'Āneñjasappāya·Suttaṁ'* ('To the Imperturbable Sutta'), The Buddha explains how the bhikkhu practises vipassanā on the fourth jhāna, and immaterial jhānas, and for that reason may be reborn on one of those jhāna planes. The Buddha explains also that a bhikkhu with the Formations-Equanimity Knowledge may not attain Nibbāna, because he delights in and becomes attached to that equanimity: accordingly, his insight knowledge produces rebirth. The Buddha explains this same process in M.II.ii.4 *'Mahāmālukya·Suttaṁ'* ('The Mahāmālukya Sutta') where He refers to the delight for samatha and vipassanā as Dhamma-lust *(Dhamma·rāga)*, and Dhamma-delight *(Dhamma·nandi)*. PsM.I.ix.56 *'Saṅkhār·Upekkhā·Ñāṇa·Niddeso'* ('Exposition of Formations-Equanimity Knowledge') PD.I.ix.318 explains: 'The ordinary person's delighting *(abhinandato)* in formations-equanimity defiles consciousness, is an obstacle to meditation, is an obstruction to further penetration *(paṭivedha)*, is a cause for future rebirth *(ayatiṁ paṭisandhiyā paccayo hoti)*.' The same for the Noble Disciple trainee. PsA explains that the productive kamma is wholesome, and the defilement only a supporting cause *(upatthambhaka·paccaya)*: and it refers only to the trainee/Stream Enterer/Once Returner without jhāna. The one with

jhāna/Non-Returner is reborn in the Brahma world, with existence craving *(bhava·taṇhā)* as supporting cause.

[182] The Buddha explains it in, for example, D.ii.9 *'Mahā·Sati·Paṭṭhāna·Suttaṁ'* ('The Great Mindfulness-Foundation Sutta'): 'And, bhikkhus, what is Right Concentration? Here, a bhikkhu detached from sensual desires, detached from unwholesome mental states, enters and remains in the first jhāna.... And with the subsiding of application and sustainment, by gaining inner tranquillity and oneness of mind, he enters and remains in the second jhāna .... And with the fading away of delight, he remains imperturbable, mindful and discerning ... he enters the third jhāna. And, having given up pleasure and pain, and with the destruction of former gladness and sadness, he enters and remains in the fourth jhāna .... This is called Right Concentration.'

[183] In A.V.I.iii.5 *'Anuggahita·Suttaṁ'* ('The "Assisted" Sutta'), The Buddha condenses the fifteen things of conduct *(caraṇa)* into five: 1) morality *(sīla)*, 2) learning *(sūta)*, 3) discussion *(sākaccha)*, 4) samatha, 5) insight *(vipassanā)*. See likewise the things necessary to attain the four discriminations, under, for example, 'The Golden Venerable Mahākaccāna', p.277.

[184] In D.iii.7 *'Lakkhaṇa·Suttaṁ'* ('The Characteristic Sutta'), The Buddha explains the kamma that produced the thirty-two characteristics of His body. The Subcommentary explains that His practice of conduct leads to good destinations, encountering the dispensations of Buddhas. The practice of wisdom means He understands the Dhamma.

[185] The Buddha said to him: 'But you, foolish man, have misrepresented us by your wrong grasp, and injured yourself, and accumulated much demerit; for this will lead to your harm and suffering for a long time.' And The Buddha asked the bhikkhus: 'What do you think, bhikkhus? Has this bhikkhu Sāti (son of a fisherman) kindled even a spark of wisdom in this Dhamma and Vinaya?'

[186] In M.I.iv.5 *'Cūla·Saccaka·Suttaṁ'* ('The Small Saccaka Sutta'), Saccaka challenged The Buddha by declaring that the aggregates are self. But when questioned by The Buddha, He was forced to admit that this was impossible. Even though he admitted defeat, he did not embrace The Buddha's teaching. Saccaka is discussed also at endnote 262, p.353.

[187] See, for example, also D.iii.2 *'Udumbarika·Suttaṁ'* ('The Udumbarika Sutta'). There, a wanderer Nigrodha and his followers listen respectfully to The Buddha explain how He trains His disciples. They acknowledge that the Buddha's training is superior to theirs. But even though The Buddha invites them to undertake the training, none of them do. By contrast, for example, the fire-ascetic Uruvela Kassapa and his disciples give up their own training and train under The Buddha (See 'Happy Uruvela Kassapa', p.282).

[188] The Buddha explains kamma by way of when they take effect, in A.VI.vi.9 *'Nibbedhika·Suttaṁ'* ('The Penetrating Sutta'): 'And what, bhikkhus, is the result of kamma? Threefold, bhikkhus, is the result of kamma, I declare: effective as a present thing [in this life], or effective upon rebirth [in the next life], or effective upon a subsequent occasion [in a life subsequent to that].' Thus the four types of kamma as given in, for example, VsM/AbS: 1) PRESENTLY-EFFECTIVE KAMMA *(diṭṭha·dhamma·vedanīya·kamma)*: *diṭṭha* (visible/apparent/present) + *dhamma* (thing) + *vedanīya* (effective/to be experienced); 2) SUBSEQUENTLY-EFFECTIVE KAMMA *(upapajja·vedanīya·kamma)*: *upapajja* (rebirth) + *dhamma·vedanīya*; 3) INDEFINITELY-EFFECTIVE KAMMA *(apar·āpariya·vedanīya·kamma)*: *apara* (following/next/subsequent) + *apara* (the next after the next/beyond) + *vedanīya·kamma*; 4) LAPSED KAMMA *(ahosi·kamma)*: *ahosi* (there existed/ was). Lapsed kamma covers non-resultant kamma of past, present, and future: 'There was kamma *(ahosi kammaṁ)*, there was not kamma result *(n·āhosi kamma·vipāko)*... there is not kamma result *(n·atthi kamma·vipāko)*... there will not be any kamma result *(na bhavissati kamma·vipāko)*.' See further under 'The Workings of Kamma Past—Present—Future', p.162.

[189] The *Dhamma·Pada* verse is: 'Here he is tormented, hereafter he is tormented: the evil-doer is tormented in both places. "I have done evil" torments him. More he is tormented when to an unhappy destination he is gone.'

[190] Discussing The Buddha's explaining that it is impossible for a Noble Disciple with evil intent to draw a Tathāgata's blood, VbhA.XVI.x.809 *'Paṭhama·Bala·Niddeso'* ('Exposition of the First Power') DD.XVI.x.2152 explains that with an attack on the Tathāgata there is no flow of blood with breaking of the skin. Thus, even though the blow was as if with an axe, the bleeding was only inside, which in English is a bruise.
[191] The Buddha explains it in, for example, S.II.I.iii.5 *'Bhūmija·Suttaṁ'* ('The Bhūmija Sutta') (also A.IV.IV.iii.1 (171) *'Cetanā·Suttaṁ'* ('The Volition Sutta')): 'And thus, Ānanda, through ignorance's remainderless fading away and cessation, the body... the speech... the mind it is no more, by which cause arises internally that happiness&suffering. The field it is no more... the site it is no more... the base it is no more... the circumstance it is no more.' See also quotation endnotes 312, p.359, and 315, p.360.
[192] See, for example, S.I.iii.10 *'Dutiya·Aputtaka·Suttaṁ'* ('The Second "Childless" Sutta'), and next endnote.
[193] In A.III.II.ii.10 *'Uposatha·Suttaṁ'* ('The Uposatha Sutta'), The Buddha explains that if one observes the eightfold Uposatha (keeping the eight precepts on a full-moon/new-moon day), one may as a result enjoy supreme happiness as a deva, with a life span of, for example, 9 million, 36 million, 576 million, up to 9,216 million human years.
[194] That is, temperature-born materiality *(utuja·rūpa)* such as money, gold, and silver, etc (see 'The Four Origins of Materiality', p.97. The Buddha explains other types of immediate result from offering *(sandiṭṭhika dāna·phala)* in, for example, A.VII.vi.4 *'Sīha·Senāpati·Suttaṁ'* ('The General-Sīha Sutta'): the generous offerer is the one 1) Arahants first have compassion for; 2) first visit; 3) first teach the Dhamma; 4) first receive alms from; 5) the generous offerer gains a good reputation; 6) gains self-confidence in assemblies; 7) is reborn in a happy, deva world.
[195] The four achievements are analysed in DhPA.x.17 *'Sukha·Sāmaṇera·Vatthu'* ('The Case of Sukha the Novice'). It relates the case of one villager who for three years works for a rich man in order to gain a bowl of the most superior and expensive rice. When he has completed his task, however, a Paccekabuddha appears, and instead he offers the Paccekabuddha the bowl of rice. When the rich man hears of his deed, he shares with him half of all his wealth, wishing to receive half of the merit gained. And when the king hears of the deed, he also gives him much wealth, and gives him the title of treasurer.
[196] MiP.V.iii.3 *'Kusal·Ākusala·Balavatara·Paṇho'* ('Wholesome/Unwholesome Predominance Question') lists a number of cases where an offering gave an immediate result: 1) Puṇṇa (just discussed; also called Puṇṇaka (AA/DPA)); 2) Queen Gopālamātā (she sold her own hair, and with the money offered food to the Venerable Mahākaccāna and other Arahants, and then became chief queen to a King Udena (AA)); 3) the female devotee Suppiyā (she cut a piece out her own thigh to make soup for a sick monk, and the next day the wound was completely healed (Vin.Mv.)); 4) the flower-girl Mallikā (she offered her food to The Buddha, and that day became chief queen to King Pasenadi (see 'Queen Mallikā', p.182)); 5) the garland-maker Sumana (he offered eight handfuls of flowers to The Buddha, and that day became rich (DPA)); 6) The Brahmin Ekasāṭaka (he offered his only upper robe to The Buddha, and that day became rich (DPA)).
[197] This phenomenon is explained by The Buddha in, for example, the suttas of S.II.viii *'Lakkhaṇa·Saṁyutta'* ('The Lakkhaṇa Section'). See 'Unwholesome Habitual Kamma', p.181.
[198] In M.II.iii.1 *'Te·Vijja Vacchagotta·Suttaṁ'* ('The Threefold Knowledge Vacchagotta Sutta'), The Buddha explains to Vacchagotta the wanderer: 'When I recollect the past ninety-one aeons, Vaccha, I do not recall any Ājīvaka [member of fatalist sect of ascetics] who, on the dissolution of the body went to heaven, with one exception, and he held the doctrine of kamma *(kamma·vādī)*, the doctrine of action *(kiriya·vādī)*.' Also, in M.II.-iv.3 *'Maghadeva·Suttaṁ'* ('The Maghadeva Sutta), The Buddha describes how one King Maghadeva's practice of jhāna (outside a Buddha's Dispensation) leads to rebirth in the Brahma world: 'He was a righteous king who ruled by the Dhamma... he led the holy life.... By developing the four divine abidings [jhāna of loving-kindness, compassion,

sympathetic joy, and equanimity]... he passed on to the Brahma world.... But that type of good practice does not lead to... Nibbāna, only to rebirth in the Brahma world.'

[199] King Ajātasattu refers to the teacher in D.i.2 *'Sāmañña·Phala·Suttaṁ'* ('The Asceticism-Fruit Sutta'). The Buddha discusses this view also in M.II.iii.6 *'Sandaka·Suttaṁ'* ('The Sandaka Sutta').

[200] In his account of this teaching, King Ajātasattu includes two more statements here: 'There is no action by oneself, there is no action by others, there is no manly action.' (D.i.2 *'Sāmañña·Phala·Suttaṁ'* ('The Asceticism-Fruit Sutta'))

[201] King Ajātasattu refers to the teacher in D.i.2 *'Sāmañña·Phala·Suttaṁ'* ('The Asceticism-Fruit Sutta'). The Buddha discusses this view also in M.II.iii.6 *'Sandaka·Suttaṁ'* ('The Sandaka Sutta').

[202] The Pali is here *padāni*, which according to the commentary means two things: 1) good conduct *(su·sīla)* and bad conduct *(du·ssīla)*, 2) body *(sarīra)*.

[203] In the section on view-clinging *(diṭṭh·upādāna)*, DhSA.iii.1221 *'Duka·Nikkhepa·Kaṇḍaṁ'* ('Twos Summarizing Section') E.493*f* explains that holding this view, one knows one can make offerings, give alms, make sacrifices, but one believes there is no fruit, or result from doing so; one knows the ten courses of unwholesome/wholesome kamma exist (see 'The Courses of Kamma', p.119), but one believes they produce no result; in the other world, one grasps the view that this world does not exist, and in this world, one grasps the view that the other world does not exist; one knows there is a mother and father, but believes it makes no difference how one behaves towards them; one believes there is no rebirth; one does not believe there are any ascetics or Brahmins whose practice is suitable; and one does not believe that there is such a thing as a Buddha who by His own insight is able to explain this world and the other world. DA.i.2 *'Sāmañña·Phala·Suttaṁ'* ('The Asceticism-Fruit Sutta') explains that in not believing in this world or another world, one believes all beings are annihilated in the world where they exist. DṬ.ibid. explains that one believes kamma brings one nowhere else, and all are annihilated where they are, without being reborn anywhere else. One believes the arising of a being is like the arising of a bubble: one does not come here, after having passed away elsewhere. And one believes that only fools teach the doctrine of offering; fools offer, whereas the wise take.

[204] For example, in M.III.ii.7 *'Mahā·Cattārīsaka·Suttaṁ'* ('The Great-Forty Sutta'), The Buddha explains that with Right View one knows that this view is wrong view: 'And how is Right View the forerunner? One understands wrong view as wrong view, and Right View as Right View: this is one's Right View. And what, bhikkhus, is wrong view? [see quotation at 'To Hold Wrong View', p.126].'

[205] The Buddha explains the interstices in S.V.XII.v.6 *'Andhakāra·Suttaṁ'* ('The Darkness Sutta'): 'There are, bhikkhus, world interstices, spaces, untouchable [by the world-systems], dark and gloomy, where the light of the moon and sun so glorious, so powerful, has no effect.' And in, for example, D.ii.1 *'Mahā·Padāna·Suttaṁ'* ('The Great-Lineage Sutta'), He explains that according to a law of nature, when (in his last life) a Buddha-to-be descends from the Tusitā deva-world into his mother's womb, light appears throughout the ten-thousand world system, so powerful that these interstices are lit up. The commentary to that sutta explains how between every three world spheres there is an interstice, just as there is an interstice between three cart-wheels that touch, and it is so dark there that eye consciousness cannot arise.

[206] In M.III.iv.6 *'Mahā·Kamma·Vibhaṅga·Suttaṁ'* ('The Great Kamma-Analysis Sutta'), The Buddha explains that the person who abstains from killing, theft, sexual misconduct, lies, slander, harsh speech, prattle, and is without covetousness, ill-will, and wrong view may still be reborn in an unhappy destination, even in hell: 'Either earlier he accomplished an evil kamma to take effect as pain, or later he accomplished an evil kamma to take effect as pain, or at the time of death, he held and undertook wrong view.' Likewise, He explains that the person who has accomplished evil kamma and held

wrong view may be reborn in a happy destination owing to earlier kamma, or because he at the time of death gave up the wrong view.

207 The Buddha gives a detailed explanation of the four means to power in S.V.VII.ii.10 *'Vibhaṅga·Suttaṁ'* ('The Analysis Sutta'). He explains also that they serve as the basis for developing the psychic powers*(abhiññā)*: walking on water, flying, the divine ear, recollecting many hundred thousand past lives, the divine eye, etc. And they serve as the basis for Arahantship.

208 The Buddha explains this in, for example, M.I.iii.6 *'Pāsa·Rāsi·Suttaṁ'* ('The Mass of Snares Sutta') (also called *'Ariya·Pariyesanā·Suttaṁ'* ('The Noble-Search Sutta')). The place of rebirth for the two teachers is given in that sutta's commentary.

209 He was the Brahma who urged the newly enlightened Buddha to teach (M.I.iii.6 *'Pāsa·Rāsi·Suttaṁ'* ('The Mass of Snares Sutta') (also called *'Ariya·Pariyesanā·Suttaṁ'* ('The Noble-Search Sutta')). On several subsequent occasions he appeared before The Buddha (e.g. M.II.ii.7 *'Cātumā·Suttaṁ'* ('The Cātumā Sutta'), and S.V.III.ii.8 *'Brahma-·Suttaṁ'* ('The Brahma Sutta')).

210 In both Vin and S, it is presented as having occurred over a number of occasions, but the commentary explains it was on only one occasion. The different beings that were seen are presented separately in the texts only for the sake of clarity.

211 DhPA.i.11 *'Dhammika-Upāsaka·Vatthu'* ('The Case of Dhammika the Devotee'). The verse uttered by The Buddha is: 'Here he rejoices, hereafter he rejoices: the maker of merit rejoices in both places. He rejoices, he exults, having seen the purity of his own kamma.'

212 The Buddha describes these devas in, for example, D.i.1 *'Brahma·Jāla·Suttaṁ'* ('The Supreme Net Sutta').

213 In A.V.II.V.10 (100) *'Kakuda·Thera·Suttaṁ'* ('The Kakuda-Elder Sutta'), a former bhikkhu, reborn as a deva, informs the Venerable Mahāmoggallāna (whose attendant he was) about the Venerable Devadatta's desire to take over the Sangha, and the loss of his psychic powers (mentioned also Vin.Cv.vii.333 *'Devadatta·Vatthu'* ('The Case of Devadatta')).

214 The Buddha gives this teaching also to one the Venerable Mālukyaputta in S.IV.I.x.2 *'Mālukyaputta·Suttaṁ'* ('The Mālukyaputta Sutta'). The Venerable Mālukyaputta elaborates the brief teaching, which is approved of and repeated by The Buddha. It is also explained by the Venerable Mahācunda in S.IV.I.ix.4 *'Channa·Suttaṁ'* ('The Channa Sutta').

215 In A.I.XIV.iii.216 *'Etad·Agga Vagga: Tatiya·Vaggo'* ('Chapter on "This is the Chief": Third Chapter'), the Buddha's declares him chief of those who comprehend a brief teaching.

216 DhPA.i.12 *'Cakkhupāla·Tthera·Vatthu'* ('The Cakkhupāla-Elder Case'). For the verse uttered by The Buddha, see endnote 64, p.233.

217 The queen's slave Khujjuttarā (see 'The Slave-Woman Khujjuttarā', p.191), who was usually with her, was at that time absent. UdA.ibid. explains that she escaped because she had not been one of the group who had tried to burn the Paccekabuddha.

218 In S.IV.I.II.iv.4 *'Channa·Suttaṁ'* ('The Channa Sutta') The Buddha discusses the suicide of the Venerable Channa with the Venerable Sāriputta. And The Buddha says: 'When one, Sāriputta, this body lays down, and another body grasps*(aññañ·ca kāyaṁ upādiyati)*, that is blameworthy, I declare*(tam·ahaṁ sa·upavajjoti vadāmi)*.' And He adds: 'Blamelessly*(anupavajjaṁ)* was the knife used by the bhikkhu Channa.' But after the incident of the five hundred bhikkhus, The Buddha says: 'It is improper*(ananucchavikaṁ)*, bhikkhus, of these bhikkhus, it is irregular*(ananulomika)*, it is unsuitable*(appaṭirūpaṁ)*, it is not the ascetic's way*(a·ssāmaṇakaṁ)*, it is unallowable*(akappiyaṁ)*, it is not to be done*(a·karaṇīyaṁ)*. How could those bhikkhus themselves deprive themselves of life, and deprive also one another of life?'

[219] In M.II.iv.1 *'Ghaṭikāra·Suttaṁ'* ('The Ghaṭikāra Sutta'), The Buddha describes how He in a past life was the Brahmin student Jotipāla, and his friend was the potter Ghaṭikāra, who was a Non-Returner. One day, Ghaṭikāra eight times suggested they should go and visit The Buddha Kassapa. And seven times Jotipāla said: 'Enough, my dear Ghaṭikāra. Really, what is the use of seeing that bald-head ascetic *(Alaṁ, samma Ghaṭikāra. Kiṁ pana tena muṇḍakena samaṇakena diṭṭhena)*?' Ap.XXXIX.x.92-93 *'Pubba·Kamma·Pilotika·Buddha-Apadānaṁ'* ('Tatters of Previous Kamma Buddha-Narrative') explains that because of this contemptuous speech, the Bodhisatta Gotama practised austerities *(dukkaraṁ)* with great effort for six years in Uruvelā. By seeking this wrong practice, the Bodhisatta suffered great physical suffering, and his enlightenment was delayed for six years. In M.I.iv.6 *'Mahā·Saccaka·Suttaṁ'* ('The Great Saccaka Sutta'), The Buddha describes the extreme sufferings that He experienced when He as the Bodhisatta practised austerities. And the subcommentary refers to the explanation in Ap. just mentioned.

[220] Here, Māra troubles the Venerable Mahāmoggallāna. To warn him of the danger of troubling an Arahant, the Venerable Mahāmoggallāna explains what happened to him when he himself was a Māra, this Māra Dūsī: details from the commentary.

[221] In M.I.iii.2 *'Alagadd·Ūpama·Suttaṁ'* ('The Snake Simile Sutta'), The Buddha warns the bhikkhus against reacting in these ways to the same kind of conduct from others.

[222] See previous endnote.

[223] The Buddha explains dependent origination in, for example, S.II.I.i.10 *'Gotama-·Suttaṁ'* ('The Gotama Sutta').

[224] This view is described by The Buddha in S.III.III.i.8 *'Mahā·Diṭṭhi·Suttaṁ'* ('The Great View Sutta'). It is described also by King Ajātasattu in D.i.2 *'Sāmañña·Phala·Suttaṁ'* ('The Asceticism-Fruit Sutta').

[225] A.III.III.ii.7 *'Kammanta·Suttaṁ'* ('The Work Sutta') Here, The Buddha lists three types of failure: 1) work failure (the ten courses of unwholesome kamma); 2) livelihood failure (wrong livelihood); 3) view failure (disbelieving the workings of kamma, rebirth, other planes of existence, and that there are ascetics and Brahmins (such as The Buddha) who teach these things, have seen them for themselves). The Buddha lists also the three opposites: work achievement, etc.

[226] In A.VI.vii.3 *'Mitta·Suttaṁ'* ('The Friend Sutta'), The Buddha explains that it is impossible for one with bad friends to achieve morality, to fulfil the training, and to forsake sensual-, material-, and immaterial lust *(rāga)* (the three types of existence). Conversely, with good friends, those things are possible.

[227] Many Pali Texts mention the ten royal qualities *(dasa rāja·dhamme)*: 1) offering; 2) morality; 3) charity; 4) uprightness; 5) gentleness; 6) discipline; 7) non-anger; 8) non-cruelty; 9) patience; 10) non-opposition (cooperation) (e.g. J.xxi.534 *'Mahā·Haṁsa-·Jātakaṁ'* ('The Great-Goose Jātaka')).

[228] In A.IV.II.ii.10 *'A·Dhammika·Suttaṁ'* ('The "Unrighteous" Sutta'), The Buddha explains how a ruler's unrighteousness leads to unrighteousness in the ministers, leading to it in Brahmins and householders, leading to it in town&country dwellers. And He explains that one effect is irregular seasons, and irregular ripening of crops. In the opposite case, He explains that there is the opposite effect.

[229] In D.ii.5 *'Janavasabha·Suttaṁ'* ('The Janavasabha Sutta'), it is explained that at King Bimbisāra's death, the people lamented his death, because he had given them happiness and his righteous rule had made their lives easy.

[230] In A.I.x *'Dutiya·Pamād·Ādi·Vaggo'* ('Second Negligence Etc. Chapter'), The Buddha explains that when bhikkhus teach non-Dhamma *(A·Dhamma)* as Dhamma, and Dhamma as non-Dhamma; non-Vinaya as Vinaya, and Vinaya as non-Vinaya; and the things not taught by The Buddha as taught by The Buddha, and the things taught by The Buddha as not taught by The Buddha; they teach to the many's detriment and suffering, etc. The opposite is the case if bhikkhus teach non-Dhamma as non-Dhamma, Dhamma as Dhamma, etc. (A.I.xi *'A·Dhamma·Vaggo'* ('Non-Dhamma Chapter'))

[231] Vin.Mv.i.6 *'Pañca·Vaggiya·Kathā'* ('Discussion of the Group of Five'). It is explained that after The Buddha had taught S.V.XII.ii.1 *Dhamma·Cakka·Ppavattana·Suttaṁ'* ('The Dhamma-Wheel Setting-in-Motion Sutta'), He cried with joy: 'Indeed you understand *(aññāsi vata)*, dear Koṇḍañña *(bho Koṇḍañño)*; indeed you understand, dear Koṇḍañña.' This was because the venerable one had attained Stream Entry. He is in the commentaries also called the elder Aññākoṇḍañña and Aññātakoṇḍañña.

[232] In S.V.XI.iv.7 *'Mahānāma·Suttaṁ'* ('The Mahānāma Sutta'), The Buddha explains that one becomes a devotee *(upāsaka)* by taking refuge in The Buddha, Dhamma, and Sangha. And one becomes possessed of morality *(sīla·sampanna)* by undertaking the five precepts. See further endnote 104, p.239.

[233] In, for example, S.IV.viii.8 *'Saṅkha·Dhama·Suttaṁ'* ('The Conch-Trumpeter Sutta'), The Buddha explains how one who has accomplished one of the ten unwholesome courses of kamma is able to overcome it by first accepting that it was a wrong thing to do, by then abstaining from doing it in the future, and by then developing liberation of mind (jhāna) by the four divine abidings: loving-kindness, compassion, sympathetic joy, and equanimity. And He explains: 'Any measurable kamma [sensual-sphere kamma], it does not stay there, it does not persist there.' The commentary explains that 'The (immeasurable) fine-material/immaterial-sphere kamma disables the sensual-sphere kamma from producing its result, and produces its own result: rebirth in the Brahma world.

[234] LIFE SPAN IS DOWN TO TEN YEARS: for the Buddha's explanation of this phenomenon, see 'Deterioration of Human Life', p.214.

[235] The Buddha explains this in M.III.iii.9 *'Bāla·Paṇḍita·Suttaṁ'* ('The Fool&Sage Sutta').

[236] In M.III.iii.9 *'Bāla·Paṇḍita·Suttaṁ'* ('The Fool&Sage Sutta'), The Buddha explains how the fool goes from hell to hell, eventually to emerge, and then be thrown back into the Great Hell.

[237] This is a reference to the Buddha's simile in A.III.I.iv.4 *'Nidāna·Suttaṁ'* ('The Causation Sutta'): 'Suppose, bhikkhus, there are seeds unbroken, unrotten, by wind&heat unweathered, fertile, well-embedded in a good field, in well-tilled earth sown. Should the deva the right rain give, then, bhikkhus, those seeds to growth, increase and abundance will come. So too, bhikkhus, whatever greed-done kamma, greed-born, greed-caused, greed-sprung, wherever that individual is reborn there that kamma matures. Where that kamma matures, there that kamma's result he experiences: either as an immediate thing, or upon rebirth, or some other [life] on the way. [... hatred-done... delusion-done....]' The opposite holds true if a man takes the seeds and burns them to ashes, which he disperses in wind or water, for they shall never come to growth, etc. That would be the result of the four types of Path Knowledge, performed out of non-greed, non-hatred, and non-delusion. See also The Buddha's metaphor of black and white kamma at endnote 282, p.355.

[238] In M.I.v.4 *'Cūḷa·Vedalla·Suttaṁ'* ('The Small Catechism Sutta'), the Arahant bhikkhunī Dhammadinnā explains to her former husband the three-fold training in relation to the Noble Eightfold Path: 'Right Speech, Right Action, and Right Livelihood: these things comprise the morality grouping. Right Effort, Right Mindfulness, and Right Concentration: these things comprise the concentration grouping. Right View and Right Intention: these things comprise the wisdom grouping.' She explains also that these factors do not necessarily comprise the Noble Eightfold Path (which is possessed only the Noble One): 'The three groupings are not included by the Noble Eightfold Path, friend Visākha, but the Noble Eightfold Path is included by the three groupings.'

[239] The division of morality-, mind-, and view-purification is taken from M.I.iii.4 *'Ratha·Vinīta·Suttaṁ'* ('The Chariot-Relay Sutta'). The *Visuddhi·Magga* is designed accordingly.

[240] In M.III.iii.9 *'Bāla·Paṇḍita·Suttaṁ'* ('The Fool&Sage Sutta'), The Buddha explains how the sage is reborn in heaven, and when he after a long time is reborn as a human being, it is into a high-class family that he is reborn, with much wealth, and he is very good-looking, enjoys many luxuries, and conducts himself well through body, speech, and mind. As a result, he is again reborn in a happy destination, even in heaven.

IV — 'The Small Kamma-Analysis Sutta'
('Cūḷa Kamma·Vibhaṅga·Suttaṁ')[666]

INFERIOR AND SUPERIOR HUMAN BEINGS

There is a sutta in the *Majjhima·Nikāya* called the 'The Small Kamma-Analysis Sutta'.[667] We shall now explain the workings of kamma with reference to that sutta. The sutta begins:

On one occasion the Blessed One was dwelling at Sāvatthi in Jeta's Grove, Anāthapiṇdika's Park. Then the Brahmin student Subha, Todeyya's son, went to the Blessed One, and exchanged greetings with him. After exchanging pleasantries, he sat down at one side and asked the Blessed One:

'Master Gotama, what is the root and cause why human beings are seen to be inferior*(hīna)* **and superior***(paṇīta)***? For people are seen to be**

[1-2] **short-lived and long-lived,**
[3-4] **sickly and healthy,**
[5-6] **ugly and beautiful,**
[7-8] **uninfluential and influential,**
[9-10] **poor and rich**
[11-12] **low-born and high-born,**
[13-14] **stupid and wise.**

What is the root and cause, Master Gotama, by which human beings are seen to be inferior and superior?'[668]

Why did Subha ask these questions? According to the commentary,[669] his late father, the Brahmin Todeyya, had been King Kosala's minister*(Purohita)*, and had been of extreme possessiveness*(macchariya)*. Owing to his extreme possessiveness, he was at death reborn in the womb of a bitch living in his own house. One day, when The Buddha went for alms by Subha's house, the dog barked. The Buddha scolded it, calling it Todeyya. Subha was greatly offended, but The Buddha proved to him that the dog was his own reborn father: The Buddha got the dog to dig up some treasure Todeyya had buried. This proof inspired Subha with faith in The Buddha, and moved him to approach The Buddha, and ask about the workings of kamma.

---

666 Reference numbers in italics refer to sutta quotations, etc. in endnotes beginning p.303.

667 M.III.iv.5 *'Cūḷa·Kamma·Vibhaṅga·Suttaṁ'* ('The Small Kamma-Analysis Sutta')

668 Here, inferior and superior refers to each side of the seven pairs of questions: seven inferior and seven superior. The VsM.xiv.496 *'Atīt·Ādi·Vibhāga·Kathā'* ('Discussion of the Past, etc. Classification') PP.xiv.193 explains: 'It is inferior where it arises as an unprofitable result, and it is superior where it arises as a profitable result.'

669 For details, see the sutta's commentary.

First, The Buddha answered Subha's question in brief:[670]

Kamma owners*(kamma·ssakā)*, **student, are beings, kamma heirs***(kamma·dāyādā)*, **kamma-born***(kamma·yonī)*, **kamma-bound***(kamma·bandhū)*, **and kamma-protected***(kamma-·ppaṭisaraṇā)*.

Kamma distinguishes beings, that is, as inferior*(hīna)* **and superior***(panīta)*.

Subha did not understand The Buddha's explanation. So he asked The Buddha please to explain in detail:

I do not understand in detail the meaning of Master Gotama's statement, which He spoke in brief without expounding the meaning in detail.

I should be happy if Master Gotama would teach me the Dhamma so that I might understand in detail the meaning of Master Gotama's statement.

Why did The Buddha explain in such a way that His listeners were unable to understand? Because the Brahmins were very proud: they thought they were the wisest of all people. And The Buddha knew that if He gave His answers in detail first, they might say they had already known the answer. To avoid this, He always gave them an answer in brief first, so as to humble their pride.

When Subha had admitted to not understanding the brief answer, and asked for a detailed answer, his pride was humbled, and only then did The Buddha give a detailed explanation. He explained the cause for each of the fourteen results one by one. He said:

Then, student, listen, pay good attention: I shall speak.

The Fourteen Ways

One Is a Killer

Here, student, a woman or man is a killer of beings; cruel, bloody-handed, engaged in slaying and attacking, without mercy towards living beings. Because of accomplishing and undertaking such actions, she or he at the breakup of the body, after death, in perdition, in a bad destination, in an infernal place, in hell is reborn.

But if she or he, at the breakup of the body, after death, in perdition, in a bad destination, in an infernal place, in hell is not reborn, if she or he as a human being returns, then wherever she or he is reborn, she or he is short-lived.

This is the way, student, that leads to a short life, namely, one is a killer of beings; cruel, bloody-handed, engaged in slaying and attacking, without mercy towards living beings.

Rebirth as a human being is always the result of wholesome productive kamma, and rebirth in a woeful state is always the result of unwholesome productive kamma. Hence, if the conclusive volition of killing functions as productive kamma to produce rebirth, it will produce rebirth in a woeful state. But if, despite the kamma of killing, a wholesome productive kamma functions as productive kamma to produce a human rebirth, the preceding and succeeding volitions (before and after the killing) will function as frustrating kamma in the course of that human life. They will frustrate the productive kamma that produced the human re-

---

[670] The Buddha explains this same principle in M.II.i.7 *'Kukkuravatika·Suttaṁ'* ('The Dog-Duty Ascetic Sutta'). There, He explains that the kamma one has as a certain being accomplished in one life determines one's rebirth as another being in a future life: 'Therefore, Puṇṇa, a being's rebirth is owing to a being: one is reborn according to what one has done. Thus, Puṇṇa, "Kamma heirs are beings", do I declare.'This is what the Commentators call the Kamma-Ownership Knowledge*(Kamma·Ssakata·Ñāṇa)*. See 'The Five Types of Knowledge', p.58. See also quotation endnote 126, p.242.

birth by direct opposition, and eventually one will intercept it: the wholesome productive kamma will not sustain the human being's life, and she or he will be short-lived. The human being will meet with adversities that are in the same way directly opposed to a long life, and that will in some way or other result in a premature death.[671/*241*]

This principle of direct opposition holds true for all cases where The Buddha explains unwholesome kamma that matures in that life's continuance *(pavatti)*.

THE VENERABLE MAHĀMOGGALLĀNA'S PAST PARRICIDE

A good example of killing leading to rebirth in hell, and a short life as a human being is the Venerable Mahāmoggallāna.[*242*] In a past life, he lived with his wife and blind parents. His wife did not want to look after the blind parents, and told him many malicious lies about them, complaining about how troublesome they were. Finally, she asked him to kill his blind parents, and he agreed.[672] Pretending that he was going to take them to another village, he took them to a forest in a bull cart. Inside the forest, he pretended to be a gang of bandits, and began to beat his parents with the intention to kill them.

As he set upon them, however, his parents cried out that bandits were attacking, and that he (their son) should not try to save them but escape. Their selfless compassion and love for him moved him so much that he stopped beating them. Afterwards he was overwhelmed by remorse.

How many unwholesome kammas did he accomplish with this act? If he beat his parents for only five minutes, billions and billions of mental processes would have arisen, with billions and billions of impulsions, each with the most reprehensible, evil volition of wanting to kill his own parents: billions and billions of unwholesome kammas. But also before he beat his parents, when planning how to kill them, did he accomplish billions and billions of unwholesome kammas. And after beating them, whenever he recollected his evil act, and was overwhelmed by remorse and unhappiness, did he accomplish billions and billions of unwholesome kammas. The maturing of the volition of each of those billions and billions of impulsions would produce the weightiest results in future lives.

Hence, at his death, the volition of a seventh unwholesome impulsion (in one of those billions of unwholesome mental processes) functioned as subsequently-

---

[671] MA explains that with the conclusive volition *(sanniṭṭhāna·cetanāya)* of killing (when all factors for killing are fulfilled: see 'A Course of Unwholesome Kamma', p.128) one is reborn in hell *(niraye nibbattati)* (the kamma functions as productive kamma, and MṬ explains that the result is sure to be most severe *(accanta·kaṭuka)*). But with the preceding&-succeeding volitions *(pubb·āpara·cetanāhi)*, the life-span may be shortened in two ways: 1) The volitions preceding/ succeeding the actual killing may function as interruptive kamma *(upacchedaka·kammena)* (MṬ: interceptive kamma *(upaghātaka·kamma)*), interrupting the wholesome kamma that has produced another human life, leading to an untimely death. 2) If killing preceded/ succeeded the wholesome kamma that produced a certain human rebirth, that wholesome kamma will not be superior *(uḷāraṁ na hoti)*, which means it is incapable of producing a long-life rebirth-link *(dīgh·āyuka·paṭisandhiṁ)*. Thus even though the life-span is short, the early death is timely, because the merit that produced the human life has been exhausted. For VsM's explanation of timely/untimely death, see subsequent endnote 241, p.303. See also 'Productive Kamma', p.186, 'Interceptive Kamma', p.194, and 'Inferior/Superior', p.60.

[672] Killing a parent is one of the unwholesome weighty kammas: see 'Unwholesome Weighty Kamma', p.170.

effective productive kamma to produce rebirth in hell. The volition of the middle-five unwholesome impulsions in those billions of unwholesome mental processes functioned as indefinitely-effective productive kamma to produce rebirth in hell again and again, and he went through horrific sufferings in hell for millions of years. And identical kammas produced many adversities for him in subsequent lives. When a wholesome kamma functioned as productive kamma to produce a human rebirth, the kamma of trying to kill his parents functioned as directly opposed unwholesome, frustrating kamma, so that he met with adversities conducive to a premature death. Sometimes the unwholesome kamma functioned as interceptive kamma, and he was beaten to death: for over two hundred lives, he was killed by having his skull smashed to pieces.

Nevertheless, from the time of Buddha Anomadassī till the time of our Buddha (one incalculable and a hundred thousand aeons), he accumulated the perfections *(pāramī)* to become second chief disciple to our Buddha. Such perfections are wholesome kammas, and when his pāramī matured, he became an Arahant and second chief disciple to our Buddha, chief in psychic power.[673]

Even so, despite being such a superior Arahant, his life was cut short, and he attained Parinibbāna, again with his skull and bones smashed into little pieces. How?

As The Buddha's Dispensation grew, day by day, The Buddha and His disciples received more and more honour and hospitality from the people. As a result, other teachers and their disciples received less and less. They held a grudge against the Venerable Mahāmoggallāna, because they thought he with his superior psychic powers was responsible. So they hired bandits to go and kill the Venerable Mahāmoggallāna. Thus, their grudge against him was a supporting cause for his parricide kamma to produce its result.

Over seven days, the bandits came to his dwelling to kill him. But the Venerable Mahāmoggallāna knew their intention with his psychic power, and with his psychic power, he disappeared from his dwelling: he went out of the key-hole. On the seventh day, however, he was unable to disappear: his parricide kamma functioned as frustrating kamma to stop him from attaining jhāna, and he could not exercise his psychic powers. Then an identical kamma functioned as interceptive kamma, and the bandits beat him to death, till his bones were smashed completely. And then they left him. But he did not die. He was able again to enter jhāna, and exercise his psychic powers. Using his psychic powers, he was then able to go and ask The Buddha for permission to enter Parinibbāna, to return to his dwelling, and to enter Parinibbāna there.

When he became an Arahant, the Venerable Mahāmoggallāna's mind was purified through the destruction of all defilements: greed-rooted defilements, hatred-rooted defilements, and delusion-rooted defilements.[674] Defilements were responsible for all the unwholesome kamma he had accomplished. And because of the unwholesome kamma he had accomplished, he had to go through immense suffering. Such are the workings of kamma.

[673] PSYCHIC POWERS: see footnote 239, p.82.

[674] DEFILEMENTS: for the ten defilements, see footnote 126, p.46.

Such workings of kamma are why The Buddha said in the second *'Gaddula-·Baddha'* sutta:[675]

Therefore, bhikkhus, one should reflect repeatedly upon one's own mind: 'For a long time this mind has been defiled by lust, by hatred, and by delusion.'

By mental defilement, bhikkhus, beings are defiled; by mental purification, beings are purified.

We shall be giving many other examples of how one's life is cut short owing to past unwholesome kamma: Tambadāṭhika the executioner (whom we mentioned before), the demon Nanda, the Venerable Pūtigattatissa, etc. We shall discuss them later on.[676]

Now, please listen to The Buddha's second explanation to Subha.

One Is Not a Killer

But here, student, a woman or man abandoning the killing of beings, is an abstainer of the killing of beings: with laid down rod, laid down knife, gentle and merciful towards all living beings, she or he dwells kind and compassionate. Because of accomplishing and undertaking such actions, she or he at the breakup of the body, after death, in a good destination, a heavenly world is reborn.

But if she or he, at the breakup of the body, after death, in a good destination, a heavenly world is not reborn, if she or he as a human being returns, then wherever she or he is reborn, she or he is long-lived.

This is the way, student, that leads to a long life, namely, abandoning the killing of beings, one is an abstainer of the killing of beings: with laid down rod, laid down knife, gentle and merciful towards all living beings, one dwells kind and compassionate.

In this case, to abstain from killing is a wholesome kamma that may function directly as productive kamma to produce either a heavenly rebirth or a long human life.

The wholesome kamma referred to here is mundane wholesome kamma, which is practice of the three merit-work bases *(puñña·kiriya·vatthu)*. We discussed them earlier:[677]

1) Offering *(dāna)*.
2) Morality *(sīla)*: for laypeople it is the five, eight or ten precepts. The first precept is always 'from killing to abstain *(pāṇātipātā veramaṇī)*'. For bhikkhus and bhikkhunis, morality is the Vinaya rule, which includes a precept against killing a human being, and a precept against killing any other being.
3) Meditation *(bhāvanā)*: that is samatha meditation, which is either access concentration or jhāna, and insight meditation, which is to know and see the impermanence, suffering, and non-self of ultimate mentality *(paramattha·nāma)* and ultimate materiality *(paramattha·rūpa)* of past, future, and present, internal and external, gross and subtle, superior and inferior, far and near.

---

675 S.III.I.x.8 *'Dutiya·Gaddula·Baddha·Suttaṁ'* ('The Second Clog-Bound Sutta'), quoted p.30.

676 For details on Tambadāṭhika, see 'Tambadāṭhika the Executioner', p.183, and for the killing-kamma that functioned as interceptive kamma to cut off his present life, see 'The Avenging Courtesan', p.272.

677 For details, 'The Merit-Work Bases', p.66*ff.*

The higher practise of mundane wholesome kamma is knowledge and conduct *(vijjā·caraṇa)*. We discussed it earlier:[678]

1) Conduct *(caraṇa)* is fifteen things: morality, faculty restraint, moderation in food, devotion to wakefulness, faith (which includes habitual practice of offering), mindfulness, conscience, shame, great learning, energy, wisdom, and the four jhānas.
2) Knowledge *(vijjā)* is insight knowledge *(vipassanā·ñāṇa)*, up to the Formations-Equanimity Knowledge *(Saṅkhār·Upekkhā·Ñāṇa)*.

   As we discussed earlier, insight meditation that produces rebirth is included under conduct, and insight meditation that does not produce rebirth is included under knowledge.

Such wholesome kammas may function as productive kamma to produce a deva life. If the conclusive volition of abstinence from killing produces a human life, it will be a long and trouble-free human life. The preceding and succeeding volitions (before and after the abstinence) may also function as reinforcing kamma to work in a similar way.[679]

This principle of similarity holds true for all the cases where The Buddha explains wholesome kamma that matures in that life's continuance *(pavatti)*.

LONG-LIVED BHIKKHUS

Good examples of gentleness and mercifulness leading to a long life are some of the long-lived bhikkhus of the past. The Venerable Mahākassapa, and the Venerable Ānanda attained Parinibbāna (final cessation) at the age of a hundred and twenty, the Venerable Anuruddha at the age of a hundred and fifty, and the Venerable Bākula went into Parinibbāna at the age of a hundred and sixty.[680]

THE VIRTUOUS VENERABLE PAÑCASĪLA SAMĀDĀNIYA

Another example is the Venerable Pañcasīla Samādāniya:[681] we mentioned him briefly before.[682] In our Buddha's Dispensation, he attained Arahantship with the four discriminations *(paṭisambhidā)*.[683] To be able to do that, he needed to have

---

[678] For details, see 'Knowledge and Conduct', p.137.

[679] MA explains that with the conclusive volition *(sanniṭṭhāna·cetanāya)* of non-killing (the actual act of abstinence: see examples in footnotes 197/198, p.71) one is reborn in the deva world *(deva·loke nibbattati)* (the kamma functions as productive kamma). But with the preceding&succeeding volitions *(pubb·āpara·cetanāhi)*, the life-span will become long in two ways: 1) The volitions that preceded/succeeded the actual non-killing may function as reinforcing kamma *(upatthambhaka·kammaṁ)*, reinforcing the wholesome kamma that has produced the human life, leading to a long life. 2) Because no killing preceded/succeeded the other wholesome kamma that produced the human rebirth, that wholesome kamma will be superior *(uḷāraṁ hoti)*, which means it is capable of producing a long-life rebirth-link *(dīgh·āyuka·paṭisandhiṁ)*. See also 'Productive Kamma' (p.186), 'Interceptive Kamma' (p.194), and 'Inferior/Superior' (p.60).

[680] DA.ii.1 (§5-7) *'Mah·Āpadāna·Suttaṁ'* ('The Great Lineage Sutta'). It explains also that The Buddha's chief patroness, Visākhā passed away at the age of a hundred and twenty.

[681] Ap.I.iii.4 *'Pañcasīla·Samādāniya·Tthera·Apadānaṁ'* ('The Pañcasīla-Samādāniya-Elder Narrative')

[682] See 'The Venerable Pañcasīla Samādaniya', p.228.

[683] FOUR DISCRIMINATIONS: 1) meaning discrimination *(attha·paṭisambhidā)*, 2) Dhamma discrimination *(Dhamma·paṭisambhidā)*, 3) language discrimination *(nirutti·paṭisambhidā)*, 4) perspica-

(Please see further next page.)

practised superior knowledge and conduct *(vijjā·caraṇa)* in the Dispensation of previous Buddhas: as we just mentioned, that includes insight meditation up to the Formations-Equanimity Knowledge *(Saṅkhār·Upekkhā·Ñāṇa)*.

For example, in Buddha Anomaddassī's Dispensation,[684] Pañcasīla Samādāniya was a poor man. Even so, he purified his morality by observing the five precepts for about a hundred thousand years, without breaking a single precept. Based on that morality, he developed strong, powerful concentration, as well as insight up to the Formations-Equanimity Knowledge *(Saṅkhār·Upekkhā·Ñāṇa)*. That made his morality pure and flawless.

How then do concentration and insight purify one's morality? The defilements *(kilesa)* are the decisive supporting causes *(upanissaya)* for bodily bad conduct *(kāya-·du·ccarita)* and verbal bad conduct *(vacī·du·ccarita)*. But they are suppressed by strong and powerful jhāna concentration *(samādhi)*. And when there is such concentration, there can also be insight knowledge *(vipassanā·ñāṇa)*. Insight knowledge knows and sees all formations *(saṅkhāra)* in oneself and the outside world, as impermanence *(anicca)*, suffering *(dukkha)*, and non-self *(an·atta)*. This insight suppresses the defilements, making one's mind pure and taintless. And if one with such a mind practises offering *(dāna)*, and morality *(sīla)* (if one with such a mind observes the five, eight, or ten precepts, etc.), those acts also become pure and taintless, which means they are most powerful.

This type of most powerful purification of morality was what Pañcasīla Samādāniya did for about a hundred thousand years. At his death, he reflected on his flawless virtue, which meant that at the time of death, his mind was full of joy and happiness. And that 'virtue kamma' functioned as productive kamma to produce rebirth in a heavenly world. And identical kammas functioned as similar productive kammas, so that he went from one deva world to another, and up and down between the heavenly worlds and the human world.

In every one of those lives he achieved three things:

1) Long life *(dīgh·āyu)*
2) Great wealth and sensual pleasures *(mahā·bhoga)*
3) Sharp wisdom *(tikkha·paññā)*

Everyone is always looking for these things: also today everyone is looking for these things. How do you achieve them?

1) By cultivating morality *(sīla)*: the five, eight or ten precepts.
2) By cultivating concentration *(samādhi)*: the four fine-material-, and four immaterial jhānas.
3) By cultivating wisdom *(paññā)*: insight knowledge *(vipassanā·ñāṇa)*.

Thus are the workings of kamma. Such workings of kamma are why The Buddha said in the second *'Gaddula·Baddha'* sutta:[685]

Therefore, bhikkhus, one should reflect repeatedly upon one's own mind: 'For a long time this mind has been defiled by lust, by hatred, and by delusion.'

By mental defilement, bhikkhus, beings are defiled; by mental purification, beings are purified.

---

city discrimination *(paṭibhāna·paṭisambhidā)*, knowledge of the previous three knowledges. (VsM.xiv.428 *'Paññā·Pabheda·Kathā'* ('Discussion of Wisdom Categorization') PP.xiv.21-26)

[684] See 'Appendix 2: The Lineage of Buddhas', p.365.

[685] S.III.I.x.8 *'Dutiya·Gaddula·Baddha·Suttaṁ'* ('The Second Clog-Bound Sutta'), quoted p.30.

You should, therefore, be inspired to put forth effort to practise these three trainings in this Buddha's Dispensation.

Āyu-Vaḍḍhana Kumāra Lives Long

Let us then take another example of someone who lives long: Āyuvaḍḍhana Kumāra. The Buddha says in the *Dhamma·Pada*:[686]

To the one always obeisant and virtuous, always the elders worshipping, four things increase: life*(āyu)*, **beauty***(vaṇṇo)*, **happiness***(sukhaṁ)*, **strength***(balaṁ)*.

If one is gentle and kind, compassionate towards all beings, and always honours and respects one's elders and betters, one's life improves in those four ways:

1) Life*(āyu)*: one's life span increases.
2) Beauty*(vaṇṇa)*: one's complexion becomes clearer.
3) Happiness*(sukha)*: one's health and comfort improves.
4) Strength*(bala)*: one's vigour and stamina increase.

The *Dhamma-Pada Commentary* explains life span with an example.[687] Suppose someone has accomplished a wholesome kamma that produces a human rebirth with a life span of fifty years. And in his human life he always honours and respects his elders and betters: those who are elder by age, and better by character, that is, by morality, concentration, and wisdom. Paying respect in this way, he accomplishes billions of wholesome kammas. Then if, when he is twenty-five, an unwholesome frustrating or interceptive kamma matures, threatening his life span, those wholesome 'respect kammas' intercept the unwholesome kamma, and he lives up to his full life span, fifty years. A good example of this is the Āyuvaḍḍhana Kumāra.[688]

Once, there were two hermits who lived together for many years. Then one of them left, and got married. When his wife had delivered a son, he and his family visited the other hermit and paid obeisance to him. The hermit said, 'May you live long', to the parents, but he said nothing to the boy. The parents asked the hermit why he had said nothing, and the hermit told them the boy would live only seven more days. And he said he did not know how to prevent the boy's death, although The Buddha might know.

So the parents took the boy to The Buddha. When they paid obeisance to The Buddha, He too said, **May you live long** to the parents, but nothing to the boy: and He too predicted the boy's coming death. Then, to prevent the boy's death from taking place, He told the parents to build a pavilion at the entrance to their house. And He told them to put the boy on a couch in the pavilion, to listen to protective chants*(paritta)* recited by bhikkhus. Then for seven days, The Buddha sent eight or sixteen bhikkhus to recite protective chants. On the seventh day, The Buddha Himself came to the pavilion. With Him came also devas from the whole universe: they came to listen to Dhamma taught by The Buddha. At that time, an evil demon*(yakkha)* Avaruddhaka, was at the entrance, waiting for a chance to take the boy away. But since devas of greater power had come, Avaruddhaka had to move back till eventually he was twelve leagues away from the boy. And all night the recitation of protective chants continued, protecting the boy. The next day, the boy was removed from the couch, and made to pay obeisance to The Buddha.

---

[686] DhP.viii.9 *'Sahassa·Vagga'* ('Thousands Chapter')

[687] DhPA.viii.8 *'Āyu·Vaḍḍhana·Kumāra·Vatthu'*, ('The Case of Āyuvaḍḍhana Kumāra')

[688] ibid.

This time, The Buddha said, **May you live long** to the boy. And when asked how long the boy would live, The Buddha said he would live up to a hundred and twenty years. So the boy was given the name Āyuvaḍḍhana Kumāra (*āyu* = life; *vaḍḍhana* = increasing; *kumāra* = boy).

If we analyse this case, we understand that a wholesome kamma functioned as productive kamma to give Āyuvaḍḍhana Kumāra rebirth as a human being. We understand also that a more powerful unwholesome interceptive kamma was going to intercept the result of his wholesome rebirth kamma, so that he would die after only one week as a human being. But by listening to the protective chants recited by the bhikkhus, and later by also The Buddha, past wholesome kamma of habitually honouring and respecting his elders and betters reinforced his 'human rebirth' kamma. That reinforcing kamma was so powerful that his life span increased from the expected one week to one hundred and twenty years. Such are the workings of kamma.

Such workings of kamma are why The Buddha said to Subha, Todeyya's son:[689]

Kamma distinguishes beings, that is, as inferior and superior.

Now, please listen to The Buddha's third explanation to Subha.

One Is a Tormentor

Here, student, a woman or man is a tormentor of beings, with the hand, with a stone, with a stick, or with a knife. Because of accomplishing and undertaking such actions, she or he at the breakup of the body, after death, in perdition, in a bad destination, in an infernal place, in hell is reborn.

But if she or he, at the breakup of the body, after death, in perdition, in a bad destination, in an infernal place, in hell is not reborn, if she or he as a human being returns, then wherever she or he is reborn, she or he is much sick.

This is the way, student, that leads to much sickness, namely, one is a tormentor of beings, with the hand, with a stone, with a stick, or with a knife.

Mischievous Nanda

A good example of going to hell because of striking someone with the hand, is the case of the demon*(yakkha)* Nanda.[690] Once, the Venerable Sāriputta was sitting in the moonlight, and his newly shaven head shone in the moonlight. As he was entering a meditative attainment, Nanda, a demon, struck him on the head out of mischief and anger. The force of the blow was such that had he struck a mountain peak, the peak would have split. But because the Venerable Sāriputta was protected by his attainment, he felt only a slight touch on his head. Nanda's unwholesome kamma, however, functioned as presently-effective productive kamma. He cried out, 'I am burning! I am burning!' and disappeared from the earth, instantly to reappear in the great hell.

Here, we need to understand that this did not happen owing to any power of the Venerable Sāriputta's:[243] it happened solely because of the power of Nanda's unwholesome kamma. Such are the workings of kamma. Such workings of kamma are why The Buddha said in the second *'Gaddula·Baddha'* sutta:[691]

Therefore, bhikkhus, one should reflect repeatedly upon one's own mind: 'For a long time this mind has been defiled by lust, by hatred, and by delusion.'

---

689 Quoted p.258.
690 U.iv.4 *'Yakkha Pahāra·Suttaṁ'* ('The Demon-Blow Sutta')
691 Quoted p.30.

By mental defilement, bhikkhus, beings are defiled; by mental purification, beings are purified.

Nanda was unable to control his mind, unable to refrain from trying to harm the Venerable Sāriputta. As a result he was reborn in hell. If you want to avoid rebirth in hell, you should try to control your mind, so you can abstain from all unwholesome kammas.

The Cruel Bird-Catcher

Another good example of harming other beings is the Venerable Pūtigattatissa.[692] In Buddha Kassapa's Dispensation,[693] when the life span was many thousands of years, he was a bird-catcher (fowler) called Sākuṇika. Whenever he caught many birds, he would not kill them. Instead, he would break their wings and legs so they could not escape. He did this over many thousands of years. And in that same life, he once filled an Arahant's bowl with delicious food, did the fivefold obeisance,[694] and aspired for Arahantship.

At death, the unwholesome kamma of tormenting and killing birds over many thousands of years functioned as productive kamma to produce rebirth in hell: there he suffered much torment over millions of years. In our Buddha's Dispensation, however, his alms kamma matured as productive kamma to produce rebirth as a human being again. Because of his aspiration for Arahantship, he ordained as a bhikkhu. But his unwholesome kamma of harming and killing so many beings functioned as frustrating kamma, to weaken his alms kamma, so it could not maintain his health and life as a bhikkhu.

One day, he became much sick. Boils formed on his whole body. They grew bigger and bigger every day, and pus oozed out of them till his whole body was full of oozing sores. And he became known as the elder 'Putrid-Body Tissa'*(Pūti·Gatta·Tissa·Thera)*. Then, after some time, his bones began to disintegrate. And his fellow bhikkhus, unable to look after him, abandoned him.

When The Buddha discovered him, He with His own hand cleaned the Venerable Pūtigatta with warm water, and changed his dirty robes. This produced pleasant feeling in Venerable Pūtigatta, and his mind became calmer and calmer. The Buddha then gave him a short Dhamma talk, and while listening to the Dhamma talk, the Venerable Pūtigatta was able to contemplate the nature of impermanence*(anicca)*, suffering*(dukkha)*, and non-self*(an·atta)* in formations. And, at the end of the Dhamma talk, he was an Arahant. His mind was free of lust, hatred, and delusion. Such are the workings of kamma.

Such workings of kamma are why The Buddha repeated in the second *'Gaddula·Baddha'* sutta:[695]

Therefore, bhikkhus, one should reflect repeatedly upon one's own mind: 'For a long time this mind has been defiled by lust, by hatred, and by delusion.'

By mental defilement, bhikkhus, beings are defiled; by mental purification, beings are purified.

Now, please listen to The Buddha's fourth explanation to Subha.

---

692 DhPA.iii.7 *'Pūti·Gatta·Tissa·Tthera·Vatthu'* ('The Pūtigattatissa-Elder Case')

693 See 'Appendix 2: The Lineage of Buddhas', p.365.

694 FIVEFOLD OBEISANCE: a traditional Indian form of obeisance, with the two hands, the two knees, and the forehead touching the ground.

695 S.III.I.x.8 *'Dutiya·Gaddula·Baddha·Suttaṁ'* ('The Second Clog-Bound Sutta'), quoted p.30.

ONE IS NOT A TORMENTOR

But here, student, a woman or man is not a tormentor of beings, with the hand, with a stone, with a stick, or with a knife. Because of accomplishing and undertaking such actions, she or he at the breakup of the body, after death, in a good destination, a heavenly world is reborn.

But if she or he, at the breakup of the body, after death, in a good destination, a heavenly world is not reborn, if she or he as a human being returns, then wherever she or he is reborn, she or he is not much sick.

This is the way, student, that leads to being without much sickness, namely, one is not a tormentor of beings, with the hand, with a stone, with a stick, or with a knife.

The wholesome kamma of not harming and killing beings may function directly as productive kamma to produce either a long heavenly life, or a long human life without much sickness. If one accomplishes also other wholesome kammas, such as three merit-work bases (offering *(dāna)*, morality *(sīla)*, and samatha and vipassanā meditation *(bhāvanā)*) one's conduct is further purified. And if one's meditation includes the four divine abidings *(cattāro brahma·vihārā)*, one's conduct is purified even further. The four divine abidings are:[244]

1) Loving-kindness *(mettā)*: wishing that all beings be happy.
2) Compassion *(karuṇā)*: wishing that all beings not suffer.
3) Sympathetic joy *(muditā)*: rejoicing in the happiness and success of other beings.
4) Equanimity *(upekkhā)*: looking at all beings with detachment.

When one practises these four divine abidings up to access concentration or jhāna, those kammas may function as most powerful productive or reinforcing kammas to produce either a long heavenly life, or a long and healthy human life. The reason is that as one undertakes to accomplish such kammas, and as one accomplishes them, one's mind is inclined to see beings free from danger; inclined to see beings free from mental and physical suffering; inclined to see beings well and happy; and inclined to see beings long-lived etc. Such kammas of goodwill can (when they mature) produce health and longevity in a human life. Therefore, if you want to be healthy and long-lived, then purify your morality, do not harm or kill beings, and cultivate the four divine abidings *(cattāro brahma·vihārā)*. The Buddha says namely:[696]

Fulfilled, bhikkhus, is the virtuous one's mental aspiration because of the purity of morality.

THE HEALTHY VENERABLE BĀKULA

A good example of such purified morality together with the four divine abidings is the Venerable Bākula.[697] One incalculable and a hundred thousand aeons ago, he was a learned Brahmin. Then, wishing to promote his own welfare in future lives, he took up the hermit's life in the forest. There, he gained skill in the eight attainments and five mundane psychic powers.[698] And then he spent his 'precious time'[245] enjoying jhāna happiness.

---

[696] A.VIII.I.iv.5 *'Dān·Ūpapatti·Suttaṁ'* ('The Alms&Rebirth Sutta'): see endnote 59, p.36.

[697] M.III.iii.4 *'Bākula·Suttaṁ'* ('The Bākula Sutta')

[698] EIGHT ATTAINMENTS: four fine-material and four immaterial jhānas; psychic powers: see footnote 239, p.82.

At this time, The Buddha Anomadassī had appeared in the world.[699] One day Bākula listened to a Dhamma talk by The Buddha, and then took refuge in the Triple Gem.

One day The Buddha fell sick with stomach trouble, and Bākula offered Him medicine, and cured Him. Bākula's offering fulfilled four factors:

1) He, the offerer, was virtuous. Furthermore, his virtue was reinforced by the eight attainments and five mundane psychic powers, for they had suppressed his hindrances for a long time. Also, he had taken refuge in the Triple Gem.
2) The receiver of the offering, The Buddha, was the most virtuous kind of person in all the world.
3) The offering, the medicine, had been righteously obtained from the forest.
4) Bākula, the offerer, had a happy, taintless mind before offering, while offering and after offering. At that time, his mind was free from defilements. He sought nothing from The Buddha: he sought only pāramī.[700] He knew the result of his kamma would be great, because he possessed the divine eye, the divine eye that knows the workings of kamma.

In the *'Dakkhiṇā·Vibhaṅga'* sutta, The Buddha explains that such kamma as fulfils these four factors is of great result, and is sure to produce its full result:[701]

[1] **When a virtuous person offers a gift,**
[2] **righteously obtained,**
[3] **to a virtuous person,**
[4] **with trusting heart, placing faith that the result of kamma is great,**
that gift will come to full fruition, I declare.

Bākula's offering fulfilled these four conditions, which means it would come to full fruition.

Then, when The Buddha had recovered and was again well, Bākula went to see The Buddha, and made an aspiration. He said to The Buddha:

Venerable Sir, the Tathāgata recovered because of my medicine. Because of this kamma, may no illness appear in my body in any life even for a few seconds.

Because of his pure and powerful kamma and aspiration, he never experienced any illness in any life, not even for a few seconds. Such are the workings of kamma.

Such workings of kamma are why The Buddha said in the *'Dān·Ūpapatti'* sutta:[702]

Fulfilled, bhikkhus, is the virtuous one's mental aspiration because of the purity of virtue.

If you want to accomplish superior kammas when you make an offering, you should emulate Bākula's example.

In Buddha Anomadassī's Dispensation,[703] for about a hundred thousand years, Bākula accomplished many pāramī, including jhāna-pāramī. He maintained his jhāna up to the time of death, so it became a wholesome weighty kamma, and he was reborn in the Brahma world.[704] For incalculable aeons, he was reborn

---

[699] See 'Appendix 2: The Lineage of Buddhas', p.365.
[700] PĀRAMĪ: see footnote 146, p.56.
[701] M.III.iv.12 *'Dakkhiṇā·Vibhaṅga·Suttaṁ'* ('The Gift-Analysis Sutta')
[702] A.VIII.I.iv.5 *'Dān·Ūpapatti·Suttaṁ'* ('The Alms&Rebirth Sutta'): see endnote 59, p.36.
[703] See 'Appendix 2: The Lineage of Buddhas', p.365.
[704] WHOLESOME WEIGHTY KAMMA: for details, see 'Wholesome Weighty Kamma', p.175.

sometimes in the deva world, and sometimes in the human world, and never did he experience any illness.

In Buddha Padumuttara's Dispensation,[703] Bākula was a householder in the city of Haṁsāvatī. When he heard The Buddha had declared a certain bhikkhu chief disciple in health, he made an aspiration to become such a chief disciple in a future Buddha's Dispensation. To that end he accomplished many wholesome kammas, such as offering different types of requisite to The Buddha and Sangha. The Buddha Padumuttara saw that Bākula would accomplish the required pāramī to fulfil his aspiration, and prophesied that it would take place in The Buddha Gotama's Dispensation. Throughout his hundred-thousand year long life, Bākula accomplished many wholesome kammas such as offering alms, practising morality, and practising samatha and vipassanā meditation up to the Formations-Equanimity Knowledge *(Saṅkhār·Upekkhā·Ñāṇa)*.[705]

Before Buddha Vipassī's Dispensation,[703] he was reborn in Bandhumatī, where he also became a hermit. When the Bodhisatta had become Buddha, Bākula also in that life met The Buddha, and took refuge in the Triple Gem. But although he had faith in The Buddha, he was still unable to give up his hermit's life. Even so, he would listen to Dhamma talks by The Buddha, and for about a hundred thousand years, he practised samatha and vipassanā meditation in his forest dwelling, according to The Buddha's instructions. Furthermore, with his psychic powers, he would collect herbs from the forest, make medicine, and offer it to sick bhikkhus. Doing this, his volition *(cetanā)* was to cure sick bhikkhus: once, he cured many bhikkhus who had become sick because of odours from poisonous flowers. Again in that life, he maintained jhāna up to the time of death, which meant that again he was reborn in the Brahma world. And for about ninety-one aeons, he went from deva life to deva life, and sometimes to a human life.

In The Buddha Kassapa's Dispensation,[703] he was a human being, and accomplished much wholesome kamma by renovating old monastic buildings, and again helping sick bhikkhus become well. Owing to this, and owing also to his previous kamma of having helped Anomadassī Buddha become well, Bākula enjoyed long lives and perfect health in every life.

Before the appearance of our Buddha Gotama, he was reborn in Kosambī, to the family of a councillor. One day, while being bathed by his nurse in the waters of the Yamunā river, he slipped into the water, and was swallowed by a large fish: but he did not die. His life was preserved owing to the power of his purity in this his last life; it was a case of psychic power diffused by knowledge *(ñāṇa·vipphāra iddhi)*.[706] This psychic power appeared in him because his many pāramī were such now that he could not die without having attained the Arahant Path-Knowledge: this was for sure his last death.[707]

The fish that had Bākula inside was caught by a fisherman, and sold to the wife of a councillor in Bārāṇasī. When the fish was cut open, the child was found unharmed, and the councillor's wife adopted the child as her own son. When the story reached Kosambī, Bākula's parents went to Bārāṇasī and claimed their child. But his adoptive mother refused to give him up. Their case was presented to the king, and he decreed that Bākula should be shared by both families: that is why

---

[705] FORMATIONS-EQUANIMITY KNOWLEDGE: see p.113.

[706] Also called 'Attainment by Intervention of Knowledge'. It is one of the ten supernormal powers *(iddhi)*.

[707] VsM.xii.373 *'Iddhividha·Niddeso'* ('Exposition of the Psychic Powers') PP.xii.27

his name was Bākula (*bā* = two/both; *kula* = families).[708] After a prosperous life, he was eighty, Bākula heard the Dhamma of our Buddha, again gained faith in the Triple Gem, and this time he ordained as a bhikkhu. Within eight days of his ordination he became an Arahant with the four discriminations*(paṭisambhidā)*.[709]

Bākula was by The Buddha declared chief disciple in good health. He was also one of the four bhikkhus in our Buddha's Dispensation with great psychic power *(mah·ābhiññā)*.[710] He was a monk for eighty years, and when one hundred and sixty years old, he entered Parinibbāna (final cessation) sitting on his pyre. His long life and perfect health were all due to his kamma, accomplished in previous lives, based on purification by morality.

Here, we should like to discuss the workings of kamma a little bit. When Bākula offered medicine to The Buddha Anomadassī, his desire to see The Buddha healthy was very strong: his volition*(cetanā)* was very strong. And when, in The Buddha Vipassī's Dispensation, he cured the many bhikkhus, his desire to see them healthy was again very strong: his volition was again very strong. The desire to see virtuous people become healthy is very wholesome kamma, and functions as either productive or reinforcing kamma that will keep one healthy in future lives.

Do you want to be reborn in heaven? Do you want to have a long and healthy human life? If you do, you should try to be a woman or man who does not injure and kill other beings. Instead, you should try to do as the Venerable Bākula.

- You should purify your conduct by observing morality.
- You should offer medicine and medical treatment to virtuous people with all your heart, that is, without expecting anything in return from the receivers.
- You should cultivate samatha and vipassanā meditation with success, and be sure to master the four divine abidings.

Injuring and killing other beings is done because of defilements. They do not produce rebirth in heaven, and do not produce a long and healthy human life: they produce only rebirth in the woeful states, and a short and troubled human life. Such are the workings of kamma.

Such workings of kamma are why The Buddha said:[711]

Fulfilled, bhikkhus, is the virtuous one's mental aspiration because of the purity of virtue.

Now, please listen to The Buddha's fifth explanation to Subha.

One Is Angry, Very Irritable

Here, student, a woman or man is an angry one, very irritable. Spoken to even a little bit, she or he is abusive, troublesome, offended, stubborn, and shows anger, hatred and resentment. Because of accomplishing and undertaking such actions, she or he at the breakup of the body, after death, in perdition, in a bad destination, in an infernal place, in hell is reborn.

But if she or he, at the breakup of the body, after death, in perdition, in a bad destination, in an infernal place, in hell is not reborn, if she or he as a human being returns, then wherever she or he is reborn, she or he is ugly.[712]

---

[708] MA explains that just as both *dvā·vīsati* and *bā·vīsati* mean 'twenty-two', so both *dvi·kulo* and *bā·kulo* mean two families.

[709] FOUR DISCRIMINATIONS: see footnote 683, p.262.

[710] The other three were the Venerable Sāriputta, Venerable Mahāmogallāna, and the bhikkhunī Bhaddakaccānā Yasodharā.

[711] A.VIII.I.iv.5 *'Dān·Ūpapatti·Suttaṁ'* ('The Alms&Rebirth Sutta'): see endnote 59, p.36.

This is the way, student, that leads to ugliness, namely, one is an angry one, very irritable. Spoken to even a little bit, one is abusive, troublesome, offended, stubborn, and shows anger, hatred, and resentment.

SCOWLING PAÑCAPĀPĪ

A good example of anger leading to ugliness is Pañcapāpī.[713] She was daughter of a poor man of Bārāṇasī. Her hands, feet, mouth, eyes, and nose were very ugly, which was why she was called Pañcapāpī (the one with five defects). But one thing about her was very good: her touch. Her touch was extremely pleasant. That was owing to kamma accomplished in a previous life.

In a past life, she was also daughter of a poor man of Bārāṇasī. And one day a Paccekabuddha went for alms in Bārāṇasī to get some clay for the walls of his dwelling.[714] When he saw Pañcapāpī preparing clay, he stopped in front of the house and stood silently. She guessed what he wanted, and gave him an angry look. Even so, she offered him a lump of clay. The offering was a wholesome kamma, but associated with anger. Although it functioned as a productive kamma to produce a human rebirth, her anger functioned as a frustrating kamma to make her look very ugly. Identical offering kamma functioned at the same time as reinforcing kamma to make her touch extremely pleasant. In the end, that kamma gave good results.

One day she happened to touch Baka, the king of Bārāṇasī. Her touch was so pleasant, he went mad with desire. And he visited her in disguise, and married her. But he was afraid to make her his chief consort, because she was so ugly: he was afraid people would mock him. So he arranged for many men of Bārāṇasī to feel her touch, and they all went mad with desire. After that, he was able safely to make her his chief consort. But the other consorts became jealous, and arranged for her to be cast adrift in a boat. She was rescued by one King Pavariya, who claimed her as his property. The two kings were prepared to go to war over her, but agreed to let Pañcapāpī live one week at a time with each king. Such are the workings of kamma.

Such workings of kamma are why The Buddha said to Subha:

Kamma distinguishes beings, that is, as inferior and superior.

ABUSIVE SUPPABUDDHA

Another good example of anger leading to ugliness is Suppabuddha, the poor leper of Rājagaha. He practised the threefold training under The Buddha. He purified his conduct by observing the precepts, he listened to the Dhamma with respect, and he practised samatha and vipassanā meditation. One day, listening to The Buddha teach Dhamma, he became a Stream Enterer *(Sot·Āpanna)*: a Stream Enterer who was a leper. How did he become a leper? What type of kamma was responsible?[715]

The bhikkhus asked The Buddha this question, and The Buddha explained. In a previous life, Suppabuddha was the son of a treasurer, a wealthy merchant in

---

[712] The Buddha explains this also to Queen Mallikā: see 'Queen Mallikā', p.192.

[713] JA.XXI.iv.4 *'Kuṇāla·Jātaka·Vaṇṇanā'* ('Description of the Kuṇala Jātaka')

[714] It was custom in ancient India for ascetics etc. to go for alms outside the time for going for almsfood, when they needed other material requisites.

[715] U.v.3 *'Suppabuddha·Kuṭṭhi·Suttaṁ'* ('The Suppabuddha-Leper Sutta'): described also in DhPA.vi.6 *'Suppabuddha·Kuṭṭhi·Vatthu'* ('The Case of Suppabuddha the Leper').

Rājagaha. One day, he was going to the pleasure park with many attendants. He was looking forward to showing off his wealth, and to have people pay respect to him. But as he was approaching the pleasure park, he saw that nobody paid any attention to him: all the people were paying attention to the Paccekabuddha Tagarasikhī. As Suppabuddha was walking along, he accumulated many unwholesome kammas, because he was disappointed. He was angry that people did not notice him, but paid respect to the Paccekabuddha. The Paccekabuddha was wearing a rag-robe. So when Suppabuddha came up to the Paccekabuddha, he spat, and said: 'Who is this leper, in a leper's robe wandering about!' Then he turned his left side to him, and went away.

Afterwards, on that day and later, he recalled the scene with anger, again and again. Proud of being son of a treasurer, he in this way accomplished many billions of unwholesome kammas. At death, one of those kammas functioned as productive kamma, and produced rebirth in hell. In hell, he underwent horrific sufferings over many millions of years. In our Buddha's Dispensation, a wholesome kamma functioned as productive kamma to produce rebirth as a human being. But his human happiness was frustrated by 'leper kammas', and he became a wretched leper in Rājagaha.

Such workings of kamma are why The Buddha said in the *'Kokālika'* sutta:[716]

When a person has taken birth, an axe is born inside his mouth with which the fool cuts himself by uttering offensive speech.

In this life, however, Suppabuddha obtained the blessing of Stream Entry *(Sot-·Āpatti)*. He went to see The Buddha, paid obeisance, and took refuge in the Triple Gem. On his way back to the city, a demon in the guise of a cow gored him to death. This was the same demon that killed Tambadāṭhika the executioner, Pukkusāti, and the ascetic Bāhiya Dārucīriya: we mentioned them earlier.[717] Why did the demon kill these four men?[718]

The Avenging Courtesan

The four men killed by that demon had in a past life been sons of wealthy merchants. The demon that now killed them in the guise of a cow was a female demon *(yakkhinī)*: she had in that life been a courtesan whom the four men had taken to the pleasure garden. Having taken their pleasure with her, they killed her and took her jewels, and the money they themselves had paid her. At her death, she vowed vengeance on them. And she killed them over a hundred lives.

Now, Suppabuddha had in the infinite past accomplished an infinite number of unwholesome kammas. Abusing the Paccekabuddha, and afterwards remembering the event with anger, as well as taking part in the killing of the courtesan, with those two actions alone, he had accomplished an infinite number of unwholesome kammas: some would mature as productive kammas, some as reinforcing kammas, some as frustrating kammas, and some as interceptive kammas. The interceptive kammas were kammas to be experienced in some subsequent

[716] S.I.VI.i.10 *'Kokālika·Suttaṁ'* ('The Kokālika Sutta'). Kokālika was a monk who criticized the Venerable Sāriputta and the Venerable Mahāmoggallāna. For that kamma, he developed a terrible skin disease, died and was reborn in the Lotus Hell *(Padumo Niraya)*. In that sutta, The Buddha explains that the life-span there is almost infinitely long.

[717] For Tambadāṭhika the executioner, see p.183, and p.211. For Pukkusāti, see p.217, and for Bāhiya Dārucāriya, see p.195.

[718] DhPA.vi.6 *'Suppabuddha·Kuṭṭhi·Vatthu'* ('The Case of Suppabuddha the Leper')

life*(aparāpariya·vedanīya·kamma)*: one now intercepted the wholesome productive kamma that had produced his rebirth as human being. But it could not make its own result arise, because all unwholesome kammas productive of rebirth in woeful states lapsed as a result of his Stream-Entry Path Knowledge. The interceptive kamma did, however, allow another wholesome productive kamma to produce rebirth in Tāvatiṁsā heaven. Such are the workings of kamma.

Now, please listen to The Buddha's sixth explanation to Subha.

One Is Not Angry, Not Irritable

But here, student, a woman or man is an unangry one, not irritable. Spoken to even a lot, she or he is not abusive, not troublesome, not offended, not stubborn, and does not show anger, hatred, and resentment. Because of accomplishing and undertaking such actions, she or he at the breakup of the body, after death, in a good destination, a heavenly world is reborn.

But if she or he, at the breakup of the body, after death, in a good destination, a heavenly world is not reborn, if she or he as a human being returns, then wherever she or he is reborn, she or he is good looking.

This is the way, student, that leads to good looks, namely, one is an unangry one, not irritable. Spoken to even a lot, one is not abusive, not troublesome, not offended, not stubborn, and does not show anger, hatred, and resentment.

The Loving-Kind Venerable Subhūti

A good example of friendliness leading to beauty is the Venerable Subhūti.[719] In Buddha Padumuttara's Dispensation,[720] he was born into a rich family and was called Nanda. Later he became a hermit, the leader of forty-four thousand hermits *(isi)*.[721] They dwelt in a forest near a big mountain, developed samatha, and all became expert in the eight jhānas and five mundane psychic powers.[722]

One day, The Buddha and a hundred thousand Arahants came down from the sky to visit them. The hermits were so pleased, they used their psychic powers within minutes to collect flowers, and spread flowers for the visitors to sit upon. The visitors seated themselves, and then entered the cessation attainment*(nirodha·samāpatti)*, the temporary cessation of mentality and consciousness-born materiality.[723] And then for seven days, Nanda stood behind The Buddha holding a canopy of flowers over Him. My audience, please see how great his perseverance was! All the time accumulating wholesome kammas, he did not move for seven days! He did not lie down. He did not take any food. He did not go to the toilet. And his mind was fully concentrated. This was possible only because he was expert in the eight attainments, and the five mundane psychic powers. With fully concentrated mind he stood behind The Buddha, holding a canopy of flowers over Him for seven days.

You may try to imagine the number of wholesome kammas that arose. Even within a snap of the fingers many thousand million wholesome mind-door processes arise and perish, each with seven impulsions, each of which have volition,

---

[719] AA.I.xiv.2 *'Subhūti·Tthera·Vatthu'* ('The Subhūti-Elder Case')

[720] See 'Appendix 2: The Lineage of Buddhas', p.365.

[721] Their hermithood was not the state of living alone, but the state of living in the forest, far from society.

[722] EIGHT ATTAINMENTS: four fine-material and four immaterial jhānas; psychic powers: see footnote 239, p.82.

[723] CESSATION ATTAINMENT: see footnote 436, p.158.

which is kamma. We may thus understand that the wholesome kammas which arose in Nanda's mind-door processes were beyond counting.

The kammas of Nanda's mental processes were sensual-plane wholesome phenomena*(kām·āvācāra kusala dhamma)*. And of the seven impulsions, the middle five impulsions are the most powerful: indefinitely-effective kammas*(aparāpariya·vedanīya·kamma)*, to be experienced in any future life after the subsequent life up to one's final Nibbāna. Such kammas can for a very long time produce the most sublime results on the sensual plane.

When The Buddha and other Arahants emerged from the cessation attainment, it was the most auspicious time to make offerings to them.[724] And the hermits offered The Buddha and Sangha fruits and flowers, righteously obtained from the forest. Then The Buddha asked one of the bhikkhus, proficient in receiving offerings, and proficient in loving-kindness jhāna*(mettā·jhāna)*, to give an inspirational talk*(anumodanā)*.[725]

At the end of the inspirational talk, all the hermits became Arahants, except Nanda. Why? Because his attention had been fixed on the eminence of the teaching bhikkhu. So he did not attain a Path*(Magga)* or Fruition*(Phala)*.

When he discovered that bhikkhu's eminent qualities, Nanda resolved that he too should reach such eminence. His resolution was accompanied by five factors:

1) His morality was purified and shone like a pearl, and was accompanied by the eight attainments and psychic powers.
2) His offerings had been righteously obtained.
3) His jhāna had suppressed the defilements of lust, anger, and conceit, so that his mind was clear and taintless before offering, while offering and after offering: He did not expect anything from The Buddha and Sangha.
4) Since he possessed the psychic power of the divine eye, he had clearly seen and understood the workings of kamma: that meant he had full faith in that the results of kamma would be great.
5) The receivers were an unsurpassed field of merit, because they were all Arahants, and one was also a Buddha. Furthermore the offerings had been made to them at the most auspicious time, because they had just emerged from the cessation attainment*(nirodha·samāpatti)*.

With these factors, it was certain that Nanda's resolution would come true. And indeed, Buddha Padumuttara prophesied that Nanda would as a bhikkhu under The Buddha Gotama become proficient in loving-kindness jhāna and eminent in receiving offerings.

In spite of his faith in The Buddha, Nanda was unable to become a bhikkhu, because he was too attached to his hermit's life. But he would very often go and see Buddha Padumuttara, and listen to the Dhamma. And he practised samatha and vipassanā under The Buddha's instruction. He emphasized the loving-kindness jhānas, and based on them, he practised insight meditation up to the Formations-Equanimity Knowledge*(Saṅkhār·Upekkhā·Ñāṇa)*.[726] And owing to his skill in the jhānas, he was able also to maintain his jhāna up to the time of death, which

---

[724] For an explanation of the most auspicious time to make an offering to an Arahant, see also 'Present Result from Wholesome Kamma', p.157.

[725] INSPIRATIONAL TALK: see footnote 445, p.160.

[726] FORMATIONS-EQUANIMITY KNOWLEDGE: see p.113.

meant one of his jhāna kammas became a weighty kamma that functioned as productive kamma to produce rebirth in the Brahma world.[727]

Here, we should like to discuss the workings of kamma a little bit in relation to dependent origination *(paṭicca samuppāda)*. After Nanda had made his offering of fruit and flowers to The Buddha and Sangha, Nanda resolved to become a bhikkhu, proficient in loving-kindness jhāna, and eminent in receiving offerings. But this resolution was based on ignorance and craving. How?

Our body and mind comprise only ultimate materiality and mentality. If we see them as that, our view is right, Right View *(Sammā·diṭṭhi)*, which is insight knowledge *(vipassanā·ñāṇa)*. But if we see our materiality and mentality as a man, woman, bhikkhu or bhikkhunī, this is wrong, wrong view *(micchā·diṭṭhi)*, accompanied by ignorance *(avijjā)* or delusion *(moha)*. This means that Nanda's view of a bhikkhu proficient in loving-kindness jhāna, and eminent in receiving offerings was a manifestation of ignorance and delusion. Dependent on that deluded view, he resolved to become a bhikkhu, proficient in loving-kindness jhāna, and eminent in receiving offerings, which is craving *(taṇhā)*. And his repeated craving, holding fast to the life of a bhikkhu, was clinging *(upādāna)*. Ignorance, craving and clinging are called the round of defilements *(kilesavaṭṭa)*, because they are the defilements that produce the round of rebirths *(saṁsāra)*.[728]

Dependent on ignorance, craving, and clinging Nanda accomplished superior wholesome kammas: he offered fruit and flowers to The Buddha, and to the Sangha, the unsurpassed field for merit in the world *(anuttaraṁ puñña·kkhettaṁ lokassa)*.[729] Such wholesome kammas are volitional formations *(saṅkhāra)*. They are impermanent because as soon as they arise they perish. But in one's continuity of mentality-materiality, they remain as a potency: that potency can produce a result at any time. In the kamma-cause section *(kamma·paccaya uddesa)* of the ***Paṭṭhāna*** (***Causal Relations***), this potency is called kamma.[730] And the volitional formations *(saṅkhāra)* and kamma are called the kamma round *(kamma·vaṭṭa)*: the kamma that produces the round of rebirths.

Altogether there are five causes for the round of rebirth:

1) ignorance .... *(avijjā)*	4) formations (of kamma) .... *(saṅkhāra)*
2) craving .... *(taṇhā)*	5) existence
3) clinging .... *(upādāna)*	(of kammic potency) .... *(bhava)*

This principle applies whenever we discuss the maturing of kamma.

Nanda's powerful offering kamma was further reinforced by his strong and powerful loving-kindness jhāna *(mettā jhāna)*. And how did his loving-kindness jhāna become so strong and powerful? One reason was that when practising samatha and vipassanā, he had emphasized the development of loving-kindness jhāna. And based on his loving-kindness jhāna, he had practised insight meditation: that way his insight knowledge became clear, deep, profound, and strong and powerful.[246] And vice-versa, owing to his insight knowledge, his loving-kindness jhāna also became firm, strong, and powerful. According to the ***Paṭṭhāna***, samatha and vipassanā are strong and powerful mutually decisive supporting

[727] See 'Wholesome Weighty Kamma', p.175.
[728] See further 'Wishing for Rebirth', p.15.
[729] UNSURPASSED FIELD FOR MERIT IN THE WORLD: this is one of the nine qualities by which The Buddha describes the Sangha. See, for example, quotation endnote 39, p.25.
[730] POTENCY: see footnotes 5, p.1, 56, p.15, and 'Kammic Potency', p.375.

causes *(upanissaya paccaya)*.[731] How? He entered loving-kindness jhāna. Emerging from it, he immediately contemplated the jhāna formations as impermanence *(anicca)*, suffering *(dukkha)*, and non-self *(an·atta)*. Then he entered loving-kindness jhāna again, and again emerged from it, and again contemplated the jhāna formations as impermanence, suffering, and non-self. This procedure he practised again and again. Owing to this type of repeated practice, both his loving-kindness jhāna and insight meditation became firm, strong, and powerful. Furthermore, loving-kindness jhāna is the direct opposite of anger, which was why his mind was usually free from anger. Whenever he practised samatha and vipassanā, especially anger, but also other defilements were long suppressed. They were also suppressed by his psychic powers. All these practices made his mind very pure, and owing to that superior purity, it was certain that he would succeed in his resolve to become a bhikkhu proficient in loving-kindness and eminent in receiving offerings. Finally, since Nanda had practised samatha and vipassanā for about a hundred thousand years, his will power became very strong. Any wish he made could come true because of his will power: will power is volition *(cetanā)*, which is kamma.

Buddha Padumuttara prophesied that Nanda would become a bhikkhu proficient in loving-kindness jhāna and eminent in receiving offerings in our Buddha's Dispensation. Nanda was then reborn as the son of a rich man called Sumana, who was a faithful devotee *(upāsaka)* of The Buddha, and younger brother to Anāthapiṇḍika, The Buddha's chief patron *(dāyaka)*. Nanda was in that life called Subhūti ('one of good looks') because of his beauty and good looks. His good looks were the result of his previous wholesome kamma, which had been free of defilements, especially free of anger.

On the day that his elder brother Anāthapiṇḍika offered the Jetavana monastery to The Buddha and Sangha, Subhūti listened with respect and attention to The Buddha's inspirational talk. It filled him with such faith in the Dhamma that he wanted to ordain. Being the son of a faithful disciple of The Buddha, he went forth from a believer's home to homelessness. After his ordination, he mastered the two Vinaya Rules (the bhikkhu and bhikkhunī rules). And having obtained a meditation subject from The Buddha, he went to the forest to live and meditate. There he developed insight and attained Arahantship based on loving-kindness jhāna. Teaching the Dhamma without distinction[732] or limitation, he was declared chief bhikkhu in living in remoteness and peace *(araṇa·vihārī)*, and in being worthy of gifts *(dakkhiṇeyya)*.[733] His strong and powerful loving-kindness jhāna (the foundation for his insight meditation), had enabled him to live in peace and remote from defilements for a long time.

The Pali Texts say that when he went for alms in the village, he would enter loving-kindness jhāna at every door, which meant every offering made to him was of superior merit.

Once, in the course of his wandering, he came to Rājagaha. And the king, King Bimbisāra, promised to build him a dwelling place for the rains. But the king forgot, and the Venerable Subhūti meditated in the open air. The result was that no rain fell in Rājagaha. When the king discovered why, he quickly had a leaf hut built. As soon as the Venerable Subhūti entered the hut, and seated himself on

---

[731] DECISIVE SUPPORTING CAUSE: see footnote 597, p.205.

[732] WITHOUT DISTINCTION: teaching with no preference of audience.

[733] A.I.XIV.ii.201-202 *'Etad·Agga Vagga: Dutiya·Vaggo'* ('Chapter on "This is the Chief": Second Chapter')

the bed of hay, rain fell. His mind was so purified with loving-kindness jhāna, and supramundane knowledge that even the devas helped protect him from getting soaked by rain. Such are the workings of kamma.

Such workings of kamma are why The Buddha said in the second *'Gaddula·Baddha'* sutta:[734]

Therefore, bhikkhus, one should reflect repeatedly upon one's own mind: 'For a long time this mind has been defiled by lust, by hatred, and by delusion.'

By mental defilement, bhikkhus, beings are defiled; by mental purification, beings are purified.

THE GOLDEN VENERABLE MAHĀKACCĀNA

Another good example is the Venerable Mahākaccāna.[735] In our Buddha's Dispensation, he was born in Ujjenī, in the family of a King Caṇḍapajjota's chaplain. He was called Kaccāna because of his golden complexion, and also because Kaccāna was the name of his clan *(gotta)*. He became one of our Buddha's most eminent disciples, declared chief in elaborating what The Buddha had taught in brief.

Why was his complexion golden? And how did he achieve that distinction as a bhikkhu? Responsible were his accomplished kammas.

In Buddha Padumuttara's Dispensation,[736] he was reborn into a very rich family. One day he went to the monastery, and stood at the edge of the audience listening to a Dhamma talk by The Buddha. And he saw The Buddha confer upon a bhikkhu (also called Kaccāna) the distinction of chief disciple in elaborating and analysing Dhamma explained in brief by Buddha. Deeply impressed, he resolved also to win that distinction in a future Buddha's Dispensation. With this intention, he invited The Buddha and hundred thousand large Sangha, and made a grand offering *(mahā·dāna)*: it lasted seven days. On the seventh day, he prostrated himself at the feet of The Buddha and said: 'Bhante, as a result of this seven-day-long grand offering, I do not wish for any other bliss. But I do wish to secure the title of the bhikkhu who seven days ago was declared chief of those who elaborate and analyse what has been taught by The Buddha in brief.'

Another account of Mahākaccāna's past[737] explains that in Buddha Padumuttara's Dispensation, he built a lotus-shaped cetiya[738] called Paduma (lotus). It was covered with gold, and had a throne inside with a canopy made of gold, jewels, and hair from the camarī-horse.[739]

---

[734] S.III.I.x.8 *'Dutiya·Gaddula·Baddha·Suttaṁ'* ('The Second Clog-Bound Sutta'), quoted p.30.

[735] AA.I.xiv.1 *'Mahākaccāna·Tthera·Vatthu'* ('The Mahākaccāna-Elder')

[736] See 'Appendix 2: The Lineage of Buddhas', p.365.

[737] Ap.I.iv.3 *'Mahākaccāna·Tthera·Apadānaṁ'* ('The Mahākaccāna-Elder Narrative')

[738] CETIYA: Pali for stupa/pagoda.

[739] CAMARĪ-HORSE: the Himalayan yak. Its tail is very precious.

In that Dispensation, over a hundred thousand years, Mahākaccāna accomplished also many other wholesome things, such as:[740]

- Mastery of the texts*(pariyatti)*: learning The Buddha's Word off by heart *(Buddha·Vacanassa pariyāpuṇanaṁ)*, reciting the Pali*(Pāḷyā sajjhāyo)*.
- Hearing*(savana)*: learning the Dhamma thoroughly, with care and respect.
- Inquiry*(paripucchā)*: discussing knotty passages in the Texts, Commentaries, etc.
- Past practice*(pubba·yoga)*: practising samatha and vipassanā up to the Formations-Equanimity Knowledge*(Saṅkhār·Upekkhā·Ñāṇa)*.[741]

In Buddha Kassapa's Dispensation,[742] he was a householder of Bārāṇasī.[743] After The Buddha's Parinibbāna, a splendid cetiya was being built over The Buddha's remains, in the shape of a solid rock of gold. And the Venerable Mahākaccāna donated bricks of gold worth a hundred thousand: and he made an aspiration that in future births he should have a golden complexion.

As we can see, all these wholesome kammas that the Venerable Mahākaccāna accomplished in past lives were all pure, all dissociated from anger or any other defilements. Some of those wholesome kammas functioned as productive kamma, some as reinforcing kamma, and almost all were to be experienced in some subsequent life. And some of them matured to function as productive kammas in our Buddha's Dispensation.

We can then analyse the Venerable Mahākaccāna's case in accordance with the workings of kamma.

A 'brick kamma' functioned as productive kamma to produce his last rebirth, as a human being. It produced the five resultant aggregates at the rebirth-linking moment, and identical kammas maintained his five aggregates through the course of life. Identical kammas functioned also as wholesome reinforcing kammas, to produce a long life, health, happiness, and a golden complexion. The wholesome kammas responsible for all these results depended on his past ignorance, craving, and clinging.

When he met our Buddha, The Buddha gave him a Dhamma talk. At the end of the talk, Mahākaccāna attained Arahantship together with the four discriminations *(paṭisambhidā)*:[744] his wholesome kammas (pāramī) accomplished in previous Buddhas' Dispensations as well as in our Buddha's Dispensation had matured.

Later, when The Buddha bestowed titles of eminence on the bhikkhus, He declared:[745]

---

740 This is the standard practice for attaining the four discriminations: VbhA.xv.718 *'Saṅgaha·Vāra·Vaṇṇanā'* ('Description of Summary Part') DD.xv.1955; VsM/VsMṬ.xiv.429 *'Paññā·Pabheda·Kathā'* ('Discussion of Wisdom Categorization') PP.xiv.28-31. See also endnote 183, p.250.

741 FORMATIONS-EQUANIMITY KNOWLEDGE: see p.113.

742 See 'Appendix 2: The Lineage of Buddhas', p.365.

743 AA.I.xiv.1 *'Mahākaccāna·Tthera·Vatthu'* ('The Mahākaccāna-Elder Case')

744 FOUR DISCRIMINATIONS: see footnote 683, p.262.

745 A.I.XIV.i *'Etad·Agga Vagga: Paṭhama·Vaggo'* ('Chapter on "This Is the Chief": First Chapter') The Commentary explains that The Buddha's declaration rested on the Venerable Mahākaccāna's elaboration of: 1) M.I.ii.18 *'Madhu·Piṇḍika·Suttaṁ'* ('The Honey-Ball Sutta'), 2) M.III.iv.3 *'Mahā·Kaccāna·Bhadd·Eka·Ratta·Suttaṁ'* ('The Mahākaccāna An-Excellent-Night Sutta'), 3) SuN.v *'Parāyana Vagga'* ('Final Chapter').

This is the chief, bhikkhus, of my bhikkhu disciples who can elaborate the briefly spoken, and analyse the meaning, that is, Mahākaccāna.

Fulfilled now was the aspiration Mahākaccāna had made in Buddha Padumuttara's Dispensation.

Do you want to be handsome and beautiful? Do you want to have a golden complexion? If you do, you should try to be a woman or man who never gets angry or irritated: even when criticised a lot, you must not get offended, not get angry, not be hostile, and not be resentful. If you want to be handsome and beautiful, you must not display anger, hatred, and bitterness. Such things are defilements and they do not produce beauty: they produce only ugliness.

Based on morality, you should cultivate samatha and vipassanā, and cultivate especially the four divine abidings *(cattāro brahma·vihārā)*: loving-kindness, compassion, sympathetic joy, and equanimity. The four divine abidings suppress anger and other defilements. The Buddha says that is how you may attain beauty.

You should not forget, however, that all formations are impermanent. All formations are impermanent, suffering, and non-self, be they beautiful or ugly, attractive or unattractive. So you should try not only to acquire beauty and a golden complexion, you should also try to acquire a beautifully pure mind, that is, you should also try to attain Arahantship. If you do as the Venerable Subhūti and Venerable Maha-Kaccāna, you will succeed. Such are the workings of kamma.

Such workings of kamma are why The Buddha says in the *Dhamma·Pada*:[746]

> **Carefulness** *(appamāda)* **is the path of Deathlessness;**
> **carelessness** *(pamāda)* **is the path of Death;**
> **the careful do not die;**
> **the careless are as the dead.**

Now, please listen to The Buddha's seventh explanation to Subha.

ONE HARBOURS ENVY

Here, student, a woman or man is an envious one. Gain, honour, respect, reverence, obeisance, and homage [received by] **another, she or he envies and begrudges, harbouring envy. Because of accomplishing and undertaking such actions, she or he at the breakup of the body, after death, in perdition, in a bad destination, in an infernal place, in hell is reborn.**

But if she or he, at the breakup of the body, after death, in perdition, in a bad destination, in an infernal place, in hell is not reborn, if she or he as a human being returns, then wherever she or he is reborn, she or he is without influence.[747]

This is the way, student, that leads to lack of influence, namely, one is envious. Another's [received] **gain, honour, respect, reverence, obeisance, and homage, one envies and begrudges, harbouring envy.**

Envy causes many problems in society.[247] Women and men who cannot control their envy and grudging do not conduct themselves well, do not conduct themselves according to the Dhamma.

[746] DhP.ii.1 *'A·Ppamāda·Vaggo'* ('Carefulness Chapter'). The Pali cannot satisfactorily be duplicated in English: *a* (non-) + *pamāda* (negligent/careless) = non-negligent = careful, attentive, heedful, etc.

[747] The Buddha explains this also to Queen Mallikā: see 'Queen Mallikā', p.192.

THE ENVIOUS VENERABLE TISSA

A good example of envy leading to rebirth in hell, and no influence as a human being, is the Venerable Losaka Tissa:[748] we mentioned him briefly in connection with destination failure *(gati·vipatti)*.[749] In Buddha Kassapa's Dispensation,[750] he was a bhikkhu. And he lived in a hermitage belonging to a rich man: the rich man was his chief patron. One day an Arahant arrived. The rich man liked the Arahant's appearance so much that he asked the Arahant please to stay in the hermitage, and promised to look after him: the Arahant agreed to stay.

In the evening, the rich man brought flowers, scents, etc. for the new bhikkhu. He listened to the new bhikkhu teach Dhamma, and left with much ceremony. And he invited both bhikkhus to his house for the next day's meal. When the Venerable Losaka Tissa saw the Arahant receive so much attention, he became very envious.

Next day, the Venerable Tissa did not want the Arahant to come for the meal. So he only struck the gong very lightly with his fingernail, and then went to the rich man's house alone. But the Arahant had read the Venerable Losaka Tissa's mind, and had already left the hermitage at dawn. When the rich man asked where the other bhikkhu was, the Venerable Losaka Tissa said he was a lazy, good-for-nothing bhikkhu. After the venerable one had eaten, the rich man washed his bowl, refilled it with food, and asked the Venerable Losaka Tissa please to give it to the other bhikkhu. But on his way home, the Venerable Losaka Tissa threw the food into a hole, and covered it with embers from a newly burned field: this act of envy was unwholesome kamma.

When the Venerable Losaka Tissa returned to the hermitage, he discovered that the Arahant had left. Then he was overcome with much remorse, and not long after, he died. At death, the 'envy kamma' functioned as near-death kamma to produce rebirth in hell. This meant that all the wholesome kammas he as a bhikkhu had accomplished, over twenty thousand years, were intercepted by his envy kamma, and were unable to produce their result. Once he was in hell, many identical 'envy kammas' functioned as reinforcing kamma, to increase and prolong his sufferings in hell.

When he eventually escaped from hell, yet other 'envy kammas' matured, to function as unwholesome productive kammas to be experienced in some subsequent life. Owing to destination failure *(gati·vipatti)*,[751] he became a demon *(yakkha)* in five hundred successive births: in each life, he never had enough to eat. Then in another five hundred successive births, he became a dog, again never with enough food to eat. And in every subsequent life, not only did he never have enough to eat, he suffered also many other hardships. My audience, just see the workings of kamma!

Finally, however, in his last life, the wholesome kammas he had accomplished in The Buddha Kassapa's Dispensation met the right conditions to mature: they functioned as productive kammas to produce rebirth as a human being. But they were intercepted by his envy kamma. How?

---

748 JA.I.v.1 (41) *'Losaka·Jātaka·Vaṇṇanā'* ('Description of the Losaka Jātaka')

749 See 'Destination Failure Enables Unwholesome Kammas', p.220.

750 See 'Appendix 2: The Lineage of Buddhas', p.365.

751 See 'Destination Failure Enables Unwholesome Kammas', p.220.

In our Buddha's Dispensation, he was reborn as the son of a fisherman in a village called Kodala. And he was given the name Losaka Tissa. And from the day of his conception, everyone in the village suffered various hardships. When they discovered why, they drove Losaka's family out. Then, as soon as Losaka could walk, his mother put a potsherd in his hand, and sent him out to beg. As a small boy, he wandered about uncared for, picking up morsels of rice like a crow. One day, when he was seven years old, the Venerable Sāriputta saw him. The Venerable Sāriputta felt sorry for him, and ordained him as a novice. But the Venerable Losaka Tissa was always unlucky: wherever he went for alms, he received only little. Also in that life, he never had a proper meal. Even so, practising the threefold higher training, eventually he became an Arahant. Why? In Buddha Kassapa's Dispensation, over twenty thousand years, he had fulfilled sufficient pāramī to attain Arahantship. But, even as an Arahant, he never had a proper meal. When people put food into his bowl, it disappeared: his pāramī produced his receiving alms, but his envy kamma intecepted them, and the food disappeared. The cause was his act of throwing away food offered to an Arahant, because he had been jealous of the Arahant: he had envied and begrudged the Arahant's gains, and his receiving honour, respect, reverence, obeisance and homage from the rich man.

One day, the Venerable Sāriputta saw that the Venerable Losaka Tissa would that night enter Parinibbāna. So he decided to make sure that the Venerable Losaka Tissa should on his last day have a proper meal. He went with the Venerable Losaka to Sāvatthi for alms, but no one even noticed them. So he told the Venerable Losaka Tissa to return to the monastery and wait there. Then the Venerable Sāriputta went for alms alone, received food, and had the food sent to the Venerable Losaka in the monastery. But the people ate all the food themselves, so the Venerable Losaka Tissa still went without food. And by the time the Venerable Sāriputta discovered what had happened, it was already afternoon: bhikkhus cannot eat regular food in the afternoon. So the Venerable Sāriputta went to the king's palace, and obtained a bowl of *catu·madhura* (honey, oil, butter, and sugar).[752] He returned to the monastery, and then asked the Venerable Losaka to eat it out of the bowl as he held it: otherwise it would disappear. Owing to the Venerable Sāriputta's compassion and efforts, that day, for the first time in his life, the Venerable Losaka Tissa had a full belly. And that night he attained Parinibbāna, the final cessation.

In every life Losaka was without influence, because of the power of his envy kamma. It functioned as productive kamma to produce unhappy rebirths, and in every unhappy rebirth, his envy kamma functioned as reinforcing kamma to deprive him of food. When finally a wholesome kamma functioned as productive kamma to produce a human rebirth, and wholesome kamma matured to provide an opportunity for food, his envy kamma functioned as interceptive kamma to make the food somehow disappear. But finally, his past and present pāramī matured: that is, his samatha and vipassanā kammas matured, and he attained Arahantship. Soon after attaining Arahantship, he attained Parinibbāna, and that kamma intercepted all the kammas that could function as productive kamma to produce rebirth. All mental and physical sufferings ceased without remainder, and there would be no more rebirth. A shrine was erected over his ashes.

---

[752] *CATU·MADHURA*: bhikkhus are by their rule disallowed to eat after noon. They are, however, allowed to eat these four items for medical reasons. The same applies novices, and for those nuns and lay devotees who observe the eight/nine/ten precepts.

Thus are the workings of kamma. Such workings of kamma are why The Buddha said in the second *'Gaddula·Baddha'* sutta:[753]

Therefore, bhikkhus, one should reflect repeatedly upon one's own mind: 'For a long time this mind has been defiled by lust, by hatred, and by delusion.'

By mental defilement, bhikkhus, beings are defiled; by mental purification, beings are purified.

Now, please listen to The Buddha's eighth explanation to Subha.

One Does Not Harbour Envy

But here, student, a woman or man is an unenvious one. Gain, honour, respect, reverence, obeisance, and homage [received by] **another, she or he does not envy and does not begrudge, not harbouring envy. Because of accomplishing and undertaking such actions, she or he at the breakup of the body, after death, in a good destination, a heavenly world is reborn.**

But if she or he, at the breakup of the body, after death, in a good destination, a heavenly world is not reborn, if she or he as a human being returns, then wherever she or he is reborn, she or he has great influence.

This is the way, student, that leads to great influence, namely, one is not envious. Another's [received] **gain, honour, respect, reverence, obeisance, and homage, one does not envy and does not begrudge, one does not harbour envy.**

Happy Uruvela Kassapa

A good example of non-envy leading to great influence is the Venerable Uruvela Kassapa. He was one of three fire ascetics who together with their disciples ordained under our Buddha.

In Buddha Padumuttara's Dispensation,[754] he was a householder.[755] One day he saw The Buddha declare the bhikkhu Sīhaghosa chief disciple in having a great following *(mahā·parivārāna)*. When he heard how this bhikkhu received much gain, honour, respect, reverence, obeisance and homage, Uruvela Kassapa was not envious, he did not begrudge him it, he did not harbour envy over it, on the contrary, Uruvela Kassapa's whole body was filled with joy and happiness for the bhikkhu: this is what we call *muditā* (sympathetic joy). This attitude of mind was of great benefit to Uruvela Kassapa. It helped him later to attain higher rebirths. At his last rebirth, it helped him attain Arahantship.

In fact, Uruvela Kassapa's happiness for the bhikkhu was such that he wished for the same honour in a future Buddha's Dispensation. Towards that end, he accomplished many wholesome kammas:[756]

- He purified his virtue, by observing the five precepts.
- He made offerings to The Buddha and Sangha.
- He memorized The Buddha's Word, learned the Dhamma thoroughly, with care and respect; discussing knotty passages in the Texts, Commentaries, etc.
- He practised insight meditation up to the Formations-Equanimity Knowledge *(Saṅkhār·Upekkhā·Ñāṇa)*.

---

[753] S.III.I.x.8 *'Dutiya·Gaddula·Baddha·Suttaṁ'* ('The Second Clog-Bound Sutta'), quoted p.30.

[754] See 'Appendix 2: The Lineage of Buddhas', p.365.

[755] ApA.Iiv.8 *'Uruvela·Kassapa·Tthera·Apadānaṁ'* ('The Uruvela-Kassapa-Elder Narrative')

[756] This is the standard practice required for attaining the four discriminations: see p.277.

We should like now to analyse this according to the principle of dependent origination *(paṭicca samuppāda)*. If Uruvela Kassapa had understood that the bhikkhu Sīhaghosa was composed of ultimate materiality and mentality, there would have been Right View *(Sammā·diṭṭhi)*, for according to reality *(yathā·bhūta)*, there is only ultimate materiality and mentality: there is no such thing as a bhikkhu or bhikkhunī. Thus, he perceived the Venerable Sīhaghosa as a bhikkhu with a large following because of ignorance *(avijjā)*. Dependent on that ignorance, he wished himself to become a bhikkhu with a large following in a future Buddha's Dispensation: that was craving *(taṇhā)* for life as such a bhikkhu. Again and again, he craved for life as such a bhikkhu: that was clinging *(upādāna)*. Towards that end, he accomplished many wholesome kammas, by offering *(dāna)*, purifying his morality *(sīla)*, studying the Dhamma, and practising samatha and vipassanā meditation *(bhāvanā)*; they were wholesome volitional formations *(saṅkhāra)*. But such wholesome kammas are impermanent. As soon as they arise, they perish. Nonetheless, in his continuity of mentality-materiality, there remained the kammic potency *(kamma satti)*.[757]

Altogether there were five past causes for continued rebirth:

1) ignorance .... *(avijjā)*	4) formations (of kamma) .... *(saṅkhāra)*
2) craving .... *(taṇhā)*	5) existence
3) clinging .... *(upādāna)*	(of kammic potency) .... *(bhava)*

Some of the wholesome kammas (the wholesome volitional formations) functioned then as productive kammas, some as reinforcing kammas, and some as frustrating kammas: almost all of them were indefinitely-effective kammas *(aparāpariya·vedanīya·kamma)*, to be experienced in future lives. And, indeed, in future lives he gained great influence.

In one such subsequent life, Uruvela Kassapa was born as the younger stepbrother of Buddha Phussa: their father was a King Mahinda.[758] There were also two other brothers. Once, the three brothers quelled some troubles at the border to the kingdom. As a reward, the king allowed them for three months to support The Buddha and Sangha. It was a Sangha of a hundred thousand bhikkhus: an unsurpassed field of merit. They appointed three of their ministers to make all the arrangements.[759] They themselves observed the ten precepts, stayed close to The Buddha, listened to Him teaching Dhamma, and practised samatha and vipassanā whenever they could.

These kammas produced superior results, and the three brothers were reborn now as devas, now as men, over many lives. In their last life, they were reborn into a Brahmin family, of the name Kassapa. They learned the three Vedas, and became matted-hair fire-ascetics, each with a following of disciples. They practised self-torment *(atta·kilamatha)*, and worshipped a sacred fire.

Uruvela Kassapa was chief. He lived at Uruvela on the banks of the Nerañjarā River, with five hundred disciples. Farther down the river lived his brother, Nadī Kassapa, with three hundred disciples. And yet farther down lived Gayā Kassapa, with two hundred disciples: the three brothers had altogether one thousand fire-ascetics.

---

[757] KAMMIC POTENCY: see footnotes 5, p.1, 56, p.15, and 'Kammic Potency', p.375.

[758] AA.I.xiv.4 *'Uruvela·Kassapa·Tthera·Vatthu'* ('The Uruvela-Kassapa-Elder Case')

[759] In Buddha Gotama's dispensation, they became King Bimbisāra, the householder Visākha, and the Venerable Raṭṭhapāla.

Not long after His enlightenment, The Buddha visited Uruvela Kassapa.[760] The Buddha asked Kassapa if He could stay in the chamber of the sacred fire. Kassapa warned him not to, because there was also a fierce *nāga* (dragon) that spewed fire and smoke. But The Buddha stayed there anyway. And with His psychic powers, The Buddha overpowered first that nāga and then another nāga nearby. Kassapa was much impressed by The Buddha's psychic powers. He invited The Buddha to stay and promised to provide The Buddha with food every day. The Buddha then stayed in a grove nearby for three months. In that time, He displayed his psychic powers many times, and each time Kassapa was impressed. But Kassapa thought he was himself an Arahant, and thought The Buddha was not an Arahant, so he did not try to learn anything from The Buddha. The Buddha could read Kassapa's mind, and waited for the right time: He waited until Kassapa should be ready to learn from Him.

Finally, when the time was right, The Buddha told Kassapa that neither was Kassapa an Arahant, nor did Kassapa know the way to Arahantship. Kassapa was very surprised. But because he had by now gained faith in The Buddha, he thought it was probably true. And humbly he asked for ordination. The Buddha asked him to tell his disciples of his decision, and to let them make their own decision: they all decided to become bhikkhus as well. All five hundred cut off their matted hair, and threw it into the Nerañjarā River, together with their sacrificial utensils. And then they were all ordained. Seeing the hair and utensils floating down the river, Nadī Kassapa and Gayā Kassapa came to inquire what happened, and then they and their disciples also ordained. Then they went wandering with The Buddha. At Gayāsīsa The Buddha taught them 'The "Burning" Sutta' *('Āditta-·Suttaṁ')*,[761] by which all one thousand bhikkhus attained Arahantship.

From Gayāsīsa, The Buddha and the new Arahants went to Rājagāha.[762] Then, in the presence of King Bimbisāra and a crowd of people, Uruvela Kassapa declared his discipleship to The Buddha.

Uruvela Kassapa was so called because he was ordained at Uruvela, and to distinguish him from other Kassapas.[763] When he was a fire-ascetic, he had one thousand disciples. And when he ordained under The Buddha, they all followed him. One such disciple of Uruvela Kassapa was, for example, the Venerable Belaṭṭhasīsa. He had followed Uruvela Kassapa in ordaining as a bhikkhu, and later became the Venerable Ānanda's preceptor. Many of Uruvela Kassapa's disciples ordained others. In that way, his following grew even larger. Hence, when The Buddha declared the chief bhikkhus, He declared Venerable Uruvela Kassapa chief bhikkhu in having a large following.[764]

Do you want to have great influence? If you do, you should try to be a woman or man who does not envy or begrudge the gain, honour, respect, reverence, obeisance and devotion received by others. Instead you should rejoice: that is what we call sympathetic joy. Such are the workings of kamma.

---

[760] Vin.Mv.i.12 *'Uruvela·Pāṭihāriya·Kathā'* ('Discussion of the Uruvela Miracles')

[761] Ibid., also S.IV.I.iii.6 *'Āditta·Suttaṁ'* ('The "Burning" Sutta').

[762] Vin.Mv.i.13 *'Bimbisāra·Samāgama·Kathā'* ('Discussion of the Bimbisāra-Meeting')

[763] Kassapa is a clan name, and there were a number of bhikkhus of that clan.

[764] A.I.XIV.iv.224 *'Etad·Agga Vagga: Catuttha·Vaggo'* ('Chapter on "This is the Chief": Fourth Chapter')

Such workings of kamma are why The Buddha said to Subha, Toddeya's son:[765]

Kamma distinguishes beings, that is, as inferior and superior.

Now, please listen to The Buddha's ninth explanation to Subha.

One Does Not Make Offerings

Here, student, to ascetics or Brahmins*(samaṇa·brāhmaṇa)***, a woman or man is not an offerer of food, drink, clothing, transport, garlands, scents, ointments, beds, dwellings, and lamps. Because of accomplishing and undertaking such actions, she or he at the breakup of the body, after death, in perdition, in a bad destination, in an infernal place, in hell is reborn.**

But if she or he, at the breakup of the body, after death, in perdition, in a bad destination, in an infernal place, in hell is not reborn, if she or he as a human being returns, then wherever she or he is reborn, she or he is poor.[766]

This is the way, student, that leads to poverty, namely, to ascetics and Brahmins, one is not an offerer of food, drink, clothing, transport, garlands, scents, ointments, beds, dwellings, and lamps.

Here, although one is able to make offerings, one does not do so because of stinginess, because of possessiveness*(macchariya)*: although one is perhaps even rich, one does not make any offerings. Such kamma produces rebirth in a woeful state, and if one is reborn as a human being, one will be poor.

The Miserly Brahmin Todeyya

A good example of such possessiveness leading to an unhappy birth is the father of the young man The Buddha is here talking to, the Brahmin student Subha. We mentioned his father earlier, the Brahmin Todeyya. He was chaplain to King Pasenadi of Kosala, and was extremely rich.

The Brahmin Todeyya had accomplished wholesome kammas in the past, and one of them functioned as productive kamma, to make him extremely rich in this life. But although he was now very rich, he was also extremely possessive and miserly.[767] He always told his son, Subha, not to give anyone anything. He told Subha to collect his property like the honey bee, which collects honey drop by drop, or like the ant, which collects grain by grain of earth to make an ant-hill. Hence, although The Buddha and Sangha often stayed at Sāvatthi, Todeyya never made any offerings. And (as we mentioned earlier) owing to his extreme attachment for his property, Todeyya was at death reborn as a dog, to a bitch in his own house.

When the dog died, he was reborn in hell. One possessiveness kamma had functioned as a productive kamma to produce rebirth as a dog, and now another, identical, possessiveness kamma functioned as interceptive kamma to cut off that productive kamma's result, and make its own result arise: rebirth in hell.

Do you want to avoid being reborn as a dog? Do you want to avoid being reborn in hell? If you do, you should try to be a woman or man who is not possessive, stingy or miserly. And you should try to remove any great attachment you may have for your property by practising samatha and vipassanā.

---

765 See extended quotation, p.258.

766 The Buddha explains this also to Queen Mallikā: see 'Queen Mallikā', p.192.

767 Being in this way unable to enjoy one's wealth is also the result of giving with stint: see endnote 248, p.303.

Please remember the envious Venerable Losaka Tissa. He was not only jealous, he was also possessive: he did not want to share his patron's favours with others. As a result, although he managed to escape from hell, at every human rebirth, he was poor. Such are the workings of kamma.

Such workings of kamma are why The Buddha said in the second *'Gaddula·Baddha'* sutta:[768]

Therefore, bhikkhus, one should reflect repeatedly upon one's own mind: 'For a long time this mind has been defiled by lust, by hatred, and by delusion.'

By mental defilement, bhikkhus, beings are defiled; by mental purification, beings are purified.

Now, please listen to The Buddha's tenth explanation to Subha.

One Makes Offerings

But here, student, to ascetics and Brahmins a woman or man is an offerer of food or drink, clothing, transport, garlands, scents, ointments, beds, dwellings, and lamps.[769] **Because of accomplishing and undertaking such actions, she or he at the breakup of the body, after death, in a good destination, a heavenly world is reborn.**

But if she or he, at the breakup of the body, after death, in a good destination, a heavenly world is not reborn, if she or he as a human being returns, then wherever she or he is reborn, she or he is wealthy.

This is the way, student, that leads to wealth, namely, to ascetics and Brahmins one is an offerer of food or drink, clothing, transport, garlands, scents, ointments, beds, dwellings, and lamps.

The Venerable Sīvali

A good example of such generosity leading to wealth is the Venerable Sīvali.[770] In Buddha Padumuttara's Dispensation,[771] he resolved to become chief bhikkhu in receiving gifts, like one of Buddha Padumuttara's chief disciples, the Venerable Sudassana. To this end, Sīvali gave alms for seven days to The Buddha and the Sangha of a hundred thousand bhikkhus. The result of this kamma was very big indeed. Why?

At that time, the human life span was a hundred thousand years, and the majority of people observed the precepts, and purified their virtue. And Sīvali understood that, owing to the purity of virtue, the wish of a virtuous one comes true.[772] To that end, he made offerings to The Buddha and Sangha; memorized The Buddha's Word, learned the Dhamma thoroughly, with care and respect; discussed knotty passages in the Texts, Commentaries, etc.; and practised insight meditation up to the Formations-Equanimity Knowledge *(Saṅkhār·Upekkhā·Ñāṇa)*. This is the standard of practice for those who attain Arahantship with the four discriminations *(paṭisambhidā)*.[773]

---

768 S.III.I.x.8 *'Dutiya·Gaddula·Baddha·Suttaṁ'* ('The Second Clog-Bound Sutta'), quoted p.30.

769 These ten items are called the ten bases for offering *(dasa dāna·vatthu)*.

770 AA.I.xiv.2 *'Sīvali·Tthera·Vatthu'* ('The Sīvali-Elder Case')

771 See 'Appendix 2: The Lineage of Buddhas', p.365.

772 See quotation p.270.

773 FOUR DISCRIMINATIONS: See footnote 683, p.262. For the standard practice required, see p.277.

So if we analyse Sīvali's seven-day long offering of alms, we see:

- It was associated with morality *(sīla)*, concentration *(samādhi)*, and wisdom *(paññā)*.
- The recipients were The Buddha and a Sangha of a hundred thousand bhikkhus: an unsurpassed field of merit in the world.
- The offerings had been righteously obtained.
- Sīvali's mind was happy, clear, and taintless, before offering, while offering, and after offering. He did not expect anything in return from The Buddha and Sangha.
- Because Sīvali had practised insight meditation, he understood dependent origination. That meant he had full faith that the result of this kamma would be great.[248]

For these reasons, the virtue of his offering was so great that his wish would certainly come true. Hence, Buddha Padumuttara prophesied that, in Buddha Gotama's Dispensation, Sīvali would become chief bhikkhu in receiving offerings.

In Atthadassī Buddha's Dispensation,[774] Sīvali was a King Varuṇa.[775] When The Buddha entered Parinibbāna (final cessation), Sīvali made great offerings to the Bodhi tree, and later died under it. At death, he was reborn in the *Nimmānaratī* deva world.[249] Thirty four times he was a king among men, with the name Subāhu.

In Vipassī Buddha's Dispensation, Sīvali was a householder living near Bandhumatī.[776] Once, the people competed with the king in making the most splendid offering of alms to The Buddha and Sangha of sixty thousand bhikkhus. For this offering, Sīvali gave honey, curds, and sugar to feed all the recipients. And he said to The Buddha: 'Bhagavā, I do not by this aspiration wish for another result except that in the future, in a Buddha's Dispensation, also I (like your foremost placed bhikkhu) should become chief in gains.'

In our Buddha's dispensation, he was born into the family of a Licchavi Mahāli. His mother was daughter of the king of Koliya, and was called Suppavāsā. Being reborn into such a rich family, was the result of a powerful productive kamma of an indefinitely-effective kamma *(aparāpariya·vedanīya·kamma)*. But that wholesome kamma was frustrated by an unwholesome kamma. How? Sīvali spent seven years and seven months in his mother's womb.[777] Before he was delivered, his mother was in labour for seven days. She thought she was going to die. So she asked her husband please to go and do obeisance to The Buddha in her name. The Buddha made a declaration:

May Suppavāsā the Koliya-daughter be happy: in comfort, may she deliver a healthy boy.

As soon as The Buddha had uttered those words, Suppavāsā delivered a healthy boy, Sīvali. Afterwards, she made offerings to The Buddha and the Sangha for seven days.

Owing to the reinforcement of a wholesome indefinitely-effective kamma, Sīvali was from birth highly gifted. The Venerable Sāriputta talked with him on the day of his birth, and with his mother's permission, ordained him.[778] Sīvali's meditation

---

[774] See 'Appendix 2: The Lineage of Buddhas', p.365.
[775] TGA.I.vi.10 *'Sīvali·Tthera·Gāthā·Vaṇṇanā'* ('Description of the Sīvali-Elder Verses')
[776] AA.I.xiv.2 *'Sīvali·Tthera·Vatthu'* ('The Sīvali-Elder Case')
[777] DhPA.xxvi.32 *'Sīvali·Tthera·Vatthu'* ('The Sīvali-Elder Case')
[778] ApA.lv.3 *'Sīvali·Tthera·Apadānaṁ'* ('The Sīvali-Elder Narrative')

subject was the seven-year suffering he had endured in his mother's womb. Thus, at the shaving of Sīvali's head, he attained the first Path&Fruition, Stream Entry *(Sot·Āpatti)*, when the first lock of hair fell; he attained the second Path&Fruition, Once-Return*(Sakad·Āgāmī)*, when the second lock of hair fell; and he attained the third Path&Fruition, Non-Return*(An·Āgāmi)*, when the third lock of hair fell.[250] Then, after his ordination, he went and lived in a secluded hut. Again meditating on his seven-year suffering in his mother's womb, he practised insight meditation, and became an Arahant with the four discriminations*(paṭisambhidā)*.[779] This was because of his pāramī: he had practised samatha and vipassanā up to the Formations-Equanimity Knowledge*(Saṅkhār·Upekkhā·Ñāṇa)* in the Dispensations of previous Buddhas.[780]

As we just explained, Sīvali spent seven years in his mother's womb, and it took his mother seven days to deliver him: it was great suffering for him and his mother, and was caused by past indefinitely-effective unwholesome kamma that functioned as frustrating kamma.

Once, when our Bodhisatta was king of Bārāṇasī, the king of Kosala waged war against him.[781] The king of Kosala killed the Bodhisatta, and took his queen. But the Bodhisatta's son escaped through a sewer. Later, he returned with a great army to give battle. His mother, hearing of his plans, sent a message saying he should blockade the city instead. After seven days, the citizens of the city captured the king of Kosala, cut off his head, and brought it to the prince.

That prince was the continuity of mentality-materiality that later became known as Sīvali in our Buddha's Dispensation, and his mother then was his mother now. Their 'blockade kamma' was the frustrating kamma that prolonged Sīvali's time in the womb, and his delivery.

The Buddha related this story, to explain to the bhikkhus why Suppavāsā's pregnancy lasted so long. Such workings of kamma are why The Buddha repeated in the second *'Gaddula·Baddha'* sutta:[782]

Therefore, bhikkhus, one should reflect repeatedly upon one's own mind: 'For a long time this mind has been defiled by lust, by hatred, and by delusion.'

By mental defilement, bhikkhus, beings are defiled; by mental purification, beings are purified.

Later, the Venerable Sīvali was by The Buddha declared chief bhikkhu in receiving offerings.[783] And once, when The Buddha went to visit Khadira-Vaniya Revata, the Venerable Sāriputta's youngest brother, He took the Venerable Sīvali with him, because the road was difficult, and food difficult to get: with the Venerable Sīvali's wholesome reinforcing 'generosity kamma', there was always enough food for everyone.[784]

---

779 FOUR DISCRIMINATIONS: see footnote 683, p.262.

780 FORMATIONS-EQUANIMITY KNOWLEDGE: see p.113.

781 JA.I.x.10 (100) *'A·Sāta·Rūpa·Jātaka·Vaṇṇanā'* ('Description of the Not-Pleasure-Seeking Jātaka')

782 S.III.I.x.8 *'Dutiya·Gaddula·Baddha·Suttaṁ'* ('The Second Clog-Bound Sutta'), quoted p.30.

783 A.I.XIV.ii.207 *'Etad·Agga Vagga: Dutiya·Vaggo'* ('Chapter on "This is the Chief": Second Chapter')

784 DhPA.vii.8 *'Khadira·Vaniya·Revata·Tthera·Vatthu'* ('The Acacia-Forest Revata-Elder Case')

Another time, to test his merit, the Venerable Sīvali went to the Himalayas with five hundred other bhikkhus.[785] The devas provided for them in abundance. On the mountain Gandhamadana, a deva called Nagadatta gave them milk rice for seven days. Sīvali's constant supply of alms was the result of his previous generosity kamma: wholesome reinforcing kamma to be experienced in some subsequent life. Thus are the workings of kamma.

Now, please listen to The Buddha's eleventh explanation to Subha.

One Is Stubborn and Proud

Here, student, a woman or man is stubborn, proud. To one who should be paid obeisance to, she or he does not pay obeisance; for one for whom one should stand up, she or he does not stand up; to one to whom one should give a seat, she or he does not give a seat; for one for whom one should make way, she or he does not make way; one to be honoured, she or he does not honour, one to be respected, she or he does not respect, one to be revered, she or he does not revere, one to be paid homage to, she or he does not pay homage to. Because of accomplishing and undertaking such actions, she or he at the breakup of the body, after death, in perdition, in a bad destination, in an infernal place, in hell is reborn.

But if she or he, at the breakup of the body, after death, in perdition, in a bad destination, in an infernal place, in hell is not reborn, if she or he as a human being returns, then wherever she or he is reborn, she or he is low-born.

This is the way, student, that leads to a low birth, namely, one is stubborn and proud. To one who should be paid obeisance to, one does not pay obeisance; for one for whom one should stand up, one does not stand up; to one to whom one should give a seat, one does not give a seat; for one for whom one should make way, one does not make way; one to be honoured, one does not honour, one to be respected, one does not respect, one to be revered, one does not revere, one to be paid homage to, one does not pay homage to.

Who, then, are those to be honoured, respected, revered, and paid homage to? One's elders and betters. First of all, Fully Enlightened Buddhas, Paccekabuddhas, and Noble Disciples *(Ariya·Sāvaka)*.[786] For a layperson, one's elders and betters include one's mother and one's father, ascetics and Brahmins, and the head of the clan.[251]

The Scavenger Sunīta

A good example of such pride leading to rebirth in hell, and low birth as a human being is the Venerable Sunīta. Once, in a past life, he met a Paccekabuddha who was on his almsround in the village. When he saw the Paccekabuddha, he spoke to him with contempt, criticizing his way of life. He said: 'You have hands and feet like everyone else. You should work for your living like the rest of us. If you have no skill, then you should earn your living by collecting scraps and waste in a bucket.'

Sunīta did not pay obeisance to one who should be paid obeisance to, he did not respect, revere and honour one to be respected, revered and honoured. Instead, he spoke with contempt to such a one, a Paccekabuddha. He accomplished many unwholesome kammas. Some functioned as productive kammas, some as frustra-

---

785 AA.I.xiv.2 *'Sīvali·Tthera·Vatthu'* ('The Sīvali-Elder Case') & TGA.I.vi.10 *'Sīvali·Tthera·Gāthā·Vaṇṇanā'* ('Description of the Sīvali-Elder Verses') & ApA.lv.3 *'Sīvali·Tthera·Apadānaṁ'* ('The Sīvali-Elder Narrative')

786 See commentary to the sutta under discussion.

ting kamma. When he died, one such productive kamma did indeed produce rebirth in hell. We may thus understand that in one's wandering in the round of rebirth, not to pay obeisance to, not to respect, revere and honour those worthy of it is very dangerous.

When Sunīta finally escaped from hell, and was again reborn as a human being, he was in many lives reborn into a family of the lowest caste: in each life, he was reborn into a family of scavengers. His 'disparaging-a-Paccekabuddha' kammas functioned as frustrating kamma, to bring misfortune into his every human life. In each life, he worked out a miserable life as a scavenger, collecting scraps and waste in a bucket. And just as he had in the past regarded the Paccekabuddha, so now did people regard him with loathing, and treat him with contempt. He had to honour, respect, revere, and pay homage to everybody, young and old, with humility and patience, because his livelihood depended on their goodwill and compassion.

Nonetheless, Sunīta had also accomplished sufficient wholesome kammas and pāramī to attain Arahantship. When they matured, one of them functioned as a productive kamma to produce his human rebirth at the time of our Buddha's Dispensation.

In our Buddha's Dispensation, he was again reborn into a family of scavengers, in Rājagaha. And again, people regarded him with loathing, and treated him with contempt. But one day, however, The Buddha saw that Sunīta had accomplished sufficient pāramī to attain Arahantship. So, at dawn, together with five hundred bhikkhus, The Buddha passed by where Sunīta was sweeping and cleaning the street. When Sunīta saw The Buddha, he was filled with joy and awe. Unable to remove himself, he stood with his back against the wall, with his hands clasped in obeisance.

The Buddha approached him, and asked in a soft and friendly voice if he would like to become a bhikkhu. Sunīta expressed great joy, and The Buddha ordained him with the words:

Come bhikkhu*(Ehi bhikkhu!)***! Well proclaimed is the Dhamma! Live the holy life for suffering's complete destruction!**

Then The Buddha took the Venerable Sunīta to the monastery, and taught him a meditation subject. The Venerable Sunīta developed the eight attainments, and five psychic powers*(abhiññā)*: with insight meditation, he attained the sixth psychic power, destruction of the taints, Arahantship.[787] After that, many Brahmas, devas, and men came to pay homage to him, and he gave them teachings regarding his way to attainment. Such are the workings of kamma.

Such workings of kamma are why The Buddha said in the *'Kokālika'* sutta:[788]

When a person has taken birth, an axe is born inside his mouth with which the fool cuts himself by uttering offensive speech.

THE BARBER UPĀLI

Another good example of how disrespect leads to a low birth is the Venerable Upāli Thera. In Buddha Padumuttara's Dispensation,[789] Upāli was a very rich Brah-

---

[787] EIGHT ATTAINMENTS: four fine-material and four immaterial jhānas; psychic powers: see footnote 239, p.82.

[788] See footnote 716, p.272.

[789] See 'Appendix 2: The Lineage of Buddhas', p.365.

min called Sujāta. He lived in Haṁsāvatī, which was the birthplace of Buddha Padumuttara.[790] Once, The Buddha came to Haṁsāvatī to see His father, the nobleman Ānanda, to teach him the Dhamma. At that time, Sujāta saw an ascetic Sunanda hold a canopy of flowers over The Buddha for seven days. He also heard The Buddha declare that Sunanda would, in Gotama Buddha's Dispensation, become the famous Venerable Puṇṇa Mantāniputta.[791] And Sujāta developed the desire to see the future Buddha Gotama. Then he heard Buddha Padumuttara declare that one bhikkhu Pātika was chief of those who master the monastic rule *(Vinaya·dhāra)*. And Sujāta aspired to gain this honour himself in Buddha Gotama's Dispensation.

To that end, he made offerings to The Buddha and Sangha. Especially, at great expense, he had a monastery constructed: it was called Sobhana. Apart from making offerings, Sujāta also memorized The Buddha's Word, learning the Dhamma thoroughly, with care and respect; he discussed knotty passages in the Texts, Commentaries, etc.; and practised insight meditation up to the Formations-Equanimity Knowledge *(Saṅkhār·Upekkhā·Ñāṇa)*.[792]

Two aeons earlier, however, as Sunanda, the son of a nobleman, he accomplished a serious unwholesome kamma. One day riding to the park on an elephant, he met the Paccekabuddha Devala. Owing to pride over his noble birth, he spoke rudely to the Paccekabuddha. And immediately he felt fierce heat in his body. Later, he went to see the Paccekabuddha together with a large following, and asked for forgiveness. Only then did the heat leave his body. In his final rebirth, this 'rudeness kamma' functioned as frustrating kamma, and his wholesome productive kamma was able to produce only a low birth into human society. He was born into a barber's family in Kapilavatthu, and worked for the Sakyan princes.

When The Buddha left Kapilavatthu, he stayed at the Anupiya Grove. There, many Sakyan young men came and ordained as bhikkhus.[793] Also six Sakyan princes: Bhaddiya,[794] Anuruddha, Ānanda, Bhagu, Kimila, and Devadatta. Upāli went with the princes, and they left him all their valuables. But he realized that if he returned to Kapilavatthu with all those valuables, the other Sakyans might think he had murdered the princes. So he left the valuables in the grove, and joined the princes to himself become a bhikkhu. At their ordination, the princes asked The Buddha please to ordain Upāli first, so as to humble their own pride.

As a bhikkhu, the Venerable Upāli one day asked The Buddha for a meditation subject, so that he might go and dwell in the forest alone.[795] But The Buddha refused to let him go. The Buddha explained that in the forest the Venerable Upāli would learn only meditation, but if he dwelt with the Sangha near The Buddha, he would learn also the Dhamma. So the Venerable Upāli stayed with

---

790 Ap.II.iii.6 *'Upāli·Tthera·Apadānaṁ'* ('The Upāli-Elder Narrative')

791 The Venerable Puṇṇa Mantāniputta: he was by The Buddha Gotama declared chief Dhamma speaker *(Dhamma·kathika)* (A.I.XIV.i.196 *'Etad·Agga Vagga: Paṭhama·Vaggo'* ('Chapter on "This is the Chief": First Chapter'). In M.I.iii.4 *'Ratha·Vinīta·Suttaṁ'* ('The Chariot Relay Sutta'), he explains to the Venerable Sāriputta that the path to Arahantship is seven successive purifications. The *Visuddhi·Magga* is designed accordingly.

792 This is the standard practice required for attaining the four discriminations: see p.277.

793 Vin.Cv.vii.1.331 *'Cha·Sakya·Pabbajjā·Kathā'* ('Discussion of the Six Sakyans' Going-Forth'), and DhPA.i.12 *'Devadatta·Vatthu'* ('The Case of Devadatta').

794 Prince Bhaddiya's case is discussed just following.

795 AA.I.xiv.4 *'Upāli·Tthera·Vatthu'* ('The Upāli-Elder Case'), and ApA and TGA.

The Buddha, meditated, and learned the Dhamma. In due course, he attained Arahantship with the four discriminations *(paṭisambhidā)*.[796] And The Buddha Himself taught the Venerable Upāli the entire 'Vinaya Basket *(Vinaya·Piṭaka)*': the *Vinaya* is the rule for bhikkhus and bhikkhunis. The Venerable Upāli attained great distinction as a bhikkhu, and was by The Buddha declared chief bhikkhu in knowledge of the *Vinaya*.[797] At the first council, in Rājagaha, just as the Venerable Ānanda recited the Dhamma, so did the Venerable Upāli recite the *Vinaya*:[798] all issues regarding the *Vinaya* were resolved by him. Such are the workings of kamma.[799]

Such workings of kamma are why The Buddha said to Subha Todeyya's son:

Kamma distinguishes beings, that is, as inferior and superior.

Now, please listen to The Buddha's twelfth explanation to Subha.

One Is Not Stubborn, Not Proud

But here, student, a woman or man is not stubborn, not proud. To one who should be paid obeisance to, she or he pays obeisance; for one for whom one should stand up, she or he stands up; to one to whom one should give a seat, she or he gives a seat; for one for whom one should make way, she or he makes way; one to be honoured, she or he honours, one to be respected, she or he respects, one to be revered, she or he reveres, one to be paid homage to, she or he pays homage to. Because of accomplishing and undertaking such actions, she or he at the breakup of the body, after death, in a good destination, a heavenly world is reborn.

But if she or he, at the breakup of the body, after death, in a good destination, a heavenly world is not reborn, if she or he as a human being returns, then wherever she or he is reborn, she or he is high-born.

This is the way, student, that leads to a high birth, namely, one is not stubborn, not proud. To one who should be paid obeisance to, one pays obeisance; for one for whom one should stand up, one stands up; to one to whom one should give a seat, one gives a seat; for one for whom one should make way, one makes way; one to be honoured, one honours, one to be respected, one respects, one to be revered, one reveres, one to be paid homage to, one pays homage to.

The Highborn Venerable Bhaddiya

Here, the Venerable Bhaddiya is a good example of how obeisance, honour, respect and homage paid to those worthy of it leads to a high birth. He was son of Kāḷigodhā, the leading Sakyan lady of the nobility: that is why he was also called *Kāḷigodhā·Putta·Bhaddiya* (Kāḷigodhā-Son Bhaddiya). The Buddha declared him chief among bhikkhus of a high family *(uccā·kulika)*.[800] He resolved to gain this distinction in Buddha Padumuttara's[801] Dispensation.[802] At that time he had been born into a very wealthy family. In that life, he offered alms and other requisites

---

[796] FOUR DISCRIMINATIONS: see footnote 683, p.262.

[797] A.I.XIV.iv.228 *'Etad·Agga Vagga: Paṭhama·Vaggo'* ('Chapter on "This is the Chief": First Chapter')

[798] Vin.Cv.XI.i.439 *'Saṅgīti·Nidānaṁ'* ('Council Introduction')

[799] For a similar case of such disrespect towards one's elders/betters, see 'The Slave-Woman Khujjuttarā' p.191.

[800] A.I.XIV.i.193 *'Etad·Agga Vagga: Paṭhama·Vaggo'* ('Chapter on "This is the Chief": First Chapter')

[801] See 'Appendix 2: The Lineage of Buddhas', p.365.

[802] Ap.I.v.3 *'Kāḷigodhā·Putta·Bhaddiya·Tthera·Apadānaṁ* ('The Kāḷigodhā-Son Bhaddiya-Elder Narrative')

to The Buddha and Sangha, all the time doing obeisance to The Buddha and Sangha, honouring, respecting, revering and paying homage to The Buddha and Sangha. He memorized The Buddha's Word, and learned the Dhamma thoroughly, with care and respect; he discussed knotty passages in the Texts, Commentaries, etc.; and he practised insight meditation up to the Formations-Equanimity Knowledge *(Saṅkhār·Upekkhā·Ñāṇa)*.[803]

In the interval between Kassapa Buddha and Buddha Gotama he was once a householder in Bārāṇasī.[804] When he heard Paccekabuddhas took their meals on the bank of the Ganges, he had seven stone seats made, and put there for them to sit on. In that way, he honoured, respected, revered, and paid homage to the Paccekabuddhas, and in a way, offered seats to those worthy of a seat. It was only one of the many wholesome kammas that later produced a high noble birth.

In his last birth, he was born to a ruling family of Sakyan royalty *(rājā)* in Kapilavatthu, our Buddha's birthplace. Bhaddiya himself ruled a Sakyan principality. At that time, Anuruddha was his great friend. When Anuruddha asked his mother to allow him to become a bhikkhu, she said she would allow it only if Bhaddiya became a bhikkhu too. And Anuruddha managed to persuade Bhaddiya to give up his royal life within seven days.[805] It is said that Bhaddiya attained Arahantship with the three knowledges *(te·vijjā)*[806] in the first rainy season retreat after his ordination.[807]

Soon after attaining Arahantship, under a tree in a lonely spot, dwelling in the bliss of Nibbāna, the Venerable Bhaddiya would often exclaim:[808]

Oh, what happiness! Oh what happiness!

His fellow bhikkhus thought he was thinking about his past as a prince in the palace, and reported it to The Buddha. But to The Buddha he explained that when he was a ruler, he was always fearful and nervous, even though there were guards inside the palace and outside. But now, having renounced all, he was free from all fear.

Owing to previous wholesome kammas, Bhaddiya had been king for five hundred births and received eminence in this last life. Though there were others of a higher rank in the nobility, The Buddha declared him to be foremost among bhikkhus of noble birth because he had been born of the leading Sakyan lady, because he had renounced his position as king, and because he had been king for five hundred lives successively.[809]

Do you want a high rebirth? If you do, you should try to be a woman or man who is not stubborn and proud. If you want a high rebirth:

- To those one should pay obeisance to, you should pay obeisance.
- For those one should stand up for, you should stand up.

---

[803] This is the standard practice required for attaining the four discriminations: see p.277.

[804] Ibid. and TGA.II.xvi.7 *'Kāḷigodhā·Putta·Bhaddiya·Tthera·Gāthā·Vaṇṇanā'* ('Description of the Kāḷigodhā-Son Bhaddiya-Elder Verses').

[805] Bhaddiya was one of the Sakyan princes who gave all their valuables to Upāli their barber. See 'The Barber Upāli', p.290.

[806] Vin.Cv.vii.1.331 *'Cha·Sakya·Pabbajjā·Kathā'* ('Discussion of the Six Sakyans' Going-Forth')

[807] ibid.; THREE KNOWLEDGES: see footnote 239, p.82.

[808] ibid.

[809] A.I.XIV.i.193 *'Etad·Agga Vagga: Paṭhama·Vaggo'* ('Chapter on "This is the Chief": First Chapter')

- To those one should give a seat to, you should give a seat.
- For those one should make way for, you should make way.
- To those whom one should honour, respect, revere and pay homage to, you should honour, respect, revere, and pay homage.

One's elders and betters are first of all,[810] Fully Enlightened Buddhas, Pacceka-buddhas, and Noble Disciples *(Ariya·Sāvaka)*.[252] And for a layperson, one's elders and betters include one's mother and one's father, ascetics and Brahmins, and the head of the clan.[811]

Please do not forget, stubbornness and pride are defilements. Defilements do not produce a high birth, they produce a low birth. Such are the workings of kamma. Such workings of kamma are why The Buddha said to Subha:

Kamma distinguishes beings, that is, as inferior and superior.

Now, please listen to The Buddha's thirteenth explanation to Subha.

One Is Not an Inquirer

Here, student, having approached an ascetic or Brahmin *(samaṇa·brāhmaṇa)*, **a woman or man is not an inquirer.** [She/he asks not]**: 'What, Venerable Sir, is wholesome; what is unwholesome? What is blameful, what is blameless?**[253] **What should be practised, what should not be practised? What, by my doing it, is to my long-term detriment and suffering, or else, what, by my doing it, is to my long-term benefit and happiness?' Because of accomplishing and undertaking such actions, she or he at the breakup of the body, after death, in perdition, in a bad destination, in an infernal place, in hell is reborn.**

But if she or he, at the breakup of the body, after death, in perdition, in a bad destination, in an infernal place, in hell is not reborn, if she or he as a human being returns, then wherever she or he is reborn, she or he is stupid.[812]

This is the way, student, that leads to stupidity, namely, having approached an ascetic or Brahmin, one is not an inquirer. [One asks not]**: 'What, Venerable Sir, is wholesome; what is unwholesome? What is blameful, what is blameless? What should be practised, what should not be practised? What, by my doing it, is to my long-term detriment and suffering, or else, what, by my doing it, is to my long-term benefit and happiness?'**

Here, one does not appear in a bad destination because one fails to ask questions about right conduct. One appears in a bad destination because one conducts oneself badly. And one does so because of stupidity, because one does not know the difference between bad and good conduct, one does not know the results of bad and good conduct. One does not know those things because one has not inquired into them. That way, one does not know how to conduct oneself well, and one conducts oneself badly, contrary to the Dhamma: one commits unwholesome kammas that function as unwholesome productive kamma to produce undesirable results, or function as unwholesome interceptive kamma, or unwholesome frustrating kamma, to cut off and oppose the desirable results of wholesome kammas.

We may thus understand that this the thirteenth explanation given by The Buddha to Subha is in fact included in all the unwholesome actions we have so far discussed: to kill, to steal, to engage in sexual misconduct, to drink beer and wine, etc., to tell lies, to slander, to speak harshly, to prattle, to covet, to harbour

---

[810] See commentary to the sutta under discussion.

[811] For the future non-honouring of elders and betters, as predicted by The Buddha, see endnote 251, p.304.

[812] In Pali *du·ppañño*: 'bad/wrong wisdom'.

ill-will, and to hold wrong view. When we do all these bad things, it is because of stupidity, because we do not know they are bad, because we do not have faith in or knowledge of the workings of kamma.

Here, of course, good examples are all the examples we have so far discussed, of people doing that which is unwholesome, that which is blameful, that which should not be practised, that which by their doing it, led to their long-term detriment and suffering. We discussed the Venerable Mahāmogallāna's shortened life span: in a past life, he tried to beat his parents to death. For that he went to hell for a very long time. Afterwards, he was beaten to death in many lives, even in his last life. Then there was the demon *(yakkha)* Nanda: he struck the Venerable Sāriputta on the head. For that, he was swallowed up by the earth to be reborn in hell. And the Venerable Pūtigattatissa's terrible sickness: in a past life, he broke the wings and legs of many birds to prevent them from escaping. For that, he went to hell for a very long time. Afterwards, he was reborn as a human being, and became a bhikkhu. But he developed boils all over his body, and his bones disintegrated. And Pañcapāpī 's ugliness: in a past life, she gave a Paccekabuddha an angry look. For that, she was reborn ugly. And Suppabuddha's ugliness: in a past life, as son of a treasurer, he abused a Paccekabuddha. For that, he went to hell for a very long time. And in our Buddha's Dispensation, he was reborn as a human being, to become a wretched leper. Then there was the Venerable Losaka Tissa's lack of influence: in a past life, he was unable to control his envy towards an Arahant, and threw away the Arahant's food. For that, he went to hell for a long time. And in every life after that, he suffered many hardships, with never enough food to eat. Even in his last life, when he had become a bhikkhu and Arahant, he never received enough food to eat. We discussed also Subha's father, the rich Brahmin Todeyya's poverty. He was miserly, and never gave alms. For that, he was reborn as a dog. Afterwards, he was reborn in hell. And the Venerable Sunīta's low birth: in a past life, also he was rude to a Paccekabuddha. For that, he went to hell. Afterwards, he was again and again reborn as a human being in the lowest caste, a scavenger. And the Venerable Upāli's low birth: in a past life, also he abused a Paccekabuddha. For that, when he was reborn as a human being in our Buddha's Dispensation, it was into a barber's family. All those people did those bad things because of stupidity.

STUPID PRINCE SUPPABUDDHA

We can take yet an example of stupidity: Suppabuddha the Sakyan prince. He was brother to The Buddha's mother, Mahāmāyā, and father to Yasodharā, Prince Siddhattha's wife. He was also Devadatta's father.

Prince Suppabuddha was born into a royal family. As we just discussed, The Buddha says the way to such a high birth is that one is without stubbornness and pride, and that one honours, respects, reveres and pays homage to those who deserve it. We may thus understand that Prince Suppabuddha had accomplished such wholesome kammas in the past, and that one of them functioned as a productive kamma to produce his royal birth. But at the end of his life, that wholesome productive kamma was intercepted by an unwholesome kamma, to produce rebirth in hell. How?

Prince Suppabuddha bore two grudges against The Buddha.[813] One grudge he bore on account of his daughter Princess Yasodharā: she had been Prince Siddh-

[813] DhP.ix.12 *'Suppabuddha·Sakya·Vatthu'* ('The Case of Suppabuddha the Sakyan')

attha's wife. And in order to become Buddha, Prince Siddhattha had left his wife and child, to go forth. Another grudge Prince Suppabuddha bore against The Buddha was on account of his son Devadatta. When Devadatta developed the desire to become leader of the Sangha, The Buddha had an announcement made in the city, dissociating Himself and the Sangha from Devadatta.

So one day, in order to make mischief, Prince Suppabuddha decided to block The Buddha's almsround. On the road where The Buddha had been invited to accept alms, Prince Suppabuddha sat down drinking liquor. When The Buddha and Sangha arrived, the bhikkhus told Suppabuddha that The Teacher had come. But Suppabuddha refused to make way for The Buddha. Several times the bhikkhus told him, and each time he refused to make way for The Buddha.

Why did Prince Suppabuddha commit this unwholesome kamma? Because he did not know it was unwholesome. Why did he not know it was unwholesome? Because he never approached an ascetic or Brahmin to find out what was unwholesome and wholesome, to find out what was blameful and blameless, to find out what would be to his detriment and suffering, and to find out what would be to his benefit and happiness. Prince Suppabuddha had never made any effort in that way. The result was stupidity. Because of his stupidity, he refused to make way for a Fully Enlightened Buddha: he refused to honour, respect, revere, and pay homage to The Buddha. Because of his stupidity, he accomplished many unwholesome kammas.

The Buddha turned back. And Suppabuddha sent a man to hear what The Buddha might say. On his way back, The Buddha smiled. And the Venerable Ānanda asked Him why He smiled. The Buddha explained that in seven days, Suppabuddha would be swallowed up by the earth at the foot of his stairway. Suppabuddha's man heard what The Buddha said, and immediately told Suppabuddha. Suppabuddha then decided he would prove The Buddha wrong. So he had all his personal belongings carried to the top floor of his house, the seventh floor. Then he had the stairway removed, and all the doors locked. On each floor, he had two strong men posted. He told them that if he were to come down, they should make him go back.

Seven days after Suppabuddha had blocked The Buddha's way, Suppabuddha's state horse escaped from its stable. Only Suppabuddha could control the horse. So he moved towards the door. The doors opened, the stairway returned to its place, and the guards threw him down the stairway, from the top floor to the bottom. At the bottom of the stairway, he was swallowed up by the earth, and reborn in Avīci Hell. The wholesome kamma that had functioned as productive kamma to produce rebirth as a human being, and to sustain his human life, was intercepted by his unwholesome kamma of refusing to make way for one whom one should make way for: in this case a Fully Enlightened Buddha, the most virtuous of all beings. That unwholesome kamma then produced its own result, which was rebirth in hell.

Here again, we need to understand that Prince Suppabuddha's rebirth in hell was not the result of anything The Buddha did:[254] The Buddha did not smile because of ill-will; The Buddha was not happy to see how Suppabuddha would suffer. The Buddha smiled because He saw that Suppabuddha's kamma would for sure bring its result, no matter what Suppabuddha did. And the result came solely because of the power of Suppabuddha's unwholesome kamma. Thus are the workings of kamma. Such workings of kamma are why The Buddha repeated in the second *'Gaddula·Baddha'* sutta:[814]

Therefore, bhikkhus, one should reflect repeatedly upon one's own mind: 'For a long time this mind has been defiled by lust, by hatred, and by delusion.'

By mental defilement, bhikkhus, beings are defiled; by mental purification, beings are purified.

Now, please listen to The Buddha's fourteenth explanation to Subha.

One Is an Inquirer

Here, student, having approached an ascetic or Brahmin, a woman or man is an inquirer. [She or he asks]**: 'What, Venerable Sir, is wholesome; what is unwholesome? What is blameful, what is blameless? What should be practised, what should not be practised? What, by my doing it, is to my long-term detriment and suffering, or else, what, by my doing it, is to my long-term benefit and happiness?' Because of accomplishing and undertaking such actions, she or he at the breakup of the body, after death, in a good destination, a heavenly world is reborn.**

But if she or he, at the breakup of the body, after death, in a good destination, a heavenly world is not reborn, if she or he as a human being returns, then wherever she or he is reborn, she or he is very wise.

This is the way, student, that leads to great wisdom, namely, having approached an ascetic or Brahmin, one an inquirer is. [One asks]**: 'What, Venerable Sir, is wholesome; what is unwholesome? What is blameful, what is blameless? What should be practised, what should not be practised? What, by my doing it, is to my long-term detriment and suffering, or else, what, by my doing it, is to my long-term benefit and happiness?'**

Also here, one does not appear in a good destination because one asks questions about right conduct. One appears in a good destination because one conducts oneself well. And one does so because of wisdom, because one knows the difference between bad and good conduct, because one knows the results of bad and good conduct. One knows those things because one has inquired into them. That way, one knows how to conduct oneself well, and one conducts oneself well, according to the Dhamma: one accomplishes wholesome kammas that function as wholesome productive kamma to produce desirable results, or function as wholesome interceptive kamma, or wholesome frustrating kamma, to cut off and oppose the undesirable results of unwholesome kammas.

We may thus understand that this the fourteenth explanation given by The Buddha to Subha is in fact included in all the wholesome actions we have so far discussed: not to kill but to be kind and compassionate, not to steal, not to engage in sexual misconduct, not to drink beer and wine, etc., not to tell lies, not to slander, to speak politely, not to prattle, not to covet, not to harbour ill-will, and to hold Right View. When we do all these good things, it is because we know they are good, because we have faith in or knowledge of the workings of kamma.

Here, of course, good examples are all the examples we have so far given of people doing that which is wholesome, that which is blameless, that which should be practised, that which by their doing it, led to their long-term benefit and happiness: not to kill, not to harm other beings, not to be angry and irritable, not to be envious, to make offerings, and not to be stubborn and proud.

We discussed the virtuous Venerable Pañcasīla Samādāniya, and long-living Āyuvaḍḍhana Kumāra. We discussed the Venerable Bākula: he was never ever

[814] S.III.I.x.8 *'Dutiya·Gaddula·Baddha·Suttaṁ'* ('The Second Clog-Bound Sutta'), quoted p.30.

sick, and passed into Parinibbāna when he was a hundred and sixty years old. Then there was the Venerable Subhūti: he was very good-looking, and proficient in loving-kindness. The Venerable Mahākaccāna was also very good-looking: he was also chief disciple in analysing and elaborating the Dhamma explained in brief by The Buddha. We discussed also the Venerable Uruvela Kassapa: he was chief disciple in having a great following. And the Venerable Sīvali: he was chief disciple in receiving gifts. Venerable Bhaddiya: he was chief disciple of high birth. These were just a few examples of the many who gained much benefit and happiness through many, many thousand lifetimes: now they were reborn as human beings, now as devas. And they practised under past Buddhas.

What was their practice?

- They observed the precepts.
- They purified their conduct.
- Based on that virtue, they made offerings to ascetics and Brahmins.
- They learned The Buddha's Word off by heart.
- They learned the Dhamma thoroughly, with care and respect.
- They discussed knotty points, and the explanations in the texts, commentaries, etc.
- They practised samatha and vipassanā up to the Formations-Equanimity Knowledge*(Saṅkhār·Upekkhā·Ñāṇa)*.[815]

This practice is also what is called knowledge and conduct*(vijjā·caraṇa)*. We discussed it earlier:[816]

1) Conduct*(caraṇa)* is fifteen things: morality, faculty restraint, moderation in food, devotion to wakefulness, faith (which includes habitual practice of offering*(dāna)*), mindfulness, conscience, shame, great learning in theory and practice, energy, wisdom, and the four jhānas.
2) Knowledge*(vijjā)* is insight knowledge*(vipassanā·ñāṇa)*. That is, knowing and seeing the impermanence, suffering, and non-self of ultimate mentality*(paramattha·nāma)* and ultimate materiality*(paramattha·rūpa)*, of past, future, and present, internal and external, gross and subtle, superior and inferior, far and near. The highest mundane insight knowledge is the Formations-Equanimity Knowledge*(Saṅkhār·Upekkhā·Ñāṇa)*.

   As we discussed earlier, insight meditation that produces rebirth is included under conduct, and insight meditation that does not produce rebirth is included under knowledge.

Why did all those people do all those good things? Because of wisdom. And that wisdom came from having inquired about the difference between bad and good conduct, and having inquired into the results of bad and good conduct: in short, wisdom comes from having inquired into the workings of kamma with faith and respect. As a result, under our Buddha, these people also practised, and gained the highest benefit of all, Arahantship.

The Inquiring Venerable Mahākoṭṭhika

Let us then take one more example of someone who gained the highest benefit of all: the inquiring Venerable Mahākoṭṭhika. In Buddha Padumuttara's Dispensa-

[815] This is the standard practice required for attaining the four discriminations: see p.277.

[816] For details, see 'Knowledge and Conduct', p.137.

tion,[817] he was a rich householder.[818] One day, he heard The Buddha declare a bhikkhu chief in mastery of the four discriminations *(paṭisambhidā)*.[819] And he aspired for similar honour for himself in a future Buddha's Dispensation. To that end, he invited The Buddha and a hundred thousand bhikkhus for an almsgiving that lasted seven days. At the end of the almsgiving, he offered each one of them three robes.

Furthermore, he memorized The Buddha's Word; he learned the Dhamma thoroughly, with care and respect; he discussed knotty passages in the Texts, Commentaries, etc.; and he practised insight meditation up to the Formations-Equanimity Knowledge *(Saṅkhār·Upekkhā·Ñāṇa)*. At that time the human life span was a hundred thousand years. So for a hundred thousand years, he accomplished these superior kammas, pāramī. The *Visuddhi·Magga* explains that this is the way of practice for those who attain Arahantship together with the four discriminations.[820] And the Venerable Mahākoṭṭhika was chief among such Arahants.

In his last life, he was born into a very rich Brahmin family of Sāvatthi. He became very skilled in the Vedas. But after hearing a Dhamma talk by The Buddha, he became a bhikkhu. He meditated, and soon became an Arahant. Having asked many questions of The Buddha and of his fellow bhikkhus, he became extremely skilled in the four discriminations *(paṭisambhidā)*. The Buddha declared him foremost among those skilled in the four discriminations *(catasso paṭisambhidā)*.[821] This was chiefly owing to his very analytical and skilful discussion of Dhamma with the Venerable Sāriputta in the *'Mahā·Vedalla'* sutta.[822] In this sutta, the Venerable Mahākoṭṭhika asks exceedingly deep and profound questions: for example, he asks about stupidity and wisdom; he asks about wisdom and consciousness; he asks about consciousness, feeling, and perception; he asks about wisdom, direct knowledge and full understanding; and he asks about how (on the one hand) the different kinds of liberation can be seen as different in meaning and different in name, and how (on the other hand) they can be seen as one in meaning and different in name. There are in the Pali Texts many other instances of the Venerable Mahākoṭṭhika discussing Dhamma with the Venerable Sāriputta: usually he would ask the questions, but sometimes also the Venerable Sāriputta would ask the questions. There are also suttas where the Venerable Mahākoṭṭhika discusses Dhamma with The Buddha Himself, one where the Venerable Ānanda asks him questions, and one where he discusses Abhidhamma with other bhikkhus.

The Venerable Sāriputta, second only to The Buddha Himself, held the Venerable Mahākoṭṭhika in high regard. He expresses his high regard in three stanzas:[823]

Being peaceful and restraining himself,
Being an expert speaker of unconceited calm,
He shakes off unwholesome dhammas
Like the wind blows leaves off a tree.

Being peaceful and restraining himself,

---

[817] See 'Appendix 2: The Lineage of Buddhas', p.365.
[818] AA.I.xiv.3 *'Mahākoṭṭhita·Tthera·Vatthu'* ('The Mahākoṭṭhita-Elder Case')
[819] FOUR DISCRIMINATIONS: see footnote 683, p.262.
[820] See p.277.
[821] A.I.XIV.i.218 *'Etad·Agga Vagga: Tatiya·Vaggo'* ('Chapter on "This is the Chief": Third Chapter') '
[822] M.I.v.3 *'Mahā·Vedalla·Suttaṁ'* ('The Great Catechism Sutta')
[823] TG.xvii.2 *'Sāriputta·Tthera·Gāthā'* ('The Sāriputta-Elder Verses')

Being an expert speaker of unconceited calm,
He removes unwholesome dhammas
Like the wind blows leaves off a tree.

Being composed and free from trouble,
Being purified and unstained,
Being virtuous and wise,
He is one who makes an end of suffering.

Do you want to be wise? If you do, you should try to do as the Venerable Mahākoṭṭhika. You should try to be a woman or man who visits ascetics and Brahmins.

- You should ask them: 'What is wholesome? What is unwholesome?'
- You should ask them: 'What is blameful? What is blameless?'
- You should ask them: 'What should be practised? What should not be practised?'
- You should ask them: 'What kamma is to my long-term detriment and suffering, and what kamma is to my long-term benefit and happiness?'

Why do you need to do this? Because if you do not understand what is wholesome to do, and what is unwholesome to do, you will not try to do wholesome things, and you cannot avoid doing unwholesome things. There may be things that are wholesome for you to do. But you may never do them, because you do not understand that they are wholesome to do. If you do not understand that they are wholesome to do, you will not want to do them, will you? And there may be things that are unwholesome for you to do. But you may do them again and again, again because you do not understand that they are unwholesome to do. If you do not understand that they are unwholesome to do, you will not want to avoid doing them, will you? So, as a disciple of The Buddha, it is very important to understand what is wholesome, what is unwholesome; what is blameful, what is blameless; what is to be practised, and what is not to be practised, etc.[255]

Then, when you have learned the difference between wholesome and unwholesome kamma, you should try to understand it with your direct insight knowledge. This means:

- You should try to restrain yourself from accomplishing unwholesome kamma, of body, speech, and mind.
- You should try to restrain yourself from doing what is blameful, through body, speech, and mind.
- You should try to restrain yourself from practising that which should not be practised, through body, speech, and mind.

Instead, you should try to do things that are to your long-term benefit and happiness. What are those things? Only wholesome kammas:

- You should observe the precepts and purify your conduct.
- Based on that virtue, you should make offerings to ascetics and Brahmins.
- You should learn The Buddha's Word off by heart.
- You should learn the Dhamma thoroughly, with care and respect.
- You should discuss knotty points, and the explanations in the Texts, commentaries, etc.
- You should practise samatha and vipassanā up to the Formations-Equanimity Knowledge *(Saṅkhār·Upekkhā·Ñāṇa)*.

That way, you first understand the wholesome and unwholesome by learning knowledge, and then you understand them by your direct insight knowledge.

Then will you understand that all these things are wholesome kammas; they produce wisdom and happiness. But they produce only mundane wisdom and happiness. If you want the highest wisdom and happiness, if you want to achieve permanent happiness, you should try to attain Arahantship: that is best.

CONCLUSION

Now, please listen to The Buddha's summary of the fourteen explanations He gave to Subha.

Thus indeed, student,

[1] **the practice that leads to a short life leads to a short life;**
[2] **the practice that leads to a long life leads to a long life;**
[3] **the practice that leads to much sickness leads to much sickness;**
[4] **the practice that leads to being without much sickness leads to being without much sickness;**
[5] **the practice that leads to ugliness leads to ugliness;**
[6] **the practice that leads to good looks leads to good looks;**
[7] **the practice that leads to lack of influence leads to lack of influence;**
[8] **the practice that leads to great influence leads to great influence;**
[9] **the practice that leads to poverty leads to poverty;**
[10] **the practice that leads to wealth leads to wealth;**
[11] **the practice that leads to a low birth leads to a low birth;**
[12] **the practice that leads to a high birth leads to a high birth;**
[13] **the practice that leads to stupidity leads to stupidity;**
[14] **the practice that leads to wisdom leads to wisdom.**

And The Buddha repeated His brief explanation of kamma:

Kamma owners, student, beings are kamma heirs, kamma-born, kamma-bound, and kamma-protected.

Kamma distinguishes beings, that is, as inferior and superior.

We have given examples of the results of these fourteen ways of conduct. In the examples, you saw eminent Mahātheras who had accomplished pāramī in their previous lives. They accomplished wholesome kammas such as purifying their virtue, making offerings, learning the Texts, and cultivating samatha and vipassanā meditation. And as we explained many times, the cause of such wholesome kammas is ignorance, craving, and clinging. And just as ignorance, craving, and clinging are varied, so are the wholesome kammas varied. With that variety of kamma consciousnesses *(kamma·viññāṇa)*, variety of consciousnesses associated with kammic potency, there is a corresponding variety in the way they are experienced: either in this same life, or in a subsequent life. This principle of variety applies also to the maturing of unwholesome kammas.

We hope that, after listening to all these stories, you may understand how beings are varied because of the variety of their past kamma. We hope also that you may understand that the variety of kamma is rooted in the variety of ignorance, craving, and clinging.[824/*256*] The variety of kamma rooted in the variety of

[824] VsM.xvii.593 *'Avijjā·Paccayā·Saṅkhāra·Pada·Kathā'* ('Discussion of the Ignorance-as-Cause-Formations Phase') PP.xvii.63 explains: 'His non-abandonment of... ignorance about the four truths in particular prevents him from recognizing as suffering the kind of suffering called the fruit of merit, which is fraught with the many dangers beginning with birth, ageing, disease, and death, and so he embarks upon the formation of merit classed as bodily, verbal, and mental formations in order to attain that [suffering], like one desiring celestial nymphs jumps over a cliff. Also not seeing how that fruit of merit

(Please see further next page.)

ignorance, craving, and clinging, produces the variety of beings, who according to reality *(yathā·bhūta)* are nothing more than the five clinging-aggregates.

---

reckoned as pleasure eventually breeds great distress owing to the suffering in its change and that it gives little satisfaction, he embarks upon the formation of merit of the kinds already stated, which is the condition for that very [suffering in change], like a moth that falls into a lamp's flame, and like the man who wants the drop of honey and licks the honey-smeared knife-edge. Also not seeing the danger in the indulgence of sense-desires, etc., with its results, [wrongly] perceiving pleasure and overcome by defilements, he embarks upon the formation of demerit that occurs in the three doors, like a child who plays with filth, and like a man who wants to die and eats poison. Also, unaware of the suffering due to formations and suffering-in-change [inherent] in kamma results in the immaterial sphere, owing to the perversions of [wrongly perceiving them as] eternal, etc., he embarks upon the formation of the imperturbable which is a mental formation, like one who has lost his way and takes the road to a goblin city. So formations exist only when ignorance exists, not when it does not.' See also 'Dependent Origination', p.109, and endnotes 74, p.234 and 76, p.20.

ENDNOTES CHAPTER IV
(SUTTA REFERENCES ETC.)

[241] VsM.viii.167 *'Maraṇa·Ssati·Kathā'* ('Discussion of Death-Mindfulness') PP.viii.2-3 explains that there are two types of death.

1) timely death *(kāla·maraṇaṁ)*: 1.1) by exhaustion of merit *(puñña·kkhayena)*: exhaustion of the rebirth-link producing kamma's maturation of result, even though the conditions for attaining the (full) life span still exist. 1.2) by exhaustion of life span *(āyu·kkhayena)*: exhaustion of the 100-year lifespan of men of the present time, since: i) there does not exist destination achievement *(gati·sampatti)* (VsMṬ: as that of devas); ii) time achievement *(kāla·sampatti)* (as at the beginning of the aeon); iii) nutriment achievement *(āhāra·sampatti)* (superior nutriment as have the Uttarakurus, etc.), etc. (see 'Achievement', p.210). 1.3) by exhaustion of both *(ubhaya·kkhayena)*.

2) untimely death *(akāla·maraṇaṁ)*: by way of kamma-interrupting kamma *(kamm·upacchedaka·kamma·vasena)* (= interceptive kamma *(upaghātaka·kamma)*). 2.1) death of those with their continuity cut off by such kamma as is capable of making one fall *(cāvana·samatthena)* from one's station in that very moment, such as Māra Dūsi, King Kalābu, etc. (VsMṬ: also the demon Nanda *(Nanda·yakkha)*, and the student Nanda *(Nanda·māṇavaka)*). 2.2) death of those with their continuity cut off by assault from a homicide, etc. (or by an accident, illness, etc.). The examples given under 2.1 are some of those who were swallowed up by the earth because of their immediately preceding evil kamma. DhpA.v.10 *'Uppalavaṇṇa·Ttherī·Vatthu'* ('The Uppalavaṇṇa-Elderess Case') describes this happening to the student Nanda, after he had raped the Arahant bhikkhuni Uppalavaṇṇa: for the remaining examples, see index, p.387.

[242] The Pali Texts give two versions of this story. DhPA.x.9-12 *'Daṇḍa·Vagga'* ('The Violence Chapter') explains that he killed his parents even as they cried out for him to save himself. JA.v.522 *'Sarabhaṅga·Jātaka·Vaṇṇanā'* ('Description of the Sarabhaṅga Jātaka') explains that he repented as they cried out, and did not kill them.

[243] This point is discussed in MiP.IV.i.1 *'Kat·Ādhikāra·Saphala·Pañho'* ('Question about Fulfilment of the Complete-Result'). Also discussed is the case of Prince Suppabuddha, who obstructed The Buddha's almsround: see 'Stupid Prince Suppabuddha', p.295.

[244] The Buddha discusses the four divine abidings in, for example, D.i.13 *'Te·Vijja·Suttaṁ'* ('The Three-Sciences Sutta'), and A.III.II.ii.5 *'Kesamutti·Suttaṁ'* ('The Kesamutti Sutta').

[245] In Myanmarese, 'precious time' is the time in which good people do good things. It derives from A.III.III.v.10 *'Pubbaṇha·Suttaṁ'* ('The Morning Sutta'). There, The Buddha explains that those who do good deeds *(su·caritaṁ caranti)* through body, speech and mind, in the morning, at noon, and in the evening/night, their morning, noon, and night is good. That means their constellation, luck, etc. are good *(su)*: good moment *(su·khaṇo)*, good instant *(su·muhutto)*. Also in SuN.ii.4 *'Maṅgala·Suttaṁ'* ('The Blessing Sutta'), The Buddha speaks in this way of 'luck' as good kamma by body, speech, and mind.

[246] The Buddha explains how the four divine abidings may serve as the basis for vipassanā in, for example, M.II.ii.4 *'Mahā·Mālukya·Suttaṁ'* ('The Great Mālukya Sutta': see endnote 268, p.353), and A.VIII.II.ii.3 *'Saṁkhitta·Suttaṁ'* ('The "Brief" Sutta'), as does the Venerable Ānanda in M.II.i.2 *'Aṭṭhakanāgara·Suttaṁ'* ('The Aṭṭhakanāgara Sutta').

[247] In his 'Towards Eternal Peace', prepared for delivery at the United Nations, the Most Venerable Pa-Auk Tawya Sayadaw explains how wars are caused by possessiveness *(issā)* and envy *(macchariya)*: his text is based on The Buddha's explanation to Sakka, in D.ii.8 *'Sakka·Pañhā·Suttaṁ'* ('The Sakka's Questions Sutta').

[248] In A.V.III.v.8 *'Sa·Ppurisa·Dāna·Suttaṁ'* ('The True-Man's Offering Sutta'), The Buddha explains five ways in which the True Man makes an offering. The primary result for all of them is wealth, but there can be also a secondary result. That is, 1) if one makes offerings with faith (AA: in the efficacy of offering and in its result), it leads also to good

looks; 2) if one makes offerings with respect, one's children/wife/slaves/servants/workers will pay attention to what one says, and understand; 3) if one makes offerings at the right time (AA: not waiting till one's old age), much wealth will come to one early in life; 4) if one makes offerings without stint, one will enjoy superior sensual pleasures; 5) if one makes offerings without harming oneself or others, one will not lose wealth to elements/kings/ thieves/unloved heirs. The opposite give the opposite results.

[249] *NIMMĀNARATI:* the fifth of the six deva worlds in the sensual world. The Buddha mentions it in, for example, A.III.II.ii.10 *'Uposatha·Suttaṁ'* ('The Uposatha Sutta').

[250] Just before one is ordained, one's hair and beard are shaved off. And one is usually instructed to reflect on the repulsiveness of one's hair of the head, hair of the body, nails, teeth and skin, as the shaving takes place. When the candidate's pāramī are right, this first meditation may provide the right conditions for such kamma to mature by which the candidate attains a Path&Fruition. Sīvali, however, was instructed to meditate on his seven-year suffering in the womb.

[251] In D.iii.3 *'Cakka·Vatti·Sīha·Nāda·Suttaṁ'* ('The Wheel-Turning Lion's-Roar Sutta'), The Buddha explains that whereas in His day those who honour their elders and betters are praised/honoured, in the future, those who do not do so will be praised/honoured.

[252] Making offerings with respect leads not only to wealth but also to receiving respect from family and associates: see endnote 248, p.303.

[253] BLAMEFUL *(sāvajjaṁ)*/BLAMELESS *(an·avajjaṁ)*: in M.II.iv.8 *'Bāhitika Sutta'* ('The Cloak Sutta'), the Venerable Ānanda explains blameful conduct as bodily/verbal/mental conduct that is criticized by the wise, that is unwholesome, that harms oneself, another, or both, that increases unwholesome things and decreases wholesome things, and that has painful results. Blameless conduct is the opposite. In A.IV.V.iv.4 *'Sāvajja·Suttaṁ'* ('The "Blameful" Sutta'), The Buddha defines the blameful as such conduct for which one is put in hell, including blameful view. Blameless is the opposite, for which one is put in heaven. And in A.X.III.iv.7 *'Sāvajja·Suttaṁ'* ('The "Blameful" Sutta'), He defines the blameful as wrong view/intention/speech/action/livelihood/effort/mindfulness/concentration and vice-versa.

[254] This point is discussed in MiP.IV.i.1 *'Kat·Ādhikāra·Saphala·Pañho'* ('Question about Fulfilment of the Complete Result'). Also discussed is the case of the demon who struck the Venerable Sāriputta on the head. (See 'Mischievous Nanda', p.265.)

[255] In, for example, M.I.v.6 *'Mahā·Dhamma·Samādāna·Suttaṁ'* ('The Great Undertaking-Things Sutta'), The Buddha explains: 'Here, bhikkhus, the uneducated ordinary person, who does not see Noble Ones [etc.] ... the things to be followed does not understand *(sevitabbe dhamme na jānāti)*; the things not to be followed does not understand *(a·sevitabbe dhamme na jānāti)*; the things to be engaged in *(bhajitabbe dhamme)* does not understand, the things not to be engaged in does not understand.... [She/he these things not knowing] follows things not to be followed; does not follow things to be followed; engages in things not to be engaged in; does not engage in things to be engaged in.' Contrariwise the Noble Disciple who does see Noble Ones, etc. And then The Buddha explains the four ways of undertaking things *(dhamma·samādānāni)*: 1) that presently painful *(paccuppanna·dukkhaṁ)*, and with a future painful result *(āyatiñ·ca dukkha·vipākaṁ)*; 2) that presently pleasant *(paccuppanna·sukhaṁ)*, and with a future painful result; 3) that presently painful, and with a future pleasant result *(āyatiṁ sukha·vipākaṁ)*; 4) that presently pleasant, and with a future pleasant result. And then The Buddha explains that because the uneducated ordinary person does not understand the type of thing which undertaken leads to a painful result, nor the type of thing that leads to a pleasant result, she/he follows it, does not avoid it *(a·parivajjayato)*, and then experiences the unpleasant result. And the Noble Disciple then again contrariwise.

[256] The Buddha explains it in, for example, A.IV.IV.iii.1(171) *'Cetanā·Suttaṁ'* ('The Volition Sutta'): 'A body there being, bhikkhus, there arises in oneself bodily-volition rooted happiness and suffering [speech/mind there being, there arises in oneself verbal/mental-volition rooted happiness/suffering]: and with ignorance as cause.'

V — Creating a Human Being

Introduction

Now that we have discussed the workings of kamma in much detail, and have gained better understanding of the subject, let us now return to the suttas we were discussing before: the *'Gaddula·Baddha'* suttas, about the clog-bound dog. We said we would return to them, to finish discussing them.[825]

You will remember how, in both *'Gaddula·Baddha'* suttas, The Buddha discusses the round of rebirth *(saṁsāra)*, the running on of beings from rebirth to rebirth. Let us quote The Buddha's words again:

Inconceivable is the beginning, bhikkhus, of the round of rebirth. A first point is not known of ignorance-hindered beings fettered by craving, rushing on and running about.

Now you may better understand what The Buddha means with these words.

As you will remember, in the first *'Gaddula·Baddha'* sutta, The Buddha then explains that in the distant future the oceans of the world will dry up and evaporate, Sineru, the king of mountains, will burn up and be destroyed, and the great earth itself will burn up, and be destroyed. And The Buddha explains that even so the continuous rebirth of beings will not come to an end:

Not even then, bhikkhus, is the suffering of ignorance-hindered beings fettered by craving (who rush on and run about) brought to an end, I declare.

Then, in both *'Gaddula·Baddha'* suttas, The Buddha speaks of a dog that is clog-bound, tied to strong post or pillar:

Suppose, bhikkhus, a dog was clog-bound, and to a strong post or pillar was bound close.

In the first *'Gaddula·Baddha'* sutta, The Buddha explains how the dog can only go round and circle round the post or pillar. And He explains how, in the same way, the uneducated ordinary person *(assutavā puthu·jjano)* can only go round and circle round the five aggregates. The reason is that the uneducated ordinary person regards the five aggregates as self in twenty different ways: materiality as self, self as having materiality, materiality as in self, self as in materiality, and the same for feelings, perception, formations, and consciousness. These twenty ways of looking at the five aggregates are a manifestation of what The Buddha calls the identity view *(sakkāya·diṭṭhi)*.

We cling to the identity view because of ignorance *(avijjā)* and craving *(taṇhā)*. Hence, we can only go round and circle round the five aggregates, which is merely to go round and circle round suffering *(dukkha)*. This going round and circling round is the round of rebirth *(saṁsāra)*.

In the second *'Gaddula·Baddha'* sutta, The Buddha again describes a clog-bound dog tied to a strong post or pillar. But you will remember that He there instead describes how the dog walks always close to that post or pillar, stands close to it, sits close to it, and lies down close to it. And again The Buddha compares the dog to the uneducated ordinary person. This time, The Buddha explains that the uneducated ordinary person regards the five aggregates as: 'This is mine' because of craving; 'This I am' because of conceit; and 'This is my self' because of

---

[825] S.III.I.x.7 *'Gaddula·Baddha·Suttaṁ'* ('The Clog-Bound Sutta'): see "I —'The Clog-Bound Sutta'", p.1*ff.* S.III.I.x.8 *'Dutiya·Gaddula·Baddha·Suttaṁ'* ('The Second Clog-Bound Sutta'): see "II — 'The Second Clog-Bound Sutta'", p.29*ff.* Discussion of the two suttas was interrupted p.35.

the identity view. Because of ignorance, craving, and the identity view, when the uneducated ordinary person walks, stands, sits, or lies down, he does so close to the five aggregates.

Then The Buddha refers to a fantastic picture that some wanderers travelled around with: it was therefore known as the 'wandering picture'. The Buddha explains that the picture is fantastic only because of the mind. And He explains that the mind is even more fantastic than the picture created by the mind. Then He refers to the fantastic variety of beings in the animal world. And He explains that their fantastic variety is also owing to the mind: the mind being even more fantastic. At each simile, The Buddha advises the bhikkhus repeatedly to reflect on the workings of the mind. Let us repeat His words:

Therefore, bhikkhus, one should reflect repeatedly upon one's own mind: 'For a long time this mind has been defiled by lust, by hatred, and by delusion.'

By mental defilement, bhikkhus, beings are defiled; by mental purification, beings are purified.

SUPPOSE, BHIKKHUS, A PAINTER, OR A MAKER OF PICTURES

Having explained the fantastic nature of the mind with the simile of the fantastic painting, and the simile of the animal world, The Buddha goes on to describe how a painter may make a picture:

Suppose, bhikkhus, a painter, or a maker of pictures, with paint or with lac, with turmeric or indigo or crimson,[826] on a well-polished board, or a wall or cloth canvas, were to make a woman's figure or a man's figure, full-featured and limbed.

Now, Buddha compares the painter with the uneducated ordinary person *(assutavā puthu·jjano)*:

So too, bhikkhus, the uneducated ordinary person,
[1] **producing** [anything], **he merely materiality produces,**
[2] **producing** [anything], **he merely feeling produces,**
[3] **producing** [anything], **he merely perception produces,**
[4] **producing** [anything], **he merely formations produces,**
[5] **producing** [anything], **he merely consciousness produces.**

Now, an uneducated ordinary woman or man accomplishes bodily actions, verbal actions, or mental actions every moment of the day, every day. When such actions are intentional, they will be either unwholesome or wholesome volitional formations *(saṅkhāra)* that possess a kammic potency. They are rooted in the defilements ignorance *(avijjā)*, craving *(taṇhā)*, and clinging *(upādāna)*. And so long as the uneducated ordinary woman or man does not practise the way leading to the remainderless cessation of those defilements (does not undertake the threefold training: morality, concentration, and wisdom), so long will the kammic potency of those many different actions always continue to produce its results.[827] And what are the results of those actions?

---

[826] LAC: red colouring secreted by certain insects; TURMERIC: yellowish-brown colouring from plant; INDIGO: blue colouring from plant; CRIMSON: red colouring from certain insects.

[827] In this regard, see quotation endnote 312, p.359.

Merely the five clinging-aggregates *(pañc·upādāna·kkhandha)*:

1) materiality .... *(rūpa)*	4) formations .... *(saṅkhāra)*
2) feeling .... *(vedanā)*	5) consciousness .... *(viññāṇa)*
3) perception .... *(saññā)*	

These five clinging-aggregates are ultimate truth *(paramattha·sacca)*. But according to conventional truth *(sammuti·sacca)*, the five clinging-aggregates are a woman or man. And according to conventional truth, a woman or man can be beautiful or ugly: unwholesome kammas produce an ugly woman or man, wholesome kammas produce a beautiful woman or man.

Thus,[828] when one accomplishes unwholesome or wholesome kammas, one is like an artist creating the figure of a man or a woman on a well-polished board or wall or canvas. The unskilled painter creates an imperfect, ugly figure of a woman or man, whereas the skilled painter creates a perfect, beautiful figure of a woman or man. In the same way, the foolish, uneducated ordinary person accomplishes unwholesome kammas, whereas the Noble Disciple *(sutavā Ariya·Sāvaka)* accomplishes wholesome kammas. Both of them create their figure on the canvas of ***saṁsāra*** (the endless round of rebirth), but one paints on the rough canvas of difficult rebirth in the human world, and unhappy rebirth in the animal world, the ghost world, and the hells etc., whereas the other paints on the smooth canvas of fortunate rebirth in the human world, and happy rebirth in the deva worlds.

Let us then look at some examples of the figure one may create.

The Jealous Venerable Jambuka's Picture

There is the picture painted by the bhikkhu, the Venerable Jambuka.[829] Just like the Venerable Losaka Tissa, whom we discussed earlier,[830] the Venerable Jambuka was a bhikkhu in Buddha Kassapa's Dispensation. He also lived in a hermitage, where a local patron looked after him. And here too, an Arahant one day arrived. The patron liked the Arahant's appearance very much, and paid him much attention. He offered a delicious meal, and excellent robes. He sent a barber to shave him, and sent him a bed to sleep in. When the Venerable Jambuka saw the visitor receive all this attention, Jambuka became very jealous: he could not control his mind, and was overwhelmed by jealousy. He went to the Arahant's dwelling and reviled him. He said:

- 'It would be better for you to eat excrement, than to eat food in this layman's house;
- it would be better for you to tear your hair out with a palmyra comb, than to let his barber cut it for you;
- it would be better for you to go naked, than to wear robes offered by him;
- it would be better for you to sleep on the ground, than to sleep in a bed offered by him.'

The Arahant, not wishing to be the cause of Jambuka's misconduct, left the hermitage the next day.

Owing to jealousy, Jambuka accomplished billions of unwholesome kammas. They would in due course mature, and produce their respective result: some

---

[828] The following explanation is derived from the commentary and subcommentary to the 'The Clogbound Sutta'.

[829] DhPA.v.11 *'Jambuka·Tthera·Vatthu'* ('The Jambuka-Elder Case')

[830] See 'The Envious Venerable Tissa', p.279.

would function as unwholesome productive kammas, some as unwholesome reinforcing kammas, some as unwholesome frustrating kammas, and some as unwholesome interceptive kammas. Unable to control his mind, Jambuka had painted the picture of an ugly man on the canvas of unhappy rebirth in the hells, and difficult rebirth in the human world.

At death, the meditation that Jambuka had practised for twenty thousand years was to no avail, for his jealousy kamma functioned as unwholesome productive kamma to produce rebirth in Avīci Hell. There he underwent the horrific sufferings of beings in that hell. He remained there in the very, very long interval between Kassapa Buddha's Dispensation and Gotama Buddha's Dispensation. When he finally escaped from that hell, and was reborn as a human being, the jealousy kamma frustrated the wholesome kamma that produced his rebirth as a human being.

The wholesome kamma that he had accomplished in Buddha Kassapa's Dispensation produced rebirth to rich parents in Rājagaha. But his jealousy kamma frustrated it so that from infancy he would eat only excrement. He would never wear any clothes, but would go about as naked as a newborn child. He would not sleep on a bed, only on the ground. And when he grew older, his parents had him ordained under the naked ascetics: they pulled his hair out with a palmyra comb. But when they discovered that he ate excrement, they expelled him. So he lived as a naked ascetic, practising all types of austerities. He made people believe he existed on air, and that the only offerings he accepted were butter and honey placed on the tip of his tongue with the tip of a blade of grass. In this way, he became very famous. But actually, at night, he secretly ate excrement from the public latrines.

Now you may compare his past kamma with the present results. Jambuka said all those bad things to the Arahant. But regardless of what he said, the Arahant did not eat excrement; the Arahant did not tear his hair out with a palmyra comb; the Arahant did not go about naked; and the Arahant did not sleep on the ground. As a direct result of having spoken like that to the Arahant, however, Jambuka now did all those disgusting things.

When Jambuka was fifty-five years old, The Buddha saw that Jambuka's pāramī were ready to mature. And He went to spend the night in a cave near Jambuka's abode. During the night, Jambuka saw mighty Brahmas and devas come to pay homage to The Buddha. He was so impressed that the next day he asked The Buddha for a teaching. The Buddha told him about the past evil deeds that now condemned Jambuka to practise austerities for so long, and advised him to give up his evil ways. As The Buddha was speaking, Jambuka grew ashamed of his nakedness, and The Buddha gave him a bathing-cloth to wear. At the end of the talk, Jambuka realized the Arahant Path&Fruition Knowledges. Then the inhabitants of Aṅga and Magadha came to pay him homage and make offerings. He displayed a psychic power, and then paid homage to The Buddha, acknowledging his discipleship to The Buddha. Such are the workings of kamma.

Such workings of kamma are why The Buddha said in the *'Kokālika'* sutta:[831]

When a person has taken birth, an axe is born inside his mouth with which the fool cuts himself by uttering offensive speech.

Now, please listen to how the beautiful Ciñcamāṇavikā painted her picture.

[831] See footnote 716, p.272.

Ciñca-Māṇavikā's Picture

Ciñcamāṇavikā was a very beautiful and intelligent female wanderer *(paribbājikā)*.[832] As The Buddha's Dispensation grew, day by day, The Buddha and His disciples received more and more honour and hospitality from the people. As a result, other teachers and their disciples received less and less, including Ciñcamāṇavikā's order of ascetics. So they persuaded her to try to discredit The Buddha; to pretend to visit The Buddha at the Jetavana monastery.

First Ciñcamāṇavikā would let herself be seen going towards the monastery in the evening, and spend the night in the quarters of another order nearby. The next morning, she would then let herself be seen as if returning from the monastery. When people asked her where she had been, she would say she had spent the night with The Buddha. In this way, she began to paint the picture of an ugly woman, on the rough canvas of hell.

After some months, she tied a block of wood to her belly, pretending to be pregnant. Then, to complete her painting, she approached The Buddha as He was teaching a large crowd, and blamed Him for not looking after her properly in her pregnancy. The Buddha replied:

Sister, whether what you have said is the truth or is untruth, only I and you know.

At this time, Sakka (king of the devas) discovered what was taking place. And he sent down four devas. Taking the form of four mice, they severed the cords that bound the block of wood to Ciñca's belly. It fell down and cut off her toes. The people drove her out of the monastery, and when she stepped outside the gate, the earth opened up, and she was swallowed up by the fires of Avīci Hell. Her picture was now complete: the five aggregates of a being in hell.

Wholesome kamma that Ciñca had accomplished in a past life functioned as productive kamma to produce a human rebirth in our Buddha's Dispensation. But her stronger 'defaming-a-Buddha kamma' functioned now as interceptive kamma, to make its own result arise: rebirth in hell. Identical unwholesome kammas would then function as reinforcing kammas, to increase and prolong her sufferings in hell.[833] Thus are the workings of kamma.[834]

Such workings of kamma are why The Buddha said in the second *'Gaddula-·Baddha'* sutta:[835]

Therefore, bhikkhus, one should reflect repeatedly upon one's own mind: 'For a long time this mind has been defiled by lust, by hatred, and by delusion.'

By mental defilement, bhikkhus, beings are defiled; by mental purification, beings are purified.

The Texts explain that The Buddha was in this way accused of having broken His morality, because He had Himself in a past life slandered a Paccekabuddha.[836]

---

[832] DhPA.xiii.9 *'Ciñcamāṇavikā·Vatthu'* ('The Case of Ciñcamāṇavikā')

[833] See 'The Principle of Identity', p.203.

[834] In Ap.XXXIX.x.70-72 *'Pubba·Kamma·Pilotika·Buddha-Apadānaṁ'* ('Tatters of Previous Kamma Buddha-Narrative'), The Buddha explains that He suffered this accusation because He as one Nanda (the disciple of a Paccekabuddha called Sabbābhibhu) levelled similar accusations at His teacher.

[835] S.III.I.x.8 *'Dutiya·Gaddula·Baddha·Suttaṁ'* ('The Second Clog-Bound Sutta'), quoted p.30.

[836] UA.iv.8 *'Sundarī·Sutta·Vaṇṇanā'* ('Description of the Sundarī Sutta')

Now, please listen to how a bhikkhunī had in a former life painted a picture. You can decide for yourselves whether it is a beautiful picture or not.

GRUDGING CŪḶASUBHADDĀ'S PICTURE

Once, there was a bhikkhunī who acquired the Birth-Recollection Knowledge *(Jāti·Ssara·Ñāṇa)*: knowledge of past births. And she saw that she had once been the wife of our Bodhisatta. Then she wanted to see if she had been a good wife to the Bodhisatta. But she saw that she had in fact caused his death. And she burst into tears in the midst of a crowd of people. Then The Buddha related what had happened.[837]

In that life, the Bodhisatta was an elephant called Chaddanta. He was the king of a herd of eight thousand elephants. And he had two chief queens: Mahāsubhaddā and Cūḷasubhaddā. All the elephants lived in the Kañcanagūhā cave on the banks of Lake Chaddantā.[838] That is in the Himalayas. At that time the Himalayas were covered in forests.

One day in the spring, when the elephants were in a sāla forest enjoying themselves, King Chaddanta gave one of the sāla trees a heavy blow with his body. Cūḷasubhaddā was standing upwind, and received a shower of dry twigs, leaves, and red ants, but Mahāsubhaddā was standing downwind, and received a shower of flowers. It was an accident, but even so, Cūḷasubhaddā got upset, complained bitterly, and held a grudge against Chaddanta.

Another time, the elephants were playing in the lake. And one elephant offered Chaddanta a large lotus flower. He gave it to Mahāsubhaddā. This also upset Cūḷasubhaddā, and she held a second grudge against Chaddanta. With those two grudges as cause, Cūḷasubhaddā trained in morality. Always wanting to be the best in everything, she achieved very pure morality. Her ill-will towards Chaddanta manifested only as ill-will, not as the breaking of any precept.

Then one day King Chaddanta and all the elephants offered wild fruits and requisites to five hundred Paccekabuddhas. When Cūḷasubhaddā offered her fruits, she made a certain aspiration; she painted a certain picture.

First of all, her offering had the four factors for a superior offering.

- She understood that the Paccekabuddhas were of the highest virtue, an unsurpassed field of merit.
- She and all the other elephants were virtuous.
- She had obtained her offering righteously, in the forest.
- She had full faith in that the result of this kamma was great, and reflected on it before offering, while offering, and after offering.

She also understood that a virtuous one's aspiration comes true because of its purity.[839] Accordingly, she painted the perfect image of a woman, complete in all its features. She made five aspirations:

'Venerable Sir, because of this merit, at death,

[1] May I be reborn into King Madda's family as a princess!

[2] May my name be Subhaddā!

---

[837] JA.I.xvi.4 (514) *'Chaddanta·Jātaka·Vaṇṇanā'* ('Description of the Chaddanta Jātaka')

[838] KAÑCANAGŪHĀ: a cave in the Himalaya mountains, mentioned several times in the Pali Texts; CHADDANTĀ: a lake nearby (mentioned by The Buddha in, for example, A.VII.vii.2 *'Satta·Sūriya·Suttaṁ'* ('The Seven-Suns Sutta'): see note 23, p.5).

[839] See quotation, p.267.

[3] May I become the chief consort of the king of Bārāṇasī!
[4] May I be able to persuade the king of Bārāṇasī into fulfilling my every desire!
[5] May I be able to send a hunter to cut off Chaddanta's tusks!'

Why did she want to be reborn into King Madda's family as a princess? She understood that physical beauty is necessary for high social status, and very important if she was to persuade a man to fulfil her every desire: rebirth into King Madda's family would produce both. She wanted to become chief consort to the king of Bārāṇasī, because she knew he was the most powerful of kings. So it is that the painting of a woman, complete in all its features, may appear in the human world according to the painter's desire.

As a result of the merit she had made, she was indeed reborn in King Madda's family as a princess, and got the name Subhaddā. Later she became the king of Bārāṇasī's chief consort. Having now become the most powerful king's chief consort (the most superior woman), one would have thought she would have given up her grudge against an animal who was living in the forest. But, she was unable to forgive Chaddanta, unable to control her mind: she nursed her old grudge, and still wanted to have his tusks cut off.

Therefore, whenever you accomplish unwholesome kamma, please try always to recall this story. Why? Because when the kamma matures, it is not easily overcome.

Subbhadā had all the hunters of the kingdom summoned. And one Sonuttara was chosen for the task: he was the future Devadatta.[840] And, because she knew Chaddanta had great respect for the yellow-robed Paccekabuddhas, Subhaddā told Sonuttara to put on a yellow robe: that way Chaddanta would not harm him.

After seven years, seven months, and seven days, Sonuttara reached Chaddanta's dwelling place. He dug a pit, covered it, and waited inside. As the elephant passed over the pit, he shot him with a poisoned arrow. Then Chaddanta charged Sonuttara, but seeing the yellow robe, he restrained himself. When he heard Sonuttara's story, he showed him how his tusks could be cut off. But Sonuttara was not strong enough to saw them through. So Chaddanta himself took the saw with his trunk. And even though he was wounded, and suffering terrible pain from the cuts already made into his jaws, he sawed through the tusks, gave them to the hunter, and died. Subhadda's picture was now complete.

The magical power of Chaddanta's tusks enabled Sonuttara to return to Bārāṇasī in seven days. When Subhaddā heard that her scheme had resulted in the death of her former beloved and husband, she died of a broken heart.

From this story, we may understand that the desire for revenge brings only agitation, even self-destruction. We may understand that we should instead cultivate forgiveness, and let go of all resentment. To hold ill-will is to do oneself harm greater than the harm others can do. Such are the workings of kamma.

Such workings of kamma are why The Buddha repeated in the second *'Gaddula·Baddha'* sutta:[841]

Therefore, bhikkhus, one should reflect repeatedly upon one's own mind: 'For a long time this mind has been defiled by lust, by hatred, and by delusion.'

---

840 See 'The Venerable Devadatta', p.152.

841 S.III.I.x.8 *'Dutiya·Gaddula·Baddha·Suttaṁ'* ('The Second Clog-Bound Sutta'), quoted p.30.

By mental defilement, bhikkhus, beings are defiled; by mental purification, beings are purified.

MAHĀPADUMA PACCEKABUDDHA'S PICTURE

Then there is the picture painted by Mahāpaduma, the Paccekabuddha-to-be.[842] In Buddha Kassapa's Dispensation,[843] he was a bhikkhu. At that time, he had already developed the pāramī for becoming a Paccekabuddha over two incalculables and a hundred thousand aeons. And as a bhikkhu in Buddha Kassapa's Dispensation, he further developed such pāramī over about twenty thousand years.

One of his wholesome kammas functioned as productive kamma, to produce rebirth as a son of a treasurer in Bārāṇasī. He became a treasurer too, and in that life he committed adultery. At death, an 'adultery kamma' functioned as productive kamma, to produce rebirth in hell. And when he eventually escaped from hell, an indefinitely-effective wholesome kamma functioned as productive kamma, to produce rebirth now as a treasurer's daughter. While she was in her mother's womb, an adultery kamma functioned as an unwholesome frustrating kamma, so that she and her mother suffered a lot of burning sensations. She always remembered this suffering. Furthermore, even though wholesome kamma produced a beautiful appearance, it was frustrated by adultery kamma so that she met much hatred, from even her parents. Later again, when she was given in marriage, the adultery kamma again functioned as frustrating kamma, so that although she was beautiful, intelligent and long-suffering, even her husband hated her, and did not care for her.

My dear audience, please always remember this story, for the sufferings she met reflected exactly the sufferings of those who are victims to adultery.

One day, owing to his hatred for her, her husband even went to the fair with another woman. In tears, she said to him: 'Even if a woman were the daughter of a universal king, she would still live for her husband's happiness. What you do breaks my heart. If you do not want to take care of me, please send me back to my parents. But if you love me, you should take care of me. You should not behave like this.' And she begged her husband to take her to the fair, and he told her to make preparations. This she did, but on the day of the festival, she heard that her husband had already gone to the fair. So she followed him with her servants, bringing the food and drink that she had prepared. On the way, she met a Paccekabuddha who had emerged from the cessation attainment *(nirodha·samāpatti)*.[844]

She descended from her carriage, took his bowl, filled it with food, and offered it to him. When her offering had been accepted, she took hold of a bundle of lotuses, and painted a picture by making five aspirations:

'Venerable Sir,

[1] in every future life, may I be reborn in a lotus!

[2] In every future life, may I be the colour of a lotus!

[3] In every future life, may I become a man!

[4] May everybody who sees me love me as they love this lotus flower!

---

[842] ApA.I.ii.95 *'Pacceka·Buddha-Apadāna·Vaṇṇanā'* ('Description of the Paccekabuddha Narrative')

[843] See 'Appendix 2: The Lineage of Buddhas', p.365.

[844] CESSATION ATTAINMENT: see footnote 436, p.158.

[5] May I know the Dhamma that you know!'

Why did she make these aspirations? She wanted to be reborn in a lotus, because she had already undergone much suffering in her mother's womb. She wanted to have the colour of a lotus, because she liked very much the colour of lotuses. Her life as a woman had caused her much misery, so she wanted to become a man. Nobody had loved her, not even her parents, so she wanted to be loved by everybody who saw her. Lastly, she had developed sufficient pāramī to become a Paccekabuddha, so there was a strong desire to become a Paccekabuddha. In this way, she painted the picture of a perfect man complete in all his features on the canvas of *saṁsāra*, the round of rebirth.

The wholesome kamma of her offering functioned as presently-effective kamma *(diṭṭhadhamma vedanīya kamma)* that intercepted the frustrating adultery-kamma, and produced its own results. Her husband, who suddenly remembered her, sent for her, and from then on not only he but also everybody else showed her much love.

The wholesome kamma of her offering functioned also as subsequently-effective kamma to give her rebirth as a male deva in a lotus in the deva world. He was called Mahāpaduma. He was reborn in the deva worlds over and over again, sometimes as a highborn deva, sometimes as a lowborn deva. In his last birth, at the suggestion of King Sakka, he was born in a lotus in a pond in the park of the king of Bārāṇasī. His queen was childless. She saw the lotus in the pond, picked it, and found the child inside as if in a casket. She adopted the child, and brought him up in great luxury. Everybody who saw him loved him very much. The king issued a proclamation saying that any harem which could feed the baby Prince Mahāpaduma, would receive a thousand coins. For that reason, there was much entertainment in the palace on his account: twenty thousand women entertained him. Prince Mahāpaduma's rebirth into the royal family was again one of his 'offering-to-a-Paccekabuddha kammas' that functioned as productive kamma, and all these different types of happiness were identical kammas that functioned also as reinforcing kammas.

When the prince was about thirteen years old, he became disenchanted with all the entertainment, because his perfections*(pāramī)*, for the attainment of Paccekabuddhahood were now mature, ready to produce their results.

One day, while playing outside the palace gate, he saw a Paccekabuddha. He warned him not to enter the palace as anyone who entered would be forced to eat and drink. The Paccekabuddha turned away. Afterwards, the boy was remorseful, in case the Paccekabuddha had been offended. So he went by elephant to the Paccekabuddha's dwelling, to ask for forgiveness. Coming near, he descended from the elephant and went on foot. Closer to the Paccekabuddha's dwelling, he dismissed his attendants and went on alone. He found the Paccekabuddha's cell empty. Then he sat down, developed insight, and became a Paccekabuddha. All taints were destroyed. The permanent liberation of mind was achieved. Thus are the workings of kamma.

Such workings of kamma are why The Buddha repeated in the second *'Gaddula·Baddha'* sutta:[845]

Therefore, bhikkhus, one should reflect repeatedly upon one's own mind: 'For a long time this mind has been defiled by lust, by hatred, and by delusion.'

---

[845] S.III.I.x.8 *'Dutiya·Gaddula·Baddha·Suttaṁ'* ('The Second Clog-Bound Sutta'), quoted p.30.

By mental defilement, bhikkhus, beings are defiled; by mental purification, beings are purified.

PRINCESS SUMANĀ'S PICTURE

Then there is the picture painted by Princess Sumanā (Jasmine).[846] During The Buddha Vipassī's Dispensation,[847] she was once reborn into a very rich family. And, after her father had passed away, the people obtained the king's permission to entertain The Buddha and his hundred thousand bhikkhus. The first one to do so was a general *(senāpati)*, and for that reason Sumanā's mother was unhappy. So Sumanā promised her that they would still be the first ones to entertain The Buddha and Sangha.

Sumanā filled a golden bowl with delicious milk-rice, and covered it with another bowl. She then tied jasmine garlands round both bowls, and with some slaves went to the general's house.

On the way, she was stopped by his men, but persuaded them to let her pass. As The Buddha approached, she said she wished to offer him a jasmine garland, and put the two vessels into his alms bowl. The Buddha accepted, and gave her offering to a layman devotee to carry to the general's house. Sumanā then painted the image of a virtuous woman, complete in all its features on the canvas of the human and deva worlds. She made three aspirations:

1) 'May my livelihood in every subsequent birth be without worry and longing!'
2) 'May everyone love me as they love jasmine flowers!'
3) 'May my name be Sumanā!'

When The Buddha arrived in the general's house, He was first served soup. But He covered his bowl, and said he had already received milk-rice. Then the layman who carried Sumanā's golden bowls served the milk-rice to The Buddha and to the bhikkhus. The milk-rice was enough to serve The Buddha and a hundred thousand bhikkhus. This miracle happened owing to Sumanā's strong wholesome volition. After The Buddha and the Sangha had eaten the milk-rice, they then ate the main meal, offered by the general. At the end of the meal the general asked who had offered the milk-rice. Being told, he invited Sumanā to his house, and made her his chief consort.

In every subsequent life, she was known as Sumanā, and on the day of her birth, a shower of jasmine flowers fell knee-deep, all owing to her former wholesome kamma functioning as productive and reinforcing kamma to be experienced in subsequent lives.

In her last birth, in Buddha Gotama's Dispensation, she was reborn as Princess Sumanā, sister of King Pasenadi of Kosala. When Anāthapiṇḍika offered the Jetavana monastery to The Buddha and Sangha, Sumanā was seven years old. She attended the ceremony together with five hundred companions: they all brought vases, flowers, and other offerings for The Buddha. After The Buddha's Dhamma talk, Sumanā became a Stream Enterer *(Sot·Āpanna)*.

Once, together with five hundred royal maidens in their royal chariots, she went to see The Buddha, to ask him about the workings of offering *(dāna)*. We shall explain His answers in brief.

---

[846] AA.V.I.iv.1 *'Sumana·Sutta·Vaṇṇanā'* ('Description of the Sumana Sutta')

[847] See 'Appendix 2: The Lineage of Buddhas', p.365.

She asked The Buddha whether there is any difference between two disciples who both have faith, morality, and insight, but one makes offerings*(dāna)* and the other does not. The Buddha explained that when reborn in the deva-world or human world, the offerer is superior in life span, beauty, happiness, honour and power. And if they become bhikkhus, the offerer is invited to receive many requisites. But if they both attain Arahantship, there is no difference in their attainment of Arahantship.

Sumanā wanted to become a bhikkhunī, but delayed it to look after her grandmother.[848] Then when Sumanā was of mature age, her grandmother passed away. And Sumanā went with King Pasenadi to the Jetavana monastery, to ordain. She brought such things as rugs and carpets, which she presented to the Sangha. The Buddha taught her and King Pasenadi Dhamma, and she became a Non-Returner*(An·Āgāmī)*. Then she sought ordination. Seeing that her knowledge was mature, The Buddha uttered a verse of Dhamma. And at the end of the verse, Sumanā attained Arahantship. And then she ordained as a bhikkhunī.

CONCLUSION

That was our last example of how accomplishment of kammas may be likened to an artist painting the figure of a man or a woman on a canvas. The unskilled painter creates an imperfect, ugly figure of a woman or man, whereas the skilled painter creates a perfect, beautiful figure of a woman or man. In the same way, the foolish uneducated ordinary person accomplishes unwholesome kammas, whereas the educated Noble Disciple*(sutavā Ariya·Sāvaka)* accomplishes wholesome kammas. Both of them create their figure on the canvas of ***saṁsāra*** (the endless round of rebirth), but one paints on the rough canvas of difficult rebirth in the human world, and unhappy rebirth in the animal world, the ghost world, and the hells etc., whereas the other paints on the smooth canvas of fortunate rebirth in the human world, and happy rebirth in the deva worlds. That is according to conventional truth*(sammuti·sacca)*.

According to ultimate truth*(paramattha·sacca)*, according to reality*(yathā·bhūta)*, all that has been created is suffering*(dukkha)*, the five clinging-aggregates*(pañc·upādāna·kkhandha)*:[849]

1)	materiality	*(rūpa)*	4)	formations	*(saṅkhāra)*
2)	feeling	*(vedanā)*	5)	consciousness	*(viññāṇa)*
3)	perception	*(saññā)*			

That is what The Buddha explained in the second *'Gaddula·Baddha'* sutta:

So too, bhikkhus, the uneducated ordinary person,
[1] **producing** [anything]**, he merely materiality produces,**
[2] **producing** [anything]**, he merely feeling produces,**
[3] **producing** [anything]**, he merely perception produces,**
[4] **producing** [anything]**, he merely formations produces,**
[5] **producing** [anything]**, he merely consciousness produces.**

According to conventional truth, in the human realm, these five clinging-aggregates are a woman or man. And according to conventional truth, a woman or

---

848 TīGA.i.16 *'Vuḍḍha·Pabbajita·Sumanā·Therī·Gāthā·Vaṇṇanā'*

849 In His first teaching, (S.V.XII.ii.1 *Dhamma·Cakka·Ppavattana·Suttaṁ'* ('The Dhamma-Wheel Setting-in-Motion'), The Buddha explains: 'In short, the five aggregates of clinging are suffering*(dukkha)*.'

man can be beautiful or ugly: unwholesome kammas produce an ugly woman or man, wholesome kammas produce a beautiful woman or man. But whether they are beautiful or ugly, whether they are inferior or superior, they are in all cases impermanent *(anicca)*, suffering *(dukkha)*, and non-self *(an·atta)*.

So long as one's volition produces kamma, so long does one continue to run on in the round of rebirth: unwholesome kammas result in rebirth and the acquisition of aggregates, that is, suffering; wholesome kammas also result in rebirth and the acquisition of aggregates, which is also suffering. But The Buddha is here talking about mundane kammas *(lokiya·kamma)*. It is different with supramundane kammas *(lokuttara·kamma)*. Why? Because supramundane kammas lead to the remainderless cessation of kamma: the unworking of kamma. That is what we shall now discuss. We shall return to the second *'Gaddula·Baddha'* sutta.[850]

[850] S.III.I.x.8 *'Dutiya·Gaddula·Baddha·Suttaṁ'* ('The Second Clog-Bound Sutta'). Discussion of this *'Gaddula·Baddha'* sutta was interrupted p.309.

VI — The Unworking of Kamma[851/852]

After discussing how the uneducated ordinary person is able only to produce aggregates, The Buddha then discusses the characteristics of the five aggregates.

Is Materiality Permanent or Impermanent?

Let us listen to Him discuss materiality *(rūpa)*:

What do you think, bhikkhus, is materiality permanent *(nicca)* **or impermanent** *(anicca)***?**
(Impermanent, Venerable Sir.)
And what is impermanent, is it suffering *(dukkha)* **or happiness** *(sukha)***?**
(Suffering, Venerable Sir.)
Then what is impermanent, suffering, a changing thing *(vipariṇāma·dhamma)***, is it proper to regard that as: 'This is mine** *(etaṁ mama)***; this I am** *(es·oham·asmi)***; this is my self** *(eso me attā)***'?**
(Certainly not, Venerable Sir.)

In the same way, The Buddha discusses the remaining four aggregates: the feeling-, perception-, formations-, and consciousness aggregate. And, of course, in all cases, the bhikkhus confirm that it is improper to regard either of the aggregates as: 'This is mine, this I am, this is my self.' That is namely how the uninstructed ordinary person regards the five aggregates.

How then, are the five aggregates impermanent, suffering, and non-self?

Impermanence

The characteristic of impermanence *(anicca)* is the arising, perishing, and changing of formations: having existed, they cease to exist.[853] As we discussed earlier,[854] the materiality aggregate *(rūpa·kkhandha)* comprises sub-atomic particles that in Pali are called *rūpa·kalāpa*s. If we develop jhāna or access concentration, the light of wisdom arises.[855] With that light of wisdom, one may be able to discern the elements of the *kalāpa*s, and see that as soon as they arise, they perish. The feeling- *(vedanā·)*, perception- *(saññā·)*, and formations aggregate *(saṅkhāra·kkhandha)* comprise mental factors *(cetasika)*: they arise and perish together with consciousness, the consciousness aggregate *(viññāṇa·kkhandha)*. And as we have mentioned now many times,[856] within one snap of the fingers, very many thousand million consciousnesses arise and perish. With proper vipassanā meditation, based on jhāna or access concentration, one may see this directly with one's own insight knowledge. One will directly see how the five aggregates are in fact nothing more than impermanence *(anicca)*. Happiness cannot be found in something that is impermanent. That is why The Buddha says the five aggregates are suffering *(dukkha)*.*[257]*

---

851 The Unworking of Kamma: the undoing of kamma, the making it ineffective, bringing it to nothing.
852 Reference numbers in italics refer to sutta quotations, etc. in endnotes beginning p.353.
853 VsM.xxi.740 *'Upakkilesa·Vimutta-Udaya·Bbaya·Ñāṇa·Kathā'* ('Discussion of Corruption-Free Arise&Perish Knowledge') PP.xxi.6
854 See 'Ultimate Materiality', p.92.
855 See 'The Light of Wisdom', p.88.
856 See, for example, 'The Workings of the Mind', p.41.

Suffering

The characteristic of suffering *(dukkha)* is continuous oppression by arising and perishing.[857] Painful feelings of the body are suffering and painful feelings of the mind are suffering. But also pleasant feelings are suffering, because they are impermanent, which means they will change: when they change, there is suffering. The same with equanimous feelings. They too are impermanent, which means they will also change.[258] And according to conventional truth, when the five aggregates arise at rebirth, impermanence arises as ageing, sickness,[259] and death. And at the next birth, it is again ageing, sickness, and death, etc. Thus the five aggregates are impermanent, and changing all the time: that means they are suffering. Ultimately, they can never comprise happiness.[257] That is why The Buddha says the five aggregates are a burden *(bhāra)*:[858] He even says they are Māra.[859]

Non-Self

The characteristic of non-self *(an·atta)* is that the five aggregates are beyond control.[260] One cannot decide, for example: 'I want the five aggregates to be like this, not like that!' Or, 'In this life, I want to see, hear, smell, taste, touch only pleasant objects! No pain, no change, and no ageing, sickness and death, please!' We cannot control the five aggregates in that way. So how can we say there is a self? That is why The Buddha asks the bhikkhus whether it is proper to regard the five aggregates as: **'This is mine** *(etaṁ mama)*; **this am I** *(es·oham·asmi)*; **this is my self** *(eso me attā)*.' And the bhikkhus agree by saying it is certainly not proper to regard the five aggregates in that way.

Clinging to Suffering

Here we need to understand that when one delights in the five aggregates, it means one in fact delights in suffering.[261] When one regards the five aggregates as associated with a self, it means one in fact regards suffering as self, and one clings to suffering as self:[262] one takes suffering as one's refuge. Doing so, one cannot ever understand the Noble Truth of Suffering. If one does not understand the Noble Truth of Suffering, one cannot ever understand the Noble Truth of the Origin of Suffering, or the Noble Truth of the Cessation of Suffering: that means one will never escape suffering. Like the dog bound to the post, one will always be bound to the five aggregates. One will continue being reborn again and again to renewed birth, renewed ageing, renewed sickness, and renewed death.[263] So it is not difficult to understand that it is improper to regard the aggregates as associated with a self.

---

[857] VsM.ibid.

[858] S.III.I.iii.1 *'Bhāra·Suttaṁ'* ('The Burden Sutta')

[859] S.III.II.i.1 *'Māra·Suttaṁ'* ('The Māra Sutta')

THEREFORE, BHIKKHUS, ANY WHATSOEVER MATERIALITY

Having established how the aggregates should not be regarded, The Buddha then explains how the aggregates rightly should be regarded, according to reality *(yathā·bhūta)*, with Right Wisdom *(Sammā·Paññā)*, that is, insight wisdom *(vipassanā·paññā)*:

Therefore, bhikkhus, any whatsoever materiality,
[1-3] **past, future, or present** *(atīt·ānāgata·paccuppannaṁ)*,
[4-5] **internal or external** *(ajjhattaṁ vā bahiddhā vā)*,
[6-7] **gross or subtle** *(oḷārikaṁ vā sukhumaṁ vā)*,
[8-9] **inferior or superior** *(hīnaṁ vā paṇītaṁ vā)*,
[10-11] **far or near** *(yaṁ dūre santike vā)*,
all this materiality *(sabbaṁ rūpaṁ [evam·etaṃ])*, **in this way is to be regarded according to reality and with Right Wisdom as: 'This is not mine** *(n·etaṁ mama)*, **I am not this** *(n·eso·ham·asmi)*, **this is not my self** *(na meso attā)*.'

In the same way, The Buddha explains how the remaining aggregates should be regarded with insight knowledge: the aggregate of eleven categories of feeling, and the aggregates of eleven categories of perception, formations, and consciousness.[860] To be able to discern them one needs, of course, to have developed the light of wisdom, which arises with jhāna or access concentration.[861] Otherwise one cannot discern the five aggregates, for they can be discerned only by the wisdom eye *(paññā·cakkhu)*.[264]

What do these eleven categories mean? Let us discuss them one by one, first with relation to the aggregate of eleven categories of materiality *(rūpa)*.[862]

MATERIALITY

Earlier we discussed materiality *(rūpa)*. It is:[863]

- The four great essentials *(mahā·bhūtā)*: earth-, water-, fire-, and wind element.
- Materiality derived from the four great essentials *(mahā·bhūtānaṁ upādāya·rūpaṁ)*:[864] twenty-four kinds of materiality, such as colour, odour, flavour, nutritive essence, life faculty, heart-materiality, sex-materiality, and translucent materiality.

1-3) MATERIALITY PAST, FUTURE, OR PRESENT

By **any whatsoever materiality** *(yaṁ kiñci rūpaṁ)*, The Buddha means all materiality without exception. By **any whatsoever materiality, past, future, or present** *(atīt·ānāgata·paccuppannaṁ)*, He means past, future, or present materiality seen in four ways:

1) According to extent *(addhā)*, materiality that arose before the arising of this life's rebirth-linking consciousness is past (materiality of past lives). Materiality that arises after the arising of this life's decease consciousness is future

---

[860] See also quotation at 'The Five Clinging-Aggregates', p.91.
[861] For details, see 'The Light of Wisdom', p.88.
[862] All details taken from The Buddha's explanations in Vbh.I.i *'Suttanta·Bhājanīyaṁ'* ('Suttanta Classification') and from VbhA/VbhT; VsM.xiv.447 *'Rūpa·Kkhandha·Kathā'* ('Discussion of Materiality Aggregate') PP.xiv.73 & VsM.ibid.493-503 *'Atīt·Ādi·Vibhāga·Kathā'* ('Discussion of the Past, etc. Classification') PP.ibid.185-210.
[863] For details, see 'Ultimate Materiality', p.92.
[864] DERIVED MATERIALITY: so-called because it derives from, depends upon, the four great essentials. The Texts compare it to plants, which grow dependent on the earth.

materiality (materiality of future lives). And materiality that arises in-between is present materiality (materiality in the course of this life).[865]

2) According to continuity *(santati)*, materiality of one series of generations of temperature- or nutriment-born rūpa-kalāpas is present; of a previous series is past; and of a subsequent series is future.[866] Consciousness-born materiality born of one mental process or one attainment is present, of a previous mental process, etc., is past; of a subsequent is future. Kamma-born materiality is past, future and present according to the materiality that supports it.
3) According to period *(samaya)*, materiality that arose as a continuity in one minute, during one morning, evening, day, etc., is present. Previous materiality is past, and subsequent is future.
4) According to moment *(khaṇa)*, materiality of one arising, standing, and dissolution is present. Previous such materiality is past, and subsequent is future.

Here, of course, for the practice of insight *(vipassanā)*, only the momentary past, future, and present apply.[867] To see materiality according to reality is to see only ultimate materiality: the individual element of each type of rūpa-kalāpa as it arises, stands, and dissolves. That means the Noble Disciple discerns the impermanence, suffering, and non-self nature of materiality moment by moment in the present life, in the past lives that have been discerned, and in the future lives that have been discerned.[868] And the same for temperature-, nutriment-, and consciousness-born materiality moment by moment, and in the smaller periods of present, past and future.

4-5) MATERIALITY INTERNAL OR EXTERNAL

Materiality internal or external *(ajjhattaṁ vā bahiddhā vā)*: here, The Buddha is referring to one's own materiality as internal, and others' materiality as external. Also, the internal bases (eye-, ear-, nose-, tongue-, and body base) are internal, whereas their objects (the external bases: sight-, sound-, odour-, flavour-, and tangible base) are external. And here again, we need to remember that the eye base is not the lump of flesh sitting in the eye socket: that is a concept. According to reality, it is non-existent.[869] One cannot do vipassanā on things that do not exist. When The Buddha speaks of the eye, the eye element, the eye door, and the eye base, He means the eye translucency *(cakkhu·pasāda)*: the tenth element of eye decad-kalāpas: that is the existent eye.[870] The same for the other bases.

---

[865] Explaining present extent, VsM.xiii.416 *'Pakiṇṇaka·Kathā'* ('Discussion of the Miscellaneous') PP.xiii.114 refers to M.III.iv.1 *'Bhaddeka·Ratta·Suttaṁ'* ('The Excellent-Night Sutta'), but see endnote 147, p.244.

[866] SERIES OF GENERATIONS: for details, see 'The Four Origins of Materiality', p.97.

[867] VsM.xiv.494 *'Atīt·Ādi·Vibhāga·Kathā'* ('Discussion of the Past, etc. Classification') PP.ibid.191 explains that only the momentary is not illustrative *(ni·ppariyāya)*, as it is actual and real. But the others are illustrative *(sapariyāya)*, as they serve only to make clear and explain.

[868] VsMṬ.xx.725 *'Udaya·Bbaya·Ñāṇa·Kathā·Vaṇṇanā'* ('Description of the Discussion of the Arise&Perish Knowledge') explains that having seen the arising and perishing of formations in the present, one then sees it in past and future.

[869] See footnote 280, p.93.

[870] In Vbh.II.156 *'Āyatana·Vibhaṅgo'* ('Base Analysis'), The Buddha explains: 'Therein, what is the eye base? The eye that, deriving from the four great essentials, is translucent, belonging to oneself, invisible, impingent… this is the eye, this is the eye element,

(Please see further next page.)

6-7) MATERIALITY GROSS OR SUBTLE

Materiality gross or subtle*(oḷārikaṁ vā sukhumaṁ vā)*: here, The Buddha is referring to the twelve bases as gross: eye-, sight-, ear-, sound-, nose-, odour-, tongue-, flavour-, and body-, and tangible base. They are gross because they impinge upon each other: a sight impinges upon the eye, and eye consciousness arises, etc. The remaining types of materiality (such as nutritive-essence, life faculty, heart-materiality, and sex-materiality) do not impinge, which means they are seen as subtle.

8-9) MATERIALITY INFERIOR OR SUPERIOR

Materiality inferior or superior*(hīnaṁ vā paṇītaṁ vā)*: here, The Buddha is referring to materiality of superior and inferior beings: a Brahma's materiality is superior to a sensual-sphere deva's materiality; a human being's materiality is inferior to a sensual-sphere deva's materiality, but superior to a ghost's materiality, which is superior to an animal's materiality, etc. The same applies to the external materiality in their realms of existence. And material things that civilized people consider agreeable and inoffensive are superior, whereas the things they consider disagreeable and offensive are inferior.[871] In terms of vipassanā practice, however, materiality that arises owing to unwholesome kamma is inferior, whereas materiality that arises owing to wholesome kamma is superior.

10-11) MATERIALITY FAR OR NEAR

Materiality far or near*(yaṁ dūre santike vā)*: here, The Buddha is referring to materiality in terms of space*(okāsa)*.[872] Thus, one's own materiality is near, whereas another's materiality is far. Materiality inside one's room is near, whereas materiality outside on the monastery grounds is far. Materiality on the monastery grounds is near, whereas materiality outside is far. Materiality within the country is near, materiality outside the country is far, etc.

That concludes our explanation of the eleven categories of materiality which make up the materiality aggregate. One needs to contemplate all those categories of materiality as impermanent, suffering, and non-self. Then there are the eleven categories of feelings that make up the feeling aggregate.

FEELINGS

The Buddha speaks of feelings in many ways. The main way is the three types of feeling*(vedanā)*:[873]

1) Pleasant feeling*(sukha·vedanā)*
2) Painful feeling*(dukkha·vedanā)*
3) Neither-painful-nor-pleasant feeling*(a·dukkha·ma·sukha·vedanā)*: that is, neutral feeling.

---

this is the eye faculty, this is a world, this is a door....'

871 VbhA.ibid refers here to accountants, chief ministers, lords, men of property, and merchants. And it explains that although pigs may be happy to eat dung, and unhappy to lie down on a fine couch, they confuse the agreeable with the disagreeable because of perception-perversion. See 'The Four Perversions', p.330.

872 subtle materiality is far, because it is difficult to discern, and gross materiality is near, because it is easy to discern

873 M.II.i.9 *'Bahu·Vedaniya·Suttaṁ'* ('The Many Kinds of Feeling Sutta')

1-3) FEELINGS PAST, FUTURE, OR PRESENT

Whatever feeling past, future, or present*(atīt·ānāgata·paccuppannā)*: here again, The Buddha is referring to all feelings without exception. By **past**, **future** and **present**, He means the same four as with materiality.

1) According to extent*(addhā)*, feelings that arose before the arising of this life's rebirth-linking consciousness are past (feelings of past lives). Feelings that arise after the arising of this life's decease consciousness are future feelings (feelings of future lives). And feelings that arise in-between are present feelings (feelings in the course of this life).
2) According to continuity*(santati)*, feelings of one mental process or attainment, or with one object, are present; of a previous mental process, etc., are past; of a subsequent are future. For example, the feeling that arises while seeing a certain Buddha image, while making a certain offering, while listening to a certain Dhamma talk, etc. are present.[874] Such previous events are past, and such subsequent events are future.
3) According to period*(samaya)*, feelings that arose in one minute, during one morning, evening, day, etc., are present. Previous feelings are past, and subsequent future.
4) According to moment*(khaṇa)*, the feeling of one arising, standing, and dissolution of consciousness is present. Previous such feelings are past, and subsequent are future.

4-5) FEELINGS INTERNAL OR EXTERNAL

Feeling internal or external*(ajjhattā vā bahiddhā vā)*: here, The Buddha is referring to one's own feelings as internal, and others' feelings as external.

6-7) FEELINGS GROSS OR SUBTLE

Feeling gross or subtle*(oḷārikā vā sukhumā vā)*: here, The Buddha means feelings seen in four ways:

1) According to species*(jāti)*: for example, unwholesome feelings are gross, whereas wholesome feelings are subtle. But wholesome feelings are gross compared to resultant feelings, whereas the Arahant's feelings (which are functional) are subtle.
2) According to individual essence*(sabhāva)*: painful feeling is gross, whereas pleasant- and neutral feeling is subtle. But painful- and pleasant feeling is gross whereas neutral feeling is subtle.
3) According to person*(puggala)*: the feelings of one who has jhāna is subtle because there is only one object, whereas the feelings of one with no jhāna is gross because there are many objects.
4) According to mundane and supramundane*(lokiya·lokuttara)*: feelings associated with defilements are gross, whereas feelings dissociated from defilements are subtle.

When discerning feelings in this way, one must not confuse the categories: for example, according to species, bodily pain is a subtle feeling because it is indeterminate (neither unwholesome nor wholesome), but according to individual essence it is gross because it is painful.

---

[874] VsMṬ says it is present even it if it lasts the whole day.

There are many other ways in which one may categorize feelings as gross and subtle. For example:

- Feelings associated with hatred are gross, whereas those associated with greed are subtle.
- Those associated with long-lasting hatred are gross, whereas those associated with brief hatred are subtle.
- Those associated with greed and wrong view are gross, whereas those associated with greed and no wrong view are subtle.
- Feelings of the sensual sphere are gross, whereas those of the fine-material sphere are subtle, although they are gross compared with feelings of the immaterial sphere.
- Feelings associated with offering are gross, whereas feelings associated with morality are subtle, although they are gross compared with feelings associated with meditation.
- Feelings associated with inferior offering, morality, or meditation are gross, whereas feelings associated with superior offering, morality, or meditation are subtle.
- The solely painful feelings in hell are gross, whereas painful feelings in the animal world are subtle, but they are gross compared to painful feelings in the ghost world, and so on up to the highest of the sensual-sphere deva worlds, where painful feelings are only subtle. And the same for pleasant feelings, from the animal world up to the fourth jhāna Brahma plane, and the solely equanimous feelings of the highest Brahma plane, the fifth-jhāna plane, and the immaterial planes.

8-9) FEELINGS INFERIOR OR SUPERIOR

Feeling inferior or superior*(hīnā vā paṇītā vā)*: here, gross feelings are inferior, and subtle feelings are superior.

10-11) FEELINGS FAR OR NEAR

Feeling far or near*(yā dūre santike vā)*: here, gross and inferior feelings are far from subtle and superior feelings. But gross and inferior feelings are near other gross and inferior feelings, and subtle and superior feelings are near other subtle and superior feelings.

That concludes our explanation of the eleven categories of feelings which make up the feeling-aggregate. One needs to contemplate all those categories of feeling as impermanent, suffering, and non-self.

The eleven categories of perception, formations and consciousness should be understood in the same way as the eleven categories of feelings.

The Buddha says each aggregate of these eleven categories is to be regarded *(daṭṭhabbaṁ)* according to reality*(yathā·bhūta)*, and with Right Wisdom*(Samma·Ppaññāya)* as: **'This is not mine, not this am I, this is not my self.'** That is His instructions for vipassanā meditation.

THE COMPREHENSION KNOWLEDGE

Such knowledge of the impermanent, suffering, and non-self nature of the five aggregates, is what we call the Comprehension Knowledge*(Sammasana·Ñāṇa)*: we mentioned it before.[875] It is knowledge of the three characteristics of all groupings. That is:

- comprehending the impermanent, suffering, and non-self nature of the six internal bases (eye-, ear-, nose-, tongue-, body-, and mind base);
- comprehending the impermanent, suffering, and non-self nature of the six external bases (sight-, sound-, odour-, flavour-, tangible-, and dhamma base);
- comprehending the impermanent, suffering, and non-self nature of the eighteen elements (the eye-, ear-, nose-, tongue-, body-, and mind element; the sight-, sound-, odour-, flavour-, tangible-, and dhamma element; and the eye-, ear-, nose-, tongue-, body-, and mind-consciousness element);
- comprehending the impermanent, suffering, and non-self nature of the twelve factors of dependent origination (ignorance, volitional formations, consciousness, etc.).

One contemplates the three characteristics of the five aggregates in this way over and over again.

The Arise&Perish Contemplation Knowledge

As one's insight knowledge becomes deeper and deeper, there then arises the Arise&Perish Contemplation Knowledge*(Udaya·Bbay·Ānupassanā·Ñāṇa)*. With this knowledge, one knows and sees the causal and momentary arising and perishing of the five aggregates at every consciousness moment from the rebirth-linking consciousness up to the death consciousness of every past life one has discerned. One knows the same for this life, and all the future lives one has discerned, up to one's **Parinibbāna**. One knows and sees how the five aggregates are in this way possessed of impermanence, suffering, and non-self. And one knows this also of the insight consciousnesses by which one has known and seen this. Everywhere one looks, in the entire universe, one sees only the arising and passing away of aggregates: their impermanence, suffering, and non-self nature. Again, one contemplates the arising and perishing of the five aggregates in this way over and over again. When one's insight knowledge becomes sharp and bold, one concentrates on only the dissolution of the five aggregates.

The Dissolution-Contemplation Knowledge

With the Dissolution-Contemplation Knowledge*(Bhaṅg·Ānupassanā·Ñāṇa)*, one no longer pays attention to the arising stage of the five aggregates: one pays attention only to their dissolution stage. Again, one practises in this way over and over again. Regarding the aggregates in this way, one gains more powerful knowledge of how they are all possessed of impermanence, suffering, and non-self. Everywhere one looks, in the entire universe, all one sees is dissolution. And one pays attention also to the dissolution of the consciousnesses that with insight know the dissolution of the aggregates.[876]

---

[875] The insight knowledges discussed here are summarized under 'The Sixteen Insight Knowledges', p.111.

[876] VsM.xxi.742 *'Bhaṅg·Ānupassanā·Ñāṇa·Kathā'* ('Discussion of the Dissolution-Contemplation Knowledge') PP.xxi.13 explains: 'Hence the Ancients said: "He sees with insight both the known and the knowledge".'

As one contemplates the five aggregates in this way, again and again, one's insight knowledge becomes stronger and stronger, and eventually the five aggregates appear fearsome to the yogi, because all the time they break up like pottery, all the time they are dispersed like fine dust. If you watch the surface of a river during heavy rain, you will see water bubbles all the time appearing and bursting: that is how the five aggregates now appear to the yogi.[877] Here again, one contemplates the dissolution of the five aggregates in this way, over and over again. As one's insight knowledge becomes more and more profound, seeing the five aggregates dissolve ever and ever again, one eventually becomes disenchanted with the five aggregates.[265]

THUS SEEING, BHIKKHUS

Disenchantment with the five aggregates is the next stage described by The Buddha in the second *'Gaddula·Baddha'* sutta:[878]

Thus seeing, bhikkhus, the educated Noble Disciple *(sutavā Ariya·Sāvako)*
[1] **with this very materiality is disenchanted** *(rūpasmim·pi nibbindati)*;
[2] **with this very feeling is disenchanted** *(vedanāya·pi nibbindati)*;
[3] **with this very perception is disenchanted** *(saññāya·pi nibbindati)*;
[4] **with these very formations is disenchanted** *(saṅkhāresu·pi nibbindati)*;
[5] **with this very consciousness is discenchanted** *(viññāṇasmim·pi nibbindati)*.

When the educated Noble Disciple has become disenchanted with the five aggregates, it means she or he has become dissatisfied with the five aggregates. She or he no longer delights in them, is no longer enchanted by them: be they the aggregates of a human being, a deva, a Brahma, etc.[266] With the arising of such disenchantment, the mind inclines towards Nibbāna. Let us see how this change takes place.

THE EDUCATED NOBLE DISCIPLE IS DISENCHANTED

Disenchantment with the five aggregates has three aspects:[879]

1) The five aggregates appear as fearsome: that is the Fearsomeness-Appearance Knowledge *(Bhayat·Upaṭṭhāna·Ñāṇa)*.
2) Because the five aggregates are fearsome, one realizes they are dangerous: that is the Danger-Contemplation Knowledge *(Ādīnav·Ānupassanā·Ñāṇa)*.
3) Because the five aggregates appear as fearsome and dangerous, one becomes disenchanted with them: that is the Disenchantment-Contemplation Knowledge *(Nibbid·Ānupassanā·Ñāṇa)*.

---

[877] The similes have been taken from VsM.ibid.748/PP.ibid.27: see also 'The Five Voidness Similes'.
[878] S.III.I.x.8 *'Dutiya·Gaddula·Baddha·Suttaṁ'* ('The Second Clog-Bound Sutta')
[879] VsM.xxi.755 *'Nibbid·Ānupassanā·Ñāṇa·Kathā'* ('Discussion of the Disenchantment-Contemplation Knowledge') explains that seeing formations as fearsome and dangerous is the same as becoming disenchanted with them: 'Hence the Ancients said: "Knowledge of Appearance as Fearsome while one only has three names: it saw all formations as fearsome, thus the name 'Appearance as Fearsome' arose; it aroused [the appearance of] danger in those same formations, thus the name 'Contemplation of Danger' arose. It arose, becoming disenchanted with those same formations, thus the name 'Contemplation of Disenchantment' arose." Also it is said in the text [PsM.I.v.227/PD.I.v.81]: "Understanding of Appearance as Fearsome, Knowledge of Danger and Disenchantment: these things are one in meaning, only the letter is different."'

The five aggregates of past, future, and present, of all worlds, appear as fearsome, because inevitably they dissolve. The *Visuddi·Magga* explains it with a simile.[880] Say a woman's three sons had offended the king, and he ordered them to be executed. And the woman went to the execution. When they had cut the eldest son's head off, they set about cutting the middle son's head off. Seeing the eldest son's head already cut off, and middle son's head about to be cut off, the mother lost all hope for the youngest son. She knew he would also have his head cut off. Her eldest son's head having been cut off is like one's having seen past aggregates cease. The middle son's head being cut off is like one's seeing present aggregates ceasing. And the mother's knowledge that the youngest son's head would also be cut off is like one's knowing that future aggregates will also cease. That is how there arises the Fearsomeness-Appearance Knowledge *(Bhayat·Upaṭṭhāna·Ñāṇa)*.

This does not mean that fear and terror arise in the yogi:[881] just knowledge about the inevitable dissolution of the aggregates. If one saw three charcoal pits, they would look fearsome: one would know that no matter which charcoal pit one were to fall into, one would suffer great pain unto death. But that mere knowledge would not make one afraid. In the same way the aggregates of past, future, and present look fearsome, but one is not for that reason afraid. Whatever aggregate one contemplates, it appears fearsome because one sees it as oppressed by dissolution. For that reason also, the five aggregates appear as dangerous.[882]

Wherever one looks, there is no safety to be found. The three types of existence (sensual-, fine-material-, and immaterial existence) appear dangerous, the four great essentials (the earth-, water-, fire, and wind element) appear dangerous, the six internal bases (eye-, ear-, nose-, tongue-, body-, and mind base) appear dangerous, and the six external bases (sight-, sound-, odour-, flavour-, tangible-, and mind-object base) appear dangerous. All destinations appear dangerous: burning with what The Buddha calls the eleven fires.[267] That is, the hells, the animal world, the ghost world, the human world, the sensual-deva realms, the Brahma realms, and the immaterial realms, wherever the rebirth consciousness can arise, all destinations appear to the yogi as burning, blazing and glowing with the fire of lust, the fire of hatred, the fire of delusion, the fires of birth, ageing, and death, and the fires of sorrow, lamentation, pain, displeasure, and despair. The aggregates appear as aggregates of danger, without anything satisfactory, without anything substantial. The Buddha says they appear as a disease *(roga)*, as a tumour *(gaṇḍa)*, as a dart *(salla)*, as misery *(agha)*, as an affliction *(ābādha)*, as only danger *(ādīnava)*:[268] nothing else. That is how there arises the Danger-Contemplation Knowledge *(Ādīnav·Ānupassanā·Ñāṇa)*.

Now we shall ask you one question. What are all these dangerous things? Can we describe them all as one thing only? Yes, we can. We may say that all these things are just the workings of kamma. That is, the accomplishment of kamma,

---

[880] VsM.xxi.750 *'Bhayat·Upaṭṭhāna·Ñāṇa·Kathā'* ('Discussion of the Fearsome-Appearance Knowledge') PP.xxi.30
[881] VsM.ibid.751/PP.ibid.32
[882] VsM.ibid.752 *'Ādīnav·Ānupassanā·Ñāṇa·Kathā'* ('Discussion of the Danger-Contemplation Knowledge') PP.ibid.35-36.

and the results of kamma: the resultant mentality-materiality.[883] That is in fact what now appears dangerous to the yogi.

THE DANGER OF THE WORKINGS OF KAMMA

What do we do when we are in danger? We seek safety, refuge, and shelter from the danger. The workings of kamma now appear as fearsome and as suffering to the yogi. He sees them therefore as dangerous, and he sees safety *(khema)* and happiness *(sukha)* as somewhere with no workings of kamma. And the only place with no workings of kamma is in the State of Peace *(Santi·Pada)*, Nibbāna.[269]

In practical terms, what does the yogi see as fearsome and suffering, and what as safety, happiness, and Nibbāna?[884]

- Arising *(uppāda)* in this life because of past kamma *(purima·kamma)* is fearsome and suffering, whereas non-arising *(an·uppāda)* in this life is safety, happiness, and Nibbāna.
- The occurrence *(pavatta)* of these results of kamma is fearsome and suffering, whereas non-occurrence *(a·pavatta)* of these results of kamma is safety, happiness, and Nibbāna.
- The sign *(nimitta)* of formations is fearsome and suffering, whereas the signless *(animitta)* is safety, happiness, and Nibbāna.
- Accumulation *(āyūhana)* of kamma is fearsome and suffering, whereas non-accumulation *(an·āyūhana)* of kamma is safety, happiness, and Nibbāna.
- Rebirth-linking *(paṭisandhi)* into the next life is fearsome and suffering, whereas no rebirth-linking *(a·ppaṭisandhi)* into a future life is safety, happiness, and Nibbāna.
- The destination *(gati)* of rebirth-linking is fearsome and suffering, whereas no destination *(a·gati)* for rebirth-linking is safety, happiness, and Nibbāna.
- Generation *(nibbatti)* of the aggregates is fearsome and suffering, whereas no generation *(anibbatti)* of the aggregates is safety, happiness, and Nibbāna.
- Re-arising *(upapatti)* of the results of kamma is fearsome and suffering, whereas no re-arising *(an·upapatti)* of the results of kamma is safety, happiness, and Nibbāna.
- Birth, ageing, sickness, death, sorrow, lamentation, pain, displeasure, and despair are fearsome and suffering, whereas no birth, no ageing, no sickness, no death, no sorrow, no lamentation, no pain, no displeasure, and no despair is safety, happiness, and Nibbāna.

Once the arising, standing, and perishing of the aggregates are in this way seen as fearsome and suffering, and the non-arising, non-standing, and non-perishing of the aggregates is seen as safety, happiness, and Nibbāna, it means one is disenchanted with formations, and one's mind inclines naturally towards Nibbāna.[270]

---

[883] In Vbh.vi.234 *'Paṭicca·Samuppāda·Vibhaṅgo'* ('Analysis of Dependent Origination'), The Buddha explains this as kamma existence *(kamma·bhava)*: meritorious-, demeritorious-, and imperturbable formation of kamma. It produces rebirth existence *(upapatti·bhava)*, which is the foundation of the rebirth consciousness in the appropriate realm: the human/fine-material realms, the woeful realms, and the immaterial realms respectively. See also quotations endnotes 65, p.233 and 74, p.234.

[884] This list has been taken from PsM.I.8 *'Ādīnava·Ñāṇa·Niddeso'* ('Exposition of the Danger Knowledge') PD.I.viii.300-305: quoted in VsM.ibid.752 *'Ādīnav·Ānupassanā·Ñāṇa·Kathā'* ('Discussion of the Danger-Contemplation Knowledge') PP.ibid.37. The elaborations are from VsM.ibid.753/PP.ibid.38-42.

That is how there arises the Disenchantment-Contemplation Knowledge *(Nibbid-·Ānupassanā·Ñāṇa).*

As one then continues to contemplate the impermanence, suffering, and non-self of the five aggregates of past, future, present, internal or external, gross or subtle, inferior or superior, far or near, eventually one develops equanimity towards the five aggregates.

EQUANIMITY TOWARDS THE FIVE AGGREGATES

Equanimity towards the five aggregates has also three aspects:[885]

1) There arises the desire and longing to renounce and give up the five aggregates: that is the Release-Longing Knowledge *(Muñcitu·Kamyatā·Ñāṇa).*
2) With the desire for release there is repeated, and increasingly profound, reflection on the five aggregates as devoid of permanence, devoid of happiness, devoid of self, and devoid of beauty: that is the Reflection Knowledge *(Paṭisaṅkh·Ānupassanā·Ñāṇa).* It is the means for release.
3) With the longing for release and the increasingly profound reflection on the voidness of the five aggregates, one sees that they are full of faults: that is the Formations-Equanimity Knowledge *(Saṅkhār·Upekkhā·Ñāṇa).* At this stage, one no longer looks upon the five aggregates as either delightful or fearsome: one looks upon them with equanimity, which means one has finally become detached from them.

We have mentioned the Formations-Equanimity Knowledge very many times. All the Arahants we have discussed were able to attain Arahantship because they developed this knowledge many times in the past, under previous Buddhas. It is the highest mundane insight knowledge there is. If one's pāramī are mature, the next step is the actual attainment of Nibbāna, with Stream Entry.

THE FOUR PERVERSIONS

It is very important to understand this stage of enlightenment. Why? Because this stage marks the big change from being the uneducated ordinary person *(assutavā puthu·jjano)* to becoming an educated Noble Disciple *(sutavā Ariya·Sāvako)*: you will remember how The Buddha discusses these two types of person in the beginning of both *'Gaddula·Baddha'* suttas.[886]

The uneducated ordinary person is enchanted with the five aggregates, thinking they are aggregates of permanence, happiness, self, and beauty. Because of ignorance *(avijjā),* the uneducated ordinary person's understanding of the world (the five aggregates) is distorted; perverted by the four perception-perversions *(saññā·vipallāsa),* the four consciousness-perversions *(citta·vipallāsa),* and the four view-perversions *(diṭṭhi·vipallāsa).*[887]

---

[885] VsM.xxi.778 *'Saṅkhār·Upekkhā·Ñāṇa·Kathā'* ('Discussion of the Formations-Equanimity Knowledge') PP.xxi.79 explains: '...the Ancients said: "This knowledge of equanimity about formations is one only and has three names. At the outset it has the name of Release-Longing Knowledge. In the middle it has the name Reflection Knowledge. At the end, when it has reached its culmination, it is called the Formations Equanimity Knowledge."' The elaborations are from VsM.ibid.780/PP.ibid.80-81.

[886] See 'The Uneducated Ordinary Person', p.6, and 'The Educated Noble Disciple', p.16.

[887] PERVERSION *(vipallāsa)*: 'With distorted apprehension as characteristic is perversion.' *Netti·ppakaraṇa·Pāḷi* IV.52 *'Desanā·Hāra·Sampāto'* ('Discourse on Connotative-Assemblage') *The Guide* IV.ii.492

They are:[271]

1) The perception, consciousness, and view that in the impermanent *(anicce)* there is permanence *(nicca)*.
2) The perception, consciousness, and view that in suffering *(dukkhe)* there is happiness *(sukha)*.[888]
3) The perception, consciousness, and view that in non-self *(an·atta)* there is self *(atta)*. Earlier, we discussed The Buddha's analysis of the uneducated ordinary person's twenty views of self.[889]
4) The perception, consciousness, and view that in the foul *(asubha)* there is beauty *(subha)*.

Thus, the uneducated ordinary person seeks safety and happiness in herself or himself (internal five aggregates), in her or his mother and father, husband and wife, daughters and sons, friends, property, etc. (external five aggregates).[272] Thus, the uneducated ordinary person's perverted understanding of reality makes Nibbāna undesirable: she or he does not want to stop.

CONTEMPLATING VOIDNESS

At this advanced stage of vipassanā meditation, however, one works towards seeing the five aggregates with Right Wisdom *(Samma·Ppaññā)*. One contemplates the five aggregates according to reality *(yathā·bhūta)* as void *(suñña)*.[273] Now, by 'void', The Buddha does not mean that the five aggregates, twelve bases, etc., do not really exist; He does not mean that everything is an illusion: that is wrong view.[274] What does not exist is five aggregates that are permanent, stable, eternal, and not subject to change. And what does in reality exist is five aggregates that are impermanent, suffering, and subject to change.[275] That means they are devoid of permanence, devoid of happiness, devoid of self, and devoid of beauty.

THE FIVE VOIDNESS SIMILES

In the *'Pheṇa·Piṇḍ·Ūpama'* sutta, The Buddha uses five similes to explain how the bhikkhu contemplates the voidness of the five aggregates.[890] First He explains that if one were to see a lump of foam floating down the Ganges River, and one were to examine it carefully, one would see that it was only hollow, only insubstantial. And He compares it to insight meditation on materiality:

So too, bhikkhus, whatever kind of materiality there is, whether past, future, or present; internal or external; gross or subtle; inferior or superior; far or near, if a bhikkhu were to see it *(passeyya)*, **contemplate it** *(nijjhāyeyya)*, **and carefully investigate it** *(yoniso upaparikkheyya)*; **as he saw it, contemplated it, and carefully investigated it, it would appear to him void only, hollow only, insubstantial only. For what substance could there be in materiality?**

That is how The Buddha says one should practise insight *(vipassanā)* on the materiality aggregate. Then He describes how rain falling on water produces water bubbles. If one examines such bubbles, one sees that a bubble arises, then bursts, having no substance. And He compares it to insight meditation on the feelings aggregate:

So too, bhikkhus, whatever kind of feeling there is, whether past, future, or present;

---

[888] For an example, see footnote 871, p.323.
[889] See 'The Twenty Types of Identity View', p.12.
[890] S.III.I.x.3 *'Pheṇa·Piṇḍ·Ūpama·Suttaṁ'* ('The Lump-of-Foam Simile Sutta')

internal or external; gross or subtle; inferior or superior; far or near, if a bhikkhu were to see it, contemplate it, and carefully investigate it; as he saw it, contemplated it, and carefully investigated it, it would appear to him void only, hollow only, insubstantial only. For what substance could there be in feeling?

That is how The Buddha says one should practise insight meditation *(vipassanā-·bhāvanā)* on the feelings aggregate. Then He explains how the bhikkhu practises insight meditation on the eleven categories of perception: they appear to him as void, hollow, and insubstantial as a mirage. And when the bhikkhu contemplates the eleven categories of formations, they appear to him as void as the trunk of a banana tree. You know, a banana tree has a false trunk: it consists of many rolls. If one removes the many rolls, one will find nothing inside. Lastly, The Buddha explains that when the bhikkhu practises insight meditation on the eleven categories of consciousness, they appear to him as void as a magician's illusion, a mere trick, devoid of substance. That is how The Buddha says one should practise insight meditation on the five aggregates.

At this stage, one's insight knowledge is greatly strengthened by one's having contemplated the five aggregates as fearsome and dangerous, and one's having become disenchanted with the five aggregates.

Void of Self and Anything Belonging to Self

Then, as one contemplates the aggregates as void, one understands that they are void of self ('This is my self') as well as void of anything belonging to self ('This is mine').[891] One does not see a self of one's own ('my self');[892] one does not see a self that belongs to another, for example, one's mother ('I am my mother's child'), one's brother ('I am my brother's sibling'), or a friend ('I am my friend's friend'). One does not see another as having a self that belongs to oneself, for example, one's mother ('This is my mother'), one's brother ('This is my brother'), or a friend ('This is my friend'). In the same way one does not see a self that belongs to any property, or any property that has a self.[893]

This understanding of voidness of self, voidness of self's property, voidness of substance, etc., one extends to the world:[276] that is, the six internal and external bases, the five aggregates, the six types of consciousness, contact, feeling, perception, volition, craving, application, and six types of sustainment, the six elements, ten kasiṇas, thirty-two parts of the body, the eighteen elements, the twelve factors of dependent origination, etc., of past, future, and present.[277]

Let One Look on the World as Void, Mogharāja

When one looks upon the world in this way, The Buddha says one cannot be seen by the king of death: Māra. The Buddha explained it once to an ascetic

---

[891] Here, VsM.ibid.760/PP.ibid.53 quotes M.III.i.6 *'Āneñjasappāya·Suttaṁ'* ('The Imperturbable-Wards Sutta'): 'Again and further, bhikkhus, a Noble Disciple, gone to the forest, or gone to the foot of a tree, or gone to a secluded place, reflects in this way: "Void is this of self or of what belongs to self."'

[892] Here, VsM.ibid. again quotes M.III.i.6 *'Āneñjasappāya·Suttaṁ'* ('The Imperturbable-Wards Sutta'): 'Again and further, bhikkhus, a Noble Disciple reflects in this way: "I am not anywhere anyone's possession, nor is there anywhere my possessing of anyone [I belong to no one, and no one belongs to me]."'

[893] VsA.ibid. and MA.ibid. explain that this refers to voidness of self and property of self in both internal and external aggregates.

called Mogharāja.[894/278] He had asked The Buddha how he should look upon the world, in order to escape death. The Buddha's answer was a verse:

> **Let one look on the world as void***(suññato)*, **Mogharāja, always mindful;**
> **Giving up the self view, one may thus outrun death;**
> **Who looks upon the world in this way, the king of death does not see.**

The world*(loka)*: this is the five clinging-aggregates. **Let him look on the world as void***(suññato)*: this means he should look upon the five clinging-aggregates as devoid of permanence, devoid of happiness, devoid of self, and devoid of beauty. **Always mindful**: this means he should always remember to see these four types of voidness in the five clinging-aggregates. If one contemplates the world in this way, one gives up **the self view***(attānu·diṭṭhi)* (the personality view*(sakkāya·diṭṭhi)*), and then may one **outrun death. Who looks upon the world in this, the king of death does not see**:[279] the king of death (Māra) cannot see the one who looks upon the world in this way.[280]

When the yogi contemplates the five aggregates in this way, again and again, his insight improves, and gradually he abandons both fearsomeness and delight towards the five aggregates: instead, he looks upon them with equanimity. He looks upon them as neither 'I', nor as 'mine', nor as 'self'. To explain this, The Buddha uses the simile of the man who has divorced his wife, and has therefore become indifferent towards her.[895]

Divorce from the Five Aggregates

Suppose a man were married to a lovely, desirable, charming wife. And suppose he was so in love with her that it was unbearable for him to be without her for even a moment. If he saw her chatting, joking, and laughing with another man, he would be disturbed and displeased, even unhappy. Why? Because he was looking upon her as 'she is mine', and he was dependent on her alone for his happiness.

Then later he might discover that she had many faults. And he would divorce her. Once divorced, he would no more look upon her as 'mine'. And if he now saw her chatting, joking, and laughing with another man, he would not be disturbed and not displeased, but indifferent and uninterested. Why? Because he no longer looked upon her as 'she is mine'. He was now independent of her for his happiness.

In the same way, the yogi looks upon the five aggregates as impermanent, suffering, and non-self. Then, having seen that there is nothing to look upon as 'I' or 'mine' or 'self', one no longer looks upon them as fearsome or delightful. Instead, one becomes indifferent, and looks upon them with equanimity.

His Mind Retreats, Retracts, and Recoils

When one knows and sees in this way, one's mind retreats, retracts, and recoils from the three types of existence*(bhāva)* (sensual-, fine-material-, and immaterial

---

[894] VsM.xxi.765 *'Saṅkhār·Upekkhā·Ñāṇa Kathā'* ('Discussion of the Formations-Equanimity Knowledge') PP.xxi.60 quotes this verse from SuN.v.15 *'Mogharāja·Māṇava·Pucchā'* ('Young Brahmin Mogharāja's Questions').

[895] The simile is given in VsM.ibid.766/PP.xxi.61-62. It has been taken from M.III.1 *'Devadaha·Suttaṁ'* ('The Devadaha Sutta'). There, The Buddha gives this simile to illustrate the bhikkhu's developing equanimity towards those things that give rise to suffering.

existence). Just as drops of water retreat, retract, and recoil on a lotus leaf that slopes a little, so too one's mind retreats, retracts, and recoils from not only the hells, the animal world, and ghost world, but also the human world, and even the sensual deva-realms, and fine-material-, and immaterial Brahma realms. Just as a bird's feather or a piece of sinew thrown on a fire retreats, retracts, and recoils, so too one's mind retreats, retracts, and recoils from wherever the rebirth consciousness can arise. In this way there arises in him what is called the Formations-Equanimity Knowledge *(Saṅkhār·Upekkhā·Ñāṇa)*.[281]

SEEING NIBBĀNA AS PEACEFUL

At this point, if one's pāramī are ready to mature, one's mind may retreat, retract, and recoil from the five aggregates, no longer pay attention to the five aggregates, **and advance towards the state of peace, seeing Nibbāna as peaceful, taking Nibbāna as object.** If not, one must again and again contemplate the five aggregates as impermanent, suffering, and non-self:[896] even for years. Doing so, eventually one's five controlling faculties will become mature, and one's insight **knowledge will take only Nibbāna as object,** and there arises the first Path&Fruition *(Magga·Phala)*.

Let us now discuss the workings of Path&Fruition.

PATH&FRUITION

There are four Path Knowledges *(Magga·Ñāṇa)* with each their respective Fruition Knowledge *(Phala·Ñāna)*. They are supramundane impulsion consciousnesses *(javana)*, **which take only Nibbāna as object.** As we discussed before, impulsion consciousnesses are volitional formations *(saṅkhāra)*: they perform kamma. While each volitional formation arises and perishes, there remains in that same mentality-materiality continuity the kammic potency *(kamma·satti)*. That potency enables the volition factor of the volitional formations to mature as a kamma result *(kamma·vipāka)* in the future: either in this life or another. A Path Knowledge functions as presently-effective kamma, with its result arising in the next mind moment as its respective Fruition Knowledge *(Phala·Ñāna)*: for example, the Stream-Entry Fruition Knowledge is the kammic result of the Stream-Entry Path Knowledge.

The kamma of a Path Consciousness is unique, however. Why? Take the volition of a mundane consciousness: whether it is volition of the sensual realm (such as the unwholesome volition of killing, stealing, etc., or the wholesome volition of offering, morality or meditation), or it is wholesome volition of the fine-material or immaterial realms, it possesses kammic potency. That potency may mature to produce rebirth into a new existence. It may also mature to produce good or bad results in the course of an existence. But the volition of a Path Consciousness does not work that way. Because it takes the supramundane object Nibbāna as object (the Unformed Element *(Asaṅkhata·Dhātu)*), it destroys defilements, it destroys the kammic potency of one's volition stage by stage: with the Arahant Path-

[896] VsM.ibid.767/PP.ibid.65 explains that so long as the Formations-Equanimity Knowledge is immature, it may be attained very many times in the infinite past. When finally mature, it is called Emergence-Leading Insight *(Vuṭṭhāna·Gāminī·Vipassanā)*, for it emerges from formations to take Nibbāna as object. It may be compared to a land-finding crow. Seeing land, the crow flies in that direction; not seeing land, it returns to the ship: likewise, the mature knowledge seeing Nibbāna as peaceful, emerges unto Nibbāna; the immature knowledge not seeing Nibbāna as peaceful remains with formations.

Knowledge, all defilements will have been destroyed, and the kammic potency of one's volition will have been destroyed completely. One's volition is then purely functional.[282] It is most wonderful.

When we practise jhāna, the jhāna kammas suppress the defilements for a long time: one hour, two hours, etc. And when we practise superior vipassanā, the vipassanā kammas do the same. This is what The Buddha calls mind liberation *(ceto·vimutti)* that is temporary*(sāmāyika)*.[283] But after some time, the defilements reappear. Yes? Even the superior vipassanā kammas that we have just discussed, such as the Formations-Equanimity Knowledge: it is a most superior wholesome kamma, and when it arises, there are no defilements. But as we have discussed, one may progress up to that insight knowledge in the Dispensation of many Buddhas, and still the defilements will return, and one will be reborn countless times.

Why do the defilements re-arise? Because they have only been suppressed. They still exist as latencies*(anusaya)*.[900] Hence, samatha and vipassanā are only temporary liberation from the defilements: mundane liberation*(lokiyo vimokkho)*.[901]

3d: **Mental Phenomena***(nāma·dhamma)* **at the Arising of Supramundane Consciousness** *(Lokuttara·Citta)*[897]

JHĀNA[898]	1st	2nd	3rd	4th	5th
CONSCIOUSNESS*(citta)*	■	■	■	■	■
MENTAL FACTORS*(cetasika)*					
Universals*(sabba·citta·sādhāraṇa)*					
1. contact*(phassa)*	■	■	■	■	■
2. feeling*(vedanā)*	■	■	■	■	■
3. perception*(saññā)*	■	■	■	■	■
4. volition*(cetanā)*	■	■	■	■	■
5. one-pointedness*(ek·aggatā)*	■	■	■	■	■
6. life faculty*(jīvit·indriya)*	■	■	■	■	■
7. attention*(manasikāra)*	■	■	■	■	■
Miscellaneous*(pakiṇṇaka)*					
1. application*(vitakka)*	■				
2. sustainment*(vicāra)*	■	■			
3. decision*(adhimokkha)*	■	■	■	■	■
4. energy*(viriya)*	■	■	■	■	■
5. joy*(pīti)*	■	■	■		
6. desire*(chanda)*	■	■	■	■	■
Beautiful Universals*(sobhana·sādhāraṇa)*					
1. faith*(saddhā)*	■	■	■	■	■
2. mindfulness*(sati)*	■	■	■	■	■
3. conscience*(hiri)*	■	■	■	■	■
4. shame*(ottapa)*	■	■	■	■	■
5. non-greed*(a·lobha)*	■	■	■	■	■
6. non-hatred*(a·dosa)*	■	■	■	■	■
7. ever-evenness*(tatra·majjhattatā)*	■	■	■	■	■
8. tranquillity of [mental] body[899]*(kāya·passaddhi)*	■	■	■	■	■
9. tranquillity of consciousness*(citta·passaddhi)*	■	■	■	■	■

Please continue next page.

Path Kammas, however, do not suppress defilements: because Path Kammas take the Unformed Element as object, they <u>destroy</u> defilements. When a defilement such as wrong view has been destroyed by the Stream-Entry Path

---

[897] The table has been designed according to the combination system *(saṅgaha·naya)*: all combinations of mental phenomena. (AbS.ii.36-37 *'Lokuttara·Citta·Saṅgaha·Nayo'* ('Supramundane Consciousness Combination-System') CMA.ii.19-20, and AbS.ii.33-34 *'Sobhana·Cetasika·Sampayoga·Nayo'* ('Beautiful Mental-Factor Association-System') CMA.-ii.17.)) One column is one type of consciousness, with mental factors shaded.

[898] A Path Knowledge is always associated with jhāna: minimum the first jhāna. See table '1e Supramundane Resultant Consciousness', p.343.

[899] TRANQUILLITY OF [MENTAL] BODY/CONSCIOUSNESS: see footnote 150, p.56.

[900] LATENCIES: see footnote 145, p.55.

[901] PsM.I.v.213 *'Vimokkha·Kathā'* ('Discussion of Liberation') PD.I.v.31

Knowledge, wrong view will not arise again in our mentality-materiality continuity: it is impossible. Not in the remainder of this life, not in the next life, not even if we are reborn for another seven lives.

As we progress from one Path Knowledge to another, more and more fetters, hindrances, defilements, etc. are destroyed: from the very gross to the very subtle. Eventually, absolutely all defilements are destroyed without remainder. And at the arising of the Arahant Path-Knowledge *(Arahatta·Magga·Ñāṇa)*, no defilement of any kind will ever arise again.

THE FOUR PATH KNOWLEDGES

Let us then discuss how the Path Knowledges liberate one from defilements stage by stage, until one is completely liberated from defilements at Arahantship.[903]

STREAM ENTRY

The first Path Knowledge, the Stream-Entry Path Knowledge *(Sot·Āpatti·Magga·Ñāṇa)*, destroys three fetters *(saṁyojana)*: the identity view *(sakkāya·diṭṭhi)*, scepticism *(vicikicchā)*, and rule&rite adherence *(sīlabbata-·parāmāsa)*. The Stream Enterer has now unshakeable faith in The Buddha, Dhamma, and Sangha, unshakeable faith in the threefold training, unshakeable faith in past lives, unshakeable faith in future lives, unshakeable faith in past and future lives, and unshakeable faith in dependent origination.[904] That means the Stream Enterer is no longer able to hold a wrong view about the workings of kamma.[905]

Continued from previous page.

Mental Phenomena *(nāma·dhamma)* **at the Arising of Supramundane Consciousness** *(Lokuttara·Citta)*

JHĀNA	1st	2nd	3rd	4th	5th
Beautiful Universals *(sobhana·sādhāraṇa)*					
10. lightness of [mental] body *(kāya·lahutā)*					
11. lightness of consciousness *(citta·lahutā)*					
12. flexibility of [mental] body *(kāya·mudutā)*					
13. flexibility of consciousness *(citta·mudutā)*					
14. wieldiness of [mental] body *(kāya·kammaññatā)*					
15. wieldiness of consciousness *(citta·kammaññatā)*					
16. proficiency of [mental] body *(kāya·pāguññatā)*					
17. proficiency of consciousness *(citta·pāguññatā)*					
18. rectitude of [mental] body *(kāy·ujukatā)*					
19. rectitude of consciousness *(kāy·ujukatā)*					
Abstinences *(viratī)*					
1. Right Speech *(Sammā·Vācā)*					
2. Right Action *(Sammā·Kammanta)*					
3. Right Livelihood *(Sammā·Ājīva)*					
Non-Delusion *(a·moha)*					
1. WISDOM FACULTY *(paññ·indriya)*[902]					
Total mental phenomena	37	36	35	34	34

Furthermore, with the arising of the Stream-Entry Path is the arising of the Noble Eightfold Path *(Ariya Aṭṭhaṅgika Magga)*: that means there arises Right Speech *(Sammā*

---

[902] WISDOM FACULTY: here, it is Path&Fruition Knowledge/Wisdom: the Stream-Entry-, Once-Return-, Non-Return-, or Arahant Path&Fruition Knowledge/Wisdom. They know Nibbāna. See 'The Five Types of Knowledge', p.58.

[903] VsM.xxii.830 *'Pahātabba·Dhamma·Pahāna·Kathā'* ('Discussion of the Abandoning of the Things to Be Abandoned') PP.xxii.64-75

[904] See quotations endnotes 32, p.24, and 54, p.28.

[905] See quotation endnote 51, p.27.

Vācā), Right Action*(Sammā Kammanta)*, and Right Livelihood*(Sammā Ājīva)*.[284] That means the Stream Enterer is no longer able to kill, to steal, to engage in sexual misconduct, to tell a lie, and is no longer able to drink beer&wine liquor. She or he is also no longer able to engage in possessiveness*(macchariya)*.

Such greed and hatred that can lead to an unhappy rebirth will have been destroyed: she or he is no longer able to accomplish unwholesome kamma of the kind that leads to an unhappy rebirth.

Furthermore, the Stream-Entry Path Knowledge functions as interceptive kamma to cut off all unwholesome kammas (earlier in this life, and in the infinite past) that could mature at death to produce an unhappy rebirth:[906] either an unwholesome subsequently-effective kamma, or an unwholesome indefinitely-effective kamma. Such kammas will all have lapsed.

Stream Entry is not the end of the training, however. The Stream Enterer is still a trainee*(sekha)*,[907] and The Buddha says she or he must not rest content with Stream Entry: effort must be made in this life to attain Arahantship.[285]

What is the Stream Enterer's duty? To do as before:[286] one must contemplate the five aggregates as devoid of permanence, happiness, self, and beauty. Then when one's pāramī mature, one may progress to the second Path Knowledge.

If, however, one dies as a Stream Enterer*(Sot·Āpanna)*, only a wholesome kamma will be able to produce rebirth: either in the human world or in a heavenly world. Wherever it be, one must again contemplate the five aggregates as devoid of permanence, happiness, self, and beauty. And one will for sure attain Arahantship within seven lives, either as a human being, deva or Brahma. How soon depends on one's effort and pāramī.[287]

Once-Return

The second Path Knowledge, the Once-Return Path Knowledge*(Sakad·Āgāmi·Magga·Ñāṇa)*, destroys no defilements, but further weakens the fetters of sensual greed, and hatred. And the Once Returner*(Sakad·Āgami)* will for sure attain Arahantship within two lives, either as a human being, deva, or Brahma. How soon depends on her or his effort and pāramī.[288]

Then again, be it in the human world or a heavenly world, the Once Returner's duty is to contemplate formations as devoid of permanence, happiness, self, and beauty. Then when one's pāramī mature, one may progress to the third Path Knowledge.

Non-Return

The third Path Knowledge, the Non-Return Path Knowledge*(An·Āgāmi·Magga·Ñāṇa)*, destroys any remaining sensual greed (sensual lust), and hatred, including remorse. One is no longer able to engage in sexual conduct, or slander, harsh speech, or ill-will.

The Non-Returner*(An·Āgāmi)* is so called because the Non-Return Path Knowledge functions as interceptive kamma to cut off all kammas (earlier in this life, and in the infinite past) that could mature at death to produce rebirth in the sensual realm: either wholesome subsequently-effective kammas, or wholesome indefi-

---

[906] See quotation endnote 56, p.28.

[907] See also 'Eight Noble Individuals', p.16.

nitely-effective kammas. They will all have lapsed. The Non-Returner will never return to the human or sensual deva worlds.

At the death of a Non-Returner, only a jhāna kamma will be able to produce rebirth: in the Brahma world. And he[908] will for sure attain Arahantship as a Brahma in a subsequent life. How soon depends on his effort and pāramī.[289] And again, his duty is to contemplate formations as devoid of permanence, happiness, self, and beauty. Then when his pāramī mature, he may progress to the fourth Path Knowledge.

ARAHANT

The fourth Path Knowledge, the Arahant Path-Knowledge *(Arahatta·Magga·Ñāṇa)*, destroys all greed for fine-material- *(rūpa·)*, and immaterial existence *(arūpa·bhava)*, sloth&torpor *(thina·middha)*, conceit *(māna)*, restlessness *(uddhacca)*, and ignorance *(avijjā)*. One is no longer able to engage in prattle or covetousness.[290] In short, the Arahant Path-Knowledge has completely destroyed greed *(lobha)*, hatred *(dosa)*, and delusion *(moha)*,[909] completely destroyed ignorance *(avijjā)* and craving *(taṇhā)*.

As we have discussed many times now, for there to be kamma, there needs to be ignorance and craving: without ignorance and craving, there is no kamma. So the Arahant's actions do not produce kamma: neither unwholesome kamma nor wholesome kamma; neither presently-effective-, subsequently-effective-, nor indefinitely-effective kamma. The Arahant's volition is purely functional *(kiriya)*.

The Arahant Path-Knowledge functions as interceptive kamma to cut off any remaining kammas that could mature at death to produce any whatsoever kind of rebirth. Such kammas will all have lapsed. At the death of an Arahant, there is no rebirth: anywhere.[910] Not in the sensual realm, not in the fine-material realm, not in the immaterial realm: and here we must remember that a Buddha is also an Arahant.[911]

THE UNWORKING OF KAMMA

The Arahant is called a non-trainee *(a·sekha)*,[912] meaning an adept, because she or he has completed the threefold training: morality *(sīla)*, concentration *(samādhi)*, and wisdom *(paññā)*. When this training is complete, one's mind is purified of the defilements. That is the Dispensation/Teaching of Buddhas *(Buddhāna Sāsanaṁ)*.

The Buddha explains it in a verse:[913]

Sabba·pāpassa a·karaṇaṁ, kusalassa upasampadā.
sa·citta·pariyodapanaṁ, etaṁ Buddhāna Sāsanaṁ.

---

[908] BRAHMAS ARE ONLY MALE: according to The Buddha, it is impossible for a Brahma to be female: see footnote 111, p.43. For why this is so, see footnote 123, p.45.

[909] The Buddha explains this many times; see, for example, quotations endnotes 33, p.24, and 173, p.248.

[910] See table '3e: Dependent Origination from Life to Life', p.349.

[911] When He explains the nine qualities of a Perfectly Self-Enlightened Buddha *(Sammā·Sam·Buddha)*, The Buddha gives Arahantship as the very first (e.g. D.II.3 *'Mahā·Pari-nibbāna·Suttaṁ'* ('The Great-Parinibbāna Sutta')). This quality of His is explained in VsM.vii.125-130 *'Buddh·Ānussati'* ('Buddha Recollection') PP.vii.4-25.

[912] The uneducated ordinary person is in this classification called a neither trainee nor non-trainee *(n'eva·sekha·n·ā·sekha)*.

[913] DhP.xiv.5 *'Buddha·Vaggo'* ('Chapter on Buddha')

All evil not doing, the wholesome acquiring,
One's mind purifying: this is The Buddhas' Teaching.

The Buddhas teach one to do no evil. That is morality training: it is wholesome kamma *(kusala kamma)*. And The Buddhas teach one to purify one's mind. That is concentration training (samatha), and wisdom training (vipassanā): concentration is wholesome kamma, and wisdom is wholesome kamma. As we have now explained many times, the escape from suffering requires that one has accomplished these three types of wholesome kamma over many lives. Then, when one's pāramī mature, one's mind is purified stage by stage by the four Path Knowledges: they are the most powerful of all wholesome kammas, because they destroy all unwholesome and wholesome kammas that are able to produce rebirth. When one's mind is purified by the ultimate Path Knowledge, the Arahant Path-Knowledge, one's actions no longer possess any kammic potency: one's actions are then purely functional *(kiriya)*.

Thus, we may say that by accomplishing many wholesome kammas over many lives, eventually one destroys kamma.[914] We may say that by the workings of wholesome kamma, one achieves the unworking of kamma.[291] Then has one done what needs to be done *(kataṁ karaṇīyaṁ)*.

[914] This is why The Buddha says wholesome kamma leads to the end of kamma: see quotation endnote 88, p.237.

5e: **The Path Process** *(Magga·Vīthi)* *

CONSCIOUSNESS MOMENT *Citta·Kkhaṇa*	(Before the mental process) ⇒⇒…⇒⇒	⇒	⇒	⇒	⇒	⇒	⇒	⇒	⇒	(After the mental process) ⇒⇒…⇒⇒
OBJECT *Ārammaṇa*	Previous Life's Near-Death Object	Impermanence/Suffering/Non-Self Characteristic of Materiality/Mentality‡				The Signless, the Discontinuance, the Unformed, Cessation, NIBBĀNA⅄				Previous Life's Near-Death Object
CONSCIOUSNESS *Citta*	Life-Continuum	Mind-Door Adverting	Impulsion *Javana*							Life-Continuum
			Preparation	Access	Conformity	Change-of-Lineage	Path	1st Fruition	2nd Fruition	
	Bhavaṅga ↑|↓	*Mano·Dvār·Āvajjana* ↑|↓	*Parikamma* ↑|↓	*Upacāra* ↑|↓	*Anuloma* ↑|↓	*Gotrabhu* ↑|↓	*Magga* ↑|↓	*Phala* ↑|↓	*Phala* ↑|↓	*Bhavaṅga* ↑|↓
	Resultant *Vipāka*	Functional *Kiriya*	Kamma				Kamma	Resultant *Vipāka*		Resultant *Vipāka*
	Mundane *Lokiya*						Supramundane *Lokuttara*			Mundane *Lokiya*

* All details given here are based on VsM.xxi.760-804 *'Saṅkhār·Upekkhā·Ñāṇa-'—'Anuloma·Ñāṇa·Kathā'* ('Discussion of the Formations-Equanimity Knowledge' — 'Discussion of the Conformity-Knowledge') PP.xxi.64-134; VsM.xxii.806-812 *'Paṭhama·Magga·Ñāṇa·Kathā'—'Sotāpanna·Puggala·Kathā'* ('Discussion of the First Path-Knowledge'—'do. Stream-Enterer Person') PP.xxii.1-21, & DhSA.I.iii.277-358 *'Lokuttara·Kusala·Vaṇṇanā'* ('Description of the Supramundane Wholesome') E.289-319.

‡ This is insight consciousnesses *(vipassanā·citta)* which is a sensual-sphere consciousness *(kām·āvacara·citta)*. It takes one of the three characteristics of ultimate materiality/mentality of the sensual sphere, or ultimate mentality (jhāna mentality) of the fine-material/immaterial sphere. If it is the non-self characteristic, the Path is the Void Liberation *(Suññato Vimokkho)*; if it is the impermanence characteristic, the Path is the Signless Liberation *(Animitto Vimokkho)*; if it is the suffering characteristic, the Path is the Desireless Liberation *(Appaṇihito Vimokkho)* (VsM.xxii.802-803/PP.xxi.121-127).

⅄ The Signless *(Animittaṁ)*, Discontinuance *(Appavattaṁ)*, Unformed *(Visaṅkhāraṁ)*, Cessation *(Nirodhaṁ)*, NIBBĀNA *(Nibbānaṁ)* (VsM.xxii.806/PP.xxii.5).

Notes for Table 5e 'The Path Process'

- One consciousness lasts one consciousness moment*(citta·kkhaṇa)*, with three stages: arising*(uppāda)*↑, standing*(ṭhiti)* |, dissolution*(bhaṅga)*↓.
- Before and after a mental process, arises a number of life-continuum consciousnesses.[915]
- The Stream-Entry Path-Process does not arise on the immaterial plane (See explanation p.176). But the Once-Return-, Non-Return-, and Arahant Path-Process arises on either the sensual-, fine-material-, or immaterial plane.
- Cognition follows a fixed procedure, according to the natural law of the mind *(citta·niyāma)*. Thus, the procedure of the Path Process is:[916]

1) A mind-door adverting consciousness: it takes the same insight object as the preceding Formations-Equanimity Knowledge.

2-4) Three preparatory impulsions with the same object:

i) Preparation*(parikamma)*[917]
ii) Access*(upacāra)*
iii) Conformity Knowledge*(anuloma)*

Their repetition prepares the way for transition from insight knowledge with the formed as object to the Path&Fruition Knowledges with the Unformed as object. Thus they may be said to function as preparation for, access to and conformity with the Change of Lineage.

5) Change-of-Lineage Knowledge:[918] it takes Nibbāna as object, and marks the transition of knowledge from the ordinary-person lineage*(puthu·jjana·gotta)* to the Noble lineage*(Ariya·gotta)*.

6) Path Knowledge:[919] it takes Nibbāna as object, and is the first arising of the supramundane Noble Eightfold Path in one continuity of mentality-materiality, whereby certain defilements are destroyed: all have been destroyed with the Arahant Path. The Path Consciousness is an absorption consciousness, minimum the first jhāna.[920/292]

7-10) Two or three Fruition Consciousnesses: they also take Nibbāna as object, and are the direct result of the Path Kamma. With practice, one may enter into the fruition attainment for longer periods of time: up to seven days (See table '5d: The Jhāna-Attainment Process', p.178).

---

[915] LIFE-CONTINUUM CONSCIOUSNESS: for details, see footnote 306, p.107, and table '5a: Death and Rebirth', p.52.

[916] For a discussion on the maturing of the Formations-Equanimity Knowledge, see footnote 896, p.334. For the mental phenomena at the arising of the various process consciousnesses, see 'Mental Phenomena of the Mind-Door Process', p.150.

[917] In one of keen faculties, the preparation consciousness does not arise: there are only three impulsions before the Change of Lineage. In that case, three Fruition Consciousnesses arise. (VsM.xxii.811/PP.xxii.16)

[918] CHANGE-OF-LINEAGE KNOWLEDGE: it takes Nibbāna as object, but is not supramundane, because it does not destroy defilements. And in preparation to a higher path, it is called cleansing*(vodāna)*, because one is in that case already a Noble One.

[919] PATH KNOWLEDGE: this knowledge's primary result is the Fruition Knowledge. The secondary result is destruction of defilements (VsM.xxii *'Ñāṇa·Dassana·Visuddhi·Niddeso'* ('Exposition of the Knowledge&Vision Purification' PP.xxii.) See also 'Stream Entry', p.336.

[920] For details, see table '1e Supramundane Resultant Consciousness', p.343.

The Reviewing Knowledges*

After the Fruition Consciousnesses, there is sinking into the life-continuum *(bhavaṅga)*. Then, in accordance with the natural law of the mind *(citta·niyāma)*, there arise the Reviewing Knowledges *(Paccavekkhaṇa·Ñāṇa)*. That is five reviewings:

1) Path Reviewing .... *(Magga·Paccavekkhaṇa)*
2) Fruition Reviewing .... *(Phala·Paccavekkhaṇa)*
3) Destroyed-Defilements Reviewing .... *(Pahīna·Kilesa Paccavekkhaṇa)*
4) Remaining-Defilements Reviewing .... *(Avasiṭṭha·Kilesa Paccavekkhaṇa)*
5) Nibbāna Reviewing .... *(Nibbāna·Paccavekkhaṇa)*

All five reviewings follow the same procedure, although Nos.3 and 4 (destroyed- and remaining Defilements) may not take place.‡ An Arahant never reviews the defilements remaining, for in her/his case, all defilements will have been destroyed.

CONSCIOUSNESS MOMENT *Citta·Kkhaṇa*	(After Path Process) ⇒...⇒	1⇒	2⇒8⇒	⇒...⇒	1⇒	2⇒8⇒	⇒...⇒	1⇒	2⇒8⇒	⇒...⇒
OBJECT *Ārammaṇa*	Previous Life's Near-Death Object	Path Reviewing *Magga·Paccavekkhaṇa*		Previous Life's Near-Death Object	Fruition Reviewing *Phala·Paccavekkhaṇa*		Previous Life's Near-Death Object	Nibbāna Reviewing *Nibbāna·Paccavekkhaṇa*		Previous Life's Near-Death Object
CONSCIOUSNESS *Citta*	Life-Continuum *Bhavaṅga* ↑|↓	Mind-Door Adverting *Mano·Dvār·Āvajjana* ↑|↓	Seven Impulsions *Javana* ↑|↓	Life-Continuum *Bhavaṅga* ↑|↓	Mind-Door Adverting *Mano·Dvār·Āvajjana* ↑|↓	Seven Impulsions *Javana* ↑|↓	Life-Continuum *Bhavaṅga* ↑|↓	Mind-Door Adverting *Mano·Dvār·Āvajjana* ↑|↓	Seven Impulsions *Javana* ↑|↓	Life-Continuum *Bhavaṅga* ↑|↓

* VsM.xxii.812/PP.xxii.21 (For sutta references, see VsM.xxi.805/PP.xxi.135.)

‡ Ibid. mentions M.I.ii.4 *'Cūḷa·Dukkha·Kkhandha·Suttaṁ'* ('The Small Suffering-Aggregate Sutta'). There, one Mahānāma (Once-Returner) does not know why greed-rooted consciousnesses still arise in him: it is because the third and fourth reviewing knowledges have not arisen for him. When discerning mentality, however, one may be able to see which defilements have been destroyed and which remain.

1e: **The Supramundane Resultant Consciousness***(Lokuttara·Vipāka·Citta)**

DOOR	FRUITION CONSCIOUSNESS	ASSOCIATED WITH	OBJECT
mind-	1. Stream-Entry 2. Once-Return 3. Non-Return 4. Arahant	1st supramundane jhāna 2nd supramundane jhāna 3rd supramundane jhāna 4th supramundane jhāna 5th supramundane jhāna	Nibbāna

Even though they are the result of wholesome kamma, these types of resultant consciousness are never called wholesome-resultants*(kusala·vipāka)*, since that term refers only to the unrooted wholesome resultants: see table, p.64.

FRUITION CONSCIOUSNESS: the Fruition Consciousness is the result of its corresponding and immediately preceding Path Consciousness*(Magga·Citta)*: for example, the Stream-Entry Path Consciousness is the supramundane wholesome consciousness, and the Stream-Entry Fruition Consciousness is the corresponding supramundane resultant consciousness. See 'The Path Process' above.

ASSOCIATED WITH: the supramundane resultant consciousnesses arises associated with the mental factors of one of the five jhānas.

1st supramundane jhāna: if the insight knowledge's object is a first-jhāna phenomenon, the Path&Fruition are first supramundane jhāna (eight-factored Path). If the object is a material phenomenon or sensual-sphere mental phenomenon, then even though the object is dissociated from any jhāna factors, the Path&Fruition are associated with the five factors of the first supramundane jhāna, even if one has no previous mundane jhāna.

2nd supramundane jhāna: if the object is a second-jhāna formation, the Path&Fruition are second jhāna with an only seven-factored Path, because there is no application*(vitakka)* (application is a first-jhāna factor, and corresponds to Right Intention*(Sammā Saṅkappa)*, a Path factor).

3rd/4th/5th supramundane jhāna: in the same way, if the insight knowledge's object is a third-jhāna formation, the Path&Fruition are third jhāna, etc.

(DhSA.i.277-358 *'Lokuttara·Kusala·Vaṇṇanā'* ('Description of the Supramundane Wholesome') E.289-319). See also quotation, endnote 292, p.355.

When the supramundane consciousnesses are reckoned according to the five jhānas, they make twenty supramundane wholesome consciousnesses and twenty supramundane resultant consciousnesses.

The Buddha ends the second *'Gaddula·Baddha'* sutta explaining how the educated Noble Disciple*(sutavā Ariya·Sāvako)* has done what needs to be done. Let us listen to his explanation.

DONE IS WHAT NEEDS TO BE DONE

You will remember how The Buddha first explained that the educated Noble Disciple practises vipassanā on the eleven categories of five aggregates, regarding them according to reality and with Right Wisdom as: 'This is not mine, I am not this, this is not my self.' Seeing them as in this way void, the educated Noble Disciple becomes disenchanted with the five aggregates. Let us take it from there again:

Thus seeing, bhikkhus, the educated Noble Disciple
[1] **with this very materiality is disenchanted;**
[2] **with this very feeling is disenchanted;**
[3] **with this very perception is disenchanted;**
[4] **with these very formations is disenchanted;**

[5] **with this very consciousness is discenchanted.**
- **Disenchanted, he is dispassionate; dispassionate, he is liberated.**
- **Liberated, there is the knowledge: 'I am liberated.'**
- **He knows: 'Consumed is birth; lived is the holy life; done is what needs to be done; there is nothing further beyond this.'**

In practical terms, what does it mean?[921]

- **He is dispassionate***(virajjati)*: here, The Buddha is referring to the Path Knowledge.
- **Dispassionate, he is liberated***(virāgā, vimuccati)*: here, The Buddha is referring to the Fruition Knowledge.
- **Liberated, there is the knowledge***(ñāṇa)*: **'I am liberated***(vimuttaṁ)*': here, The Buddha is referring to the Reviewing Knowledge*(Paccavekkhaṇa·Ñāṇa)*. After the arising of the Path&Fruition Knowledges, there is always Reviewing Knowledge: reviewing what has been achieved.[922]
- **He knows: 'Consumed is birth***(khīṇā jāti)***; lived is the holy life***(vusitaṁ Brahma·cariyaṁ)***; done is what needs to be done***(kataṁ karaṇīyaṁ)***, there is nothing further beyond this***(n·āparaṁ itthattāya)*:[923] The Buddha explains this in another way in the first *'Gaddula·Baddha'* sutta.[924] There He says:

  [1] **He is released from materiality***(parimuccati rūpamhā)***;**
  [2] **he is released from feeling***(parimuccati vedanāya)***;**
  [3] **he is released from perception***(parimuccati saññāya)***;**
  [4] **he is released from formations***(parimuccati saṅkhārehi)***;**
  [5] **he is released from consciousness***(parimuccati viññāṇamhā)***;**
  he is released from birth, from ageing&death, from sorrow, from lamentation, from pain, from displeasure, and from despair*(parimuccati jātiyā jarā·maraṇena sokehi paridevehi dukkhehi domanassehi upāyāsehi)***.**
  'He is released from suffering', I declare*(Parimuccati dukkhasmā'ti vadāmi)***.**

This is Arahantship.

Is it good? Yes, it is very good! It is the best: it is the ultimate happiness*(parama sukha)*.[925] Buddhas arise in the world for this reason. This is why Buddhas teach The Buddhas' most superior Dhamma teaching *(Buddhānaṁ sāmukkaṁsikā Dhamma·desanā)*.[293] It is found only in the teaching of Fully Enlightened Buddhas.[294] It is for this They teach the Four Noble Truths.[926] Because it is only by fully understanding the Four Noble Truths that one may achieve the liberation that is perpetual, not temporary*(a·sāmāyikaṁ)*: that is, supramundane liberation*(lokuttaro vimokkho)*, the highest being the Arahant Path&Fruition Knowledges.

---

[921] The following analysis has been taken from SA.II.I.vii.1 *'Assutavā·Suttaṁ'* (The "Uneducated" Sutta').

[922] See 'The Reviewing Knowledges', p.342.

[923] DA.i.2 *'Sāmañña·Phala·Suttaṁ'* ('The Asceticism-Fruit Sutta') explains: CONSUMED IS BIRTH: the birth that would have arisen if the Arahant Path-Knowledge had not arisen has been consumed. LIVED IS THE HOLY LIFE: whereas the good, ordinary person and the seven trainees 'live' the holy life, the Arahant has 'lived' the holy life. DONE IS WHAT NEEDS TO BE DONE: the tasks to be done by the Path Knowledges have been done. THERE IS NOTHING FURTHER BEYOND THIS: there is nothing further to be done with regard to developing the Path, or, there are no further aggregates beyond the present ones (see in this connection also quotation from the *Saṅkhār·Ūpapatti'* sutta, endnote 59, p.36).

[924] See 'He Does Not Go Round the Five Aggregates', p.18.

[925] DhP.xv.8 *'Sukha·Vagga'* ('Chapter on Happiness')

[926] The Buddha's most superior Dhamma teaching: see p.137.

We shall now ask you: what is the Arahant's duty? To observe the Vinaya,[295] to learn and teach the Dhamma as taught by The Buddha,[296] so that others may learn the Dhamma taught by The Buddha, and themselves attain a Path&Fruition:[297] that is the Arahant's duties, while she or he waits for Parinibbāna.[298]

To prevent any misunderstandings, let us then discuss the Arahant's Parinibbāna.

The Two Types of Parinibbāna

The Buddha speaks of two types of Parinibbāna:[299]

1) The Nibbāna element with remainder*(sa·upādisesā Nibbāna dhātu)*: here, as we mentioned before, the four Path Knowledges take the Unformed Element *(Asaṅkhata·Dhātu)* as object. Doing so, they destroy the defilements stage by stage. And with the fourth Path Knowledge (the Arahant Path-Knowledge *(Arahatta·Magga·Ñāṇa)*), there is the remainderless cessation of defilements: that is, they no longer arise, ever.[927] Hence, this type of Parinibbāna is also called defilements Parinibbāna*(kilesa·Parinibbāna)*.[928]

   With the defilements Parinibbāna there is the destruction of lust*(rāga·kkhayo)*, the destruction of hatred*(dosa·kkhayo)*, and the destruction of delusion*(moha·kkhayo)*.[929] That means the five causes for future rebirth have been destroyed: ignorance, volitional formations, craving, clinging, and the existence of kammic potency have ceased to be: the Arahant's volition is therefore only functional*(kiriya)*.[300] And all the kammas accomplished before Arahantship, which had the power or potency to produce a new existence lapse.[301] But the Arahant's aggregates have not ceased; they still remain. If the Arahant is a human being or a sensual-realm deva, there are still consciousness, mentality-materiality, the six bases (eye-, ear-, nose-, tongue-, body-, and mind base), contact, and feeling. The human Arahant still has consciousness established in the human world, in the sensual sphere, and still experiences physically painful feelings*(dukkha·vedanā)*, pleasant feelings, and neutral feelings. But because all defilements have been destroyed, she or he does not experience mentally unpleasant feelings*(domanassa·vedanā)*.[302]

2) The Nibbāna element without remainder*(an·upādisesā Nibbāna dhātu)*: here, the aggregates cease. Hence, this is also called aggregates Parinibbāna*(khandha·Parinibbāna)*. But if it is a human Arahant, there remains one type of materiality aggregate: temperature-born materiality*(utuja·rūpa)*, which is the human corpse: if the corpse is cremated, there may remain material relics*(dhātu)*.[303]

   The five results that are the present rebirth have now ceased. For the Arahant of the human or sensual-realm deva, it is the remainderless cessation of consciousness, mentality-materiality, the six bases (eye-, ear-, nose-, tongue-, body-, and mind base), contact, and feeling. Here again, 'remainderless cessation' means no further arising. The Arahant's decease consciousness arises, stands and perishes, and then there is no further arising of

---

[927] This means the latencies have been destroyed: see footnote 145, p.55.

[928] DEFILEMENTS PARINIBBĀNA: e.g. VbhA.XVI.x.809 *'Paṭhama·Bala·Niddeso'* ('Exposition of the First Power') DD.XVI.x.2173. The Most Venerable Sayadaw points out that this is in fact not really Nibbāna, but is explained as such by The Buddha as a method of teaching*(pariyāya)*.

[929] The Buddha explains it many times. See, for example, quotation endnotes 33, p.24, and 173, p.248.

consciousness. It means all suffering has ceased without remainder: physically painful feelings *(dukkha·vedanā)*, mentally painful feelings, pleasant feelings, and neutral feelings. The remainderless cessation of defilements and the kammic potency is the cause, and the remainderless cessation of the five aggregates is the effect.[930/304]

Our Buddha's defilements Parinibbāna took place at Uruvelā, beside the Nerañjarā River at the foot of the Bodhi Tree: there, He realized the Unformed Element, Nibbāna, with His four Path&Fruition Knowledges. He lived on for forty-five years, teaching the Dhamma. Many times He suffered physical pain and discomfort, because of digestive problems. And when Devadatta caused a splinter of rock to strike The Buddha's foot, The Buddha suffered great physical pain.[931] But He endured the pain, mindful, and discerning, without suffering mental pain.[932] Then, when our Buddha was eighty years old, between the two lines of sal *(sāla)* trees in Kusināra, His aggregates Parinibbāna took place.

Only with the attainment of one's aggregates Parinibbāna has one put an end to all suffering, because there is no re-arising of any aggregate: the Arahant attains Parinibbāna with consciousness unestablished *(apatiṭṭhita)*.

To prevent any misunderstandings, let us then discuss consciousness established *(patiṭṭhita)* and consciousness unestablished *(apatiṭṭhita)*.

Consciousness Established and Unestablished

Consciousness Established

Let us begin by repeating the beginning of the two *'Gaddula·Baddha'* suttas:

Inconceivable is the beginning, bhikkhus, of the round of rebirth. A first point is not known of ignorance-hindered beings fettered by craving, rushing on and running about.

As we have already mentioned, The Buddha is here discussing the round of rebirth *(saṁsāra)*. It is the rushing on from one world to another (birth now as a human being, then a deva, then an animal, then again a human being, etc.), and the running about within one world (again and again birth as a human being, or again and again birth as a deva, etc.).

Birth

What is birth? It is the arising of resultant aggregates:[305] they arise as the result of past kamma.[933] The Buddha speaks of birth also as descent *(okkanti)* (descent of consciousness).[306] And He speaks of birth as consciousness established *(viññāṇa patiṭṭhita)*, which is the same thing: the arising and establishment of the rebirth-linking consciousness *(paṭisandhi·citta)*. The rebirth-linking consciousness is a resultant conciousness *(vipāka·citta)*, and it takes as object the kamma, kamma sign *(kamma·nimitta)* or destination sign *(gati·nimitta)* cognized by the near-death process *(maraṇ·āsanna·vīthi)* of the preceding life.[934]

As we have explained before, consciousness does not (cannot) arise alone. It arises always together with the three other mental aggregates, feeling *(vedanā)*,

930 See table '3e: Dependent Origination from Life to Life', p.349.
931 See 'The Venerable Devadatta', p.152.
932 S.I.IV.ii.3 *'Sakalika·Suttaṁ'* ('The Splinter Sutta')
933 See 'The Resultant Dhammas', p.44.
934 See table '5a: Death and Rebirth', p.52.

perception*(saññā)*, and formations*(saṅkhāra)*: they are mental factors*(cetasika)*.[935/307] When a being is born in the sensual realm (the hells, the animal world, the ghost world, the human world, and the sensual-realm deva worlds), or in the fine-material realm (the Brahma world), the rebirth-linking consciousness depends on materiality*(rūpa)*: that makes the five aggregates*(pañca·kkhandha)*.[308]

FIVE-, FOUR-, AND SINGLE-CONSTITUENT EXISTENCE

In the Pali Texts,[936] rebirth of a being in the sensual- and fine-material worlds is called five constituent existence*(pañca·vokāra·bhavo)*. In such a case, the rebirth-linking consciousness*(paṭisandhi·citta)* is established together with resultant mentality-materiality*(vipāka·nāma·rūpa)*.[309]

When a being is born in the immaterial world, however, the rebirth-linking consciousness is established together with only feelings, perception, and formations: there is no materiality. Therefore, such rebirth is called four-constituent existence *(catu·vokāra·bhavo)*.

And when a being is reborn in the impercipient world, only matter is established. Therefore such rebirth is called single-constituent existence*(eka·vokāra·bhavo)*. But because the impercipient being*(asaññā·satta)* has not uprooted the latencies, impercipient existence is followed by re-establishment of consciousness. How? When the impercipient being's material life faculty is cut off, in the next mind moment there is the maturing of an adventitious indefinitely-effective kamma from that being's past: it establishes a rebirth consciousness in the human world, which is five-constituent existence.[937/310] That is how there is the establishment of consciousness (rebirth), in the three spheres of existence: the sensual-, fine-material, and immaterial sphere.

Is there rebirth anywhere else? No. The Buddha says the highest existence is rebirth in the highest plane of the immaterial sphere: the plane of neither-perception nor non-perception.[938]

After the rebirth consciousness is established, what happens?

---

[935] See further 'Things Impossible for Consciousness to Do', p.350.

[936] VsM.xvii.647 *'Upādāna·Paccayā·Bhava·Pada·Vitthāra·Kathā'* ('Detailed Discussion of the Clinging-as-Cause-Existence Phase') PP.xvii.253-255. It quotes The Buddha's explanation in Vbh.vi.234 *'Paṭicca·Samuppāda·Vibhaṅgo'* ('Analysis of Dependent Origination').

[937] The impercipient being's near-death object in the previous life is a kasiṇa object, with strong revulsion for mentality. And there is rebirth of only materiality: no mentality, rebirth-, or decease consciousness, or near-death process (for details, see subsequent endnote 310, p.359). *'Pañca·Ppakaraṇa Anu·Ṭīka'* ('Sub-Subcommentary of Five Expositions') *'Paccaya·Paccanīy·Ānuloma·Vaṇṇanā'* §190 explains that this principle applies both to impercipient existence (which is always followed by sensual-sphere existence), and immaterial existence (which may be followed by another immaterial existence on the same or a higher plane), or by sensual-sphere existence. See table '5a: Death and Rebirth', p.52.

[938] In M.III.i.6 *'Āneñjasappāya·Suttaṁ'* ('The Imperturbable-Wards Sutta'), The Buddha explains that the chief [existence-] clinging*(upādāna·seṭṭhaṁ)* is clinging to existence in the base of neither-perception nor non-perception. MA.ibid. explains that this refers to rebirth there: it being the chief and highest plane of existence. In Vbh.ibid., The Buddha speaks thus of percipient existence (all types of existence other than the next two), impercipient existence, and neither-percipient nor non-percipient existence.

THE STREAM OF CONSCIOUSNESS

After the rebirth consciousness is established, the life-continuum consciousnesses *(bhavaṅga·citta)* arise one after the other: they take the same past object as the rebirth-linking consciousness, and are also resultant consciousnesses. The stream of life-continuum consciousnesses is arrested only when there arises a mental process *(citta·vīthi)*: either a five-door process *(pañca·dvāra·vīthi)*, or a mind-door process *(mano·dvāra·vīthi)*. Such a mental process comprises resultant consciousnesses *(vipāka·citta)*, functional consciousnesses *(kiriya·citta)*, and impulsion consciousnesses *(javana)*. As we have discussed earlier, the impulsion consciousnesses of a non-Arahant produce kamma: they are also called kamma consciousness *(kamma·viññāṇa)*.

That way, from the beginning of a life (the rebirth-linking consciousness *(paṭisandhi·citta)*) up to the end of that life (the decease consciousness *(cuti·citta)*), there is established a stream of consciousness *(viññāṇa·sota)*. And together with each consciousness arise also the mental factors (feeling, perception, and formations), as well as materiality. We have thus consciousness, mental factors, and materiality arising and perishing one after the other like a river.[311]

The last consciousness in one life is the decease consciousness *(cuti·citta)*: it takes the same past object as the rebirth-linking consciousness and life-continuum consciousnesses, and it is also a resultant consciousness. Then, so long as one is still one of the **ignorance-hindered beings fettered by craving**, the decease consciousness is followed by yet another rebirth-linking consciousness: in the very next mind moment. The stream of consciousness is not broken. It establishes itself in a new set of mentality-materiality: that is rebirth of a new 'being'. For example, a human being's decease consciousness arises and perishes, and then a new rebirth-linking consciousness may be established in another world, maybe the animal world or a deva world: that is **rushing on** from one world to another. The new rebirth-linking consciousness may also be established in a new mother's womb: that is **running about** within one world.[312]

A being who in this way rushes on and runs about is in fact merely the establishment of a stream of consciousness. It may be established in, for example, the sensual sphere, and flow there maybe over many lives. It may be established as the mentality-materiality of a human being, and then as the mentality-materiality of a deva, etc. Then maybe it stops flowing in the sensual sphere, and establishes itself in the fine-material sphere, flowing there for many lives too. Again, it may stop flowing in that sphere, and continue flowing in the human world again, etc.[313]

The two main causes for the establishment of consciousness are ignorance *(avijjā)* and craving *(taṇhā)*. Without ignorance and craving, the kammic potency *(kamma·satti)* cannot establish consciousness in any sphere. We have discussed this many times.

With the Arahant Path-Knowledge, there is the remainderless cessation of ignorance and craving. That means ignorance and craving will never arise again: it is the defilements Parinibbāna *(kilesa·Parinibbāna)*. With the remainderless cessation of ignorance and craving, the kammic potency of present volition ceases to be: we may say it is the complete unworking of present kamma. But the kammic potency of past kamma still works, which means the Arahant's stream of consciousness continues, and consciousness is still established. Consciousness is no longer established, however, in the production of kamma.[314] The impulsion consciousnesses that arise no longer produce kamma: the Arahant's volition is purely functional.

CONSCIOUSNESS UNESTABLISHED

Then we shall ask you a question. If ignorance and craving are the reason why consciousness is established in one of three realms again and again; if ignorance and craving are why a being is reborn again and again (now here, now there), what happens when ignorance and craving have been destroyed? What happens when the cause for consciousness's establishment has been destroyed?

It is very easy: when the cause for consciousness's establishment has been destroyed, consciousness is not established: when consciousness is not established, it is unestablished *(appatiṭṭhita)*.[939]

At the dissolution of the Arahant's decease consciousness (at the Arahant's death), the stream of consciousness is unestablished in this world or another world.[940] It is the complete unworking of kamma past, present, and future.

At the Arahant's death, there is no further flow of consciousness: that is the aggregates Parinibbāna *(khandha·parinibbāna)*.[941] As The Buddha says at the end of the second *'Gaddula·Baddha'* sutta, the Noble Disciple knows: **Consumed is birth** *(khīṇā jāti)*.[942/315]

3e: **Dependent Origination from Life to Life***

(one life) NON-ARAHANT		(next life) NON-ARAHANT		(last life) FROM ARAHANTSHIP		PARINIBBĀNA
» results »‡	causes »⅄	» results »	causes »	» results »|	~~causes~~ *	~~results~~
	IGNORANCE		ignorance		~~IGNORANCE~~	
consciousness	FORMATIONS »	CONSCIOUSNESS	formations »	consciousness	~~FORMATIONS~~	~~CONSCIOUSNESS~~
mentality-materiality		MENTALITY-MATERIALITY		mentality-materiality		~~MENTALITY-MATERIALITY~~
six bases		SIX BASES		six bases		~~SIX BASES~~
contact		CONTACT		contact		~~CONTACT~~
feeling »	craving	FEELING »	CRAVING	feeling »|	~~craving~~	~~FEELING~~
	clinging		CLINGING		~~clinging~~	
(BIRTH	existence »	(birth	EXISTENCE »	(BIRTH	~~existence~~	~~(birth~~
AGEING&DEATH) »		ageing&death) »		AGEING&DEATH) »|		~~ageing&death)~~

* E.g. A.III.II.ii.1 *'Titth·Āyatana·Suttaṁ'* ('The Sectarian Doctrines Sutta' quoted p.109). Here, The Buddha teaches in two ways: according to custom *(vohāra·desanā)*, and according to ultimate truth *(param·attha·desanā)*. Birth/ageing&death are according to custom. They correspond to the five factors consciousness /mentality-materiality/six bases/contact/feeling, which are according to ultimate truth. For the process going from life to life, see, for example, The Buddha's explanation, endnote 313, p.357.

---

[939] UNESTABLISHED CONSCIOUSNESS: see quotation, endnote 324, p.361.

[940] See endnote 311, p.357.

[941] VsM.xxii.836 *'Pahātabba·Dhamma·Pahāna·Kathā'* ('Discussion of the Abandoning of the Things to Be Abandoned') PP.xxii.88 explains: '... the clansman disenchanted with the occurrence of the aggregates undertakes to develop the four Paths in his own continuity.... Then his aggregates-continuity *(khandha·pavattiyaṁ)* is rendered incapable of prolonging the continuity to a subsequent existence. It is now unproductive of future existence since all the kinds of kamma beginning with bodily kamma are now merely functional.... Being without clinging, he inevitably attains with the cessation of the last consciousness the complete Nibbāna, like a fire with no more fuel.'

[942] See table '3e: Dependent Origination from Life to Life', p.349.

‡ Results in the life of both a non-Arahant and Arahant: kamma formations in a past life result in the arising of a rebirth consciousness, and subsequent consciousnesses in that life, and the simultaneous arising of mentality-materiality, the six bases, contact, and feeling. In D.ii.2 *'Mahā·Nidāna·Suttaṁ'* ('The Great Causation Sutta'), The Buddha explains that in one life one can go only as far back as the arising of mentality-materiality and consciousness at rebirth: 'Thus far the round [of rebirth] goes as much as can be discerned in this life, namely to mentality-materiality together with consciousness.'
⅄ Causes in non-Arahant's life: the non-Arahant is possessed of ignorance. Hence, when there is feeling, there is craving, and clinging, owing to which there is existence of the kammic potency, formations of kamma. This means there is at death the arising of a rebirth consciousness.
★ Causes in Arahant's life: because there is no ignorance, there is no craving, and no clinging, which means there is no further existence of the kammic potency, no formations of kamma. This means there is at death no arising of a rebirth consciousness. Until then, the five results are still in operation.

No Establishment in Nibbāna

Then we may think the Arahant's stream of consciousness is established in Nibbāna. But that is impossible. Why? Because

- according to the Buddha's Teaching Nibbāna is devoid of five-constituent existence, four-constituent existence, and single-constituent existence;
- according to the Buddha's Teaching, Nibbāna is devoid of coming, going, and staying, and devoid of rebirth and decease.[316]
- according to the Buddha's Teaching, in Nibbāna the four great essentials are unestablished, and mentality as well as materiality completely stops *(asesaṁ uparujjhati)*.[317] It is the cessation of the world *(loka·nirodha)*, which is the non-arising of the five aggregates, non-arising of the six internal and external bases, etc.[318]

Things Impossible for Consciousness to Do

Now, it is important not to get a wrong view about this: please understand that consciousness unestablished does not mean that consciousness exists without being established anywhere; it does not mean that Nibbāna is unformed consciousness, awareness or mind; it does not mean that Nibbāna is unconditioned consciousness or unconditioned awareness, unconditioned mind, pure consciousness or awareness independent of an object. According to the Buddha's Teaching, such a thing does not exist.

Let us summarize the things that, according to the Buddha's Teaching, are impossible for consciousness to do:

- According to The Buddha's Teaching, it is impossible for consciousness to arise without an object, independently of an object, independently of causes; it is impossible for consciousness to be unconditioned; it arises dependent upon an internal base (eye-, ear-, nose-, tongue-, body-, or mind base), and an external base (sight-, sound-, odour-, flavour-, tangible-, or dhamma base).[319]
- According to The Buddha's Teaching, it is impossible for consciousness to arise alone; it arises always with associated mental factors.[943]

[943] See quotation endnote 307, p.358.

- According to The Buddha's Teaching, it is impossible for consciousness to be permanent; it is formed *(saṅkhata)*, and has therefore an arising stage, a standing stage, and a dissolution stage.*[320]*
- According to The Buddha's Teaching, it is impossible for consciousness to be Nibbāna, for consciousness is possessed of the three characteristics: impermanence, suffering, and non-self. While Nibbāna is also non-self, it is not possessed of impermanence, or suffering.[944] Consciousness is one of the five aggregates, the Noble Truth of Suffering.*[321]* Thus, Nibbāna cannot be consciousness, for Nibbāna is the Noble Truth of the Cessation of Suffering.*[322]*

When we remember these simple facts about consciousness, it is not difficult to understand that when The Buddha says the Arahant passes away with consciousness unestablished, it means consciousness no longer arises.[945]

Please remember what The Buddha says about the Arahant bhikkhu in the first *'Gaddula·Baddha'* sutta:[946]

[1] **He is released from materiality** *(parimuccati rūpamhā)*;
[2] **he is released from feeling** *(parimuccati vedanāya)*;
[3] **he is released from perception** *(parimuccati saññāya)*;
[4] **he is released from formations** *(parimuccati saṅkhārehi)*;
[5] **he is released from consciousness** *(parimuccati viññāṇamhā)*;

he is released from birth, from ageing&death, from sorrow, from lamentation, from pain, from displeasure, and from despair.

'He is released from suffering', I declare.

WHERE DOES THE ARAHANT GO?

In this connection, a common question regarding the Arahant is: 'Where does the Arahant go after her or his Parinibbāna?' 'What is her or his destination?' Then we shall ask you another question: if you light a candle, there is a flame. When the candle has burned down, where does the flame go? What is your answer? It goes nowhere: the wax and the wick burned up and the flame expired. There is no going anywhere: the Arahant does not go anywhere.*[323]*

When we say a Buddha or other Arahant 'enters into Parinibbāna', it does not mean they enter into a place: it is a figure of speech. Just as we say, 'I went to sleep', it does not mean we went anywhere. The Arahant's Parinibbāna does not mean she or he goes anywhere. The Arahant's Parinibbāna means there is no re-arising of consciousness after the dissolution of the decease consciousness: consciousness is unestablished.*[324]* That is why The Buddha says of the Arahant:[947]

> *Ayaṁ, bhikkhave, bhikkhu na katthaci upapajjati.*
> **This bhikkhu, bhikkhus, is not anywhere reborn.**

Māra does not know the Arahant's coming and going, because Māra cannot see where the rebirth consciousness has been established, because it has nowhere been established.*[325]* We may, for example, look for a certain word on a page. But if that word has not been written on that page, we cannot see it, can we?

Please remember the last stanza of the *'Ratana'* sutta: we quoted it earlier. When The Buddha was reciting the *'Ratana'* sutta, a lamp near Him expired. And in the last line of the sutta, The Buddha compared Arahants to such an expired

---

[944] See quotation endnote 270, p.354.
[945] See table '3e: Dependent Origination from Life to Life', p.349.
[946] Quoted at 'He Does Not Go Round the Five Aggregates', p.18.
[947] M.III.ii.10 *'Saṅkhār·Ūpapatti·Suttaṁ'* ('The Formations-Rebirth Sutta')

lamp *(padīpo)*. He said:[948]

Nibbanti dhīrā yath·āyaṁ padīpo.
Steadfast, they expire as this lamp.

CONCLUSION

We hope that by this explanation there is no doubt about consciousness unestablished. If any doubt remains, please allow us to suggest that you see it all with your own direct knowledge. First undertake morality *(sīla)*. Then develop concentration *(samādhi)*, until your mind is full of bright, brilliant, and radiant light of wisdom. Then use that light of wisdom systematically to practise materiality meditation *(rūpa·kammaṭṭhāna)* and mentality meditation *(nāma·kammaṭṭhāna)*.

When it is complete, you will have attained the Mentality-Materiality Definition Knowledge *(Nāma·Rūpa·Pariccheda·Ñāṇa)*. Then discern dependent origination, and attain the Cause-Apprehending Knowledge *(Paccaya·Pariggaha·Ñāṇa)*.[949] With that knowledge, you will have overcome all and any doubt about the establishment of consciousness in the three realms: that is why it is called Doubt-Overcoming Purification *(Kaṅkhā·Vitaraṇa·Visuddhi)*.[326]

If you then practise vipassanā on the five aggregates of past, future, and present, internal and external, gross and subtle, inferior and superior, far and near, your pāramī may mature, and you will attain a Path&Fruition. Then continue practising until you attain Arahantship: the defilements Parinibbāna.

Then at the end of that life, you will attain the aggregates Parinibbāna. Then will you know for yourself the true meaning of 'consciousness unestablished'.

JUST AS, BHIKKHUS, A LOTUS, BLUE, RED, OR WHITE

So long as your Arahant consciousness is yet established, you may abide in the world like a lotus. Do you know what it means to abide in the world like a lotus? Please listen to The Buddha explain a Buddha's or other Arahant's abiding in the world:[950]

Just as, bhikkhus, a lotus, blue, red, or white, though born in the water, [and] **grown up in the water, when it reaches the surface, it stands there unwetted by the water.**

Just so, bhikkhus, though born in the world, [and] **grown up in the world, having overcome the world, the Tathāgata**[327] **abides unwetted by the world.**

Do you want to be like a lotus? Now you know what to do.

The very first thing for you to do is to develop strong and powerful faith[951] in the workings of kamma as explained by The Buddha. With that faith and understanding, you may then accomplish superior wholesome kammas. With the working of those kammas, you may eventually attain the unworking of kamma.

May you accomplish the unworking of kamma as soon as possible.
May you attain consciousness unestablished as soon as possible.
May you become like a lotus as soon as possible.

---

[948] The last stanza of the *'Ratana'* sutta is quoted on p.154.

[949] These knowledges are explained under 'The Two Preparatory Insight Knowledges', p.90.

[950] S.III.I.x.2 *'Puppha·Suttaṁ'* ('The Flower Sutta')

[951] Faith *(saddhā)* is the first of the five faculties *(indriya)*.

ENDNOTES CHAPTER VI
(SUTTA REFERENCES ETC.)

[257] See also, for example, S.III.I.ii.4 *'Yad·Anicca·Suttaṁ'* ('The What-is-Impermanent Sutta'): 'Materiality [feeling, etc.], bhikkhus, is impermanent. What is impermanent it is suffering. What is suffering is non-self.' Mentioned VsM.ibid./PP.xxi.7.
[258] These are the three types of suffering discussed by The Buddha in S.V.I.vii.5 *'Dukkhatā·Suttaṁ'* ('The Sufferings Sutta'): discussed also at 'Insight Meditation', p.88.
[259] In S.III.I.i.1 *'Nakulapitā·Suttaṁ'* ('The Nakulapīta Sutta'), the Buddha explains that the only reason one might say one's body was healthy is foolishness *(bālyaṁ)*.
[260] The Buddha discusses this aspect of the five aggregates in, for example, his discussion with the philosopher Saccaka in M.I.iv.5 *'Cūla·Saccaka·Suttaṁ'* ('The Small Saccaka Sutta').
[261] The Buddha explains this in, for example, S.III.I.iii.8 *'Abhinandana·Suttaṁ'* ('The "Delighting" Sutta'): 'Whoever, bhikkhus, delights in materiality [etc.], he delights in suffering.'
[262] In M.I.iv.5 *'Cūla·Saccaka·Suttaṁ'* ('The Small Saccaka Sutta'), The Buddha asks the philosopher Saccaka: 'What do you think, Aggivessana? When one sticks to suffering, turns to suffering, cleaves to suffering, and regards suffering as "This is mine, this am I, this is my self", could one ever comprehend suffering, or dwell with suffering having been fully exhausted?' 'How could one, Gotama, Sir? Indeed not, Gotama, Sir.' Saccaka is mentioned also at endnote 186, p.250.
[263] The Buddha explains this in, for example, S.III.I.iii.9 *'Uppāda·Suttaṁ'* ('The "Arising" Sutta'): 'Whatever, bhikkhus, arising, standing, regeneration, and manifestaton of materiality [etc.] is the arising of suffering, the standing of disease, and the manifestation of ageing&death.' See also the Buddha's analysis of the First Noble Truth in D.ii.9 *'Mahā·Sati·Paṭṭhāna·Suttaṁ'* ('The Great Mindfulness-Foundation Sutta').
[264] In Iti.III.ii.2 *'Cakkhu·Suttaṁ'* ('The Eye Sutta'), The Buddha explains: 'Three, bhikkhus, are the eyes. What three? The fleshly eye, the divine eye, the wisdom eye.'
[265] The Buddha explains this in, for example, A.VI.x.7 *'Anavatthita·Suttaṁ'* ('The "Unstable" Sutta'): 'By having seen six advantages, bhikkhus, it is enough for a bhikkhu to establish the perception of impermanence *(anicca·saññā)* in all formations without restriction. What six? "[1] All formations will appear unstable to me, [2] and nothing in the whole world will my mind find pleasure in, [3] and my mind will rise above the whole world, [4] and my mind will become inclined towards Nibbāna, [5] and my fetters will tend towards abandonment, [6] and I shall become possessed of the supreme state of an ascetic *(sāmañña)*."'
[266] In A.X.I.iii.9 *'Paṭhama·Kosala·Suttaṁ'* ('The First Kosala Sutta'), The Buddha explains that the Noble Disciple sees how King Pasenadi of Kosala, the highest human being changes; sees how the different kinds of sensual-realm devas change; sees how the different kinds of fine-material devas change; sees how the different kinds of immaterial-realm beings change; and sees how also very skilful meditators change. Seeing how all these high beings change, the Noble Disciple becomes disenchanted with the high, let alone the low, and develops insight as explained here.
[267] The Buddha uses the simile of the eleven fires in Vin.Mv.i.12 *'Uruvela·Pāṭihāriya·Kathā'* ('Discusssion of the Uruvela Miracles'), and S.IV.I.iii.6 *'Āditta·Suttaṁ'* ('The "Burning" Sutta'). And in S.V.XII.v.3 *'Mahā·Pariḷāha·Suttaṁ'* ('The Great-Conflagration Sutta'), He explains that those ascetics and Brahmins who do not understand the Four Noble Truths delight in and accomplish kamma that leads to birth, ageing, death, etc. Having done so, they are then burned by those eleven conflagrations.
[268] These three metaphors are referred to in VsM.ibid. The Buddha uses them in M.II.ii.4 *'Mahā·Mālukya·Suttaṁ'* ('The Great Mālukya Sutta'), when He explains how the bhikkhu develop the fine-material-, and immaterial jhānas, and then practises vipassanā on the materiality and mentality associated with them. He then becomes disenchanted with

them, and progresses as explained here. Also, throughout His Teachings, The Buddha speaks of the gratification, danger of, and escape from sensual pleasure, the elements, and the five aggregates. For example, in S.III.I.iii.5 *'Assāda·Suttaṁ'* ('The Enjoyment Sutta'), He explains: 'Whatever happiness and pleasure arises dependent on materiality [etc.]: this is enjoyment of materiality [etc.]. Any materiality [etc.] is impermanent, suffering, a changing thing: this is the danger in materiality [etc.]. The abandonment of desire and lust, the removal of desire and lust for materiality: this is the escape from materiality.' And in the following sutta, He explains that so long as He did not directly know the enjoyment, danger and escape from the five aggregates, so long did He not claim to be enlightened. See also endnote 272, p.354.

[269] The Buddha explains this in, for example, A.VI.x.8 *'Ukkhittāsika·Suttaṁ'* ('The Raised-Sword Sutta'): 'By having seen six advantages, bhikkhus, it is enough for a bhikkhu to establish the perception of suffering *(dukkha·saññā)* in all formations without restriction. What six? "[1] The disenchantment perception *(nibbida·saññā)* towards all formations will be established in me, in the same way as towards an executioner with raised sword, [2] and my mind will rise above the whole world, [3] and I shall become one who regards Nibbāna as Peace *(Santa)*, [4] and my latencies will tend towards uprooting, [5] and I shall become one who has fulfilled his duty, [6] and I shall have attended to the Teacher *(Satthā)* with loving-kindness practice."' See also quotation, endnote 272, p.354.

[270] In A.III.I.v.7-8 *'Saṅkhata [-A·Saṅkhata]·Lakkhaṇa·Suttaṁ'* ('The Formed [-Unformed] Characteristic Sutta', The Buddha explains: 'Three, bhikkhus, are the formed characteristics of the formed. What three? Arising is known, perishing is known, change in standing is known.' - '... the unformed characteristics of the Unformed ... Arising is not known, perishing is not known, change in standing is not known.' See also quotation endnote 34, p.24.

[271] The Buddha explains these four perversions in A.IV.I.v.9 *'Vipallāsa·Suttaṁ'* ('The Perversion Sutta'): 'Four, bhikkhus, are these perversions of perception... of consciousness ... of view. What four? [1] In the impermanent there is permanence....[2] In suffering there is happiness. [3] In non-self there is self.... [4] In the foul there is beauty.'

[272] In M.I.iii.6 *'Pāsa·Rāsi·Suttaṁ'* ('The Mass of Snares Sutta') (also called *'Ariya·Pariyesanā·Suttaṁ'* ('The Noble-Search Sutta')), The Buddha describes this as the ignoble search *(an·ariyā pariyesanā)*: 'And what, bhikkhus, is the ignoble search? Here, one himself a born thing, seeks that which is also born; himself an ageing... ailing... mortal... sorrowing... defiled thing, seeks that which is also ageing... defiled thing.' And He explains the object of the ignoble search: 'wife and children, men and women slaves, goats and sheep, fowl and pigs, elephants and cattle, horses and mares, gold and silver.' The Noble Search, on the other hand, He explains as one who, having understood the danger *(ādīnava)* in those things, seeks the Unborn, Unageing, Unailing, Deathless, Sorrowless, Unsurpassable safety from bondage, Nibbāna. See in this connection further 'The Danger of the Workings of Kamma', p.329.

[273] This is one of the many ways The Buddha says one should regard the five aggregates in M.II.ii.4 *'Mahā·Mālukya·Suttaṁ'* ('The Great Mālukya Sutta'): see further endnote 268, p.353.

[274] In S.II.I.ii.5 *'Kaccānagotta·Suttaṁ'* ('The Kaccānagotta Sutta'), The Buddha explains that all wrong views can be grouped into two: '"All exists", Kaccāna, this is one extreme. "All does not exist", this is the second extreme.' He then teaches the middle way, which is dependent origination.

[275] The Buddha explains the existent and non-existent in, for example, S.III.I.x.2 *'Puppha·Suttaṁ'* ('The Flower Sutta'): 'Matter [etc.] that is permanent, stable, eternal, not subject to change: this the wise in the world agree upon as not existing, and I too say that it does not exist.... Matter [etc.] that is impermanent, suffering, and subject to change: this the wise in the world agree upon as existing, and I too say that it exists.'

[276] The Buddha explains the world in, e.g. S.IV.I.viii.9 *'Loka·Pañhā·Suttaṁ'* ('The World-Question Sutta'): 'The eye, bhikkhu, is crumbling, sights are crumbling, eye conscious-

ness is crumbling, eye contact is crumbling, and whatever feeling (either painful or pleasant or neither·painful·nor·pleasant) arises with eye contact as cause, that too is crumbling... the ear... tongue... body... mind.... It is crumbling, bhikkhu, that is why it is called the world.'

277 The Buddha explains this in, A.VI.x.9 *'A·Tammaya·Suttaṁ'* ('The "Unconcerned" Sutta'): 'By having seen six advantages, bhikkhus, it is enough for a bhikkhu to establish the perception of impermanence *(anicca·saññā)* in all formations without restriction.What six? "[1] I shall be unconcerned about the whole world, [2] and 'I'-makings will stop in me, [3] and 'Mine'-makings will stop in me, [4] and I shall become possessed of extraordinary knowledge, [5] the root *(hetu)* will be become clearly known to me, [6] and the things arisen with the root."'

278 He was a pupil of King Pasenadi's chaplain Bāvarī. Bāvarī was too old to go and see The Buddha, and sent sixteen of his students to see the Buddha and ask questions, including Mogharāja.

279 In DhP.xiii.4 *'Loka·Vagga'* ('Chapter on the World'), The Buddha says this in connection with two of the similes just mentioned: 'As a bubble seen, as a mirage seen, one who regards the world in this way, the king of death does not see.'

280 Describing the Arahant in M.I.iii.2 *'Alagadd·Ūpama·Suttaṁ'* ('The Snake Simile Sutta'), The Buddha explains: 'The bhikkhu with thus liberated mind, bhikkhus, the devas with Indā, with Brahmā, and with Pajāpatī, seeking, do not find: "Dependent on this is the *tathāgata's* [Arahant's] consciousness." What is the reason? Right then, bhikkhus, the *tathāgata* is unknowable, I declare.' The commentary explains that the devas are unable to discover the object of his insight consciousness, and Path&Fruition consciousnesses.

281 In A.VII.v.6 *'Dutiya·Saññā·Suttaṁ'* ('The Second Perception Sutta'), The Buddha explains how proper development of the perception of foulness *(asubha·saññā)* counters thoughts of sexual intercourse *(methuna·dhamma)*; that of death *(maraṇa·saññā)* counters attachment to life *(jīvita·nikanti)*; that of the repulsiveness of food *(āhāre paṭikūla·saññā)* counters craving for taste *(rasa·taṇhā)*; that of discontent with the whole world *(sabba·loke anabhirata·saññā)* (AA.ibid.: sensual-/fine-material-/immaterial world) counters thoughts of the 'wonderful' world *(loka·citresu)*; and that of impermanence *(anicca·saññā)* counters thoughts of gain, honour, and fame *(lābha·sakkāra·siloka)*. In each case, He explains that when the perception is properly developed, then, just as a bird's feather or a piece of sinew thrown on a fire retreats, retracts, and recoils, so too one's mind retreats, retracts, and recoils from the object, giving rise either to equanimity *(upekkhā)* or disgust *(pāṭikulyatā)*. And for each He adds that it is of great fruit and benefit, is related to the Deathless *(Amat·ogadha)*, and terminates in the Deathless *(Amata·pariyosāna)*. This passage is partly quoted in VsM.ibid.766/PP.xxi.63. For an example of this practice, see 'Māra Dūsī', p.200.

282 In A.IV.V.iv.2 *'Vitthāra·Suttaṁ'* ('The Detailed Sutta'), The Buddha speaks of four types of kamma, using the metaphor of black/white: 1) one accomplishes harmful kamma, is reborn in a harmful world, and experiences harmful contacts and feelings, as beings do in hell = black kamma with a black result; 2) one accomplishes harmless kamma, is reborn in a harmless world, and experiences harmless contacts and feelings, as beings do in the Brahma world = white kamma with a white result; 3) one accomplishes harmful&harmless kamma, is reborn in a harmful&harmless world, and experiences harmful&harmless contacts and feelings, as beings do in the human world, some deva worlds, and some lower beings = black&white kamma with a black&white result; 4) one accomplishes the volition (AA = Path Volition *(magga·cetanā)*) to abandon black, white and black&white kamma and its result, which leads to the destruction of kamma *(kamma·kkhaya)* = non-black & non-white kamma with non-black & non-white results. See also the Buddha's explanations endnotes 300, p.358, 315, p.360, and His simile of the seeds planted in a field, endnote 237, p.255.

283 In M.III.iii.2 *'Mahā·Suññata·Suttaṁ'* ('The Great Voidness Sutta'), The Buddha explains that a bhikkhu who enjoys company with other bhikkhus is neither capable of

ever entering into the mind-liberation that is temporary *(sāmāyika)* nor the one that is not temporary *(a·sāmāyika)*.

[284] The Venerable Ānanda explains it in M.II.i.3 *'Sekha·Suttaṁ'* ('The Trainee Sutta'): 'Here, Mahānāma, a Noble Disciple is moral, by the Pātimokkha restraint restrained he lives, possessed of conduct and resort, in the slightest faults seeing fearsomeness, undertaking to train in the training precepts. That is how, Mahānama, a Noble Disciple is possessed of morality.' And in A.VIII.ii.9 *'Pahārāda·Suttaṁ'* ('The Pahārāda Sutta'), The Buddha explains how the Noble Disciple never transgresses any precept He has laid down: 'Whatever precept has by Me been made known to my disciples, that they do not transgress even for life's sake.' Further, in A.VIII.iv.9 *'Abhisanda·Suttaṁ'* ('The Flow Sutta'), The Buddha explains: 'Here, bhikkhus, a Noble Disciple abandons killing, abstains from killing... theft ... sexual misconduct... lies... he abstains from beer&wine liquor, which is a foundation for carelessness, [as he does so] he gives to countless beings safety ... friendliness ... benevolence.'

[285] In M.I.iii.9 *'Mahā·Sār·Opama·Suttaṁ'* ('The Great Heartwood-Simile Sutta'), The Buddha explains: 'So this holy life, bhikkhus, does not have gain, honour, and renown for its benefit, nor the attainment of virtue for its benefit, nor the attainment of concentration *(samādhi)* for its benefit, nor knowledge and vision for its benefit. But it is this unshakeable liberation of mind that is the goal, bhikkhus, of this holy life, its heartwood, its end.'

[286] In S.III.I.xii.10 *'Sīlavanta·Suttaṁ'* ('The "Virtuous" Sutta'), the Venerable Sāriputta explains that the virtuous bhikkhu must attend carefully to the five aggregates as impermanent, suffering, a disease, etc. Doing so, he may attain Stream Entry. And the Stream Enterer, Once Returner, and Non-Returner must each do the same to attain their next Path. Even the Arahant, he says, should do so, although there is nothing he needs to do, for it leads to a pleasant dwelling in this life (the fruition-/cessation attainment, both which require preceding vipassanā practice).

[286] In S.V.IV.iii.4 *'Eka·Bījī·Suttaṁ'* ('The One-Seeder Sutta'), The Buddha explains three types of Stream Enterer: 1) one attains Arahantship at the end of seven rebirths in the human and heavenly worlds; 2) one does so at the end of two to six rebirths in a good family; 3) one does so after only one rebirth in the human or heavenly worlds (explained also in, e.g. A.III.II.iv.7 *'Dutiya·Sikkhā·Suttaṁ'* ('The Second Training Sutta')).

VbhA.xviii.1028 *'Āyu·Ppamāṇaṁ'* ('Lifespan Reckoning') DD.xviii.2594-2596 further explains that the Stream Enterer/Once Returner reborn in the fine-material or immaterial sphere does not return to the sensual sphere, and is called a Jhāna Non-Returner *(Jhāna·An·Āgamino)*. The jhāna plane attained depends on the jhāna most familiar *(paguṇa)*, one's aspiration *(patthanā)*, or any other jhāna attained at the time of death *(maraṇa·samaye)*.

[288] ONCE RETURNER: there are five types: 1) a human being attains the Once-Return Path& Fruition, and attains Arahantship in the next life as a human being; 2) a human being attains the Path&Fruition, and attains Arahantship in the next life as a heavenly being; 3) a heavenly being attains the Path&Fruition, and attains Arahantship in the next life as a heavenly being; 4) a heavenly being attains the Path&Fruition, and attains Arahantship in the next life as a human being; 5) a human being attains the Path&Fruition, passes the next life as a heavenly being, and attains Arahantship only in the subsequent life as a human being.(PuPA.ii.34 *'Ekaka·Niddesa·Vaṇṇanā'* ('Description of the First Exposition') & VsMṬ.xxii.814 *'Tatiya·Magga·Ñāṇa·Kathā·Vaṇṇanā'* ('Description of the Discussion of the Third Path Knowledge')). But when The Buddha speaks of a Once Returner, usually He means one who returns to human existence: No. 5 above. See also explanation from VbhA in previous endnote.

[289] NON-RETURNER: all are reborn in the fine-material sphere (the Brahma world). There are five types: 1) one attains Arahantship halfway through that Brahma life; 2) one attains Arahantship in the second half of that Brahma life, even on the point of death; 3) one attains Arahantship without exertion; 4) one attains Arahantship with exertion; 5) one passes from one Brahma world to another, living out the whole life span (from a third of an aeon up to 16,000 aeons: each time, it is a jhāna kamma in the one life that

functions as subsequently-effective productive kamma to give him his next Brahma rebirth), and reaching the highest of the five pure abodes, the *Akaniṭṭha* world. There he attains Arahantship (S.V.IV.iii.4 etc., as endnote 287, p.356).

VbhA.xviii.1028 *'Āyu·Ppamāṇaṁ'* ('Lifespan Reckoning') DD.xviii.2593 further explains that one who attains Non-Return in the sensual deva world does not remain, but takes a fine-material existence: because there is no other suitable place for one without sensual desire. See also endnote 295, p.357.

In D.ii.1 *'Mahā·Padāna·Suttaṁ'* ('The Great-Lineage Sutta'), The Buddha speaks of visiting the pure abodes, and being told by many thousand Non-Returners still abiding there of the past Buddha's dispensation during which they attained their Path&Fruition.

[290] In D.iii.6 *'Pāsādika Sutta'* ('Delightful Sutta'), The Buddha explains nine things that the Arahant is incapable of doing: 1) killing, 2) stealing, 3) incelibacy, 4) lying, 5) storing up things for sensual pleasure like a householder, 6) doing something out of desire, 7) out of hatred, 8) out of delusion, 9) out of fear.

[291] Thus, The Buddha explains that kamma with the three wholesome roots leads to the ending of kamma: see quotation, endnote 88, p.237. In A.IV.IV.i.9 *'Bhikkhunī·Suttaṁ'* ('The Bhikkhunī Sutta'), the Venerable Ānanda explains how craving *(taṇhā)* to attain Arahantship overcomes craving. And in S.V.VII.ii.5 *'Uṇṇābha·Brāhmaṇa·Suttaṁ'* ('The Uṇṇābha Sutta'), he explains how desire *(chanda)* to attain Arahantship overcomes desire. (For details in this regard, see footnote 597, p.205.)

[292] In M.III.v.7 *'Mahā·Saḷ·Āyatanika·Suttaṁ'* ('The Great Sixfold-Base Sutta'), The Buddha explains that when the Noble Eightfold Path arises, 'These two things occur concurrently yoked: samatha [Right Concentration] and vipassanā [Right View].' The commentary explains that they arise at the same time.

[293] The Buddha explains it in, for example, M.I.iv.5 *'Cūḷa·Saccaka·Suttaṁ'* ('The Small Saccaka Sutta'): 'Attained to Nibbāna is the Blessed One: He teaches the Dhamma for attaining to Nibbāna.'

[294] The Buddha explains it in, for example, D.ii.3 *'Mahā·Parinibbāna·Suttaṁ'* ('The Great-Parinibbāna Sutta')) 'In whatever Dhamma and Vinaya the Noble Eightfold Path is not found, there no [one] ascetic is found. There no second ascetic is found. There no third ascetic is found. There no fourth ascetic is found.' See also quotation, endnote 39, p.25.

[295] In M.II.iii.1 *'Te·Vijja·Vacchagotta·Suttaṁ'* ('The Triple-Science Vacchagotta Sutta'), The Buddha explains that a lay-arahant must either ordain or attain Parinibbāna: 'Vaccha, there is no householder who, without abandoning the fetter of householdership, on the breakup of the body has made an end of suffering.' VbhA.xviii.1028 *'Āyu·Ppamāṇaṁ'* ('Lifespan-Reckoning') DD.xviii.2593 also explains that since the sensual-sphere deva world is unsuitable for an Arahant (and since a deva cannot become a bhikkhuni/bhikkhu), the sensual-sphere deva who attains Arahantship attains Parinibbāna at the same time.

[296] The Buddha explains this in D.ii.3 *'Mahā·Parinibbāna·Suttaṁ'* ('The Great-Parinibbāna Sutta'): 'The Four Foundations of Mindfulness, the Four Right Efforts, the Four Bases of Success, the Five Faculties, the Five Powers, the Seven Factors of Enlightenment, the Noble Eightfold Path. These, bhikkhus, are the things of which I have direct knowledge and have taught, which you should learn well, cultivate, develop, practise much, so that this holy life *(brahma·cariya)* is established, and long endures, for the many's welfare, for the many's happiness, out of compassion for the world, for the benefit, well being, and happiness of devas and human beings.' These things are also called the Thirty-Seven Requisites of Enlightenment *(Satta·Tiṁsa·Bodhi·Pakkhiya·Dhamma)*.

[297] In D.ii.3 *'Mahā·Parinibbāna·Suttaṁ'* ('The Great-Parinibbāna Sutta'), The Buddha explains to a wanderer: 'And if, Subhadda, bhikkhus were to rightly to dwell *(sammā vihareyyuṁ)*, the world would not be void of Arahants.' The commentary explains that 'rightly to dwell' means the Stream Enterer teaches others how to attain the Stream-Entry Path& Fruition, the Once Returner teaches others to how to attain the Once-Return Path&Fruition, etc. And the one who is as yet only practising samatha and vipassanā for the at-

tainment of a Path&Fruition should teach that. Also in Vin.Mv.I.8 *'Māra Kathā'* ('Māra Discussion'), The Buddha says to His first sixty Arahant Disciples: 'Freed am I, bhikkhus, from all snares, both divine and human. And you too, bhikkhus, are freed from all snares, both divine and human. Wander, bhikkhus, for the many's welfare, for the many's happiness, out of compassion for the world, for the benefit, well being, and happiness of devas and men. Let not any of you go together. Teach, bhikkhus, the Dhamma, which in the beginning is lovely, in the middle is lovely, and in the end is lovely.'

[298] The Venerable Sāriputta explains this in TG.xvii.2 (1002) *'Sāriputta·Tthera·Gāthā'* ('The Sāriputta-Elder Verses'): 'I do not delight in life, I do not delight in death; I await the time [of Parinibbāna], like a government servant [waits for] his wages.'

[299] The Buddha explains the two types of Nibbāna element in Iti.ii.8 *'Nibbāna·Dhātu·Suttaṁ'* ('The Nibbāna-Element Sutta'), : '[1] Here, bhikkhus, a bhikkhu is an Arahant... In him, still established are the five faculties [eye/ear/nose/tongue/body] through which... he experiences sensations pleasant and unpleasant, undergoes pleasure and pain. In him, the end of lust, hatred, and delusion, bhikkhus, is called "Nibbāna with clung [aggregates] remainder...." [2] Here, a bhikkhu is an Arahant.... In him, in this very life, all things that are sensed [sights/sounds/odours/flavours/touches/other things] have no delight for him: they have become cool. This is called "Nibbāna without clung [aggregates] remainder."

[300] In A.X.IV.ii.8 *'Kamma·Nidāna·Suttaṁ'* ('The Kamma-Causation Sutta'), The Buddha explains: 'With greed-... hatred-... delusion destruction, there is kamma-causation destruction *(kamma·nidāna·saṅkhayo)*.' See also endnote 282, p.355.

[301] In M.I.iv.9 *'Mahā-Assapura·Suttaṁ'* ('The Great Assapura Sutta'), The Buddha explains that a bhikkhu is an ascetic *(samaṇa)* when evil, unwholesome things that defile, produce renewed existence, are harmful, result in suffering, lead to future birth, ageing-&death are appeased.

[302] In S.III.I.i.1 *'Nakulapitā·Suttaṁ'* ('The Nakulapitā Sutta') The Buddha explains this to one Nakulapitā: 'Even though my body be afflicted, my mind will not be.' Afterwards, the Venerable Sāriputta explains to him that this is achieved by not identifying with the five aggregates, and being rid of the defilements: only then does bodily pain not give rise to mental pain.

[303] In S.II.I.vi.1 *'Pari·Vīmaṁsana·Suttaṁ'* ('The Thorough Investigation Sutta'), The Buddha explains that 'mere bodily remains are seen.'

[304] There are cases, however, of one attaining both types of Parinibbāna at the same time. The Buddha explains such a case in A.VII.ii.6, 7, 8 *'Aniccā... Dukkhā ... Anatt-·Ānupassī·Suttaṁ'* ('The Impermanence... Suffering... Non-Self Contemplation Sutta').

[305] The Buddha explains birth in, for example, D.ii.9 *'Mahā·Sati·Paṭṭhāna·Suttaṁ'* ('The Great Mindfulness-Foundation Sutta'): 'And what, bhikkhus, is birth? The birth of the various beings into the various orders of beings, their being born, descent, production, the appearance of the aggregates, the acquisition of the sense bases: this is called birth.'

[306] The Buddha explains it in, for example, D.ii.2 *'Mahā·Nidāna·Suttaṁ'* ('The Great Causation Sutta'): 'I have said: "Because of consciousness, there is mentality-materiality *(viññāṇa·paccayā nāma·rūpaṁ)*," and this is the way it should be understood. If consciousness, Ānanda, were not to descend into the mother's womb, would mentality-materiality develop there?'

[307] The Venerable Sāriputta explains this in M.I.v.3 *'Mahā·Vedalla·Suttaṁ'* ('The Great Catechism Sutta'): 'Feeling, perception, and consciousness, friend: these things are conjoined, not disjoined, and it is impossible to separate each of these things from the others in order to describe the difference between them. For what one senses, that one perceives, and what one perceives that one is conscious of.' See also next endnote.

[308] The Buddha explains this in *'Upaya·Suttaṁ'* ('The Assumption Sutta'): 'Whoever, bhikkhus, were to say thus: "As separate from materiality... feelings... perception... separate

from formations, I shall make known consciousness's coming or going, or decease, or re-arising, or growth, or increase, or completion," that is not possible.' See also previous endnote.

[309] The Buddha explains it in, for example, D.ii.2 *'Mahā·Nidāna·Suttaṁ'* ('The Great Causation Sutta'): 'I have said: "Because of mentality-materiality, there is consciousness *(nāma·rūpa·paccayā viññāṇaṁ),*" and this is the way it should be understood. If consciousness, Ānanda, did not obtain establishment in mentality-materiality *(nāma·rūpe·patiṭṭhaṁ na labhissatha),* would there then be an arising and existence of birth, ageing, death and suffering?' The Buddha is here referring to the cause of mentality-materiality within one life (see quotation footnote ‡ under table '3e: Dependent Origination from Life to Life', p.349): if one goes beyond the one life, the cause of consciousness is formation, which is the kammic potency of a kamma formed in a past life.

[310] In D.i.1 *'Brahma·Jāla·Suttaṁ'* ('The Supreme Net Sutta'), the Buddha explains that as soon as perception arises in such impercipient beings, they vanish. Someone may be reborn as human being after such an existence, and be unable to recall that past life. They may then teach that birth occurs by chance. And in A.IX.I.iii.4 *'Satt·Āvāsa·Suttaṁ'* ('The Abode-of-Being Sutta'), The Buddha mentions impercipient beings as one of nine types of abode. Then in Vbh.XVIII.ii.3 *'Asañña·Sattā'* ('Impercipient Beings') BA.XVIII.-ii.1017, He explains: 'At the impercipient-being devas' moment of rebirth, one aggregate manifests: the materiality aggregate. Two bases manifest: the sight base, the dhamma base. Two elements manifest: the sight element, the dhamma element. One truth manifests: the truth of suffering. One faculty manifests: the material life faculty. Impercipient-being devas manifest without root, without nutriment, without contact, without feeling, without perception, without volition, without consciousness.' And VbhA.xviii.1027 *'Āyu·Ppamāṇaṁ'* ('Life Span') DD.xviii.2588 explains further: 'For some, after going forth in a sectarian sphere and seeing a fault in consciousness because lusting, hating and being deluded depend upon consciousness, imagine that: "The consciousnessless state is good, this is nibbāna in the present existence;" and they generate the fading away of greed for perception and developing the fifth attainment in conformity therewith, they are reborn there. At the moment of their rebirth, the materiality aggregate alone is reborn. If he is reborn standing, he stands only; if reborn sitting, he sits only; if reborn lying down, he lies only. They remain for five hundred aeons like painted statues. At their end the material body vanishes; sensual-sphere perception arises. Through the arising of that perception here [in this sensual sphere] those deities notice that they have passed away from that body.'

[311] In D.iii.5 *'Sampasādanīya·Suttaṁ'* ('The Faith-Inspiring Sutta'), the Venerable Sāriputta explains how The Buddha teaches the meditator to know both the uninterrupted *(abbocchinnaṁ)* flow of consciousness *(viññāṇa·sota)* in this world established *(patiṭṭhita),* and in another world established. For details, see footnote 306, p.107, and table '5a: Death and Rebirth', p.52.

[312] In, S.II.I.ii.9 *'Bāla·Paṇḍita·Suttaṁ'* ('The Fool&Sage Sutta') The Buddha explains that because the fool does not destroy ignorance and craving, he is reborn: 'Because the fool has not lived the holy life for the complete destruction of suffering. Therefore, with the breakup of the body, the fool fares on to [another] body *(kāy·ūpago).* Faring on to [another] body, he is not released from birth, ageing, and death.' But destroying ignorance, the sage is no longer reborn: 'Because the sage has lived the holy life for the complete destruction of suffering. Therefore, with the breakup of the body, the sage does not fare on to [another] body. Not faring on to [another] body, he is released from birth, ageing, and death.' See also quotations endnote 191, p.251, and 315, p.360.

[313] The Buddha explains this in, for example, A.III.II.iii.6 *'Paṭhama·Bhava·Suttaṁ'* ('The First Existence Sutta'): 'Sensual-element [sensual-sphere kamma-] result, and, Ānanda, kamma not existing, would any sensual existence be manifest?... Fine-material element [fine-material sphere kamma-] result... and kamma not existing, would any fine-material existence be manifest?... Immaterial element [immaterial-sphere kamma] result... and

kamma not existing, would any immaterial existence be manifest?' ('Surely not, Venerable Sir.') 'In this way, Ānanda, kamma is the field, consciousness is the seed, craving the moisture. For ignorance-hindered beings fettered by craving in the inferior element [sensual] ... in the middle element [fine material]... in the superior element [immaterial], there is consciousness established *(viññāṇam patiṭṭhitaṁ)*. Thus, in the future, there is re-existence of rebirth.'

[314] In S.II.I.vii.4 *'Atthi·Rāga·Suttaṁ'* ('The There-Is-Lust Sutta') and SA.ibid., The Buddha explains that with delight and craving for the nutriments edible food/contact/mental volition/consciousness, consciousness becomes established there by kamma that can produce rebirth. Wherever the resultant rebirth-consciousness then is established, there is descent of mentality-materiality, which means there is new production of kamma, which means there is production of re-existence *(atthi āyatiṁ puna·bbhav·ābhinibbatti)*. The opposite holds true of the Arahant, whose consciousness does not become established in the four nutriments by kamma, which means there is no resultant rebirth-consciousness to become established anywhere, which means there is no descent of mentality-materiality, no new production of kamma, which means no production of re-existence *(natthi āyatiṁ puna·bbhav·ābhinibbatti)*.

[315] The Buddha explains it also in, for example, S.II.I.vi.1 *'Pari·Vīmaṁsana·Suttaṁ'* ('The Thorough-Investigation Sutta'): 'But when a bhikkhu has abandoned ignorance and aroused true knowledge... he does not accomplish a meritorious formation (of kamma), or a demeritorious formation, or an imperturbable formation... When there are utterly no formations, with the cessation of formations, would [rebirth] consciousness be discerned?' ('No, Venerable Sir.') 'When there is utterly no consciousness... no mentality-materiality ... no six bases... no birth, with the cessation of birth, would ageing&death be discerned?' ('No, Venerable Sir.') See also quotation endnotes 191, p.251, 282, p.355. and 312, p.359.

[316] In U.viii.1 *'Paṭhama Nibbāna Paṭisaṁyutta·Suttaṁ'* ('First Nibbāna-Related Section Sutta'), The Buddha explains: 'Truly, there is a base, where there is neither earth, nor water, nor fire, nor air, nor the infinite-space base, nor the infinite-consciousness base, nor the nothingness base, nor the neither-perception nor non-perception base; where there is not this world, nor another world, not either moon or sun. This I call neither coming, nor going, nor staying, nor decease, nor rebirth. It is quite without establishment, without continuity, and without object.'

[317] In D.i.11 *'Kevaṭṭa·Suttaṁ'* ('The Kevaṭṭa Sutta'), The Buddha describes Nibbāna as: 'Invisible cognition, infinite, everywhere a landing-place, here water, earth, fire, and wind gain no footing. Here long and short, small and large, fair and foul; here mentality and materiality, completely stops; with consciousness's cessation, here this stops.' DA explains: INVISIBLE COGNITION = Nibbāna in the sense that it is cognizable by the Noble Path Knowledges, not by eye consciousness; infinite = not limited by arising, perishing and standing, no North, South, East, and West; EVERYWHERE A LANDING-PLACE (the further shore *(pārima tīra)*) = can be reached anywhere, using any of the forty meditation-subjects; WITH CONSCIOUSNESS'S CESSATION: the cessation of kamma consciousness, and the cessation of the Arahant's final consciousness. In this connection, The Buddha explains in A.VIII.ii.9 *'Pahārāda·Suttaṁ'* ('The Pahārāda Sutta'): 'Even if many bhikkhus attain to the Nibbāna of the Nibbāna element without remainder, not by that is the Nibbāna element's emptiness or fullness known.'

[318] In S.I.II.iii.6 *'Rohitassa·Suttaṁ'* ('The Rohitassa Sutta'), The Buddha refers to the five aggregates as the world *(loka)*, and to Arahantship as the cessation of the world. And in S.II.I.v.4 *'Loka·Sutta'* ('The World Sutta'), The Buddha explains the origin of the world: 'In dependence on the eye and sights, arises eye consciousness. The meeting of the three is contact [etc. through the factors of dependent origination]. This, bhikkhus, is the origin of the world.' And He says the same for the other six types of internal base, external base, and consciousness. Conversely, with the remainderless dispassion and

cessation of craving, the subsequent factors cease, and, 'This, bhikkhus, is the disappearance of the world.' See also quotation endnote 50, p.27.

[319] The Buddha explains it in, for example, M.I.iv.8'Mahā·Taṇhā·Saṅkhaya·Suttaṁ' ('The Great Craving-Destruction Sutta'): 'In many discourses have I stated consciousness to be dependently arisen, since without a cause there is no origination of consciousness.... Consciousness is reckoned by the particular cause dependent upon which it arises.' He then explains how eye consciousness depends on the eye and sights, etc. (see previous endnote). And: 'When consciousness arises dependent on the mind and other things *(dhamma)*, it is reckoned as mind consciousness.' Nibbāna, being a thing other than the five material external bases (being a thing of the sixth external base), is cognized by mind consciousness.

[320] In S.III.I.x.2 *'Puppha·Suttaṁ'* ('The Flower Sutta'), The Buddha explains: 'Consciousness that is permanent, stable, eternal, not subject to change: this the wise in the world agree upon as not existing, and I too say that it does not exist.' See also quotation endnote 143, p.244, and 270, p.354.

[321] The Buddha explains this throughout His Teaching, for example, in His first teaching, (S.V.XII.ii.1 *'Dhamma·Cakka·Ppavattana·Suttaṁ'* ('The Dhamma-Wheel Setting-in-Motion Sutta'), He says: 'In short, the five clinging-aggregates are suffering *(dukkha)*.'

[322] In S.V.IV.v.10 *'Āpaṇa·Suttaṁ'* ('The Āpaṇa Sutta'), The Buddha discusses the Noble Disciple's development of the five faculties with the Venerable Sāriputta. And He says: 'Indeed, Sāriputta, of any Noble Disciple of faith, of firm energy, of established mindfulness, and of concentrated mind, it is to be expected that he will understand in this way: "Inconceivable is the beginning of the round of rebirth. A first point is not known of ignorance-hindered beings fettered by craving, rushing on and running about. But with ignorance's, the mass of darkness's, remainderless fading away and cessation, this is the peaceful place, this is the superior place, namely, the calming of all formations, the forsaking of all grounds [for rebirth], the destruction of craving, dispassion, cessation, Nibbāna. That wisdom of his, Sāriputta, that is his wisdom faculty."' See also dependent origination in negative order, quoted p.110.

[323] A wanderer called Vacchagotta also asks this question in M.II.iii.2 *'Aggi·Vacchagotta·Suttaṁ'* ('The Fire&Vacchagotta Sutta'): 'When a bhikkhu's mind is liberated thus, Master Gotama, where is he reborn?... Then is he not reborn... both reborn and not reborn... neither reborn nor not reborn, Master Gotama?' In all cases, The Buddha says the question does not apply. That is because there is simply no re-arising of consciousness: to speak of an Arahant not being reborn is an instance of the annihilation view. Afterwards, The Buddha explains as the Most Venerable Sayadaw does here, with the fire simile. Also in S.IV.x.9 *'Kutūhala·Sālā·Suttaṁ'* ('The Debating Hall Sutta'), The Buddha explains: 'Just as a fire burns with fuel but not without fuel, so, Vaccha, I declare rebirth for one with fuel, not for one without fuel [the fuel of rebirth is ignorance and craving].'

[324] UNESTABLISHED CONSCIOUSNESS: The Buddha uses this term in, for example, S.I.IV.iii.3 *'Godhika·Suttaṁ'* ('The Godhika Sutta'). It describes how, after the Venerable Godhika has attained Parinibbāna, The Buddha and some bhikkhus go to his dwelling. There is a dark cloud moving around nearby. And the Buddha says: 'That, bhikkhus, is Māra the Evil One looking for the consciousness of the clansman Godhika, wondering: "Where has clansman Godhika's consciousness been established?..." With unestablished consciousness, bhikkhus, the clansman Godhika has attained complete Nibbāna.' The same thing happens after the Parinibbāna of the Venerable Vakkali, mentioned p.7. For Māra's not knowing the coming and going of the Arahant, see 'Māra Dūsī', p.200.

[325] Thus, in, for example, D.i.1 *'Brahma·Jāla·Suttaṁ'* ('The Supreme Net Sutta'), The Buddha explains: 'Just as, bhikkhus, when the stalk of a bunch of mangoes has been cut, all the mangoes hanging on it go with it, just so the Tathāgata's link with existence has been cut. As long as the body subsists, devas and human beings will see Him. But at the breakup of the body, and the exhaustion of the life span, devas and human beings will see Him no more.'

[326] In S.II.I.ii.5 *'Kaccānagotta·Suttaṁ'*, The Buddha explains that with knowledge of dependent origination one no longer doubts that what arises is only suffering, and what ceases is only suffering: see quotation endnote 166, p.247. And He says: 'His knowledge *(ñāṇa)* about this is not because of another *(a·para·paccayā)*. It is in this way, Kaccāna, that there is Right View *(Sammā Diṭṭhi hoti)*.'

[327] *TATHĀGATA*: The Buddha uses this to refer to Himself, although in some contexts, He uses it to refers to any Arahant, as here, and in quotation endnote 280, p.355. In, for example S.III.I.ix.4 *'Anurādha·Suttaṁ'* ('The Anurādha Sutta'), the term is: '*tathāgato*, the supreme man *(uttama·puriso)*, the ultimate man *(parama·puriso)*, the one who has attained the ultimate *(parama·pattipatto)*.'

APPENDIX 1: THE FORTY MEDITATION SUBJECTS

The forty meditation subjects taught by The Buddha,[952] for the development of samatha meditation, with some sutta references.[953]

Kasiṇa	+	Foulness	+	Recollection	+	Divine Abiding	+	Immaterial	+	Perception	+	Defining	=	Total
10	+	10	+	10	+	4	+	4	+	1	+	1	=	40

Ten Kasiṇas

D.ii.2 *'Mahā·Nidāna·Suttaṁ'* ('The Great Causation Sutta')
M.II.iii.7 *'Mahā·Sakuludāyi·Suttaṁ'* ('The Great Sakuludāyi Sutta')

Ten Foulnesses

D.ii.9 *'Mahā·Sati·Paṭṭhāna·Suttaṁ'* ('The Great Mindfulness-Foundation Sutta')
M.III.ii.9 *'Kāya·Gatā·Sati·Suttaṁ'* ('The Body-Related Mindfulness Sutta')

Ten Recollections:

Buddha, Dhamma, Sangha

D.ii.3 *'Mahā·Parinibbāna·Suttaṁ'* ('The Great-Parinibbāna Sutta')
S.I.XI.i.3 *'Dhajagga Suttaṁ'* ('The Standard Sutta')

Virtue

D.ii.3 *'Mahā·Parinibbāna·Suttaṁ'* ('The Great-Parinibbāna Sutta')
A.III.II.ii.10 *'Uposatha·Suttaṁ'* ('The Uposatha Sutta')

Generosity

A.VI.i.10 *'Mahānāma·Suttaṁ'* ('The Mahānāma Sutta')

Devas

A.III.II.ii.10 *'Uposatha·Suttaṁ'* ('The Uposatha Sutta')
A.VI.i.10 *'Mahānāma·Suttaṁ'* ('The Mahānāma Sutta')

Death

A.VI.ii.9 *'Paṭhama·Maraṇa·Ssati·Suttaṁ'* ('The First Death-Recollection Sutta')
A.VI.ii.10 *'Dutiya·Maraṇa·Ssati·Suttaṁ'* ('The Second Death-Recollection Sutta')

Body-Related Mindfulness[954]

D.ii.9 *'Mahā·Sati·Paṭṭhāna·Suttaṁ'* ('The Great Mindfulness-Foundation Sutta')
M.III.ii.9 *'Kāya·Gatā·Sati·Suttaṁ'* ('The Body-Related Mindfulness Sutta')

Mindfulness-of-Breathing

D.ii.9 *'Mahā·Sati·Paṭṭhāna·Suttaṁ'* ('The Great Mindfulness-Foundation Sutta')
M.III.ii.9 *'Kāya·Gatā·Sati·Suttaṁ'* ('The Body-Related Mindfulness Sutta')

Peace[955]

M.II.ii.4 *'Mahā·Mālukyāputta·Suttaṁ'* ('The Great Mālukyāputta Sutta')
A.X.I.i.6 *'Samādhi·Suttaṁ'* ('The Concentration Sutta')

---

[952] VsM.iii.47 *'Kamma·Ṭṭhāna·Ggahaṇa·Niddeso'* ('Exposition of the Meditation-Subject Obtainment') PP.iii.104-105.

[953] The sutta references given are only examples: there are more suttas that mention these meditation subjects.

[954] In the *Visuddhi·Magga*'s listing, body-related mindfulness refers specifically to meditation on the thirty-two parts of the body. The term body-related mindfulness, however, is used by the Buddha in many ways. Thus, in M.III.ii.9 *'Kāya·Gatā·Sati·Suttaṁ'* ('The Body-Related Mindfulness Sutta'), for example, The Buddha explains it as the exact same fourteen body-contemplations (incl. meditation on the thirty-two parts of the body) that He explains in D.ii.9 *'Mahā·Sati·Paṭṭhāna·Suttaṁ'* ('The Great Mindfulness-Foundation Sutta'), as well as the four material jhānas: at each explanation He says: 'That too is how a bhikkhu develops body-related mindfulness.'

[955] This is recollecting the qualities of Nibbāna.

Four Divine Abidings

Loving-Kindness

M.I.iii.1 *'Kakac·Ūpama·Suttaṁ'* ('The Saw-Simile Sutta')
A.IV.II.ii.7 *'Ahi·Rāja·Suttaṁ'* ('The Snake-King Sutta')

Loving-Kindness, Compassion, Sympathetic Joy, Equanimity

D.i.13 *'Te·Vijja·Suttaṁ'* ('The Three-Sciences Sutta')
M.II.iv.3 *'Maghadeva·Suttaṁ'* ('The Maghadeva Sutta')
A.III.II.ii.5 *'Kesamutti·Suttaṁ'* ('The Kesamutti Sutta')[956]

Four Immaterials

The Boundless-Space Base, The Boundless-Consciousness Base, the Nothingness Base, the Neither-Perception nor Non-Perception Base

D.ii.2 *'Mahā·Nidāna·Suttaṁ'* ('The Great Causation-Sutta')
M.I.iii.6 *'Ariya·Pariyesanā·Suttaṁ'* ('The Noble-Search Sutta')[957]
M.III.i.6 *'Āneñjasappāya·Suttaṁ'* ('The Imperturbable-Wards Sutta')
A.IX.I.iv.5 *'Jhāna·Suttaṁ'* ('The Jhāna Sutta')

One Perception

Nutriment

S.V.II.viii.3 *'Āhāre·Paṭikūla·Suttaṁ'* ('The Nutriment-Repulsiveness Sutta')
A.X.II.i.6 *'Paṭhama·Saññā·Suttaṁ'* ('The First Perception Sutta')
A.X.II.i.7 *'Dutiya·Saññā·Suttaṁ'* ('The Second Perception Sutta')

One Defining

Four Elements

D.ii.9 *'Mahā·Sati·Paṭṭhāna·Suttaṁ'* ('The Great Mindfulness-Foundation Sutta')
M.III.ii.9 *'Kāya·Gatā·Sati·Suttaṁ'* ('The Body-Related Mindfulness Sutta')

---

[956] Also known as 'The Kālāma Sutta'.
[957] Also called *'Pāsa·Rāsi·Suttaṁ'* ('The Mass of Snares Sutta').

Four incalculables and one-hundred thousand aeons ago, a hermit Sumedha resolved to become a Buddha. He did this in the presence of The Buddha Dīpaṅkara. The Buddha Dīpaṅkara prophesied that he would eventually become The Buddha Gotama. From then till his attainment of Buddhahood as The Buddha Gotama, the Bodhisatta developed his pāramī. That included training under twenty-four different Buddhas: sometimes as a hermit, sometimes as a bhikkhu, or a Brahmin, a king, a lord, a superior animal, a deva, or yakkha.

The twenty-four Buddhas are explained in *The Buddha·Lineage Text (Buddha·Vaṁsa·Pāḷi)*. It explains their birth, life span, status, the name of their parents, the name of their wives and children, their life span, way of renunciation, the duration of their efforts to attain Buddhahood, their teaching of the *'Dhamma·Cakka·Ppavatthana·Suttaṁ'* ('The Dhamma-Wheel Setting-in-Motion Sutta'),[958] and the name of their Chief Disciples and chief lay-disciples. Each account explains also where they went into Parinibbāna, and how their relics were distributed.

Included in *The Buddha·Lineage Text* is The Buddha's prophecy of the next Buddha, The Buddha Metteya:[959]

24) The Buddha Dīpaṅkara	11) The Buddha Atthadassī
23) The Buddha Koṇḍañña	10) The Buddha Dhammadassī
22) The Buddha Maṅgala	9) The Buddha Siddhattha
21) The Buddha Sumana	8) The Buddha Tissa
20) The Buddha Revata	7) The Buddha Phussa
19) The Buddha Sobhita	6) The Buddha Vipassī
18) The Buddha Anomadassī	5) The Buddha Sikhī
17) The Buddha Paduma	4) The Buddha Vessabhū
16) The Buddha Nārada	3) The Buddha Kakusandha
15) The Buddha Padumuttara	2) The Buddha Koṇāgamana
14) The Buddha Sumedha	1) The Buddha Kassapa
13) The Buddha Sujāta	The Buddha Gotama
12) The Buddha Piyadassī	The Buddha Metteya

The six Buddhas before The Buddha Gotama are explained by our Buddha also in *'Mah·Āpadāna·Suttaṁ'* ('The Great-Lineage Sutta'). He explains, for example:[960]

958 The Buddha Gotama's version of this sutta is found in S.V.XII.ii.1.

959 The Buddha Gotama mentions the coming of The Buddha Metteya also in D.iii.3 *'Cakka·Vatti·Sīha·Nāda·Suttaṁ'* ('The Wheel-Turning Lion's-Roar Sutta').

960 (D.ii.1) The Buddha knows this by His own knowledge, and also because Non-Returners in the pure abodes describe to him the past dispensation during which they attained their Path&Fruition.

Name	Appearance	Status	Human Life span (years)
6) The Buddha Vipassī	91 aeons ago	Noble	80,000
5) The Buddha Sikhī	31 aeons ago	Noble	70,000
4) The Buddha Vessabhū		Noble	60,000
3) The Buddha Kakusandha	present aeon	Brahmin	40,000
2) The Buddha Koṇāgamana		Brahmin	30,000
1) The Buddha Kassapa		Brahmin	20,000
The Buddha Gotama		Noble	100

EDITOR'S NOTE
(Second Revised Edition)

The Workings of Kamma was over several years prepared by the Most Venerable Pa-Auk Tawya Sayadaw and various of his bhikkhu disciples at Pa-Auk Tawya Forest Monastery, Myanmar: as a *Dhamma·dāna*, for the many's welfare and happiness. The Sayadaw checked whatever his editors had prepared, including the final manuscript. But owing to continuous visitors, the Sayadaw could never find sufficient peace to check the final manuscript well and thoroughly.

During a meditation retreat abroad, however, the Sayadaw found sufficient peace properly to check the entire book, and he made some amendments. The most notable ones were:[961/*328*]

- The **Arahant's consciousness** may be knowledge dissociated*(ñāṇa·vippayutta)*: see p.57 <1st ed., p.57>.
- The **wholesome resultant consciousness** that is unrooted may function not only as a process-separate consciousness (already discussed), but also as a process consciousness (added to the discussion): see notes under table, p.63.
- The factor of **great learning***(bāhu·sacca)* under 'Conduct*(caraṇa)*', includes the first two insight knowledges: knowing and seeing ultimate mentality/materiality/their origin. See, for example, p.138 <1st ed., p.133>.
- In the first edition's explanation of the five-door process, it said the **'knowing'** of an object taken by a five-door process 'takes place at the fifth subsequent mental processes' <p.143>, which was not only ungrammatical, but also disagreed with the subsequent explanation of visual cognition <p.145>. Thus, it should say that the knowing of a five-door object 'takes place at the **fourth** and subsequent mental processes.' See in this edition p.147.
- In the first edition, it said that of the many thousand million **first-impulsion volitions** arising during one particular kamma, only one is able to produce its result in this life: but there is no such restriction. That restriction exists only for subsequently-effective kamma. See under 'Presently-Effective Kamma' and 'Subsequently-Effective Kamma', p.151 <1st ed., p.146>, and at every other mention of presently-effective kamma, especially under 'The Workings of Kamma Past/Present/Future', p.162*f*<1st ed., p.158>.
- The **table** describing **the attainment of jhāna** covers both fine-material and immaterial jhāna. In the first edition, 'the counterpart sign' was given as object, which does not apply to the immaterial jhānas. Hence, the object is now described as 'Jhāna Object', and the table is now called 'The Jhāna-Attainment Process': see p.178 <1st ed., 'The Absorption Process', p.174>.
- Under **The Kaṇṇamuṇḍa Devī** (p.189) <1st ed., p.183>, it said a 'wholesome kamma' gave her rebirth as a beautiful mansion-ghost: this was meant to refer only to her beauty. It could, however, be misconstrued to refer to her having become a ghost. Thus, it is now: 'Her unwholesome kamma of lying about her adultery gave her rebirth as a mansion-ghost*(vimāna·peti)*. But because of wholesome kamma, she was beautiful....'
- **King Ajātasattu** will in the distant future become a Paccekabuddha called Vijitāvī, not Vijita: see, for example, p.191 <1st ed., p.187>.

---

[961] For changes made since the first printing of the second revised edition, see subsequent endnote 328, p.378.

- Regarding **the five hundred bhikkhus** who were killed either by themselves or another, the Most Venerable Sayadaw (and the commentary) emphasizes that those who were Noble Ones did not kill themselves or kill another: this emphasis has been added: see p.199*ff*<1st ed., p.194*ff*>.
  Having become aware that there are those who disbelieve the workings of kamma in this story, the Sayadaw has also elaborated upon it, so as to help such readers overcome their scepticism.
- The name of the first human being to attain Stream Entry in this Dispensation is in the *'Dhamma·Cakka·Ppavattana'* sutta given as **Aññāsikoṇḍañña**, although he is in the Texts referred to also as Aññākondaññā (the name given in the first edition): see p.216 <1st ed., p.211>.
- Resolution of **the Venerable Bākula**'s name should be: *bā* = two/both; *kula* = families: see p.267*ff*<1st ed., p.268>.
- The discussion of **Nanda**'s kamma while honouring The Buddha said: 'And of the seven impulsions, the middle five impulsions are the most powerful: kammas to be experienced in some subsequent life, subsequent to the next life.' The middle five are, however, indefinitely-effective kammas, to be experienced in a life after the subsequent life: see p.273*ff*<1st ed., p.272>.
- The **Stream Enterer/Once Returner** who is reborn in the fine-material or immaterial sphere does not return to the sensual sphere, and is called a Jhāna Non-Returner*(Jhāna·An·Āgamino)*: see explanation in endnote 287, p.354 <1st ed., endnote 34, p.357>.

Other amendments were elaborations for the sake of greater accuracy (see, for example, the two factors for **wrong view** now elaborated, p.129<1st ed., p.124>; the distinction between **conclusive volition and preceding&succeeding volitions**, under for example 'Function of Effect', p.186 <1st ed., p.181>; and the new description of how the **body is maintained by nutriment**, under 'Nutriment-Born Materiality', p.103 <1st ed., p.100>), and some more examples.

The editor has also improved some of the tables (further improved by the Sayadaw, and also finally approved by him), and has added a few more example stories (see, for example, The Parsimonious Millionaire, p.34). Owing to many difficulties with the proof of the first edition (owing to an unstable computer program), the footnotes and endnotes have now been made to run on from page to page, and are both referred to by numbers: regular and italicized respectively.

The Sayadaw has reported that 'many foreigners' have 'criticized' him because his editor refers to him as **the Most Venerable Sayadaw**. The Sayadaw has thus been questioned: 'Are you the most venerable person in the whole world?' Such a reading of 'Most Venerable', however, has no basis in Standard English.[962]

[962] MOST: PHR (*Longman's Dictionary of the English Language*): '*adv* 2 very *<shall ~ certainly come>* *<her argument was ~ persuasive>* NOTE 1 As an intensifier meaning "very", *most* is generally used only with adjectives and adverbs conveying a judgment of feeling or opinion *<a most handsome gift>* *<he argued most persuasively>*'. MW: 'adv. ... 2 to a very great degree <was ~ persuasive>. POD: 'adv. To a great or the greatest degree or extent or amount (esp. with adjj. & advv. To emphasize or, with *the*, to form superlative...).' PHR (*Usage and Abusage* Eric Partridge) 'MOST AND VERY *Most* can properly (though rather formally) mean "very", as well as meaning "more than all the others".' *Fowler's Modern English Usage* Revised Third Edition by R.W. Burchfield, Oxford University Press, Oxford, 2004: '*Most* governing an adj. frequently has an intensive rather than a superlative function.' Thus the term is used in, for example, *On the Path to Freedom* (Buddhist Wisdom Centre, Selangor, Malaysia) p.441: 'The Most Venerable *Ovadacariya*

(Please see further next page.)

Since such an expression of reverence and respect for the most venerable author of *The Workings of Kamma* is fully in line with the Teachings of The Buddha, many readers have approved of it as only natural, only proper, and even wonderful. For that reason, and in order to avoid causing offence to those many readers, this most venerable term of reference has been left untouched.[963]

From a retreat in the USA came a most valuable contribution from successful yogis. They pointed out that '**translucent**' is in fact more accurate than 'transparent', to describe the counterpart sign in, for example, mindfulness of breathing; to describe the 'ice-block' appearance of the body during successful four-elements meditation; and to describe *pasāda·rūpa* (now translated 'translucent materiality').[964] This is confirmed by the *Visuddhi·Magga*'s comparing the counterpart sign to a mirror, to mother of pearl, and to the full moon, and its comparing transparent materiality to a pellucid mirror: they are all translucent things rather than transparent ones.[965]

For the first edition, there was no one at Pa-Auk to proof-read the manuscript. For this new edition, however, there were several, which has meant the great number of small mis-typings, copy-paste oversights, other oversights, etc. of the first edition has been vastly reduced.

The Most Venerable Sayadaw found it most difficult to read the first edition unless it was enlarged, and also reported that he had received complaints from 'many' readers that the script was too small, even though it was in fact noticably larger than standard script. Therefore, the font was changed to *Tahoma,* and the Sayadaw has arranged with the most generous donors from Singapore (who together with a group in Malaysia will publish the second edition) that a special edition enlarged to A4 be published. Anyone wishing to acquire a copy may contact the Singapore group. (A special edition has/will not be published, after all.)

the editor

Sayadaw Bhaddanta Panditabhivamsa [sic] '; and on p.442: 'The Most Venerable Aggamahapandita Mahasi Sayadaw'; and on the cover of their *The Great Chronicle of Buddhas*: 'The Most Venerable Mingun Sayadaw Bhaddanta Vicitta Sārābhivaṁsa.' In the same way, 'Most Reverend' is used in the Christian church to refer respectfully to and address an archbishop or cardinal.

963 See The Buddha's words under 'One Is Not Stubborn, Not Proud' (p.292), and 'One Does Not Harbour Envy' (p.282), as well as footnote 665 (p.231), and 'Reference to The Buddha, Etc.' (in this edition, p.372).

964 TRANSLUCENT (translucency/translucence): PHR 'permitting the passage of light: e.g. A clear, transparent <*glass and other ~ materials*> B transmitting and diffusing light so that objects beyond cannot be seen clearly <*a ~ window of frosted glass* > <*~ porcelain* > [L *translucent-, translucens,* prp of *translucre* to shine through, fr *trans-* + *lucēre* to shine ...]' TRANSPARENT: PHR 'having the property of transmitting light without appreciable scattering, so that bodies lying beyond are entirely visible [ME, fr ML *transparent-, transparens,* prp of *transparēre* to show through, fr L *trans-* + *parēre* to show oneself - more at APPEAR]'

965 VsM.iv.57 *'Bhāvanā·Vidhānaṁ'* ('Meditation Directions') PP.iv.31 describes the kasiṇa counterpart sign: 'The counterpart sign appears as if breaking out from the learning sign, and a hundred times, a thousand times more purified, like a looking-glass disk drawn from its case, like a mother-of-pearl disk well polished, like the moon's disk coming out from behind a cloud, like cranes against a thunder cloud.' And VsM.xiv.447 *'Rūpa·Kkhandha·Kathā'* ('Discussion of the Materiality-Aggregate') PP.xiv.73 explains that the five types of translucent materiality *(pasāda·rūpaṁ)* are so-called because they are like a pellucid mirror-surface *(vippasannattā ādāsa·talaṁ).*

EDITOR'S NOTE
(First Edition)

When the Most Venerable Pa-Auk Tawya Sayadaw teaches the Dhamma, the Pali is his authority. Hence, the explanations and examples given in this book can in their full version be found in the Pali Texts, for which source references are given in footnotes. Hence also, the editing of this book has been governed by faith in, respect for, and deference towards the Pali, in the unsceptical spirit of the author.

In preparing the book for publication, one editor has inserted endnotes (located at the end of each chapter, indicated by a reference number in italics) with sutta references and quotations, etc. Also various charts have been inserted to make the text clearer: they are all the independent work of one editor, based on data in the Pali Texts.

Certain orthographical and stylistic points need to be mentioned.

PALI SPELLING

The spelling of some Pali words is in Myanmarese[329] not the same as in the Sinhalese (used in Romanized Pali): here, the Myanmarese version has been adopted. Hence:

MYANMARESE	SINHALESE	ENGLISH TRANSLATION
*ānāpāna·***ss***ati*	*ānāpāna·***s***ati*	mindfulness-of-breathing
*th***ī***na*	*th***ī***na*	sloth
*v***ī***riyaṁ*	*v***i***riyaṁ*	energy

DIACRITICS AND INFLECTION

In accordance with Standard English, Pali words (being foreign) are written in italics: excepting such words that have become 'naturalized', such as 'Buddha', 'Arahant', 'Pali', 'Sangha', and 'vipassanā'. But Sanskrit loanwords such as *dharma* or *karma* have nowhere been resorted to.

Pali words are also written with all diacritics: for example, *mettā* rather than *metta*, *ñāṇa* rather than *nana*, or *ñana*. And usually the uninflected stem is given: for example, *saṁsāra* rather than, for example, *saṁsāro*; *ñāṇa* rather than, for example, *ñāṇaṁ*.

PALI COMPOUNDS

Translation of the Pali has (in so far as it accords with Standard English) been kept as close to the Pali as possible: to maintain the same semantic emphasis. For clarity and brevity's sake (as well as to familiarize the reader with the Pali original) Pali compounds have been kept as compounds, with dots to indicate the compound's individual elements: e.g. *Kamma·Ssakata·Ñāṇaṁ*, which is translated 'Kamma-Ownership Knowledge' instead of 'Knowledge of the Ownership of Kamma'; *upādāna·kkhandha*, which is translated 'clinging aggregate' instead of 'aggregate of clinging'; *Saṅkhār·Upekkhā·Ñāṇaṁ*, which is translated 'the Formations-Equanimity Knowledge' instead of 'the Knowledge of Equanimity towards

Formations'; and *avijjā·nīvaraṇānaṁ sattānaṁ*, which is translated 'ignorance-hindered beings' instead of 'beings hindered by ignorance'.

REFERENCE TO THE BUDDHA, ETC.

In accordance with the Most Venerable Sayadaw's overriding reverence, respect and veneration for The Buddha, Dhamma and Sangha,[966] and in accordance with The Buddha's teachings on kamma,[967] The Buddha and anything related to Him is written with a honorific initial capital letter: **T**he Buddha; **H**e said; **H**is **T**eaching, etc. For the same wholesome reasons, all Noble Ones or anything related to their attainments, are also written with an initial capital letter: **N**oble **D**isciple, **S**tream **E**ntry, **O**nce-**R**eturner **P**ath, **A**rahant **F**ruition **C**onsciousness, etc. Likewise, reference to elders of the past, or an editorial reference to the author of this book, is preceded by the honorific title in standard usage: the Venerable, or the Most Venerable.

TRANSLATIONS[330]

INDIVIDUAL WORDS AND PHRASES

Readers of the manuscript voiced the necessity for a discussion about translation of certain Pali words and phrases.[968/331]

Beer&Wine Liquor*(surā·meraya·majja)*

According to the ingredients and manufacturing processes given in the Pali,[969] *surā* is equivalent to the English 'malt liquor',[332] and *meraya* equivalent to the English 'vinous liquor':[333] both fermented, and distillable.[334]

Surā is milled-grain malt*(piṭṭha·surā)*, bread malt*(pūva·surā)*, rice malt*(odana·surā)*,[335] with yeast added*(kiṇṇa·pakkhittā)*, or with ingredients blended*(sambhāra·saṁyuttā)*. *Meraya* is flower liquor*(pupph·āsava)* (sap/oil/honey*(madhu)* from the honey tree *(madhuka)*, palmyra*(tāla)*, coconut palm*(nāḷikera)*, etc.), fruit liquor*(phal·āsava)* (jack-/bread fruit*(panasa)*, grape*(muddika)*, etc.), sugar liquor*(guḷ·āsava)* (sugar-cane juice *(ucchurasa)*, etc.), honey liquor*(madhv·āsava)*,[970/336] or with ingredients blended*(sambhāra·saṁyutta)*.[337] *Majja* is a generic term for liquor, spirituous-, intoxicating drink. That makes: *surā·meraya·majja* = malt and vinous liquor, which is all kinds of liquor. Unfortunately, these two English terms are not in common usage, which is why the translation here is 'beer&wine liquor':[338] also covering all kinds of liquor.

---

[966] Every evening, at Pa-Auk Forest Monastery, the bhikkhus chant a twenty-six verse long Pali Text that honours The Buddha: *'Nama·Kkāra·Pāḷi'* ('Homage-Paying Text').

[967] See quotation at 'One Is Not Stubborn, Not Proud', p.292, and quotation on superiority/ equality-/inferiority conceit, endnote 81, p.235.

[968] The endnotes refer to definitions given in standard English dictionaries, etc.

[969] E.g. Vin.Pāc.V.vi.2 *'Surā·Pāna·Sikkhā·Padaṁ'* ('Malt-Drink Training-Precept') and commentary, DṬ.iii.8 *'Siṅgālaka·Suttaṁ'* ('The Siṅgālaka Sutta'), and VbhA.xiv.703 (DD.xiv.-1905) *'Sikkhā·Pada·Vibhaṅga'* ('Training Precept Analysis').

[970] This is also explained as liquor from grape juice*(muddikā·raso)*.

Conscience*(hiri)*

The Pali analyses conscience*(hiri)* and shame*(ottappa)* together:[971] 'It has conscientious scruples about bodily misconduct, etc., thus it is conscience. This is a term for modesty. It is ashamed of those same things, thus it is shame. This is a term for anxiety about evil. Herein, conscience has the characteristic of disgust at evil, while shame has the characteristic of dread of it. Conscience has the function of not doing evil and that in the mode of modesty, while shame has the function of not doing it and that in the mode of dread. They are manifested as shrinking from evil in the way already stated. Their proximate causes are self-respect and respect of others. A man rejects evil through conscience out of respect for himself, as the daughter of a good family does; he rejects evil through shame out of respect for another, as a courtesan does. But these two states should be regarded as the Guardians of the World.'[972]

Hiri is thus modest and disgusted at evil because of self-respect. That makes it equivalent to the English 'conscience'[339] or 'conscientiousness'.[340] A popular translation is 'shame', which is better suited for *ottappa.*[973]

Dependent Origination/'Because of Ignorance', etc.

Dependent origination*(paṭicca·samuppāda)* is analysed at length in the *Visuddhi·Magga.*[974] What is emphasized throughout is that it is not simple arising, one after the other. Hence, it should in English really be 'dependent co-arising' (*sam·* = co- + *uppāda* = arising). The factors arise in association: some sequentially and some concurrently, etc., although no factor can be left out. Nonetheless, this translation has not been chosen, but the less perfect 'dependent origination': the meaning is perfectly in accord with *paṭicca·samuppāda* although the equivalence is not.

Furthermore, the Most Venerable Pa-Auk Tawya Sayadaw emphasizes that ignorance causes volitional formations, volitional formations cause consciousness. The workings of the factors of dependent origination are to be seen at work, not to be inferred as working. That is, when the yogi discerns dependent origination, she or he discerns the dynamic working of one thing causing another thing: she or he does not merely infer the condition for a thing's arising. Hence, rather than the popular translation, 'with ignorance as condition, formations arise,', etc., the Sayadaw's preferred translation of *avijjā paccayā, saṅkhāra* is the straightforward 'because of ignorance, formations arise,' etc.[341]

---

[971] VsM.xiv.466 *'Saṅkhāra·Kkhandha·Kathā'* ('Discussion of the Formations-Aggregate') PP.xiv.142

[972] A.II.I.i.9 (9) *'Cariya·Suttaṁ'* ('The Conduct Sutta')

[973] See 'Shame', p.376.

[974] VsM.xvii.574-580 *'Paṭicca·Samuppāda·Kathā'* ('Discussion of Dependent Origination') PP.xvii.7-24

Faith *(saddhā)*

There are four kinds of *saddhā*:[975]

1) Religious faith *(āgamana·saddhā)*,[342] which is comprehensive faith in the Teachings of The Buddha, possessed by Bodhisattas and Noble Disciples.
2) Acquired faith *(adhigama·saddhā)*, which is acquired by realization of a Path&-Fruition *(Magga·Phala)*.
3) Determined faith *(okappana·saddhā)*,[976] which is unreserved/absolute conviction by which one relies and depends on The Buddha, Dhamma, and Sangha. It is unshakeable *(acala)* faith in the qualities of The Buddha, Dhamma, and Sangha, with an attitude described as: 'It is so *(evam·etaṁ)*.' Such faith is essential for full commitment to the threefold training (morality, concentration, and wisdom).
4) Inspired faith *(pasāda·saddhā)*, which is non-committal liking and respect for the Teachings of The Buddha. It is insufficiently strong not to alternate with scepticism, and liking/respect for also teachings of other teachers. It cannot support full commitment to the threefold training, although it can support great offerings, and even ordination.[977]

The only word faithful to *saddhā* is thus 'faith'.[343] In certain quarters, however, the English word 'faith' has become restricted to mean a weak and unwholesome state of mind, akin to superstition, blind credulity, or restricted solely to mean theistic faith. *Saddhā* is then translated as 'confidence'. Since such a restricted meaning of 'faith' finds no corroboration in Standard English, that translation has here not been considered: it is (as just seen) too narrow and shallow. *Saddhā* reaches from existential surrender to the tenets of a certain religion, which govern one's conduct and thought (and cannot be translated as mere 'confidence'), to reserved regard for such tenets, some of which one may bow to more or less, given the circumstances (which can be translated as mere 'confidence'). Thus *saddhā* may manifest as belief, blind credulity, conviction, confidence, devotion, knowledge, superstition, and trust, etc.: in English the word is 'faith'. Hence, one can have confidence in many teachers, but faith in only one.

The only real difference between the English 'faith' and the Pali *'saddhā'* is that 'faith' can refer to belief in religions that are based on wrong view, whereas *'saddhā'* refers only to faith in the religion based on the view of a Fully Enlightened Buddha. The objects of such faith are eight: The Buddha, Dhamma, Sangha, the

---

[975] When asked by one Prince Bodhi how long it takes for a bhikkhu under training to realize Nibbāna, The Buddha gives five striving factors necessary for success. The first is faith, which is also the first of the five faculties. The other four striving factors are: 2) good health/ digestion; 3) honesty/sincerity towards teacher and companions; 4) energy in abandoning unwholesome things and undertaking wholesome things, with firm perseverance; 5) superior knowledge regarding the arising&perishing of formations (see under 'The Sixteen Insight Knowledges', p.111). Each factor is explained by MA.II.iv.5 *'Bodhi·Rāja·Kumāra·Suttaṁ'* ('The Royal-Son Bodhi Sutta').

[976] The subcommentary to D.ii.3 *'Mahā·Parinibbāna·Suttaṁ'* ('The Great-Parinibbāna Sutta') describes determined faith as having plunged into *(ogāhetvā)* and entered upon *(anupavisitvā)* the bases of faith *(saddheyya·vatthuṁ)* (Buddha/Dhamma/Sangha), and occurring with the attitude of, 'It is so' *(evam·etan'ti)*.

[977] DhSA.12 *'Kām·Āvacara·Kusalaṁ Niddesa·Vāra·Kathā'* ('Discussion of Sensual-Sphere Wholesome Exposition Part') E.IV.ii.191-192

threefold training, past lives, future lives, past&future lives, and dependent origination.[978]

Kammic Potency *(kamma·satti)*

To explain this term, the Most Venerable Pa-Auk Tawya Sayadaw always uses the simile of a mango tree. There may be a mango tree in a garden. At present it bears no fruits. But when the conditions are right, it will bear fruits: it has the power or potency to bear mango fruits. But if we examine the mango tree, we cannot identify that potency. It is neither to be found in the leaves, nor the twigs, the branches, the trunk or the roots.[979] Yet it cannot be denied that it exists.[344]

In the same way, when unwholesome or wholesome kamma has been accomplished, there remains in that same mentality-materiality continuity the power or potency for that kamma to produce a result. It is neither mentality nor materiality, but it produces resultant mentality and kamma-born materiality.

In translating *satti*, 'force' has been avoided, since that refers to strength or energy, an active thing that brings to bear, and exerts change, rather than a capacity or potency which may or may not produce a result (may or may not become a force).[345] 'Force' could (and does) therefore give rise to (or reinforce) the very common misunderstanding that kamma is somehow 'stored', and 'underlies' the mentality-materiality continuity.[980] Better translations are 'ability', 'capacity', 'potential', although they are all rather weak, being too abstract. 'Power' is an apt translation,[346] but is used to translate *bala*.[981] Equally apt, although perhaps not as commonly used, is 'potency', which has been preferred over 'potential', as it is stronger.[347]

Materiality *(rūpa)*

As the first of the five clinging-aggregates, The Buddha is referring to ultimate materiality: the four essentials and derived materiality.[982] The Most Venerable Pa-Auk Tawya Sayadaw (having taken it from Bhikkhu Ñāṇamoli's *Path of Purification*), almost only uses 'materiality'.[348] Other popular translations are 'matter' or 'form'. Whereas 'materiality' and 'matter' may be said to be equivalent, 'form',[349] has not been considered: it suggests the delusions of material compactness,[983] even Platonic/Aristotelian wrong view. Furthermore, *rūpa* includes the fire element (temperature), and the wind element, as well as odour, flavour, nutritive essence, and life faculty, neither of which can be said to possess, constitute or even suggest form.

Mentality *(nāma)*

As the four immaterial clinging-aggregates, The Buddha is here referring to ultimate mentality *(paramattha·nāma)*. The Most Venerable Pa-Auk Tawya Sayadaw

---

978 EIGHT OBJECTS OF *SADDHĀ*: see quotations regarding the uneducated ordinary person's objects of scepticism, endnote 18, p.22.

979 The meditator who has penetrated to ultimate materiality can, however, see that when the fruit appears and grows, it is temperature-born materiality that initially arises from temperature-born materiality of the tree.

980 See footnote 56, p.15.

981 See quotation at 'The Buddha's Knowledge of Kamma&Result', p.39.

982 FOUR ESSENTIALS/DERIVED MATERIALITY: see 'The Twenty-Eight Types of Materiality', p.105.

983 See 'The Three Types of Material Compactness', p.95.

(having taken it from Bhikkhu Ñāṇamoli's *Path of Purification*) uses almost only 'mentality'.[350] Other popular translations are 'mind' or 'name'. 'Mentality' and 'mind' may be said to be equivalent, although in common usage 'mind' can imply the delusions of mental compactness,[984] which 'mentality' does not do. 'Name' has not been considered, as it belongs to the realm of concepts*(paññati)*, rather than the ultimate realities of consciousness and mental factors that The Buddha is referring to.[351]

Possessiveness*(macchariya)*

The Pali defines *macchariya* as follows:[985] 'Concealment of obtained or obtainable personal gain is the characteristic. Not tolerating that others share one's property is the function. Shrinking or contraction is the manifestation. One's own gain is the proximate cause. It is to be regarded as mental warping.' It is thus equivalent to the English 'possessiveness'.[352] It may also be translated as 'stinginess', which has not been chosen, because stinginess means also that one is averse to spending one's property.

The Buddha gives five kinds of possessiveness:[986]

1) dwelling possessiveness*(āvāsa·macchariya)*
2) family possessiveness*(kula·macchariya)*
3) gains possessiveness*(lābha·macchariya)*
4) beauty possessiveness*(vaṇṇa·macchariya)*[987]
5) Dhamma possessiveness*(Dhamma·macchariya)*.

They are all about something one already possesses or is about to possess, which one does not want to share with others. Hence, the popular translation 'avarice' has not been considered, not least because avarice is greed-rooted, while *macchariya* (possessiveness) is hatred-rooted.[353]

Shame*(ottappa)*

Ottappa is anxious about evil, and dreads evil, because of respect for others.[988] It is thus equivalent to the English 'shame' (although there can be some overlap with 'conscience').[354] Other translations are 'fear of shame', 'fear of blame', and 'fear of wrongdoing' (which misses the respect for others). These fears are already inherent in the single word 'shame', which is why those translations have not been chosen.

Sympathetic Joy*(muditā)*

Muditā is rejoicing in another's success, being unenvious. It is a happy equivalent to the English 'commiseration':[355] the opposite of the German loanword *schadenfreude*.[356] German has also the exact equivalent, *mitfreude* ('con-felicity'/'con-gratulation'),[357] which word has not become a loanword in English.

---

[984] See 'The Four Types of Mental Compactness', p.107.

[985] VsM.xiv.487 *'Saṅkhāra·Kkhandha·Kathā'* ('Discussion of the Formations Aggregate') PP.xiv.173

[986] A.V.V.vi.4 *'Pañca·Macchariya·Suttaṁ'* ('The Five [Kinds of] Possessiveness Sutta')

[987] The commentary explains that *vaṇṇa·macchariya* refers to two things: bodily beauty *(sarīra·vaṇṇa)* (one is physically beautiful, and wants no one else to be so); quality beauty *(guṇa·vaṇṇa)* (one possesses such qualities as make one famous, and wants no one else to possess such qualities).

[988] See quoted analysis at 'conscience', p.373.

Since no true equivalent exists in English, one needs to contrive a paraphrase. Popular translations are: 'altruistic joy', 'appreciative joy', and 'empathetic joy'.[358] Rare translations are 'gladness', and 'congratulation'.[359] The least flawed paraphrase would seem to be another popular translation: 'sympathetic joy'. Even though 'sympathy' is commonly used to mean participation in the other's feelings, empathy, and feeling sorry or pity for the other, it also refers to the ability to respond to something good or bad that has happened to another:[360] although not perfect, this translation is unlikely to be misunderstood.

For any errors, oversights, inconsistencies, incoherences, ambiguities, etc., the various editors beg forgiveness.

The last of a series of editors
Pa-Auk Forest Monastery

ENDNOTES EDITOR'S NOTE

[328] Since the first printing of *The Workings of Kamma Second Revised Edition*, the following changes have been made:
CORRIGENDA
- p.45—Kamma-born materiality: the eighteenth should be: 'Kamma-born space ⇨ The space element*(ākāsa·dhātu)* that defines and delimits kamma-born material clusters *(rūpa·kalāpa)*.'
- p.48—table 2a 'Mental Phenomena at the Arising of Greed-Rooted Consciousness': the fourth, fifth, and sixth type of unmprompted consciousness should be without joy*(pīti)*, unshaded.
- p.49—table 2b 'Mental Phenomena at the Arising of Hatred-Rooted Consciousness': the second column should be the same as the third and fourth, with nineteen mental phenomena. Likewise, the sixth column should be the same as the seventh and eighth columns, with twenty-one columns.
- p.50—table 2c 'Mental Phenomena at the Arising of Delusion-Rooted Consciousness': the mental factor restlessness is associated with all unwholesome types of consciousness, which is why it is included in the mental phenomena at the arising of the delusion-rooted consciousness associated with scepticism, making in all sixteen mental phenomena.
- p.64—table 1b 'The Wholesome Resultant Unrooted Consciousness': the feeling for body consciousness should be happiness. The feelings for investigation consciousness should be: pleasure — equanimity — pleasure — equanimity — equanimity.
- p.148—table 5c 'The Mind-Door Process': there is no past life-continuum, etc., before a mind-door process, only the regular life-continuum.
- p.149—Notes to table 5c 'The Mind-Door Process': 'It is from the fourth mind-door process onwards that the concept is known' (as explained in notes to the five-door process).
- p.178—table 5d 'The Jhāna-Attainment Process': as for p.146, since this is type of mind-door process.
- p.179—Notes to table 5d 'The Jhāna-Attainment Process': '2nd immaterial jhāna... it is ~~a kamma,~~ an ultimate phenomenon.... 4th immaterial jhāna... it is ~~kamma,~~ an ultimate phenomenon.'
- p.180—table 1d 'The Fine-Material Sphere and Immaterial Sphere Resultant Consciousness': the object of all four immaterial jhānas is a kamma sign.
- p.340—table 5e 'The Path Process': as for p.146, since this is a type of mind-door process.
- p.25, endnote 40; p.241, endnote 122; p.356, endnote 284—the bhikkhu's morality: it should be his seeing fearsomeness in the 'slightest faults*(aṇumattesu vajjesu)*' (plural).

AMENDMENT Describing the arising of mental phenomena in DhS, The Buddha says that upon the occasion*(samaya)* when an certain type of consciousness*(cittaṃ)* has arisen*(uppannaṃ hoti)*, there is contact*(phasso hoti)*, there is feeling*(vedanā hoti)*, there is perception *(saññā hoti)*, there is volition*(cetanā hoti)*, there is consciousness*(cittaṃ hoti)*, etc. As DhS is the source text for AbS, and better to conform with The Buddha's usage, the titles to the various tables 'Mental Phenomena of [such and such] Consciousness' have been amended to 'Mental Phenomena at the Arising of [such and such] Consciousness'. This amendment has also been made in the text here and there. See, for example, titles of tables listing mental phenomena at the arising of consciousness with one of the three unwholesome roots, p.48*ff.*

ADDITION The source reference for the Sayadaw's description of the procedure for cognition has been added: see footnote 405, p.149.

[329] According to the *Longman Dictionary of Contemporary English*, Pearson, Longman, 2005, and *New Oxford Spelling Dictionary: the Writer's and Editor's Guide to Spelling*

and Word Division, Oxford University Press, 2005, 'Myanmarese' is now standard English.

[330] In translating, the editor has referred to the following translations of the following texts: *Vinaya·Piṭaka* ~ *Book of the Discipline*, I.B. Horner, M.A., PTS (Pali Text Society, Oxford/London); *Dīgha·Nikāya* ~ *Dialogues of The Buddha*, Rhys Davids, PTS, and *The Long Discourses of the Buddha*, Maurice Walshe, WP (Wisdom Publications, Boston)); *'Brahma·Jāla·Suttaṁ'* and commentary ~ *The Discourse on the All-Embracing Net of Views*, Bhikkhu Bodhi, BPS (Buddhist Publication Society, Kandy); *'Samañña·Phala·Suttaṁ'* and commentary ~ *The Discourse on the Fruits of Recluseship*, Bhikkhu Bodhi, BPS; *Majjhima·Nikāya* ~ *Middle Length Sayings*, I.B.Horner, PTS, and *The Middle Length Discourses of the Buddha*, Bhikkhu Ñāṇamoli/Bodhi, WP; *'Mūla·Pariyāya·Suttaṁ'* and commentary ~ *The Discourse on the Root of Existence*, Bhikkhu Bodhi, BPS); *Saṁyutta·Nikāya* ~ *Kindred Sayings*, various translators, PTS, and *The Connected Discourses of The Buddha*, Bhikkhu Bodhi, WP; *Aṅguttara·Nikāya* ~ *Gradual Sayings*, various translators, PTS, and *Numerical Discourses of the Buddha*, Nyanaponika Thera/Bhikkhu Bodhi, Vistaar Publications, New Delhi; *Dhamma·Pada·Attha·Kathā* ~ *Buddhist Legends*, Eugene Watson Burlingame, PTS; *Udāna* and *Itivuttaka* ~ *The Udāna & The Itivuttaka*, John D. Ireland, BPS; *Milinda·Pañhā* ~ *The Questions of King Milinda*, I.B. Horner M.A., PTS; *Thera·Gāthā* and *Therī·Gāthā* ~ *Psalms of the Early Buddhists*, Mrs Rhys Davids M.A., PTS; *Peta·Vatthu·Aṭṭha·Kathā* ~ *Elucidation of the Intrinsic Meaning*, U Ba Kyaw, PTS; *Vibhaṅga* ~ *The Book of Analysis*, Paṭhamakyaw Ashin Thiṭṭhila (Seṭṭhila) Aggamahāpaṇḍita, PTS (mispelled 'Thiṭṭila'). Referred to has also been *Buddhist Dictionary* by Nyanatiloka Mahathera, BPS, and the *Dictionary of Pāḷi Proper Names* by G.P. Malasekera, D.Litt., Ph.D., M.A. (Lond.), O.B.E. The translations mainly referred to, however, have been translations by Bhikkhu Ñāṇamoli (quotations from which have been taken directly with only rare changes), published by PTS, as well as his translations of certain suttas in the following publications by BPS: *The Buddha's Words on Kamma*, and *The Lion's Roar*. See also 'Bibliographical Abbreviations etc.', p.383.

[331] The standard English dictionaries referred to are: CTCD: *Chambers Twentieth Century Dictionary*, Editor A.M.Macdonald OBE BA(Oxon): W&R Chambers Ltd.: 1972 (British); MW: *Merriam-Webster's Collegiate Dictionary*, 10 Ed., Merriam-Webster, Incorporated, 2001 (American); PHR: *Penguin Hutchinson Reference Library*, Helicon Publishing and Penguin Books Ltd, 1996 (British); POD: *The Pocket Oxford Dictionary*, H.W. Fowler: Clarendon Press: 1924 (British); RHU: *Random House Unabridged Dictionary* (American); WNW: *Webster's New World Dictionary: Third College Edition*, Eds. Victoria Neufeldt, David Guralnik, Cleveland & New York, 1988 (American). Also referred to is EB: *Encyclopaedia Britanicca 2002 Deluxe Edition CD-ROM*, britannica.co.uk 2002 (American Ed.), and two dictionaries by Aggamahāpaṇḍita A.P. Buddhadatta Mahāthera, BEP: *Concise English-Pāli Dictionary*, Motilal Banarsidass Publishers Private Limited, Delhi, 1997, and BPE: *Concise Pāli-English Dictionary*, The Colombo Apothecaries' Co., Ltd., Colombo, 1968.

[332] MALT: POD 'Barley or other grain prepared by steeping & germination or otherwise for brewing & distilling... *m. liquor*, made from malt by fermentation' LIQUOR: '*malt... liquor...* beer &c.' RHU '2. any alcoholic beverage as beer, ale, or malt liquor, fermented from malt.' In Pali malt is referred to by several other terms: BEP:'"malt" *aṅkurita-yava* [sprouted barley], *surā·kiṇṇa* [malt ferment/yeast], *yava·surā* [barley/corn-malt, also under 'beer' and 'ale']'.

[333] VINOUS: CTCD 'pertaining to wine: like wine: caused by or indicative of wine.' POD 'Of or like or due to wine.' LIQUOR: '*vinous... liquor...* wine.' RHU 'resembling, or containing wine.'

[334] DISTILLED LIQUOR: (EB) brandy, whisky, rum, or arrack are obtained by distillation from wine or other fermented fruit juice (e.g. grapes, apples, peaches) or plant juice (e.g. sugarcane/beets/potatoes) or from various grains (barley, corn, rice, rye) that have first been brewed into beer. The process has existed since ancient times.

[335] (EB) In Russia, beer is made from rye bread, and in China, Japan, and Korea, it is made from rice. In Africa, it is made from many different kinds of grain.
[336] (EB) Honey liquor is in English called 'mead', a liquor fermented from honey and water, sometimes with yeast added, very similar to table wine: it was once widespread in Europe: PHR '[ME *mede*, fr OE *medu*; akin to OHG *metu* mead, Gk *methy* wine].' BPE '"mead" *madhu·pāna* [honey drink].'
[337] BPE: '"vine/grape" *muddikā*, and "vinous/grape wine" *muddik·āsava* [vinous liquor].'
[338] BEER: CTCD 'an alcoholic beverage made by fermentation, in which the yeast settles to the bottom ... the generic name of malt liquor, including ale and porter.' RHU '1. an alcoholic beverage made by brewing and fermentation from cereals, usually malted barley, and flavored with hops and the like... 2. any of various beverages, whether alcoholic or not, made from roots, molasses or sugar, yeast, etc.' BPE "beer" *yava·surā* [barley/-corn malt]. WINE: MW '2: the usu. fermented juice of a plant product (as a fruit) used as a beverage.' RHU '1. the fermented juice of grapes, made in many varieties... 3. the juice, fermented or unfermented, of various other fruits or plants, used as beverage.' BPE: see endnote 337, p.380.
[339] CONSCIENCE: CTCD '[L. *cōnscientia*, knowledge—*cōnscire*, to know well, in one's own mind—*con-*, inten., *scīre*, to know.]' MW: '1a: the sense or consciousness of the moral goodness or blameworthiness of one's own conduct, intentions, or character together with a feeling or obligation to do right or be good b: a faculty, power or principle enjoining good acts... 3: conformity to the dictates of conscience: conscientiousness.' WNW: '1 a knowledge or sense of right and wrong, with an urge to do right: moral judgement that opposes the violation of a previously recognized ethical principle and that leads to feelings of guilt if one violates such a principle.' Bhikkhu Ñāṇamoli, in his *Dispeller of Delusion, The Guide, Path of Discrimination, Path of Purification*, and *Pali-English Glossary of Buddhist Technical Terms*, also translates *hiri* as 'conscience', and *ottappa* as 'shame'.
[340] Used by Professor Pe Maung Tin M.A. in *The Expositor* (E)
[341] Used by the Most Venerable Paṭhamakyaw Ashin Thiṭṭhila (Seṭṭhila) in his translation of the second book of the Abhidhamma, *The Book of Analysis (Vibhaṅga)*, PTS (Luzac & Company, Limited, London) 1969.
[342] RELIGION/RELIGIOUS: although in English, 'religion' refers to an attitude of faith/devotion towards a god or something supernatural, and the teachings of a church, the term may legitimately be used to describe the attitude of faith/devotion that arises with regard to the Teachings of The Buddha. Thus: PHR '[religion] 1 of or showing faithful devotion to an acknowledged ultimate reality or deity [here, to the Teachings of The Buddha]... 2 of, being, or concerned with (the beliefs or observances of a) religion 3 committed or dedicated to the service of a deity or deities <*the ~ life*> [here, the threefold training]' POD '[religion] system of faith and worship; human recognition of superhuman controlling power [here recognition of truth of the Dhamma]... effect of this on conduct ...[religious] imbued with religion... devout; of or concerned with religion.'
[343] FAITH: CTCD 'belief in the truth of revealed religion: confidence and trust in God: the living reception of religious belief.... [M.E. *feith, feyth*—O.Fr. *feid*—L. *fidēs—fidēre* to trust]' PHR '2a(1) belief and trust in and loyalty to God 2a(2) belief in the traditional doctrines of a religion 3a something that is believed with strong conviction; esp a system of religious beliefs <*the ~ of our fathers*>' POD 'belief in religious doctrines esp. as affecting character.'
[344] The Most Venerable Sayadaw has had it suggested that modern science's identification of the mango tree's genetic code constitutes such a potency: it has, however, been considered untenable to put an equation between code and potency.
[345] FORCE: CTCD '[Fr., —L.L. *fortia*—L.*fortis*, strong.]' MW '1a (1): strength or energy exerted or brought to bear... active power <the *~s* of nature>.'

[346] POWER: CTCD: 'ability to do anything—physical, mental, spiritual, legal, etc.: capacity for producing an effect... potentiality... [O.Fr. *poer* (Fr. *pouvoir*)— L.L. *potēre* (for L. *posse*) to be able.]' MW '1a (1): 'ability to act or produce an effect... (3).... possession of ability to wield force '

[347] POTENCY: 'CTCD 'power: potentiality... [L. *potēs*, *-entis*, pr.p. of *posse*, to be able — *potis*, able, *esse*, to be.]' MW '1a: force, power ... c: the ability or capacity to achieve or bring about a particular result 2: potentiality 1.'

[348] MATERIALITY: CTCD 'L. *māteriālis—māteria*, matter.' POD 'adj. Composed of or connected with matter, not spirit (*the m. universe*; *m. phenomena... the m. theory of heat*, that it is a substance)... materiality n.' MW '1: the quality or state of being material 2: something that is material.' RHU '1. material nature or quality. 2. something material.'

[349] FORM: RHU '*Philos.* a. the structure, pattern, organization, or essential nature of anything b. structure or pattern as distinguished from matter.' PHR 'form 1a the shape and structure of something as distinguished from its material, colour, texture, etc... 2 *philosophy* the essential nature of a thing as distinguished from the matter in which it is embodied: e.g. 2a often cap IDEA [Platonic Idea], [ME *forme*, fr OF, fr L *forma*, perh modif of Gk *morphē* form, shape]'

[350] MENTALITY: CTCD 'mind.' RHU 'that which is of the nature of the mind or of mental action.' WNW: 'mental capacity, power or activity; mind.'

[351] NAME: CTCD 'that by which a person or a thing is known or called: a designation. [O.E. *nama*; Ger. *name*; L. *nōmen*.]' POD 'Word by which individual person, animal, place, or thing, is spoken of or to... word denoting any object of thought.' PHR '1a a word or phrase whose function is to designate an individual person or thing.'

[352] POSSESSIVENESS: CTCD 'extreme attachment to one's possessions.' RHU '[possessive] 'desirous of possessing, esp. excessively so: *Young children are so possessive they will not allow others to play with their toys.*' This is the very example given by the Most Venerable Pa-Auk Tawya Sayadaw, when explaining *macchariya*. 'Stingy/mean/niggardly/parsimonious/tightfisted/miserly' can also have this as a general rather than specific meaning (PHR). Thus, possessive children is one example given in RHU's entry for 'stingy': 'unwilling to share, give, or spend possessions or money: *children who are stingy with their toys*.'

[353] AVARICE: CTCD 'eager desire for wealth: covetousness. [L. *avāritia—avārus*, greedy-—*avēre*, to pant after.]' POD 'Greed of gain, cupidity' RHU 'insatiable greed for riches; inordinate, miserly desire to gain and hoard wealth.'

[354] SHAME: CTCD 'the humiliating feeling of having appeared unfavourably in one's own eyes, or those of others, as by shortcoming, offence, or unseemly exposure, or a similar feeling on behalf of anything one associates with oneself... susceptibility to such feeling; fear or scorn of incurring disgrace or dishonour; modesty; bashfulness.' POD 'feeling of humiliation excited by consciousness of guilt or shortcoming or being ridiculous or having offended against propriety or modesty or decency, restraint imposed by or desire to avoid this.' WNW: '1a painful feeling of having lost the respect of others because of the improper behaviour, incompetence, etc. of oneself or another 2 a tendency to have feelings of this kind, or a capacity for such feeling.'

[355] COMMISERATE: CTCD 'to feel or express compassion for: to pity... commiserative, feeling or expressing sympathetic sorrow. [L. *com-*, with, *miserārī*, to deplore—*miser*, wretched.]'

[356] *SCHADENFREUDE*: CTCD 'pleasure in others' misfortunes.'

[357] See *'muditā'* in *Buddhistisches Wörterbuch (Buddhist Dictionary)*, by the Venerable Ñāṇatiloka, Verlag Beyerlein & Steinschulte, Stammbach-Herrnschrot, 1999.

[358] ALTRUISTIC JOY: altruism is action governed by regard for others. Hence, this would mean one rejoices out of regard for the other, which is not equivalent to *mūditā*; appreciative joy: this fails to mention that the joyous appreciation is of another's success; empathetic joy: this means one enters into the other's feelings, which is alien to *mūditā*.

359 GLADNESS: this fails to mention that it is gladness over another's success; congratulation: this is in standard usage restricted to expression of joy at the other's success: MW '[L *congratulatus*, pp. of *congratulari* to wish joy, fr. *com-* <with> + *gratulari* to wish joy, fr. *gratus* pleasing] 1 *archaic*: to express sympathetic pleasure at (an event) 2: to express vicarious pleasure to (a person) on the occasion of success or good fortune.'

360 SYMPATHETIC JOY: CTCD 'sympathy... affinity or correlation whereby one things responds to the action of another... sympathetic... induced by sympathy.... [Gr. *sympatheia—syn*, with, *pathos*, suffering]' POD '(of pain [joy] &c.) caused by pain [joy, etc.] to some one else....'

Bibliographical Abbreviations etc.
(Used in Source References)[989]

A.	*Aṅguttara·Nikāya (Numerical Collection)*
AA.	*Aṅguttara·Nikāya-Aṭṭhakathā*[990] *(— Commentary)*
AbS.	*Abhidhammattha·Saṅgaho (Abhidhamma Compendium)*
Ap.	*Apadāna·Pāḷi (Narrative Text)*
ApA.	*Apadāna·Aṭṭhakathā (— Commentary)*
AṬ.	*Aṅguttara·Nikāya Ṭīkā (Numerical Collection Subcommentary)*
CMA.	*A Comprehensive Manual of Abhidhamma*[991]
D.	*Dīgha·Nikāya (Long Collection)*
DA.	*Dīgha·Nikāya·Aṭṭhakathā (— Commentary)*
DAṬ.	*Dīgha·Nikāya-Abhinava·Ṭīkā (– Newest Subcommentary)*
DD.	*The Dispeller of Delusion*[992]
DhP.	*Dhamma·Pada (Dhamma Word)*
DhPA.	*Dhamma·Pada·Aṭṭhakathā (— Commentary)*
DhS.	*Dhamma·Saṅgaṇī (Dhamma Compendium)*
DhSA.	*Dhamma·Saṅgaṇī·Aṭṭhakathā (— Commentary)*
DhSṬ.	*Dhamma·Saṅgaṇī·Mūla·Ṭīkā (— Root Sub·commentary)*
E.	*The Expositor*[993]
Iti.	*Iti·Vuttaka·Pāḷi (Thus It Was Said Text)*
J.	*Jātaka·Pāḷi (Jātaka Text)*
JA.	*Jātaka·Aṭṭhakathā (— Commentary)*
KhP.	*Khuddaka·Pāṭha·Pāḷi (Minor Reading)*
KhPA.	*Khuddaka·Pāṭha·Aṭṭhakathā (— Commentary)*
M.	*Majjhima·Nikāya (Middle Collection)*
MA.	*Majjhima·Nikāya·Aṭṭhakathā (— Commentary)*
MiP.	*Milinda·Pañha·Pāḷi (Milinda Question Text)*
MR.	*The Minor Readings*[994]
MṬ.	*Majjhima·Nikāya·Ṭīkā (— Sub·commentary)*
P.	*Paṭṭhāna·Pāḷi (Causal Relations)*
PaD.	*Param·Attha·Dīpanī*[995] *(Manuals of Ultmate Reality)*
PD.	*Path of Discrimination*[996]

---

[989] For details on the source references, and examples, see next section.
[990] The Pali titles for the commentaries are: AA = *Manoratha·Pūraṇī*; DA = *Su·Maṅgala-·Vilāsinī*; DhSA = *Aṭṭha·Sālinī*; MA = *Papañca·Sūdanī*; SA = *Sārattha·Ppakāsinī*; VbhA = *Sa·Mmoha·Vinodanī*
[991] CMA: English translation of *Abhidhammattha·Saṅgaha* edited and with notes by Bhikkhu Bodhi, Buddhist Publication Society, Kandy, Sri Lanka.
[992] DD: English translation of *Vibhaṅga-Āṭṭhakathā* by Bhikkhu Ñāṇamoli, Pali Text Society, Oxford, England.
[993] Exp: English translation of *Dhamma·Saṅgaṇī·Āṭṭhakathā* by Professor Pe Maung Tin M.A., Pali Text Society, London, England.
[994] MR: English translation of *Khuddaka·Pāṭha-Aṭṭhakathā* by Bhikkhu Ñāṇamoli, Pali Text Society, Oxford, England.
[995] PaD: 'manual' by the Most Venerable Ledi Sayadaw (1846-1923). References are to paragraph number in the edition on the *Chaṭṭha Saṅgāyana CD-ROM*:see footnote 1000, p.385.
[996] PD: English translation of *Paṭisambhidā·Magga* by Bhikkhu Ñāṇamoli, Pali Text Society, Oxford, England.

PED.	*The Pali Text Society's Pali·English Dictionary*[997]
PP.	*Path of Purification*[998]
PsM.	*Paṭisambhidā·Magga (Discrimination Path)*
S.	*Saṁyutta·Nikāya (Connected Collection)*
SA.	*Saṁyutta·Nikāya·Aṭṭhakathā (— Commentary)*
SuN.	*Sutta·Nipāta (Sutta Book)*
TG.	*Thera·Gāthā·Pāḷi (Elder's·Verses·Text)*
TGA.	*Thera·Gāthā·Aṭṭhakathā (— Commentary)*
TīG.	*Therī·Gāthā·Pāḷi (Elderess's·Verses·Text)*
U.	*Udāna (Inspiration)*
Vbh.	*Vibhaṅga (Analysis)*
VbhA.	*Vibhaṅga·Aṭṭhakathā (— Commentary)*
VbhṬ.	*Vibhaṅga·Ṭīkā*[999] *(— Sub·commentary)*
Vin.Cv.	*Vinaya Cūḷa·Vagga (Monastic Rule: Small Chapter)*
Vin.Mv.	*Vinaya Mahā·Vagga (Monastic Rule: Great Chapter)*
Vin.Pāc.	*Vinaya Pācittiya·Pāḷi (—: Expiable Text)*
Vin.Pār.	*Vinaya Pārājika·Pāḷi (—: Defeat Text)*
VsM.	*Visuddhi·Magga (Purification Path: Commentary)*
VsMṬ.	*Visuddhi·Magga·Mahā·Ṭīkā (— Great Sub·commentary)*

[997] PED: by T.W.Rhys Davids, F.B.A., D.Sc., Ph.D., LL.D. D.Litt., and William Stede Ph.D., Pali Text Society, Oxford, England.

[998] PP: English translation of *Visuddhi·Magga* by Bhikkhu Ñāṇamoli, Buddhist Publication Society, Kandy, Sri Lanka.

[999] The Pali titles for the sub-commentaries are: VbhTi = *Mūla·Ṭīkā*; VsMṬ = *Param·Attha Mañjūsā*

Source References

The source references are according to the standard divisions in the Pali:[1000]

Nikāya	*Vagga*	*Saṁyutta*	*Vagga*	*Sutta*
(Collection	Book	Section	Chapter	Sutta)

For example:[1001]

S.III.I.x.7				
S.	**III.**	**I.**	**x.**	**7**
***S**aṁyutta·Nikāya* *(Connected Collection)*	*'Khandha·Vagga·Pāḷi'* ('Aggregate-Chapter Text')	*'Khandha·Saṁyutta'* ('Aggregate Section')	*'Puppha·Vaggo'* ('Flower Chapter')	*'Gaddula·Baddha·Suttaṁ'* ('The Clog-Bound Sutta')

M.III.iv.5			
M.	**III.**	**iv.**	**5**
***M**ajjhima·Nikāya* *(Middle Collection)*	*'Upari·Paṇṇāsa·Pāḷi'* ('Further Fifty Text')	*'Vibhaṅga·Vagga'* ('Analysis Chapter')	*'Cūḷa·Kamma·Vibhaṅga·Suttaṁ'* ('The Small Kamma-Analysis Sutta')

DhP.ii.1		
DhP.	**ii.**	**1**
***Dh**amma·**P**ada* *(Dhamma Path)*	*'A·Ppamāda·Vagga'* ('Non-Negligence Chapter')	First Verse

VsM.xvii.587 (PP.xvii.43)		
VsM.	**xvii.**	**587**
***Vis**uddhi·**M**agga* *(Purification Path)*	*'Paññā·Bhūmi Niddesa'* ('Wisdom-Ground Description')	Section 587
(PP.	**xvii.**	**43)**
***P**ath of **P**urification*	'Description of the Soil in Which Understanding Grows'	Section 43

[1000] All source references are according to the *Chaṭṭha Saṅgāyana CD-ROM*, Version 3.0, Vipassana Research Institute, Dhamma Giri, Igatpuri-422 403, India.
[1001] Please note also references to section numbers in VsM *(Visuddhi·Magga)*, and DhSA *(Dhammasaṅgaṇī-Āṭṭhakathā)*, the last examples.

DhSA.I.i.1 (E.135)			
DhSA.	**i.**	**iii**	**1**
***Dh**amma·**S**aṅgaṇī **A**ṭṭha·Kathā* (*Dhamma·Compendium Meaning·Discussion)*	*'Citt· Uppāda· Kaṇḍo'* ('Consciousness-Arising Grouping')	*'Kām·Āvacara· Kusala·Pada· Bhājanīyaṁ'* ('Sensual-Sphere Wholesome-Factor Association')	*'Akusala· Kamma·Patha· Kathā'* ('Unwholesome Kamma-Course Discussion')
(E.			**135)**
*The **E**xpositor*			p.135

Index

The main headings are in bold script. For the main discussion of a subject, reference is made only to the first page: the discussion may therefore continue onto the next page or more.

The many sutta references in the endnotes are not referred to in the index, as such endnotes may be found under the related subject. For example, the index entry 'abandonment*(pahāna)*, -discipline, five types' refers to an analysis of abandonment as (1) substitution (with five examples), (2) suppression, (3) eradication, (4) subsiding, and (5) escape. It has been taken from DhSA.iii.1007 (E.451-456), and MA.I.i.1 *'Mūla·Pariyāya·Suttaṁ'* ('The Root-Theme Sutta'). Included in that listing are references to eight endnotes that quote pertinent sutta passages.

Abbreviations

- (fnote123) = footnote 123
- (enote231) = endnote 231
- tbl = table
- qtn = quotation

A

B

D

E

F

L

M

W

Made in United States
North Haven, CT
06 January 2023

30673162R20250